DIRECTING

FILM TECHNIQUES
AND
AESTHETICS

Fifth Edition

DIRECTING

FILM TECHNIQUES AND AESTHETICS

Fifth Edition

Michael Rabiger
Mick Hurbis-Cherrier
Illustrated by Gustavo Mercado

Focal Press
Taylor & Francis Group

NEW YORK AND LONDON

First published 2013
by Focal Press
70 Blanchard Road, Suite 402, Burlington, MA 01803

Simultaneously published in the UK
by Focal Press
2 Park Square, Milton Park, Abingdon, Oxon OX14 4RN

Focal Press is an imprint of the Taylor & Francis Group, an informa business

Library of Congress Cataloging in Publication Data
Rabiger, Michael.
  Directing : film techniques and aesthetics / Michael Rabiger, Mick Hurbis-Cherrier.—5th ed.
    p. cm.
  Includes index.
  1. Motion pictures—Production and direction. 2. Motion pictures--Aesthetics. I. Hurbis-Cherrier, Mick. II. Title.
  PN1995.9.P7R26 2013
  791.4302′33—dc23   2012027180

ISBN: 978-0-240-81845-0 (pbk)
ISBN: 978-0-203-07238-7 (ebk)

Typeset in Sabon LT Std
by MPS Limited, Chennai, India
www.adi-mps.com

Printed and bound in the United States of America by Sheridan Books, Inc. (a Sheridan Group company)

CONTENTS

PART 2: THE STORY AND ITS DEVELOPMENT

PART 3: THE DIRECTOR AND THE SCRIPT

PART 4: AUTHORSHIP AND AESTHETICS

PART 5: A DIRECTOR'S SCREEN GRAMMAR

PART 7: PRODUCTION

CONTENTS FOR THE COMPANION WEBSITE

www.directingbook.com

PROJECTS
    Director's personal themes projects
        Will help you identify your personal themes and develop your artistic voice as a director (from Ch. 1).
    Shooting and editing projects
        These projects explore a variety of techniques of expression and filmmaking skills.
    Outcomes assessment forms
        These forms are used with the shooting and editing projects to measure the development of your skills.
    Film analysis projects
        These film study projects will exercise your ability to examine image composition, editing, sound, and lighting technique in films.

WORKFLOW CHARTS
    A collection of common project workflows from shooting to distribution and a *Workflow Worksheet* to help determine your specific workflow.

FORMS AND LOGS
    Download: Storyline analysis form / Storyboards / Location scouting report / Budget form / Call sheet / Script breakdown / Camera and sound logs / Sound spotting sheet

AESTHETICS AND GENRE QUESTIONNAIRES
    Designed to help you uncover your film's full aesthetic potential.

PROJECT CHECKLISTS
    Stage-by-stage summaries derived from the chapters that serve as reminders for each phase of the production process.

MISCELLANEOUS
    An actor prepares (for Chapter 21)
    Production safety notes, publications, and links
    Teaching notes

FILMOGRAPHY
    Full citations and distributor information for all films mentioned in this book.

WEB RESOURCES
    Links to all websites mentioned in this book and more.

BIBLIOGRAPHY

INTRODUCTION

Here is a practical, comprehensive film manual for the aspiring film director. To find a friendly and comprehensive text that can help you learn film directing has been difficult, except of the technological kind. There has always been a lot of anecdotal material—better known as war stories—but almost nothing prescriptive, practical, and encouraging. Here is a book that explains the procedures using analogies, exercises, and illuminating mentorship. Like none other, this book prepares you for the thought processes, feelings, judgments, and techniques that a director needs throughout the demanding and fascinating experience of practicing the craft.

Using digital cameras and computers, the novice can now at low cost experiment, improvise, solve problems collaboratively with cast and crew, revise earlier solutions, and treat crises as disguised opportunities. A guerrilla approach like this—common in documentary but foreign to the cost-driven norms of the features industry—means you are empowered as a low-budget independent to produce cutting-edge creativity.

By recognizing that you can only learn from doing, this book offers a great range of hands-on projects as learning tools and talks to you like a colleague. You will find few warnings, and much encouragement: simply *do* it and learn, we say.

Learning to make films that speak with your own voice and identity will engage your head, your hands, and your heart. This is the artistic experience as it's lived through filmmaking—a way of life that you can make your own, and one that will test and enhance every aspect of your life for decades to come.

This, the 5th edition, brings together the latest trends and terminology that the director must know, while avoiding the extensive particularities of equipment that nowadays can be found elsewhere in satisfying depth. The core knowledge here is the human, psychological, and technical knowledge that any director needs, knowledge that will remain current for a very long time to come.

WHAT'S NEW

In this, the 5th edition, virtually every chapter has been revised, updated, and re-organized for a more streamlined and integrated approach. These developments expand and emphasize all that is enduringly central to the director's creative and logistical responsibilities, no matter how much the technologies of sound, image, and editing may change in the future.

Critical and aesthetic:

- All illustration graphics are new.
- Film examples and references are completely updated and expanded to include recent independent and international films, as well as those considered classics.
- New discussion exploring the elements of naturalistic and stylistic aesthetic approaches.
- New discussion of the narrative power of lighting and the lens—including many film examples of shot size, perspective, focus, and exposure.
- Greater emphasis on the narrative, emotional, and tonal implications of composition, mise-en-scène, continuity shooting and editing, long take shooting, point-of-view sequences, and camera handling.

Dramaturgy:

- Revised and expanded sections on the basics of drama include thorough analyses of *The King's Speech* (Academy Award for Best Original Screenplay, 2010), *The Fighter* (Academy Award nomination for Best Original Screenplay, 2010) and *The Messenger* (Academy Award nomination for Best Original Screenplay, 2009) among many other examples and references.
- Considerations specifically for the short film added to the "The Story and its Development."

Project development:

- New discussions of the director's approach to script analysis and development.
- The "Director's Screen Grammar" section, thoroughly revised and expanded, includes new examples of cinematic storytelling techniques.

Preproduction:

- Expanded discussion of collaboration between the director and principal creative crew (Cinematographer, Art Director, Sound Mixer).
- Updated discussion of workflow and comparative advantages to digital or film acquisition.

Production:

- Updated discussion and examples on lighting techniques.
- New section on film production safety, set protocol and etiquette.

NOW AVAILABLE ON THE BOOK'S WEBSITE

To enhance this book's portability, some material has been shifted to the book's website (www. directingbook.com) for simple downloading. Teachers will like the fact that they can be edited or augmented at will. There you will find:

- Suggested production and film analysis exercises.
- Checklists and project assessment forms.
- Analytical questionnaires.

- Updated forms and logs for all phases of a project (including a short film budget form, location scouting forms, storyboards, camera and sound logs, SFX spotting sheets and more).
- Links to other websites, in particular those concerned with safety on the set.

PREPARATION VS. EXECUTION

You may wonder why a film directing book devotes the majority of chapters to the thinking, planning, and arrangements prior to the production phase. Much teaching experience has taught us that beginners often assume that a director needs mainly to know screen techniques and filmmaking technology. This is not so, because cameras, equipment, and techniques are not an alchemy that can transform lead into gold. Instead they are magnifying devices that enlarge equally whatever is present or lacking. Fiction is a very difficult genre to make credible, and when beginners' work falls short, the reasons are usually because:

- The story is imitative and lacks dramatic unity, individuality, and the force of conviction. Film stories need originality, momentum in the narrative, and something worthwhile and deeply felt to say.
- The film's world and characters aren't credible. The director needs greater understanding of actors, acting, dramatic structure, and the psychological processes of human perception that underlie film language.
- The film is theatrically based on dialogue and lacks an understanding of the visual and aural forms that make the cinema the powerful force that it is.

For all these common faults there are remedies, and this book takes the bull by the horns from its first pages. It tells you clearly and succinctly what a director must know for every phase of fiction production, how professionals handle each of the tasks in the process, and what you can do to put moving, deeply felt stories on the screen.

The thinking, analysis, procedures, and disciplines you learn here can prepare anyone truly dedicated for a life as a professional in the film industry.

LOCATING HELP

You can find information by going to:

- The Index.
- The Contents for the Part covering the filmmaking stage you're at.
- The books and websites suggested throughout each chapter for further research.

OUR COLLABORATION

Michael Rabiger writes: The organization and writing in this book evolved from a new collaboration between myself (as the original writer) and the distinguished teacher, filmmaker, and writer

Mick Hurbis-Cherrier, whose production experience, teaching, and involvement with contemporary fiction cinema are all more current than my own. Since so much information about film technology, techniques, and equipment now exists in specialized texts and on the Internet, we decided to concentrate more on the experiential core of the director's art. For me it has been a stimulating delight to debate methods and explanations every step of the way, and undoubtedly the book has shed some of its girth.

Anyone writing a book like this one stands on the shoulders of all the professional communities to which he has ever belonged. The largest of these in my case include Pinewood and Shepperton Studios, the BBC, and Granada TV—all in England. Many of my ideas about film education grew from decades of working with students at Columbia College Chicago, and shorter residencies at New York University and other film schools around the world. For this edition we benefited from advice and criticism from film industry and teaching colleagues including Ben Benesh; Jacqueline Frost, California State University, Fullerton; Gary Goldsmith, formerly of University of Southern California; Dewi Griffiths, Red Sea Institute Jordan and UK; Robert Lewis, California State University, Northridge; Simon Tarr, University of South Carolina; Patrick Titley, University of Leeds; George Chun Han Wang, University of Hawaii. Through the years I have benefited greatly from advice, help, and criticism from colleagues in Columbia College Chicago's Film/Video Department: Doreen Bartoni, Robert Buchar, Judd Chesler, Gina Chorak, Sandy Cuprisin, Dan Dinello, Chap Freeman, Paul Hettel, T.W. Li, Joan McGrath, Chris Peppey, Emily Reible, Joe Steiff, Diego Trejo, Jr., and Wenhwa Ts'ao.

I must also mention Tod Lending of Nomadic Pictures, Milos Stehlik of Facets Multimedia, and Elinor Actipis formerly of Focal Press. Also thanks to my son Paul Rabiger of Cologne, Germany; daughters Joanna Rabiger of Austin, Texas, and Penelope Rabiger of London; and the good folks at Focal Press whose unfailing support, good humor, and solid work are always inspiring. Lastly, I must thank to my wife and closest friend Nancy Mattei, who puts up philosophically with the writing that I so much like doing.

Mick Hurbis-Cherrier writes: Working as a new co-writer on one of the beloved classic texts in this field was at first a daunting proposition, but ultimately an immensely rewarding experience. Although I was not one of the lucky students to have had Michael Rabiger as an instructor, it was my great fortune to have benefited from his profound knowledge, generosity, and gentle guidance throughout our collaboration on this 5th edition. So much so that I can now say I have enjoyed this esteemed professor's mentorship.

Sincere thanks go to the team at Focal Press, especially former Senior Editor Elinor Actipis who got this edition rolling, and current Senior Editor Dennis McGonagle who, with project manager Carlin Reagan and production editor Emma Elder, saw it through to the end.

I would also like to join Professor Rabiger in thanking the external reviewers—their meticulous evaluation and invaluable suggestions unquestionably helped to make this edition the strongest one yet.

I am grateful to the many people who generously provided expertise, advice, materials, or time toward this new edition. This includes Tracey Bussell and Newmarket Press, Nichole Kizer of Copper Post, Ramin Bahrani, Thelma Schoonmaker, Paul Thompson, Ken Dancyger, Tom Ashton,

Maya Sheppard, Htat Htut, Melissa Hill, John Dougless, Rick Litvin, Debra Tolchinsky, David Tolchinsky, Kristiina Hackel, and Hamp Overton.

I would like to extend a very warm thanks to the students from various universities who responded to my call for production photos. I am grateful for the time they took from their projects to submit photos. They include Felix Thompson, Andrew Knudsen, Ariel Rudnick, Catrin Headstrom, Amanda Sabater, and Mallory Schwartz from New York University; Hannah Janal from Columbia University; Jac Reyno from Northwestern University; Jared Stanton and Josue Martinez from the University of New Orleans, Debbie Camper, Sonya Dunn, Carles Boles, and Nicole Haddock from American University, Washington; Carey Hu, Melissa Hill, Miles Adgate, and Nick Vega, from Hunter College—CUNY.

I am extraordinarily lucky to work with so many, energetic, knowledgeable, and experienced colleagues at the Department of Film and Media Studies at Hunter College. I am thankful for the support of President Jennifer Raab, Provost Vita Rabinowitz, Dean Eric Koch, Department Chair Jay Roman, and film program head Joel Zuker. I am especially grateful to my colleagues Andrew Lund, Shanti Thakur, Ivone Margulies, Joe McElhaney, Marty Lucas, Kelly Anderson, Michael Gitlin, Renato Tonelli, and Peter Jackson who were all willing to devote time to helping with this book through technical support, material support, advice, criticism, encouragement, and in some cases, close and extensive readings of text.

My enduring gratitude goes to my wife Katherine Hurbis-Cherrier whose support, expertise, advice, and energy made this book (and so much more) possible; and to my colleague Gustavo Mercado who not only illustrated this edition, but always remained cheerfully "on call" whenever I needed advice, confirmation, a fresh perspective, or some quick research throughout the writing of this edition.

PART 1

THE DIRECTOR AND ARTISTIC IDENTITY

PART 1-1 ——

Student Director Auriel Rudnick on the set of *Fitted*.

PART 1-2 ——

Student Director Patrick Ng on the set of *Real Talk*.

CHAPTER 1

THE WORLD OF THE FILM DIRECTOR

CINEMA ART AND YOU

Cinema is the great art form of our time. It provides popular entertainment and is the preeminent forum for ideas and self-expression. Occupying the place of the theater in Elizabethan times, or the novel in the 19th and early 20th centuries, the cinema is where dreams of every shape and meaning take hold of the contemporary mind. The cinema leaps national and cultural barriers as no medium has ever done before, and the best films excite hearts and minds as only good art can. We each have particular stories to tell, and I shall show you that you do too.

No limit exists to the number of films the world can consume, so if you can direct outstanding screen work, you can make a job for yourself. This won't be simple or easy, and the competition is stiff. But if you can sustain passion for the work, this book will help you succeed no matter whether you've done ten years in the film industry or are just starting out.

Learning to direct films is like learning to conduct an orchestra. Most conductors learn an instrument, master music, and then learn to conduct—which means coordinating an ensemble of top-notch musicians. And although conductors are not virtuosic on every instrument, they must understand the musical range and expressive capabilities of each instrument in their orchestra. Most who direct get there by mastering one key craft such as screenwriting, cinematography, or editing, but they must also have a general understanding of the other crafts and how they interrelate in the service of telling a cinematic story. Which area you should choose to specialize in will emerge as you roll up your sleeves, use this book, and get an all-around immersion. You may do this in film school with fellow students, or outside it working with a few committed friends. In either case, getting a taste of the broader world of film production will greatly inform your abilities and perspective as you eventually move into the realm of the director.

Superb, affordable digital technology now makes high-quality filmmaking possible on any budget, and distribution through video sharing services and online short film competitions assures a ready outlet and audience. However, while the technical means for directing films[1] have never been more accessible, learning to truly express yourself in the cinema is complex because it involves all the other arts combined. You'll need to investigate how the other arts contribute to film and how each acts on us. To make your mark, you will need strong, clear, and critical ideas about the condition of your times. To open up interior spaces and existential questions in your audience's imagination, you must aim beyond the ordinary. Good films invite us to dream, to exercise our judgment, and to draw on our feelings and intuitions. Film is a continuously evolving art form, and it needs energetic and original people driving it. The groundwork to begin this is already in you. As I shall show, you already have an established artistic identity that awaits discovery.

THE DIRECTOR

WHO DIRECTS

Steven Spielberg, Souleymane Cissé, Kathryn Bigelow, Todd Haynes, Lucrecia Martel, Spike Lee, Fatih Akin, Florian Henckle Von Donnersmarck, Chan-Wook Park, Courtney Hunt, Abbas Kiarostami, Hirokazu Koreeda, Jason Reitman, Kar-Wei Wong, Jean-Pierre Jeunet, Mira Nair, Claire Denis, Pedro Almodovar... people who direct films come in all human types and from all continents, cultures, backgrounds and personal experiences. Filmmakers may emerge from any corner of the world, any subculture and any background. However, the task of film directing is formidable and doing it well takes determination, resourcefulness, creativity and tenacity. A director must have strong ideas about the human condition, a passion to express these ideas and a mountaineering capacity for filmmaking's grueling process. It also requires an ability to collaborate and an understanding of how to get the best out of a creative team.

Don't listen to anyone who says you are (or are not) talented. I've taught thousands, and "talent" can be a flash in the pan. What matters more is your quality of effort, dogged persistence, and that you love the work. Nobody can predict who will do well. If entry tests could spot potential, then Britain's National Film and Television School would never have rejected Mike Figgis and the German Film & Television Academy would have eagerly welcomed R.W. Fassbinder as a student.

If you really want to direct, find a way to do it and do not give up.

BASIC RESPONSIBILITIES AND PERSONAL TRAITS

A director answers to the producer and is responsible for the details, quality, and meaning of the final film. A film team (cast and crew) is made up of a number of creative and technical collaborators. The director's job is to coordinate this collective expertise and inspire its creative energy into producing a single, stylistically unified and coherent cinematic story. Ideally, this story will ultimately connect with an audience and move them in some way.

During preproduction this requires writing or working with writers; envisioning the film's scope, purpose, identity, and meaning; finding appropriate locations that advance the dramatic

---

[1] When I speak of filmmaking or directing a "film," I include film and digital media together as by this time in the history of the art form, they are thoroughly integrated in all aspects of moviemaking.

meaning and atmosphere of the film; auditioning and casting actors; assembling a crew (though this may be done with the producer or unit production manager, if you have one); developing both cast and script through rehearsals; developing the technical and stylistic approach with the various department heads (camera, sound and art departments).

During production (the shooting of the film), the director essentially performs two functions: stage the scene for the camera and assure that the performances are strong, consistent and appropriate. The first task involves directing the crew and the second, directing the actors. If the director, actors and crew do their work properly in preproduction, everyone arrives on the set with a good idea of what they need to do to get the film in the can—this allows the director to stay loose, keep their eyes and ears open and perhaps improvise, rework, improve, or reconceive scenes along the way if the realities of production on location suggest improvements.

During postproduction and distribution, the director usually oversees the creative aspects of the editing and finalization of the project. In the commercial film world, the director collaborates with an editor to deliver a "director's cut" to the producer who in turn has the authority to make changes—and they usually do. In the independent and student film world, the director works with an editor to guide the film through all the editing stages. Additionally, the director has to make themselves available for promoting the production in festivals and other distribution and promotion circuits during its early run.

Ideally, a director is broadly knowledgeable in the arts; possessed of a lively, inquiring mind; likes delving into people's lives and looking for hypothetical links and explanations; is methodical and organized even if outwardly informal and easygoing; able to scrap prior work if assumptions become obsolete; and possessed of endless tenacity when searching out great ideas, techniques, people, and performances. The better directors are able to be articulate and succinct in communication; make instinctive judgments and decisions; get the best out of people without being dictatorial; speak on terms of respectful equality with a range of specialists; and understand technicians' problems and inspire their best efforts. In short, a film director is a leader, and as a leader must exude authority, build trust, communicate abstract ideas clearly, and inspire good work.

If this sounds superhuman, it should also be mentioned that many excellent directors are also obstinate, private, awkward, and idiosyncratic. During production, most directors sooner or later show signs of insecurity (depression, manic energy, low flash point, panic, irresolution). If that is not enough to puzzle crew members, the director's inflamed mental state during production will generate superhuman energy that pushes everyone's patience to the limit. They often sink into acute doubt and anxiety during shooting; suffer sensory overload and find choice painful; and, at the end of a production, go into postpartum depression and/or physical illness.

The truth is that giving birth to a story for the screen is an intoxicating business. Whoever does it fully and completely is living existentially—that is, entirely in the present and spending each precious moment as if it were their last. This is especially true after an initial success: thereafter you face artistic and professional extinction every step of the way. Like stage fright, the dread and exhilaration of the chase may never go away. But the sign of any worthwhile experience is that it both attracts and scares you.

For all this, you will have to develop the self-knowledge, humility, humor, and self-discipline that command respect. Probably, you will acquire these qualities from endless mistakes, because in filmmaking a lot of learning is negative learning. As you mature as an artist over years, you come to understand better and better how to fulfill the emotional, psychological, and intellectual needs of the common person—that is, your audience. Happily, the members of that audience are a lot like yourself.

LEADERSHIP: COLLABORATION AND VISION

> As a director, I'm a sort of human lens through which everyone's efforts are focused. A big part of my job is making decisions about how all the great talent that I'm working with blends into a single consciousness.[2]
>
> —Christopher Nolan

People think directing must be the ultimate in self-expression, but the cinema earned its preeminent place because it is a collective, not an individualist's medium. Making a feature film takes directors, writers, actors, cinematographers, art directors, editors, sound designers, makeup artists—creative craftspeople of every kind, all working together (Figure 1-1).

To complete the Noah's ark, there are producers, distributors, exhibitors, and financiers who make filmmaking possible because they insist that it find a paying audience. Each specialist yields the greater part of his or her life to making a contribution, and cinema's strength and appeal come from the collaborative interplay at the core of this process. Ingmar Bergman likened it to the great undertakings in the Middle Ages when teams of international craftsmen—specialists who never even bothered to leave their names—gathered in crews to build the great European cathedrals. The cinema, he says, is today's version of such collective endeavor, and from each emerges something greater than the sum of its parts.

It is the director who sets the creative tone for a film production, and an intelligent director will not bear the burden of making an entire film themselves; instead they take advantage of the experience, expertise, and creative sensibilities of the team around them. Cinematographers, actors, art directors, and editors often work on multiple films in a single year, of all sorts, while a director is lucky to make

FIGURE 1-1 ——————————————————

Christopher Nolan with Hillary Swank and production crew during the shooting of *Insomnia* (2002).

[2] Christopher Nolan—director of *Memento, Insomnia, Batman Begins, The Prestige, The Dark Knight*—in *American Cinematographer*, January 2007 (back cover).

one film in three years. These specialists have faced many challenges. Soliciting their creative and technical suggestions not only shows respect to the many professionals on the project, but will also win respect for the director. A director need not take every suggestion offered, but the act of inviting and considering ideas from creative personnel generates more possibilities for success and makes everyone feel personally invested in the project. This inspires people to give their very best and every director should strive for it.

In addition to a director's capacity for collaboration, a central quality of their effectiveness as a leader is the confidence to have a strong vision for a project. As the overseer of all the creative activity on a film project, the director maintains the bird's eye view of the film and ensures that all the component parts (image, performance, sound, and editing) work together to achieve an integrated, cohesive, and expressive motion picture. To this end, a director must conceive and clearly articulate an overarching vision for the film: the thematic goals, the stylistic approach, and the overall emotional tone and resonance. All the principal collaborators will take their cues from these central ideas. The ability to devise and communicate a clear creative roadmap for the project is at the core of a director's authority and is the basis for the trust that the cast and crew must have in their leader.

ART, IDENTITY, AND COMPETITIVENESS

Some enter the arts in search of self-affirmation. This is treacherous ground, for it suggests that art and therapy are synonymous. They overlap, but have different purposes. Art does work in and for the world, whereas therapy is self-directed and seeks relief from doubt or unhappiness. Self-affirmation in the guise of art leads down the slippery slope of self-display. Living as we do in a celebrity culture, we have a great need to be special and different. Hindu belief is interesting here, for Self in their philosophy is *that which you share with all creation*. A Hindu shares his or her identity with a tree, a mountain, a bird, a crippled child. The Western idea of Self is by contrast very isolating. Most people trying to create films actually subscribe to both ends of the spectrum. They want to be individual and recognized, but also to create something universal and meaningful to others.

If you are asking, "Does all this philosophy and psychology stuff really matter?" then I have to answer, yes, I think it does, because what you believe will determine whether you are happy and productive working in a collective medium like film. Filmmaking offers a close link to a communal identity in that it's not really the expression of a single individual, rather we always make film with others. When film students fail, it's seldom because they can't handle the work or the technology. It's usually because they can't work as equals with others. Problems arise from control issues, competitiveness, authorial stinginess, or a refusal to make or keep commitments. As a result, the project itself takes a back seat to personal conflicts and squabbles. When generosity of spirit is lacking, it's the movie that suffers most.

It's important to understand that you establish your reputation as a filmmaker and collaborator from your very first efforts, even if it's in film school. If you are known as someone who is obstinate, closed minded, and dictatorial, you will not find many people willing to

FIGURE 1-2 ———————————

Bob Teitel and George Tillman Jr., a producer/writer/director team who established their partnership in film school.

FIGURE 1-3 ———————————

Director Ramin Bahrani and DP Michael Simmonds, a collaborative relationship which has lasted four films and counting. Here they are lining up a shot for *At Any Price* (2012).

share their talents with you. On the other hand, if you establish a reputation as someone with strong ideas who also creates an atmosphere of artistic excitement, mutual respect and hard work, then you'll attract the most serious minded people around you. Anyone can modify their asocial habits if it matters enough, and some of the group work in film schools exists to sort through and conquer these problems, and to help students locate their best partners. George Tillman, Jr. and Bob Teitel, the writer/producer/director team responsible for *Men of Honor* (2000), the *Barbershop* films (2002, 2004), and *Notorious* (2009) were students who met in my college's second-level production course (Figure 1-2). After leaving college, they began their professional output with *Soul Food* (1997) and have worked successfully together ever since.

It's common that the creative group you've cultivated in film school becomes the one you rely on when you're making your first professional projects, but close collaborative relationships can also originate outside film school. Director Ramin Bahrani first met cinematographer Michael Simmonds while he was writing the screenplay for his first feature film *Man Push Cart* (2005). Bahrani was impressed with a film Simmonds had shot and asked if he would look at his screenplay. Simmonds, in turn, was impressed by the script and decided to join the project. Since that first meeting, Bahrani and Simmonds have collaborated on every one of Bahrani's subsequent projects (four feature films and one short to date) (Figure 1-3). Here's how Simmonds characterizes their creative relationship.

There are no "meetings" but rather a consistent dialogue which has continued for eight years and counting. It is a collaboration based on mutual respect and a common desire to make the best films we can. [...] No creative statement is off-limits between the two of us. Of course as the director he has no obligation whatsoever to use the idea I may bring to the table, but I know he has thought about it and taken the idea seriously.[3]

Countless working relationships come from similar beginnings and persist over decades. This is how you build your own creative community from your very first film. People find who they need and make the relationships that work, and these form an integral part of your identity as an artist.[4]

IDENTIFYING YOUR THEMES

From the very first film you make, you are simultaneously expressing and developing your artistic voice. Choosing a subject that excites your imagination, assessing its meaning, and determining how and why it connects with an audience is a process you will undertake at the beginning of every project. Remember, on every project you will devote a great deal of time, physical effort, emotional investment, creative energy, and often hard cash, so it is important for you to rigorously explore which type of stories you care deeply about.

I often ask my students to name a film they wish they had made and tell me why. One student named *Frozen River* by Courtney Hunt because he liked the way the director made an emotionally moving and suspenseful film that was also keenly aware of social issues. He was also inspired by the power and immediacy of the low-budget, realist production style. Another student named *The Thin Red Line* because of the way it explored the intense and deeply personal experience of war in a poetic and metaphysical style. She explained that "most films in this genre are about a specific war, but this one seems to be about all wars." Yet another named *Sleepless in Seattle*. This student had significant stress in his life; he worked full time for very little income, his father and brother were both serving in the Iraq war at the time, and he was taking care of his mother who had recently suffered a stroke. Here is how he explained why he chose *Sleepless in Seattle*, "When I saw that movie, it just made me feel good and that's what I want to do for people. I want them to feel good for a little while." Social realism, metaphysical poetry and making people feel good—three different ideas for how films can connect and enrich other people's lives yet all of these impulses are legitimate because they are honest and specific to each young filmmaker who found inspiration in them.

---

[3] *Spotlight: Cinematographer Michael Simmonds On Working Collaboratively With Ramin Bahrani.* Movie City News Blogs, Kim Voynar, Moviecitynews.com (March 22, 2011).

[4] I am indebted to my Buddhist colleague Dean Doreen Bartoni for enlightening conversations around this subject, as well as to her example of egoless leadership at Columbia College Chicago.

Whether you write your own stories, work from someone else's script, or choose something to adapt, you will always face these central questions:

- What kind of subjects should I tackle?
- What can I be good at?
- What is my artistic identity?
- What are my unique skills?
- What do I believe can be my contribution to the art form?

Each new film project should be about something meaningful to you, not just an exercise in basic skills. If it isn't, you'll be deferring authorship in pursuit of technical excellence—which is a common mistake. Human beings are by nature seekers, and though everyone's quest is different, everyone seeks fresh chapters of meaning during their journey through life. The stronger and more articulate you are in committing to this quest, the more intense your work is likely to be. Those with dramatic life experience (say, of warfare, survival in labor camps, or of being orphaned) seldom doubt what subject to tackle next. But for anyone whose life seems ordinary, finding the keys to your undoubted sense of mission can be baffling. You face a conundrum: you can't make art without a sense of identity, yet it is identity you seek by making art.

IDENTITY, BELIEF, AND VISION

Film students, asked if they really have stories to tell, are apt to find the question insulting. Surely, to direct, you just need to learn the tools of cinema, and the rest follows! A year or two later, they are anxiously casting around for a decent project.

From your first efforts, I believe you must *tell stories expressing ideas and values about the lives around you*, or your films will be hollow and give audiences nothing to which they can respond. No matter how competently you handle the tools and the medium, your storytelling will be colorless and meaningless.

How, then, can you prepare to make compelling screen fiction? Actually, your options already exist and simply need uncovering. Here's the secret: your life has marked you in unique ways, and these marks—whether you know it or not—will determine how you live your life, what quests you pursue, and what you are equipped to say with passion and authority through a story.

So what are these marks, and how do you recognize them? Everyone has had the experience of suddenly discovering a pattern to some part of their life, and of feeling the rush of relief and excitement that comes from seeing what has been driving them. Once upon a time, when most people lived in small settlements, everyone saw how you acted over time, and could connect this with your temperament and history. This is still true in farming communities. Lacking those reflections from others, we see our own tendencies only with effort and difficulty. Yet to a large degree, those marks make our destiny, for as Heraclitus said, "a man's character is his fate."[5]

---

[5] Heraclitus (*c.*540–*c.*480 BC).

I did not stumble over this truth until I was in my thirties. As part of a study program, I was required to watch all my documentary films and write a self-assessment. My films were about very different topics, so I was astonished to discover there was a common theme linking them all. It was that "most people feel imprisoned, but the inventive can adapt, rebel, and escape." How can you make 20 films and not be aware of such a constant theme? Rather easily, I have to say. And where did the theme come from? The answers came sailing in like homing pigeons. During World War II, my middle-class family relocated to an English agricultural village. For several years, my father, a foreigner, was away serving on merchant ships, and my mother found nothing in common with her rural neighbors. So I had to contend with kids jeering at the way I spoke. I was derided, my possessions envied, and sometimes I was ambushed. Never doubting that we were "better" than the local people, I had to accept that I was different, unacceptable to the majority, and that fear would be a constant in life. This is something I would have to handle alone because adults were too busy. At home, I was one person; outside it, I had to become another.

The common thread in my films came from my character, and my character came from having lived on both sides of a social barrier and empathizing with those in similar predicaments: the black person in a white neighborhood, the Jew among Gentiles, the child among adults. Any story with these trace elements quickens my pulse. But I'd survived into my thirties *unaware that I carried a vision of life*. This vision was of life as a succession of imprisonments, each of which, given determination and friends, one can overcome. Perhaps there's a mark of Cain in my family, for each generation seems to migrate abroad.

The stories you tell always arise from a core of belief, which is your *philosophy*. Mine, had I noted it before starting each film, would have read: "When alone in hostile territory, look for others like yourself, then together search for the right way out, because one always exists."

Each person who creates with originality carries a mark. A biography by Paul Michaud about the late François Truffaut links such films as *The 400 Blows* (1959), *Jules and Jim* (1961), *The Wild Child* (1969), and *The Story of Adèle H.* (1975) with pain Truffaut suffered as a child upon being estranged from his mother (Figure 1-4). His characters' rootless lives, their naive impracticality, and Adèle Hugo's neurotic, self-destructive hunger for love all reflect aspects of the Truffaut known to his friends. This does not reduce or "explain" Truffaut; rather, it points to an energizing self-recognition that he turned outward to develop stories of universal appeal.

Is it helpful or is it destructive to "understand" your own experience too well? Should one seek professional help in doing so? There is a different answer for each person here, but psychotherapy is hard work, and those who pursue it usually do so only to get relief from unhappiness. Making art is a little different, for it arises from burning curiosity and the need to create order and suggest meaning. You should do whatever prepares you best for this. Below are techniques for clarifying your sense of direction and the imprint your life has made on you. If this is interesting, you can explore it in greater depth in my book *Developing Story Ideas,* 2nd ed. (Focal Press, 2006).

Films appear to look resolutely outward and not inward at their makers, so many who work in film do not seek what really drives them. But if drama is to have a spark of individuality, it must come from a strenuous inner dialogue. And whatever starts with yourself and your time becomes ultimately a dialogue with your audience.

FIGURE 1-4

The desperate search for love by so many of Truffaut's main characters is said to be a heightened version of his own during his youth. Antoine Doinel (Jean-Pierre Léaud) from *The 400 Blows* (*right*, 1959), a character who would return in five subsequent films by Truffaut (*left*).

TEMPERAMENT AFFECTS VISION

Temperament, personal history and cultural factors influence how a filmmaker sees the world. A political historian sees a naval battle as the interplay of inevitable forces, with victory or defeat resulting from the technology and strategy in use and the strengths and weaknesses of the leaders. This vision can lead to a film that aims to be objective in its approach and historical in its scope. A more empathic personality, who sees history growing grassroots fashion from the action of individuals, may see this battle quite differently. Her film might go below decks to seek out the profound conflicts amongst the humans whose humble lives are at stake. She places us in the heat of battle—not to show the constants in human history or the eternal repetition of human error, but to highlight the human potential and consequences inherent in moral choice.

Your temperament will determine the stories you want to tell, the worlds you want to create, and the scale of your conflicts and themes. This comes from the marks your life has left on you so you need to explore and listen to those traces.

FIND YOUR LIFE ISSUES

The marks you carry come from a few central issues in your formative experiences. Reminders of them unfailingly arouse you to strongly partisan feelings. This is your savings bank of deepest experience, and finding how to explore and use it in your work—even if your experiences seem few and personal—can keep you creatively occupied for life. I am talking not about autobiography, but about a core of deeply-felt experiences whose themes apply to endless situations outside yourself.

Ideation—the business of defining dramatically charged ideas—begins when you set aside some quiet, self-reflective time away from the hubbub of normal life.

Then,

- Examine without judgment the marks your life has made on you.
- Write briefly how these experiences have shaped you.
- From these reflections, list:
  - The kinds of stories you are best qualified to tell
  - The kinds of characters that particularly attract you
  - The situations you find especially intriguing
  - The genre(s) you want to work in (comedy, tragedy, history, biography, film noir, etc.).
- Now go over your answers, and substitute something better for everything that is glib, super-ficial, or clichéd. Make everything sharply particular. Never settle for fuzzy generalizations. "Generalization," said the acting theorist Stanislavsky, "is the enemy of art."

Quick, reflex answers usually jump out of the pool of clichés we all carry. Consider them a starting point from which to refine and sharpen what you are reaching for. Little by little, some-thing that is itself, something you don't have to reject, will emerge. Work quietly and persistently. Stay open to surprises and changes of direction. Good ideas are not ordered into existence, they are beckoned, and the better ones hide behind a façade of stereotypes. Your job is to find them and lure them out.

At first, it seems that nothing dramatic has happened in your life to draw upon. Perhaps the tensions you have witnessed or experienced never matured into any action. But the writer's grati-fication—and it may even be the chief reward of authorship—is to make happen what should have happened, but didn't. Any event or situation that is sharply etched in your consciousness awaits shaping into something that expresses emotion and a theme or vision of life. Depending on your tastes and temperament, this may be tragic, comic, satiric, realistic, surreal, or melodra-matic. By sending the original characters and events into the confrontations and changes that might have happened, you can follow the road not taken and investigate the originals' unused potential.

Any real-life situation containing characters, events, situations, and conflicts has the elements of drama, and thus the potential to become a full-blown story. Change one or two of the main ele-ments in this borrowed framework, develop your own characters, and the meaning and impact of the entire work will begin to evolve in their own special direction. You can digress imaginatively from a biographical structure or stick more or less closely to it.

John Boorman's autobiographical *Hope and Glory* (1987) is modeled on the lives and emo-tional evolution of his family during his boyhood in World War II. With imagination, sympathy, and wit, Boorman explores his mother's unfulfilled love for his father's best friend.

In his 2007 film *Into the Wild*, Sean Penn traces the journey of Christopher McCandless, a 20-year-old college graduate who abandoned the materialism of civilization for a solitary existence in the heart of the Alaskan Wilderness. McCandless' quest for a more truthful existence was a real and tragic story, but Penn overlays it with his own emphasis, presenting this young seeker as a folk hero, a refugee from cynicism, a spiritual revolutionary who nobly maintains hope, idealism, and faith in nature (Figure 1-5).

FIGURE 1-5

Sean Penn emphasizes the nobility and idealism of Chris McCandless' (Emile Hirsch) journey into the Alaskan wilderness in his 2007 film *Into the Wild*.

Tom Hooper's *The King's Speech* (2010) is based on the true story of King George VI, "the stammering king", and his Australian speech therapist Lionel Logue. Although screenwriter David Seidler had a long and successful career before this film, *The King's Speech* was of particular significance for him because he himself developed a stutter in childhood and always viewed King George as a role model and hero.

These films make biography dramatic by developing ideas about the underlying causes of their characters' desires, goals and dilemmas. This, in turn, broadens the specific story into something which connects with a larger audience. Anyone who studies real lives knows that nothing is more mysterious or dramatic than the actual.

Keep in mind that your exploration into real lives, real stories and real events need not begin with the struggles of the King of England; your noisy neighbor, the young clerk at the local convenience store, the old cook in the cheap diner, your crazy uncle, the next person who crosses your path can all be inspiration for story material if you look closely and honestly enough.

SUBJECTS TO AVOID

Many subjects that come to mind do so because they are being pumped up by the media or lend themselves to moral propaganda. You'd also be wise to avoid:

- Worlds you haven't experienced or cannot closely research.
- Any ongoing, inhibiting problem in your own life (find a therapist—you are unlikely to solve anything while directing a film unit).
- Anything or anyone "typical" (nothing real is typical, so nothing typical will ever be interesting or credible).

- Preaching or moral instruction of any kind.
- Films about problems to which you have the answer (so does your audience).
- Anything that attracts you just because filmmakers you admire have done it. Only Martin Scorsese can make a Scorsese film, only Terrence Malick can make a Malick film and only Kelly Reichardt can make a Reichardt film. They have their artistic voices—now find yours.

Aim to reach people outside your peer group and you will be making films accessible to a wide audience. For films of a few minutes, try taking something small that you learned the hard way, apply it to a character quite *un*like yourself, and make a modest comment on the human condition. By so doing, you can avoid the self-indulgence afflicting most student films. After all, your work is going to be your portfolio, your precious reel that tells future employers what you can do. You don't want to seem a perpetual student.

DISPLACE AND TRANSFORM

For your first short films, work from events and personalities in your own life, but displace the screen version away from the originals. Fictionalizing frees you from self-consciousness and allows you to tell underlying truths that might offend the originals. Most importantly, it allows you to concentrate on developing dramatic and thematic truths instead of getting tangled in questions of taste and biographical accuracy. You can further liberate your imagination and obscure your sources by:

- Giving characters alternative attributes and work.
- Making them composites or amalgamating the attributes of two life models.
- Placing the story in a different place or epoch.
- Altering the gender of protagonists.
- Adapting the central events to something similar in effect while being different in the details.

One student director whose script told his own story—about abandoning a suburban marriage and well-paying job to become a film student—inverted the gender of his main characters and made the rebel a woman. To give her credible motivations, he had to inhabit both husband's and wife's positions, and so came to more deeply investigate what people trapped in such roles expect out of life. Displacing the actual details into a fictionalized frame forced the director into a more empathic relationship with all of the characters and raised the level of his thematic discourse.

The great method acting guru Sanford Meisner famously defined acting as "… living truthfully under imaginary circumstances." This also provides a good guide for what we as fictional narrative storytellers do. If we are to represent truthful human behavior, we inevitably work with what we have personally experienced and seen in our own lives. We can make up fictional situations, but we cannot invent human behavior. We don't need to because it surrounds us every day. We simply must keep our eyes open, take note of what we see, imagine its dramatic potential and transpose it into a new context in order to create our fictions. In the final analysis, there should exist a great deal of truth in our fictional storytelling because that's what makes it resonate with an audience.

Here are a few projects that can help you explore your own life issues and identify your personal themes. These exercises which work in tandem with the development of your artistic voice as a director are only summarized here, but you will find detailed guidelines for each on the companion website at www.directingbook.com under "projects."

The Self-Inventory

To uncover your real issues and themes, and thus what you have to say to others, make a nonjudgmental inventory of your most moving experiences. This examination will confirm which life events have formed your quest, and bring into focus the underlying issues they represent. Almost certainly you'll see that you have resonated all along to these issues in your choice of music, literature, and films, not to mention in your friendships, love affairs, and family relationships.

Alter Egos

This exercise takes another route to finding what themes, ideas, characters, and situations resonate with you by exploring characters or situations in films, plays, or books that trigger a special response in you.

Dreams and Your Preoccupations

In dreams, the mind expresses itself unguardedly using surreal, symbolic, and often highly emotional imagery. This exercise explains how keeping a log of your dreams might reveal images or associative connections that are fertile for dramatic development.

The Daily Observer

Everything we know about human behavior and how people negotiate conflict (both large and small) comes not from our invention but from what we've observed in our families, at work, among our friends and in the world around us. This exercise asks you to keep a journal of daily observations—moments, interactions, overheard dialogue, and impressions of people you come across—to help sharpen your antennae for the material that is around you every day.

THE ARTISTIC PROCESS

All artists and craftspeople agree that there is an artistic process, and that living it means traveling the most significant and exhilarating journey of your life. At the beginning, you get clues. Clues lead to discoveries. Discoveries lead to movement in your work, and movement leads to new clues. It never stops opening new doors to meaning, and keeps revealing connections to an ever larger whole.

It will happen if you find that special element that fascinates you. It might be expressed through mountaineering, the rescue of animals, something involving water and boats, or love between school friends. You explore it by producing something external to your own thoughts: the piece of expressive work. What begins as a circumscribed personal quest soon leads outward. You might take two opposing parts of your own character during a trying period of your life and make them into two sparring characters, perhaps making imaginative use of two well-known political or historical characters to do so.

This search for the truths underlying your formation and patterns starts feeding itself once you make a commitment to expressing something about it. A piece of work—whether a painting, a short story, or a film script—is both the evidence of movement and the engine of progress during the search for meanings. Your work becomes the trail of your own evolution and a reflection of your times.

Profiling favorite historical personalities, social assumptions, political events, or the temperaments of the people most influential in your life will help shape and sharpen your consciousness. By doing such things well, you can entertain and excite your audience. Whether they know it or not, they, too, are pursuing a quest and hungry to join a journey of exploration like yours.

CHAPTER 2

DEVELOPING YOUR PATH AS A DIRECTOR

Most people using this book will either be film students or the intrepid autodidact who is working independently. In both cases, filmmakers just starting out usually work with modest equipment and slender budgets. Take this as a badge of honor, for original, powerful and even revolutionary films can come from the intelligent use of simple equipment and shoestring production values. The primary reason one can be just as cinematically successful with a low-budget film as any massive studio project is that all the most critical dramatic elements for making a good film can be present with a low price tag. A good screenplay, moving performances, expressive camera work and a sensitive sound design are all achievable on practically any budget.

STARTING OUT

The film industry now accepts that new recruits come from film schools, and that they are more ambitious, educated, versatile, and knowledgeable about the cinema than any generation preceding. The question (for those that can afford it) is not whether to go to film school, but which one might be most suitable.

Film school provides a ready community of like-minded individuals with a common purpose. The compressed time frame for producing work and the near total immersion in all things cinematic allows a novice to acquire much experience very quickly. Film school also furnishes a concrete reason for making films. For most people, film school is the first (and sometimes last) time that someone (professors) will actually ask them to write scripts, make movies and demand to see their work. After film school, these emerging filmmakers must learn to make films entirely on their own initiative and then convince others to see them and want them.

But supposing you don't have the time or resources to go to film school, can you learn with friends, develop a style and a film unit without attending film school? Yes, you can, but it's not easy and it takes enormous personal initiative and self-motivation. You do not have a professor asking for your work, setting deadlines and reviewing your progress. It's entirely up to you to carve out the time and find the energy to make work which no one is asking for. Self-motivation, resourcefulness, and tenacity are the most valuable personal assets a filmmaker must develop to find success.

In the professional world the industry will not beat a path to your door (at least until you are a well-known and profit-making film director); you must prove yourself. A gifted director with no initiative will not find much work. The self-taught and self-motivated emerging filmmaker learns very quickly whether they have these qualities. If they do, then the environment is ripe for them to make a career of it. These days, self-taught filmmakers with digital equipment are in the same position as musicians making use of new recording methods in the 1960s. From them came a revolution in popular music—and profound social changes in consequence. Something similar is under way with the screen.

First, however, we must dismantle a common misperception—that all you really need do is learn about equipment and techniques. Certainly there's plenty to learn, and it's important to understand the tools if we are to express ourselves in cinema with eloquence and authority. But tools are just tools, whereas the cinema's lifeblood, where it all begins and what it all means, comes from human feeling, experience and intelligence. And don't believe those who say you must learn the tools before you can have anything to say. To direct intelligently, you'll need:

- A knowledge and love of film language and film history.
- A strong grasp of what drama is and how to use it.
- A drive to tell stories that comes from passionately held ideas about the human condition.

The first two are easy: every aspiring director loves film and enjoys learning about drama. The last, concerning authorship, is harder. Having something original to say about the business of being alive, and telling stories cinematically—those are what face most people when they look beyond equipment. Yet anyone able to use this book can open doors in their own psyche and find a fully formed artistic identity ready to guide their directing.

SHORT FILMS OR FEATURES?

Serve on a festival jury, and you quickly discover that most films disclose their limitations in the first dozen shots. The screening jury wonders (sometimes testily and aloud) why people don't make films of five minutes instead of a mind-numbing 50. Ask anybody who has judged a film competition and nearly all will agree that most films (especially shorts around 20 to 30 minutes) would have been greatly improved by being cut much shorter. Filmmaker and film professor Alexander Mackendrick (*Sweet Smell of Success*) put it this way, "Student films come in three sizes: too long, much too long and very much too long."[1]

Short films are generally defined as those between two and 30 minutes and features are those with a running time of 80 minutes or more. However, the reality of festival programming and distribution looks at the issue of running time somewhat differently. Films up to 15 minutes are very programmable because they can be screened before a feature film and, even if they are not terribly

---

[1] *On Filmmaking*, Alexander Mackendrick, Paul Cronin ed. (Faber & Faber, 2005).

strong, they do not require a significant time commitment from the audience. Films coming in at 16 to 30 minutes are much more difficult to fit into a program: if they do not connect with an audience, they become a serious waste of time. Films between 30 and 70 minutes are neither short nor features and represent a veritable no-man's land in terms of programming. It's generally thought that these films either contain a small-scale idea in an overly large package or a feature scale story without enough room. These films are nearly impossible to program and distribute. Running times of 70 minutes and above constitute a feature film, and now you're working on a scale which is the most common format for motion picture screening and distribution—however, you're also vying on an entirely different, much more competitive and immensely more expensive playing field.

Short films can easily be as profound, moving and memorable as features and they can show in a small compass your full range of production, authorship, and stylistic skills. What makes them so valuable for the emerging filmmaker is that their economy lies in shooting costs and editing time, not in brainwork. For you must still establish characters, time, place, and dramatic situation, you'll just need to set very tight limits on the story scale. These are tough disciplines to acquire, but short films offer excellent circumstances to sharpen your craft, develop your ability to work with a creative team, and to explore your artistic direction. In terms of learning, short films pay off handsomely. Even better, short films now enjoy an exceptionally wide audience beyond the festival circuit. Shorts (meaning 15 minutes and under) are custom made for web distribution through video sharing services like *YouTube* and *Vimeo*, short film streaming websites like *Triggerstreet* and *indieflix* as well as through numerous online festivals and other web-based self-distribution.

It's a puzzle why film schools don't insist more on brevity. Students and teachers alike, I suppose, are drawn into the medium by feature films, so everyone makes zeppelins when they should make kites. But your work must reach audiences if you are to get recognition; two good short films (under 15 minutes) are ten times more likely to get festival screenings than a single long one of similar quality. And when you start looking for work, successful short films are your best calling cards. Numerous directors have gained recognition for their excellent short films before moving into the world of feature films. It's a very common trajectory. Here are just a few examples:

Abbas Kiarostami made eight short films for the Iranian Institute for Intellectual Development of Children and Young Adults before making his first feature films *Where is the Friend's House* (1987) and *Close-Up* (1990) which gained him international recognition as one of the major directors of his generation. Kiarostami, who is self-taught, often describes his time making short films as his most critical and valuable learning period, one which allowed him to develop his full abilities as a director. To this day, even after nine narrative features, Kiarostami continues to produce short films, both fiction and non-fiction, as a way of exploring and expanding his craft.

Scottish filmmaker Lynne Ramsay's three short films made in 1996 and 1997 all won major festival awards and set her on her way to a career as a feature film director. Although only 15 minutes in length, her powerful short, *Gasman* (1997, Figure 2-1 *top*) fully reveals her unique skill and sensibility as a director and only a year later she went on to direct the internationally celebrated film *Ratcatcher* (1999).

South African filmmaker Neill Blomkamp made a handful of short films, some on assignment for his commercial job, including the *Landfall* series of shorts promoting a new edition of the video

FIGURE 2-1 ————————————————

Directors Lynne Ramsay and Neill Blomkamp followed a common path for emerging filmmakers; first showcasing their talents with short films before jumping into the world of feature films. *Top* Ramsay's *Gasman* and *bottom* Blomkamp's *Alive in JoBurg.*

game *Halo.* Other shorts he made in his spare time, including *Alive in JoBurg* (2006) about extraterrestrials stranded in their own ghetto community in Johannesburg. Having received much attention for his *Halo* short films, the director/producer Peter Jackson (*Lord of the Rings* film cycle) tapped him to direct a feature film based on the video game. Unfortunately, the *Halo* feature project fell apart. However, having seen Blomkamp's abilities through his short films, Jackson decided they should adapt *Alive in JoBurg* into a feature film—the result was *District 9* (2009), Blomkamp's first feature and an Academy Award nominee for Best Picture in 2010 (Figure 2-1 *bottom*).

More than just an inexpensive way to cut your teeth as a director, the short form is in and of itself a viable and expressive art form. Through short films, a filmmaker has ample opportunity to display their artistic ideas and abilities because they place high demand on your control of craft and storytelling essentials. I've included a more detailed discussion on the basic conceptual approach for short films beginning on page 70.

WORKING WITHIN SMALL BUDGETS AND LIMITATIONS

Film schools seem to promise a quick route to the film industry, and many students figure that big-budget studio productions await them right after graduation. The harsh reality is that Hollywood studio feature filmmaking is simply not a viable way to imagine one's formative efforts in filmmaking. In fact, it's probably best for the development of the director-in-training as well as for the art form that entrée into the mainstream industry is difficult. What happens is that truly creative, persistent and resolute filmmakers find another way. In the absence of the money, the stars and the industry machine, a filmmaker must get lean, smart, resourceful, innovative, and creative—and that's when things get really interesting.

Commercial feature film priorities are economically determined. Scriptwriting, though slow, is relatively inexpensive, while actors, equipment, crew and production expenses are high cost and used with military precision. Hollywood skills and intelligence are second to none, but the system requires "bankable" stars and highly developed technicians, all able to produce without delay or experiment what is usable, repeatable, and above all profitable. During a feature shoot, about 50 to 100 specialists carry forward their particular part of the communal task. Each will have begun as an apprentice in a lowly position and will have worked half a lifetime to earn senior levels of responsibility. Many come from film families and imbibed the necessary mind-set with their orange juice.

A director in the high-budget world is under pressure to shoot safe, all-purpose camera coverage that can be sorted out in the cutting room. Unless that director is a heavy hitter, he (only rarely she) must fight narrowly for what is achievable in the schedule. Thus, star vehicle films—too profitable to change from within—are often as packaged and formulaic as supermarket novels. Why? Because a box office success can return millions to its backers in a few weeks. At the very least, the film must not lose money—careers are on the line. Make no mistake, film is a *business*. This is why, in the United States especially, it is called the *film industry*. The phenomenally large financial

FIGURE 2-2

Director Christopher Nolan now works with nine-figure Hollywood budgets but launched his feature film career with *Following*, a movie made for around $6,000. Pictured is The Young Man (Jeremy Theobald) with a penchant for following strangers on the street.

investments require equally large returns and this in turn keeps the industry very conservative in its choice of material and operating procedures. Producers prefer predictable winners over the new or the personal or the exceptional. The caveat in all of this, of course, is that one doesn't even become part this world at all unless a producer has confidence that the director will deliver the product they are after—and that requires ample evidence in the form of previous films. If you doubt my words, read a few issues of the film industry's trade journal *Variety*.

Far more common for the developing or entry-level director is the low-budget (or no-budget) independent route. This is true whether you've set your sights on a career in the mainstream industry or on a life as an independent filmmaker. Either way, you will need to prove yourself with work. Hollywood luminary Christopher Nolan (*The Dark Night*, *Inception*) started his film career with the gritty, black-and-white film *Following* (1998, Figure 2-2), which, at 70 minutes, squeaked in as a feature and was purportedly made for around $6,000. But the concept and directorial execution was so solid that he was making the multi-million dollar *Memento* only two years later.

Since the beginning of cinema, innovative and thoughtful filmmakers have used the best of their creativity to turn the limitations inherent in low-budget filmmaking into creative opportunities. This is why, despite everything, independent filmmaking thrives and remains a vital incubator of new talent. The prolific independent film producer Christine Vachon of Killer Films opens *A Killer Life*,[2] her book on producing, with a string of aphorisms, among them this nugget: "Less

---

[2] *A Killer Life* Christine Vachon and Austin Bunn (Limelight Editions, 2007).

money = more control; more money = less control." What is important to understand is that, while low-budget films indeed struggle with many limitations (money, time, equipment and personnel) you can nonetheless use the freedom of flying below the radar to truly create films that tell the stories you want to tell and in the way that you want to tell them.

This brief and random list of a few American independent film directors who have worked with low budgets should reveal to you how filmmaking outside the studio system is not only viable, but is mostly where cinema's creative innovators emerge from: Martin Scorsese, Darren Aronofsky, Lisa Cholodenko, Jim Jarmusch, Robert Altman, Spike Lee, Mary Harron, David Lynch, Woody Allen, Steven Soderbergh, Miranda July, George Romero, Todd Haynes, Gus van Sant, Rebecca Miller, John Cassavetes, John Sayles, Wes Anderson … and these are only *some* of the Americans! Add to this just a few *current* luminaries of international cinema who work with small budgets: Abbas Kiarostami, Tsai Ming-Liang, Susanne Bier, Aki Kaurismäki, Lars von Trier, Ken Loach, Claire Denis, Werner Herzog, Hou Hsiao-hsien, Ermanno Olmi, Lucrecia Martel, Hirokazu Koreeda… and you can clearly see that profound filmmaking certainly does not require a Hollywood budget or the studio system.

While low-budget (or no-budget) independent filmmaking means keeping the production scale (cast and crew) somewhere between four and 20 people, there are in fact two options for choosing who you'll engage as your creative team. The first is to convince professional crew members and actors to work for minimal or no pay. The term "professional" is a broad one in this field; it simply means that they usually get paid and make a living for what they do, whether it's in the mainstream industry or as an independent professional themselves.

This approach can be tricky and requires special contracts if the professionals are union members, but that is hardly the most difficult challenge. To go this route, a filmmaker needs more than just passion for their film idea. One needs a very strong script, an equally strong vision for realizing the film and the resources to get it done. Because you are asking people to give up time during which they could be making money to support themselves, you must convince them that not only can you pull this off—but the project is something they will feel proud to be a part of.

The benefits of using professionals are obvious. They have the experience to provide useful suggestions and solutions to creative or practical dilemmas; and they work quickly, efficiently, and reliably. They deliver what they say they can deliver and they rarely make stupid blunders. However, seasoned veterans can become a challenge for the director-in-training because many professionals feel that their experience trumps the instincts of the inexperienced director. If the newbie director maintains the courage of their convictions and communicates ideas clearly and convincingly, the professional will respond by being a team player. If the young director becomes insecure and wishy-washy, the professional crew member or actor may take matters into their own hands and call the shots. In this case, the leaderless project loses its rudder and everyone starts making a different film—their own film. Faced with people who have much more experience, a young director must remain an active and confident leader who knows what they want at every moment (even if it feels like a bit of a performance at the beginning).

The other route for the low-budget filmmaker is to use aspiring professionals for their production crew and on-camera talent. Assembling a nonprofessional crew (aspiring to be professionals in their own right) usually involves finding highly motivated and knowledgeable team members who have some training but very little experience. Aspiring professionals can be recent film school graduates or practitioners who have worked in an assistant level post (for example 1st Assistant Camera) and who want to promote themselves to an elevated creative role (say Director of Photography). The benefits to going this way are many. Aspirants tend to be highly energetic, eager to please and determined to give their very best creative energy. Like you, they want a chance to prove that they are as talented as they believe they are. Also, like you, they are at the beginning of their careers and willing to work for little or no pay because they must acquire experience, credits and visible evidence of their abilities—a work reel. However, their lack of experience usually means somewhat slower work, occasional lapses in quality consistency, fewer tricks up their sleeves, and perhaps a few mistakes along the way. The challenge for the director is to shape a non-professional group into a well-knit, efficient and consistently focused creative team.

When it comes to nonprofessional actors, a director can audition those who have had some training (such as acting classes) or seek those who have never even thought about acting but fit the part simply because they are similar to a character. These people are often called non-actors because they aren't really acting—they are being themselves. I talk much more specifically about directing the cast and crew in Parts 6 and 7.

A common configuration for a low-budget director is to work with a combination of professional and nonprofessional cast and crew in the same film. Directors working on low budgets often hire experienced professionals in the principal positions (cinematographer, art director, editor, lead actors, production manager) and then fill out the team with aspiring professionals. On her 2008 film *Frozen River*, Courtney Hunt had a few trained and experienced actors (notably Melissa Leo and Misty Upham in the lead roles) while many of the smaller parts were trained non-professionals and first-time actors. Likewise, her crew included some with feature film experience and others with only a few short films on their resumes (Figure 2-3).

In the final analysis, although the budgets and production scale of a studio picture and an independent film might be vastly different, there is something common at the core of both production methods. Whether you are trying to create cinema art or produce the next blockbuster, you are always trying to reach and connect with an audience. Filmmaking is a very public art form. We do not make movies strictly for ourselves as it's much too expensive. Even working at low budgets you want your film distributed to a public; you want people to see your movie, and in some form you want your investment back so that you can make another film. This means that you must always consider

FIGURE 2-3

While making *Frozen River*, director Courtney Hunt confronted a typical challenge for the low-budget filmmaker, working simultaneously with experienced professionals, emerging talent, and first timers.

the experience of the audience and how your story will connect with them, regardless of your budget, crew size, or production scale.

THE GOOD NEWS

The number of independently financed and produced ("indie") feature-length productions keeps rising, and in the United States the Sundance Film Festival is their Mecca. They outpace studio productions in number and sometimes quality, originality, and awards. Increasingly they use digital video for its lower costs and greater flexibility, which in large part accounts for the proliferation of independent films. Ever since the early Standard Definition (SD) digital productions like Thomas Vinterberg's *The Celebration* (1998, Figure 2-4 *left*), Spike Lee's *Bamboozled* (2000), Lars von Trier's *Dancer in the Dark* (2000) and Rebecca Miller's *Personal Velocity* (2002) found wide international release and critical accolades, countless independent filmmakers have taken advantage of the relatively inexpensive and flexible format. David Lynch personally used a Sony PD150 camcorder and Apple Final Cut Pro digital technology for *Inland Empire* (2006). The difference while shooting was welcome to its cast. "We were shooting constantly", said Laura Dern. "There were no large lights to put up, and we had no need to wait between setups for coverage, because David was holding the camcorder—he would cover an entire scene in 20 minutes or an hour. The luxury was an incredible shorthand on the set. There was never any down-time" (*American Cinematographer,* April 2007).

In more recent years, the proliferation of High Definition video (HD) in all categories of video equipment, from consumer to professional, has greatly improved the image capabilities of low-cost gear and essentially erased SD video from the scene. Today, film and digital video manufacturers still remain in a battle to prove that their format has better light response and resolution—but filmmakers tend not to take sides these days. They simply shoot with what they have access to, benefiting from the consistently improving image of both formats created by this game of one-upsmanship. However, all this frantic R&D has also created a new generation of ultra-high end (and very costly) digital video formats which shoot uncompressed RAW files. Some video formats are now out of the price range of many low-budget filmmakers. With directors like Steven Spielberg and Michael Mann embracing digital technology, you know it's not because they want to shoot on a shoestring.

But there will always be a viable alternative to the elite class of digital gear. The latest entry in low cost, highly accessible production tools for the independent filmmaker is the Digital Single Lens Reflex camera (DSLR). High definition films shot with cameras costing in the hundreds of dollars (rather than the tens of thousands of dollars) are starting to get noticed. Lena Dunham's award-winning *Tiny Furniture* (2010) was shot on a micro budget using Canon's EOS 7D and a production crew numbering around 10 and we're likely to hear about many other projects like this soon (Figure 2-4 *right*).

THE BAD NEWS

Technically proficient as they may be, most independent features are unwatchable and never find a distributor. They suffer from poor writing, poor dramatic structure, poor acting, poor

FIGURE 2-4

From Vinterberg's trailblazing film *The Celebration* (*left*, shot on consumer grade SD video) to Dunham's DSLR feature *Tiny Furniture* (*right*), innovative filmmakers have always found ways to make expressive use of low cost equipment.

directing—and they sink without a trace. Open access to screen tools has produced a karaoke situation where anyone can stand up and sing—but the public won't stay to listen. So you and I squarely face the problems that follow any liberation: How to use the new freedom effectively? How best to develop one's potential? How not to run over the cliff with the herd? These are the questions that have inspired this book, but a little bit of research into those who have negotiated these treacherous and overpopulated waters is also extremely useful. Here are two examples to learn from.

The Duplass brothers' engaging *The Puffy Chair* (2005), well received at Sundance, epitomizes the strengths and handicaps of the best low-budget indie films, and few can have garnered such contradictory reviews (see www.rottentomatoes.com/m/10005108-puffy_chair/). The film is significant because it shows just how much you can achieve with a main cast of three, a $15,000 budget, a miniDV camera, and well-defined dramatic ideas. A road movie combining comedy and bittersweet lovers' scenes, it involves the confused, well-meaning Josh and his girlfriend, Emily, who yearns for commitment from him. Meaning to salvage their waning relationship, they take a long journey to pick up the puffy armchair that Josh has bought on eBay as a present for his dad's birthday. Then things start going wrong: Josh's self-involved filmmaker brother, Rhett, tags along; the deal turns out to be a scam; and the couple's relationship, vastly aggravated by Rhett's presence, runs on the rocks.

The film doesn't quite live up to the high promise of its opening scenes, reshot at the end of shooting. Its techniques are quite basic, but it has strong dramatic ideas, a clear developmental arc, and well-defined character types. It has a neat and funny setup, but the actors play their characters below their own natural intelligence, and every scene is slowed by improvised dialogue. The deficiencies lie in the lack of acting and directing skills at the scene level. There's a brief, candid, and quite inspiring interview with the Duplass brothers about their homegrown career at www.thefilm-lot.com/interviews/INTduplassbros.php. Do read it.

Another successful independent filmmaker to follow is Ramin Bahrani. As of the writing of this book Bahrani has released three low-budget films in quick succession (*Man Push Cart* (2005), *Chop Shop* (2007) and *Goodbye Solo* (2008)), each more assured and artistically accomplished than the last. Yet while Bahrani's directing instincts are clearly improving, his artistic vision, which has always been mature and insightful, has remained remarkably consistent. This is a director who has carefully considered the personal elements that make up a director's artistic voice. His interview with Reverse Shot reveals just how thoughtful and articulate he is about the personal themes and life issues he brings into each project.

Bahrani is also a director who looks for inspiration everywhere, including personal history and experiences, myths and literature, and the work of great film directors. Above all, however, Bahrani closely observes life itself: real people, in real places, going about the business of living. The strength of Bahrani's approach comes from his ability to channel his multiple inspirational sources into only a few basic, closely held, themes from film to film: especially his view of life as a relentless Sisyphean struggle which is made meaningful only by our profound connection to family and bearable by an occasional gesture of human compassion. You can read his interview at http://www.reverseshot.com/article/interview_ramin_bahrani.

THE DIRECTOR AND TECHNOLOGY

Thanks to the digital revolution, the technology of making and distributing motion pictures has transformed far more radically in the last 15 years than in the previous 100 years after the Lumière brothers first presented the 46-second *La Sortie des Usines Lumière à Lyon* in 1895. If history is any indicator, we're in for much more technological transformation at an ever quickening pace. Jumping into filmmaking now, after the first decade of the 21st century, an emerging director is inevitably faced with the critical question: how much of this technology do I actually need to know? In the section above, I briefly discussed the impact of digital shooting formats on independent film production, but how much does a director need to know about the dynamic range and color space of CCD vs. CMOS chips? Do they need to know exactly what a container format is or how to read a D-Log E graph? What about audio formats? Must a director be able to decide which sampling bit rate should be used to record sound? How deep does a director's knowledge about lens construction or lighting and electricity need to be? Should a director know how to use a 3D-LUT table? Just how much technology *must* a director know in order to be an effective motion picture storyteller?

Let's return to the analogy of the film director as a conductor of an orchestra. We said that a conductor doesn't need to be a virtuoso on all the instruments under his or her baton—but they must understand the sounds and tonal range the instruments can produce as well as the traditional and potential creative contribution the instrument makes to the ensemble. The playing itself is done by those who are experts on those particular instruments. Filmmaking is very similar. A director must understand how camera, lenses, microphones and shooting formats contribute to the tone, mood, and aesthetic impact of the film. They must know the narrative contribution, range and potential of their cinematic tools, but the actual "playing" of these tools is done by experts who know how to achieve the particular look, image or sound the film requires.

The director's primary task is to communicate their unified vision to their team of craftspeople who in turn figure out the technology necessary achieve that vision. If the director has chosen their creative team wisely then they can be confident that their collaborators will bring technical expertise to the project—hopefully an expertise that is far more substantial than the director's. However, the more a director knows of the possibilities and limitations of the equipment they have, the more they are able to communicate clearly and not ask for the impossible. So, while a director need not know everything about technology, some baseline knowledge is required to express abstract ideas in precise terms, especially in areas where technical choices have a direct effect on the look, tone and narrative impact of the film.

Here are a few examples: a director should know what various shooting formats look like in order to make an informed decision about whether shooting HD Video or super 16mm film provides the appropriate texture and response to the lighting conditions, but that director may never need to know how to load a film camera or decide if they should shoot REDCODE 28 or REDCODE 36. A director must understand thoroughly the impact that lens selection has on perspective, focus and exposure, because they are critical factors in the visual expression of the story, though a director may never need to check the rear focal flange depth (hopefully they're working with someone who *will* check the back focus). If location sound is crucial, a director must be aware of the physical production requirements a sound mixer needs to gather those sounds, so some knowledge of microphones is helpful, though a director may never need to decide if the sound gets recorded on a hard drive or a flash memory card.

Yes, more technical knowledge is good but a director infatuated with technology can, in fact, be counterproductive. Film crews want to do their jobs and want to do them well, but they do not want a micromanaging director telling them to use a cardioid instead of a super-cardioid, or to use tough opal instead of grid cloth to diffuse the lights. A director must concentrate on camera placement, directing actors and the other tasks that are squarely in the director's domain. Nothing is so dispiriting to an actor than being abandoned by the director in favor of technical camera considerations.

Throughout this book (primarily in Chapter 27) I explore those areas of technology that have an immediate and crucial impact on the creative expression of your story. This is the stuff a director should know and know well. Beyond that, leave the hard tech to the experts—share this responsibility with your creative collaborators. One can certainly conduct an orchestra playing Beethoven's Fifth Symphony, but one cannot play Beethoven's Fifth Symphony all by oneself.

PART 2

THE STORY AND ITS DEVELOPMENT

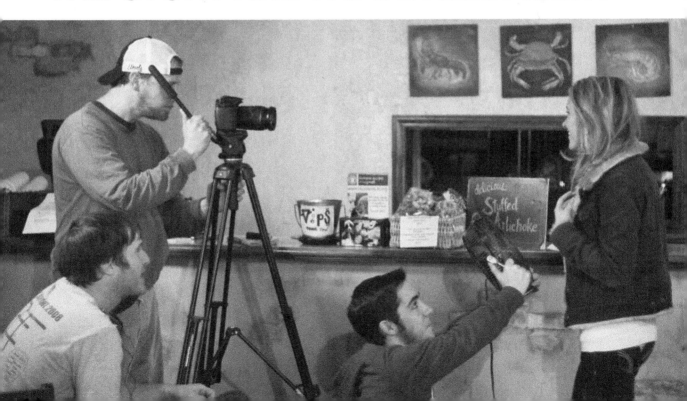

PART 2-1 ——

Director Shanti Thakur consults with DP Benjamin Wolf on the set of *Red Tulips* (2012).

PART 2-2 ——

Student Director Jared Stanton with cast and crew rehearsing a shot for *Mr. Right Thing*.

CHAPTER 3

ESSENTIAL ELEMENTS OF DRAMA

Once you have honestly explored what truly interests you—the people, places, events and cultures that make up your stories—the next stage is to find dramatic material that connects with you and to put that material into a shape that has dramatic tension and can connect with an audience on a narrative, emotional, and thematic level.

Although there are many writer/directors in the world, the director's role doesn't necessarily involve screenwriting. A director must however have a solid understanding of the basic elements of a dramatic story to do their job well—that is, to recognize a strong screenplay and explore its full potential, to stage scenes for the camera effectively, to discuss the nuances of character and narrative line with actors and crew, and in short to bring that story to life on the screen. Understanding these essential dramatic principles is critical for both the writer and director's role—and indeed for actors, editors, cinematographers and production designers as well—because they form the foundations of cinematic storytelling across the board.

DUALITY AND CONFLICT

Have you received this kind of family newsletter during the holiday season?

The Robinson News for the Year:
    Betty has completely redecorated the dining room (with an avocado theme!) after successfully completing her interior decorator course at Mallory School of the Arts. David received his promotion to area manager, but now has a longer drive to work. Terry spent the summer camping and canoeing, and thoroughly enjoyed being a camp counselor. He also learned he was accepted into Hillshire University's creative writing program. In spite of what the doctor said, Joanne has successfully adapted to contact lenses.

What makes this so tedious? Surely it's because Robinson life is presented as a series of happy, logical steps with nothing candid, spontaneous, challenging or disturbing. It's not untrue—it's just a selection method that renders the family lifeless, especially if you happen to know that David's drinking is getting worse, that Betty strongly disapproves of Terry's choice of major, and that no one seems to know why poor Joanne is steadily losing her eyesight. Family life is like a pond—calm on the surface, but containing all the forces of warring nature below the surface. So, too, is an interesting individual. This inner contradiction is our *duality*, and every active individual embodies contradictions and conflicts. By avoiding all *conflict*, the newsletter suppresses the dissent, doubt, struggle, and eccentricity that give every family dramatic tension.

Take David O. Russell's 2010 film *The Fighter* as an example. There is a reason that the title is not *The Boxer*. Although "Irish" Micky Ward's goal is to win the world championship, the film is not really about his struggles in the boxing ring, but more about the way he struggles with the warring factions among the people he loves: his brother Dicky, his mother, his father, and his new girlfriend Charlene. It's interesting how all these people seem to want the same thing—that Micky be successful in his quest for the championship—and yet there is conflict everywhere because each wants him to achieve his goal on their terms. The conflict in this film comes from the complicated and contradictory nature of Micky's family: everyone is fighting to control him, and he is fighting to gain a little control over his own life. Even though everyone "only wants what's best" for Micky, all these good intentions pose a crushing burden on the emotionally generous and vulnerable young man and threaten to knock him out of the ring. Micky's boxing career is simply the arena in which the dysfunction of his specific situation plays out. In the end, the fact that Micky is able to heal his broken family while earning some self-determination over his own life is his ultimate triumph (Figure 3-1).

DEFINING CONFLICT

Conflict *is essential to drama*, but can be defined in different ways and take many different forms. Conflict can come from external factors, from within a character, or arise from a combination of forces.

- Person versus person (external conflict)
- Person versus environment or social institution (external conflict)
- Person versus a task they are compelled to undertake (internal and external conflict)
- Person versus themselves, as in someone with conflicting traits or beliefs (internal conflict).

In all of these cases conflict can additionally be expressed in stark "right vs. wrong" moral polarities or with more relative and complexly drawn human dimensions.

Stories devised on mythic, heroic or moralistic models usually frame conflict with the clear dichotomy of good versus evil. Ridley Scott's *Gladiator* (2000), George Lucas' *Star Wars* (1977), the *Harry Potter* films, and most superhero action pictures maintain a very clear moral compass that pits good guys against bad guys. Even many films dealing with more realistic material, such as Steven Soderbergh's *Erin Brockovich* (2000), draw distinct lines between those who fight for good against those who embody evil. *Erin Brockovich* and *Gladiator* may seem at first glance to be very different films, but in terms of the clear moral struggles at the core of their conflicts they have very much in common. Both films involve a righteous protagonist who is at a serious disadvantage struggling to defeat a powerful and evil entity on behalf of the people. In *Gladiator*,

FIGURE 3-1

"Irish" Micky Ward's (Mark Wahlberg) boxing opponents are nothing compared to the battles his family puts him through.

Maximus struggles to unseat the ruthless Emperor Commodus and return Rome to the people and their representatives. Maximus must accomplish this noble feat from the impossible position of a hunted former general who is now a slave. Similarly, Erin Brockovich, a paralegal with absolutely no training in the law, is compelled to battle the rich and powerful PG&E, an industrial energy giant she believes is poisoning the groundwater and causing local residents to contract cancer. In both films, against all odds, good defeats evil and the people are saved (Figure 3-2).

Conflicts come fairly easily when you create a world of clear moral polarities, however, as you move away from mythic or heroic dramas, and develop stories about the human struggles of characters who could be your neighbors, the blunt "right vs. wrong" distinction becomes unsupportable. When you develop conflicts that reflect the way real people function, with all their psychological complexities, you need to consider more relativistic ideas about right and wrong. This is

FIGURE 3-2

As energetic, motivated heroes determined to fight for justice, *Erin Brockovich*'s titular character (*top,* Julia Roberts) and *Gladiator*'s Maximus (*bottom,* Russell Crowe) share many of the same dramatic qualities.

where conflict gets really interesting: good people can do misguided or even bad things, and bad people can have sympathetic motives or soft spots. People can undermine themselves and their noble goals or they can display motives and actions that are ambiguous, inconsistent or paradoxical. Conflicts can even involve a struggle between opposing forces in which each side has virtuous objectives and good intentions, which makes it "right vs. right"—which is complex and challenging.

As we've already discussed, the conflicts in *The Fighter* are very human and complex. Nobody is completely bad or completely good in relation to Micky's goal because everyone around Micky wants to help him become a successful fighter. But his family is bitterly divided over who should train him (father and girlfriend in one corner; and mom and Dicky in the other) and how this should be done. While we clearly see how they trap Micky in this tug of war for his future, we also understand the motivations and failings on all sides. We even sympathize with Micky's crackhead brother Dicky who desperately wants to help, but consistently messes up because his ego and addiction come first. No one in *The Fighter* is purely good or totally evil. Everyone has some good intentions and many human flaws and yet the conflicts are serious—even potentially disastrous. This makes the conflicts in *The Fighter* multidimensional and allows the film to truly connect with an audience.

ELEMENTS OF CONFLICT AND ACTION

Conflict can be large (a soldier must obey orders, but finds his conscience forbidding it) or something minor (a toddler struggles to get her little wooden chair upright). It can have strict moral polarities (*Gladiator*) or be complexly devised (*The Fighter*). But in all cases conflict must frame some important problem that must be solved and must do so in specific terms. Moral complexity and the idiosyncrasies of human psychology are not excuses for struggles to be indistinct. The writer, director, or actors cannot afford to be vague or approximate in the articulation of conflict. As the creator of drama you must find the paradigm to its central conflicts, so you will need to dig deep to achieve an understanding of your characters and their situations so you can realize their goals and motivations as precisely as possible. Until you can state confidently and specifically the nature of the conflict that your film (and even individual scenes) revolves around, you have not mastered it and will lack control over all the other dramatic elements in your film.

Let's look closer at those elements that constitute cinematic conflict. In his book *On Directing*, director and writer David Mamet breaks down a basic dramatic story this way: "[the story] consists of the assiduous application of several basic questions: What does the hero want? What hinders him from getting it? And what will happen if he does not get it?" These three story elements: *the objectives*, *the obstacles* and *the stakes* must be fully developed and in highly specific terms.

THE OBJECTIVES AND THROUGHLINES

Film characters, like human beings, only become fully alive when they have something meaningful to push against. To identify a character's conflict, we must first ask about their **objectives**: What is this character trying to get, do, or accomplish? What do they need or want? Directors regularly work with two kinds of objectives: **plot objectives** (external) and **life objectives** (internal), and there is an intimate relationship between these two.

Let's say our story has a young man whose life objective is to win the respect of his father. That's great, and something with which any audience can identify. But how would an actor perform "to win respect from my father" for the camera? His personal objective is not yet something we can film—it's entirely too internal and vague. We must develop that internal need further, in a specific and dramatic way, into something we can build a story around and photograph.

So the next question is, what *specifically* does this *particular* character need to do or accomplish in order to earn his father's respect? In other words, how can this emotional imperative be turned into visible and dramatic action? It could be to get a job, win an election, save the farm, or kill a bear. Any one of these four choices will define a different character and yield a very different film, but in all these cases the internal (often subconscious) need is revealed by the specific external task. Always remember, *objectives must be realized in specific terms*. If objectives are vague, then your conflicts will be vague and your character will be vague so that the purpose of your story remains indistinct.

An objective which informs a character's actions throughout the entire story (usually the internal/life need type of objective) is often called the character's **through-line** or **super-objective**.[1] A character's through-line acts as the emotional engine for nearly every scene and rarely changes over the course of a film. The through-line for our young man, to win his father's respect, will remain until the very end and informs every choice the young man makes. However, when we translate that internal through-line into plot action we often break it down into smaller, component goals which play out at the scene level. The through-line for our young man can be broken down into smaller plot objectives like: get a job, save the farm, take care of his brother's needs, and so on. Then, each of these plot objectives can also be further broken down into even smaller tasks along the way. Getting the job can involve: securing a job interview, getting the proper clothes for the interview, preparing for the interview, getting to the interview on time, doing well in the interview, and so on.

A director must be able to recognize and name the through-line of every character's journey in order to fully comprehend why they do what they do, and what actions will reflect their inner needs. For this reason, directors and actors spend a great deal of energy seeking the broader motivation behind a character's goals, choices, and actions.

THE STAKES

The stakes are another important aspect of the character's objective. What are the consequences if the character fails to achieve their objective? What specifically is at stake? If the objective is not a crucial one and only a mild need, then the character has little reason to struggle and all motivation and sense of purpose drains out of your film. If, on the other hand, the young man's family will lose the farm, his baby brother will not get his eye operation, and his father will disown him unless he starts working, then the young man is motivated to get a job, and if that's impossible, will perhaps resort to illegal means to get the money his family needs.

Characters become motivated when the objectives are imperative and the stakes are high. Throughout a film's development, directors and actors discuss in great depth the objectives and motivations for every character in the film as they search to "raise the stakes."

---

[1] Occasionally you'll also see the through-line called a character's "spine," as in Judith Weston's *Directing Actors* (Michael Wiese Productions, 1999).

THE OBSTACLES

Each time we settle on a specific and imperative objective, we then need to devise ways to make it difficult for our main character to achieve it. Whenever we give characters what they want quickly and easily, we have no *dramatic tension* and no film. If in his first attempt, the young man is given a great job at the local bank with benefits and bonuses, then the problem is solved, the movie is over, and we have no character and no story. So we devise **obstacles**, both internal and external, that prevent our characters from succeeding so that they must struggle to *earn their goals*. Perhaps we place our young man in a fading industrial town where there simply is no substantial work. We add that he never finished high school so that decent paying jobs are essentially closed to him. We make the folks in the town hold much animosity toward his father for some bad business in the past—so that no one is inclined to help this family out. By doing this, we are "raising the stakes."

Perhaps the only job he can find is at minimum wage in the local convenience mart, which disappoints his father more. Perhaps he's then offered an opportunity to make real money, but it's with a crew that robs homes and steals cars. Will he do it? What if that crew decides to rob the convenience mart and he's blamed for it? The possibilities are endless. By devising the right obstacles we could even create a film in which the son's best efforts, instead of keeping his family from ruin, lead to him getting arrested and destroying the family.

The important principle is that by obstructing a character's objectives you force them to do something about it, to make decisions, to take action. This in fact builds and reveals your character, for *it is through their actions that characters fundamentally show who they are*. If, faced with conflict, they choose to do nothing, or retreat, that, too, reveals who they are. We choose obstacles carefully because each one defines which aspect of our character will be revealed.

ACTION AND CHARACTER

You define the elements of your drama's conflict in order to understand with equal precision the decisions and actions your characters must take. Here "actions" do not mean mere physical activity, for they include the choices and decisions characters make, the things they say, and everything they do to change their predicament. Whether the action is powerful or subtle, what a character chooses to do (or *not* do) in pursuing their objectives reveals in unambiguous ways who that character is and how badly they need to achieve their goals.

The **strategies** characters employ reveal their specific human traits, and this is where a drama puts flesh on the bones of its storyline. If the actions of our young man trace a struggle to earn the necessary money through legal means and hard work, though they may seem at first insufficient to the goal, we get a distinct impression of him. If he eventually turns to working for the local crystal meth lab and robs the convenience store where he was once offered a job, then we've created a very different character. By choosing particular objectives and obstacles we can devise specific actions and strategies that reveal a specific, living, breathing character.

Returning to *The Fighter* and the fact that Micky's goal is to win the World Welterweight Boxing Championship: the stakes are already high and winning will bring pride to his family and his hometown. But it's still just a boxing title (external goal). However, winning would also mean that Micky could step out from the shadow of his elder brother and become his own man (internal need). With his family imploding, and the need to earn his future wife's respect by becoming

FIGURE 3-3

Having stepped out of his brother's shadow and bridged the deep divisions in his family, Micky's world championship victory means much more than a title belt.

master of his own destiny, the personal stakes are nothing less than Micky's identity and future. But an array of complications both external and internal keeps him from winning the title. The principal problem is that his family is bitterly divided over who will train him. Micky needs everyone united and behind him if he is to win, but they refuse to reconcile with one another. Added to this is that only one person has actual championship experience, and Dicky is a narcissistic junkie who cannot pull it together to help his brother. To make matters worse, one of Micky's biggest obstacles is his internal nature—he's a good boy with shaky confidence. Micky doesn't want to hurt or alienate anyone, so he's reluctant to make demands or call his own shots.

All of these complications push at Micky while he acts to achieve three seemingly mutually exclusive goals: keep his family together, impress his girlfriend, and make progress toward a title bout. When these conflicts become too much, he also struggles with an impulse to just give up on the whole thing.

With the stakes so high and the obstacles nearly insurmountable, Micky's triumph in the end is not only earned, but momentous on many levels (Figure 3-3).

To continue the exploration into the construction of dramatic characters, see "Character Development," in Chapter 8.

FROM STORY TO DRAMATIC NARRATIVE

Once upon a time there lived in Berlin, Germany, a man called Albinus. He was rich, respectable, happy; one day he abandoned his wife for the sake of a youthful mistress; he loved; was not loved; and his life ended in disaster.

This is the whole of the story and we might have left it at that had there not been profit and pleasure in the telling; and although there is plenty of space on a gravestone to contain, bound in moss, the abridged version of a man's life, detail is always welcome.

This passage opens Vladimir Nabokov's 1938 novel *Laughter in the Dark*[2] (which was adapted into a film by Tony Richardson in 1969). The very first sentence of the novel neatly summarizes the totality of the story and contains all the essential elements we've just discussed. It has a central character (the rich and respectable Albinus), who has a goal (to leave his family for the sake of his mistress, presumably to build a new life with her), and the story has conflict (he loved, but was not loved in return). The conclusion to Albinus' struggles is that his life ends in disaster (which certainly points to a theme).

So, why does Nabokov, without announcing "spoiler alert," give away his entire story in the first sentence of this novel? The second sentence explains: more important than the basic understanding of the story (what happened) is *how* we tell that story and the specific details that make up the story. When Nabokov speaks of "profit and pleasure in the telling" he's saying that the way we tell a story is what allows an audience to get something out of it (insight or understanding) and to enjoy the ride (pleasure and entertainment). Implicit here is the relationship between the storyteller and the audience. A storyteller does not simply recount a story for its own sake—rather he or she is crafting a **narrative** for the pleasure and profit of an audience. By the way, the difference between story and **plot** is that **story** constitutes the overall, chronological understanding of what happened while plot is the way in which that story unfolds. Which events you choose to portray and in what order you reveal them makes a big difference to the work's effectiveness (see Chapter 5).

For filmmakers, it's important to understand that a story in its raw form, even a good one, does not necessarily constitute compelling drama, which is the *art of shaping a story into a form that maximizes its audience's involvement and emotional engagement.* There are five broad considerations for shaping a raw story into a dramatic narrative:

1. **Specificity.** Expressing characters, objectives, conflict, and actions with vivid and revealing specificity makes them clear and memorable.

2. **Emphasis.** The character, environmental, and narrative details we choose to include, to emphasize and develop help the viewer understand precisely what the film is ultimately about.

3. **Plot.** By carefully selecting the events that define the narrative, and by arranging them in a particular order, we can maximize the audience's engagement with the story.

4. **Perspective.** Determining from whose point of view the film is mainly told strongly affects the audience's emotional engagement with the story (see Chapter 9).

5. **Tone.** The rules of the fictional universe in which we place this story establish the credibility of the story's world and its emotional framework (see Chapter 11).

---

[2] Vladimir Nabokov, *Laughter in the Dark* (New Directions Publishing: New York, 2006. First published 1938).

CHAPTER 4

SHAPING THE STORY INTO DRAMA

SHAPING THE STORY INTO DRAMA

Even small interactions with little narrative development involve dramatic content, pressure and release. This is true for two schoolgirls waiting moodily for a third to arrive, a man trying to roll a rock aside on a mountain track, or an assassin setting out to kill a president. Dramatic terminology may sound extreme and only useful for "big" subjects, but it represents a set of analytical tools that will unlock the power in everything you will ever film. Your ability to analyze, shape, and sharpen dramatic content will determine your insight into scripts, and decide your competency at directing actors.

THE BEAT

Critical to understanding the overall human dynamic of drama are small component units called **dramatic beats**. The word "beat" applied to film is widely misunderstood, for it has nothing to do with rhythm, nor is it a unit of pause or rest, as screenplay usage often suggests. A **beat** is in fact *a moment in drama producing an irreversible change of awareness in one or more characters*. It starts from a character attempting to get, do, or accomplish something. For example,

> Phil is in the last pages of a gripping novel when the phone rings from another room. Irritated, he gets up, only to find the connecting door stuck. He yanks hard but the doorknob comes away in his hand. Realizing the door is inoperable, he goes another way.

Let's convert this ten-second action into dramatic terminology:

1. Phil's **goal** or **objective** is to see how his novel ends.
2. His **situation** is that a ringing phone demands his attention. His **conflict** is between the pleasure of reading, and answering the phone. His decision and new short-term **goal** is to answer it.
3. The jammed door becomes the **obstacle** which he tries vainly to overcome.

4. A **complication** is that the doorknob breaks off, and Phil realizes that his way is blocked. This is the **beat**, and **crisis,** to his situation.

5. He **adapts** to this new obstacle by setting off through another doorway.

We can regard the whole action, from the phone ringing to Phil seeking a new solution, as a **dramatic unit**. The pivotal comedic moment when our accident-prone hero stares disbelievingly at the doorknob in his hand and realizes that he must get to the phone some other way is the *beat*, the pivotal moment of new awareness leading to a new strategy.

Think of beats therefore as "A-ha" moments, as in: "A-ha, he already knows"; "A-ha, she isn't buying my alibi"; "A-ha, I went too far and hurt him with that comment." In Phil's case it's, "A-ha, now I can't get through this door."

A dramatic unit always contains at least one beat, which is its **crisis point**. But a unit may contain several beats along the way towards the unit's crisis (as you will see below).

Once film students grasp what dramatic beats and dramatic units really are, their writing, directing and editing take a quantum leap in clarity and purpose. Of course, look for beats and dramatic units as you analyze a screenplay, but you can practice all the time by looking analytically at the life around you. For actors and for directors, the ability to see dramatic action as it takes place in the real world is their preeminent skill (see *The Daily Observer* exercise on p. 16).

Here is a true story. Not long ago, I took the subway to go shopping. I entered the opened doors with two other riders and the three of us sat fairly close to each other. At the very same moment, all of us noticed a $10 bill on the floor between the feet of a man reading a newspaper (*Beat #1: A-ha, there's money on the floor*) (*set up*). My fantasy *objective* was clear: to snatch up that $10 bill. But a quick round of glances revealed that all three of us saw it and knew the others saw it as well (*Beat #2: A-ha, I'm not alone*) (*conflict/competition*). As the train continued on its way, we kept looking at each other and back at the $10 bill and at the man reading the newspaper who was oblivious. The air around us vibrated with our common thoughts: Does it belong to the newspaper reader? Will he notice if I pick it up? Should I ask if he dropped it? (Nah, he'll just say "yes" whether it's his or not). If I grab it without asking, what will the others think of me? And what if the newspaper guy confronts me by saying it's his? Is $10 worth the hassle ($5 no, $50 yes, but $10?)? And if I don't do it right now, will one of the others grab it first? (*rising tension*). Just as one of us was about to pounce, the newspaper man shifted in his seat and unconsciously placed a foot on top of the $10 bill (*Beat #3: A-ha, I'll never get it now*) (*crisis point*). Seeing the impossibility of the situation, I simply leaned over to the newspaper guy and said, "Excuse me, I think you dropped something." He grabbed the money and thanked me and got back to his reading (*result/resolution*). I turned to my two competitors and we all smiled and shook our heads at our missed fortune (*falling tension*).

DRAMATIC UNITS

The standard elements for a dramatic unit are:

*   The **set up** initiates an issue in which we meet a central character who forms an **objective** and this provokes action. Often there is an **inciting moment** or **catalyst** to kick off the scene's action.

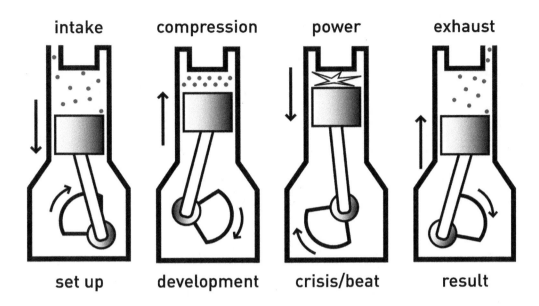

FIGURE 4-1

The internal combustion engine, John Howard Lawson's handy metaphor for a dramatic unit.

- The **development** follows the efforts of the character as he or she struggles against *obstacles* and *complications*. This, known as **rising action**, is when tension increases both for the character and the watching audience during the character's struggle.
- At the **crisis point** is the success or failure of the objective, a point where the central character realizes the change irreversibly.
- The outcome, called the **result** or **resolution,** is often accompanied by a feeling of *released tension*, and leads to new circumstances. These become the setup for the next dramatic unit.

John Howard Lawson, in his *Theory and Technique of Playwriting* (Hill & Wang: New York, 1960), has usefully likened the dramatic unit's action to the cycles of an internal combustion engine[1] (Figure 4-1).

1. The intake stage is where the engine's piston draws in explosive gases (set up: a "cycle" begins by bringing together the combustible elements of character, objective, and obstacle).
2. The compression stage builds pressure inside the cylinder (development: builds tension as characters take action and struggle against opposing forces to achieve goals).
3. At maximum cylinder pressure the ignition spark causes explosion (crisis point: the moment which sparks an irreversible change in the nature or understanding of the conflict).

---

[1] For an animation of this, go to http://auto.howstuffworks.com/engine.htm.

4. The piston is forced downward, producing power and movement, and initiating a new cycle of intake, compression, and explosion (result: energy, forward momentum, and a new situation which contributes to the set up of the next dramatic unit. Dramatic tension eases as the new combustible material for the next cycle is drawn together).

The analogy between the dramatic unit and the internal combustion engine works well because its cycles deliver power, create forward movement, and are interconnected. Developing a successful progression of dramatic units is at the core of attaining structural unity in your story. This principle assures that viewers:

1. See dramatic events connecting organically with one another
2. Feel scenes generating momentum and dramatic tension
3. Understand the motivation behind characters' feelings, decisions and actions
4. Become involved through the questions, anticipations, hopes, and revelations this approach develops in the spectator's mind.

Though the words "dramatic analysis" sound extreme (tension, conflict, crisis point, and so on) dramatic units operate over a wide expressive range, from moments of very subtle revelation all the way to events of major narrative impact.

Very often, a dramatic unit will play out within a single scene, but keep in mind that a dramatic unit can span a number of scenes—one scene being the set up, another the development, and a third being the crisis point and resolution.

DRAMATIC UNIT AND BEAT ANALYSIS

Let's look at these dramatic principles in action by dissecting the opening of the film *The King's Speech* (directed by Tom Hooper, 2010 from the screenplay written by David Seidler).[2] The first 12 minutes include five distinct, yet carefully linked dramatic beats. The year is 1925 and during the opening scene (and first dramatic unit) these script pages start with a BBC radio newsreader establishing that King George V has asked his son the Duke of York to give the closing speech at the Empire Exhibition at Wembley Stadium. It will have a live audience of over 100,000 and a radio audience of millions. The enormous scale of this public address begins the set up of the first dramatic unit which continues…

```
INT. GREEN ROOM - DAY

Nervous eyes flick towards a tunnel leading to a bright light.

CLOSE ON - BERTIE - the Duke of York, second son of the King; his handsome,
sensitive, features look terrified.

                    BBC NEWS READER (V.O.)
          The Opening Ceremony was the first occasion his
          Majesty the King addressed his subjects on the
          wireless. The close of the first Season was the
          initial time His Royal Highness the Prince of
```

---

[2] *The King's Speech* by David Seidler. Script excerpt courtesy of *The Shooting Script* (Newmarket Press, 2011).

Wales had broadcast. And today His Royal
Highness the Duke of York will give his
inaugural broadcast to the Nation and the World.

WIDEN TO REVEAL his young wife, truly an English rose.

               ELIZABETH
Time to go.

He stares straight ahead, frozen. She gives him a loving peck on the cheek,
quickly rubbing off a fleck of lipstick.

               BBC NEWS READER (V.O.)
Leading us in prayer will be the Right
Honourable and Most Reverend Archbishop of
York, Primate of all England and
Metropolitan. Now we go live to Wembley
Stadium, where His Royal Highness the Duke
of York will read his message from the King.

COSMO LANG - comes up to Bertie. Tries to be helpful but makes him more nervous.

               COSMO LANG
I am sure you will be splendid.
Just take your time.

The last bars of "God Save The King" echo down the corridor.

ROBERT WOOD, the Chief BBC Engineer on Location whispers:

               WOOD
Let the microphone do the work, sir.

Wood checks his watch.

               WOOD (CONT'D)
Thirty seconds, sir.

Bertie braces his shoulders manfully, but without an ounce of confidence, closes his
eyes, nods, opens them, and reluctantly goes through the tunnel towards the light,
like a prize-fighter entering the arena, to be greeted by the roar of the crowd.

EXT. ROYAL PODIUM - DAY

HAND-HELD CAMERA, BERTIE'S POV: far ahead, at a seemingly impossible distance, is
the huge intimidating microphone, the only thing between the terrified observer and
100,000 people.

Silence falls over the stadium.

Overhead, thick roiling clouds.

BERTIE approaches… like a death march.

Bertie's eyes widen in terror as he reaches the microphone. The red transmission
light blinks four times then glows solid red. Bertie is live.

```
INT. CONTROL ROOM, BBC BROADCASTING HOUSE - DAY

Technicians stare at dials and listen to the hiss of silence.

The Reader and Floor Manager glance at each other nervously.


EXT. SPECTATOR STAND, EMPIRE STADIUM - DAY

In the tense silence PAN THROUGH some of the crowd waiting with
growing discomfort. In particular we notice a father and son
watching intently.


EXT. ROYAL PODIUM - DAY

Bertie is frozen at the microphone. His neck and jaw muscles contract and quiver.

                        BERTIE
          I have received from his Majesty the K-K-K

[For ease of reading, Bertie's stammer will not be indicated from this point in the
script.]

The stammer careens back at him, amplified and distorted by the stadium PA system.

CU huge metal speakers.

CU soldiers at rigid attention.

CU Wood, he shuts his eyes.

CU Cosmo Lang, expressionless.

CU Elizabeth, dying.

Bertie gulps for air like a beached fish and attempts to continue:

                        BERTIE (CONT'D)
          …the King, the following gracious message…

He can't get the word out. SPLAT…the first drops of rain begin to fall.
```

Scene 1—Dramatic Unit 1

The set up for this first dramatic unit draws together combustible material: the **objective** for our central character, the Duke of York (Bertie), seems simple: he must give a speech. But the scene lines up a host of **obstacles**: the significance of the event, the "named" witnesses (his wife Elizabeth, the Archbishop Cosmo Gordon Lang, Wood, etc.), the vast audience (live and broadcast), the text of the speech and of course, the microphone itself.

The **tension** of the situation is increased during the development primarily through Bertie's nervousness, the crushing weight of expectations on him, and the unavoidable nature of his task. Time is closing in on him (from minutes to seconds to three blinks of a red light), and people urge him forward as he moves toward the crowd and the microphone. There is no backing out. Even

In the first dramatic unit of *The King's Speech*, the Duke of York (Colin Firth) must face his greatest fear, public speaking. His failure to give the Empire Exhibition speech prompts the next dramatic unit.

sincere reassurances seem to make him more, rather than less, nervous.

This tense build-up begs two critical questions. The first is character-based: why is Bertie so nervous about giving a speech? The second is dramatic: will he pull it off (Figure 4-2)?

The **crisis point** (and **dramatic beat**) comes when the mike finally goes "live" and Bertie must give his speech. Both questions are answered at this moment: we learn that Bertie has a serious vocal stammer (primary complication) and, no, he does not pull it off. In fact, he publicly humiliates himself. From this we realize that here is a royal personage who must address the public, yet cannot speak in public. The **result** of this scene and situation leads to the next dramatic unit—something must be done about Bertie's stammer.

Now let's look at subsequent dramatic units as they unfold in the film.

Scene 2—Dramatic Unit 2

The **set up** for the next dramatic unit includes Bertie's objective to overcome his stammer (the **result** or **resolution** from the previous scene) and his actions to achieve that goal; Bertie is enduring a traditional speech therapy session which includes cigarettes, more than half a dozen marbles "inserted into his mouth," and reading more text. The struggle can be characterized as, "stammer versus humiliating therapy," with the added complication of Bertie's quick temper, which culminates in the **dramatic beat**: Bertie nearly swallows the marbles, kicks the therapist out and vows to give up therapy altogether (**crisis point**). This leads Bertie to conclude that therapy doesn't work and he's stuck with his stammer (**dramatic beat**).

The **result** of Bertie's giving up hope leads directly to the next dramatic cycle in which his wife Elizabeth seeks out Lionel Logue, a highly recommended, eccentric speech therapist with unorthodox methods. Her motivation is to relieve her husband from his public humiliation.

Scene 3 and Scene 4: Dramatic Unit 3

The next dramatic unit includes two scenes (elevator and Logue's office) and four dramatic beats in which Elizabeth's overarching objective remains the same: to secure Mr. Logue's therapeutic services. The principal obstacle also remains essentially the same—she must overcome the exalted status and insulated perspective that she and her husband have as members of the royal family.

The initial scene (**set up** scene) which introduces this idea is quite elegant. Lionel's office is in the basement, Elizabeth must negotiate the elevator herself (no servants here), and at first she doesn't know how to use the thing (the conflict is "royalty versus elevator"). The **1st beat** occurs when she finally figures it out and makes it to the basement. This **result** leads to the next **obstacle** when she encounters Lionel but it also establishes new **dramatic tension**—a member of the royal family in the land of the commoners is like a fish out of water. The questions start to emerge. Can she negotiate this situation? Can she get what she wants?

In the next **scene (development)** Elizabeth speaks with Lionel in his office and tries to secure an appointment with him while hiding behind the pseudonym "Mrs. Johnson," adopted to keep him unaware of the identity of his patient-to-be. Though her false identity is unsustainable, her objective is complicated by several factors; her husband isn't there (doesn't even know she's there); and Logue's lack of the deference to which she is accustomed appalls her, as does his insistence that she play by his house rules. Lionel requires that her husband "pop by" for a personal appraisal while "Mrs. Johnson" insists that Lionel must go to her husband. The **2nd beat** pivots on Lionel refusing by saying, "My game, my turf, my rules." She realizes that the "Mrs. Johnson" strategy isn't working, which leads to the next strategy in which she lays her cards on the table (**rising tension**).

Elizabeth announces to Lionel that her husband is the Duke of York. Surely this strategy will work, she thinks. Indeed, Lionel now adopts a more deferential and formal demeanor toward the Duchess, but the new strategy does not work entirely. Lionel is an Australian and despite the royal revelation asserts that his method relies on total equality. He insists that the treatment must take place on his turf. Elizabeth realizes that there is no way around his house rules (**3rd beat** and **crisis point**). For a moment it looks as though she has failed in her objective to secure a new speech therapist for Bertie. But realizing that Lionel is her last hope (**4th beat**) Elizabeth capitulates to his rules and hires him (**resolution**). The objective is finally won and the dramatic question is answered: yes, she secures Lionel's services, but on his terms, not hers. This **result**, in turn, generates the next dramatic situation where she must overcome more obstacles to get her husband Bertie into the basement of a commoner's consultation room for more speech therapy… and so on.

One quick note—through Elizabeth, this dramatic unit (four beats) prepares us for (*foreshadows*) one of the most significant conflicts between Bertie and Lionel: the clash between royal codes of conduct versus a commoner's therapeutic method. This conflict develops into so great a problem that it threatens to derail the whole undertaking.

THE DRAMATIC ARC

The elements within each dramatic unit typically follow a pattern called a **dramatic arc** that reflects the shifting levels of intensity over time. The tension in a dramatic unit generally increases until reaching its apex at the crisis point, where there is often a release of tension as the next dramatic unit is set up. Looking at the first two dramatic units of *The King's Speech* we can clearly see the principle of the dramatic arc (Figure 4-3).

a) *Set-up:* The scale and importance of the Wembley event is established with Bertie's objective to make a speech. The

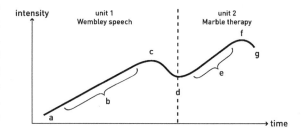

FIGURE 4-3

Dramatic arcs in *The King's Speech*, dramatic units 1 and 2.

complicating factors (the audience, the "witnesses," the text, and the microphone) are all brought into the mix.

b) *Development*: Bertie's nervousness increases as he gets nearer to air time and nearer to the microphone. Well-intentioned reassurance, facing the live audience, and standing before the microphone only make him more nervous and create more tension.

c) *Crisis point*: The red light indicates the mike is now "live." Bertie cannot deliver the speech without stammering. He fails in his task and is publicly humiliated.

d) *Result*: Bertie must do something about his problem. *Set-up:* Bertie works on his stammer with a speech therapist.

e) *Development*: Bertie struggles against a mouthful of marbles, reading aloud and trying to fulfill the demands of a traditional speech therapist.

f) *Crisis point*: Bertie nearly swallows the marbles, realizes it's not working and tosses the therapist out.

g) *Result*: Bertie gives up on speech therapy.

Although dramatic units often end with an apparent release in dramatic tension, the overall trend over time is a wave form, up and down, mounting toward ever greater tension and higher stakes. Note how Bertie's giving up on a "cure" represents a graver situation than the failure at Wembley because, in fact, he is further from his goal to speak publicly without a stammer. Each dramatic unit, and each beat within it, must steadily ramp up the consequences, struggles, tension and suspense if they are to progress into new dramatic territory, or our story will remain flat and stationary.

LEVELS OF ACTION

Drama is modular, each module nesting inside a larger one, like Russian dolls. These different modules are called **levels of action**. Their tightly interconnected nature is what assures dramatic cohesion and organic development between all of the various dramatic events and elements:

- The interactions between characters are called **moments** and the realizations that occur are called **beats**.
- Moments and beats combine into **dramatic units**, each having its own tension which culminates in a **crisis point**.
- Dramatic units combine into compound action to form scenes and sequences, which have their own **dramatic arcs**.
- Scenes and sequences combine to form acts, each in turn having its own **dramatic arc**.
- Acts combine into a whole that constitutes the dramatic arc of the work's entire storyline.

THE THREE-ACT STRUCTURE

The basic engine of the dramatic unit which we've examined (set up/development/crisis point/ result) is also reproduced at the larger dramatic levels. Each individual act contains its own set up, development (with rising action), crisis, and result leading directly to the next act. Crisis points at the act level are also commonly called **turning points**. Finally, and even more broadly, each act functions similarly in relation to the complete story so that Act I is the set up act, Act II the development act, and Act III is the result, which in the case of a film's ending is a resolution. You can expect each act to contain:

> **Act I: The set up.** Introduces characters, relationships, and situations and establishes the central problem faced by the main character, often called the *major dramatic question* (i.e. will Bertie overcome his stammer?). The *turning point* of Act 1 establishes the tenacity of the central problem—meaning, the problem will not go away on its own.
> **Act II: Development.** Escalates the complications in relationships as the main character

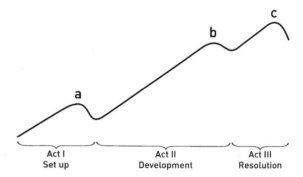

FIGURE 4-4

Graph of typical three-act structure with rising action. The first act turning point (a) comes just before the beginning of Act II and the second act turning point (b) comes just before last act. The climax of the film (c) resolves the central dramatic questions.

struggles with the obstacles that prevent solving the central problem. The situation intensifies until reaching the second *turning point* where the main character realizes that he or she must make a direct *confrontation* with the problem.

> **Act III: Resolution:** The main character finally goes toe-to-toe with the central problem (the principal opposing force) in the **climax** (*third crisis point*) and this confrontation resolves the central problem. The resolution can be favorable or unfavorable for our character, but in either case the major dramatic question is answered. How it is resolved usually consolidates the thematic underpinning of the film.

Let's do a quick three-act breakdown of *The King's Speech* and you'll see how the basic patterns of dramatic units and dramatic arcs also function at the larger structural level (Figure 4-4).

Act I

The first scene establishes the first manifestation of the central conflict, Prince Albert the Duke of York (Bertie) stammers and it's a public embarrassment. The central dramatic question quickly emerges: will Bertie overcome his stammer? Bertie's wife Elizabeth secures the Australian Lionel Logue as a "last chance" speech therapist. Lionel informs Bertie that to be relieved of his stammer he must submit to controversial methods. These include meeting in the office of a commoner, absolute equality, and exploring his personal history to uncover root causes. Prince Albert finds such subversive familiarity unacceptable and dismisses Lionel after one session—even before hearing the result of his first reading pressed onto a record.

In the next critical scene, Bertie is with his father King George V who despairs of his unruly elder son Prince David (who reigned briefly as Edward VIII) succeeding him as king. With the prince shirking his duties and the age of the radio dawning, Bertie must bear the public speaking burden after his father dies. Bertie realizes at this pivotal moment that he has no choice but to overcome his stammer. This, the **first turning point (A),** is where the central conflict takes on greater stakes. That is, his impediment is no longer a personal embarrassment, but it will now reflect on the entire monarchy.

Desperate for a solution, Bertie listens to the recording he made at Lionel's studio and hears himself speaking without stuttering for the first time. He realizes (*result*) that Lionel might hold the key to his problem.

Act II

Bertie returns to Lionel and instantly their "ground rules" clash. Bertie insists that Lionel treat only the "mechanics" of his impairment, while Lionel believes that Bertie must engage in some serious self-examination to uncover the root causes of his feelings of inadequacy that undermine his confidence and, Lionel believes, induce his stammer. The result of this very rocky relationship, in which the Prince feels that Lionel repeatedly steps over the line of propriety, is a long series of conflicts that ultimately lead to mutual respect and friendship. Throughout this Act Lionel helps Bertie with the mechanics of speech and Bertie eventually starts to look inward for deeper causes.

In the meantime, Bertie's encounters with his brother David (the Prince of Wales) and David's American divorcée lover lead him (and the viewer) to realize that David is indeed unfit to succeed his dying father. Bertie's fate as the heir to the crown is sealed when his brother abdicates. The trouble is that Bertie is set to become king before his stammer is alleviated, and he again doubts Lionel's eccentric, challenging and introspective methods.

Now that Bertie must ascend the throne, the stakes are even higher: the conflict reaches its **second crisis point (B)** at Westminster Abbey during preparations for Bertie's coronation as King George VI. Still afflicted with the stutter, Bertie learns that Lionel has no formal training or credentials as a speech therapist, and on the advice of the archbishop tries to dismiss him. But Lionel will not give in: he assures Bertie that he has insight into the deeper causes of speech impairment and has successfully treated many shell-shocked soldiers returning from World War I. He connects these cases to Bertie's situation by saying that ultimately these veterans were helped by "a friend willing to listen." With Bertie unwilling to relent and the destruction of their valuable therapeutic relationship imminent, Lionel plays insolent and blatantly disrespects the tradition of the English monarchy. Intentionally he makes Bertie so angry that he yells, "I have a right to be heard! ... I have a voice!" without a trace of a stammer. In this exchange Bertie not only realizes the method to Lionel's madness, but also that Lionel honestly believes he has the qualities to become king. In Lionel he sees the first true friend he's ever had, and against everyone's advice retains Lionel as his speech therapist. Bertie is successfully crowned King George VI.

Act III

No sooner is Bertie convinced that he has a voice and can actually be a good king than he faces the ultimate test of both his kingship and his ability to deliver a speech. England has slipped inexorably toward war with Germany and the people are unsettled by the awkward transition of power from George V to Prince David to Bertie. The times are momentous and at **the climax of the film (C)** Bertie must announce over the radio to Britain and her worldwide empire that they are entering war with Germany. At home, his speech must reassure the nation and inspire confidence in his kingship. Again Bertie must go toe-to-toe with his central problem (his stammer) and must overcome it. With the help of his friend Lionel, Bertie delivers the speech of his lifetime—powerful, profound, and one successfully bolstering his nation's courage to enter the war. In this one scene he vanquishes his stammer (external problem), and his through-line (internal need) is resolved so that he can become a worthy king.

Notice the beautiful dramatic arc of the larger architecture. The film begins with a speech and ends with a speech—but the stakes are substantially greater by the time we reach the climax. The first speech is not much more than an acute personal embarrassment for Bertie, but the final speech confirms his ability to serve as king during a time of worldwide crisis and represents a triumph of historic proportion. He accomplished the journey from one to the other through a connected series of challenges, stumbles, and victories. He earned the passage by breaking with the established rules of conduct in relation to royalty so that he could look inward, examine himself, and establish a trusting friendship. Thus the monarch and commoner find true friendship and loyalty (the theme of the film).

THE THREE-ACT STRUCTURE CAVEAT

This discussion is not intended to assert that the classical three-act structure is the only way to structure a cinematic story because there are many variations and alternative approaches that may be more appropriate for your specific story. The three-act model has in fact been roundly challenged since there are other ways to divide up a complete work into broad dramatic sections. Nonetheless, the three-act structure remains a popular structural paradigm since it provides a solid foundation for understanding how all dramatic stories are told, helps one recognize how alternative strategies work, and articulates the expectations that audiences bring to the film experience.

This discussion illustrates an even more important truth, that *drama in any form fundamentally consists of cycles of conflict, action, struggle, and change.* These patterns are reflected on the micro level of dramatic beats all the way up to the macro or architectural level of the work. A dramatic story lacking the integrity of these elements is likely to stall, fall apart, lose its purpose, and its audience. That you understand these concepts is critical to your work as a director.

ESSENTIALS OF DRAMATIZATION I: MAKING THE INTERNAL VISIBLE

Cinematic dramatization means telling a story about characters in conflict using action, dialogue and visual detail. A central principle is to draw the internal and emotional world of a character out into the open so that we can see it in action and film it. That requires transforming internal desires, feelings, needs and thoughts into goals, action, and human behavior within a carefully organized plot. Even lines of dialogue should reflect human will and volition rather than explain the story verbally.

What makes *The King's Speech* so affecting is its ability to reveal profound internal needs through specific, conflict-riddled, external tasks. The plot shows Bertie's attempts to overcome his stammer as it becomes clear that he must ascend to become King George. Bertie vows to quit the whole thing several times but keeps coming back. Why? We understand that *internally* Bertie yearns to be worthy of his father's royal legacy and a worthy king, but feels persistently unworthy. His stammer is the physical, external manifestation of this internal sense of inadequacy. To overcome his stammer therefore represents gaining the confidence to lead a nation through one of its darkest periods. Though his conscious desire (plot objective) is to overcome his stammer, the *through-line* of Bertie's story is to prove himself a worthy king, and this, with or without Lionel, is the need he brings to every situation.

ESSENTIALS OF DRAMATIZATION II: QUESTIONS AND REVELATIONS

When we dramatize a story we work hard to make the story really matter. We encourage *engagement* whenever we elicit emotional *participation* by the audience. Engagement and participation depend on the dramatist creating compelling questions and poignant revelations. This means that *good drama doesn't just deliver information, it also raises questions that need answering.* Every dramatic unit we analyzed from *The King's Speech* embodies a dramatic question:

Unit #1: Will Bertie deliver the speech? (no).

Unit #2: Can traditional therapy help him? (no).

Unit #3: Will Elizabeth figure out how the elevator functions? (yes, eventually).

Unit #4: Will Elizabeth convince a new speech therapist to help her husband? (yes, but within limits).

All these smaller questions are subsets of the movie's larger, overarching dramatic questions: Can Bertie abide by Lionel's rules? Will Bertie find the authority to serve as king? And, will Bertie ultimately overcome his stammer?

Once you have successfully created dramatic questions, then understanding a situation or a character becomes a journey of discovery for the audience, rather than one of exposition or verbal explanation. Primed with a compelling question, the audience will probe complex situations for themselves through what is revealed by the human behavior on display. This is the basis for that commonly used (and misused) phrase, *show me, don't tell me.* In other words, human behavior reveals character and conflict for our judgment, while verbal explanation simply narrates what's going on. Even dialogue should be revealing rather than explanatory, and good dialogue is usually verbal action, that is, it seeks to act on the other person and get a result. These principles are vital to engaging your audience and making them *care* about your characters and what happens to them. Why? Because this is how we all seek to understand people and situations in real life. Say you're walking in the park with a friend and you pass a man sitting on a bench. Your companion confides, "That guy is really mean," and you believe him, but you have to take his word for it. But you've seen no evidence and can't feel it. Now imagine seeing a cute little puppy scamper up to that man and playfully sniff his boot. The man kicks at the puppy and yells, "Scram, you miserable mutt." Now you understand his meanness in a profound way.

Think back to when you last became convinced that someone truly loved you, or was loyal, brave, smart or a bad teacher, or a great athlete. Surely you arrived at your conviction by witnessing and evaluating their actions, not by what they or anyone else said. Actions, they say, speak louder than words, and the first scene in *The King's Speech* provides a simple and elegant example of this. No one tells us why Bertie is so nervous at having to speak to a huge crowd. Instead the writer and director carefully shape the scene to raise the tension before we get any answers. By allowing us to discover and witness the problem for ourselves, we make a powerful emotional connection (engagement) with Bertie and his crippling embarrassment. The purpose is not just to inform us of Bertie's stammer, but for us to understand, viscerally and unforgettably, how it tears him up.

That is the purpose of drama.

CHAPTER 5

PLOT, TIME, AND STRUCTURE

So much about film's appeal is hotly debated, but, "if anything is natural," says Dudley Andrew, "it is the psychic lure of narrative, the drive to hold events in sequence, to traverse them, to come to an end."[1] Every intended film has an optimal structure, one that best conveys its dramatic issues, their working out and outcome. You begin by deciding how to organize the sequence of events and how to handle time. From this you will recognize the vessel you need to contain your story—its structure. As with all design problems, less is more, and the simplest solution is usually the strongest.

WHAT IS PLOT?

In Chapter 3 we discussed the difference between story and narrative by saying that **story** is the overall chronological progression of the complete work, and the **dramatic narrative** is the way in which that story is told, namely what details are selected and emphasized, what events are actually represented and, most importantly, in what order they are presented. This aspect of the selection and ordering of events (the sequencing of dramatic moments), is what we call the plot.

Plot is the order in which events are organized and told. Its most effective form is determined by the nature of the story and the intentions of the writer and director functioning as storyteller. As the story advances, each incident must stand in logical and meaningful relationship to what went before, and each must lead with seeming inevitability to what follows. A plot is devised, says Michael Roemer, "to manipulate, entertain, move, and surprise the audience."[2] He argues that the plot represents the rules of the universe against which the characters struggle. This explains why plot discussions always revolve around whether some event or characteristic is likely or not, and what we anticipate might happen next.

Thankfully, stories only ever show fractions of their characters' lives. So, the writer must carefully select significant incidents and actions to stress their particular angle on this particular story.

---

[1] *Concepts in Film Theory,* Dudley Andrew (Oxford University Press, 1984).
[2] *Telling Stories*, Michael Roemer (Rowan & Littlefield, 1995).

By so doing, they imply a whole world outside the purview of the plot. By concentrating our attention, a plot acts as a frame in which to enact its author's intentions.

It is entirely possible to have a fantastic story fall flat because it was expressed via a weak plot: "Why did the chicken cross the road? To get to the other side," is a classic joke with an absurdist punch line. But "To get to the other side, the chicken crossed the road" is a totally dry, banal statement of fact. No one would chuckle at this, not even a four-year-old. With stories, as with jokes, it's not only the content that counts—it's also in the delivery. You can kill a good story with a poorly conceived plot, but you cannot make a poor story engaging through intricate plot machinations. Plot is just plot: it is means rather than substance and does not constitute the primary way an audience connects with stories. We can work diligently to construct the best possible organization of events, but the most crucial elements of a dramatic work remain the characters, the conflicts, and the ultimate meaning of the whole piece. Audiences want a meaning to emerge.

CAUSE AND EFFECT

When you develop an idea for a film, the type and degree of plotting you choose depend on your beliefs about the narrative and thematic essences of the story. The emphasis on a logical plot line may be light or heavy. Some stories, such as action and mystery oriented films, usually require extensive plotting to design a tight progression of incidents and adhere to a fairly strict regimen of **cause and effect** linkage; that is, each new situation is the result of the actions in previous events: scene A causes the actions of scene B which in turn prompts the actions of scene C, and so on. This sort of plot assures the forward momentum of your story, and clarity of character motivation, from scene to scene.

We saw a good example of a tight cause and effect chain in the first six dramatic beats of *The King's Speech* in the previous chapter. Trace this chain in the three-act summary provided on pp. 49–52 and you'll see how this plot pattern creates strong forward development momentum and a clear understanding of why characters do what they do.

But character-oriented or theme-oriented stories, especially those which function deeply within real human psychology and experience, may involve an organization of events that incorporates chance, ambiguity, randomness, or irony. They may incorporate the idiosyncratic psychological imperatives of the central characters or even a quirky storyteller "voice." Such plots are neither random nor arbitrary; rather, they make sense by logic that is other than linear cause and effect.

Oren Moverman's highly regarded *The Messenger* (2009) is a good example of a different plot model. While his film maintains a steady linear chronology, it consistently reverses the cause and effect linkage when it comes to character motivation. Moverman tends to shows effects first and then slowly works toward revealing their cause hidden within the psychology of the characters. Throughout the film we witness the emotionally erratic, often baffling behavior of Sergeant Will Montgomery and the acutely rigid behavior of his commanding officer Captain Tony Stone while they fulfill their duty as an Army Casualty Notification team. Their grim mission is to inform next of kin that a son, daughter, or spouse has been killed in the line of duty. It is not until quite late in the movie that we understand precisely why Will is so emotionally delicate and Tony so tightly wound. Our understanding for how they respectively respond to their task lies in their personal

FIGURE 5-1

Even though Moverman's *The Messenger* has a steady linear chronology, it tends to show effects first and then works toward revealing their cause.

and starkly divergent experience of their wars—which doesn't emerge until very late in the film (Figure 5-1). *The Messenger* exemplifies the French film master Robert Bresson's well-known aphorism, "Let the cause follow the effect, not accompany it or precede it."

Although your film may ardently promote a sense of uncertainty or randomness in life, keep in mind that plots which depart from tight cause and effect are never truly uncertain or random. Filmmaking is highly intentional and the journey you design, from moment to moment, must make perfect sense on some level (logical, emotional, psychological, etc.).

No matter what organizing principle you choose, you must construct your event sequence to build tension and generate those all-important dramatic questions that keep an audience engaged. *The Messenger*'s tense core revolves around two dramatic questions: Why is this "hero" so emotionally delicate? And why does he so easily disregard Army protocol? It is especially puzzling that he does this by initiating a relationship with a war widow to whom he himself delivered the heartbreaking news.

FLOW AND INEVITABILITY

The well-crafted plot flows with an exhilarating sense of inevitability because it includes nothing gratuitous, facile, or unlikely. By assiduously respecting the logic of the characters and their situation, the plot generates an energizing sense of excitement at each step, stimulating the spectator to keep asking, "And now what?" This, called forward momentum in dramaturgy, is what screenwriters work hardest to accomplish. Directors must clearly comprehend the source of this momentum before they tackle the transformation of a screenplay into a motion picture.

CHARACTER-DRIVEN AND PLOT-DRIVEN STORIES

Understanding the source of plot momentum is matter of asking one simple question: At its core, what kind of film is this? Films can be essentially character-driven, plot-driven, or theme-driven.

The purpose of a **character-driven** film is to explore what it means to be human through examination, and often transformation, of a character. In this type of film, we devise our conflicts, actions and plot to reveal or transform that character over time. The momentum of such a story comes directly from the desires, decisions and reactions of the particular character under our dramatic microscope. Kathryn Bigelow's Iraq war film *The Hurt Locker* (2008) is a good example (Figure 5-2, top). In the war genre, we generally expect an action/plot oriented story, however *The Hurt Locker* is not particularly goal oriented, that is, it's not about winning a big battle or saving a particular soldier. Really it is a close examination of how the trauma of war changes the good character of a man. The central character is Sergeant William James whose

FIGURE 5-2

The plot of Bigelow's *The Hurt Locker* (top) is driven by the close examination of Sergeant James' (Jeremy Renner) psychology, while Spielberg's *Raiders of the Lost Ark* favors plot over character complexity.

duty on an Explosive Ordinance Disposal unit keeps him perpetually in an atmosphere of mortal danger and adrenalized alertness. We witness James encounter so many emotionally extreme, life-threatening moments that he becomes indifferent to death and ultimately addicted to the adrenaline rush of combat. Like all addicts, Sgt. James begins to seek out extreme conflict, endangering himself and his team. When he returns home, James finds that he cannot re-adjust to a normal civilian life and is soon back in Iraq for another fix. Although returning to a war zone seems like a paradoxical response to the end of his military obligations, we fully understand why he does it.

When a piece is character-driven, the storyteller's vision will be expressed through the actions and point of view (POV) of the character. The primary character, in essence, becomes a surrogate for the voice of the author.

When the piece is **plot-driven**, the driving momentum comes less from within the central character and more from the pattern of external forces. In fact, characters in plot-driven films need not change all that much. What is important is that they are designed to maximize the plot line's capacity to generate action, suspense, mystery, reversals, and so on. An extreme example would be Indiana Jones in *Raiders of the Lost Ark* (1981, Figure 5-2, bottom). Indie suffers no moral dilemma about what he's called on to do. He doesn't worry that taking archeological treasures infringes on the ownership rights of native populations nor does he consider the moral consequences of pilfering icons associated with deeply held religious beliefs. After the first few scenes, we know who Indie is and he remains that way for the duration of the film. Indie is a man of action: he is created to take whatever punishment the plot throws at him, and to prevail over whatever foe gets in his way—even if it's half the Nazi army.

A character in a plot-driven film is devised to maximize the possibilities for the plot to twist and turn. With this sort of approach, the storyteller's vision hinges more on dynamic situations, energetic characters, interesting locations, and the requirements of the action line of the plot.

Clearly we do not face an either/or situation: most films are a mélange of character and action orientation. However, it's important to understand where the essential source of the story is located, how and why material is generated, and what thematic ideas are moving the film from one moment to the next. We will discuss theme and thematically driven films later (see "Premise and Theme" on page 69).

FIGURE 5-3

Chandor's *Margin Call* (*left*) takes place over a 24-hour period. Istvan Szabo's *Sunshine* (*right*) depicts three generations of a Hungarian family.

ORGANIZING TIME

Every story, like every sequence of memorable events in life, has its own chronology; that is, significant happenings with a beginning, middle, and end. As we have said, they may not however be told in that order, which only makes matters more interesting. Embedded in the task of designing a plot sequence is the fundamental question—how will I handle time? Cinema has considerable temporal elasticity. The time element of a story can be greatly manipulated within the film's actual duration. So where to begin?

The first question when considering the issue of time is: How much time does this story cover? J.C. Chandor's first feature film *Margin Call* (2011) follows the actions of an investment bank's executives over a 24-hour period as they cope with a financial crisis that could ruin the company literally overnight. *The Messenger* follows Sgt. Montgomery during the last three months of his deployment (the time he is assigned to casualty notification duty), and *The King's Speech* explores the king's relationship with his therapist over a 14-year period. Istvan Szabo's *Sunshine* (1999) follows the fate of a Hungarian family over three generations, from the end of the 19th century to the Hungarian revolution of 1956 (Figure 5-3). All these films are roughly two hours long.

Whatever the time-span your story traverses, you must consider how to condense that expanse into your film's screen real time: for a short you'll have anywhere between three to 30 minutes; for a feature approximately 70–120 minutes. Given this imperative, you can see how almost all film stories must condense time by presenting only events crucial to the story, and how they must exclude whatever is extraneous or can be inferred by the audience.

WHERE TO BEGIN AND END

First ask yourself: Why am I starting this story here, at this moment rather than one hour, one day, or one week earlier or later? Where you begin should announce very clearly what this movie is about, as if you were making a contract with your audience. The slice of history Seidler presents in *The King's Speech* begins with Bertie's first ever radio address, a disaster revealing his fatal impediment to the world. The writer ignores everything in Bertie's life leading up to this moment and instead plunges us into his central conflict. Bertie's past (his *backstory*) emerges only when necessary and through occasional dialogue rather than whole scenes.

In *The Messenger*, Moverman does not start with Sgt. Will Montgomery in the Iraq war because the film is about not his war experiences but the trauma he carries well after combat. So the film starts when Montgomery is ordered to join the experienced Cpt. Stone as a two-man Casualty Notification team.

Once you've established where to begin, you need to understand very specifically where your film will end. Seidler ends after Bertie, now King George VI, successfully delivers the most important address of his life. This resolves both his ability to control his stammer and his capacity as a leader. Beginning with a disastrous speech and ending with one that is historically moving not only traces a dramatically satisfying arc but also presents a lovely symmetry. *The Messenger* ends when Sgt. Montgomery can open up and tell Cpt. Stone, now his trusted friend, exactly what happened during the firefight where he earned his "hero" status. This scene unlocks and resolves the dramatic questions surrounding the mystery and cause of his irregular behavior.

Between these poles, beginning and end, you must now carefully devise how to handle the organization through time of all the other events that make up the plot of your film.

OPTIONS FOR ORGANIZING TIME

Cinema is highly flexible when it comes to organizing the events of a story over time because films can easily move forward and backward in time, in large or small leaps. We can suspend, reverse, expand, or contract time. We can even repeat moments according to whatever works best for the story we're telling. Here are a few organizing strategies, starting with the most strictly linear approaches and moving to more temporally free-flowing options.

Real Time

Real time, something seldom tackled by film, means that events unfold without breaks, lapses, or ellipses so that the complete story has the same duration as the film's running time. Agnès Varda's *Cleo from 5 to 7* (1962) shows two uninterrupted hours in the life of a French singer, convinced she is dying of cancer, as she wanders the streets of Paris waiting for the results of a medical test. The drama of her situation justifies using real time, but usually it's difficult for feature films to overcome the conspicuousness of this device. Short films however, especially the slice of life genre, can pull off real time very successfully. Rodrigo Garcia's 2005 film *Nine Lives* presents nine portraits of women at particularly revealing moments in their lives. Each little portrait is a 10-minute, self-contained, real time short film (Figure 5-4, *left*).

Chronological Time

Far more common than real time are films that adhere to chronological time, where chronology means putting events in event order, from beginning to end. Chronological films can however be highly elliptical, meaning they elide (skip over) large chunks of time (hours, days, weeks, years)

FIGURE 5-4

Each of the nine episodes in Garcia's film *Nine Lives* (*left*) is presented in real time and without any edits. Mungiu's *4 Months, 3 Weeks and 2 Days* (*right*) leaps over hours of time in the edits between scenes that play out in real time.

thus excluding whatever is inessential. *The Messenger* and *The King's Speech,* both strictly linear films, never once present an event out of its chronological order. From Bertie's Wembley speech to the moment he returns to Logue's office after the haranguing from his father is a span of nine years (1925–1934) yet each represented event happens in chronological order.

Cristian Mungiu's *4 Months, 3 Weeks and 2 Days* (2007) tells the story of a young woman helping her friend get an abortion in Romania during Ceauşescu regime. The story takes place over one day and uses a common approach to chronological time: each scene is shot in real time (mostly one shot per scene) but the cuts between scenes skip forward by anything from minutes to hours (Figure 5-4, *right*).

Many essentially chronological films will insert a flashback here and there which disrupts the linear flow somewhat, but not significantly.

In Medias Res

In medias res, which translates as "into the middle," is a common narrative time manipulation. The story begins at some crisis point as a dramatic hook and then bounces back to the beginning. Once this flash forward opening is completed, these films usually follow a chronological progression leading back to that crisis point. In medias res usually plunges the audience into the heart of the conflict and privileges emotion and action over exposition. It also puts the audience ahead of the main character because they know what will befall the protagonist. This creates additional dramatic questions such as, how the character got from here to there.

Jon Favreau's *Iron Man* (2008) starts with Tony Stark, in a tailored suit, riding in a Humvee in the middle of Afghanistan. The vehicle comes under intense fire that kills all the marines transporting him. As Tony tries to flee the kill-zone a missile detonates, seriously injuring him. When Tony regains consciousness he discovers that he has been taken captive by an Afghan terrorist group. This blistering opening leaves us wondering: What's going on? Who is this guy? Then the plot backs up 36 hours and introduces us to Tony Stark and Stark Industries before chronologically making its way back to the firefight and beyond.

FIGURE 5-5 ——

The plot of Penn's *Into the Wild* starts with McCandless (Emile Hirsch) reaching his wilderness destination and then returns to his college graduation two years earlier, where it begins his journey step-by-step right back to his destination.

Sean Penn's *Into the Wild* (2007) begins near the end of Christopher McCandless's two-year journey to escape the corruption of modern civilization and find greater spiritual freedom. In the first 13 minutes of the film we see him arrive in the Alaskan wilderness, find the abandoned school bus which will become his shelter, and carve into a table his manifesto beginning the "climactic battle to kill the false being within ... and victoriously conclude the spiritual revolution." The plot then returns in time to McCandless's university graduation two years earlier and traces his long journey from his family's home, across the highways of America, and back to the Alaskan wilderness, where it then resumes the conclusion of McCandless' personal revolution (Figure 5-5).

Frame Narrative

Frame narratives involve a framing device within which the film's central story is told. This device most often uses a character from the central story recounting the events so that the central story (usually told chronologically) is an extended flashback. Eventually, the conclusion of the central story leads back to the framing story. Frame narratives have been used extensively through cinema's history from Robert Wiene's *The Cabinet of Dr. Caligari* (1920) to Danny Boyle and Loveleen Tandan's *Slumdog Millionaire* (2008).

David Fincher's *The Social Network* (written by Alan Sorkin, 2010) is a slightly more complex frame narrative that tells the story of Facebook's creation through two separate flashbacks. These originate from two lawsuit depositions that occurred well after the success of the company (Figure 5-6).

The device of two frame narratives allows Fincher to tell the story in retrospect and from multiple points of view (Zuckerberg's, Saverin's, the Winklevosses and the official record). Most valuably, it also allows Fincher to bridge large gaps in the story and represent only events critical to his

FIGURE 5-6

Fincher's *The Social Network* uses two separate frame narratives from which flashbacks tell the story of Facebook's creation.

particular take on the Facebook story. This excludes events concerning computer code, network development, the process of incorporation, capital investment, or company valuation and instead concentrates on the development of Mark Zuckerberg's personal relationships and inner motivations. This is precisely why the film begins with a scene between Mark and his girlfriend on their final, dreadful date. Because the scene zeroes in on Mark's character, ambitions, vulnerabilities and his humiliation, this becomes a film not about a corporation, but about a brilliant young man with human needs and fallibility, and one who must prove his worth by building a personal empire.

Parallel Time

Parallel time, also called **parallel storytelling**, involves intercutting between multiple story lines of more or less equal dramatic weight in order to create narrative and thematic associations across time and terrain. The intercutting can create disruptions in linear time, but each individual storyline usually progresses chronologically.

This technique was influenced by the novels of Charles Dickens and first applied to the cinema by D.W. Griffith, who took the technique to the extreme in his sprawling epic *Intolerance* (1916). The film spans 2,500 years of human history and follows the struggle between love and intolerance in four separate stories from four different time periods: a contemporary story (1914) of a boy wrongly accused of a crime; events from the life of Jesus Christ; the massacre of the Huguenots by the Catholics in 16th-century France; and the fall of ancient Babylon around 540 BC. The cumulative thematic effect of the four juxtaposed narratives is to assert that human history has been shaped by the struggle of love to survive in the midst of persistent intolerance (Figure 5-7).

FIGURE 5-7

Parallel storytelling has been used since the early days of cinema: from D.W. Griffith's *Intolerance* (1916, *left*) to Paul Haggis' *Crash* (2005, *right*).

The same plot strategy can be seen in Paul Haggis' *Crash* (2005) with its multiple storylines linked by the social tension surrounding issues of race and violence; and in Stephen Daldry's *The Hours* (2002) which revolves around the lives of three women from different time periods (1941, 1951, 2001). Each must confront the specter of depression and suicide in their lives. Virginia Woolf's 1925 novel *Mrs. Dalloway* serves as the central connection for the three main characters, one of which was Woolf herself.

Non-Chronological Narratives I: Subjective Time

Frequently a story's chronology is rearranged to reflect a character's subjective recall of events. This can take the form of multiple flashbacks intruding on the chronological narrative flow, each with a story line of its own. In Alain Resnais' *Hiroshima Mon Amour* (1959), the Frenchwoman and her Japanese lover are consistently invaded by memories of their respective traumas—his, the dropping of the bomb on Hiroshima; hers, punishment for a love affair with a German soldier in occupied France. These memories inject anguish into their relationship so that Resnais seems to propose that extreme lives are propelled by extreme trauma. By juxtaposing the past and present, this plot design poses questions about the effect of repressed personal history on present behavior.

More recently, Michael Mills' *Beginners* (2010) incorporates several layers of temporally fluid and interrelated flashbacks. In the present-day story, Oliver is trying to begin a romantic relationship with Anna, a French actress. The difficulty is that Oliver is grieving over the recent death of his father Hal and reeling from Hal's revelation, toward the end of his life, that he was gay. As Oliver becomes more intimate with Anna he is inundated with memories of taking care of his father while Hal struggled with terminal cancer and exulted in his new life as an openly gay man. Oliver also reflects on his parents' relationship when he was a boy, as more distant memories of himself and his mother surface. The close emotional proximity of Oliver's past with the events of his present both encourage Oliver to fall in love and cast into doubt whether anyone can truly know another (Figure 5-8).

Even more radical is the non-chronological narrative plotline in Terence Davies' celebrated *Distant Voices, Still Lives* (1985) which mimics the fluidity of human memory. Events neither follow one another in chronological or cause and effect relationship, nor follow the subjective perspective of a single character. Instead moments flow through the collective memories and multiple perspectives of a whole family. Using major events (weddings, funerals, births, etc.) and the music of the era as springboards, the connections between scenes are highly personal, loosely associative, and poetically resonant.

FIGURE 5-8

Mills' *Beginners* uses a non-chronological plot to bring together the disparate emotional currents crashing in on Oliver (Ewan McGregor) as he tries to overcome his father's death and find love for himself.

Non-Chronological Narratives II: Repeated Time

Occasionally, films will repeat events, usually to represent a new perspective or new context, or to extract a new meaning from some moment the audience assumed they understood. But few are the films that build an entire plot around event repetition. Harold Ramis' very funny *Groundhog Day* (1993) features a man trapped in a time loop. A jaded TV weatherman is sent on assignment to cover the annual emergence of groundhog Punxsutawney Phil, but finds himself waking up on the same day over and over again. Each time he relives this day he learns a little more about himself until he finally he comes to understand what he's doing wrong and can escape the time loop as a purged and happier man. This perhaps takes its inspiration from the Hindu belief that we are reincarnated into new bodies, from life to life, until we attain perfection.

The celebrated *Run Lola Run* (Tom Tykwer, 1998) repeats the same moment three times—the 20 minutes in which Lola races to save her boyfriend from gangsters who are intent on killing him. Each run traces the same journey but with very slight variations, revealing how tiny changes in one's timing and route can make enormous differences in the outcome of many people's lives (Figure 5-9, *left*).

In the case of Akira Kurosawa's classic *Rashomon* (1950) the events of a murder that occurred in a wooded grove are recounted at the trial four times (in flashback) by four witnesses: the bandit (the murder suspect), the murdered samurai (through a medium), the samurai's wife, and the woodcutter. Each version favors the perspective of the witnesses who cast themselves as blameless victims. Interestingly, this film also uses a **frame story** because the events of the trial itself are being retold by a woodcutter and a priest to a commoner as they wait out a rainstorm at the ruined Rashomon gatehouse. In other words, we are shown flashbacks within flashbacks, a plot design

FIGURE 5-9 ———

Repeated time with tiny variations reveals how small actions can have enormous consequences in Tykwer's *Run Lola Run* (*left*). Kurosawa's *Rashomon* (*right*) recounts a brief moment four times with each narrator providing a version that 'proves' their innocence.

which, given the vagaries of subjectivity and self-interest, calls into question the reliability and validity of anyone's memory or testimony.

Non-Chronological Narratives III: Reverse Chronology

As its name implies, reverse chronology involves a plot line that orders events backwards in time. Jane Campion's first full length film *Two Friends* (1986) is told entirely in reverse chronology and begins with two teenagers who appear to be estranged friends and vastly different from one another. Louise is a great student destined for a fine school while Kelly is trapped in an aimless life and into drugs. As the film traces their friendship in reverse order (over the previous year) we see them slowly converging and getting closer and we realize that only a few differences (small and large) pushed them onto radically different life paths. In Louise's case, opportunities were given to her, but for Kelly they were stripped away. At the end of the film, we see their poignant beginning: two inseparable friends, very much alike, with the same energy, intelligence and potential for the future.

A film may also mix chronological time and reverse chronology in its different story lines. In Michel Gondry's *Eternal Sunshine of A Spotless Mind* (2004) the reverse chronology of Joel Barish's memories, as they are being erased, play against the chronological story of the Lacuna Corp. procedure itself. Another example is Christopher Nolan's *Memento* (2001), which tells the story of a man suffering from short-term memory loss trying to piece his way backward to the moment of his wife's murder. One element of the plot follows events chronologically (the black-and-white sequences) and another storyline plays out in reverse chronology (the color sequences). These two storylines, moving backward and forward, converge by the end of the film at a common point. Since the viewer enters moments and locations with no notion of what came before, or why they're there, this strategy plunges the audience into the point of view of a protagonist suffering short-term memory loss (Figure 5-10).

STRUCTURE

A film's **structure** is the overall design we employ in shaping the flow of the plotline—the broader logic of the narrative design. On pp. 49–50 we discussed one very common architecture, the three-act structure that divides the plot line into three large dramatic units: there was the introductory act (introducing the major characters and conflict) the development act (tension and stakes rise as the protagonist struggles to achieve their goals), and the resolution act (the major dramatic questions are finally confronted and resolved).

FIGURE 5-10

The complex plot structure of Nolan's *Memento* integrates chronological and reverse chronological time.

However, cinematic storytelling as an art form is vastly more malleable than that. It's often been noted that Stanley Kubrick's *Full Metal Jacket* (1987) is structured in two acts: Act I being the "boot camp" section, and Act II being the battle of Hué. Like many road films, *Easy Rider* (Hopper, 1969) has an episodic structure whose incidents are not necessarily connected through cause and effect; yet each contains a facet of the central conflict, revealing that no matter how far one travels, the problems one is trying to escape (usually societal) remain ubiquitous. Wyatt and Billy are searching for the true American Dream—freedom—but discover that no matter how far they travel, they cannot escape the restrictive American "establishment." Loosely and poetically cyclical in its structure, Michelangelo Frammartino's *Le Quattro Volte* (2010) shows four cycles of life energy as it lives, passes, and transmutes into other forms: from human, to animal, to vegetable, to mineral (Figure 5-11, *left*). And Michael Hazanavicius' *The Artist* (2011) pays loving homage to the Hollywood classics of the Silent Era and fashions a traditionally melodramatic story juxtaposing the tragic fall of one movie idol (George Valentin) against the meteoric rise of another (Peppy Miller). Absolutely appropriate for the genre, the plotline follows the classic three-act structure (Figure 5-11, *right*).

Many film scholars, notably Kristin Thompson[3] and Robert McKee,[4] have argued the existence of four, five, six and eight act plot structures, but even this array seems confining. Perhaps this is because these structures emerged from an analysis after the fact of the films' creation. To discuss all the potential act structures available, though important to cinematic storytelling, is beyond the scope of this book but there are many fine texts on the bookshelves that explore this topic; the two mentioned here are a good place to start.

Screenwriter and Professor Paul Thompson once told me: "Read all the books, learn it all, and then use whatever is helpful for your own story." In other words, work organically and from the inside out. Let the content and your intentions suggest the structure rather than the other way around.

If you're writing a biopic about an avant-garde artist who spent her life breaking rules and paradigms, would it be appropriate to fit such an iconoclastic life into a tidy three-act structure?

---

[3] *Storytelling in the New Hollywood*, Kristin Thompson (Harvard University Press, 1999).
[4] *Story*, Robert McKee (It Books, 1997).

FIGURE 5-11

Subject matter determines story structure. Frammartino's lyrical *Le Quattro Volte* (*left*) has a poetically cyclical structure, while the classic three-act form fits Hazanavicius' *The Artist* (*right*) perfectly.

If your film revolves around existential themes and questions, would a logical, deterministic cause and effect story structure really exemplify that idea? However, if you were working on a lean crime thriller whose protagonist must resolve personal issues before solving the crime, the classic three-act structure might work well.

When writer/director Todd Haynes took on the task of creating a film based on the life and music of Bob Dylan, he knew that the subject himself defied both strict motivational logic and tidy structure. Instead, Haynes opted for a non-linear, collage structure in which the multiple personalities of Bob Dylan, played by six different actors, could be freely intercut (Figure 5-12). In the synopsis Haynes submitted to Bob Dylan to secure permission to fictionalize his life, Haynes is very articulate about his intentions for the film's structure,

> If a film were to exist in which the breadth and flux of a creative life could be experienced, a film that could open up as oppose to consolidating what we think we already know walking in, it could never be within the tidy arc of a master narrative. The structure of such a film would have to be a fractured one, with numerous openings and a multitude of voices, with its prime strategy being one of refraction, not condensation. Imagine a film splintered between seven separate faces—old men, young men, women, children—each standing in for spaces in a single life.[5]

In the end, the creative storyteller must struggle to thoroughly understand the essence of their own dramatic materials (characters, conflict, actions, sequencing and time considerations, and the ultimate meaning) and then to build the structural architecture that best answers the needs of their story. No matter what you decide, you must begin developing your structure from the outset: failing to do so would be like driving through a strange city without a map—you can easily get lost, waste time, and become disoriented and disheartened.

---

[5] *This is Not a Bob Dylan Movie* by Robert Sullivan. *The New York Times Magazine* (Oct. 7, 2007).

FIGURE 5-12

The radical approach to plot and characterization in Haynes's *I'm Not There* is entirely appropriate to its mercurial subject, Bob Dylan.

PREMISE AND THEME

Over the course of a film there is a lot of dramatic activity. We've got characters struggling against obstacles to achieve their goals in moments, beats, dramatic units, acts and so on. So what holds it all together? How do we know whether the story is unfolding in a unified way or if our plot starts to veer off course? This is where we go back to the beginning of it all—the concept and your themes.

The **premise** (also called the **concept** of the film) is the critical, overall idea that informs each and every scene and holds the story together. It is the heart of your story. A good premise focuses all of your narrative activity, including the main characters and the primary conflict, into a sharp sentence or two representing the engine of your story.

Theme is the underlying intellectual idea, message, statement, or moral of the film. If the concept is the heart of your story, then the theme is its soul. A theme should provide some sense of illumination about our experience as human beings. Themes are rarely expressed overtly during the course of a film, instead they are implied, emerging through the specific chemistry between the narrative elements and the directorial approach. Sometimes a film story will have one large and clear theme, like "one cannot change society, society changes you," "innocence is the first casualty of war," or "love conquers all," but very often a film will work its narrative around a number of themes that are not entirely possible to sum up in a pithy phrase, but represent an exploration into the complexities of the human condition. For example a single film can explore themes around, "how individuals respond to mortal danger" and "what it takes to be a hero."

Understanding the premise and theme(s) of your film is critical during the writing stage as well as the production phase because they serve as developmental yardsticks. Since they clarify what you as an artist want to express, concepts and themes help us determine what specific elements are necessary and germane to a particular story and what is therefore inappropriate and extraneous. We constantly return to our premise and themes to test every moment, scene, acting choice and staging idea against them. If a scene or directing choice fails to reflect the central premise or themes then there's a good chance that the scene or directing idea is unnecessary and will only prove a distraction.

The premise for *The King's Speech* could be: Albert, Duke of York, must submit to the unorthodox speech therapy of an Australian commoner if he is to take control of his physical stammer, overcome his psychological demons, and become an effective leader as king. The film's themes revolve around (1) the importance of friendship and trust in overcoming our human frailties and (2) the idea that true friendship can transcend social boundaries. It is no accident that, at the climactic moment when Bertie must give his most important speech about going to war with Germany, Lionel's last piece of advice before Bertie goes on-air live is, "Forget everything else and just say it to me. Say it to me, as a friend."

SHORT FILMS AND STORY SCALE

So far, we have discussed the essentials of dramatic storytelling by examining feature films. This is primarily because the feature-length film has become the common coin of exchange in the world of cinema and they are readily available for readers to view. This however is no reason to underestimate the importance and artistic power of the short form. True, most emerging filmmakers cut their teeth on quite a few short films before they tackle the extreme demands (and expense) of a feature. But more importantly, short films are an artistically viable form in themselves: they represent a brief and highly effective opportunity for a filmmaker to express their particular thematic and artistic sensibilities.

All the dramatic principles discussed throughout this book apply equally to short films as to features. There are however some additional considerations that come into play, and there is an extra degree of stylistic and narrative freedom that you can exploit as well. Compared to literature, a feature film is more akin to a long short story or novella than a novel and a short film is closer to a poem or song form because it requires deft characterization, a highly compressed narrative, and a fresh and focused point of view. In a short film, every element must have an especially strong reason to be included, and everything probably contributes more than one aspect to the story.

Short films can be about any subject and can be just as profound as features. Your film can be plot intensive or character oriented; it can be a farce, a dark comedy, a lyrical love letter, a social satire, an allegory about human nature, an extended joke—anything. Shorts work you hardest in the ideation area—just where most people are lazy—precisely because they tell simple stories with a strict economy of means. Of necessity, short film concepts are narrowly circumscribed because they must be expressed in a matter of minutes. Here are a few parameters for keeping your story within the appropriate scale:

- Short films are *not* feature film ideas crammed into a smaller vessel.
- Shorts revolve around a single idea, and involve a quickly recognizable situation. You won't have room for multiple story layers, developing historical context, or elements outside the basic story engine.
- Shorts usually have one main character and hinge on a single, sharp turning point that makes one moment resonate.
- Shorts use few and quickly recognizable characters. You have no time to complexly develop or slowly transform a character. If your character changes, it should result from one sharp event.
- Short film conflicts and actions should be revealing on their own without need for explication or backstory.
- Locations, imagery and actions, so critical to efficient storytelling, should be vividly evocative and revealing of character as well as theme.
- Short films often employ familiar genre elements as a form of storytelling shorthand.

SHORT FILMS AND FLEXIBILITY[6]

There are two advantages that short films enjoy over their longer counterparts. First, they do not need to sustain dramatic tension and momentum over a long period of time. Second, audiences presented with a short do not have the same conventional narrative expectations. In fact, they usually expect a short to push the narrative and stylistic envelope. Because of this, shorts enjoy a freedom of form that is often difficult for features to pull off (though clearly not impossible).

The primary advantage is that short film stories can be very successfully built around dramatic questions that are not goal/conflict oriented (or at least overtly so). When filmmakers decide to work with something other than a conflict-driven plot, they must replace the goal-oriented dramatic question, "Will the protagonist get what they are after?" with something else equally compelling. For instance:

- Mysterious or ambiguous activity that is explained in the end
- Slice of life stories that are detailed, perceptive, and revealing portraits.
- A discovery that changes the perceptions of a character or the viewer or both
- An experience that changes a character or reveals their true nature
- A story that constitutes a puzzle to be solved
- An allegorical journey
- A set up/pay-off plot structure (set up/ironic twist, set up/epiphany, set up/humorous punch line, set up/perception shift, etc.).

Here's a simple example from Rodrigo Garcia's omnibus film *Nine Lives* (2005) which comprises nine short portraits of nine different women. Maggie, a woman in her early fifties and her young daughter Maria (about nine) arrive at a cemetery and stroll to one of the graves. Along the way they talk casually about the girl's school, the cemetery, and a stray cat. When they get to the grave they set out a little picnic including sandwiches and grapes (Maria's favorite fruit). It seems like this is a regular, if infrequent, outing for them. The dramatic question is subtle—whose grave are they visiting?—and there are clues in the dialogue that it could be Maggie's father, whom she mentions in the past tense.

At the plot level there is absolutely no direct conflict to their task of getting to the grave. In fact, nothing much out of the ordinary happens as they eat, chat, and play games, except for two small details: during their picnic Maggie drinks something from her thermos that is clearly more potent than orange juice and she uses the F-word in front of her little girl. While this doesn't constitute conflict, it is rather incongruous. Eventually, Maria needs to urinate and goes behind a tree and more subtle tension enters the situation here, for Maggie responds strangely during an "I spy with my little eye ..." game, and when they play patty-cake, Maggie breaks down and cries. But her little girl is there to comfort her and Maggie lays her head on her daughter's lap. The camera

---

[6] This section derived from *Voice & Vision: A Creative Approach to Narrative Film and DV Production* (2nd ed.) by Mick Hurbis-Cherrier (Focal Press, 2011).

FIGURE 5-13

With no apparent external conflict, the *Maggie* episode from Garcia's *Nine Lives* slowly reveals the internal conflict at the heart of the story.

briefly leaves them and scans the periphery of the cemetery before returning to the picnic site, only to find Maggie now alone and folding her blanket getting ready to leave. When she makes the small gesture of laying the grapes on the gravestone, we realize that this is Maria's grave and Maggie has conjured the presence of her daughter for comfort, thus revealing her deep inner conflict (Figure 5-13).

The structure here is simple: set up/perception shift. The set up is filled with activity that seems completely commonplace. Instead of overt conflict, there are only a few peculiar moments. Then, at the very end, the filmmaker reveals the true nature of the visit and what we assumed was real and true, wasn't. Even without the usual goal-oriented plot, the perception shift is a satisfying conclusion because as we reflect on the subtle clues embedded in the story we see that it makes perfect narrative, emotional and psychological sense. A feature film would have a difficult time sustaining over an hour of mundane, conflict-free activity before making its big revelation at the end. But for *Maggie*, clocking in at 14 minutes, it works beautifully.

PART 3

THE DIRECTOR AND THE SCRIPT

CHAPTER 6

SCREENPLAY GROUND RULES

Most fiction films start with a screenplay. It should be original, well written, and make good use of cinema. As its director, you must be involved to the point of fascination with the world it creates and with the ideas it puts forward, because you are going to be married to it for a long, long time.

It is certainly not within the scope of this book to cover the craft and technique of screenwriting, since there are many good books on that topic already available. Instead, this section addresses what happens after the screenplay leaves the hands of the writer and becomes a director's film project.

Screenplays are the starting point and ongoing reference for the final film, so to understand a screenplay's function in the larger creative process, a director must know screenplay form, rules, and language. It is important to understand that the story as it exists in a screenplay is very far from being ready to film. The director must first interpret this paper manuscript and construct an appropriate and coherent fictional universe from it using images and sound. The director's initial work reading, testing, and analyzing the screenplay is critical to establishing the artistic vision that will carry all the way through the production process to the film's completion.

To create something—whether boat, chair, song, or film—you must first envision the finished article in your head. Imagining what this literary material might look like as a film begins with your very first reading.

THE WRITER IS THE WRITER, NOT THE DIRECTOR

The screenplay represents only the bones of a film in a standard, shareable form. It provides the film's basic content (characters, locations, actions, dialogue and general dramatic shape) though much of this may be changed along the way. Whoever writes the screenplay, it is folly to try and "direct the film" on the page. A film develops its full expression through the creative input of a collaborative team—its final form is not set in stone in the script. A screenwriter handing a script to a director, must leave room for the other creative talents on the crew (director, actors, cinematographers, production designers, editors, etc.) to do their jobs.

It is equally unwise for a writer/director to "direct the film" in the screenplay. Doing this only undercuts interpretive freedom down the line. It is very easy for a writer/director to become so wedded to the shortsighted directorial choices imbedded in their script that they overlook the many opportunities to improve the project during the various stages of production. Instead of benefitting from the creative collaborators around them, they set out to slavishly reproduce what they put down on paper months earlier. If you are both writing and directing you should wear your writer's hat when writing and then your director's hat when directing. This way you can approach that script with the same critical, analytical and interpretive rigor as you would a screenplay that came from another writer.

CHOOSING WHAT IS RIGHT FOR YOU

Whether your film is comedy, tragedy, horror, fantasy, or a piece for children, it should embody issues you find compelling. Even while you are learning basic film techniques and grammar, choose subjects you care about because they will give you ideas and energy rather than fatigue. Avoid scripts that preach, debate problems, or demonstrate solutions. Aim to deal, in a suitably disguised and displaced way, with whatever life has incised in your psyche. It might be racial or class alienation, fear of the dark (horror films!), rejection or a loss, a phobia, a period of intense happiness, family dynamics, or a painful love affair.

Don't let technique get confused with content. You may have a strong affinity for the visual energy of the martial arts genre, or the intricate plot weaving of a mystery, or the observational realism of slice-of-life drama—but each of these cinematic approaches can be used to tell any number of stories. Attach yourself to the story that most truly represents your experience and understanding of the world. Make use of the scars you carry from living and of your unfinished business awaiting exploration. By working with characters, themes and situations that stir you to strong and, perhaps, contradictory feelings, your work will become energized with the dynamic of creative exploration.

SCREENPLAY STAGES

Screenplays are not artworks with a final form. By their very nature they are malleable and revisable. Usually, they have already undergone multiple revisions *before* they land in a director's hands. But after that point, a script can (and often should) be re-written throughout the filmmaking process in response to what the creative personnel, resources, locations, limitations, opportunities and new perspectives contribute along the way. In reality, scripts never stop evolving, so you should expect to keep developing yours right down to the first day of shooting.

Sadly, few screenplays whether professional or beginning, are ever adequately developed. In student production groups, rewriting is frequently omitted because nobody wants to hurt the writer's feelings. In the professional world when a writer delivers a script, he or she relinquishes control over it. There is good reason for this: the director and producer must take over the script and alter it as necessary. In a community of unpaid equals you may need to be more diplomatic, so have compassion for writers who must relinquish their work—the profession's path is littered with stones, and happy writers are about as common as happy taxpayers.

Step Outline

A **step outline** (also called a **beat sheet**) is a brief sketch of the major dramatic beats of the narrative in third person, present tense prose. Step outlines describe each significant narrative moment in one or two sentences concentrating on who is in the scene and what happens. They trace the development of the essential plot line and the moves of the major characters. Their language is spare, describing scenes in broad strokes with important dialogue exchanges summarized.

Step outline for *The Oarsman*:

1. NIGHT. A shadowy figure in black tails and top hat rows a coffin in a strange, high boat along a dark canal. The rower is MORRIE (late 50s) He is serene, distant.
2. ESTABLISHING. A panoramic view of Amsterdam. 17th-century buildings lining black canals glittering with reflections. Bridges busy with pedestrian and bike traffic. The view settles on a noisy locals' bar.
3. INSIDE the bar, JASMINE, late 20s, tough, attractive, argues with her boyfriend, MARCO about another woman. Jasmine announces it's over between them, but when she tries to leave he grabs her roughly. She stares him down and he releases her.

Not all writers use step outlines: some prefer to work with treatments, but the step outline's pared down expression of the story is valuable as a screenplay analysis tool and directors use them even after the full screenplay has been written (see p. 93).

Treatment

When a writer is commissioned to write a script, the **treatment** is often the first contracted submission. It is a prose version of the plot written in the present tense. More detailed than a step outline, it can be of various lengths, but commonly devotes one paragraph per major dramatic unit. A treatment outlines the characters and their interactions; traces the conflicts, actions and resolution in the plot; and sketches in important subtexts, moods, tone and other vital aspects of the story. Dialogue exchanges are summarized, though an especially important one might be given verbatim inside quotation marks.

Usually a treatment is a writer's tool, especially with spec scripts.[1] It is an ideal way to hammer out basic story elements before getting into the complexities of fully developed scenes with dialogue, actions, and so on. The producers (along with a director if attached at this stage) use the treatment to assess story and character dynamics before moving on to a first draft screenplay.

If, as a director, you are given the opportunity to see story material in this early stage of development, suggest necessary changes right away. It's always easier to revise a treatment than a

---

[1] Short for *speculative screenplay*: a noncommissioned or unsolicited script written with the intention of sending it to producers, production companies and agents to obtain a sale or an option.

finished screenplay because the treatment makes the larger structural and character development issues far more apparent.

First Draft to Final Draft

The **first draft** is the first version in standard screenplay format with fully realized scenes and dialogue in place. A smart writer will not let too many people see this draft. Instead, through re-working, feedback from trusted colleagues, further research, and multiple re-writes the writer eventually arrives at a draft representing the work in its best light. This, the **author's draft**, is sent to producers, directors or anyone else who can move the script into the next stages of development. Writers often believe *this* to be the final draft, however this is rarely the case. The **final draft** is the version, including revision input from the producer and director, that represents the very last draft before the director breaks it down for preproduction visualization and creates the shooting script.

Shooting Script

The **shooting script** is the screenplay draft that is taken into production. It is essentially a visualized final draft, now including scene numbers and camera angles. This is the draft which is shared with the cast and crew during production. Again, script re-writes, cuts, tweaks and alterations are often made during the process of transforming the final draft into a shooting script. Often these revisions are made by the director and do not involve the writer at all.

STANDARD SCREENPLAY FORMATTING

The screenplay, certainly a dramatic manuscript, is also a technical document that must be written in a standardized format. This facilitates breaking it down for efficient production scheduling, and for everyone on the project to quickly determine what they need to do their jobs. Screenplay formatting is simple, effective, essential, and standardized. Do not invent your own.

There are several screenplay formatting software programs available for writers; some cost money (e.g. Final Draft) and others are free downloads (e.g. Celtx). Many word processing programs come with screenplay formatting templates. However, there is much more to screenplay formatting and language than margins, so it's wise to get a reliable book on formatting, like *The Complete Screenwriter's Manual* by Bowles, Mangravite, and Zorn (Allyn & Bacon). For our purposes, the following brief overview will suffice:

Tense: Screenplays are written in the third person, present tense. In other words, they are written as the film would present itself to an audience; moment by moment, scene by scene.

Typeface: Screenplays are written in 12-point Courier font. The industry has kept this standard because it assures that one page lasts approximately one minute of screen time.

Numbering: Script pages are always numbered in the upper right hand corner.

The **six manuscript elements** to all screenplays are illustrated in Figure 6-1.

INT. SCHOOL CAFETERIA — DAY

DANA places a mug of coffee on her tray next to her
books. She slides her tray down, in sync with the line of
impatient students. She stops at a heat lamp glowing over
small cartons of French fries. She picks up a carton and
contemplates the limp, greasy yellow potatoes. Dana sighs
and places the fries on her tray.

                          ED (O.S.)
               You can't live on French fries alone.

Startled, Dana turns to find Ed next to her chomping on a
banana.
                          DANA
               Do you always sneak up on people
               like that?

Ed moves alongside Dana as she progresses to the grill.

                          ED
               You were up and out so early...

Dana reads the menu above the grill.

                          DANA
               I've got classes, remember?

                          ED
               Try the Veggie Burger, it's not bad.

                          DANA
               Whose lunch is this?

                          ED
               You okay?
                    (touches Dana's arm)
               You sound tired.

Dana glares at the menu.

                          DANA
                    (hissing)
               Do not touch me.

She slides her tray away. Ed is momentarily stunned, then
catches up with her again, standing close.

                          ED
               Dana... everybody cries.

FIGURE 6-1 ——

Elements of a standard screenplay: 1) Scene heading, 2) Stage directions, 3) Character cue, 4) Dialogue,
5) Personal directions (sample page from A *Night So Long* by Lynise Pion).

1. **Scene heading**: Each scene begins with a capitalized scene heading including: (a) Interior or exterior location indication (abbreviated INT. or EXT.). (b) Specific location indication (not a description). (c) Time of day (usually only DAY, NIGHT, DAWN, or DUSK. Technically speaking, a scene is an event or exchange with unity of time and place, so if you move to a new location, you need a new scene beginning with a new scene heading (see p. 45). If you shift to another time, say day to night, or two days later, then you must begin a new scene.

2. **Stage directions**: Include description of essential actions, images and sounds, written in the present tense in the order an audience would perceive them. Paragraphing can be used to distinguish dramatic beats or shifts in visual perspective.

3. **Character cue**: Written in all capitals, this is the name of the person delivering the line of dialogue that follows. Character cues must remain consistent. Also written on this line are the indications (O.S.) for *off-screen* dialogue and (V.O.) for *voice over*, that is, speech coming from another time and place.

4. **Dialogue**: This is what the characters say, which can be past, present or future tense. Dialogue, reflecting human speech and the dramatic voice of your character, doesn't necessarily follow strict grammatical rules.

5. **Personal direction**: A very brief note of a small action that must happen on a particular line, or an indication of the specific person being addressed, if unclear from the context. Personal directions can also communicate the manner in which a line is spoken (e.g. 'whispering', 'yelling', etc.).

6. **Shot transitions** (not shown): Descriptions used *only* when unavoidable to the script's making sense. They may indicate a special relationship between scenes (e.g. temporal or graphic relationship) or shot transitions such as DISSOLVE TO: (used to indicate a transition into a flashback or fantasy sequence) or MATCH CUT TO: (used to indicate a shared graphic element from one scene to the next).

Figure 6-1 represents an author's draft screenplay, that is, a draft that the writer shares with directors and producers. Notice that there are no scene numbers and absolutely no camera cues like "CLOSE UP" or "PAN WITH". These are added later, when the screenplay enters the preproduction stage and must be broken down to create a shooting script and shot list (a step that seldom includes the writer) (see Chapter 24)

In the personal directions, there should be no emotion indications like "wistfully" or "sorrowfully." How lines are spoken depends on the interpretive concepts the actor and director develop during rehearsal. A writer can of course write a sorrowful or wistful line, but the line in its context must *read* that way without needing a personal directive. Poorly written dialogue will never ring true no matter how many emotional cues are tagged on.

True, in some scripts the writer has taken liberties and inserted camera cues and emotional indications (all normally ignored). Some writers produce scripts that are hybrid creatures that dramatize their contents by taking on some characteristics of a shooting script. These are deviations from standard practice, and written for some particular person or purpose.

CHAPTER 7

RECOGNIZING THE SUPERIOR SCREENPLAY

The minute a screenplay lands in a director's hands, the process begins of assessing its quality, potential as a movie, and feasibility as a film project. First impressions are vital, so take careful notes because at this time a director decides either to proceed with the project or to continue looking.

SCRIPT LANGUAGE AND TECHNIQUE

Professionals who read screenplays for production companies will tell you that if they find poor formatting, inappropriate script language, or sloppy typos in the first few pages, they won't bother to read the script. As one reader told me, "If they don't care enough to proofread or figure out how to format it right, why should I believe they'll be careful about writing a good story?" If you see these marks of an absolute beginner or of someone who just doesn't care—stay away.

The professionally written screenplay is fairly minimal because it aims to seed a longer creative process that is focused on a different product—a story told not with words, but mainly with images and sounds. Beyond formatting, here are a few guidelines to recognizing a technically well-written script.

STAGE DIRECTIONS

The language of stage directions should be spare yet vivid, and include only the essential locations, actions, images, and sounds necessary to tell the story. Trying to "direct on the page" results in overwriting, a tedious and even dangerous practice that conditions its readers (money sources, actors, crew) to anticipate particular, hard-edged results. The director then feels locked into trying to fulfill a vision that disallows variables, including those that contribute positively. You can recognize overwritten stage directions from far too much description of environments, blocking, and physical gestures. Directing the film on the page looks like this:

```
Bill walks into the empty office, stops just inside the door and scans the room
from left to right. The only light comes from a street lamp just outside the large,
curtainless window. The walls of the office are off-white, and the wooden floor is
strewn with file folders, papers, soda cups, pizza boxes, plastic water bottles,
ketchup packets, and crumpled napkins. Bill sees a desk in the far corner. Bill
nervously runs a forefinger round the inside of his collar. After a few seconds he
bites his lip and heads toward the desk etc. etc.
```

Because actors get important messages from how a script is written, the overprescribed, closed screenplay tells them they must conform to minutely specified actions and mannerisms. Simply describe essential actions and leave the rest to the director and actors (when to move and how to look nervous), cinematographer (where the light comes from), and set designer (wall color, furniture, and set dressing). Directors, actors, and the other creative personnel are not robots hired to fulfill a writer's vision; they are creative contributors whose specialized experience brings vital interpretive energy to a script. This would be enough:

```
Bill walks into the empty office. Even in the near dark he sees garbage strewn eve-
rywhere. Nervously he approaches the desk.
```

Give no camera or editing instructions, no author's thoughts, instructions, or comments on thematic intentions, and never describe what a character is thinking or feeling:

```
Gregg looks at Alice. He remembers her behaving like this when her father was diag-
nosed, so he's not surprised by her silence. Gregg wants to hug her, he wants to
tell her everything will be alright but he knows she needs her own time to handle
the situation and he decides to let her have some space.
```

If we were to shoot this, all a viewer would see is two people in a room, thinking. Nothing more is visible or palpable. Remember, a film can only tell its story through recordable actions, images, and sounds.

DIALOGUE AND PERSONAL DIRECTIONS

Dialogue must never replicate what the camera already shows us (such as, "I see you're wearing your heavy coat") and never repeats what is clear from the actions and behavior of the characters. If a character throws a beer bottle at her husband's head, she does not need to also yell "I am so mad at you, Fred." We get it.

Poorly written dialogue tends to be overwritten and repetitive, "Wow, thanks so much for the gift. I really appreciate the present. I mean, it's really great to get something from you. Thanks."

Dialogue should not be written to replicate accents phonetically, which becomes awkward and even insulting. Instead of writing "Zis iz zee most wonderfool feeelm," just specify that the character speaks with a thick French accent. Write the line normally and the actor will work it out. You can however imply accents through the particularities of vernacular grammar, as in this restaurant scene:

>   PIERRE
>   (strong French accent)
>   Yes, please. I am taking the waffle.
>
>   WAITRESS
>   You want the mixed fruit with that?
>
>   PIERRE
>   Yes. I would like the fruits as well.
>
>   WAITRESS
>   I'd recommend the maple syrup too.
>
>   PIERRE
>   Very good. Thank you for the advices.

Trying to "direct the film on the page" also happens in dialogue and personal directions. It may include too many little verbal tics ("Well …," "Uh …," "Um …"), may specify where an actor is supposed to pause, or dictate the emotional inflection of the line. This urge to seize control only closes interpretive doors and discourages actors from exploring the material.

FIRST ASSESSMENT

The first read-through of the screenplay is critical because it's your only opportunity to have the kind of "first impression" that an audience has. Find a place where you will not be distracted and read the screenplay from beginning to end without stopping—the way you'd watch a film in a theater. With this first read you want the broad, immediate impressions of the narrative, the characters, and the emotional impact of the movie. Try not to read the screenplay from an analytical perspective—just read for story and for pleasure. When you are done, digest it all and make notes about your first impressions:

- Did you like it?
- Did you connect with the story? How?
- What did it make you feel?
- Which characters did you care about or find fascinating?
- What was the plot about?
- What moments did you really like?
- What parts felt like a chore to get through?
- What elements didn't ring true?
- What is the piece really about beneath the surface events?

A good screenplay should convey a central idea, a thematic core that gives the story its ultimate meaning, in the very first reading. Take note of it, because this will be a guiding beacon through all the analysis and changes the script undergoes as it becomes a movie. If it's great, you must protect this original idea from getting lost or diluted. If it's weak, you must figure out ways to strengthen it in subsequent drafts.

GETTING SPECIFIC WITH MARGIN NOTES

Having noted initial impressions, read the screenplay once or twice again, looking for hard evidence for what you felt. In other words, take your responses to the questions above and ask, *where* in the script did I get these impressions and *why* did I feel the way I felt? Specifically, *what* in the script gave me those feelings or ideas? It's got to be in the script somewhere, so locate their sources.

Make margin notes in the script tracking the location of your initial impressions. That is, jot down moment by moment what you feel, think, decide, understand as you read each scene. These notes will evolve during your script analysis to reflect moment by moment what you want *your audience* to feel, think, decide, understand while watching the film.

ASSESSING CINEMATIC QUALITIES

HOW IS THE STORY TOLD?

As you look closely at where emotional and narrative impressions (or meanings) arise, you should start to see just *how* the film conveys these impressions. Does our emotional and narrative understanding come primarily through action? Did you come to conclusions or feelings by watching characters simply behave as they do? Were there points when you knew what a character was thinking without them having to say a word? Did dialogue play a role in conveying information? If so, who delivered that dialogue? Is dialogue used to explain situations, feelings and ideas or is it used more as evidence of human behavior, that is, does it show how characters act upon each other and react?

Cinema is strongest when it tells its story through revealing human behavior and actions rather than using dialogue to narrate thoughts, feelings and situations. This goes back to our discussion on pp. 52–3. Dialogue should never substitute for action; it should be used only when truly necessary, and then it should *reveal* rather than *explain*. A simple but deadly test of a script's potential is to imagine shutting off the sound to see just how much an audience would understand from what remains. What is told through behavior, and what through dialogue used as narration?

INTEGRITY OF CHARACTERS AND MOTIVES

Test the integrity of your script by tracing major events and characters backward to see if the requisite groundwork has been laid. If a cousin arrives to show off a new car, and in so doing, reveals his uncle's plan to sell the family business, that cousin needs to be established earlier, and so does the family's dependence on the business. Drama that uses coincidence, rolls out a character purely for plot requirements, or tosses in a plot-changing detail for convenience looks shoddy and contrived.

UNCOVER CHARACTER SUBTEXT

In life, people rarely deal directly with the true source of their tensions. This is because we seldom know them ourselves, or we try to hide what we know from those around us. What should happen in drama is often thus a displacement, or an alternative to the characters' underlying desires. In a scene from Alexander Payne's 2007 film *Sideways*, Miles, a divorced man, is speaking with Maya, to whom he's attracted. On the surface, Miles explains his admiration for the pinot noir grape while Maya explains how she became interested in wine. However, given what we already know about Miles' persistent loneliness, we understand something else when he describes the pinot noir grape like this:

```
                    MILES
        It's thin skinned, temperamental […]
        Pinot needs constant care and
        attention […] Only when someone has
        taken the time to truly understand its
        potential can Pinot be coaxed into its
        fullest expression. And when that
        happens, its flavors are the most
        haunting and brilliant and subtle and
        thrilling and ancient on the planet.
```

Without realizing it, Miles is in fact describing himself and posing the question to Maya: will you take the time to understand my true potential? Maya's response, which describes her thoughts on the "life of wine," confirms her sensitivity and interest in Miles. Though the dialogue is about wine, they are alluding to their attraction and love. That's called subtext (Figure 7-1, *left*).

Subtext is the unspoken (often subconscious) motivational drive behind a character's words or actions. It is directly related to the character's through-line (p. 37) especially when the internal needs are never articulated, but revealed only through behavior and context. Intelligent drama exploits the way that characters—consciously or unconsciously—hide their underlying intentions

FIGURE 7-1

Subtext suffuses these scenes from Payne's *Sideways* (*left*) and Fincher's *The Social Network* (*right*).

and concerns even as they try to achieve their goals or control a situation. By developing subtexts, a writer leaves much for discovery. Subtexts invite the audience to uncover for themselves a character's hidden life and true motivations. When director and actors know the subtexts, they can develop actions and behaviors that manifest all the tensions between inner and outer worlds.

In David Fincher's 2010 film *The Social Network* (Figure 7-1, *right*) Sean Parker is a character who aggressively insinuates himself into the emerging Facebook venture, believing (correctly) that it will make him a fortune. In the script however he never asks to become a partner. Though he acts as a sympathetic mentor to Mark Zuckerberg, his actions slowly undermine the authority of Mark's legitimate partner Eduardo Saverin by slyly encroaching on his territory. In one key scene, when Sean finds that Mark has moved to California (as Sean advised), they have this seemingly innocuous exchange:

SEAN
Where is Eduardo?

MARK
He got an internship in New York.

SEAN
Eduardo didn't come out?

The words are simple, but point to a complex subtext. In response, Mark only shakes his head, and we need no dialogue to spell it out. The audience understands that Sean and Mark both realize that Eduardo is becoming peripheral and that Sean's opportunity to usurp Eduardo's place as principal advisor and partner has arrived. The subtext to "Eduardo didn't come out?" closes his case to Mark: he is a better partner than Eduardo (because Eduardo thinks too small), and he's now a member of the team.

METAPHORIC DETAIL

Thematic nuances and screen characters' inner experiences can also be expressed through artfully chosen settings, objects and character detail. These function as symbolic or metaphoric keys to deeper issues. Is your script using these?

Symbols and symbolic action should be carefully designed, because your audience will gag on the manipulative symbol or the over-earnest metaphor. Above all, they must be organic to the world in which the characters live, or they will pop up as contrived, editorial comments. Here, locations, set design and cinematography can serve profound purposes. The parched, bleached settings in Wim Wenders' *Paris, Texas* (1984, Figure 7-2) emblematize the emotional aridity of a man searching for his lost wife and child.

FIGURE 7-2 ———————————————

In *Paris, Texas,* the desert landscape counterpoints Travis' (Harry Dean Stanton) lost and arid inner state.

FIGURE 7-3

The overwhelming power of nature creates a perfect metaphor for the elemental human passions that propel Campion's *The Piano*.

Jane Campion's *The Piano* (1993) makes an equally sharp integration of metaphor into screen drama, and sweeps the viewer up from its earliest scenes. Ada, a young immigrant Scot who won't or can't speak, arrives with her illegitimate daughter and her piano on the harsh New Zealand seashore of the 19th century. She is there to marry a man she neither knows nor loves. But he refuses to bring home her piano, so instead it goes to another man's home. Because he, not her husband, repairs her piano and listens to her music, it is to him that Ada gives her body and soul. We are in a time and place where nature is savage, love denied by decorum, and subtlety is beyond the reach of language. So the soul reaches out by way of music and suppressed eroticism. We quickly understand that the film will be dealing with the overwhelming power of nature and elemental human passions. Who could ask for a more potent canvas (Figure 7-3)?

CHECKING THE EMBEDDED VALUES

All storytelling begins from assumptions about what will be familiar and normal to the audience. Consider how gender roles and relationships were represented in movies just a few decades back. Women were secretaries, nurses, teachers, mothers, or seductresses. People of color were servants, vagrants, or objects of pity with little to say for themselves. Criminals or gangsters were ethnic types, and so on. Such stereotypes and clichés arise from *embedded values;* that is, values so familiar to the makers of a film that they pass below the radar of awareness. An excellent book written by three USC faculty members, *Creative Filmmaking from the Inside Out: Five Keys to the Art of Making Inspired Movies and Television*,[1] offers useful tools to expose unintended stereotyping. I have adapted them below. Try applying these criteria to any script you are considering.

Characters:

Class: What class of society do they come from? How are differences handled? How are other classes represented?

Wealth: Do they have money? How is it regarded? How do they handle it? What is taken for granted? Are things as they should be, and if not, how well does the film express this?

Appearances: Are appearances reliable or misleading? How important are appearances? Do the characters have difficulty reading each other's appearances?

Background: Is there any diversity of race or other background, and if so, how is this handled? Do other races or ethnicities have minor or major parts?

Belongings and work: Do we know what the characters do to sustain their lifestyle? Do their clothes, appliances, and cars belong with their characters' breadwinning ability? What do their belongings say about their tastes and values? Is anyone in the film critical of this?

Talismans: Are there important objects, and if so, what is their significance?

Valuation: For what are characters valued by other characters? Does the film question this or cast doubt on the intercharacter values?

Speech: What do you learn from the vocabulary of each? What makes the way each thinks and talks different from the others? What does it betray?

Roles: What roles do characters fall into, and do they emerge as complex enough to challenge any stereotypes?

Sexuality and gender roles: How are gender roles apportioned? If gay or transgender characters appear, how are they portrayed? If the script deals with sexuality, does it contain a range of expression, and how is it portrayed? Is it allied with affection, tenderness, and love? Or is it shown as disembodied lust? Is it true to your experience?

Volition: Who is able to change his or her situation, and who seems unable to take action? What are the patterns behind this?

Competence: Who is competent, and who is not? What determines this?

Environment:

Place: Do we know where characters come from and what values are associated with their birthplace or other origins?

Settings: Will they look credible and add to what we know about the characters?

---

[1] *Creative Filmmaking from the Inside Out: Five Keys to the Art of Making Inspired Movies and Television*, Jed Dannenbaum, Carroll Hodge, and Doe Mayer (New York: Simon & Schuster, 2003).

Time: What values are associated with the period chosen for the setting?

Home: Do the characters seem at home? What do they have around them to signify any journeys or accomplishments they have made?

Work: Do the characters seem at home with their work, and how is the workplace portrayed? What does it say about the characters?

Family dynamics:

Structure: What structure emerges? Do characters treat it as normal or abnormal? Is anyone critical of the family structure?

Relationships: How are relationships between members and between generations portrayed?

Roles: Are roles in the family fixed or do they develop? Are they healthy or unhealthy? Who in the family is critical? Who is branded as "good" or "successful" by the family, and who "bad" or "failed"?

Power: Could there be another structure? Is power handled in a healthy or unhealthy way? What is the relationship of earning money to power in the family?

Authority:

Gender: Which gender is shown to have the most authority? Does one gender dominate, and if so, why?

Initiation: Who initiates the events in the film, and why? Who resolves them?

Respect: How are figures with power depicted? How are institutions and institutional power depicted? Are they simple or complex, and does the script reflect your experience of the real thing?

Conflict: How are conflicts negotiated? What does the film say about conflict and its resolution? Who wins, and why?

Violence: Who is violent, and why? Is violence a dramatic crutch for resolving differences or for infusing superficial excitement; or is it justified? What does it say about your values when violence is gratuitous? Can conflict be negotiated in another and more artistically interesting way?

In total:

Criticism: How critical is the film toward what its characters do or don't do? How much does it tell us about what's wrong? Can we hope to see one of the characters coming to grips with this?

Approval/disapproval: What does the film approve of, and is there anything risky and unusual in what it defends? Is the film challenging its audience's assumptions and expectations, or just feeding into them?

World view: If this is a microcosm, what does it say about the balance of forces in the larger world, or macrocosm, of which it is a fragment?

Moral stance: What shape does the film's belief system take in relation to privilege, willpower, tradition, inheritance, power, initiative, God, luck, coincidence, and so on? Is this what you want?

You are not considering these questions to be politically correct, which is suffocating, but to avoid presenting something as "normal" when it just shouldn't be. This sort of investigation should also lead you to examine where you, as the author, acquired the cultural assumptions embedded in the story. Do they align with your own experiences or were they derived from other models, like other films? Ultimately, these questions will lead you to creating fresher, more authentic and vivid characters and dramatic situations.

To make fiction is to propose reality, and this is as true for fantasy as it is for realism. Do the elements you intend to work with mean what you intend? Do they align with what you'd like your audience to think about? Such considerations lie at the heart of screen authorship, and *Creative Filmmaking from the Inside Out* asks you to become fully aware of your work's ethical and moral implications. This means not just guarding against mistakes, but consciously reaching out to further your deepest intentions.

VIABILITY AND WORKING WITHIN LIMITATIONS

After several read-throughs, you should have a very good sense of whether a script connects with you. Each reading, rather than giving you fatigue, should draw you deeper in. If you find yourself becoming attached and imagining scenes, hearing voices, seeing light and movement with each reading, then you need to pause and ask a critical and sobering question: is this script do-able with my resources? Can I pull it off? Your answer should not be overly optimistic, but should reflect the reality of your situation.

DETERMINE THE STORY GIVENS

Once you've considered the narrative and emotional appeal of the story and the cinematic qualities of the script, it's time to get down to practicalities. Make a list of the narrative givens directly specified in the screenplay, including:

- Epoch (contemporary or period).
- Total time frame.
- Length of film (remember, one page equals one minute of screen time).
- Tone (naturalistic, hyperbolic, fantastic, etc.).
- Locations (where and how many).
- Character details: How many characters? Who is the main character? Who are the other major characters? Who are the minor figures with or without speaking parts? How many extras populate the environment?
- Wardrobe and essential objects (props).
- Number of scenes and time of day for each.

The list of givens should revolve around the essential elements that make the story function, and provide you with your first sense of the scale of the story and the resources necessary to bring it to the screen. You may be able to tweak the story givens somewhat, combine or eliminate characters or scenes, change a location or two, but for the most part you should list all practical story parameters.

DETERMINE PROJECT RESOURCES

Assessing a screenplay requires balancing the need to find strong material that connects with you creatively *and* finding material you can realistically accomplish. I once had a student who wanted to direct a script written by a classmate in a screenwriting class. He was very excited about it and he was right to be—it was a powerful, short screenplay. But it had a problem—one of the essential characters was a two-month-old baby. Given the script, there was no way to use a doll or a bundle of blankets with goo-goo gaa-gaa sound effects—it had to be a real baby. Though he felt confident he could "find a baby", I probably don't need to tell you that he couldn't find anyone willing to loan their new baby for his student film and he never got the project off the ground. So, always be realistic about your screenplay's requirements, and the resources you need before you commit to any project.

Financial resources: How much cash do you have to spend on the film? How much do you realistically think you can raise? Filmmaking is an expensive art form—even if you're shooting digitally (see p. 322). Do factor in other in-kind support which might offset costs (e.g. donated equipment, services, supplies and so on).

Production time: Are you limited by a school or professional deadline? Are there external limits to your cast and crew's time and availability? How experienced are you and your crew (inexperience slows the process)?

Equipment and supplies: What do you have available? What are you and your crew qualified to use? How experienced are you with the equipment?

Location, sets, props and wardrobe: Are you limited geographically? Can you create environments? Do you have access to, or can you make, all the necessary props and wardrobe?

Cast and crew: What is the size and experience level of your crew? Can you get the necessary cast?

VIABILITY AND SAFETY ISSUES

Take production safety very seriously when assessing the viability of a screenplay. Does it call for car chases or picture vehicles? Are firearms or physical stunts involved? Does anything burn? Is there water involved where electricity might be? Boats? Extreme weather? Risky locations? Any of these situations requires specialized equipment, oversight, and planning by experienced professionals, all of which costs a great deal of money (if you're even allowed by your school to include such things).[2] Look closely, does the script call for anything that might run afoul of the safety regulations of your program and school, state law, or film production unions? Does the script call for anything that pushes the boundaries of common sense (for more on production safety see p. 347)?

WORKING WITHIN LIMITATIONS

Every film project, from a student's first film exercise to huge-budget Hollywood productions, works within limitations. No matter how good your idea, if it exceeds your resources and

---

[2] Many college film programs have strict safety guidelines which restrict the use of firearms, vehicles, open flames, stunts, and other hazards. Check your school's safety guidelines and incorporate these conditions in your viability assessment as well.

FIGURE 7-4

By working creatively with material he had to hand for his first film *El Mariachi,* Roberto Rodriguez launched his directing career.

experience, you will have no movie to show in the end. From the very beginning, one must clearly understand and work with what one *has* rather than what one *wishes* one had. Only with practicality and resourcefulness will you, in fact, make movies. A filmmaker's job is to make the best film possible given the reality of their particular circumstances and resources.

You can however be a successful filmmaker with limited means; you only need be smart with the resources that you have. Accepting limitations provides great opportunities for creative expression and innovation. Here's some advice from Roberto Rodriguez who famously made his first feature film, *El Mariachi* (1992) for only $7,000 and launched his career (Figure 7-4).

> Look around you. What do you have around you? Take stock in what you have. Your father owns a liquor store—make a movie about a liquor store. Do you have a dog? Make a movie about your dog. Your mom works in a nursing home, make a movie about a nursing home. When I did *El Mariachi* I had a turtle, I had a guitar case, I had a small town and I said I'll make a movie around that.[3]

[3] Roberto Rodriguez, *10 Minute Film School.* From BBC2 *Moving Pictures* (Dir. Philip Day, 1993).

CHAPTER 8

SCRIPT ANALYSIS AND DEVELOPMENT

The purpose of script development is threefold: first to reveal, through script analysis, the essential dramatic foundations of a work including its structure, character, story logic, and theme; second, to use creative intelligence to address weaknesses or missed opportunities; third, to make advantageous adjustments according to the creative assets one acquires along the way (such as talent, crew, locations, etc.). This is all part of the director's job. Only by sustained and methodical script development can the director fully inhabit every aspect of the story, explore all its potential, and capitalize on the cinema's strengths.

Always remember that a screenplay is not written in stone and should evolve throughout the production process. As a director, you remain constantly alert to refining the material as you strengthen your interpretive angle on the story, and as you adapt to the unfolding realities of casting and shooting. Script development may involve simplifying, cutting, compressing, or expanding the material—or even wholesale rewriting. Feature films I've worked on delivered new script pages down to the day of shooting.

Script development is usually done as a collaboration between the writer and director, though on commercial films producers play a big role as well. The director is in charge of guiding the script to a form that can be successfully brought to the screen, and this is why it's especially difficult to be a writer/director: you lack the critical distance necessary to re-imagine and re-work the screenplay.

COLLAPSING THE SCREENPLAY FOR ANALYSIS

Ideation—the development of ideas—and screenwriting call on taste and instincts. A writer may freely follow inspiration, intuition, and emotional memory rather than objectivity and logic. Story analysis and editing, on the other hand, which employ critical thinking and dramaturgic skills, rely on objectivity to see the work as an audience would see it, and to judge how best to structure and cadence the work for maximal impact on a first-time viewer.

You can certainly do your analysis directly on the screenplay, especially if you're working on a short film. However, working in screenplay format, with completed scenes and dialogue, means the basic structure is usually obscured. When a screenplay presents problems (and which one doesn't?), making a **step outline** (or **beat sheet**) from it reveals the essential plot structure and makes clear the development of central characters. Any glitches in these areas will quickly become apparent. To make a step outline at this point, simply go through the script, and give each scene a brief, functional description:

1. DAY: Elliot enters the park and spots the college kid Ricky at a park bench. The kid is nervous but Elliot, promising confidentiality, convinces him to hand over the photos.
2. When Elliot leaves the park he sees Angelo's SUV again. Realizing he's being watched, he runs down an alleyway.
3. After a harrowing foot chase through the city, Angelo and his sidekick lose Elliot in the crowd.
4. NIGHT: Kelly enters her apartment. Elliot is inside waiting for her. He pointedly asks her why Angelo always knows where he'll be. Kelly insists that he leave but he's not budging—this is the one place Angelo will never look for him.
5. NIGHT: On campus, Angelo's SUV pulls up alongside Ricky. Before the kid knows what's happening, he's dragged into the SUV and taken away.

Now you can see the essential flow of the story and its underlying dramatic logic. After you've done this, you can begin questioning the function of every scene in terms of plot information, character development, and connection to other scenes. You will see very clearly where holes exist and what scenes or characters are extraneous or not working as they should. Expect to uncover potentially useful story avenues or character attributes that were not previously developed.

Some directors use an additional tool to test the integrity of plot structure and narrative flow. Print each brief scene description on a 3 × 5 index card and then lay them out on a table in order. Now experiment with changing the position of select sequences to see if you can tell the story more interestingly. Consider intercutting sequences to create parallel stories. You can also experimentally collapse scenes into other scenes or even remove some entirely. Most scriptwriting software programs provide a 3 × 5 index card format outliner for just this purpose.

To keep your analysis on track, take the time to revise the central, ruling premise of the film as it changes—that is, the core concept behind all this narrative activity (see p. 69).

Creating a step outline and a premise are vital tools in testing the integrity of a story's foundations. By making them we are in effect reverse engineering the screenplay back to the original intentions of the dramatic work and thus uncover its full potential. Often you will find more going on than the screenwriter was aware of. Especially with feature length films, initial script analysis is far more efficient using a step outline than working with the entire screenplay.

> Once we've [writer and director] agreed on the all-important question "What's this picture about?" we can start in on the details. First comes an examination of each scene—in sequence of course. Does this scene contribute to the overall theme? How? Does it contribute to the story line? To

character? Is the story line moving in an ever increasing arc of tension or drama? [...] Is the story being moved forward by the characters?

—Sidney Lumet [1]

ANALYZING PLOT AND STORY LOGIC

As discussed in Chapter 5, **plot** is the sequencing of dramatic events, and it provides the central logic and energy for how the story unfolds. The plot should generate questions in the audience's mind and maintain dramatic tension, interest and involvement. Every step the characters take should feel inevitable. Anything unsupported, arbitrary, or coincidental weakens the causal chain on which the feeling of forward momentum depends. Once you uncover how the plot works, you need only common sense and a little inspiration to make improvements. However, if your analysis reveals confusion or facile storytelling, then think carefully before taking on the script—you want a story with solid foundations to work from.

Begin the plot analysis by first laying bare the larger structural issues and then zero in on scene details. As you can see from the quote by Sidney Lumet above, script analysis boils down to assiduously posing critical questions and, of course, answering them precisely and constructively. If answers are difficult to express or unrelated to the ultimate aims of the film, then you must flag these areas as problematic and in need of further development. Here are some basic questions to get you started on your own script analysis:

Structural Level

1. What is the central dramatic question? What overall problem needs to be solved?
2. What is the relationship between the plot conflicts and the overall premise?
3. Does the central problem remain consistent or does it evolve?
4. If it evolves, in what scenes does it take on new dimensions or go in new directions?
5. How does the main character get involved in this problem?
6. Who or what represents the principal opposing force?
7. What are the steps (actions and decisions) the main character takes to solve the central problem?
8. Are these actions dynamic (do they change in intensity and effect)?
9. What questions does the plot pose along the way, and where?
10. Does the plot maintain dramatic tension?
11. How does the film end?
12. Does this conclusion meaningfully answer the central question posed at the beginning?
13. What is the larger structure of the plot? (See p. 67)
14. Is there an obvious and natural connection between this plot and a central character?
15. Are there any credibility problems?

---

[1] From *Making Movies*, Sidney Lumet (Vintage Books, 1996).

Scene and Dramatic Unit Level

After you've examined the plot in general, take a close look at each and every dramatic unit (see Chapter 4).

16. What is the objective, obstacle, and result of each dramatic unit?

17. Whose scene is it (who controls the action and direction of the scene)?

18. What is this scene accomplishing (does it develop character, move plot forward, create dramatic questions, establish tone, etc.)?

19. Does any scene repeat what another scene has already accomplished?

20. Is there a logical dramatic flow to the scenes and sequences?

21. If I remove any particular scene, what will happen to the story? What will be lost?

22. Does any scene feel out of place, inconsistent, unnecessary, or just not right?

Plot points

A *plot point* is a moment in which a story pivots into new territory or where the dramatic circumstances become amplified. This can be the introduction of an unforeseen obstacle or story force; it can be a dramatic reversal or revelation, or it can be the ironic or unintended outcome of previous actions. Plot points create delicious dramatic questions like "Oh no, what will happen now?" and they send the story in new, unexpected directions. They shake things up and demolish the predictability that any story can fall into.

A great plot point example from *The King's Speech* occurs in Act 2 when Lionel, feeling a bit too bold, touches a nerve by telling Bertie that he'd make a better king than his brother. It's honest, but also a blunder; rather than encouraging Bertie, it scares him. After reprimanding Lionel harshly, Bertie terminates his speech therapy sessions with Lionel and stalks off. The audience knows that this will result in a personal disaster for Bertie and we wonder what will happen to him now that he's cut off his only hope of controlling his stammer.

To keep dramatic tension high in your film, plot points should occur whenever the story needs them:

23. Are the plot points organic to what came before?

24. Do they come as a surprise?

25. What questions do they provoke in the viewer?

26. What is the new dramatic direction they establish?

27. How do your main characters respond to each plot point?

28. Do the plot points increase the narrative tension?

While looking at the dynamics of the plot, we must also look closely at how those dynamics reveal and develop our characters, and how they move the plot forward. Remember from p. 57, in a plot-driven story it is the story line that determines the main character, and in a character oriented story it is the character that determines the story line.[2] In either case the two should be inextricably linked.

SUBJECTIVE OR OPEN POINT OF VIEW

The issue of **point of view** (POV) and cinematic storytelling is a critical and complex one for the director. Point of view plays out on a number of important levels that are explored in greater detail in Chapter 9. However, the aspects of POV we will be examining during an initial script analysis revolve not just around whose film this is (or, who is the protagonist) but also how tightly the viewer identifies with the central character. By definition, it is the central character's objectives, decisions and actions that determine the direction of the film, so the central character gets the lion's share of screen time. How often that main character shows up in scenes tells us how closely the script invites us to identify with him or her.

A film in which the main character is in every scene has a **close, subjective point of view** because the audience discovers and understands everything in the same way the central character does. Because we experience events through him or her, this strategy elicits very strong character identification. Let's say we open our movie with the following sequence:

> District Attorney Anne Zayas is in court excoriating a notorious Mafia boss in her closing arguments. Anne is pleased when the judge sentences the boss to 30 years in prison. Leaving the courthouse, Anne gets in her car and takes off down the road. As she drives down a picturesque highway, she notices the gorgeous sunset and decides to pull over to take a photo. She steps out of her car for a better angle and as she snaps a few shots her car suddenly explodes in a massive fireball!

The explosion is a shock for the audience, as it is for Anne, because they experienced it with her. They are also likely to ask the very same questions she's asking: who is trying to kill her? Is it related to the Mafia boss case? Their investigation starts with hers. That's a sequence of scenes with a close POV and strong character identification.

A film with an **open POV** will contain scenes that do not include the central character. When the audience experiences moments without the central character, they acquire more information than the absent protagonist and this can lead to many interesting possibilities. Let's rework the opening scene:

> D.A. Anne Zayas is in court excoriating a Mafia boss while… outside in the parking lot we see a man plant a bomb in the undercarriage of a car. Back in court, Anne is pleased when the judge sentences the boss to 30 years in prison. Leaving the courthouse, we see Anne get into the car with the bomb (!) and take off down the road. As she drives down a picturesque highway, she notices the gorgeous sunset and decides to pull over to take a photo. She steps out of her car for a better angle and as she snaps a few shots, her car explodes in a massive fireball!

---

[2] Paraphrased from *Making Movies*, by Sidney Lumet (pp. 30–31).

In this version, the explosion is not a total surprise to the audience because they knew more than she did. By loosening the previously tight POV identification, we gain in dramatic suspense. The whole time Anne is in her car the viewer is wondering *when* the car will blow and if Anne will be killed. The audience may still be wondering, like Anne, who is trying to kill her—but we have more clues than she does.

Now let's say that Anne's first step is to consult with her closest colleague and most trusted friend, Frank Hill. When they get together, the audience recognizes Frank as the man who planted the bomb (!) and all sorts of new questions and tensions enter the film. That little bit of information we learned in the absence of our protagonist yields enormous amounts of dramatic material. So,

29. How does the script handle point of view? Is the central character in every scene (close, subjective) or are there scenes which exclude them (open)?

30. Is there information the viewer knows but the central character does not?

It's important to look closely at how a script handles point of view and character identification because a wayward or inconsistent dramatic POV is often the sign of a writer not in control of all their narrative tools.

CHARACTER DEVELOPMENT

Characters, like real people, reveal who they are in a multitude of ways. We judge people by the clues in their physical appearance, their body language, and their surroundings. Their actions, large and small, help us interpret their temperament, assumptions, beliefs, and goals. How a person deals with unexpected, challenging, or threatening events tells us still more about their capacity to affect situations. All these factors establish how we understand characters, both in the real world and in the fictional word of drama. Never forget that character is destiny.

STATIC AND DYNAMIC CHARACTER DEFINITION

First assess the script's characters by their *givens* (age, sex, appearance, occupation, accents, etc.), but these lead only to a static summation. Characters stuck at this level of conception feel like figures in a photomontage in which each has a single role and attitude. You see this in TV commercials, which have to sell something in 30 seconds. Each character is *typical*: a typical mother, a typical washing machine repairman, a typical holiday couple on a typical romantic beach. Homes, streets, meals, and family relations are all typical—which is to say, stereotyped. Actors faced with static characterizations struggle in vain to breathe life into their parts.

The dynamic approach moves beyond what characters "are," and focuses instead on what challenges and mobilizes them. For this, you must uncover *on multiple levels* what each character is trying to get, do, or accomplish. Trained actors know how to look for this, yet need the help of their director to find the clues embedded in their characters' words and actions, and to breathe life into their roles. To obtain a complete character portrait, a director analyzing a screenplay looks at each character's internal needs and external behavior, paying special attention to when and how the character changes.

CHARACTER AND VOICE

Consider each significant role in terms of **character** and **voice**. We spent much of Part 2 discussing how character is revealed through actions. "A character is what a character does" (action = character) is a popular screenwriting adage. *Voice*, on the other hand, is the way in which characters present themselves to the world. What they wear, the way they keep their personal environment (home, office, etc.), the car they drive, what they say about themselves and, of course, the way they speak (the words they use, accents, etc.) all reveal a great deal.

FIGURE 8-1

Throughout Coppola's *The Godfather*, Michael Corleone (Al Pacino) presents himself as a regular, mild mannered guy, but his actions reveal otherwise.

These elements of voice can be written consistent with what we understand of that character through their actions, or voice can provide further layers of complexity, even of outright contradiction. As we know, people do not always present themselves as they really are.

Michael Corleone from *The Godfather* (Coppola, 1980) is the classic example of a character with a dramatically effective discrepancy between character and voice. He presents himself as a mild mannered and noble guy. When we first see him he's dressed in his military uniform with the decorations of a war hero. He speaks softly and never reveals a hot head or violent temper like his brother Sonny. Michael wants to make the family "legitimate," he says, and after telling a story in which his father closed a deal by threatening to blow someone's brains out, he says to his girlfriend, "That's my family, Kay. It's not me." He means he's not a gangster, but after he kills the Turk Sollozzo and a police captain, the heads of the five crime families as well as his sister's husband (!), the audience becomes absolutely certain that Michael is not only a gangster—he's the Godfather (Figure 8-1).

DEVELOPMENT

No story will move us much unless its main character has to struggle, grow in awareness, and change. This important process is called a character's **development**. You will need at least one character showing some degree of development, or the story will feel pointless. Character-based drama obviously offers great opportunity for character transformation, but action-oriented films also require character evolution, even if it is only their perception of the conflict, and their reactions to it that change.

Nancy Savoca's *Dogfight* (1991, written by Bob Comfort) tells the story of Eddie Birdlace, a US Marine, during one wild night of R&R before he ships out for Vietnam. Eddie and his marine buddies plan an event called the dogfight, a large party in which the marine who brings the "ugliest" date wins a prize. One rule is that the women cannot know about the dogfight contest. At the beginning of the film Eddie is a callous jerk who brings Rose, a date he believes ugly, to the

FIGURE 8-2

Character-based films with different approaches: Savoca's *Dogfight* (*left*) edifies its lead character Eddie (River Phoenix) over time, while in Fleck's *Half Nelson* (*right*) the depth of Dan's (Ryan Gosling) problem is slowly uncovered.

dogfight. When she manages to beautify herself for a night out, he even tries to make her look worse so that he can win the prize. However, Rose discovers the true nature of the event, and castigates him and his shipmates before running home devastated. The rest of the film involves Eddie trying to make it up to her by taking her out on a proper date. For the first time he sees a woman for who she really is, and falls in love with her. Throughout Act 2, the dramatic beats are devised to re-educate the main character: moment by moment Eddie's eyes are opened as he transforms into a better man (Figure 8-2, *left*).

Another interesting type of character development involves less the transformation of a character, than developing the audience's understanding of that character through slow revelation. In other words, the full complexity of a character reveals itself over the course of the film, bit-by-bit, like peeling away the layers of an onion. Dan Dunne, the principal character in Ryan Fleck's *Half Nelson* (2006, co-written with Anna Boden) is a terrifically complex and totally engaging character who does not essentially change; however the narrative line conspires to slowly uncover his true nature, one dramatic beat at a time. In the beginning, Dan is shown to be a dedicated junior high school teacher who truly connects with his students. But after a student discovers him freebasing cocaine in the school bathroom, we begin to understand the depths of Dan's drug addiction and of his self-imposed isolation. Much of the film's tension, in fact, revolves around the audience wishing that this likeable and capable teacher would pull himself together, but in the end, he's unable or unwilling to change much (Figure 8-2 *right*).

The development of a short film's main character usually happens very quickly, often as the result of a single transformative moment because there is not time for a slow or complex evolution. In some shorts, character development may only be minor and symbolic, but the fact that it exists is the sign of mature storytelling.

INTERNAL THROUGH-LINE

As you conduct your analysis, watch for evidence of an internal, connecting through-line of development. Can you detect a subtext from the external evidence? Can you sense what might be driving this character below the level of the plot? Writers do not necessarily devise character through-lines while they work—yet, if they remain true to human nature, internal through-line will emerge as each character negotiates conflict. It is the job of the director to seek these out.

CHARACTER ANALYSIS

It's often best to start your character analysis at the scene level. By tracing their immediate goals you will uncover the characters' development, moment by moment. To uncover a character's identity, voice, agency and dynamism apply the following questions to each significant dramatic unit and significant character.

Scene and Dramatic Unit Level

1. Whose scene is it (from whose POV)?
2. What is this character trying to get or do, moment by moment and short term?
3. What does this character bring to this moment from previous scenes?
4. What are the obstacles this character is facing (internal and external)?
5. How does each character try to overcome or adapt to each obstacle? What strategies do they employ and what choices do they make?
6. What do the actions and choices they make reveal about them?
7. What new situation is this character facing?
8. As a result of this new moment of development, has our understanding of this character changed?
9. Has this character's goals changed as a result of this moment?

When the answers become consistent, you sense you are completing a connect-the-dots puzzle. As the evidence mounts, characters should come to struggle for consistent ends and gain the dynamic qualities of living human beings. Over the whole piece, long-term goals should emerge that dominate each character's existence.

For a short film, a scene-by-scene analysis will usually suffice, but for a feature film you may want to correlate your character scene analysis with your structural plot analysis in order to uncover the broader strokes of character development.

Structural Level

10. What is this character trying to get or do in the long term?
11. What does this character want the most, and fear the most?
12. What are the larger obstacles that obstruct this character (and do they change)?

13. Does this character, on some level, create their own obstacles?

14. What tools or traits does this character have (or lack) to overcome obstacles?

15. Does internal conflict exist in the main character? If so, what is it, where does it come from, and how does it reveal itself?

16. Consider the relationship between character (what we learn from actions) and voice (what we learn from self-presentation): are they harmonious, or are there dramatically effective contradictions?

17. Does the main character change over the course of the film? If so, how and where?

18. How tight is the audience's perspective to the character POV? Does the audience know anything that the main character does not?

ESTABLISHING CHARACTER

While developing a story, you work from experience, imagination, and intuition, as well as from assumptions stored in the unconscious. Miscommunication about characters often begins from character traits that you take for granted but that your audience can't possibly know. It might be important to know that Harry is an honest man and would never perjure himself in court. The screenwriter who knows intuitively, from the very first draft, that Harry is honest can easily forget that the audience knows nothing of the sort. Harry's openness must be "established"—a frequent word in script discussions. To do this, you must create some situation early on where Harry can reveal his innate honesty in a way organic to the events—perhaps by including a scene where he returns to pay for the newspaper he has unthinkingly carried out with his groceries.

When establishing your character, think in terms of actions and behavior instead of dialogue. Harry could simply say, "Trust me. I'm honest and never lie," but when did you ever trust someone who said something like this? Action is more believable and indelible.

When a character's behavior strikes you during your analysis as confusing or arbitrary, what is often missing is an earlier moment that establishes some basic characteristics before they come into play in the plot.

DIALOGUE AND VERBAL ACTION

Writers responding to criticism are always tempted to first rework dialogue, but in fact dialogue is often the last element we put under the critical microscope. Don't bother tweaking it until you are first certain that your story is structurally sound. To analyze dialogue, leave aside the step outline and turn to the full screenplay (hopefully now revised).

How does one recognize good dialogue? Cinema dialogue aims to be vernacular speech. Whether the character is an immigrant worker, a young street punk, or an academic philosopher, each uses their own speech—broken English, street slang, or jargon-laden abstractions. Each needs his or her own dialogue characteristics. Each person's vocabulary, syntax, and verbal rhythms have to be special and unlike another's—and certainly not simply a reflection of how the author speaks.

Dialogue in life and dialogue in movies are different. In the cinema, it must sound true to life yet exclude life's verbosity and repetitiousness. The best cinema dialogue is highly succinct, but just as informal and authentically "incorrect." Getting this right takes exacting research and a careful ear. To get a sense for the natural rhythms and vocabulary of everyday speech, listen in on other people's conversations. Yes, eavesdrop. By transcribing everything you hear—complete with ums, ers, "like"s, grunts, and pauses—you will see that normal conversation is not normal at all. People converse elliptically, often at cross-purposes and never in the tidy ping-pong of stereotypical drama. In real life, little is denoted (said directly) and much is connoted (alluded to in a roundabout way). Silences are often the real "action" during which extraordinary currents flow between the speakers. I once overheard two man-boys in a coffee shop conversing just like this:

— Dude, I gotta ... it's just ... go, you know? Go!

— You are totally, like, running away, dude ... that's like ... knowwhatimsaying?

— Naw, dude, I'm not doin' that sh*t. I'm leaving, that's it, you know ... it's ... whatcanIsay? Opportunities, and, you know.

— C'mon dude, I mean, Germany?

— Well, yeah ... dude, What's the ... it's no different than anything else. And I told her that ... I told her ... I was like ... phew ... that's it. Yeah ... whatever ...

— Dude, man ... I mean, like ... I don't know.

Good movie dialogue attempts to remove what is redundant, yet retain, or even strengthen, the sense and idiosyncrasies. This way, voices become strongly defined and their subtexts more vivid. This is the secret of masters such as Paddy Chayefsky, Paul Schrader, Nora Ephron, Mike Leigh, Woody Allen, Quentin Tarantino, Charlie Kaufman, Ruth Prawer Jhabvala and so on. By truly listening, then abbreviating and sharpening, they capture the keys to other people's behavior and thinking. Here's what would appear in a screenplay.

```
                    MAN-BOY #1
        Dude, I gotta go. Just go!

                    MAN-BOY #2
        You're totally running away.
        You know that?

                    MAN-BOY #1
        I'm not running away. I'm just leaving.
        That's it. Opportunities.

                    MAN-BOY #2
        C'mon. Germany?

                    MAN-BOY #1
        It's no different than anywhere else.
        And I told her I told her, that's it.

                    MAN-BOY #2
        I don't know, dude.
```

Using the word "dude" tells us a lot about a character's voice, but repeating it in *every* sentence can become unintentionally comical in a movie—even if that was how these guys "really" talked.

VERBAL ACTION

The best dialogue is **verbal action** because the speaker *uses words to get or accomplish something*. It is pressure applied even as it seeks to deflect pressures the speaker is experiencing. Active and structurally indispensable to the scene, good dialogue is never verbal arabesque or an editorial explanation of what is visible. Least of all is it verbal padding. Ted Tally's screenplay for *The Silence of the Lambs* (Demme, 1991) is masterful for its use of verbal action—nearly every line of dialogue intends to elicit information, hides intentions, proves worthiness, or tries to gain dominance. Clarice Starling's first encounter with Dr. Chilton, the egotistical director of the asylum that holds Hannibal Lecter, does not go well. In his office Chilton quickly makes a pass at her:

> CHILTON
> You know, we get a lot of detectives here, but I can't ever remember one so attractive […] Will you be in Baltimore overnight? Because this can be quite a fun town if you have the right guide.
>
> CLARICE
> I'm sure it's a great town, Dr. Chilton, but my instructions are to talk to Lecter and report back this afternoon.

Chilton's line reveals that he does not take her seriously as a law enforcement professional. But when she swiftly but carefully rejects his advance, he turns mean by explicitly undercutting her abilities:

> CHILTON
> Crawford's very clever using you […] Pretty young woman to turn him on. I don't believe Lecter's even seen a woman in eight years and ohhh are you ever his taste - so to speak.
> CLARICE
> I graduated from UVA doctor, it is not a charm school.

Chilton's insinuation that Clarice has no professional abilities beyond her use as sexual bait is intentionally insulting. He wants her to know she is a novice and he is her superior. You can

FIGURE 8-3 ——————————————

Dr. Chilton (Anthony Heald) from Demme's *The Silence of the Lambs* uses words as aggressive action in an attempt to dominate Clarice Starling.

see from her retort that this entire encounter is essentially a verbal boxing match. Each time Chilton aggressively asserts his authority and dominance over Clarice, she reveals her capacity to deftly parry the challenges of a sexist schmuck (Figure 8-3).

REPLACING DIALOGUE WITH ACTION

When analyzing dialogue, always question whether the writer is using dialogue to communicate ideas when they might better be expressed through action. On the whole, action is more efficient, interesting, and convincing than verbal explanation. However, actions are sometimes more than what a character does to accomplish their objectives. Some non-verbal activities or moments can be extremely revealing. A student of mine once wrote a scene in which a teen-aged sister gives unsolicited advice to her resistant 10-year-old brother. The original scene involved the siblings sitting on the porch of their house and just talking it out. The sister kept giving advice, the brother saying he wasn't interested and wanting to be left alone, and the sister expressing her frustration with his obstinacy. Not only was the scene far too long, but it felt flat because they just sat there, hands on knees, articulating in clear terms how they felt.

The solution was to totally reconceive the scene, first by moving it to the boy's bedroom (his personal space). His sister enters without knocking and launches into her advice (a nice action to show her officiousness). In response, the boy starts playing a video game involving loud gunshots and explosions (effectively shutting her out with an action). When she pauses for a response to her advice he says nothing—his full concentration remains on the game (showing her and us that he's not interested in anything she has to say). The sister gets up and storms out of the room (revealing her frustration). The boy then puts the game away and calmly shuts the door.

This scene not only diminished from three pages to one, but said everything it had to say in a far more efficient and memorable way.

As a matter of craft, try to substitute action for every issue handled verbally. It may mean looking for strong actions that reveal intentions and feelings so that actors need not articulate them, but it may also simply involve replacing a line like, "I told you not to mention that in front of my parents," with a sharp look from one character to the another. Sometimes an action or activity can heighten tension by concealing rather than revealing a character's true feelings. Such suppression is very human because it reveals inner and outer dimensions, the conscious and the unconscious, the public and the private. Directors commonly ask writers at this stage to replace dialogue with action or visual activity.

TESTING DIALOGUE

To initially assess dialogue, first read the lines aloud, listening to the sound of your own voice and asking:

1. Is every word and every phrase in the character's particular vernacular?
2. What is this character trying to do or get with these words?
3. Are the words explaining, displaying, or hiding feelings?
4. Does the dialogue constitute behavior or exposition (for exposition, see below)?
5. Does the dialogue carry a compelling subtext (a deeper underlying connotation)?
6. Could it be made more subtextual (allusive and indirect) instead of "on the nose" (evident and obvious)?
7. Does it make the listener speculate or respond emotionally?
8. Is anything awkward for an actor to articulate?
9. Can it be briefer, by even one syllable, and remain effective?

The next test is to have an informal **table reading** with a **scratch cast**; that is, a reading from beginning to end with trained actors who are not necessarily the cast. Table readings allow a director to just listen—a valuable perspective. Actors are very attuned to the flow and purpose of dialogue so you can explore these questions with them. During this reading you want to concentrate on the language of the dialogue, not its performance, so actors should not attempt to play the emotions fully. Instead, instruct them to read at half intensity, meaning relatively flat.

If the script is fairly well advanced, consider holding the reading with a small, invited audience who will tell you candidly what they think. In discussion with both actors and audience, be ready to wholeheartedly justify every word of dialogue and every stage direction in the script. Sometimes you cannot, because you discover new aspects during this process—and that's the purpose of holding a dramatic reading.

CHECKING EXPOSITION

Exposition is information needed by the audience in order to understand the story. This might be medical or legal information, but it could also be information about a character from before the film begins. This kind of expository information is called **backstory**.

Short films should always be conceived, as much as possible, with no exposition or backstory so that they are narratively self-contained. Some feature films incorporate very little exposition while others require substantial amounts. *Erin Brockovich* (Soderbergh 2000) requires the audience to understand the scientific details and public health consequences of the toxic waste hexavalent chromium, as well as the procedures of a class action lawsuit. The film also provides some backstory about Erin's personal history and past marriages so we understand what drives her to succeed. All these expository details are handled deftly by screenwriter Susannah Grant (Figure 8-4 *left*).

FIGURE 8-4

Soderbergh's *Erin Brockovich* (*left*) skillfully delivers reams of necessary exposition, while Scott's *Thelma & Louise* (*right*) remains coy by not being explicit about backstory.

Exposition poses a problem for the writer because it's not story with a momentum, it's explanation. Efforts to shoe-horn raw exposition into a scene often stand out as clunky, inorganic passages in which the audience feels the writer feeding them information. The most important questions to ask when you come across exposition are:

1. Do I really need this exposition?
2. Do I really need all of it?
3. Do I really need it right now (or can it be drip-fed in less obvious increments through multiple scenes)?

A poorly written screenplay will frontload the story with exposition in the belief that the audience must know all the facts before they can understand the story. An experienced dramatist knows that you always go with emotion before facts. If the story is compelling, you can actually do away with facts that add very little. During the turning point scene in Ridley Scott's 1991 film *Thelma & Louise* (written by Callie Khouri, Figure 8-4 *right*), Louise walks across the parking lot of a cowboy dancehall and discovers the man with whom Thelma was dancing is now trying to rape her. Louise holds a gun on him and he lets Thelma go—but before the women walk away he hisses a crude insult at Louise. She turns and shoots him dead. Now Thelma and Louise are fugitives. As the women flee, always just one step ahead of the law, Detective Slocum discovers that something happened to Louise in Texas. In a phone conversation where Slocum is trying to get Louise to turn herself in he says "I know what happened to you in Texas. The judge will take what happened in Texas into consideration." But never is there any explicit expository dialogue or flashback that explains what exactly happened to Louise. The audience doesn't need to know—in fact, it's probably more powerful left to their imaginations.

Here are a few principles when working with necessary exposition:

1. Reveal facts about characters through visuals or action as much as possible (expository dialogue is always awkward).

2. Do not create characters or scenes for the sole purpose of communicating exposition (e.g. therapists asking "tell me what's going on and how you feel about it," neighbors who come over to "talk about it," concerned mothers who say "tell me everything, dear.") Every character, action, and scene must make some dramatic contribution to the story beyond dragging out facts.

3. Hide verbal exposition in scenes that have a strong dramatic purpose (or are funny).

4. Motivate the exchange of exposition. There must be a compelling dramatic reason for one character to tell another this information and it should be organic to the scene. It's poor exposition if a defense lawyer says to the prosecutor, "My client is going to take the Fifth Amendment. That means that he doesn't have to testify at his own trial." Both lawyers obviously know the law so there is no reason to spell it out. However, the writer can motivate the exposition by placing it in a dramatic scene between the defense lawyer and the defendant's frantic mother:

— "Don't worry. I'm going to have your son take the Fifth Amendment."
— "Fifth what? What's that?"
— "It just means they can't make your son testify at his own trial. They'll never get him on the stand."

ASSESSING ENVIRONMENTAL DETAIL

LOCATIONS

The writer indicates the locations for a film, but they are too important to take for granted or leave poorly defined. Locations can add a great deal of information, context, and even thematic meaning to each scene and the story as a whole. Neutral, bland settings stop a film from ever reaching below the surface of the story. Inappropriate locations are worse, because they compel the audience to struggle with plausibility at every scene change. Carefully consider each location to assess what it can add to each scene's content.

J.C. Candor's low budget 2011 film *Margin Call* is about major figures in an investment firm discovering they are holding on to assets that may ruin them. Their moral dilemma is whether to hold on to toxic assets and watch the company fold, or to sell them off before anyone discovers they're junk. Naturally, the preponderance of the film takes place in the offices and board rooms of an investment bank. At a critical plot point the firm's CEO appeals to Sam Rogers, the firm's best sales manager, to direct his team to dump the toxic assets—a strategy to which Sam is morally opposed. This pivotal scene could have been set in the CEO's office but Chandor made a brilliant choice and set it instead in the men's bathroom (Figure 8-5).

Not only does it even out the power differential between them so that Rogers feels free to speak his mind, but toilets and what goes down them are a good dumping metaphor, and we're reminded that behind the money, power and headlines are just human beings who, like all of us, must use the facilities from time to time. It humanizes the world-altering decisions taking place

FIGURE 8-5 ————————————————————

Location as metaphor. A high finance deal takes place in the men's bathroom in Chandor's *Margin Call*.

and reminds us that economic shifts are not forces of nature, but choices made by ordinary people—sometimes in unlikely places.

SOUND

An area of cinematic storytelling routinely overlooked by beginners is sound. Most neophyte filmmakers only think about it during postproduction, when it's often too late. More experienced filmmakers, on the other hand, incorporate sound during the scripting process as an element of story, tone and mood. I am not talking about score music, I mean the sounds of the location, sounds that reveal things, sounds that hide things, sounds providing irony, emotion or information, or sounds that drive the story forward. Make a practice of reading through the screenplay exclusively for sound and its potential in the telling of the story or in establishing tone.

As an example, return to *The King's Speech* script pages on p. 46. Notice that just as Bertie begins his fated speech, revealingly stammering badly on the word "K-K-King," Seidler writes "The stammer careens back at him, amplified and distorted by the stadium PA [public address] system." It's devastating because the already self-conscious Bertie is brutally confronted by his own "defect." He hears exactly how every stuttered consonant, verbal falter and gasp for breath is being broadcast to the world (see discussion of *The Man Who Knew Too Much* on p. 178).

By carefully using evocative and revealing locations and their sound possibilities, you can hurl the audience into the emotional heart of a situation. When this process begins in the script development stage, it can continue in the preproduction (locations), production (locations and sound), and postproduction stages (sound).

INVITING A CRITICAL RESPONSE

To shoot an imperfectly developed screenplay is to open a Pandora's box of problems. Trying to cure them later, as they become apparent in the editing stage, is heartbreaking. It's important, therefore, that you expose your work at different stages to criticism from readers or audiences who know little to nothing about the project. Objective critique is crucial, and often energizing, because it usually generates fresh perspectives on the work. Although raw critical feedback can be frightening, it helps confirm how well each aspect of your film is reaching a first-time audience.

We've already discussed the table reading as one procedure for gaining valuable feedback (p. 106) but another is to send your script-in-progress for comments from several trusted *readers*.

It's important that they not be personally involved in the project beyond wanting to help you make a good film. Here are a few tips for using readers effectively:

- Find mature readers whose values you share and respect.
- Find readers with some sense of how to read a screenplay.
- Ask for an overview understanding of the script.
- Ask about their impressions of each character and which they find compelling.
- Ask what they believe is driving each main character, and what they believe each is trying to achieve.
- Ask which scenes are particularly effective or involving.
- Ask which are not effective or involving.
- Ask if they found anything confusing or implausible.
- Ask if they remained engaged throughout, or if they stopped caring at any point.
- Ask what they think the film as a whole is about.

Important from this is to learn what impressions a first-time reader gets from the page. If your reader says, "I thought Frank was an insensitive bully" then you can decide if that's what you want, in which case it's a positive response. If the assessment is not what you had in mind, then you must figure out how to rework the character.

By cultivating astute critical feedback, you aim to acquire a complete and accurate sense of what your audience knows and feels at each stage of the proposed film. What is *not* useful is to hear about the film readers would themselves have made from similar material. Remember, it's your film and you must guard its integrity. I recently wrote a stylish, low-budget gangster film on commission, and a reader (not chosen by me) told me that *The Godfather* was the greatest film ever made. My script was problematical for him because my main character wasn't enough like Michael Corleone. He even told me what Michael would do in each scene! He was right. My character wasn't like Michael Corleone; he wasn't supposed to be.

INCORPORATING CRITICISM

In a mass medium, the director's job is to be understood by a wide audience and to captivate. This begins with your first critics. If you resist criticism and argue with your critics instead of just listening, you are probably insecure. If you agree with almost everything and set about a total rewrite—or worse, scrap the project—it means you are *very* insecure. If, however, you continue to believe in what you are doing, and recognize some truth in what your critics say, you are progressing nicely.

Never make changes hastily or impulsively. Let the criticism sit for a few days, then see what you can accept as valid. You do not need to accept or reject everything wholesale; use what is useful and discard the rest.

Be cautious about responses from family or intimates. They often want to hide your flaws from public view. Almost as damaging is their loving, across-the-board praise, whether earned or not. So, show your work to friends and family after it's finished, and only in the company of a general audience, whose responses will greatly help your people in theirs.

ASSESS AND REASSESS

The purpose of all this close analysis and development is, of course, to discover the latent dramatic power of the screenplay and to devise a rewrite strategy after each round to ensure that every moment functions to enrich the whole. In some cases rewrites can be relatively minor, but the director and writer should not be afraid to tackle substantial changes if it can truly improve the integrity of the project.

Seidler's *The King's Speech* took 50 drafts (going from screenplay, to stage play and back to screenplay). The final drafts came only weeks before shooting because a diary by Lionel Logue surfaced with notes about his treatment of the king. Clearly, such new information had to be incorporated. Director Tom Hooper said of the diary's impact on subsequent re-writes:

> There were snippets of wonderful dialogue. Most famously, at the end of the final speech, Logue turns to the king and says, "You still stammered on the 'W,'" and the king says, "Well, I had to throw in a few so they knew it was me," which always gets a huge laugh... Also, my search was originally "What is the epiphany, what is the moment in the therapy where he (Bertie) makes the breakthrough"? And it was a detail from the diaries—that Bertie and Logue were alone in a room when he delivered the speech—that made me think that maybe the epiphany isn't about therapy, it's about friendship.[3]

During your screenplay rewrites, update your step outline and premise, or you will lose track of the meaning of the piece as a whole. Your work will subtly change and may even take on new thematic focus. This is a truly magical aspect of narrative art and it doesn't end here—every stage in the filmmaking process, right up to the final edit, presents new opportunities to distill more meaning and impact from the film.

Along the way, keep your audience strongly in mind. This means not exploiting them or making easy or cynical compromises, but trying to work toward a final script that investigates some human dilemma, prompts pertinent questions and ideas, and challenges conventional thought. Remember from pp. 39–40 that Nabokov advises us that, in the telling of a story, we should always keep in mind the "profit and pleasure" of the audience. When you succeed, it will resonate afterward in the hearts and minds of your viewers, and may even change their lives a little. That is art's work in the world.

---

[3] *Q&A with 'King's Speech' director Tom Hooper*, by Walter Addiego, *San Francisco Chronicle*, Feb. 4, 2011.

PART 4

AUTHORSHIP AND AESTHETICS

PART 4-1 ————————————————————————————————————

Matthew S. Nagy (DP) and Morgan Pavlovic (AC) frame a tricky mirror shot for student director Tony Gioconda's film *Gift*.

PART 4-2 ————————————————————————————————————

A film crew using atmospheric smoke and a jib arm.

CHAPTER 9

CINEMATIC POINT OF VIEW

The most important thing a director needs is a point of view. When you see a movie, if you're alert, it's the thinking that went on behind the movie that's interesting, really. The rest is just … scenery. Even the script. In the first ten or fifteen shots of a film you can usually tell whether the director's thinking and what he's thinking about.

—Oliver Stone[1]

Once a director has thoroughly analyzed the screenplay for dramatic and narrative integrity, their work has only just begun. A director is a Storyteller whose medium is not the screenplay, but the screen. The visual compositions, performances, lighting, sound, setting, and the juxtaposition of images are the director's tools and means of expression. The tonal and stylistic designs latent in the screenplay start taking shape as soon as you can separate the interlocking aspects of film discourse, and give each a functional name. This section, along with Part 5, will help equip your cinematic storytelling toolbox so you can make the successful transition from script to screen.

TELLING STORIES ON FILM

The philosopher and filmmaker Michael Roemer begins his provocative survey of narrative like this:

Every story is over before it is begun. The novel lies bound in my hands, the actors know all their lines before the curtain rises, and the finished film has been threaded onto the projector when the houselights dim.

Stories appear to move into an open, uncertain future that the figures try to influence, but in fact report a completed past they cannot alter. Their journey into the future—to which we gladly lend ourselves—is an illusion.[2]

---

[1] From *Moviemakers' Master Class*, Laurent Tirard (Faber and Faber, 2002).
[2] *Telling Stories: Postmodernism and the Invalidation of Traditional Narrative*, Michael Roemer (Rowman & Littlefield, 1995).

Standing like an authorial puppet master behind these illusory figures is the invisible figure of the cinema Storyteller, whose part is yours to play as the director. You determine your movie's vision of the universe through making aesthetic decisions, and these derive from:

- The nature and requirements of the story
- The tone and mood suggested by the story and its themes
- The nature and purpose of the main characters
- Their changing points of view inside the story
- The plot and how it is presented in time (structure)
- The associations of space, environment, and time period
- The Storyteller's intended impact on the audience.

These aspects relate to each other in a confusingly circular way, but I shall argue that point of view (POV) is pivotal, and makes as good a starting point as any.

POINT OF VIEW IN LITERATURE

In literature, a story's narrating POV has two basic sources. One is **omniscient POV**, and belongs to the Storyteller standing outside the story; the other is **subjective POV**, and belongs to a character within it. For both, the type of person, their outlook and point of view, are inextricably linked.

The *omniscient narrator* has unrestricted movement in time and place. Like God, he or she while revealing the story's events can see into every aspect of the characters' past, present, and future. The *self-effacing narrator* is also omniscient, but leaves us to make our own interpretations through showing the tale neutrally and without comment.

The *character within the story POV* offers a more partisan, subjective, and limited perspective that is routed through what that character experiences, sees, hears, and (mis)understands. He or she can be:

- A *naive narrator* unaware of all the implications in his or her situation
- A *knowing narrator* who may pretend naïveté, but be more astute than he or she cares to show
- An *epic hero*, such as Odysseus or Superman, who is cunning, heroic, or superhuman.

The character within the story sometimes addresses the reader directly and can have omniscient powers, as in the "tall tale" convention in which the narrator affects great knowledge and ability.

There are two types of literary narrative: *simple narrative*, which is functional and supplies an exposition of events, usually in chronological order; and *plot-driven narrative*, which entertains by generating suspense. This type of narrative often reorders story chronology to reveal events according to the story's type and plot strategy.

To generate anticipation and involvement in the reader, storytelling aims to generate *suspense* or *narrative tension*. This arises from predicaments the characters must face, attitudes they take, and from the author's critical attitude toward the characters. Getting us involved, making us *identify* with the characters, makes us buy into the stakes for which they play. Often tension is raised by withholding information or creating disorientation—familiar from the mystery story, where the reader must interpret clues and spot the killer.

POINT OF VIEW IN FILM

A point-of-view shot is a camera angle taken from a character's physical location in the scene (see p. 185), but the broader issue of cinematic point of view (POV) is rather less tangible. As with point of view in literature, you know it because it somehow makes you share a character's feelings and predicaments, an effect easier to describe than account for. Harder still is to say how to write, direct, and control it.

Film language—unlike the printed page, which obligingly stands still as you analyze it—moves in a flow of dynamic images that are subtly modified by words, symbols, sounds, color, movement, and music. However complex it is, POV is nevertheless within its director's sphere of influence.

Compared with literature, the screen has both advantages and handicaps. Cinematography can set up a situation and a gripping mood in seconds, avoiding literature's lengthy tracts of exposition, but photography's inclusiveness can present a bewildering array of detail. James Monaco says that the "insistently descriptive nature of the film image inundates both subject and subtext with irrelevant detail. Ideas and authorial clarity are therefore harder to achieve." Terrence Malick's *Days of Heaven* (1978) is a beautiful and moving film on a big screen, but only from the reduced image of a TV viewing did I grasp its underlying themes and allusions.

Film must use framing, blocking (choreographing the subject and camera), and editing to keep the eye where it needs to be. In film realism, the camera often uses an omniscient POV with occasional forays into individual characters' viewpoints, but let's look at the wide array of POV options available to filmmakers, and see what they offer as authorial tools. We're going to start close on the particularities of the main character, and then back away, ending with the audience's broad, onlooker perspective.

CENTRAL CHARACTER, ONE POINT OF VIEW

The single main character is by far the most common internal narrative POV. Main characters and their issues are established by exposing the audience to the events that put a central character under revealing pressure. Audience members merge with them through empathy and identification. Tony Richardson's *A Taste of Honey* (1961) focuses like a documentary on a provincial teenager in the grim industrial cityscape of Manchester. After her mother takes off with a new boyfriend, she gets pregnant and must struggle to survive. Often led by raw emotion, she bears some responsibility for what happens. Then lonely and abandoned by the baby's father, she is befriended by a nurturing homosexual boy. Thus, through the interaction of her character, social class, environment, and sheer chance, her destiny takes shape under the sympathetic gaze of the audience.

IMPLIED CHARACTER POV

Most films more or less follow the lead of omniscient literature, and imply POV by involving the audience in the concerns and changing awareness of whoever is at the center of the work. Dorothy as she sets off down the yellow brick road in Victor Fleming's *The Wizard of Oz* (1939) is a good example. As she passes through a bewitched landscape, we share her shocks and insecurities, and rejoice when she overcomes difficulties. Dorothy is joined by the Cowardly Lion, the Tin Man, and the Scarecrow, each an alter ego whom she inspires to continue, but who actually represents a threatened aspect of her own psyche. At the end, when she awakens, we understand that Dorothy has been reordering aspects of herself while dreaming, and that her quest has been to reconcile the anxieties of her waking life. What a beautiful vision!

SUBJECTIVE CHARACTER POV

Because events are experienced through the filter of the central character's perceptions, a director portrays the events of the story by drawing upon the central character's high degree of subjectivity. Thus **subjective character POV** takes into account both the immediate emotional perspectives of the main character and those that are more broadly psychological. These, in turn, influence content and form, and show up in a number of ways:

- Subjectivity may be explicit, in the form of a character who speaks as a narrator directly to the audience, either through first person voice-over narration as with Ryan Bingham in Jason Reitman's *Up in the Air* (2009, Figure 9-1), or through the much rarer direct camera address by one such as the titular character in *Amélie* (Jeunet, 2001).

- Subjective POV characters are often present in every scene in the film. However, any information the audience learns is necessarily restricted to that learned by the central character. Ryan in *Up in the Air* is in every scene and we encounter all the other characters as he encounters them. We accompany him through every step of his developing relationships and in the end discover along with him the stunning truth that the woman he's fallen in love with is married and has children. So deeply does this strategy plunge us into Ryan's subjectivity that no words are necessary to understand the impact this revelation has upon him.

FIGURE 9-1

The POV of Reitman's *Up In The Air* is strongly established as being from Ryan Bingham's (George Clooney) perspective.

- A deeply subjective film may feature a retrospective POV, meaning the body of the film is perhaps a diary or exploration of memory.

- Expressive mise-en-scène (directing, compositions, scene design, and blocking) and sound design contribute heavily to immersing us in a character's psychological state (see Part 5).

- Personal POV shots (see p. 185) help connect an audience to a character's emotional reactions or internal state of mind and help create a strong sense of subjective perspective.

- Also possible, but rarely used, is the subjective camera POV, where the camera directly represents what the character is seeing—as if we were looking through their eyes. All other characters interacting with the central character thus look directly into the camera (and directly at the audience). Julian Schnabel's *The Diving Bell and the Butterfly* (2007) uses this technique extensively to powerful effect.

Keep in mind that the single-character implied POV and subjective POV are not isolated approaches. Many films will mix and match these as the narrative requires. Films employing an implied POV will often flip into a deeply subjective mode when the main character negotiates particularly emotional, pivotal, or climactic scenes. Jonathan Demme's *The Silence of the Lambs* introduces expressionistic framings and sound design to bring us into Clarice Starling's subjectivity whenever the pressure on her becomes especially intense (Figure 9-2).

MULTIPLE CHARACTERS, MULTIPLE POVS

Dual main characters: The subjects in Penn's *Bonnie and Clyde* (1967), Malick's *Badlands* (1974), and Scott's *Thelma and Louise* (1991) are partnerships involving two equally important POV characters. All three films involve outlaws and road journeys ending in self-destruction. In the first two works, the dramatic tension revolves around the fugitive couple's relationship, whereas *Thelma and Louise* explores two differing women's perspectives on the same dilemma. In the end they converge into a shared understanding of women and society.

Ryan Fleck's *Half Nelson* (2006) also has two character POVs, but the perspectives come through two characters of very different social position: Dan Dunne, a white, middle-class junior high school teacher and Drey, his 13-year-old African American student whose single mother is struggling to make ends meet. But as the film candidly explores the extent of Dan's drug addiction and Drey's inexorable fall into a criminal life, they become near equals in peril. By creating two vulnerable and uncertain characters struggling with forces beyond their control, Fleck assiduously avoids kitsch sentiment or simple moral polarities in order to reveal how empathy can connect people across age, class, sex, and racial divides.

FIGURE 9-2

Demme's careful framings in *The Silence of the Lambs* bring the viewer into Clarice Starling's (Jodie Foster) subjectivity, as in this uncomfortable frame that pushes her into the corner as Lecter burrows into her psyche on their first meeting.

Multiple characters: Robert Altman's *Nashville* (1975) and *Gosford Park* (2001, Figure 9-3) have casts reaching into double figures, and there is no dominant POV. Each

FIGURE 9-3

Like other Altman films, *Gosford Park* explores relationships and hierarchies in a special corner of society.

character is a thread in a social fabric, and each film focuses on the patterns that emerge from group situations.

This concern with collective life and multiple narrative perspectives also emerges in Soderbergh's *Traffic* (2000) and Gaghan's *Syriana* (2005). Both explore the interconnectedness of people, economies, actions, and consequences up and down a sociological scale.

When POV migrates from character to character, we gain access to a range of people's needs, feelings and awarenesses. Shifts of POV between characters give empathic insight into multiple characters' thoughts and feelings, and portray a fuller and more complex (and even divergent) understanding of the events of the narrative. Joe Wright's 2007 film *Atonement* gains great dramatic complexity by repeating critical events from two different subjectivities, each highly charged emotionally: the immature and bewildered perspective of Briony, a 13 year-old with a vindictive nature and a child's crush on the much older Robbie; and Robbie himself, as he falls into a passionate romance with Briony's older sister Cecilia. There are also occasional forays into Cecilia's POV as well, rounding out the complete story of this tragic triangle, a fateful night, and a lie that destroys three lives (Figure 9-4).

Subsidiary or alternative POVs: In addition to films with the full-fledged, multiple POVs of central characters, drama can also switch briefly to subsidiary POVs whenever it augments or refreshes the viewer's perceptions. Sometimes seeing through a minor character's or an antagonist's

FIGURE 9-4

A critical moment in the film *Atonement*, as seen by 13-year-old Briony (Saoirse Ronan) whose POV is one of three represented in the movie.

perspective for a brief moment leads us to know more than the main character, which can multiply narrative possibilities and heighten suspense. A similar effect can also be achieved through parallel action—that is, by cutting to another story strand happening concurrently.

So enigmatic was the historical Oskar Schindler that Spielberg's *Schindler's List* (1993) sees him mostly through the eyes of those around him. Good fiction uses minor characters, and shows that they, too, have lives, feelings, and agendas to fulfill.

THE DIRECTOR'S POV: FROM CONCERNED OBSERVER TO STORYTELLER

The kindly angels in Wim Wenders' *Wings of Desire* (1987, Figure 9-5) keep Berliners under empathic observation.

Cinema itself is like one of these angels, following and observing characters as it does while they live their lives. Let's call this perspective that of the **Concerned Observer**, because he is involved, invisible, and weightless like a spirit. Feeling for the characters, the observer leaves the periphery to fly into the center of things, always searching for greater significance and larger patterns of meaning beyond the mere witnessing of activity.

Developing empathy with the characters and knowledge of them, the Concerned Observer comes to identify with them in their unfolding difficulties, and tries profoundly to understand them. It is a part we all play in life, so it feels familiar, and it is a role that every director must

FIGURE 9-5

In *Wings of Desire*, everyone has a guardian angel looking over his shoulder who can sympathetically observe, but cannot intervene.

actively adopt in making films. Through the perspective of the Concerned Observer we register the competing dramatic tensions, perspectives, objectives, appeals, and sensibilities of all the dramatic characters as they negotiate the plot and conflicts of the film. This POV guides us each time we must choose where to place the camera, who or what to emphasize at any particular moment, when to cut away, when to hold on an action or reaction, and for how long. The Concerned Observer role helps us discover and visualize the heart of any dramatic interaction. But however well the Concerned Observer can see, hear, and sympathize with the characters, he or she, like one of Wenders' angels, cannot intercede or express an opinion. This is a handicap.

OBSERVER INTO STORYTELLER

The Concerned Observer can however turn into the proactive **Storyteller** by going several steps farther and arranging the events, and modulating the narrative emphasis, for the instruction and entertainment of an audience. Through aesthetic choices, developing the sense of environment, tone, context, and subtext, the Storyteller instills a thematic resonance to all that occurs throughout the story. The wise Storyteller makes it all add up to something so that the dramatic journey has achieved "pleasure and profit in the telling" (p. 39). What we see on the screen is not free-functioning, autonomous truth such as we'd see on any street corner, but an artful construct filtered through a temperament—the Storyteller/director's temperament.

You wouldn't know this from most commercial cinema or television, which is perfectly professional and absolutely without individuality. You can work hard to make your film look professional and it can still be faceless. David Mamet thinks of such work "as a supposed record of what real people really did," that is, something like a newsreel report. The Concerned Observer and the Storyteller roles are explored in greater depth in Chapter 16, but to direct screen work with a distinctive voice, you must act in at least four different ways:

1. **Define:** Make it your priority to tell a good story in a special and particularly cinematic way, and in a defined genre. You'll need a clear definition of your approach, one that enthuses people. You can go only where you aim to go.

2. **Take control:** You must direct the filmmaking process, not become controlled by its fascinating technology. To stay in control, you'll need a clear and unshakeable idea of the underlying premise and themes of the film, and a strongly visualized design to express them. You'll also need the ability to communicate those concepts to your collaborators and by sheer obstinacy get them realized during production. If you don't, the crew and the actors will take over, and the tail will wag the dog.

3. **Impose a Storyteller:** You must impress a strong storytelling "voice" on your film, the kind that lends enchantment to all effective storytelling. This voice may not exactly be yours—though it emerges from your sensibilities and personal preoccupations—for the Storyteller is really a character that you alone define and that you alone play privately and to the hilt. This character's eyes, ears, mind, and movement are a Storyteller's sparkling stream of consciousness made manifest in your film. In the next chapter, on film grammar, we'll see all the tools with which this can be done.

4. **Stay the course:** Many details change during a film project: the script gets rewritten; actors, cinematographers, set designers, editors, and sound designers can bring surprising interpretations to the material; locations change; and the rigorous process of film production imposes limitations of its own. But the director must hold on tightly to the story's central premise and thematic underpinnings, which are the foundation for all the aesthetic choices of the Storyteller. It's the beacon the directors can never lose sight of, or they risk veering off course and losing the unifying thread of the story and the attention and goodwill of an audience. Theme in most films is rarely stated in direct terms by the characters; it resides in the culmination of all the dramatic activity and the aesthetic approach the director brings to the story.

What you need is to find that original idea, that spark. And once you have that it's like fishing: you use that idea as bait, and it attracts everything else. But as a director, your main priority is to remain faithful to that original idea. [...] Every decision matters, however small. And every element can make you move a little forwards or a little backwards. You have to be open to new ideas, but at the same time, you must always stay focused on your original intention. It is a sort of standard against which you can test the validity of every new suggestion.

—David Lynch[3]

---

[3] From *Moviemakers' Master Class*, Laurent Tirard (Faber and Faber, 2002).

The source of the Storyteller's viewpoint is never very evident, because it is hidden behind the choices that express it. These aesthetic and stylistic choices regarding performance, location, tone, sound, and pace serve as proxies for the Storyteller's POV on the content of the narrative. And though all films have directors, their authorship is necessarily more collective and collaborative than individual, like music from a conductor.

AUDIENCE POV

There is one last POV still to be considered—that of the audience, which assesses the Storyteller, his or her cinematic tale, and whatever the film expresses. Viewers always bring their personal perspective and this can be a powerful filter since it is always shifting. Individually and collectively, audience members bring their own cultural and historical experiences: a religiously educated audience, for instance, won't automatically accept that an anarchist can have powerful and altruistic morals. Western audiences will have difficulty understanding the suicidal agony of an Asian student who must go to his parents with a B grade instead of an A, and so on. A plainly honest film about the traumas of war, like Moverman's *The Messenger* (2009), will be understood one way by civilians and another way by veterans, and still another way by people who have lost loved ones to warfare. Though you cannot as a director control the audience's perspective, it is something you must be aware of and work with.

POV IS LIKE RUSSIAN DOLLS

Film point of view is a bit like the enclosing and embracing nature of Russian dolls—one containing the others. Its most restricted level of subjectivity is that of a character, whereas its most embracing is that of the audience.

- The main character's POV embraces that of the subsidiary characters, but the subsidiary characters also have feelings and views.
- Each character holds up a mirror to the others.
- The Storyteller's POV encloses all the characters' POVs.
- The audience's POV encloses the Storyteller's and characters' points of view.

PLANNING A POINT OF VIEW

Difficult to control but important to influence, POV sets the aesthetic agenda for practically everything. In run-of-the-mill films, it emerges by default from the subject at hand and the idiosyncrasies of the team making the film. You must take a far more deliberate approach. The most practical is to decide what thematic statement you want your story to make, and then to work on developing all the subjectivities you can draw from the characters, their world, and their Storyteller. Each provides an interpretive lens through which you can legitimately enhance meaning.

CHAPTER 10

FORM AND STYLE

The screenplay is content rather than form. Form is how that content appears on the screen and form should never be approached as a merely functional vehicle. A film that delivers a memorable and intriguing impact usually has a form special to the story's purpose and themes. Norman McLaren's short *Neighbours* (1952) makes stunning use of pixilation. This creates a powerfully allegorical tone and enhances the film's theme about men, possessions, and territory. Chris Marker's unforgettable futuristic fable *La Jetée* (1962) is told entirely in still photos with just a few seconds of movement in a single mysterious shot (Figure 10-1).

Possibilities in form, seemingly unlimited, are to a large extent circumscribed by the narrative requirements, logic, and tone suggested by the story. By determining the ruling point of view and purpose, you can choose the genre, imagery, and even camera angles that best serve your authorial intentions. Let's see how this might work.

Say you are planning a short film about a holdup in a grocery store. First decide the controlling point of view, which could be that of the store owner, a nearsighted old man out buying a lottery ticket, the off-duty policeman getting a loaf of bread, or the robber himself. The robbery acquires a different significance for each, because each person would be in a different frame of mind and notice different things.

Point of view suggests the choice of lenses and camera positions—all contributing to the cumulative impressions that add up to a particular person's way of seeing. Lighting would flow from the time of day, mood, type of store, and kind of interaction. How the camera is handled (static positions, handheld, mounted

FIGURE 10-1 ⸻

By using still images almost exclusively, Marker's *La Jetée* incorporates concepts of the cinematic form itself into the themes of the film.

on a dolly) would also flow from point of view and the kind of comment the director wants to make. You might additionally choose particular set dressing, and the particular characteristics of a film stock or video image. Then, in the final film, you might edit the events in or out of their chronology. That is, the crime need not be shown in chronological order—you might show it in discontinuous portions—as remembered by a survivor, or perhaps in stage-by-stage retrospect in the court case following the arrest of the robber. Different witnesses might have conflicting versions of key actions, and so on.

In fact, screen order is also subservient to the controlling point of view. For ultimately the whole film is filtered through the Storyteller, whose agenda and purpose are distinct from any held by the characters. The Storyteller might concentrate on one character's experience or shift narrative focus between three of the characters, treating each as equally important.

Good formal choices are made from close analysis, instincts and making concrete decisions.

THE STORYTELLER'S VISION

Audiences know instinctively that *good fiction is not a reproduction of life, but an enactment of ideas about it*. If your topic is robbery, be provocative about what robbery means—socially, culturally, or emotionally. Ask yourself:

- Who carries out robbery, in what way, and why?
- Why am I attracted to this basic situation—does it have roots in an analogous experience of mine?
- What moves characters to act, and what does the incident say about life and living?
- What do I want my audience to see, consider, wonder about during each phase of my film?
- How do the locations, visual aesthetic, and sound design of the film contribute to the story I am telling and what I want to express?

This kind of interrogation, natural enough while one watches drama, is something you must make happen during the writing, designing, shooting, and editing stages. Calculating how to reveal the story's events, what questions the audience must ponder and at what points, are how the Storyteller uses their powers of entertainment.

The elements of cinematic form that directors harness to tell their stories are contained within four broad areas: **visual design, sound design, performance style,** and **editorial style**. It is no surprise that film production teams are built around these particular aesthetic areas.

VISUAL DESIGN

A film gains power whenever its thematic concerns emerge visually rather than through dialogue exchanges. A film's visual design is a combination of the **art direction** (locations, set dressing, costuming, props, and make-up); and the **cinematography** (recording format, lighting, exposures, choice of lenses, focus, camera angles, and movements).

FIGURE 10-2

Jeunet's stylistic approach to *Amélie* establishes a warmly nostalgic and romantic tone which complements the magical nature of the story.

Ingmar Bergman's *The Seventh Seal* (1956), set in the Middle Ages when people's hearts were ruled by superstition and fear of the plague, tells much of its story amid gloomy forests and severe shorelines (see Figure 13-7b). The dark figures and low-key, high-contrast black-and-white photography prime us to anticipate the mixture of magic and superstitious terror at the heart of an epoch when life was "nasty, brutish, and short."[1]

At the other end of the stylistic spectrum, Jean-Pierre Jeunet's *Amélie* (2001, Figure 10-2) tells its story in an ultra-vivid, sepia-tinged Paris—a city oozing with romance, beauty and nostalgia. It is a semi-fantastic city filtered through Amélie's sweet-hearted, melodramatic, and longing subjectivity. Jeunet said, "we cleared the streets of all cars, cleaned the graffiti off the walls, replaced posters with more colorful ones, etc. Let's just say I tried to exert as much control as I could upon the city's aesthetic quality."[2]

The visual palette (photography, costumes and settings) includes deep greens and reds that, along with the warm, soft lighting approach, provides a painterly impression. Wide-angle lenses deepen the space to include as much of the lush architectural detail as possible, and sweeping camera movements thrust the viewer down cobblestone streets, through 19th-century train stations, into quaint Parisian cafés, and over the grey rooftops of this magnificent city. Jeunet produced a perfect visual complement to the tenderly romantic story of Amélie's selfless acts of kindness, ones that eventually earn her true love. See Chapter 23, for further discussion of visual design.

---

[1] Thomas Hobbes (1588–1679).

[2] The Writing Studio Conversations: *Talk With Jean-Pierre Jeunet* (writingstudio.co.za).

SOUND DESIGN

I have always believed that sound is half of what makes a film work. You have the image on one side, the sound on another and if you know how to combine them properly, then the whole is stronger than the sum of its parts.

—David Lynch[3]

Summon for yourself the feelings that go with these sounds: the cooing of doves floating in through a sunny bedroom window, footfalls in a church, children distantly playing hide-and-seek, the insistent dripping of water in a dank basement, or muffled weeping in a darkened room. They work miraculously on our imagination and receptivity. Robert Bresson said, "The eye sees, but the ear imagines."[4]

Sound design is the total aural universe of the movie. It includes sounds we record on location and sounds added later in postproduction. Here are its principal elements:

- **Speech,** which includes **dialogue** recorded on location with the picture (**sync sound**), dialogue we dub in later in postproduction (**ADR**[5]), and **voice-over** narration.
- **Sound effects** include noises recorded in sync on location, those recorded later in postproduction (**Foley effects**) and those gathered from sound libraries (**hard effects**).
- **Ambient sounds** or **atmospheres** (such as playground, airport terminal, crowded restaurant) associated with the environment of a location. They can be recorded at the actual location, or if inadequate, added in postproduction by substituting sound tracks from a sound library.
- **Music** can be recorded at the location in sync, but this rarely happens. More often, it is added later from pre-recorded material or music composed specifically for the edited film. When music has a visible source in the film, like a juke box playing in a bar scene, it is called **source music**. When music emerges from outside the narrative world to underscore a scene with a specific mood or emotional tone, it is called **score music**.

Two other concepts are critical to understand the flexibility of the sound universe. One is **diegetic** sound, meaning all sounds that come from the world of the scene we are watching. This includes characters' dialogue, their footfalls on the pavement, the traffic noise behind them and the car radio booming music as it passes—all are part of the world of the scene. **Non-diegetic** sounds are heard by the audience, but not by the characters in the film because non-diagetic sound does not come from the world of the scene we are watching but has been authorially applied to it. The most common is score music, but another is **voice-over.** It comes from without and implies editorializing. In his 2009 film *The White Ribbon*, Michael Haneke introduces voice-over narration from an omniscient perspective, which we later discover is from one of the characters in the film, many years older, reflecting back on the events (Figure 10-3).

---

[3] From, *Moviemakers' Master Class*, Laurent Tirard (Faber and Faber, 2002).

[4] Robert Bresson, *Notes on the Cinematographer* (Los Angeles: Green Integer, 1997).

[5] Automatic dialogue replacement (ADR) is the practice of re-recording dialogue under acoustically controlled conditions in postproduction to sync with the picture.

FIGURE 10-3

The voice-over in Haneke's *The White Ribbon* begins from an omniscient perspective, until we learn that it originates from the retrospective thoughts of one of the characters.

Mark Webb's *500 Days of Summer* (2009) incorporates the voice of an omniscient Storyteller who is not part of the internal world of the story—a literary device seldom used in film.

Sound design is a storytelling tool that a director uses as part of a film's overall aesthetic approach; sound should not be used as a cosmetic applied late in the film's development. Sound designer Randy Thom complains that he is usually brought into a production just after it has been edited as wall-to-wall dialogue—leaving him room to add nothing. To capitalize on the tone, mood and meaning that sound can add, he recommends screenwriting for sound. That is, characters should listen; sound should occasionally lead the picture, and quiet spaces should exist to deliberately withhold information so that narrative momentum becomes channeled through sound.

Sound design can be especially effective to define POV as it can discretely but efficiently transition our attention from an objective soundscape to one emanating from the subjectivity of a character. In Elem Klimov's remarkable *Come and See* (1985, Figure 10-4) the central character, a Belorussian boy who has joined a rag-tag group of resistance fighters during World War II, is caught in a German air raid. Having survived an initial barrage of bombs, he emerges from his shelter to look for the girl who is hiding in the forest with him.

The sound design switches from the objective sounds of the explosions, to the aural perspective of the boy who has been deafened by the blasts. The soundtrack is dominated by a high

FIGURE 10-4

Klimov's *Come and See* uses subjective sound to immerse the audience into the visceral experience of combat.

pitched ringing and when he cries out the girl's name, he (and we) can barely hear his voice. The soundtrack remains within his aural POV for some time until his hearing is restored.[6]

Michel Chion's book *Audio-Vision: Sound on Screen* (New York: Columbia University Press) and Thom's "Designing a Movie for Sound" at www.filmsound.org are two first-rate resources for anyone wanting to understand more about the power of sound design.

PERFORMANCE STYLE

The extremes of performance style are often expressed as **naturalistic** and **stylized**. Naturalistic performances are those in which the actor inhabits their role (dialect, voice, gestures, posture and so on) in a thoroughly natural manner so that audiences accept him or her as a real person. The performances in Asghar Farhadi's *A Separation* (2011, Figure 10-5, *left*) convince us that the two families at the center of the conflict are real and their struggles actual.

Stylized performances, on the other hand, highlight the act of performance and include mannerisms (dialect, voice, gestures, and so on) that are deliberately exaggerated or surreal. Good examples are the vividly amplified characters in Tim Burton's *Edward Scissorhands* (1990, Figure 10-5, *right*) or those in the Coen Brothers' *The Big Lebowski* (1998).

Between these two extremes are myriad nuanced approaches, but all directors strive for performances that are "believable" and "convincing" within the genre of their film—even when calling attention to themselves. Depending on the tone, genre, and stylistic approach you establish for your film there is a wide range of approaches to performance that an audience will find credible. Although highly stylized, we believe in Edward Scissorhands because he exists in a fairytale world full of outsize characters. We fear for the fate of this good and vulnerable boy in a similar way that we fear for the fate of the good and vulnerable 11-year-old daughter in *A Separation*.

EDITORIAL STYLE

Although editing is a postproduction procedure, its style and rhythms constitute a major aesthetic and authorial component that you must consider from the beginning of the conceptualization process. Production and postproduction, shooting, and editing are intimately linked and are best conceived holistically.

---

[6] This same technique was later used by Steven Spielberg in the Omaha Beach sequence of *Saving Private Ryan* (1998).

FIGURE 10-5

Despite their completely different stylistic approaches, Farhadi's naturalistic *A Separation* (*left*) and Burton's stylized *Edward Scissorhands* (*right*) manage to make us feel great sympathy for their central characters.

- **Continuity style** production is a traditional system of shooting and editing that use multiple shots and angles edited together to construct coherent time, space, and action. It allows the Storyteller a high degree of control over the dramatic shape, POV, rhythms, and emphases of a scene, and renders authorial intervention invisible. Through the invisible, guiding hand of the Storyteller, continuity style invites the audience into an easy emotional identification with characters. It is so prevalent that all other approaches are often just lumped into "non-continuity style."

FIGURE 10-6

Garcia's *Nine Lives* is made up of nine carefully choreographed one-shot scenes each lasting nearly 10 minutes.

- **Long-take style** presents continuous time and action without employing the illusions of the continuity system. Extended moments or even entire scenes are played out in real time using long, unedited shots. This can involve a static camera observing the action or a moving camera actively selecting characters or details, not unlike the emphasis available through continuity style. The power of the long-take technique is its immediacy which invites the viewer to feel immersed in the unfolding and uninflected action. This technique also benefits the actors, who can unfurl an extended, unbroken emotional thread, though getting a whole take that is successful from beginning to end can be painfully difficult. Rodrigo Garcia's *Nine Lives* (2005, Figure 10-6), comprises nine, one-shot scenes each lasting nearly 10 minutes. Each is a self-contained short narrative centered on a revealing a transitional moment in a woman's life.

FIGURE 10-7

Jump cuts in Godard's *Breathless*, a radical technique in 1960, are today a familiar part of the cinematic language.

Long-take style places you squarely in the heart of a dramatic situation and simply lets you inhabit the unfolding scene without the intervention of cuts to different angles and shots.

- **Jump-cut style** departs from both continuity and long-take styles by accentuating spatial and temporal disjunctions from angle to angle. While the result is a more self-conscious approach to storytelling, there is a certain "honesty" implied by the director in revealing the artifice and construction of the film. A great benefit to this style is the direct and edgy energy that jump cutting brings to a dramatic scene. Jean Luc Godard famously introduced this technique in his 1960 film *Breathless* and it has been used extensively by many directors up to this day, including Lars Von Trier and Wong Kar-Wai (Figure 10-7).

- **Associative and intellectual** editing creates overt thematic, intellectual, emotional, or political connections between shots not necessarily related by spatial or temporal links. This didactic style of editing is associated with the Soviet masters of early cinema like Sergei Eisenstein and Dziga Vertov, but is commonly used today in highly stylized films like Darren Aronofsky's *Requiem for a Dream* (2000).

The editing style you choose can have a profound effect on the tone of your film, particularly on the emotional and intellectual involvement of the audience. However, this list is not intended to insinuate that one approach must be used to the exclusion of the others. Film language has evolved to the point where most films employ an eclectic approach to editing style. There is a place for both emotion and intellect in any film. Depending on the content and point of view, your film may call for a different language at different points. Even conservatively conceived films employing a straightforward continuity style often include non-continuity editing techniques for particularly elevated or revealing dramatic moments.

Obviously, this overview only scratches the surface of the expressive power and flexibility in using different editing approaches and narrative style. There is more detail in Chapters 33 and 34, but for greater depth, try Ken Dancyger's book, *The Technique of Film and Video Editing* (Focal Press, 2010).

RHYTHMIC DESIGN

All well-told stories rely on rhythm. An audience's involvement is best sustained by variety. William Shakespeare—who supported a large company of actors by satisfying the tastes of the common people—juxtaposes very different textures and rhythms in the course of elaborating a theme. He switches from action to monologue to comedy, intersperses long and short scenes, group scenes, duologues and soliloquies. So as you design your narrative, make us pass through a succession of perspectives and moods by refreshing the ear and eye with variations and comparisons. You can also do this by varying your film's dramatic pressure—increasing or relaxing the tension through rhythmic changes. Bergman says, "Film is mainly rhythm; it is inhalation and exhalation in continuous sequence."[7] If the idea of rhythmic design seems limited to music or sound such as footsteps and clocks ticking, consider how many other rhythmic elements are present:

- Shots: length, composition and movement in the frame
- Pacing of shots within a sequence and sequences in relation to those before and after
- Scene alternation (changes from night to day for instance)
- Emotional rhythms (ebbs and flows)
- Camera movement
- Ambient sound, sound effects, speech patterns and breathing patterns
- Performance pace (according to mannerisms, temperament, predicament, etc.).

Rhythms important to cinema language emanate from multiple sources at any given time. Experienced editors and directors are acutely sensitive to the combined effects of rhythms, and know as instinctively as any musician when their "orchestration" is or isn't working.

DIRECTORIAL STYLE

Godard said, "Style is just the outside of content, and content the inside of style, like the outside and inside of the human body—both go together, they can't be separated."[8] A film's style emerges from the dramatic requirements of the screenplay, and also reflects its makers and their identity. Any film by Lynch, Almodóvar, Kiarostami, Ramsay, the Coens, or Jeunet is immediately recognizable. It's not only the content, kind of tale, or forms that each tends to choose, but also the fact that

---

[7] Introduction to *Four Screenplays of Ingmar Bergman* (Simon & Schuster, 1960).
[8] Richard Roud, *Jean-Luc Godard* (Secker & Warburg, 1967), p. 13.

their work has their personality and taste written all over it. It is this last, virtually uncontrollable element that is properly known as style. Just as you can influence but not choose your own identity, so you should let your film identity, or style, emerge from the content. If you serve each controllable aspect of your film well, people will come to recognize something they will call your style.

CHAPTER 11

TONE: NATURALISTIC AND STYLIZED APPROACHES

Taken together, the aesthetic and stylistic elements listed in the previous chapter (visual style, sound design, editorial style and performance style) establish the tone and credibility of the world of the film. They establish, in other words, the rules of your cinematic universe.

It's important to keep in mind that film is a *construct* of reality—not reality itself. A great miracle of the cinematic art form is its ability to create a vast range of believable realities. The contemporary Paris represented in Jeunet's *Amélie* is not the Paris represented in Mathieu Kassovitz' gritty and violent *La Haine* (1995). And yet both are believable, given the context of their respective worlds. David Lynch's suburbs in *Blue Velvet* are vastly different from the suburbs in John Hughes' *Ferris Bueller's Day Off*. Woody Allen's New York will never look remotely like that of Martin Scorsese.

The aesthetic and stylistic palette from which a director paints arises from the narrative and dramatic elements of the screenplay. Within that, as discussed in the previous chapter, the director also influences the tone by way of their temperament and vision for the story.

One other stylistic influence comes to us however from the history of our artistic medium—it is called **genre**.

GENRE AND STYLE

All art grows out of what went before it, so any film you care to make will veer toward a particular type and aesthetic area, have a prevailing mood, and draw on a circumscribed language with which it speaks to its audience. In French, the word *genre* simply means kind or type, but 'genre' in the film lexicon describes groups of movies that belong to a recognizable cinematic type. According to Timothy Corrigan and Patricia White:

[Movies] rely on repetitions and rituals that allow audiences to share expectations and routines. Besides the myriad characters and stories we find at the movies, we frequently experience these movie repetitions in a film genre, an organization and categorization of film according to repeated subjects, icons and styles. Grounded in audience expectations about characters, narrative and visual style, a film genre is a set of conventions and formulas repeated and developed through film history.[1]

Most films fall under genre categories and contain familiar types of characters, conflicts, situations, actions, and subtexts that are often older than the cinema. Each genre promises a world running under familiar rules and limitations. Genre also indicates more than a story type, since the elements of tone that make up a narrative convention also suggest common stylistic approaches to telling those stories. For example, *film noir* is a genre of betrayal, violence and sexuality. It is a cinematic universe that conjures up dark psychological impulses and is closely associated with a particular visual style (urban, dark, gritty—a world of shadows) and performance style (hard edged and direct). One can trace this characteristic aesthetic from Tourneur's *Out of the Past* (1947) and Welles' *A Touch of Evil* (1955, Figure 11-1 *top*) through to Fincher's *Se7en* (1995) as well as most of the work of Christopher Nolan including *The Dark Knight* (2008).

FIGURE 11-1 ——————————————————

The romantic comedy, on the other hand, steers clear of violence or dark psychological impulses and their associated imagery. The "rom-com" suggests an emotional and romantic world rendered in a bright, clean, vivid aesthetics and performances that are humorously broad and breezy. The contemporary rom-com has its roots in the screwball comedy genre, like Howard Hawk's *Bringing up Baby* (1938, Figure 11-1 *bottom*) and the aesthetic look and performance style has remained consistent right up to films like *Crazy, Stupid Love* (2011).

Ghost stories, science fiction, Westerns, social realism, melodramas, musicals[2] and so

Many film genres suggest visual styles. Film noir conjures a world of dark shadows, as exemplified in Welles' *A Touch of Evil* (*top*) while the screwball comedy calls to mind a bright, lighthearted aesthetic, as in Hawks's *Bringing up Baby* (*bottom*).

---

[1] From *The Film Experience*, Timothy Corrigan, Patricia White (Bedford: St. Martin's, 2004).
[2] A useful list of genre types can be found in *Alternative Scriptwriting* by Ken Dancyger and Jeff Rush (Focal Press, 2006).

on are all historically associated with stylistic conventions that a director can either tap into or subvert in order to make a thematic point. Either way, the audience's stylistic expectations are a powerful point of reference for a director.

Today, fewer films fall strictly into traditional genre definitions. More often than not you'll see genre conventions mixed —as in Ridley Scott's *Blade Runner* (1982) (sci-fi and film noir) or subverted—as in Kelly Reichardt's revisionist Western, *Meek's Cutoff* (2010, Figure 11-2). It is quite common to see traditional genre styles being borrowed, mixed, adapted and subverted in order to tell stories in fresh ways. Even if your film falls into no specific genre, you can certainly draw on these visual styles and benefit from the overtones and associations they elicit.

FIGURE 11-2

Pure genre films are seldom seen these days. Most are now mixed, subverted, or like Reichardt's Western, *Meek's Cutoff*, revised for a contemporary perspective.

NATURALISM

Naturalism is a stylistic approach that attempts to make the locations, sounds and actions of the cinematic universe appear as closely as possible like the world we inhabit in everyday life. It strives to erase the notion that a fictional world is being created for the camera and seeks to convince us instead that the camera is simply capturing events occurring in the real and familiar world. At its best this can generate a potent immediacy akin to the experience of watching a documentary film; we don't reflect on the fiction or artistic design but accept the story as one that simply exists.

However, there is nothing natural about narrative cinema, which is always a highly controlled and artificial process. To work with a naturalistic tone, one must understand the basic conventions and cinematic codes whose artifice imbues a fictional world with "real world" immediacy. These are some of the aspects:

Art Direction: Settings in naturalistic films are common, recognizable places that never feel constructed or "art directed" for the camera (even though they often are). Costumes and props are not elaborate, and typical of what this character would own or wear in the real world.

Camera work: In general, naturalistic films are shot from a fairly objective perspective and avoid visual extremes suggesting directorial interpretation. Distortion through the use of wide-angle lenses, elaborate camera moves that involve dollies or cranes, complexly designed mises-en-scène are eschewed for a camera style more often resembling simple observation. This can include long-take shooting and other practices common to the documentary tradition, like *cinéma vérité*'s use of handheld cameras, zoom lenses, and occasionally wayward focusing.

Lighting: Naturalistic films may use only available light, that is, light customarily present at a given location such as sunlight, table lamps, or overhead fluorescent bulbs, etc. Many films discretely add movie lights to boost exposure to acceptable levels—using a 1,000-watt movie light, for example, to replicate the glow of a TV screen, which itself provides very little light. Such lighting is carefully placed to augment natural light sources and is called "motivated lighting" because every movie light has a real-world reference determining its angle, color, and intensity (see Chapter 27 for more on lighting approaches).

Performance: Characters in naturalistic films reflect the kind of people we know or have heard about in the world around us. Naturalistic performances use dialects, mannerisms, gestures, and emotions to help us believe that this is a real person in a real world. Often **non-actors** similar in personality, culture, and profession to the intended characters will use improvised conversation rather than memorized lines. Thus non-actors don't really act, but are simply themselves within the fictional situation established by the director. In this type of film, professionally trained actors must work hard to achieve a similar degree of freshness and uninflected spontaneity.

Editing approach: Traditional continuity style editing (p. 179) must be used sparingly in highly naturalistic films because nothing can be used to suggest actors performing the same scene from multiple camera angles. A more usual aesthetic is to use long takes from a static or, more often, handheld camera and to punctuate sequences with jump cuts.

Sound Design: Sounds are usually limited to those natural to the scene, without overt embellishment. Likewise score music is used judiciously and with extreme subtlety—if at all.

A case study for the naturalistic style is Lance Hammer's *Ballast* (2008, Figure 11-3). Set in an economically depressed region of the Mississippi Delta, it tells the story of the bitter aftermath

FIGURE 11-3

Director Lance Hammer employed a strict naturalistic approach in his film, *Ballast*, which included using non-professional actors in all the principal roles.

to a man's suicide and its effect on his wife, son and brother. The principal settings are common and unadorned: the forlorn piece of property with two miserable shacks that the deceased man and his brother shared, and the family convenience store where they worked. The camerawork is entirely handheld and uses available light exclusively. Most remarkably, the principal cast are all non-actors from the region, and their costumes could have come from their own wardrobes. Hammer never showed them a script so that their language was always their own. When asked about the method he used to "bring out" the amazing performances of the leads, Hammer responded,

> It really wasn't about bringing something out; it was about preventing them from putting something out there that wasn't them. So my singular goal in the direction of actors, was to have the actors behave as they are at all times… I wanted *them*.[3]

Despite *Ballast*'s detached tone, and visual and aural austerity, the film unfolds with the slow burn of repressed emotions mixed with the human need to do more than survive, the need for love.[4]

Many stylistic conventions of naturalism emerged from the work of the Italian Neo-realist filmmakers of the 1940s and 1950s who shot their films primarily in the streets of post-World War II Italy, and used real people from circumstances similar to those of the characters. Films like Roberto Rossellini's *Rome Open City* (1945) and Vittorio DeSica's *Umberto D.* (1952) continue to make an enormous impact on generations of filmmakers. This influence you see in the films of Ken Loach (from *Kes*, 1969 to *Sweet Sixteen*, 2002) and the Dardenne Brothers' (from *La Promesse*, 1996 to *The Kid with a Bike*, 2011). They in turn have subsequently influenced a newer generation of filmmakers including: Lance Hammer, Zhang Ke Jia, (*Still Life*, 2006), Ramin Bahrani (*Chop Shop*, 2007), and So Yong Kim (*Treeless Mountain*, 2008, Figure 11-4).

At its most rigorous, naturalism blurs the line between documentary and fiction. The first episode in Abbas Kiarostami's *Ten* (2002, Figure 11-5) is a single long shot of a boy arguing with his mother over her recent divorce while she drives him to swimming practice. Although staged, the 17-minute scene

FIGURE 11-4 —————————

A new generation of directors, like So Yong Kim in her powerful film *Treeless Mountain*, have continued in the tradition of naturalistic films started by the Italian neo-realists.

---

[3] From The Filmlot interview with Lance Hammer, www.thefilmlot.com
[4] Go to www.reverseshot.com/article/interview_lance_hammer for more on the stylistic approach to *Ballast*.

derives so much of its content from the real life situation between the two "characters" (truly a mother and son coping with a recent divorce) that it's practically impossible to decide whether this is documentary or fiction.

STYLIZATION

Stylizing anything means heightening it—characters, settings, or story language—to accentuate its impact beyond what we recognize is normal.

Partially stylized: Most films told from the implied, single-character POV expose us only sparingly to the POV character's subjective perspective. Their drama is usually shown from a more detached and omniscient standpoint, but occasionally and at especially dramatic moments the perspective can shift to a more stylized mode. In the famous shower scene in *Psycho* (1960), we temporarily merge with the killer's eye-line after he begins stabbing. Then the POV switches to the last agonized images seen by Marion Crane. This brief foray into immediate, limited perceptions—first of the killer, then of his victim—is reserved for the starkest moment in the film, when Alfred Hitchcock boldly disposes of his heroine. After the killer flees, we are left with the Storyteller's point of view—alone with the body in the motel room. In this passage—a tour de force of stylized mise-en-scène and editing—Hitchcock makes his audience into privileged collaborators by raising their awareness above that of the characters.

Omniscient cinema will often resort to a stylized POV as a storytelling inflection to indicate, say, a character's temporary imbalance (euphoria, fear, insecurity, etc.), or to share confidential information with the audience as a novelist might do in a literary aside. This information (symbolic objects, foreshadowing devices, special in-frame juxtapositions) is often withheld from the characters, and heightens tension by making us anticipate what the characters do not yet know.

Hyperbolic style: Somewhere between naturalism and highly stylized approaches is the universe of hyperbole. Films in this mode exaggerate their visual and aural designs and performance style to the point where they are excessively vivid without entirely detaching from the real world. Parody and satire rely heavily on hyperbole, but so do films which aim to establish such an ironic tone toward their subject that we are driven to look beneath the surface of people, places and events. The hyperbolic approach, which looks real, but a little too much so, is the stock in trade for directors like the Coen Brothers, Wes Anderson, Terry Gilliam, David Lynch, and Alexander Payne, whose 1999 film *Election* finds the perfect hyperbolic/ironic tone in its visual and performance style. Its filmic universe is just a bit too bright, too clean, too direct, and too intense. We can believe in it, but not quite; this makes us seek the larger, darker meaning behind the utterly banal topic of a high school student government election (Figure 11-6).

FIGURE 11-5

At its most rigorous, naturalism blurs the line between documentary and fiction, as in Abbas Kiarostami's *Ten*.

FIGURE 11-6

Hyperbole presents a slightly exaggerated world which encourages the audience to look beneath the surface of events, as in Payne's highly ironic *Election*.

FIGURE 11-7

Robert Wiene's *The Cabinet of Dr. Caligari* drew on expressionistic trends in the visual arts of the period (*left*). *A Clockwork Orange* owes its origins to early 20th-century German Expressionism (*right*).

Highly stylized: German Expressionist film, epitomized by Robert Wiene's *The Cabinet of Dr. Caligari* (1919, Figure 11-7 *left*), borrowed its style from contemporary developments in the graphic arts, which explored a nightmarishly altered reality. It was a trend that reflected the zeitgeist of inter-war Germany and foreshadowed the encroaching Nazi regime. Characters may have unnatural skin texture or move without shadows in a world of oversized, distorted architecture and machinery. F.W. Murnau's *Nosferatu* (1921) and Fritz Lang's *Dr. Mabuse* (1922) sought to create the same unhinged psychology with a more subtle use of the camera. They made their political and satirical comment much as Oskar Kokoschka, George Grosz, and Edvard Munch were doing in the 1920s and 1930s through the graphic arts.

Some more contemporary films also construct a highly stylized world. Stanley Kubrick's strange, violent *A Clockwork Orange* (1971, Figure 11-7, *right*) is a picaresque tale played out by painted grotesques in a series of surreal contemporary settings. Even if you quickly forget what the film is about, the visual effect is unforgettable, and undoubtedly has its origins in German Expressionism earlier in the century.

In highly stylized films the camera work, compositions, lenses and exposures can be quite obtrusive—they do, after all, constitute a major and overt component of the expressionistic look. Figure 11-7 reveals just how stylized lighting also helps create the fantastic tone of the fictive world. Because lighting is used to make strong visual, emotional or even thematic statements it does not need to tether itself to the strict "motivated lighting" technique of naturalism (see Chapter 27 for more on lighting styles).

Futurism: No discussion of stylization would be complete without mentioning journeys into the imagined future. Lang's *Metropolis* (1926) is the classic, but there is no shortage of other examples. Jean-Luc Godard's *Alphaville* (1965), Kubrick's *2001* (1968), François Truffaut's *Fahrenheit 451* (1966), Ridley Scott's *Blade Runner* (1982), and Terry Gilliam's *Brazil* (1986) all hypothesize "what if" worlds of the future. Each shows grave distortions in the social, sexual, or political realms that put characters under duress. Plucked from the familiar and invited to respond as immigrants in a world operating under totalitarian assumptions, we are often shown the fascism of governments made omniscient through technology. In the drive to create a doomsday thesis, secondary characters are often unindividualized, flat characters. Such storytelling explores collective anxieties, and the future seems reserved for nightmares about the individual isolated during a breakdown in collective control.

Stylized environments: Stylization often intensifies a film's specific period and setting, or even the terrain of a character's psychology. Pier Paolo Pasolini's *The Gospel According to St. Matthew* (1964) uses cinematography and costuming to make the film redolent of Renaissance painting. Roman Polanski's chilling *Repulsion* (1965, Figure 11-8, *left*) is told from the deeply subjective POV of its paranoid heroine Carol, who is descending into madness. True to her psychological perspective, Carol's apartment becomes the embodiment of threatening evil. Though you know that events are projections of her deluded mind, the result is a sickeningly unpleasant sense of her psychotic vulnerability.

Joann Sfar's film *Gainsbourg: A Heroic Life* (2010) adopts a larger-than-life, often surreal visual style that tosses aside the objectivity of most bio-pics. More in the style of the graphic novel that he adapted (and which he himself created), Sfar goes so far as to include La Gueule, a grotesque caricature alter ego representing the entertainer's subconscious fears and compulsive provocation. Though Sfar's fantastic visual excesses distort some facts, they perfectly

FIGURE 11-8

Extreme stylization. Polanski's *Repulsion* draws us into experiencing Carol's (Catherine Deneuve) delusional mind as it slips into madness (*left*). Sfar created the grotesque caricature La Gueule to physically represent Gainsbourg's (Eric Elmosnino) compulsively provocative behavior.

reflect the spirit of Gainsbourg's life and reputation—excessive, brilliant, controversial, and tortured (Figure 11-8, *right*).

DISTANCING AND SUSPENDING DISBELIEF

The children's story opening, "Once upon a time..." attests how readily we suspend disbelief and accept the wildly stylized worlds of anything filtered by time, distance, or memory. Burton's *Edward Scissorhands* (1990) draws on this fairytale trope by having an old woman narrate her fantastic story to a young girl as a bedtime story, beginning with "A long time ago ..." Period films also fall readily into this category. Ang Lee's athletic fable *Crouching Tiger, Hidden Dragon* (2000, Figure 11-9) is set in ancient China where, as we completely accept, the laws of physics are suspended for those martial arts masters able to transcend the limits of the physical universe.

Cinema set in the past continues the oral tradition in which historical events or personages become legend, that is, they can be freely shaped and embellished to serve the narrator's artistic, social, or political purpose.

Settings in the past or distant future transport us far from the banality of contemporary life, but careful use of music can do something similar. It can serve as a distancing mechanism so that your film can be set in the present and still make everyday transactions seem heightened and nonrealistic. When used to counterpoint, rather than illustrate or heighten what we see, music carries its own powerful message and imposes its own patterning of emotion. Jacques Demy's *The Umbrellas of Cherbourg* (1964) tells a conventional small-town love story, but uses striking color schemes, lyrical compositions by Michel Legrand, and balletic

FIGURE 11-9

Because *Crouching Tiger, Hidden Dragon* is remote in time and place, we readily accept its enchanted, operatic world where rivals can fight amongst the treetops.

camera movement. All the dialogue is sung, giving the effect of a realistic operetta (if that's not an oxymoron). It's a cinema masterpiece showing how surely music can provide an embracing social, emotional, and historical foundation, one that dislodges unexpectedly strong emotions in the viewer.

Form and Aesthetics Questionnaire

The companion website www.directingbook.com contains a detailed questionnaire that will help you uncover the aesthetic and stylistic designs latent in your screenplay. The inquiry begins with asking for your beliefs, and ends with how you intend to affect your audience. Like the rest of this book, it assumes the artistic process is a delivery system for something intended to do work in the world.

PART 5

A DIRECTOR'S SCREEN GRAMMAR

PART 5-1 ——

Student director Jacqueline Reyno with DP Travis LaBella on location in South Dakota for the film *Language of the Unheard*.

PART 5-2 ——

Director Werner Herzog slating a shot on location for *Rescue Dawn* (2006).

CHAPTER 12

FILM LANGUAGE

As children, we learn to speak because language is a tool to accomplish things. My eldest daughter's first sentence was, "Meat, I like it"—effective, if a little shaky in syntax. All languages operate under conventions, and screen language began developing in the 1890s when camera operators and actors competed to put elementary stories before paying audiences. Soon movies became big business, and the actors and camera operators were joined by directors and editors. A production line had evolved needing greater division of labor.

Most of today's screen language emerged in the first two decades of silent cinema. Separately, through trial and error in each world film center, filmmakers felt their way toward a movie grammar that would eventually merge into a global language. In the early years of the 20th century in United States, directors like Charlie Chaplin and D.W. Griffith were consolidating many of the early experiments by shooting, editing, and codifying the "classic Hollywood" continuity style. In post-revolutionary Russia of the 1920s, filmmakers needed an efficient common language to communicate with a vast, multilingual, and mostly illiterate population, so they made a concerted effort to formulate screen language based on the accumulation of thematic meaning from shot to shot.

Throughout the 20th century, innovative filmmakers like Maya Deren, Orson Welles, Alfred Hitchcock, Jean-Luc Godard, Satyajit Ray, Sergei Parajanov, Chantal Akerman, Federico Fellini, Akira Kurosawa, and Raul Ruiz (to name only a few) continued to infuse fresh contributions into the film language as did the great national film movements like German Expressionism, Italian Neo-realism, the French New Wave, New German Cinema, Dogme 95 and Hong Kong martial arts cinema. Toward the end of the 20th century, avant-garde film, video art, music videos, independent filmmakers around the globe and even commercial ads borrowed from the existing film language and added still more techniques to our ever evolving and expanding art form.

In short, like any language, cinema is evolving to facilitate the stories we want to tell and using forms that are novel, striking, and contemporary. And while new storytelling techniques are being adopted all the time, not a single technique in the history of cinema has become obsolete. The language of narrative cinema began in 1895 with the presentation of the first motion picture

FIGURE 12-1

Every cinematic technique ever used is still viable today. The complete *L'Arroseur Arrosé (1895, left)* plays out in a single take, an approach employed in Haneke's *Code Unknown* over 100 years later (*right*).

to employ a performance for the camera, *L'Arroseur Arrosé* by the Lumière Brothers (Figure 12-1, *left*). This simple comedy is about a boy who steps on a gardener's hose and cuts off the water supply. When the puzzled gardener inspects the nozzle, the boy releases the water into the gardener's face. As with all films before the 20th century, this short film was presented in a single unedited take.

Now, in the 21st century, the single long-take technique still exists as a viable, expressive, and commonly used part of cinema's screen grammar: it can be seen in films like Rodrigo Garcia's *Nine Lives* (2005) and Michael Haneke's *Code Unknown* (2000, Figure 12-1, *right*) which includes many extended scenes unfolding in real, unedited time.

Film is universally accessible because it plays to the full arsenal of human perception—that is, the juxtaposition of images, actions, and sounds, as well as spoken and written language for which all humans are hardwired. A film language that relies on something so common should be easy to use, and using it superficially is not difficult. But making it really move an audience takes a special understanding and thoughtful implementation. Film grammar is not something arbitrary, because it literally makes or breaks the identity of what you put on the screen. What makes using it so tricky is that we don't normally pay attention to our perceptual and emotional processes. From birth, they work to automatically feed our feelings, and our feelings feed our actions, so we live in happy ignorance of how all this works—until, that is, we try to make an effective film.

FILM LANGUAGE AND STORYTELLING

The literary or oral storyteller seeks to affect the listener by a selective presentation of bygone events. Think of how a comedian might describe a wedding. Through the telling, he aims to evoke in the reader's imagination a funny event that has already happened.

Cinematic storytelling, however, is always "now," and appears to show us an unmediated, ongoing present. Although you can temporarily force the past tense into what the audience sees and hears, film always settles back into the present tense. Yet how can you retell something that seems to be unfolding at that very moment? This is film's paradox, its sleight of hand. It is an artfully constructed "now" in which the camera observes, reacts, and navigates the events as they seem to happen. In reality, of course, a selective intelligence is silently guiding our eyes and ears just as any literary mediator would. This is the film Storyteller at work—and creating this effortless narrative is the job of the director. The director *is an unseen presence through whose creative intelligence we perceive unfolding events and who is palpably alert to their significances, meaning, and ironies.*

The job of a film director has many facets. Directors do indeed work with actors to put flesh and blood on the characters and create dramatic interactions in a screenplay, but a film director is also a visual Storyteller, translating the literary material of a screenplay into images and sequences that communicate all the narrative, emotional and thematic dimensions of the story. Because visualization is at the core of the director's craft, a director must understand the essential expressive power and flexibility of the image, how it implies meaning and emotion, and how it can be modulated to accomplish specific dramatic aims.

In the visual language of cinema the two basic visual elements for creating and communicating specific meaning (what a viewer sees and understands) are the **shot** and the **edit**.

The shot, like the word in written language, communicates something specific; but through editing we connect shots together to create compound meaning just as we string words together to create sentences, paragraphs and chapters. The director's most fundamental tools of expression are first to create shots that are precisely expressive on their own and, second, to construct sequences of shots that, through their relationship to one another, accumulate the complex meanings necessary to tell an effective visual story.

THE SHOT AND MISE-EN-SCÈNE

The **shot** is the smallest unit of the film language. A shot is a single running image unbroken by an edit. Shots can be as short as a few frames or as long as your format allows before you run out of film or data storage space. The "hallway fight" scene in Chan-wook Park's *Old Boy* (2003) shows Oh Dae-su battling over a dozen adversaries in one single shot that lasts nearly four minutes. On the other hand, in the "Hard Luck Round 13" fight sequence in *Raging Bull* (1980), Martin Scorsese and editor Thelma Schoonmaker compile over 50 shots in less than a minute for the moment when Jake offers himself to a barrage of punches from Sugar Ray Robinson.

Every shot, regardless of length, contains information. Everything visible within the frame of each shot (subjects, actions, movements, objects, setting, backgrounds) gives each shot its meaning as does the way they are visually presented (lighting, color, texture, spatial relationships and compositional aspects). This concept is known as **mise-en-scène** (a term derived from a French theatrical phrase meaning "placed in the scene").

A shot's mise-en-scène can either be very simple or densely informative, depending on what you need it to convey. Examine the first shot in Jason Reitman's *Young Adult* (2011) in which we

FIGURE 12-2

Intelligent use of mise-en-scène can reveal enormous amounts of information very quickly, as with the introduction of Mavis (Charlize Theron) in Reitman's *Young Adult*.

see the main character Mavis (her introduction)(Figure 12-2). It is a short pan scanning a small apartment bedroom in the daytime. We see a dusty television tuned to a reality TV show where an attractive young woman is talking about her low self-esteem. The walls are empty. We see an old pink DVD player, dirty clothes and towels tossed carelessly in the corner and every horizontal space cluttered with old cosmetics, perfume bottles, and junk. Through a window we see a city skyline. The shot settles on a sleeping woman dressed in sweat pants and a t-shirt and lying on top of her rumpled blanket. Her left hand is resting on a side table where we see a wine bottle, wine glass, vodka bottle and rocks glass.

The evidence in this one shot already communicates a great deal about the character. She lives in a small, modest apartment in the city, is not a great housekeeper and has paid little attention to furnishing her space. We imagine she has had a rough night of drinking, probably alone. She seems to have passed out with the TV on before getting into bed. Nothing indicates this is an anomaly, since all this looks routine for her.

Through careful attention to mise-en-scène detail Reitman has communicated volumes of story and character information—all in a single shot.

CREATING COMPLEX MEANING IN AN IMAGE

Unlike a painted image, which is inevitably inflected by the vision and technique of the artist creating it, or the literary image that is conjured through carefully selected words, the photographic image has the disadvantage of being excessively literal and blunt. A shot of a dog is, well, a dog. A filmmaker must work hard to overcome this literalness if they are to impart any degree of complexity, poetry, or allegorical significance. For that dog to be a hound from hell, or the embodiment of pure loyalty, you must carefully consider your treatment of that image or it won't resonate the way you want. **Image denotation** and **connotation** refer to how we register an image's meaning. Denotation is what an image is (a dog); connotation is what it seems to mean (the embodiment

FIGURE 12-3 ——

A carefully composed mise-en-scène is worth a thousand words. This frame alone from Kubrick's *Lolita* reveals Humbert's complex and perverse situation.

of loyalty). The Storyteller's *intention* behind any image is delivered through a combination of its content and its form.

The meaning of a shot arises from carefully selected mises-en-scène and the embedded cultural associations that combine to direct the spectator along a particular path of speculation. Figure 12-3 is a frame from Stanley Kubrick's *Lolita* (1962). It shows Humbert making love to his wife Charlotte (note the obvious placement and lighting of the wedding band). Superficially the shot's intention is to show Charlotte's enjoyment, but that is only what the shot denotes. The inclusion of Lolita's carefully placed photograph (even though slightly out of focus) and Humbert's precisely angled head (even though his face is not visible) make this average love-making shot connote something far more complex and sinister. The mise-en-scène details encourage us to read into the scene that Humbert can only make love to his wife while fantasizing about her 14-year-old daughter—a twisted sexual dynamic that is going on behind poor Charlotte's back. In fact, this shot confirms what we've only suspected up to this point, that Humbert only married Charlotte so he can pursue her daughter.

The crucial concept behind mise-en-scène is that everything in a shot is placed there purposefully, because every detail in the frame can add highly significant story information and emotional context.

THE EDIT AND MONTAGE

Through editing, we can place shots next to each other so that the meaning in each becomes inflected, even multiplied, by the other shots around it. By arranging shots in a particular way we can contextualize each individual image and create meanings that are greater than the sum of its parts. This concept is known as **montage** (from a French word that simply means editing). Broadly defined, montage is the technique by which meaning is suggested by the accumulation of information in an edited sequence.

Central to understanding how montage works is the concept of **juxtaposition**, which simply means placing shots next to each other so that you highlight a link or contrast between the content of each. It's essential to understand that viewers do not interpret each image alone, but instinctively create connections and meanings between them. For example, the shot from *Young Adult* in Figure 12-2 is preceded by a shot of a tall building. We do not just read these two shots as, "here is a building, now here is a woman sleeping on a bed." Instead, we fill in additional information to conclude that the woman in her bedroom is in that building.

The most famous examples of this phenomenon are the film experiments by Lev Kuleshov in the early 1920s in which he juxtaposed the same emotionally neutral shot of a man's expressionless face with various images. When juxtaposed with a bowl of soup, people saw a hungry man; when juxtaposed with a child's coffin, people read his expression as sorrowful. Each new juxtaposed image inflected the man's neutral expression with a different emotion.

FIGURE 12-4 ⸻

The Kuleshov effect in Hitchcock's *Rear Window*. Is Jeff (James Stewart) smiling at the puppy in the basket or leering at the young dancer?

Alfred Hitchcock referred to the Kuleshov effect, as it is known, when discussing the image associations he employed in *Rear Window* (1954, Figure 12-4):

FIGURE 12-5

In Lang's *M*, the emotionally devastating moment of Elsie's murder is created using only one repeated word, "Elsie," and six carefully composed and juxtaposed shots.

> This is actually the purest expression of a cinematic idea...
>   In the same way [as Kuleshov], let's take a close-up of Stewart looking out of the window at a lit-tle dog that's being lowered in a basket. Back to Stewart, who has a kindly smile. But if in the place of the little dog you show a half-naked girl exercising in front of her open window, and you go back to Stewart again, this time he's seen as a dirty old man[1]!

Young Adult's connection was spatial (that building contains this woman), while the association in the Kuleshov and Hitchcock juxtapositions are emotional. The possibilities do not end there, and we will see more juxtaposition types in Chapter 16.

When you start to string more than two images together, the juxtapositions and associations can build into very complex meaning indeed. In his film *M* (1921) Fritz Lang creates an emotionally devastating moment out of only six shots which, on their own, mean very little (Figure 12-5). (a) A mother leans out of her window to call out to her little girl, "Elsie!" (b) an empty staircase,

[1] *Hitchcock*, Truffaut (revised edition) (Simon & Schuster, 1985).

(c) an empty attic space, (d) an empty chair at the dinner table, (e) Elsie's ball rolls out of the bushes, (f) a balloon, given to Elsie earlier by a friendly man, is tangled in electrical wires. A powerful alchemy occurs because Lang shows the toys that are no longer in Elsie's possession, and the places where Elsie should be, but is not. Without seeing anything explicit, we understand that Elsie has become the latest victim of the child killer we know is on the loose—and it's utterly shattering.

CINEMATIC SPACE AND TIME

While a film may represent physical and temporal reality, it is in fact a highly flexible and artificial construction of space and time—a construction so familiar, however, that few viewers are ever consciously aware of the extreme manipulations taking place. Film commonly abridges space as well as time in the interest of narrative compression. A protagonist suddenly remembering at lunch that he forgot to feed his parking meter might be shown in three brief shots: (a) leaping out of his chair, (b) his feet running downstairs, and then (c) arguing on the street with a cop who's filling out the citation. Because a viewer will infer what's been left out, they will have the impression of experiencing the protagonist's full journey (from apartment to street) even though only a few key actions in a few representative locations were actually represented (see Chapter 16).

AUTHORIAL POINT OF VIEW

Image connotations and juxtapositions working in tandem not only communicate complex meaning but cause us to infer the human sensibility that chose to notice these particular details. We experience the empty spaces connoting the absence of the girl, the balloon implying her victimization, each in its particular context. This, along with the choice of subject and its treatment, becomes the authorial point of view, the Storyteller's sense of what matters.

Cinema is a living language with an ever-expanding vocabulary—the fundamentals in this section are just the beginning of how we speak in film. Just as in writing, cinematic language can be bland or expressive, prosaic or poetic, utilitarian or profound. Visual eloquence begins from appreciating the basic vocabulary and creative possibilities of film language. And the best place to begin is with the frame.

CHAPTER 13

THE FRAME AND THE SHOT

In Chapter 10 we explored how form is the manner in which you choose to present content. Image composition is one of the primary vehicles by which you project ideas and dramatize relativity and relationship, and thus effective composition is vital to expressing yourself with visual precision. It makes not only the subject (content) accessible, but heightens the viewer's perceptions and stimulates his or her imaginative involvement, like the accurate and vibrant language from the pen of a good poet.

COMPOSITIONAL AXES OF THE FRAME

All aesthetic decisions concerning shot composition begin with the dimensions of the frame. The **aspect ratio** of a film frame refers to the relationship between the **x-axis** (width of the frame) and the **y-axis** (height of the frame). Aspect ratios are predetermined by the shooting format you use. Early theatrical cinema and standard 16mm film had an aspect ratio of 1.33:1—that is, it was 1.33 units wide to every 1 unit high—a nearly square frame (see Figure 12-5 and 13-7b). Until the early part of the 21st century, broadcast television also maintained these proportions. Widescreen aspect ratios were first developed in the 1950s, and today's standard cinema aspect ratios are 1.66:1 (Europe) and 1.85:1 (United States). The recent revolution in high-definition television (HDTV) has created the new and wider aspect ratio of 1.78:1 (also called 16×9). Cinemascope aspect ratio, used primarily for theatrically projected films with a need to create broad vistas, has a super-wide frame of 2.39:1.

For all practical purposes the 1.33:1 aspect ratio is now obsolete as a shooting format. As you can see in Figure 13-1, the three main widescreen aspect ratios (1.66:1, 1.85:1, 1.78:1) are similar as a compositional canvas. Although the compositional frame is essentially a two-dimensional canvas, the audience perceives a third dimension, depth, called the **z-axis**. The illusion of depth is a powerful compositional element that can be emphasized or de-emphasized by using depth cues (p. 157) and lens selection (p. 361) according to the aesthetic requirements of your shot.

ESSENTIAL PRINCIPLES OF COMPOSITION

CLOSED AND OPEN FRAMES

When we frame a shot we are representing a small portion of a larger environment. A shot that contains all necessary narrative information is called a **closed frame**, while one that calls attention to or relies on **off-screen space** for meaning is called an **open frame** shot. Alluding to unseen space can be a powerful narrative tool especially when it allows sound to suggest the world beyond what is visible. Early in Lynne Ramsay's *We Need to Talk about Kevin* (2011, Figure 13-2), the central character Eva rushes to her son's high school where some unspecified crisis is in progress. As she searches for her son amid a panicked crowd and police cars, she is stopped cold at the sight of something. Is it her son? Is it a body? What is she looking at? We don't know, because what she sees remains off-screen. All we see is her reaction, but what we hear coming from off-screen is the sound of a power saw. Because the shot is framed to withhold critical information, it creates mystery and suspense.

FIGURE 13-1

The most common aspect ratios in cinema (see Figure 13-7b for an example of the seldom used 1.33:1 aspect ratio).

FIGURE 13-2

Open frame. The use of off-screen space in this scene from Ramsay's *We Need to Talk About Kevin* creates a central mystery.

DEEP FRAMES, SHALLOW FRAMES

Shots that accentuate the illusion of depth are referred to as **deep frames,** while shots that flatten the space along the z-axis are called **flat frames.** Each type of shot has its own expressive value. The several compositional techniques used to control the perception of depth in the frame are called **depth cues.**

- **Relative size** is the depth cue that arises from the way we judge the sizes of objects in the real world. By their relative size, we judge how far apart they must be in the near and far planes of the frame. In Figure 13-3, *right,* the fact that the two little girls are smaller than the boy's head extends the perception of z-axis space because we understand that, in order to appear so small, they must be far away (in the background) from the boy, who is in the foreground.

- **Receding planes** is another depth cue in which objects are placed along foreground, mid-ground, and background along the z-axis. In Figure 13-3, *right,* the doors and ceiling lamps serve this function.

- **Objects overlapping** where objects along the z-axis (depth) overlap and partially obstruct each other (foreground details covering background objects) is another strong depth cue. Even a small detail included in the foreground can immediately create a deeper frame.

- Composing your image with **receding diagonal lines** also provides a powerful depth cue. For example, a row of buildings shot head on will line the horizontal axis of the frame in a flat row, but adjust the camera position left or right so that you're shooting the row on the diagonal and now they will appear to be receding along the z-axis. The converging diagonal lines in Figure 13-3, *right,* provide a very strong indication of depth as they are receding toward a central point.

- Finally, focus can play a crucial role in a viewer's perception of depth. An image with **deep focus** allows a viewer to perceive fine detail deep into the frame, extending the significance of the z-axis, while shallow focus flattens the background and isolates limited planes along the z-axis (see Figures 27-22 and 27-23). The capacity to control the range of focus along the z-axis depends on technical aspects of the lens and is a creative tool we'll explore more thoroughly in Chapter 27.

FIGURE 13-3

This flat frame from Lucas' *THX-1138* (*left*) intentionally suppresses indicators that imply depth while Kubrick uses several depth cues for this deep frame in *The Shining* (*right*).

FIGURE 13-4

A balanced frame from Ozon's *8 Femmes* (*left*), and an unbalanced frame in *The Constant Gardener* (*right*), reflecting Justin's (Ralph Fiennes) emotional state as memories of his murdered wife overtake him.

BALANCED AND UNBALANCED FRAMES

All objects in a frame carry a certain degree of visual weight. Their size, volume, brightness and color all give them greater or lesser prominence. When that visual weight is evenly distributed within a frame, we have a **balanced frame**. When composed with similar elements in perfect equilibrium the image is not only balanced, but **symmetrical** (Figure 13-4, *left*). When only one edge of the composition is loaded with objects or detail, we have the effect of an **unbalanced frame**. Saying balanced and unbalanced is not a judgment of a good or poor composition since an unbalanced image, with all the instability and unease it evokes, may be the best choice for what you're trying to express (Figure 13-4 *right*).

THE RULE OF THIRDS

Like other art forms, cinema has developed a few classical principles for "harmonious" composition, many of which come from other visual arts and long pre-date moviemaking. One of the oldest and most prevalent is the **rule of thirds**, a compositional principle that begins by dividing your frame into thirds, both horizontally and vertically, with imaginary lines along the x-axis and y-axis. The intersections of these lines create what are called **sweet spots**, each indicating four exceptional areas to place your subject to ensure a dynamic composition (Figure 13-5).

When the subject is a person, we commonly place the eyes near the top third sweet spot. This provides extra room in front of the subject to accommodate the direction in which they are moving or looking (regardless of shot size). This is known as giving your subject **moving space** or **looking room**.

Consider the rule of thirds as a starting point only for your compositions. Narrative intentions and requirements of the moment must always trump "rules" like this. However, knowing what is

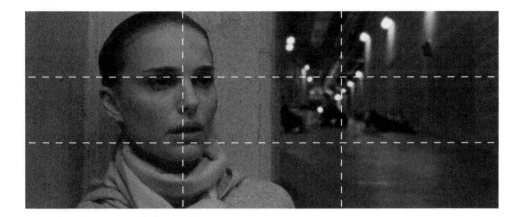

FIGURE 13-5

The rule of thirds compositional principle. Placing eyes near one of the top third "sweet spots" allows looking room, as in this frame from Aronofsky's *Black Swan*.

classically harmonious can help you devise intentionally uncomfortable and uneasy compositions that serve particular narrative needs, as with Figures 9-2 and 13-4, *right*.

CAMERA HEIGHT

One way to tell the work of a novice filmmaker is when camera angles fail to vary. Static shots are always taken from the default height of the tripod, and handheld shots are positioned wherever the camera operator's shoulder happens to be. Understanding what the visual dynamics of camera height can contribute is important because it determines the visual relationship the viewer has with your characters.

The **eye-level shot** (Figure 13-6, *middle*) places the camera at eye level to the subject no matter what their position: sitting, standing or lying on the ground. Well-conceived eye-level shots can be powerful because they place us in the direct line of sight of a character—which can be acutely confrontational or empathetic as a position. Poorly designed eye-level shots can simply be dull. Placing the camera higher than eye level creates a **high-angle shot** (Figure 13-6, *top*), looking down. Positioning the camera below eye-level produces a **low-angle shot** (Figure 13-6, *bottom*).

The steeper the angle of the camera (high or low), the more you emphasize the z-axis (depth). Many film manuals like to assert that low-angle shots convey power and high-angle shots emphasize the powerlessness of a subject—and though this may be true in some circumstances, you should look beyond such facile associations. Camera angles, subtle or extreme, convey many different moods or ideas depending on the narrative context. They can also be used in a fairly utilitarian way, for example a high-angle shot over a writer's shoulder can be used to show what that person is writing on the page and give the audience the feeling of peering over their shoulder.

COMMON SHOT SIZES

Another creative variable crucial to the director's visual vocabulary and storytelling toolbox is **shot size,** which refers to the size of the subject in your frame. You can alter it in two ways: by changing the proximity of the camera to your subject (moving closer or farther) or through optics (changing the magnification power of your lens). These two solutions yield very different compositions and I will discuss the differences in the lens section later in the book (see p. 364).

When directors visualize each dramatic moment in the script, they choose the shot size that best communicates the narrative, emotional, and thematic meaning for each moment. Shot size plays an important role in creating the emotional connections between audience and characters, and the frame of reference is the human form. However, the following shot designations work in principle for nonhuman subjects as well (Figure 13-7).

- *Extreme long shot* (ELS): A wide view of location, setting, or landscape (frame-a). If there are characters in this shot, the emphasis remains on their surroundings or their relationship to the environment.

- *Long shot* (LS): A shot that contains the human figure from head to toe. This works well when you need to show larger physical movements and activity. Location and setting are very visible and provide a context for the character (frame b).

- *Medium long shot* (MLS): Frames your subject from approximately the knees up with the background still quite visible (frame c). Larger physical movement and body "attitude" are emphasized in this shot.

- *Medium shot* (MS): Frames from approximately the waist up (frame d). This shot is good for smaller physical actions, posture, and facial expressions, yet maintains some connection with the setting. However, the environment is no longer prominent since the viewer is now drawn closer to the subject.

FIGURE 13-6

A high-angle shot (*top*), an eye-level shot (*middle*) and a low-angle shot (*bottom*) from Jane Campion's *Sweetie.*

FIGURE 13-7

Common shot sizes by abbreviation: (a) ELS from Haneke's *The White Ribbon*, (b) LS from Bergman's *The Seventh Seal*, (c) MLS from Kaurismäki's *Le Havre*, (d) MS from Kurosawa's *Rashomon*, (e) MCU from Thornton's *Samson and Delilah*, (f) CU from Soderbergh's *Sex, Lies, and Videotape*, (g) ECU from Romanek's *One Hour Photo*.

FIGURE 13-8

A two shot (*left*) and a group shot (*right*) from Ayoade's *Submarine*.

- *Medium close-up* (MCU): This framing, also called a "head and shoulders shot," frames from the chest or shoulders up (frame e). The emphasis here is on the subject's facial expressions, but it also shows any physical "attitude" carried in the shoulders. This shot brings us into the personal space of a character.

- *Close-up* (CU): Places primary emphasis on the face (or other part of the body) (frame f). Small details in features and expression are the subjects of this very intimate shot. A close-up brings us into the character's intimate space and underscores object details when narrative emphasis is important.

- *Extreme close-up* (ECU): A stylistically potent shot that isolates a very small detail or feature of the subject (frame-g). Strangely, moving this close to a human subject can create an abstraction because it leaves too many features off-screen and thereby obscures emotions. ECUs create such a strong and graphic emphasis on minute details that objects often take on thematic or symbolic weight.

- *Two shots and group shots*: The two-shot frame features two subjects. Shots including more than two people are called *group shots* (Figure 13-8).

SHOT SELECTION

One of the principle duties of a director is to determine how to visually present every moment in the script, and this means choosing shots. As you can see, shot size greatly determines visual and narrative emphasis, the relationship between the subject and environment, and the emotional connection between a viewer and a character at any given dramatic moment. Here are four basic considerations a director takes into account when imagining shot sizes:

- *Function:* Considering a shot's utility, we choose the image size according to what we want the audience to see. Showing the grace and athleticism of a dancer requires a long shot. A medium shot of a few soldiers will not show the awesome strength of an army, but an extreme long shot can reveal their vast numbers. A close-up is best to show a flicker of emotion crossing someone's face in a reaction shot—any wider and it may not be detected.

- *Importance:* Related to function is "Hitchcock's rule" of composition stating that the size of an object in the frame should be directly related to its importance in the story at that moment.[1] Giving an object great visual prominence focuses audience attention on that object and cues us to its narrative importance. At a critical dramatic moment in *Atonement* (Wright, 2007) a MLS two shot could have easily shown Robbie handing Briony a letter to give to her sister Cecilia, but director Joe Wright cuts to a CU of the letter at the moment it changes hands. This shows its extreme importance as *the letter* that will destroy everyone's lives (Figure 13-9).

- *Emotion:* Shot size can be used to elicit a specific emotional response or make a connection between a character or situation. As mentioned earlier, close shots reveal the emotion in facial details, while longer shots can withhold emotional attachment.

- *Theme or concept:* Frame size of a single shot can also imply a thematic idea or conceptual approach or, if used consistently, the concept behind an entire film. The very first shot of Ray, the central character in Courtney Hunt's *Frozen River* (2010, Figure 13-10, *top*), is an extreme

FIGURE 13-9 ————————————

"Hitchcock's rule" in Wright's *Atonement*. The size of the letter in the frame reflects its importance in the scene.

FIGURE 13-10 ————————————

The unflinching ECU during Ray's (Melissa Leo) introduction in *Frozen River* (*top*) and the persistent use of ELS's in Koreeda's *Mabarosi* (*bottom*) indicate very different conceptual approaches to representing hardship and emotional pain.

---

[1] This term is taken from *Cinematography: Theory and Practice*, by Blain Brown (Focal Press, 2011). The concept itself is derived from Hitchcock's discussions with François Truffaut in *Hitchcock/Truffaut* (Simon & Schuster, 1985).

close up that plainly shows her tears, the stress lines and the red blotches on her face—even her dirty fingernails. From shot size alone the director's message is clear: the film will be a very close, direct, and unflinching look at this woman's struggles and conflicts. Hirokazu Koreeda's *Mabaroshi* (1995, Figure 13-10, *bottom*), on the other hand is primarily in long shots and extreme long shots, and traces the profoundly emotional journey of a young woman grieving the death of her husband. Because we rarely get a clear look at Yumiko's face, we never enter her intimate emotional space, and Koreeda is implying that we can never understand this sort of deeply personal sorrow. Never can we approach or truly share it, leaving Yumiko isolated with her anguish.

FIGURE 13-11

Sometimes we chose a framing because it just looks stunning. Frame from Boyle and Tandan's *Slumdog Millionaire*.

- *Formal:* Sometimes shot size contributes to the formal style and tone of the film (which should remain consistent). Often, we'll select a specific shot size because it helps us create a graphically compelling, engaging or seductive image (Figure 13-11).

Keep in mind that these categories are not exclusive—many shots perform multiple functions. This discussion only scratches the surface of the broader topic of shot composition and selection and for a deeper analysis of the conceptual and technical aspects of the shot, turn to Gustavo Mercado's masterful volume, *The Filmmaker's Eye: Learning (and Breaking) the Rules of Cinematic Composition* (Focal Press, 2011).

Lenses, Lighting, and Mise-en-scène

Mise-en-scène, shot composition, and the dramatic meaning of an image are also fundamentally linked to lenses and lighting. Lenses determine focus, exposure, and the visual perspective of the shot, and lighting determines visual emphasis and mood. Together, they greatly determine the aesthetic qualities and tone of a film. No discussion of mise-en-scène or composition is complete without exploring the impact of lens choice and lighting aesthetics. Go to Chapter 27 for a detailed discussion of these two vital aspects of the director's visual and expressive palette.

CHAPTER 14

THE MOVING CAMERA

Figure 13-10, *bottom* from *Mabaroshi* is a **static composition**, meaning the camera and subject remain fixed. There is some movement as the character turns the pages of her book, but the essential composition does not change. However, entirely new compositional principles and visual dynamics come into play if either the subject or camera moves significantly during a take: shot emphasis can shift; a balanced composition can become disturbingly unbalanced, or camera movement in any direction can create entirely new compositions with completely new subjects. The shot in Figure 13-10, *top* from *Frozen River* actually begins as an ECU of a tiny rose tattoo on a woman's toe, and then the camera slowly moves up her pink house robe, catches her hands holding a pack of cigarettes, and eventually reveals the worried face of the main character Ray. Subject movement within a static frame or altering the frame through camera movement creates a **dynamic composition**.

CAMERA MOVEMENTS FROM A FIXED POSITION

Camera moves which occur from a fixed spot, whether mounted on a tripod or handheld by a stationary camera operator, are called **pivot camera moves** and there are two principle pivot moves, the **pan** and the **tilt**.

- **The pan** (short for panorama shot) is a camera move that scans the scene by moving the frame horizontally, similar to the way we swivel our heads left and right. Direction is specified as "pan left" or "pan right." As with all moving shots, using a pan requires you to know what subject you intend to frame from the beginning to the end of the move. A pan shouldn't search around aimlessly looking for its frame. Panning shots are commonly used to shift the view of a scene **from** one subject **to** another: doing this in a single shot establishes a clear spatial connection. For example, a shot on a person arriving at their front door then pans across the street to reveal someone watching them. A pan connects the two subjects spatially in a way that two juxtaposed shots cannot. Pans also let you simply **follow** a subject moving horizontally over time and terrain, such as a person walking from their car to their front door. You can see an

FIGURE 14-1

Scorsese and camera movement: this one scene from *Goodfellas* starts with a tilt up and then uses both a pan from/to (*top frames*) and a follow pan (*bottom frames*).

example of both types of pans in a single shot in Martin Scorsese's *Goodfellas* (1990) (Figure 14-1). Henry and Tommy wait outside a diner. Pan right *from* the gangsters *to* a truck pulling into the parking lot, then pan left, *following* the driver of the truck as he gets out and walks past the two gangsters. Once Henry and Tommy are back in the frame, the camera pans right again, *following* them to the truck—which they casually steal.

- **The tilt** shot pivots the camera vertically, up and down, and reproduces the action of tilting your head up and down. Direction is indicated as "tilt up" or "tilt down." As with the pan shot, we can tilt to **follow** a subject moving vertically through space, such as a rocket lifting off; or **from** one subject **to** another, such as tilting from a mountain climber up to the summit that is her goal. Michel Hazanavicius' *The Artist* (2011) has a tidy movement combining both: a tilt up shifts the frame *from* a pile of newspapers with headlines announcing the 1929 stock market crash *to* the worried face of George Valentin. But the tilt also *follows* the glass of whisky that George picks up from the newspapers and brings to his mouth for a hefty swig (Figure 14-2). The move nicely connects the bad news George is getting and the two causes of his downfall—he's broke and drinking heavily.

- **The zoom** shot is technically an optical effect rather than a bona fide camera move, but looks like a move because it alters the frame significantly during a shot, either by "zooming in" (increasing focal length and size of the subject) or "zooming out" (decreasing focal length and subject size) using a variable focal length lens. Zoom shots magnify all objects in the frame equally while also changing the x-axis and y-axis the field of view. Though a zoom enlarges or diminishes a subject, it does not feel dynamic, meaning that it does not give the viewer the sensation of truly traveling through space (see *dolly shot* below).

DYNAMIC CAMERA MOVEMENTS

A **dynamic camera** is one which alters the frame by moving through the space of the scene—up, down, forward, sideways, backward, or a combination of these. These give the viewer the sensation of moving through space because of kinesthetic cues associated with walking, running, approaching, following, ascending, descending, retreating, and so on. Dynamic camera moves can infuse a moment with enormous energy, but they often require special equipment, like dollies and tracks, extra crew to move the camera smoothly, and extra time to set up and rehearse the move.

FIGURE 14-2 —————————————

A beautiful tilt camera move in Hazanavicius' *The Artist* that loads the frame with revealing information.

- **The tracking** (or **trucking**) **shot** is a horizontal camera movement that follows a moving subject either alongside, from behind, or from in front by moving the camera backwards. Movie lovers cherish the great long-take tracking shots such as the three-and-a-half minute opening of Orson Welles' *A Touch of Evil* (1958) or the hilarious seven-minute traffic jam tracking shot in Jean-Luc Godard's *Weekend* (1967), but less flamboyant tracking shots are more common. *Amélie* has a lovely tracking shot after the title character has anonymously changed a man's life for the better. The move implies she feels a moment of perfect harmony by tracking her as she crosses the beautiful Pont des Arts bridge in Paris. At first the camera precedes her,

FIGURE 14-3 ———

Jeunet's *Amélie* uses dynamic camera moves throughout, including this energetic dolly shot following Amélie (Audrey Tautou) across the Pont des Arts.

tracking slowly backwards, then as she overtakes the camera, it moves alongside her, and in the end the camera is following her (Figure 14-3).

- **The dolly shot** allows the camera to move closer or farther from an object (often stationary). Direction is indicated as "dolly in" or "dolly out" or also commonly "push in" or "pull out." Dollying is similar to zooming because the size of the subject changes. However, because the focal length of the lens remains constant, the perspective changes along the length of the move and promotes a strong sense of moving through space. A dolly move can change frame size on a subject significantly (for example, from long shot to a medium close-up). Of course, this can be accomplished by editing from LS to MCU, but a continuous camera move tends to infuse the moment with extra dramatic weight (see Figure 14-8 for an example of a long dolly out).

A very common technique for adding dramatic punctuation to a moment is the **short dolly in** (or **short push in**). It need not change the frame much but if the timing is precise, dramatic tension intensifies and the audience is cued to imagine what the character is thinking or feeling. François Truffaut does this at a critical moment in *The 400 Blows* (1959, Figure 14-4); earlier in the day 12-year-old Antoine avoided punishment for missing school by lying to his teacher, and telling him it was because his mother died. Later on during class, Antoine's teacher is summoned out of the classroom by visitors. When Antoine turns to look, he sees his mother and father talking to the teacher. As Antoine realizes what this means, Truffaut and cinematographer Henri Decaë dolly in slightly on his stricken face (from MLS to MS)—tension ramps because we imagine Antoine thinking, "Uh-oh, I'm in big trouble now." Notice how this shot does not dolly in so much (i.e. to a CU) that we lose the additional tension of Antoine's classmates' scrutiny.

FIGURE 14-4

When timed perfectly, as in this moment in Truffaut's *The 400 Blows*, a short dolly-in can intensify an emotional situation.

- **The crane shot** raises the camera vertically up or down in relation to the subject. Crane shots can be major—moving vertically above houses, treetops or buildings over 100 feet tall—or they can be minor and rise only a few feet. Large crane shots are often used for establishing shots that situate a character in a landscape. A famous one is in Victor Fleming's *Gone With*

FIGURE 14-5

This epic crane shot in Fleming's *Gone With the Wind* alters the subject from Scarlett O'Hara (Vivien Leigh) to the massive scale of the Civil War devastation within a single shot.

the Wind (1939, Figure 14-5): Scarlett O'Hara has gone to the train station looking for Dr. Meade to help deliver Melanie's baby, but the station is now an improvised field hospital for wounded Confederate soldiers. As she searches for the doctor amid the suffering and chaos, the camera cranes up from a long shot on Scarlett to an extreme long shot, far above the scene, revealing acres and acres of dead, dying and wounded soldiers. It finally comes to rest on a tattered Confederate flag flying above the gruesome scene. A single, poignantly dynamic move communicates the severity, enormity and carnage of the civil war, utterly dwarfing Scarlett and her domestic concerns.

Epic crane shots like this require significant equipment and personnel to accomplish. But short crane shots (also called **pedestals**) are far more common, and practical for the low-budget filmmaker. A simple **jib arm** will allow you to create a crane rise of several feet which, like all dynamic moves, infuses energy into a moment. The shot from *Goodfellas* in Figure 14-1 begins with a short crane up Henry's body, starting on his slick leather shoes, moving up his tailored suit and open collared shirt, and ending on his slicked back hair and tough guy attitude. It's the first time we've seen Henry as an adult and the move emphasizes that he's grown up to be every inch the gangster he aspired to be.

- **The Steadicam shot** involves mounting the camera on a stabilizing apparatus held by a camera operator who can freely move in any direction. Steadicam shots are named after the Garrett Brown invention (circa 1976) that allowed heavy film cameras to be mounted on a stabilizing arm attached to a body brace worn by a camera operator. The articulated arm acts as a shock absorber and permits the operator freedom of movement while maintaining a steady, jitter-free frame. Today stabilizing systems are manufactured by many companies, especially for lighter DV cameras, but the Steadicam name is synonymous with a free-flowing dynamic camera movement. Steadicam shots take much practice and can mix pans, tilts, dollies and tracking moves to create long fluid shots.

The remarkable five-minute shot on the beaches of Dunkirk from *Atonement* (Wright, 2007) is a great example of the flexibility of Steadicam shots as well as the extraordinary choreography necessary to pull them off (Figure 14-6). This single shot tracks right, tracks left, tilts up, arcs around, pushes in, dollies out, and creates every imaginable shot size as it follows, loses, and relocates the lead character as he traverses the surreal environment of the British evacuation at Dunkirk.

- **The handheld camera**, like the Steadicam shot, can do any pivot or dynamic move, and in any combination. It does however introduce the human movements of the operator into the image. Even though good operators can control handheld movements to a great degree, their unsteadiness, jiggles, wayward framing, and even breathing are detectable in a handheld shot. Nonetheless, many narrative filmmakers have used these artifacts to their advantage, incorporating them into an intentional visual style that is reminiscent of cinéma vérité documentary. It is an aesthetic that feels immediate, truthful and direct, which the French New Wave and the Danish Dogme 95 directors have used

FIGURE 14-6

Long Steadicam shots, like this one from Wright's *Atonement*, require careful camera/subject choreography and lots of rehearsal.

FIGURE 14-7

The handheld camera in Bigelow's *The Hurt Locker* is used to reflect the edgy, adrenalized perspective of an army bomb squad working in a hostile environment.

extensively in their groundbreaking work. Many low-budget, independent films have embraced this inexpensive and flexible camera approach, such as the Darden Brothers' *La Promesse* (1996), Rebecca Miller's *Personal Velocity* (2002), Ramin Bahrani's *Chop Shop* (2007), Lance Hammer's *Ballast* (2008), Kathryn Bigelow's *The Hurt Locker* (2009), and Neill Blomkamp's *District 9* (2010). Despite their diversity, all incorporate the handheld look to great aesthetic advantage (Figure 14-7).

MOTIVATING THE MOVING CAMERA

Convincing camera movements, like their human-movement equivalents, never happen without a stimulus or **motivation**.

- *Subject movement-motivated*, where the shifting frame follows a traveling subject to keep them in view or adapts to a changing composition due to character movement (as in Figure 14-1)

FIGURE 14-8 ————————

The multiple revelations created by this dolly-out camera move in Gilliam's *The Fisher King* add complexity to a relatively simple moment.

- *Subject gaze-motivated*, where the camera follows the attention of a subject, moving "off their look" to show what they are looking at. This motivation ties the perspective of the camera (and therefore the viewer) to the point of view of a character.

- *Subjective camera*, where the camera is understood to be from the direct visual perspective of a character and therefore moves, seeks, and responds as they would.

- *Reveal or conceal*, a powerful dramatic device in which the camera move uncovers critical narrative details or actions that were previously located off-screen at the beginning of the shot (as in Figure 12-2). Also used as framing that leaves an activity to hide it from view.

- *Authorial-motivated*, in which the camera's "mind" actively pursues a logic of inquiry or expectation. This mode probes, explores, interrogates, and can even go ahead of the action—adding visual, emotional, and even thematic information along the way.

Camera movements generally have three phases:

- *Initial composition*: preliminary static composition making an initial mise-en-scène statement before the camera movement begins.

- *Movement*: the pre-planned re-positioning of the frame involving particulars of direction, speed, and shifting compositions.

- *Concluding composition*: coming to a rest on a static composition after the movement, and making a concluding statement.

Figure 14-8, from Terry Gilliam's *The Fisher King* (1991) shows just how much a simple camera move can accomplish in relatively little time. The initial composition is a close-up on Annie who is boldly admonishing her boyfriend Jack for treating her badly. As the camera dollies out, the composition shows more of the space. By the time we get to a medium shot of Annie, we see her at a dinner table set for two but the chair across from her is empty. She is talking to no one. We realize that Jack has stood her up once again. The 'reveal' is simultaneously funny and pitiful. But the camera doesn't stop there, it keeps pulling back to reveal more and more of the space until it finally comes to rest on an extreme long shot of Annie, looking small, lonely, and pathetic in the empty apartment—and now our hearts break for poor Annie.

CHAPTER 15

LANGUAGE OF THE EDIT

This section began with a discussion of the basic concepts of *mise-en-scène* (the meaning created by the content of a shot) and *montage* (the meaning created when we juxtapose shots). Juxtaposing images highlights a link, contrast, or relationship between shots that compounds their meaning, guides the viewer's attention and evokes associations. Juxtaposing key images, especially of significant moments, in a sequence helps to compress a lengthy process while still conveying its essence. Each chosen moment makes us imagine (that is, co-create) the progression from the previous one. Film's favorite form of juxtaposing is the cut from one image to another, but we must also consider the power of juxtaposing scene against scene, for it enables a film to fly through space and time and make narrative and thematic comparisons and contrasts.

SHOTS IN JUXTAPOSITION

There are six fundamental relationships or associations involved in image-to-image juxtapositions.

- **Spatial relationships** involve the creation and organization of film space by linking areas through a cut or sequence of shots, or by dividing large locations into smaller areas. This type of editing encourages the audience to infer a spatial whole. For example, a shot of a character getting out of bed and leaving her bedroom, juxtaposed with her entering the kitchen narrates her progress by implying that she walked through the larger space of her house.

- **Temporal edits** organize and manipulate time. Beyond simply building the chronology of events, temporal editing is commonly used to condense real time into **elliptical time**. Occasionally, temporal editing goes the other way and expands time beyond the actual duration. Temporal editing can also imply that events taking place in different locations are happening simultaneously. Using the same juxtaposition above (a character getting out of bed and then entering her kitchen) we not only compress space, but condense time by jumping over the other areas of the house between the bedroom and kitchen. We could go even further if she leaves her bedroom in her house robe, then enters the kitchen fully dressed for work (see p. 190 for the way spatial and temporal edits are used in the continuity system).

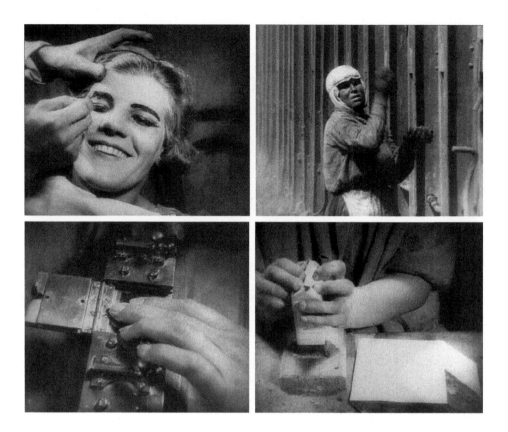

FIGURE 15-1 ———

Associative juxtapositions (*top frames*) and formal/graphic edits (*bottom frames*) in Vertov's *Man with a Movie Camera*, a film that is a veritable textbook of editing technique.

- **Narrative and emotional emphasis edits** guide the viewer's attention at precisely timed moments toward a detail in a scene in order to emphasize its narrative importance and emotional contribution to the unfolding drama. Cutting from a two shot of a young man and woman having a dinner to an ECU of the engagement ring he offers her, gives that object narrative impact. Another juxtaposition from the ring to a close-up of her reaction emphasizes her immediate emotional response.

- **Associative** (or **intellectual**) **edits** create additional meaning through provocative juxtapositions that encourage the audience to infer connections, conceptual ideas or thematic meaning not contained in each shot individually. By juxtaposing a bourgeois lady being pampered in a beauty salon with a peasant woman doing grueling work, Dziga Vertov in his 1929 film *Man with a Movie Camera* suggests that wide class disparities still existed in post-revolutionary Russia (Figure 15-1 *top*).

FIGURE 15-2

Rhythmic and graphic cutting in Aronofsky's *Requiem for a Dream*.

- **Formal/graphic cuts** establish visual and graphic links or disparities between juxtaposed shots (color, shape, composition, movement, and so on). This technique is often used to create symbolic connections or contrasts between shots. Vertov includes a long sequence in *Man with a Movie Camera* that juxtaposes numerous close-ups of hands: sharpening an axe; sewing; editing film; at a phone operator's patch board; wrapping cigarettes at a cigarette factory; working a cash register; hitting the keys of a typewriter, and playing a piano. The impression is of the continuity of manual labor and the sense that the hands of all its workers will build the new Soviet society (Figure 15-1 *bottom*).

- **Rhythmic relationships** are determined more by the length of each shot rather than the content (although movement within the frame can have an impact as well). Examples include cutting shots to fit the beats of a soundtrack, or to create a visually percussive rhythm, as with the famous drug dealing montage from Aronofsky's *Requiem for a Dream* (2000) (Figure 15-2).

These various image-to-image associations are not isolated techniques because they are often used in tandem. The example of the woman leaving her bedroom and entering her kitchen, for example, utilizes both spatial and temporal cutting. Aronofsky's "drug dealing montage" is not only rhythmic editing but uses many formal/graphic juxtapositions to elliptically represent the routine of several nights of selling drugs—so it is an example of temporal editing as well.

JUXTAPOSING SOUND AND IMAGE

Although we have been discussing image juxtapositions, we should also note that **sound juxtapositions** play a significant role in the creation of complex narrative meaning. Sound effects, music, and language can be juxtaposed against picture to create, not an imitation of reality, but a composite set of impressions for the audience to interpret. Sound becomes another tool to provide additional information (especially when it's off-screen) or as an ironic counterpoint to what is visible on the screen.

Alfred Hitchcock's *The Man Who Knew Too Much* (1956) brilliantly exploits all the possibilities of sound. In this scene (Figure 15-3), Dr. McKenna, an ordinary family doctor who unwittingly stumbles into an assassination conspiracy, goes to a taxidermist in search of his young son who has been kidnapped. McKenna is hyper-aware of the danger he's in, and as he walks down the sidewalk toward the taxidermist, he (and we) hear that his footfalls are echoing strangely. He stops and listens but all is silent. When he starts walking again, the echo delay becomes greater, and there may now be two sets of footfalls. Is he being followed? McKenna stops again, but this time the second set of footsteps continues. He waits as they get louder and soon a man rounds the

FIGURE 15-3

Hitchcock's *The Man Who Knew Too Much* exploits all the possibilities of sound and image juxtapositions.

corner and passes him at a casual stroll. McKenna looks at him with a suspicion bordering on paranoia, and the man glances back as if McKenna is nuts. This scene is so extraordinary because of the way Hitchcock uses sound as a vehicle into character subjectivity. The image we are watching is banal—a man walking down a sidewalk—but it's the sound that plunges us into the paranoia of someone entangled in a deadly conspiracy.

THE CONTINUITY SYSTEM

Continuity style shooting and editing is a system that organizes cinematic space, time, and action so that scenes unfold with no spatial or temporal confusion. It also assures that individual shots, when cut together, give the illusion of continuous time, movement and space regardless of when those shots were actually taken. The hallmark of the continuity style is to make each edit from one shot to the next as smooth and invisible as possible.

To truly understand the creative and logistical flexibility of the continuity system, it's important to remember two facts about narrative film production:

- *Narrative films are shot with a single camera.* This allows absolute control of lighting, camera angles, mise-en-scène and performance in every shot. This means that multiple angles on the same scene must be shot individually and often out of sequence. Granted, there are some exceptions: a stunt that can be performed only once might be covered with multiple cameras, but ordinarily scenes and dramatic beats are performed repeatedly for each camera angle.

- *Narrative films are rarely shot in sequential order* from the first scene to the last. Dramatic narrative production is so costly and labor intensive that shooting is organized for maximum time and money efficiency. Usually this means shooting out of order, thus shots presented in the final edit as continuous are often taken hours or days apart.

The continuity system approach aims to make all the visual elements of a scene cut together in a seamless, continuous whole, as if unfolding sequentially, no matter when they were actually shot. See Chapter 25 for more detail on production logistics.

Obviously a single, unbroken take—say a LS[1] of two people talking in an office from beginning to the end—will maintain perfect continuity. But what if you want to cut a shot into this exchange in order to create narrative or emotional emphasis? Perhaps when one character says something incendiary, you wish to insert a close-up of the other person's reaction (emotional emphasis). Maybe you want to show a close-up of a hand reaching into a pocket and pulling out a key (narrative emphasis). Or perhaps you want to show a character's impatience by having him look at the clock on the wall (character point of view). Then again, you might want to control the rhythm and intensity of the conversation by shifting between close ups of each character on specific dramatic beats.

In all these cases, the continuity system principles allow you to incorporate other shots seamlessly, invisibly and with the illusion that the scene is unfolding in continuous, sequential time. The continuity style permits great interpretive flexibility: it allows one to visually interpret a scene, create narrative emphasis, develop emotional connection, and guide the viewer's attention, all the while maintaining the illusion that the moment is unfolding of its own accord, right before the viewer's eyes.

In other words, the director can manipulate the audience's understanding while remaining hidden behind an invisible editing strategy.

THE BASIC SHOTS OF MASTER SCENE TECHNIQUE

Let's look at a simple scene, shot and edited in classic continuity style. Figure 15-4 from Hazanavicius' *The Artist* (2010) illustrates the basic principles of continuity shooting and editing for a simple two-person interaction using the **master scene technique**. The silent film star George Valentin has just been told by his producer (and studio boss) that silent movies are finished and he is no longer one of the studio's bankable stars. Meantime Peppy Miller, the ingénue whom George once mentored, has signed with the studio as one of the new faces of talking motion pictures—the next star. In their meeting, appropriately staged on a staircase in the film studio building, George is descending and Peppy is ascending (he is the falling star, she is on the rise).

The scene was created by cutting together the four traditional shots of the **master scene technique** for dramatic interactions.

- **The master shot** (*frame a*) is usually a wide shot showing both characters in the same shot. The master shot establishes the space and the proximity of the characters to one another. It also establishes the perspective from which the camera (the observer) is viewing the exchange.

- **Closer shots/reverse angles** (*frames b, c, d, and e*). Closer framings in a dialogue exchange are designed to intercut with the master shot and with each other. These can be of one subject, each subject, or subjects in groups, and they may be shot in different sizes, depending

---

[1] This chapter refers to shot sizes by their abbreviated labels, to review please see pgs. 160–162 in Chapter 13.

FIGURE 15-4

This scene from Hazanavicius' *The Artist* utilizes the basic shots of classical master scene technique: a master two shot (a), intercut with closer shots, and reverse angles (frames b, c, d, and e).

on dramatic needs. In this scene, there are two closer angles for each character: George and Peppy each have a medium long shot and a medium close-up. Notice that some shots contain a portion of the other character from the back (*frames b and c*) and these are called **over the shoulder** shots (**OTS**). Cutting back and forth between the close-up angles of two people facing each other is called **shot/reverse shot** technique because each is a reverse of the other. This is a very common editing pattern in the continuity system.

- **Reaction shots** are close shots in which a character usually does not speak. They are inserted into a scene to reveal an emotional reaction to a particularly important moment. These shots are powerful tools for creating character identification. In this scene, Peppy, not knowing that George has just been told by the studio head that he is irrelevant, optimistically announces her wish to make a movie with him. At this moment the scene cuts to a close up reaction shot of George (*frame d*) so that the audience can see that characteristic smile of his falter slightly at the cruel irony of the situation. The intimacy of the close-up frame not only assures that we'll see this subtle reaction, but it also allows us to believe that Peppy did not detect it, thus creating close identification with his predicament.

- **Insert shots** are close-ups of a scene detail that would otherwise be missed in a wider shot, for example, the insert shot of Peppy writing her phone number for George in Figure 15-6, *bottom*. **Cutaway shots** refer to details that are not directly part of the interaction, but reside somewhere in the scene. These shots usually include no part of either character, like a clock on the wall. They can often be used to serve as bridge edits that cover continuity errors. "When in doubt," one of my editors once told me, "cut to seagulls."

THE SIX PRINCIPLES OF CONTINUITY EDITING

From the basic shots in a continuity exchange, let's look at the continuity principles that allow these shots (each taken from a different angle) to cut together seamlessly and with the impression of continuous time.

1. **Continuity of mise-en-scène** (shared shot content). Common detail contained in juxtaposed shots, such as costume, hair, environment, lighting, props, character movement, must all match—or the illusion of continuity will be broken. The master shot shows Peppy in a white blouse, white skirt, and earrings standing at the newel of the staircase (*frame a*). Should any of these details be different in her MLS or MCU reverse shots, they would not flow together. If Peppy has kept her glasses on in the MLS, or stands in the middle of the staircase, or has changed her blouse… continuity is broken.

2. **Continuity of performance.** Given that contiguous shots are taken at different times, each actor must (with the help of the director) maintain the same movements and performance intensity from shot to shot. In the master shot, Peppy is bright, winning, and cheerful (*frame a*) and you see the same in both of her reverse shots (*frames c and e*). If however Peppy's bright energy falters over many takes, the close-ups might not match other material. Actor movements can also pose a problem: should reverse shots be played differently from the

master shot, it might be hard to find an edit point that maintains the illusion of an unbroken flow of action.

3. **Continuity of spatial orientation (180 degree principle).** As mentioned, the master shot establishes the proximity of the characters to one another as well as the perspective from which the camera (the observer) is viewing the exchange. These relationships take place on the **subject-to-subject axis**, and they are seen from the **camera-to-subject axis** respectively (Figure 15-5). When there are two subjects in a scene, their positioning creates a **180 degree line of action** (also called the **axis of action**, **scene axis** or simply "**the line**"). The master shot establishes from which side of that 180 degree line the camera (and therefore the audience) will observe the exchange. In Figure 15-4, *frame a*, the camera is placed so that George is looking *frame right* while talking with Peppy, who is looking *frame left* back at George. All shots for the sequence must maintain this **looking direction**. The 180 degree principle reminds us that we must stay on the same side of the 180 axis of action so that all closer shots will intercut and maintain a consistent looking direction. This is the key to seamless edits.

Imagine we were to "cross the line" and take Peppy's close-up from the other side (Figure 15-5 X) then her looking direction would be reversed. Instead of looking from *frame left* she would now be looking *frame right*—the same direction as George in the master shot. Intercut these two shots, and not only does their exchange become absurd, but all their background information changes, results that would utterly disrupt audience attention.

4. **The 20 mm/30 degree rule** addresses camera placement and puts a slightly finer point on the technique of invisible juxtapositions. This rule states that to cut from one shot to another (from master shot to a closer shot, say) one must change the angle on the scene by at least 30 degrees and alter the size of the shot significantly (by at least 20 mm, or its equivalent in camera proximity). In other words, shots must be substantially different in size and angle to juxtapose well.

The purpose of this rule is to avoid the appearance of a **jump cut**, which arises when juxtaposed shots are so similar in angle and size that one feels that a section has been removed from the scene. Compare angles and shot size differences between the master (*a*) and closer shots (*b, c, d,* and *e*) in this simple sequence from *The Artist*, and it's easy to see how it adheres to this rule (Figure 15-5).

Of course, the jump cut can deliberately depart from traditional continuity style, and has become a legitimate technique with an overt stylistic feel all its own. By signaling elision it aims to eliminate unnecessary sections of time. Jump cut technique has its own shooting principles and needs planning. It won't emerge well from poor continuity shooting.

5. **Eyeline matching** is another technique useful to continuity style shooting. More precise than general sightline direction, eyeline matching means reproducing the exact angle of a character's gaze from shot to shot. The master shot establishes that George is lower than Peppy and looking up, and that Peppy is higher than George and looking down. In their matching closer shots, George should be looking up, and Peppy looking down at precisely the same angles. Notice that camera heights, and not just camera angles, must also mimic their sightline differences. It is a common practice that helps maintain strong eyeline matching and a sense of visual connection. If the gaze of either varies, the dramatic connection and tension in a scene

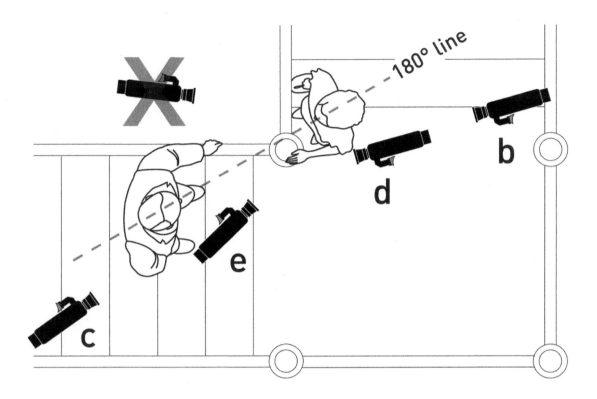

FIGURE 15-5 ——

An overhead diagram of Figure 15-4 reveals that the camera never crosses the 180 line of action (maintaining correct sightlines) and closer shots are framed according to the 20 mm/30 degree rule. The "Xed out" camera angle shows how crossing the line would have reversed Peppy's sightlines.

could be shattered, a problem that can easily occur in close reaction shots when the other actor may not be present. Without a point of focus, an actor's gaze will wander.

6. **Cutting on action** is a powerful technique for making physical movement flow across edits. Editing from one juxtaposed shot to its matching shot during a physical action shares the action from one shot to the next and has the effect of rendering the cut invisible. During *The Artist*, Peppy writes down her phone number for George (Figure 15-6) and the scene cuts to a close-up of her note pad during the writing action, then cuts back to the medium shot during her action when she lifts her pencil from the pad. These actions are fairly large, but even a tilt of the head, or a slight shift of the body can offer enough movement to create a smooth cut on action. Cutting on action requires you to shoot **overlapping action** in each shot. That is, the entire action must be repeated in both shots and in precisely the same way so that you have the option to cut anywhere within the action in the search for the best **matched action edit**.

FIGURE 15-6

A perfect cut on action creates a seamless edit between two angles in Hazanavicius' *The Artist*.

NOT JUST FOR TWO PEOPLE

The basic shots and principles of continuity style shooting and editing function not only for person-to-person exchanges, but also for person-object interactions or group interactions. A secret agent trying to defuse a bomb, a gambler watching a boxing match, or a teacher lecturing to an entire classroom of students—all these scenes can incorporate exactly the same guidelines for scene axes, camera placement, camera angles and editing points. Notice in Figure 15-6 how a new 180 degree line is established between Peppy and her note pad, and that the camera remains on one side of that axis for all shots involving her writing.

FIGURE 15-7

Creating a strong visual POV with three shots: a looking shot (*left*); a POV shot (*middle*) and a reaction shot (*right*).

VISUAL POINT OF VIEW

In Chapter 9 we discussed the importance of establishing a dramatic point of view in the screenplay. **Point of view** (**POV**), of course, has its visual equivalent too. By visually representing a character's point of view, you encourage the audience to not merely look at your character, but look *with* them as well. There are two common ways we represent point of view visually.

The **subjective shot** is a camera angle taken directly from the perspective of a character—as if the camera was their eyes (see Figure 13-8, *left*). The subjective camera is often handheld to give the feeling of human movement behind the gaze. However, as directly representative as this approach may seem, it is seldom used.[2] Its inability to show the reactions of the character through whose eyes we are seeing eliminates evidence of emotional response.

Much more common is a three-shot POV sequence that approximates the perspective of the character, yet provides much more internal emotional information. The shots in this sequence are: (1) the **looking shot,** in which the character turns and sees something; (2) the **POV shot,** which shows what that person is looking at from approximately their perspective; and (3) the **reaction shot,** in which we see how that character feels about what they have just seen.[3] The same scene from *The Artist* contains a good example. During George and Peppy's conversation, George looks over her shoulder and notices the handsome young men with whom she arrived (Figure 15-7). Already feeling old and superfluous, his reaction to these boys not only provides an enormous

---

[2] See Julian Schnabel's remarkable *The Diving Bell and the Butterfly* (2007) for extensive use of the subjective camera.

[3] The POV sequence is three shots in terms of editing, but in terms of shooting there are only two shots. The looking and reaction shots are usually done in one take, with the POV shot inserted between these moments making three shots.

amount of internal information, but because Peppy does not get a similar POV moment, we feel this is George's scene; on his way to irrelevance, he's the one with the most at stake.

The juxtaposition of the POV and reaction shots is a good example of the Kuleshov effect (see p. 152). Simply juxtaposing the handsome young men (the future) with George (fading into the past) allows the audience to infer a great deal of meaning and practically read his mind. Because of this, Jean Dujardin's (George) performance can be quite subtle, and he does not need to broadcast his feelings—we know.

Creating character POV is so crucial to building character identification that you must be careful not to squander this technique on just anyone. The ability of a character to look and send the camera (and therefore the audience's perspective) to what they are seeing is powerful. A director employs this technique to help establish a main character and the point of view of the film.

STORYTELLING STYLE AND COVERAGE

The shooting strategy and number of shots a director uses to present a scene is called **scene coverage**. Obviously, this scene from *The Artist* could have simply played out entirely in one LS master shot with no editing. Instead, Hazanavicius shot six additional angles (two MLS reverse shots, two MCU reverse shots, a CU of the note pad and a POV of Peppy's "boys"). Later, cutting these shots together, the director and editor carefully experimented so they could orchestrate the audience's attention, the emotional flow of the scene, and the POV of a dramatically critical moment.

Not every scene requires equal coverage; some are best shot from multiple camera angles (two, three, five, or even more) while others lack dramatic justification for multiple shots and require only a master shot or one moving shot. The amount of coverage for any given scene is determined by your visual conception of it. Being able to choose between several angles of the same moment gives you great flexibility in shaping the dramatic arc and molding the scene emphasis later in the editing. The motivation for cutting to a CU reverse shot, for deciding where and when to utilize the master shot, and when to use a cutaway, is largely determined by the dramatic rhythms of action, dialogue, and emotions. These were conceived in the screenplay, but achieved in the acting and liberated by the coverage and your editing.

Some films require extensive coverage because of their genre, general coverage strategy, and directorial style. The action films of John Woo are a good example. Other films, like *4 Months, 3 Weeks, 2 Days* (2007) by Cristian Mungiu adopt a "one angle per scene" approach that can produce an equally powerful emotional undercurrent. Most films, however, are a mixture of traditional continuity system coverage, some unedited scenes that play out in a single shot, and a few non-continuity edit sequences using associative, formal/graphic, and rhythmic juxtapositions or other non-continuity styles (like intentional jump cuts) to stress thematic, conceptual or stylistic points.

Decisions about coverage are initially made in preproduction, but using the modular, highly flexible mode of standard continuity coverage, your choices can develop according to the dynamics of performance and shooting. Inevitably they develop still further during the editing process as you work with the reality of your footage. Often it will contain unexpected strong moments, or weak moments or inconsistent performances that you must cut around. We will look more at how directors determine coverage in Chapter 24.

MOVEMENT AND SCREEN DIRECTION

The term **screen direction** describes a subject's direction or movement within the frame. Controlling screen direction becomes crucial when that movement flows through multiple shots. An important screen convention, related to the 180 degree axis of action for two person interactions, is that characters and their movements are generally observed from only one side of that movement so that screen direction remains consistent. Say you're on the sidewalk shooting a parade flowing down the street. In your frame a high school marching band moves from *right to left* across the screen. Now let's say that as the volunteer firefighter corps arrives, you cross the street to shoot them from the other side. The firefighters will be traveling from *left to right*. If you juxtapose these shots with one another they will be moving oppositionally, and the audience will expect the two factions to collide. Similarly, if we show two characters walking along the street, one moving from *left to right* and the other from *right to left*, a viewer will assume that these characters will soon cross paths (Figure 15-8, frames a and b). If, on the other hand we wish to create a chase (or 'follow') sequence then both characters must move across the screen in the same direction, and pass the same landmarks (Figure 15-8, frames c and d).

This same principle of screen direction applies when we trace the progress of a subject traveling toward a destination. The character in Figure 15-9 is walking from one office to another. If that journey begins with him moving left to right (*frame a*), then we understand that the destination is "over there toward the right" and every shot tracing that journey should maintain the same screen direction if we wish the audience to feel progress toward the destination (*frames b1 and c*), regardless of the actual logistics of the space. If we were to inadvertently "cross the line" and insert a shot where suddenly the subject is moving from right to left (*frame b2*), this can give the impression that he has suddenly reversed himself and is returning to the original office.

Of course, if you're representing a character that is lost, or just meandering over the course of a day, a sequence including various screen directions would successfully give us the feeling that their trajectory isn't specifically directed.

CHANGING SCREEN DIRECTION

A journey which moves in only one direction for any length of time can quickly get tedious—especially if you're tracing it over many shots. There are a number of strategies for changing screen direction while maintaining progress toward a specific destination. Figure 15-10 shows two common examples.

1. One common method is use a **neutral shot**—that is a shot with no horizontal screen direction (taken from directly on the 180 axis). If your character moves directly toward or away from

FIGURE 15-8

Cutting between characters moving in opposite directions (frames a and b) strongly suggests they will meet at some point. Cutting between characters moving in the same direction and passing similar landmarks (frames c and d) implies one is following the other.

the camera, then the subsequent shot can be from any screen direction at all (Figure 15-10, *sequence a, b1, c*).

2. Another solution is to simply show your character changing directions, like turning a corner, in a single shot. In Figure 15-10, *sequence a, b2, c*, the man enters in the background moving left to right but turns a corner and exits right to left. Now subsequent shots can proceed right to left.

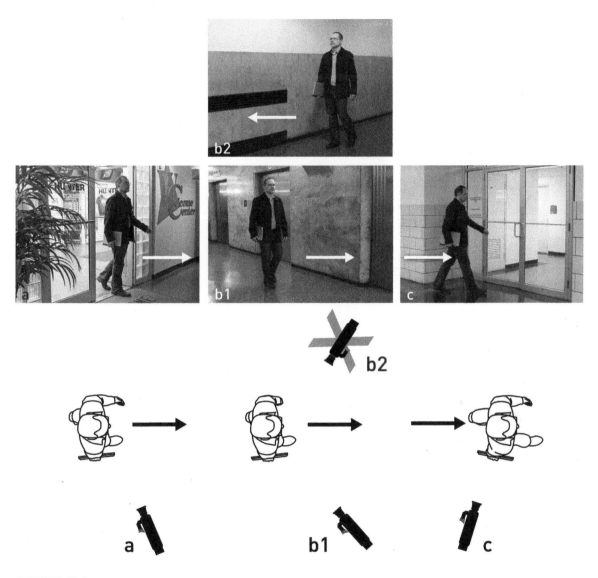

FIGURE 15-9

The movement of a subject through the frame establishes the direction of their journey and the axis of action. Crossing the line of action (*camera position b2*) reverses screen direction creating the impression that the subject is suddenly moving away from their destination.

FIGURE 15-10

Two common ways to reverse the screen direction of a subject while maintaining the feeling of forward progress. From shot (*a*) (moving screen right); cutting to a neutral shot (*b1*); or changing direction within a shot (*b2*); allows us to continue the journey toward screen left (*c*).

EDITING AND TIME COMPRESSION

Though traditional continuity style aims to rid itself of any evident contrivance, and to give the illusion of continuous time, behind these semblances the editor is regularly contracting time and occasionally expanding it. All narratives select, compress, and juxtapose their materials to intensify meaning, reveal ironies, and achieve brevity. This shorthand has become increasingly concise over time as film audiences develop an ever more succinct understanding of filmmakers' intentions.

Look at the three-shot sequence in Figure 15-9 and remove the middle shot. It still works. It's common to show a character going from point A to point B in just two shots: we could in fact show a person pulling out of their driveway in Los Angeles and pulling up to the Capitol building in Washington DC—in just two shots. However, we could also show the man traveling from one office to the other in four shots or 10 shots or even more. The important question is, how much detail of a journey do we really need to show? The answer is that we show only what is dramatically necessary. Merely getting someone from one place to another means jumping over nonessential time and terrain. Removing extraneous time and territory is called **elliptical editing** and is a common cinematic technique. Elliptical editing gives the *feel* of the complete journey without making the audience endure every step, yet the journey can still fit into the invisibility and seamlessness of continuity style.

REAL TIME AND EXPANDED TIME

Some film scenes, as we said, play out in real, unedited time, but very few films employ real time throughout. Alfred Hitchcock's *Rope* (1948), Agnes Varda's *Cleo From 5 to 7* (1962) and Aleksandr Sokurov's *Russian Ark* (2002) are three feature-length exceptions, the last of which is a remarkable 99-minute, unedited single shot that choreographs a cast of 2000, three live orchestras, 33 rooms, and covers 300 years of Russian history!

Exceptions aside, the most common use of real time is within individual scenes, with elliptical edits occurring in the transitions between scenes. This is the general strategy for Mungiu's *4 Months, 3 Weeks, and 2 Days* (mentioned earlier) in which each scene unfolds in real time, but the critical events of an entire day are shown in 113 minutes (Figure 15-11).

Extending time through the use of **slow motion** is common and used to provide extra emphasis on a particular moment. Extending time with editing is less usual and therefore highly overt and stylistic. Temporal elongation through editing usually means adding or repeating extra movements, details, duration, or terrain beyond what the audience expects of the brief moment. A great

FIGURE 15-11

Most scenes in Mungiu's *4 Months, 3 Weeks, and 2 Days* unfold in real time through long, unedited takes while edits between scenes jump forward in time.

FIGURE 15-12

In Ayoade's *Submarine*, time is suspended at the precise moment when Oliver's (Craig Roberts) teasing goes horribly wrong.

example can be seen in Richard Ayoade's 2010 coming-of-age film *Submarine* (Figure 15-12). Oliver Tate (15 years-old) is basically a good guy, but one day he tries to win the attention of Jordana (the girl with whom he's smitten) by bullying the class loser Zoe. Oliver steals Zoe's book bag and, with Jordana and a friend, plays a cruel game of "keep-away." The teasing gets out of hand and when Zoe grabs the bag to pull it from Oliver's grasp, she slips and falls into a small pond. The moment Zoe falls is suspended in time. Inside this moment Ayoade cuts together a sequence of extended shots of all four people, frozen in the moment, while Oliver muses on the significance of this incident in voice over. What should only take a fraction of second is extended to nearly 20 seconds in order to accurately reflect the very human response. In a moment of crisis, many thoughts pass through your mind in a split second.

SHOT DURATION, INFORMATION AND PERCEPTION

The issue of **shot duration** is quite different than that of temporal editing, which organizes and manipulates time. The duration of a shot on the screen depends upon the amount of information and dramatic tension it contains and thus how much actual screen time is required for the audience to assimilate it.

Imagine you are showing a series of interesting slides (paintings or photos) to an audience without comment. You move to a new image after sufficient time has elapsed for the eye to absorb the content and meaning of each picture. Some require more time than others, and this is how an audience must deal with each new shot in a film.

Unlike responding to a photograph or painting, which can be studied thoughtfully and at leisure, the film spectator must interpret the image within an unremitting and preordained forward movement in time. It is like reading a poster on the side of a moving bus: if the words and images cannot be assimilated in the given time, the inscription goes past without being understood. If, however, the bus is crawling in a traffic jam, you have time to absorb, understand, or even become critical of the poster.

There is an optimum duration for each shot to stay on the screen. It depends on the context in which the shot is seen, the complexity of its content, form, and tension, and how hard the viewer must work to extract its significance and intended meaning. Editor and director must judge each shot's essential purpose and value. Underestimate the time it takes to digest it, and critical information may be lost; overestimate it, and your audience becomes bored and restless. This does not place any value judgment on short or long shots: either can work extremely well if they are appropriate to the story, rhythm, and tone of their part in the film.

CHAPTER 16

THE HUMAN VANTAGE OF CINEMATIC LANGUAGE

Early in this section I said that the director is an unseen presence through whose creative intelligence we perceive unfolding events and who is palpably alert to their significances, meaning, and ironies. To be successful, a director must never forget that the written story and acted performances must bear a relationship and resonance with lived human experience, and that our visual technique must do so as well.

The camera's verisimilitude and tried-and-true editing patterns can make events unfold on the screen as naturally and inevitably as a rose blossoming in June. Newcomers assume that cinema's equipment, processes and techniques are the alchemy that does this. But film language is not simply a mechanical system. Using cinema intelligently and expressively means pulling sound and image away from their most blunt representational function and recognizing how film syntax can communicate the full complement of human experiences, including: physical experiences like glancing, studying, walking, chasing, rushing, trembling, falling, scanning, gliding, and spinning; emotional experiences like tension, fear, humor, anticipation, affection, loneliness, compassion, excitement; and intellectual understanding like irony, memory, metaphor, consequence, subtext, association, and theme.

To tell a story on film is to make a construct—a triangular relationship between content, Storyteller, and viewer. Thus effective storytelling does not simply apply elements of film language in a routine or generally expressive way—it harnesses cinematic language to replicate human perception and express the story from the vantage of a human heart. This is the only way a film can truly connect to an audience.

HUMAN VANTAGE

Human experience and human communication always involve a vantage (or point of view): everything you put on the screen should do so too. By this, I mean more than a political outlook or philosophy that can be learned or copied. Your point of view on, say, authority figures cannot be copied because it is too individual, too much the outcome of your individual experience. Potentially fascinating, it implies individual convictions, loyalties, and contradictions. Point of view is not a manifesto or teaching strategy, and does not need to educate or improve others. It is instead the unique awareness of a living, breathing soul, and it's always present in work loved by audiences and critics. By comparison, run-of-the-mill films are soulless. Run through the TV channels any evening to see what I mean.

Our work here is to arm you against being overwhelmed by the routines of the technology and technique, which is where soulless filmmaking begins. The best defense is to pick subjects that hold special meaning for you, and to design your storytelling around an integrated human consciousness. Paradoxically, this is often present in students' (technically naïve) first works, but departs as they acquire glossier skills. To avoid this dehumanization, you must forever keep in mind the essential connection between film language, and human perception and behavior. The perspective of the Concerned Observer (first discussed on p. 121) is our link to embedding a human vantage into every shot, sequence, and scene of our film.

THE CONCERNED OBSERVER AND THE STORYTELLER

A journalist in the field, or a witness in a court case, often relate events they witnessed in matter of fact tones as if they took no action in response and had no subjective feelings. But witnessing is never a value-neutral reception of oral and visual information: at the very least it includes an inner dialogue of ideas, feelings, memories, expectations, and judgments.

The Concerned Observer: The word "observe" has such scientific associations that I am appending "concerned" to imply the observer's feelings, associations, and ideas, all of which lead to involvement. The Concerned Observer in this book is a notional figure whose experience forms ideas and anticipations. As an example, imagine an undercover detective at a significant gathering: she would move around, picking and choosing whom to watch. She would decide whom to approach based on prior knowledge, on suspicions about each type and individual, and on what she sees happening. She would also try to discover the purpose of the gathering and what to expect next.

The Storyteller: Reporting back at headquarters, our Concerned Observer detective changes from being an informed witness to an opinionated Storyteller. A film Storyteller is seldom an identifiable person delivering a perspective in voice-over: usually he or she is an unseen presence through whose creative intelligence we perceive unfolding events and who is manifestly alert to their significances and ironies. Creating the narrative wit and emotional involvement of a Storyteller behind the events in your film is central to film directing that is evolved and not mechanical. For this to happen, a film's stream of perception must be modeled on how someone witty and perceptive experiences events, and also (less visibly) how that person engages a listener by retelling them.

CONFLICT, ATTENTION, AND THE CONCERNED OBSERVER

Consider how you follow a conversation you're observing. Sometimes you merely look toward whoever speaks next. Other times, when the talk becomes heated, you find yourself looking at the listener to see how they're going to react, not the speaker. What's going on?

THE ACTOR, THE ACTED-UPON

Any human interaction is like a tennis game. At any given moment, one player acts (serves the ball), and the other is acted upon (receives it). When we see a player prepare to make an aggressive serve, our eye runs ahead of the ball to see how the recipient will deal with it. We see her run, jump, swing her racquet, and intercept the ball. Certain she's going to succeed, our eye flicks back to see how the first player is placed to handle the return. The cycle of actor and acted-upon, now reversed, makes our eye jump ahead of the ball back to the original player. This is essentially how we unconsciously monitor all significant human interactions. A game ritualizes this interchange as a competition, but to the dramatically aware filmmaker every human interaction is equally complex and structured. Breaking this dynamic down and using it is how we tap into the perspective of the Concerned Observer.

An experienced director understands that every human being is forever trying to get, do, or accomplish something. If you intend to work in drama you must take this to heart: *everyone acts upon those around him, even when he uses the strategy of passivity*. And anytime one person acts on another, there is always an actor and an acted-upon. Usually, but not always, the situation alternates rapidly, and it is through these actions and reactions—in drama as in life—that we assess another's character, mood, and motives. We do this because this is the nearest we ever get to inhabiting another person's reality.

Sit in a café and notice how you watch two people conversing. Just like our tennis match, your sightline switches according to your notion of who is acting upon whom. As soon as you've decided how A has begun acting on B, your eye switches in mid-sentence to see how B is taking it. Depending on how B adapts and acts back, you soon find yourself returning to A. Once you grasp this very human dynamic, most shooting and editing decisions become obvious. You simply use your human expectations, moment to moment, to decide where to look next. In the end, coverage and editing decisions are visceral, with your instincts dictating where the camera eye should look at any given dramatic moment.

DIFFERENT ANGLES ON THE SAME ACTION

Is there a human vantage justification to using very different angles to cover the same action? Imagine covering the scene of a tense family meal from several very different angles. It's a familiar enough screen convention, but does it match what happens in life? In literature, it is clear that multiple points of view are not physical changes of vantage point, but shifts in psychological and emotional points of view. The same is true when this strategy is used on-screen. But film is misleading because, unlike literature, it seems to give us "real" events and a "real" vantage point. As filmmakers, we must keep in mind that film gives a *perception* of events, a "seeming" that, despite appearances, is not the events themselves.

Privileged views: As a bystander during a major disagreement between two friends, you get so absorbed that you forget all about yourself. Instead, you internally debate a series of internal agreements and disagreements, seeing first one person's point, then the other's, so that by the end you have virtually experienced each protagonist's realities. Screen language, by using physically shifting viewpoints, mimics this privileged, heightened subjectivity and signals shifts that are emotional and psychological. Film language thus mimics how an empathic observer identifies with different individual viewpoints as the exchange progresses. Giving such close attention, our sympathy and fascination migrate from person to person.

Such empathic shifts should be rooted in an identifiable point of view—either one of the characters or the Storyteller—if they are to pass as natural and integrated. By the way, nobody can maintain this state of heightened, all-encompassing concentration for long, so a film should not do so either.

ABSTRACTION

Movement from whole to part, or part to whole: Watch the shifts in your attention. They often take you to a private realm where you speculate, contemplate, remember, or imagine. While doing this, we often alter our examination from the whole to a part, or from a part to the whole—whatever suffices to occupy our reverie.

Meaningful detail: A detail registered during a period of abstraction often turns out to have symbolic meaning, or is a part that stands for the whole. Thus, a car door immersed up to the door handle in swirling water can stand for the Hurricane Katrina disaster. This oft-used filmic principle is called synecdoche (pronounced sin-ECK-doh-kee). It arises when our eye alights on something symbolic in an otherwise naturalistic scene—that is, something representative much as a scale represents justice, or, as in our example from Fritz Lang's *M* on p. 153, an empty chair and a discarded child's ball, representing a horrific murder.

Contemplation: We enter a state of abstraction for good reason. We may be taking refuge at a time of fatigue, or making an inward journey to interpret something that has just happened. Selective focus, for example, is a cinema device used to suggest this state. An object isolated on the screen, with its foreground and background thrown out of focus, strongly suggests abstracted vision. Slow motion, fast motion, elaborate camera moves, and expanded time editing are other devices that can have the same effect. In these ways, we distance ourselves and contemplate an event by dismantling reality. Only long and careful attention to the habits of your own consciousness can teach you how this works.

SUBJECTIVITY AND OBJECTIVITY

The world is full of dualities, oppositions, and ironic contrasts. You drive your car very fast at night, and then stop to look at the stars and contemplate your own insignificance under a light that has taken millions of years to reach your eye. Human attention shifts from subjectivity to objectivity, from past to present and back again, from looking at a crowd as a phenomenon, to looking at a woman's profile as she turns away into the crowd.

Screen language exists to replicate every aspect of the observer's attention as he or she stores experience. Make the shifts in the image stream of your film consistent with human consciousness, and your audience will experience an integrated being's presence—that of our invisible, thoughtful, all-seeing Concerned Observer.

SEQUENCE AND MEMORY

You are always surrounded by an everlasting flow of events, but only some are memorable. A biography takes the significant parts of a life and jumps them together. The building blocks are segments of time (the hero's visit to the hospital emergency room after a road accident), the events at a location (the high points of his residency in Rome), or of a developing idea (as he builds their home, his partner loses patience with the process). Because changes of time and space are involved, there are junctures between the narrative building blocks that must either be indicated or hidden as the story demands. These junctures are *transitions*, to be emphasized or elided (glided over).

Elision is faithful to human experience because our memory routinely jettisons whatever lacks significance. Think back on the sensations during an accident, and you'll find that recall has kept only the significant parts, virtually a shot list for a film sequence. The memory is a fine editor.

Once, at New York University, I was asked to advise Danae Elon and Pierre Chainet, students feeling defeated by their 70 hours of documentary dailies. They were astonished when I suggested they put away their laborious documentation and simply write down the sequences they remembered. What they listed was, of course, the minority of the footage that "had something." This became the core of their *Never Again, Forever* (1997), a film about the roots of the settler movement in Israel that gained the dubious distinction of starting fistfights in cinemas.

When we have a dream, or tell an experience, we recall only the peaks of what happened, seldom the troughs. The art of storytelling makes use of this trait to compress a narrative into a short compass.

SCREEN LANGUAGE IN SUMMARY

Screen language when treated like professional packaging robs its subject of soul by making life seem mechanical and banal. But when it employs a Concerned Observer's sensitivities, and is told with panache by a Storyteller, we sense the sympathy and integrity of a questing human intelligence at work. We see with eyes that are human, critical, and compelling. If, for instance, you went to your high school reunion, then saw what another participant filmed with his video camera, you would certainly see what his eyes and ears cared to notice, but more importantly, you would see *a mind and heart at work*. Cinema at its most magical always implies the feeling of an intelligence grappling with the meanings of the events it shows us.

Intelligently made fiction film implies an overarching heart and mind governing the flow of perception. Some call this the "the director's vision," but controlling how a film crew and company of actors create, this is not a simple matter, and is scarcely within individual control. Never forget that yielding too much to the industrial process of filmmaking can kill this sensibility stone dead.

We have personified the native intelligence behind a film's point of view as that of the Storyteller. This is not the robust "I" of the director, but a fictional entity arising from the collective inventiveness of everyone involved. What you see on the screen is a collective construct that is paradoxically individual in effect.

THE FILMMAKER AND RESEARCH

Learning the "how" of cinematic technique is fairly simple, but understanding the "why" of it takes deeper investigation into your own work and also the work of others. An essential component of any filmmaker's development (a process that, in fact, never ends) is to closely analyze existing films, scenes and sequences. Assiduously interrogating films that already exist is a way of reverse engineering the filmmaking process from result back to intention. Look particularly at those films that have grappled with issues and challenges that are similar to your project. Such research will ultimately help you to see with a moviemaker's eye and train you to interrogate your own directorial decisions as you move from screenplay to shooting to editing.

You will find a number of film analysis exercises, each focusing on a particular area of cinematic technique, at the companion website for this book: www.directingbook.com under "Projects." The four study projects in this online resource will raise your awareness of the essentials in image composition, editing, script analysis, and lighting. Collectively, they call upon the basics of seeing with a moviemaker's eye, and will strengthen your confidence when you begin directing.

THE FILMMAKER AND PRACTICE

Every filmmaker will agree on one point: the way to truly learn about making films is to make them. Some like to read, understand, and be thoroughly prepared before entering practical work; others (myself included) learn best by doing things in order to discover what's involved. Either way, all roads lead to getting in there and rolling camera.

So, now that you've covered the basic principles, it's time to really learn how to use them by making movies. Make a lot of short ones since video makes it cheap and easy. Production is the seat of learning in the school of hard knocks, and immersion teaches more than just technique. It forces you to develop your abilities for teamwork, organization, communication, and planning. You won't go far wrong if you remember always to pattern your filmmaking techniques around the natural processes of human perception, action, and reaction. When not filmmaking, you can always watch how you process events in life. Do this consistently, and your films will naturally take on a narrative identity all their own.

An astounding aspect of the artistic process is that once you embark, films use you to make themselves. Each film, once begun, will let you know what step to take next, step by step. Sure, you'll make mistakes, but you'll learn from them and you will get better. A lot of learning is negative learning, and making films is the only way to develop.

At www.directingbook.com ("Projects") you will find a number of short shooting and editing exercises. Each is designed to explore different techniques of expression and you can make each a vehicle for your own ideas and tastes. I have also included a list of skills you can expect to learn, discussion suggestions, and questions to help determine your work's strengths and weaknesses. These projects and their variations represent a huge filmmaking workout. Pick and choose to build the particular skills you want—there are far too many otherwise. Use them particularly to explore building a character, developing a situation, and maintaining your audience's involvement through nonverbal, behavioral means. When you can develop the disparate perspectives of the characters and build a Storyteller's overarching point of view, you are doing advanced work.

PART 6

PREPRODUCTION

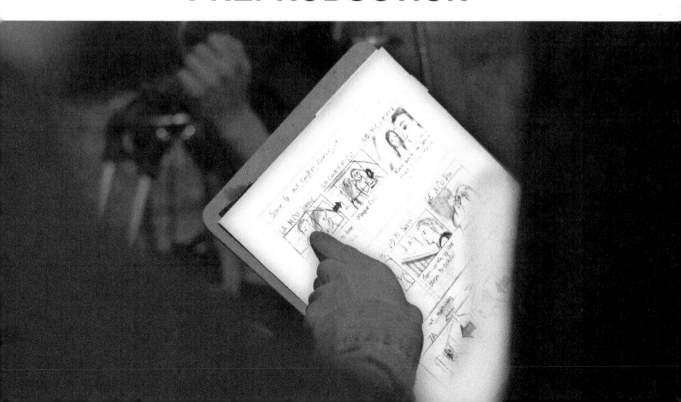

PART 6-1 ───

Director Tyler Perry giving Kathy Bates direction on the set of *The Family That Preys* (2008).

PART 6-2 ───

Consulting storyboards on the set.

CHAPTER 17

EXPLORING THE SCRIPT

INTERPRETING THE SCRIPT

We explored many tools for developing the dramatic potential of a screenplay in Chapter 8. But once major rewriting is done, script analysis becomes script interpretation as you prepare to make cinema from a literary blueprint. This requires a rather different analysis and preparation. New directors in particular nearly always under develop their scripts, a particular irony since it is their own work. Later in editing they discover all that lay latent and unused in the screenplay.

This chapter offers many tools for preproduction development. Taken together they are probably excessive, so do as much as you find useful. Short films are an excellent practice ground: they demand a full palette of skills but their restricted size lets you make several films and experiment in depth to find what works best for you. Later, when you turn to longer forms, you will have distilled this very important process to your own temperament.

TWO TYPES OF FILM, TWO KINDS OF PREPARATION

Speech and behavior represent two polarities in fiction filmmaking—and each requires a different script interpretation. They can be characterized thus:

The dialogue-driven film tells its story mainly through dialogue exchanges. For example, Billy Bob Thornton's *Sling Blade* (1996, Figure 17-1), developed from a stage play Thornton had written and acted in earlier. It concerns mentally and emotionally disabled Karl, discharged after decades of incarceration, returning to the rural community where in childhood he had murdered his mother and her lover.

The visually-driven film tells its story more through imagery and behavior. In Jean-Pierre Jeunet's *Amélie* (2001) a lonely waitress discovers that by carrying out anonymous acts of kindness, she can change people's lives for the better. It is what she does rather than what people say that tells the story.

Both films are fully realized cinema, and each conveys a powerful sense of place. The first uses absorbing and sustained dialogue exchanges, whereas the second uses a montage of short scenes

FIGURE 17-1

Dialogue-driven films, like Thornton's *Sling Blade*, rely mainly on the verbal exchange between characters to advance their narratives.

to advance the story through image and behavior rather than dialogue. Neither mode is better or more legitimate—they are simply different stories that use the screen in different ways. Each mode, however, takes a different emphasis during preparation.

The characters in the *dialogue-driven film* pursue their objectives through language and are fulfilled or frustrated at each beat. Dialogue narrates the film and provides its forward movement, so the scene dynamics lie with the players. Let's say quickly that dialogue-centered material does not have to be static and devoid of visual or behavioral interest. Characters can be in movement at work or play, and can do anything organic to the world they inhabit. With this strongly realistic type of film, the director works as one does with theater actors, digging for the meaning and rhythms of the text, and working to build the integrity of the characters.

The *visually-driven film* has fewer sustained dialogue scenes, and builds its dramatic units using a montage technique of images or short action scenes. The characters still need objectives, but the arc of each dramatic unit may be formed from several scene fragments. Like mime, comic strips, or early movies, the story is narrated more by action and images than by language. The director works to design action, behavior, composition, and editing juxtapositions—envisaging most at the writing stage, but the cinematographer's taste and inventiveness will be paramount. Afterwards, much of the film's rhythm and momentum are consolidated during editing, as in a documentary.

Both modes require fully occupied, fully realized characters busy pursuing their objectives, and both need strong design and **visualization** (the use of visual elements to reinforce intended meanings). Both benefit greatly if you initially design your film as if it were going to be silent. It is easier to allow dialogue into a strongly visualized film, than to bring a visual design to one made of static set pieces (see Chapters 23 and 24 on visual design).

HOMEWORK

Your interpretive work is going to move from the large toward the small. That is, you'll decide large-scale matters before you consider detail. First clearly articulate the premise and thematic purpose for your film; this will guide you and your partners as you explore, analyze, and break down the screenplay into various workable parts (see "Premise and Theme", p. 69)

You should arrive at decisions that you can defend with spirit and authority, because each cast member will read the script from their own character's point of view, and early readings tend to produce divergent, contradictory interpretations. You won't have all the answers ready, nor should you try. This is intensely creative and collaborative work, and your function is to shepherd your ensemble toward shared understandings. No matter how much work you put in, probing and intelligent actors will take you into unexamined areas, and that's part of the excitement in ensemble work.

SCRIPT BREAKDOWN

Take the script and make a preliminary breakdown (or cross-plot) of characters appearing in each scene, as in Figure 17-2, made for the short film *FearFall* (2001). You can see at a glance which characters each scene uses, and which scenes take place in each location. This helps plan a rehearsal schedule, and lays bare the film's pattern of interactions and underlying structures. A more advanced and detailed version will be needed for planning the shoot. If you have three scenes in the same day-care center, you shoot them consecutively to conserve time and energy, even though they are widely spaced in the story.

Scheduling and budgeting software like the industry favorite Movie Magic™ or Gorilla™ can download from popular screenplay programs like Final Draft® and help produce scheduling lists. These are the foundation for the massive coordination that a large production requires if you are to effectively integrate locations, sets, camera and sound requirements, characters, extras, stunts, wardrobe, makeup, properties, special effects, animal handlers, transportation, catering—and anything else the script calls for. See Chapter 25 for more about production logistics.

DEFINE THE SUBTEXTS AND A METAPHOR

Subtexts arise from what each character is trying to get, do, or accomplish. Every part of a well-written screenplay is a skin covering deeper layers of potential meaning. Your success as a director hinges on your ability to create their presence in the audience's mind.

Scene	Location	Script pages	Ray	Alice	Sophie	Jack	Gregg	Mia	Kurt	# of characters
1	R&A bedroom	1-2	✓	✓						2
2	Sophie's room	2-4	✓		✓					2
3	Kitchen	4-7	✓	✓	✓					3
4	Front lawn	7-8	✓	✓	✓	✓				4
5	Boardroom	8-9	✓				✓			2
6	Ray's office	9-11	✓				✓			2
7	School	12-14			✓			✓	✓	3
8	Dining room	15-18	✓							

FIGURE 17-2

A preliminary script breakdown such as this one for the short film *FearFall* (2001), links characters with scenes and can help plan rehearsals as well as visualize the underlying structures of your film.

Now try moving from macro to micro by developing a **logline** (one-sentence summary of the pitch for the production) such as "Rescuing the rescuer," "Finding out where it all started," or "No love as sweet as the first." You also need a guiding metaphor for your production. For Guillermo del Toro's *Pan's Labyrinth* (2006), one might use the metaphor of a laundry. The child Ofelia, an Alice in Francoland, launders the grinding evil of her daytime life in the dream cauldron of her imagination. Her fascist stepfather is the Evil Wizard, her mother the Babe in the Wood, the house-keeper her Guardian Angel. The faun is her Taskmaster, and the Pale Man is the terrifying Baby Eater of folktale. The fascist army forces are the black knights of evil, and the guerrillas are the decimated powers of light who are fated to become all but extinguished.

By such images, you summon and grasp the essential dynamics of any tale. Similes and metaphors are vital to clarifying your authorial purposes and enormously helpful to communicating your ideas to others.

TOOLS TO REVEAL DRAMATIC DYNAMICS

Following are ways to expose each scene's heart and soul. Bringing to light what would otherwise remain latent allows the director to fully exploit the implications of his or her material. It takes time and energy, but will fully repay your effort.[1]

STORYLINE ANALYSIS

Storyline analysis is standard procedure during preproduction, but the scene-by-scene summary surpasses the screenplay step outline (p. 94) because it defines *dramatic effect*, that is, intent and not just content. Storyline analysis builds not only the emotional integrity of the narrative, but helps you to determine the initial emphases and direction of your rehearsals with the actors. Figure 17-3 shows a typical **storyline analysis form** as it should be filled out. It creates a flowchart of your movie's content, with each sequence envisaged as a building block. Accompanying the sequence description are notes of what the sequence should contribute to the storyline.[2] Filling one out, expect to write descriptive tags concerning:

- Plot points
- Exposition (factual and set up information)
- Character definition
- Emotional consequences
- Reactions and actions that push the story forward
- Building or changing mood or atmosphere
- Parallel storytelling
- Ironic actions or juxtaposition
- Set up and foreshadowing.

Having to write so compactly makes you find the paradigm for each tag—a brain-straining exercise of the utmost value. Soon you have the whole screenplay laid out as a flowchart and will be surprised at what you learn about its structure, strengths, weaknesses, and emotional arc. Following are common failings and their likely cures:

---

[1] An additional resource is Judith Weston's *The Film Director's Intuition* (Michael Wiese Productions, 2003). Use in parallel with practical work or its excellent, always actor-oriented advice may seem overwhelming.
[2] Use the same storyline analysis form during the editing stage to get an important flowchart perspective during postproduction.

Fault	Likely cure
Expository scenes release information statically, without advancing the action or building tension.	Make the scene contribute action and movement, not just factual information. Can you drop the scene and bury the exposition in a more functional sequence?
Repetition of information.	Cut it now, or later. You may want to cover yourself and edit it out in postproduction, when audience reactions prove you don't need it.
Information released early or unnecessarily.	Withholding information is axiomatic for all drama, so it comes down to deciding how long.
Expository information comes too late.	When an audience is unduly frustrated, they may give up— another judgment call.
Confusions in time progression.	This can be disastrous, so be conservative during the shoot, knowing you can reorder time in editing if experience shows the story profits by it.
Bunching of similar scenes, events, or actions.	You'll spot this because you forced yourself to tag each scene with a premise. The cure is to drop the weaker scenes or to rewrite and assign them different purposes.
Characters disappear for long periods until needed.	This may signify having too many characters (amalgamate some?), or that some are conveniences and not properly active in their own right.
Characters are invented to serve a limited dramatic purpose.	Amalgamate, thin out cast, or reconsider who does what.
Use of coincidence to solve a dramatic problem ("Guess what, Dad: I've won the lottery!")	Something is drastically wrong with the plotting unless the piece is about the degree to which life is determined by chance. Normally coincidence should never be allowed to carry a major dramatic point.
A lack of alternation in mood or environment.	See if you can reconfigure the order or chronology of scenes, or set them in different locations, to produce a more varied progression.
Excitement too early, leading to anticlimax.	Climaxes in scenes or in whole screenplays are often wrongly placed. Try to reposition any that undercut the whole.
Similarity (and therefore redundancy) in what some scenes contribute.	Remove the weaker of the redundant material.
Multiple endings because of indecision over what (and therefore how) the story must resolve.	This problem comes from an ill-defined premise, or from having multiple and incompatible premises. If so, kill a darling or two. Because endings sometimes depend on the nuance of the playing, it may be legitimate to shoot more than one—even to include them all, depending on the genre.

STORY LINE OR EDITING ANALYSIS FORM　　　　Page ___1___

Production title _"A NIGHT SO LONG"_　　　Length _58_ mins

Editor _MURRAY TYNDALL_　　　Date _9 / 01 /2002_

Sequence definition (brief line title)	Sequence's contribution to the film's developing "argument."
Seq. # _1_　BAR SEQ: ED PRESSES HIS COMPANY ON DANA	Contributes: _ESTABLISHES ED'S & DANA'S CHARACTERISTICS AND THE SPARRING TO COME. HE PROMISES TO KEEP THEIR RELATIONSHIP PLATONIC_　Length _3_ mins _10_ secs
Seq. # _2_　GARAGE SEQ: DANA SHOWS ED HER MOTORCYCLE. EACH PROBES THE OTHER'S BACKGROUND	Contributes: _MORE CHARACTER DETAILS THAT BOTH LOVE COUNTRY MUSIC & THAT EACH CAN BE SENTIMENTAL_　Length _5_ mins _35_ secs
Seq. # _3_　LEN'S APARTMENT: DANA VISITS OLD BOYFRIEND, MAKES LOVE WITH HIM, REALIZES IT'S A MISTAKE.	Contributes: _DANA TRIES (AND FAILS) TO HAVE DISCONNECTED SEX, AND REALIZES THAT ED IS A FORCE IN HER LIFE_　Length _4_ mins _15_ secs

FIGURE 17-3

Storyline analysis is helpful to define the dramatic intent of a given scene and can guide your actor's rehearsals. Download storyline analysis forms at www.directingbook.com (under "Forms and Logs").

GRAPHING TENSION AND BEATS

Read the script several times then draw a graph to contain the changing pressures or temperatures of each scene. Time is the graph's baseline, and tension its vertical axis. Graph the overall scene in black, then try a different color for each main character. In a comedy scene between a dentist and a nervous patient, you could graph the rise and fall of the patient's anxiety, and graph also the rising and falling irritation of the dentist. Each dramatic unit within the scene culminates in a beat (or moment of decisive realization) for one or the other character. Graphing them forces you to extract essentials from the scene and reveals its hidden contours, which you can augment in rehearsals. The flowchart process may reveal similar scenes bunched together, and what the predominant mode is in the script as a whole.

Here as an example is a scene based on an experience of my father's in World War II London when food was scarce and sugar a luxury. You might even practice rehearsing and shooting this scene. As with all film treatments, it is told in the present tense.

Paul is a sailor from the docks setting out for home across London. On board ship, he has acquired a sack of brown sugar and is taking it home to his family. Food of all kinds is rationed, and what he is doing is very risky. He has the sugar inside a battered old suitcase. It is as heavy as a corpse, but he contrives to walk lightly as though carrying only his service clothing. In a busy street, one lock of the suitcase bursts, and the green canvas sack comes sagging into view. Dropping the suitcase hastily on the sidewalk, he grips it between his knees in a panic while thinking what to do. To his horror, a grim-faced policeman approaches. Paul realizes that if the policeman checks what he's carrying, Paul could go to prison. He's poised to run away, but the policeman pulls some string out of his pocket and gets down on his knees, his nose within inches of the contraband, to help Paul tie it together. Paul keeps talking until the job's done, then, thanking the policeman profusely, picks up the suitcase as if it contained feathers and hurries away, feeling the cop is going to sadistically call him back. Two streets later, Paul realizes he is free.

Figure 17-4 plots the intensity of each character's dominant emotion against the advance of time. Paul's emotions change, whereas those of the unaware policeman are simple and placid by contrast. Paul's stages of development are:

- Trying to walk normally to conceal weighty contraband
- Sense of catastrophe as suitcase bursts

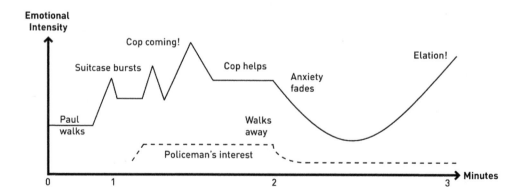

FIGURE 17-4

Plotting the tension and beats present in every scene can reveal mood patterns and the overall tone of a film.

- Assuming policeman is coming to arrest him
- Realizing his guilt is not yet apparent—all is not yet lost
- Tension while trying to keep policeman's attention off contents
- Making escape under policeman's ambiguous gaze
- Sense of joyous release when he realizes he's free.

The treatment contains some realizations that cannot be explicitly filmed without context being established in prior scenes. Missing is the knowledge of (1) the nature of the contraband, (2) the family Paul is trying to get it to, and (3) what he risks if he gets caught. For the scene to yield its full potential, this expository information would need establishing. That the sugar is going to Paul's family and not to a crime syndicate alters how the audience views him. A graph like Figure 17-4 brings clarity to where and how changes must take place in dominant emotions. It shows:

- How the actors need to create distinct rising and falling emotional pressures within their characters
- Where characters undergo major transitions, or beats
- Where the actors must externalize beats through action
- How you might visually create emotional shape through shot angles, compositions, and editing
- Where you should create visual emphasis through shot size, movement, and editing.

Actors can properly deal only with one objective and one attendant emotion at a time, and must find a credible way to transition to the next. Your directing must help them maintain the specifics of their character's consciousness, one step at a time, one objective at a time.

The policeman feels only a mild, benign interest, which falls away as the sailor with the successfully mended suitcase goes on his way. Not so for Paul. He must pretend he's an innocent man with a luggage problem. Knowing something the policeman doesn't, the audience empathizes with the sailor's anxiety and appreciates his efforts to project petty concerns. We can underscore Paul's subjectivity and raise the stakes in the scene by having the policeman appear threatening as he approaches. Paul could see the policeman testing his guilt by pretending to offer help. Late in the scene, we can release the tension by revealing the policeman's motives as benign all along. Throughout, compositions juxtaposing the bulging, insecure suitcase against the approaching policeman can visually relay the anxieties uppermost in Paul's mind. By focusing on Paul's anxieties, we make the audience identify with his problem. By switching to the policeman's point of view, we show how Paul looks to the policeman, or even how Paul thinks he looks to him. Such complexity is more interesting than the simple good versus evil dichotomy in which the main character is a rounded portrait and all others are two-dimensionally flat.

The audience is being led to participate in Paul's inner experience while seeing how he conceals what he is feeling. Actors and directors of long experience intuitively carry out this duality. For the actor lacking an instinct for this, nothing less than a detailed, moment-to-moment analysis with his director will enable him to effectively mold his character's consciousness, step by step, at the core of the scene.

Your breakdown of each dramatic unit for this scene might look like this:

Define the unit's...	By asking...	Example
Situation	What, when, and where?	During World War II, the young sailor Paul is leaving London docks with contraband sugar hidden in a suitcase.
Primary point of view	Whose experience are we sharing?	The sailor's
Secondary point(s) of view as resource	Who else's viewpoint might we share?	Bystanders', policeman's, hungry seagulls'
Main problem	What is the character trying to get, do, or accomplish?	He wants to get the sugar safely home to his family.
Conflict	Where is the main conflict?	Trying to look normal while fearing arrest for contraband.
Obstacle(s)	What is the obstacle that he or she faces?	Just when his suitcase bursts, he encounters a policeman.
Stakes	What is the price of failure?	If caught, he may go to jail.
Complications	How do the stakes rise as the situation moves toward the apex, or crisis point?	The policeman may be playing cat and mouse as he ties up the suitcase while Paul sweats. Paul starts walking away. Has he gotten away with it? He walks jauntily, in dread of hearing, "Hey you! Stop!"
Beats	How does a main character's consciousness change?	Turning into the next street, he realizes that he is free.

FIRST VISUALIZATION

A film does not find its own visual form; you have to actively impose one—and the earlier you start, the better. When you first explore the script, start seeing your project as a visual entity by making sketches and collecting representative images so that the film you want to make forms in your head. Don't be ashamed to use stick figures. Try watching other films of similar story types or genre as research, but think also in terms of particular music, and particular painters or photographers. Immerse yourself in developing the particular style and imagery that will accentuate the world your characters live in, and the way you want us to react to them. Doing this while analyzing the script means you straight away begin defining the film's **style and visual design** (see Part 4). At first, this is an instinctive, associative process, but soon you must communicate your ideas to your creative team, mainly the art director and cinematographer, who will help you design the physical and photographic look of your cinematic world in practical terms (see Chapter 23).

CHAPTER 18

CASTING

Your audience knows immediately if your film's cast is giving authentic and gripping performances, which is why casting is said to be 75 percent of any film's success. Beginning directors often cast poorly: guilty about choosing between fellow aspirants, they settle gratefully for whoever seems right and available. On a BBC film I once edited, the director had cast his wife in the main part and remained touchingly blind to her limitations. Later the poor man lost his job because of it.

This is an anxious time: you need actors enthusiastic about the character they play, who will work well with you and other cast members, and who will be loyal to the project. Acting is an intense and insecure profession, so look for actors keen to build their skills with you. Unless you have considerable budget and worldly achievements, it's unwise to direct players more experienced than you are. Nothing is scarier or riskier than to direct someone out of your league, to have a disagreement, and then find that he or she has spread disaffection and that now the whole cast doubts your judgment. Actors are nothing if not human.

OVERVIEW

In casting, as in all aspects of filmmaking, generate abundance from which you can select. You'll need character descriptions, scenes, and **sides** (selected scenes from your script) in your search for special actors. If you employ SAG (Screen Actors Guild)[1] actors, you must provide a full script 24 hours before the audition. If you are working in a film-producing area and have a considerable budget, maybe you'll use a **casting director** or **casting agency** to preselect actors. Casting specialists have knowledge of local resources and can drastically cut the time and labor it takes to find the best. Main speaking parts are called **principal casting**, while **background casting** means finding secondary or background characters such as store clerks, restaurant diners, or nursing staff. Often these can be chosen for appearance and

---

[1] In 2012 the Screen Actors Guild merged with the American Federation of Television and Radio Artists to create a single union, SAG-AFTRA.

without audition. If you're casting without specialized help, you must substitute hard work and gumshoe ingenuity, but can still find a brilliant cast. Good casting comes from:

- Searching far and wide
- Having techniques ready to elicit actors' underlying potential
- Self-knowledge about whom you should work with—and whom you should not
- Dogged persistence.

Knowing how to run auditions helps remove the crippling self-consciousness you feel about choosing between likable, hopeful people. Have your collaborators present during the process so you get a broad spectrum of reaction. Use the industry standard process of three or so stages:

1. Locate potential players. This can be through a casting call advertisement for applicants who must **submit a headshot and bio** (biography) from which you will make first audition selections (see below), or, if you issue an **open call,** all interested applicants may attend the audition.

2. Hold your **first audition**, which (with either selected applicants or the open call) should include a number from whom to choose those with the experiential, physical, psychological, and emotional suitability for your parts.

3. Invite back the most promising for **callbacks,** and use rehearsal procedures that reveal *directability*, potential under duress, and how each handles a range of representative situations.

4. In **final callbacks**, make more stringent demands, and mix and match players before settling on your final choice.

If your talent is trained and professional, follow the theater and film norms. These are abundantly described in the many websites that deal with acting and auditions. Because they are geared toward the hopeful actor, they convey much about the stress that auditioning actors experience. When you cast inexperienced players, approach the task according to your level of development and what you can expect of nonprofessionals. There's plenty of help here to follow.

POST A CASTING CALL ADVERTISEMENT

Keep your ad brief. Describe the project in one sentence and include thumbnail descriptions of all the characters you're seeking (Figure 18-1). Compressing much into few words allows the reader to infer possible physical appearances, but be sure to include shooting dates in order to eliminate anyone not available. Mention if you will consider union actors, but if so, you must abide by union rules, which sometimes allow sliding scales for student or nonprofessional productions. Provide all necessary application information and indicate whether there is any remuneration. When there is none, a DVD of finished work is a must.

When posting for an open call, include the location, date(s) and times of the auditions. If selecting actors to audition from a pool of applicants, you must give them an address and request they send a **headshot and bio**. This is an 8"×10" photo of the actor on one side and a résumé of

SEEKING ACTORS FOR SHORT FILM (NON UNION)

"A Visit from Mom" is a comedy about how a demanding mother-in-law's extended visit ultimately strengthens a family's bonds by nearly pulling them apart. Shooting begins April 10 and ends April 25.

Available Roles:

GEORGE: early 40s, conservative, medical equipment salesman, calls his father every Friday; husband of Claire.

CLAIRE: late 30s; former small-town beauty queen with a torrid past trying for conservative housewife status after a steamy divorce; met George through an online dating service and married him.

KENNY: 12, tall and thin, nervous, curious, intelligent, overcritical, obsessed with science fiction.

ANGELA: 70s, Claire's mother. Cheerful, eccentric, determined to live forever. Has a veneer of respectability that breaks down raucously after some drinks. In early life, made a fortune in something illicit.

TED: mid 60s, George's disapproving father. Car salesman, patriot, grower of prize chrysanthemums.

Compensation: No Pay. Meals, transportation and DVD copy of final film provided

To apply: Send headshot and bio by March 15 to:
Karyn Decker, #2 Belleview Rd. City, State, Zip.
or via email: Karyn@visitfrommomfilm.com

FIGURE 18-1

A casting call should provide all essential information about the project, including incisive character descriptions.

acting experience, training, and other related information on the other. Most actors with any aspirations have these ready to send in, and you'll make your first selection from these (Figure 18-2).

Post your casting call on the internet with casting services (backstage.com, actorspages.com, castingcall.com, and so on) or on more localized places like www.craigslist.com under: tv/film/ video/radio jobs. You should also advertise in the local theater auditions newspaper, in local

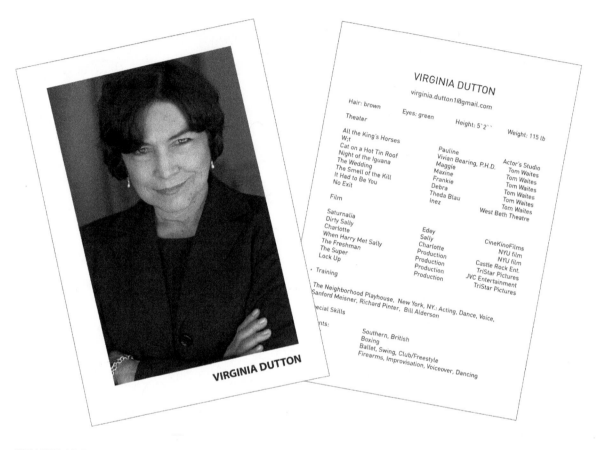

FIGURE 18-2

Most serious actors have a professional headshot and bio on hand when responding to casting calls.

newspapers, or by posting flyers on acting school or theater billboards. Be warned that large nets catch some very odd fish.

ACTIVE SEARCH FOR ACTORS

Some roles pose special challenges and require a more active approach, like Kenny and Angela from Figure 18-1 whose ages may require you to seek contacts with a line on the person you're seeking. Contact key people in theater groups. Write to the casting director, say what you are doing, and ask if he or she can grant you ten minutes for a brief chat. This person will have a wealth of information about local talent, but may fear you are poaching on their preserves.

Among knowledgeable and committed theater workers, producers (who direct in the theater) are highly knowledgeable. Film and theatre professors are good resources and will often suggest names for you to try out. If your budget is rock bottom, you will have to work really hard. People well suited to playing specific parts can always be found, but it takes ingenuity and diligence, and whoever you find may need sustained work in rehearsal.

For the character of 12-year-old Kenny, I would track down teachers producing drama in local schools and ask them to suggest boys who could play that character well. The teacher can ask the boy's parents to get in touch. This allays the nightmare that their child is being stalked by some hollow-eyed pedophile.

Older actors are more difficult to find. To cast Ted and Angela (from Figure 18-1) you should try to locate a senior citizens' theater group, but you should also try to track down special individuals whose attitude and energy can overcome lack of acting experience. For Ted, I would look among older men who have taken an active and extroverted role in life—perhaps in local politics, union organizing, entertainment, teaching, journalism, sports, or salesmanship. All these occupations require a flair for interaction and a relish for the fray.

Angela is a hard person to cast, but try looking among retired actresses or vocal women's group members such as citizens' and neighborhood activist groups—anywhere you could expect to find an older woman secure in her life's accomplishments and adventurous enough to play a boozy, earthy woman with a past.

While you cast, remind yourself periodically that, hidden among the ranks of the unremarkable, are always a few individuals whose lives are being lived with wit, intelligence, and individuality. Such people rise to prominence in the often-unlikely worlds to which exigency or eccentricity has taken them. Angela, for instance, might be the president of the Standard Poodle Fanciers Club, and Ted might be a regular entrant in comedian contests or poetry slams.

FIGURE 18-3

Casting non-actors in lead roles (like Bruno S. in Herzog's *The Enigma of Kaspar Hauser*, *left*) or alongside professional actors (like Maria Heiskanen in Troell's *Everlasting Moments*, *right*) can yield remarkable performances under the right direction.

The search for human authenticity has led Werner Herzog to cast many nonprofessionals in his films. Most famously, the central roles in *The Enigma of Kaspar Hauser* (1974) and *Stroszek* (1977) were played by the endearing Bruno S., a street singer and Berlin transport manager whose surname has remained undisclosed to protect his job (Figure 18-3, *left*).

The veteran Swedish director Jan Troell in *Everlasting Moments* (2008) very successfully mixes professional actors (lead Maria Heiskanen has many credits) and non-actors in a film developed from the true story of a working-class woman who won a camera in 1907 (Figure 18-3, *right*). In spite of the jealous resistance of her volatile, alcoholic husband, she made herself into an excellent documentary photographer. The DVD set includes an interview with Troell, a documentary about the making of the film and his methods with actors, and a documentary about the life of the photographer herself, told by her descendants.

Robert Bresson refused to cast anyone trained to act, and chose lawyers in *The Trial of Joan of Arc* (1962) to play Joan's inquisitors. Their lifetimes spent defining details gave them the right punctiliousness for cross-examination. In Bresson's *Notes on the Cinematographer* he gives a compelling rationale, akin to a documentary-making attitude, for using "models" (his word for players) uncorrupted by having performed.[2] Many filmmakers, including Abbas Kiarostami, the Dardenne Brothers, and Ken Loach have followed in his footsteps and regularly cast "non-actors" whose own lives resonated, in some fundamental way, with those of the characters.

SETTING UP THE FIRST AUDITION

From the requested headshots and bios, and from any actor contacts you've made along the way, you will make up a pool of candidates. Publicity materials are promotional tools for the actor, so they often represent a more glamorous performer than the seemingly nondescript individual who appears before you. At least they show whether the actor is broadly suitable by age, ethnicity, physical type, and acting experience. Be alert for résumé inflation—it's not a sign of good faith. Anyone experienced knows you can check their claims at prior workplaces.

With your candidate shortlist in hand, you and your assistant begin scheduling each actor into an audition slot over the course of a few days (depending on the size of your cast and response). This you can do by phone or email, but it's usually more efficient to do it by phone—the back and forth of email scheduling can burn up a lot of time. When you contact them to schedule their first audition, here is what they will want to know:

- *The project and your experience.* Be direct and realistic. Experienced actors want to know if you are legitimate, so mention where you studied (if you are a film student or graduate), what you have produced, and any exposure or awards that it garnered.

- *Time commitment and remuneration.* Be candid about the time that rehearsal and shooting will take. Cool responses or undue negotiating may result from low interest, high ego, or negative experience with other filmmakers.

---

[2] *Notes on the Cinematographer* Robert Bresson (Green Integer, 1997).

- *The role in which the actor is interested*. Determine which role the actor thinks he or she fits, what their characteristics are, and be ready to suggest trying for an alternative part.
- *What the audition will require*. A first call might ask actors to give two brief (two minutes, say) and very different monologues of their own choosing and to do a cold reading from a script. See *Monologues* and *Cold Readings* below.
- *The audition slot*. If all seems promising, give them their audition slot (date and time) with clear directions to the audition address. If you can, confirm the information via email.

THE ACTORS ARRIVE

Time your audition program to schedule arrivals at, say 15- or 20-minute intervals. Arriving actors wait in a **green room** (a holding area well away from the audition space). Have actors individually received by someone lively and pleasant who can answer questions—say, where the bathroom is—and who by their understanding manner helps allay the extreme anxiety to which actors are subject. This trusted assistant can chat informally and form an impression of each actor's interests, personality, work habits, and punctuality. Your assistant's notes can prove very helpful when it comes to decision time. As actors wait, they should be given their script sides so they familiarize themselves with the text, and if they do not have a headshot and bio, an **audition form** to complete which includes:

1. Name, street address, email address
2. Home, cellular, and work phone numbers
3. Role for which actor is trying out
4. Acting experience and references (if other than on their résumé)
5. Special interests, skills, volunteer work (if other than on their résumé)
6. This form should also have space below this information where the director will make notes during the audition.

For open casting calls, this form is essential as some people may not have a headshot and bio.[3]

CONDUCTING THE FIRST AUDITION

The actor can now be shown into the audition space where he or she will perform. Most are trying to hide how nervous and apprehensive auditions make them feel, but a warm, informal greeting and handshake during which you make eye contact help ease the sense of being judged. Introduce anyone that's in the room during the audition. If you are taping first auditions (optional) try to make light of the camera.

---

[3] A blank audition form is available on this book's companion website for you to download: www.directing-book.com ("Forms and Logs").

That an actor is very nervous is not necessarily negative since it means they attach great importance to being chosen. Give them a brief overview of the project and ask them to give their **slate** (brief self-identification such as: "Hi, my name is _____, and I'm going to play [*character's name*] from [*play*]." Later, when you are watching tapes, you will know who's who.

It's useful but not necessary to tape your first auditions, though it's mandatory for subsequent auditions. If you do, keep the camera some distance away and have the operator zoom in for facial close-ups, and take medium-shots for body expressiveness and movements.

MONOLOGUES

You will learn a lot from two brief and very different monologues taken from a work of the actor's choosing. They should show very different characters and moods, and you will commonly see:

- What material the actor thinks (rightly or wrongly) is appropriate for him- or herself and for your film
- What kind of physical presence, rhythm, and energy he or she has
- What his or her voice is like (vocal quality is extremely important)
- How differently each actor handles their character, and the emotional range that he or she can handle.

You will also see how good they are at:

- Interpreting and memorizing a text
- Acting with the whole body and not just the face
- Being instead of acting. It's essential for film actors to work outward from their character's thoughts and feelings, and not inward from analytic ideas
- Finding the character in themselves rather than imitating a type or version of someone else.

Pay attention to your every intuition—they're seldom unfounded. Could you spontaneously "see" the character the actor was playing? The choice and handling of material indicate whether the actor has developed something new for your production, or whether he has a standard repartee. It also says something about self-image, for if an actor trying out for a brash salesman chooses the monologue of an endearing wimp, that actor may already have cast himself in life as a lovable loser, reckoning that his best hope is to be funny. The quality of acquiescence that makes him unsuitable for the salesman's part may however work for the unlucky boyfriend.

COLD READINGS

Take sides from your script or scenes culled from stage plays, and make several copies. Scene choices should allow you to combine at will two men, two women, a man and a woman, an old person with someone young, and so on. Based on who is waiting, your assistant can decide which piece the available actors might read, giving them copies to study in advance as they wait in the green room. With inexperienced players, you may prefer something from theatrical repertory, and *not* scenes from your film—especially as untrained actors often internalize early impressions and these might prove hard to change subsequently. In a cold reading, you will typically see:

- Which actors have intelligent questions about their character or the piece
- Actors having to think on their feet and trying to give life to a part just encountered
- The same scene handled by more than one set of actors, and thus what each brought to the piece
- What quickness, intelligence, and creativity they can summon from the bare words on the page
- How each actor uses their voice
- Whether they understand the importance of their character's problem with other characters, and make use of this essential conflict
- Whether they grasp what their character is fighting for, and the essentials of relationship implied in the scene
- How they modify their performance when asked for changes of attitude or behavior in their character. In the next reading, you might, for instance, ask for an attitude of resentment rather than apology.

Different performances and action will leave different impressions, and often in ways that pose questions. With two characters of the same sex, try switching the actors to see how well each produces appropriate and different qualities as the new character.

ASSESSMENT

If possible, transfer audition tapes to an editing program so you can quickly contrast different performers and solicit impressions from key production members. Over time you will be assessing characteristics and adding notes to the actor's audition form:

- Suitability for a particular part (age, gender, physical type, ethnicity, etc.)
- Grasp of acting (experience, craft knowledge)
- Physical presence (features, body language, movements, voice)
- Innate character (confidence, movement, energy, sociability, attitude)
- Directability (interaction with others, flexibility, defenses, self-image)
- Commitment (work habits, motivation to act, reliability).

Casting means looking for individuals whose age and history fit them for your roles, but there are wrong and right questions to ask in pursuit of this:

1. *Does this actor fit the father in my script?* This contains an inbuilt bias because each actor is being held up against an ideal, as though the characters were already formed and each

candidate either far or close. This, like searching for the ideal spouse, invites disappointment and misjudgments.

2. *What kind of father would this actor give my film?* This anticipates myriad possibilities in the role, and lets you see the actor's physical and mental being as a new and active contribution to the process of building drama. This makes casting developmental rather than image fulfillment.

NEGATIVE CHARACTERS AND TYPECASTING

All actors have some difficulty playing negative characteristics, especially if they fear these are in their own makeup. Be careful, for it can be disastrous during shooting if an actor thinks you cast him for his own negative qualities. Villains are easier to play, but playing an insipidly stupid or nasty character may be viewed by the actor either as an interesting challenge or as a personal sacrifice. The less secure the individual, the more his doubts will fester. A sure sign of this happening is when an actor wants to upgrade his character's qualities. There are no small parts, said Stanislavsky, just small actors.

All acting is both a departure from self and an exploration of it. Most actors are cast by type, and some hate the type they fall into. Typecasting is both necessary and potentially imprisoning. Acting can be a liberation or a dive into the abyss, depending on the chemistry between actor and director. To protect yourself, try asking actors under consideration for their ideas about the cause of their character's negative traits. What can be said in his defense? How do the other characters regard him and how does he regard himself? What is his function in the world the piece represents?

How maturely the actor answers may well influence your choice.

CONCLUDING EACH AUDITION

That an actor has traveled to your audition and performed in front of a camera takes time and effort, so be sure to conclude each audition graciously. Remember, you are establishing your own reputation and may need that actor for another role in the future, if not for this particular film. So,

- Thank him or her personally.
- Give a date by which to expect news of the next round or final decision.
- Make a note of whatever was positive about their performance so you can be supportive of everyone you have to reject.

DECISIONS AFTER THE FIRST ROUND

If you have promising applicants, run the tapes of their work and brainstorm with collaborators. Discussing strengths and weaknesses usually reveals further dimensions in the candidates, not to mention insights into your crew members and their values.

You may be tempted to cast the person who gave something especially attractive at the audition. This actor may be brilliant or glib yet inflexible, developing less than does a partner whose audition was less accomplished. Try to investigate not only what an actor wants to do, but also how willingly he ventures outside customary boundaries. Most actors are fervently committed to this in principle, but performance may differ. Acting involves the whole person, not just ideas, so you may find that a genially accomplished personality, coming under the threat of the unexpected, suddenly adopts bizarre forms of self-defense and resistance. The shy but dedicated actor may be the one with the potential to grow and who makes the best candidate. During his first auditions, Marlon Brando mumbled into his shirtfront.

Small parts usually require little adaptability. To cast a surly gas station attendant for one short scene requires no potential for growth in the actor, whereas the part of the new wife inexorably realizing that her husband is deeply mother-dominated calls for extended and subtle powers of development. Her character must explore a spectrum of emotions and the actress will have to dig deeply into unpleasant, even frightening feelings. You will need someone with the openness, trust, and emotional reach to undertake a grueling rehearsal and performance process.

Now comes the agonizing part. Call everyone who auditioned and tell them whether they were selected for callback auditions. Giving the bad news to those not selected is hard on both parties; so mitigate the disappointment by saying something appreciative and positive about the person's performance. With those you want to see again, set the place and callback date for further auditioning.

FIRST CALLBACK—AUDITIONING WITH THE SCRIPT

You now need to do some additional testing. To show their range, many actors will prepare a further monologue in a different style. You can ask ahead of time for another, but callbacks mostly involve reading select scenes from your screenplay. Make sure callback actors have basic information on the story and where the scene fits in. Be ready to field questions about motivation, prior scenes, and so on. The sides should be demanding dialogue scenes, but limit the material to a couple of minutes' duration if you have many to audition. For now you are most interested in directability, so,

- Ask each actor to play his or her character in a specified way. Then give critical feedback and specific directions to develop what you saw.
- Have them play the scene again. Look for who builds on their initial performance, who holds on to what you praised yet could develop the areas you specified.
- For a further run-through, give each actor a different mood or characteristic to see what he or she can produce from an altered premise.

From here onward it's vital to tape auditions. The camera should zoom in for a variety of shots, so you can see not only how they look on camera, but also how they respond to its presence. Keep the camera running throughout to gather plenty of footage for your final decision review.

IMPROVISATION

If you are auditioning experienced actors, don't ask for improvisations (improvs) unless you have experience and can handle the situation with some confidence. It puts actors in an exposed situation and they should feel you know what you are looking for. If you decide to ask for an improv, try giving two actors brief verbal outlines of characters and a situation in the script that involves them, such as waiting for officials at a foreign border, or dealing with a car that's run out of gas in a scary neighborhood. Keep expectations low and make it enjoyable. Ask your players to improvise their own scene based on the situation in the (unseen) script. The goal is not to see how close they get to the scripted original, but how each handles the situation of interacting with another actor when the creation is spontaneous. After they have done a version, give them feedback about aspects you see developing, and ask for a further version, specifying any changes you'd like in behavior and mood. Now you can see how well they incorporate direction.

If you have only one person left to audition, test their imaginative resources by asking for an improvised phone conversation based on a situation that you specify. You should feel there's a real person on the other end. For more improvs, use the guide table under "Improv Exercises" in Chapter 22 to locate what you need to put under test.

SECOND CALLBACK

Depending on the size of the cast and time constraints, the material in this section may be incorporated with that in "First Callback," above, or handled separately as a further round.

INTERVIEW

Confirm and amplify the impressions you've formed by interviewing the individuals you like most. Give them the full script to read first, but tell players *not* to learn any lines since that might fix their performance at an embryonic stage of development. Spend one-on-one time with each actor, encourage questions, discuss their character and the script as a whole, and let them talk about themselves. Look for realism, sincerity, self-motivation, and a great interest in drama. When an actor is spontaneously excited because the script explores some issue from his or her own experience, it is a good sign. Another is when an actor feels they have something to learn from you and your project.

Be wary of those who flatter you, name-drop, seem content with superficial readings, intellectualize, are inflexibly opinionated, or make you feel they are stooping to do you a good turn. Avoid like the plague anyone you suspect will bail out when something better comes up.

MIX AND MATCH ACTORS

When you have multiple candidates for lead parts, use mix and match to find which actors combine to make the most vivid chemistry. You want to know how they interact with each other, and to see what they communicate to an audience. I once had to cast a short film about a man in his 30s who becomes involved with a rebellious teenage girl. We had to reject a more accomplished actor owing to something indefinably sinister in his manner that made the relationship disturbing. Another actor we paired with the same actress changed the balance; this gave the girl the upper hand, as the story demanded.

Sometimes two actors simply don't communicate well or are temperamentally mismatched. Actors cast to play lovers must at least like each other; if they don't, the wariness and stiffness in their playing might disable your entire film. Even when your characters are mortal enemies, you want players who are responsive and interested in each other.

MAKING FINAL CHOICES

Someone who auditions well may simply be good at auditioning but unequal to a challenging part. Conversely, someone shy or anxious might develop very well under the right direction. Every person is stamped by their life and by a mass of intangible qualities, to which you must try to respond. Your audience certainly will.

When you come to final choices, review each actor's:

- Physical and temperamental suitability
- Impact
- Imprint on the part in relation to the other actors
- Rhythms of speech and movement
- Quickness of mind and directability
- Ability at mimicry, especially when having to maintain a regional accent
- Voice quality (its associations are extremely important!)
- Capacity to hold on to both new and old instructions
- Ability to carry out his or her character's development, whether it is quick and intuitive or slower and more graduated
- Commitment to the project
- Long-term commitment to acting as an art and a discipline
- Likely patience with filming's extremely slow and disjunctive progress
- Ability to enter and reenter an emotional condition over several takes and camera angles
- Compatibility with the other actors
- Compatibility with you, the director.

Now is the time to cross-check with anyone inside or outside your project whose judgment you particularly respect.

CAMERA TEST

To confirm your choices, tape a short scene with the principal actors. Even then, you will probably remain somewhat uncertain. Look for actors who can remain in focus and interesting when their characters are thinking or listening. Show their scenes to co-workers and dig into the impressions each actor makes. When you want to cast someone your intuition says is risky, communicate your reservations tactfully but directly to the actor. You might, for instance, feel uncertain of their commitment, or sense a resistance to authority figures that could make directing them problematic.

Candid confrontation at this point shows you how the actor handles uncomfortable criticism, and paves the way should that perception later become an issue or, God forbid, should you need to replace him. Sometimes an actor who seems arrogant and egocentric will, faced with a frank reaction to his characteristics, gratefully admit that he has an unfortunate way of masking uncertainty. Suddenly you both feel closer to each other!

ANNOUNCING CASTING DECISIONS

Make final decisions by the promised date, then personally notify and thank all who took part. Give each person whatever appreciative, constructive comments you can. This signals your professionalism and maintains your good standing in the community. If you can, say in what ways they gave a great audition—but add that, unfortunately, your part doesn't fit their type. Needless to say, rejection is painful, and all the more so for those who made it across the threshold. Actors are wearily used to the pain of rejection, but a director who does it sensitively is someone definitely worth approaching in the future. Filmmaking is a village; when you return with your bucket to the well, your reputation matters.

GIVING AND TAKING

Now you have your cast, keep this in mind: more than anything, people in all walks of life crave recognition for what they can do. When a director liberates an actor's potential, or works responsibly on the deficiencies that obstruct it, the serious actor responds with love and gratitude. Sharing and honesty are important in director-actor and actor-actor relationships; they are also the best foundation for any creative working relationship. Every committed actor wants a director who can lead them into new territory. This means they develop not just in acting, but in living. Perform this function only a little, and your cast will place great faith in you and become your most enthusiastic advocate to other actors.

CHAPTER 19

ACTING FUNDAMENTALS

The innate realism of photography makes us expect psychological realism from film actors, so you'll need to understand the craft of acting, and even become something of a drama coach. Communicating with actors in an inspiring and productive way is at the core of directing and will become your lifetime's work. You will need a little acting under your belt to do this well. Acting is a well-understood craft, and what follows is a brief primer that I hope will launch you into acting and reading books about it by the master teachers (listed at the chapter end). It's usual to face a cast with different acting methods and even a mixed cast of trained and untrained talent. Here we will look at the concepts and vocabulary most familiar to trained actors, and this you will use to lead those untrained.

STANISLAVSKY

Today there are a number of approaches to acting, but all owe much to the Russian actor Konstantin Stanislavsky (1863–1938), who developed the modern understanding of the craft. He saw that some actors naturally gripped an audience, and the others who used empty gestures and histrionics did not. From interviewing those successful with audiences he winnowed out the common denominators and human psychological linkages, and developed his groundbreaking explanations. Behind these are a few vital truths that show up repeatedly and in different ways—in life as well as in acting.

The prime enemy of the actor is losing belief in what he or she is doing, which is where we shall start.

Focus, relaxation, and the interior monologue: Think how relaxed, concentrated, and boundlessly energetic you feel whenever you concentrate on something you really love to do. It might be grooming a pet, riding a skateboard, or playing an instrument in a band. People can watch you, come and go, or ignore you—and yet you remain utterly focused and effective. This mental and emotional **focus** lets you simply *be*; being preoccupied and in a state of **relaxation** blocks your internal censor from hounding out your failings. Imagine now the opposite condition: you step into a room full of strangers. Under their combined stare, you feel awkward and conscious of your body; you can barely put words together. Now add a camera pointing at you and recording everything, and your anxiety only intensifies. This is what the film actor faces.

These extremes—being focused and relaxed, or self-conscious and rigid—are the heaven and hell of the actor's existence. By using what Stanislavsky called the **magic "if"** to set the imagination going, actors can pursue their character's mental focus, and relax, become natural, alert, and present the character's "now." The audience sees a character really thinking, planning, remembering, deciding—all those actions that take place inside a living, breathing person, and that for some reason are fascinating to watch. From documentaries you know this: people are effortlessly natural simply because they are doing something normal that consumes their attention. This is the gold standard to which you aspire for your fictional characters. Actors cannot will themselves directly into this state, for that would only make them fear failure and try too hard. Instead, by pursuing all that is natural to his character the actor can abandon all the tension, ambition, ego, and self-consciousness that so cripples us.

To stay focused, many actors maintain an **interior monologue**, much as you or I do when we talk ourselves through something tricky. This helps maintain a focused consciousness and is particularly useful when the actor must repeat the same scene many times for different camera angles. When fatigue or boredom tempts the actor to cut corners, the interior monologue helps them stay focused and in the moment. In rehearsals, the director may ask the actors to externalize these interior monologues as a way to zero in on the meaning and subtexts of actions, reactions, and dramatic moments.

Losing and regaining focus: Actors cannot afford to stop thinking their character's thoughts or seeing with their character's eyes. When they do, they are apt to **lose focus**. Like drowning to divers, this is the actor's occupational hazard. The camera registers everything so minutely that the audience feels the lapse immediately as a loss of credibility. No actor loses focus without a reason: something he must say or do doesn't sit right, or something has happened to shake him out of character. A misplaced prop, a wrong line from another actor, or something in their eyeline distracting them—any of these can disrupt the actor's attention. Insecurity of all kinds—even the fear of losing focus—can lead to loss of focus, and in a moment a believable character crumbles into a beleaguered actor.

A trained actor will know how to sidestep the impending self-consciousness and **regain focus**. She only needs to look closely at something in her character's immediate circle of awareness, such as a carpet pattern or the texture of her sleeve. Because it is real and in her character's here and now, the actor's attention is stabilized. Now she can broaden her attention back out to include her character's larger spheres of awareness. All this can happen in a few seconds with no break in a conversation. Trained actors do this reflexively like a trained kayaker righting their craft instead of drowning.

The director's role in helping actors maintain focus lies in work they do together *before* the camera rolls. Understanding every line they speak is not enough for an actor; they must *believe* every line and action. What you're asking your cast to say and do must root them deep in their characters, not pull them away. Actors will tell you when a line or movement bothers them, and you must listen and respond.

Imagination, interior life, and actions: Acting is the most generous of professions because it starts from using the **imagination** to create another person's reality. We did this effortlessly as children, but as we grow up and become self-conscious it gets more difficult. Stanislavski has special techniques to encourage, relax, and therefore liberate the imagination. Characters become truthful and believable when actors maintain an **interior life** authentic to their character. The actor achieves this by disciplining and sustaining his attention, and acting on his fellow actors. Actors are called such because they *act* on each other, and then, watching and listening to other characters, allow themselves to be *acted upon*. The anxious actor, however, isolates himself inside a cocoon of preparation: he visualizes the script page instead of seeing other characters around him, and carries out premeditated, mechanical actions instead of what's appropriate to the nuance of the moment.

Justifying and the givens: While preparing a part, every action, every line, should be justified according to the **givens**; that is, all the information given or implied in the script. This includes each character's background, backstory, recent experience, life needs, plot goals, and thought processes in relation to the other characters. Whenever a section seems fuzzy and unmotivated, the director will probe this with his or her actors.

Objectives and the active voice: Characters become dramatic and interesting when they actively pursue a series of needs, each demanding to be satisfied. Even a passive central character pursues goals and **objectives**—ones that protect him from taking action or initiative. Experienced actors learn their character's objectives and stay physically and mentally busy *in character*. This helps them continuously develop in the here and now whatever their character is trying to **get, do, or accomplish**.

A character's objectives are always discussed as transitive verbs; that is, as "doing" words that each denote an action meant to affect someone. For example, "I'll scream till Dad stops the car." In life, we pursue these strategies unconsciously, but actors must consciously construct them by breaking their parts down into their character's objectives ("I will make him listen and see my side," or, "I will tear open the door and overpower the guard"). Each acting objective is formed in the **active voice**, never the passive, (for example, "I will open the door and run through", not "the door being opened, I get to pass through." A well-described objective has an action, an objective, and an outcome:

- An active verb (I will charm...)
- Someone or something that you act upon (... Marie, my brother's standoffish wife...)
- A desired and measurable outcome (... so she asks me to stay to dinner).

Using this formula, the actor transforms every aspect of their part into a series of actable goals. Note that you can't act "being angry," "being hurt," or being anything at all, because it's abstract, unspecific, and simply unplayable. Objectives not only give shape and purpose to a character's every moment, but make them fascinating to watch, and a joy for other actors to act with.

Developing the character's interior life: Each actor strives constantly to develop their character in relation to the text. From all the clues there, she decides scene by scene what her character wants, thinks, notices, remembers, and imagines. From this she uses her experience of life to decide how this character will walk, sit, stand, eat, and do everything else. This helps her to feel the weight of cutlery in her hand, smell flowers or freshly dug earth, cry out in despair, whisper encouragement, eat a banana, or open a can of food. No action is ever "in general": every action is unique to her character, unique to her character's mood at that moment, and every action creates a series of emotionally precise clues that convey the character's thoughts and feelings. Living the innermost thoughts and feelings of character culminates in whatever that character says and does in the script.

There is help in this from the other players. Every nuance of what other characters do—if the actor is truly taking this in—helps feed their character's inner life. Since every relationship (say, with one's parents, teachers, best friend, most hated enemy) evokes a different "me," characters show a range of selves to each other. A hospital cleaner, for instance, might show a tender self to her son and a tough and angry one to an abusive fellow worker. Real human beings are complex and often seem contradictory.

Business and personalizing: During rehearsal, each actor develops the physical actions that accompany all his character's aims and objectives. **Business** is all the small activities that help the actor involve the body and reveal the character's inner reality. It can literally be entrancing to watch someone eat a meal or wash the dishes when it reflects the emotional tone of the moment. A critical scene in Tom Hooper's *The King's Speech* (2010) shows the first time that Bertie (the Duke of York and future king) speaks with his speech therapist Lionel as a friend rather than an employee (Figure 19-1). It's also the first time Bertie reveals his personal life and traumatic childhood, something royals never do—especially with a commoner. During his monologue, Bertie absentmindedly pieces together one of the unfinished model airplanes built by Lionel's son. This bit of business adds complexity and poignancy to Bertie's personal disclosures; this simple boyhood activity serves to delicately imply all the normal things he was denied as a child. With this bit of business, Colin Firth transforms himself into a vulnerable little boy.

Because acting is about doing, business is described in verbs, those "doing" words such as *lowering* the eyes, *glancing* out of a window, *searching* for change in a pocket, or *recalling* a birthday kiss from a loving aunt. Interior actions are as important as exterior ones, and an actor **personalizes** by discussing their character states in the first, not the third, person. To say, "She's getting really depressed" would signify standing outside one's character, but to say, "I'm getting agitated and blaming myself for the delay" takes ownership in the here and now.

The mind-body connection: A brother will know intuitively from the way his sister eats a sandwich or sets down her bicycle when she has had a bad day. It's a fact that *no inner state exists without creating outward evidence* in a

FIGURE 19-1

Small physical activities, or business, can help reveal a character's inner traits, as seen in this key scene from Hooper's *The King's Speech*.

person's face and body. Indeed, from small facial and vocal gestures, and body language, the director has a perfect source for what the actor is thinking and feeling. An actor experiencing her character's thoughts, sensations, and emotions expresses them effortlessly and unconsciously through her physical instrument—that is, through her body, face, actions, and voice. This means that even **interior actions** such as choosing, holding back, or calculating become evident and unexpectedly interesting to watch. This I learned from studio dailies as a teenage editing assistant. The best actors remained alive and interesting during reaction shots because you saw their character's interior life continuing. Mediocre actors, on the other hand, went dead without the cover of lines or action. Having no interior life left them **indicating**, which means trying to physically and intellectually signal thought and feeling rather than experiencing it.

Communion and isolation: An actor's preparation is counterproductive if it becomes a protective cocoon. When this happens, it's called **acting in isolation**. The actor neither notices nor reacts to the query in another actor's voice, or to the glance of surprise or a slight gesture of submission. He can't—he's visualizing his lines on the printed page and trying, irrespective of the life around him, to do what he decided his character must do. In fact, that life is subtly different each time the scene is played. True, the scene and its lines are the same, but when everyone reacts to each other's more subtle, in-the-moment implications, which vary from take to take, this is the hidden life of the scene. Other characters' nuances vary every time, which makes the scene fully alive even after 10 takes. This inter-character communication is called **communion**, something vitally important for actors to maintain.

Actions and verbal actions: Getting on a bike, smiling, or slapping someone across the face are plainly **actions**, but it's important to note that dialogue is also a form of action. In her first meeting with Hannibal Lecter in *The Silence of the Lambs* (Demme, 1991) Clarice Starling points out the intricate drawings he's created in his prison cell. He responds, "That is the Duomo seen from the Belvedere. You know Florence?" Lecter is not genuinely asking if she's familiar with the city of Florence—he already knows she isn't. He's using the rhetorical question to belittle her, make her feel culturally inferior, in an effort to gain the upper hand (Figure 19-2). Acting on someone to gain or change something is called a **verbal action**: *The Silence of the Lambs* is filled with it (see p. 104). In a truly cinematic script, almost every spoken word is a verbal action.

Subtext: If a character says to someone, "So, shall I see you again?" it can imply a range of meanings, depending on the context and the character's motives. If he has a hidden agenda (hoping to get some money back) then the **subtext** might be, "Maybe I can get you to finally repay me." In other contexts the subtext might be, "You never make time for me these

FIGURE 19-2

Hannibal Lecter (in Demme's *The Silence of the Lambs*) is a perfect example of a character who uses verbal actions to control and manipulate those around him.

FIGURE 19-3

The subtext of Sean Parker's (Justin Timberlake) spiel in Fincher's *The Social Network* is to seduce Mark Zuckerberg into letting him join his nascent enterprise.

days," or "Do you still care for me?" Actors decide their character's subtexts (to lines or actions) by starting from an overall understanding of what their character and other characters are trying to achieve, and then deciding how their character handles each particular while pursuing the overall objective. Nearly every scene in David Fincher's *The Social Network* (2010) contains subtext that ultimately leads us to understand that Mark Zuckerberg's empire-building is not at all about making money—it's about the revenge of a socially unskilled kid on those socially entitled and gifted. When Zuckerberg and his partner Eduardo Saverin first meet the charismatic entrepreneur Sean Parker in a restaurant (Figure 19-3), everything Parker does and says is designed to win Zuckerberg's confidence—from ordering the food and drinks, to his advice on dropping "the" from their current company name "The Facebook." The scene subtext is, "Eduardo thinks too small for you, Mark. Pair up with me and you'll become cool and powerful too." The coup de grace comes when Parker says, "A million dollars isn't cool. You know what's cool? A billion dollars." The idea manipulating Zuckerberg's loyalties here is not "billion dollars," but "what's cool."

Obstacles, adapting and anticipating: When pursuing any goal in life, we often meet an **obstacle** and must **adapt** by altering course and finding another way forward. Dramatic characters often meet obstacles and these may be external (a locked door) or internal (fear of what the boss will say). Obstacles give the characters something to push against, and how each person adapts yields important clues to the inner workings of their character. For adaptation between characters, picture two people trying to stand up in a small boat. Each must compensate for the changes of balance caused by the movements of the other, causing feints, experiments, surprises, and mistakes. A script says nothing about these because *it is the actors' work to create whatever adaptations lead to the next line or piece of action*. In this work, the actors suggest and demonstrate; the director accepts, rejects, modifies, or asks for a new solution.

Another actor's problem is that, knowing what is coming in the text, he **anticipates** what is going to happen. A vital aspect of an actor's relaxation is giving up trying to look ahead—and to just let the scene happen. Sometimes you will hear a director invite an actor to relax by saying, "Never mind the lines, just play the scene."

Sense memory and emotional memory: In life, the bank of memories and associations we build up plays a large part in our capacity to imagine and empathize. Sensory input and memories are intimately linked—the smell of baked potatoes at home, the flapping of one's clothes at the seaside, the rough feel of rope in a gym, the song of a skylark rising ever higher into an azure sky—all these sensory memories evoke a time, place, mood, and special people. An actor reading a script correlates her character's experiences to whatever lies in her memory bank. There, she finds the analogous experiences to help imagine what a pilot does while losing control of an aircraft, what a store clerk does as she wins the lottery, or what a pensioner does on finding that she's lost her door key. Related personal experiences can be stirring emotional triggers.

Calling on sense memory, the actor recovers the specific actions he or she does under particular circumstances. Here's the extraordinary part: when authentic, *the actions themselves evoke particular emotions* in the actor. For example, practice covering your mouth in the precise way you do when you've spoken out of turn, and you will actually experience some embarrassment. Try it several times! Any natural, accompanying physical action, which is part of an actor's business, can therefore awaken **emotional memory**. Recognizing that memory is not in our heads alone, but in our bodies, our actions, and even in smell and feeling, Stanislavsky named this curious reflex *emotional memory*. Unfortunately, it's also the most misunderstood among his arsenal of discoveries about acting psychology.

Try several actions associated with strong feelings, such as shielding your face from a slap, sipping a cold drink on a hot day, stepping back from a sheer drop, walking past a gruesome road accident, or placing your hand tenderly on a child's fevered brow.

Now as an experiment try just feeling embarrassed without making any physical movement— or try summoning any other feeling. You simply can't do it, because we cannot choose to feel an emotion. Were it humanly possible, mankind could dispense with mind-altering drugs. But "business" can help you get there, which this why trained actors are constantly deciding what their characters do, moment to moment. Most people think emotions produce actions, but in acting it's the other way round. Actions the actor has chosen as authentic to the character *release authentic emotions in the actor*. Even more useful and extraordinary is that it usually happens *every time the actor performs them*, and moves an audience every time too.

You must use the sensory to access the emotional. In Marcel Proust's novel *Remembrance of Things Past*, it was the taste and smell of the little fluted cakes called *petites madeleines* that unlocked the enchanted gate to his childhood, and did so quite involuntarily.

Using the actor's emotions as the character's: When an inappropriate emotion intrudes itself upon the actor, such as pain from a headache, shock at an unexpected move by a partner, or confusion from a misplaced prop, well-trained actors, knowing how little can be hidden from an audience, learn to incorporate every genuine emotion into the character's present. The Second City improv comedy training in Chicago trains comedians to sustain their character under any and every condition. This means embracing and co-opting the invader instead of fighting a losing battle to keep it out.

By using every facet of an actor's consciousness to maintain the character's physical and mental action, and by reacting to every nuance of the other characters' behavior, the actor stays so busy every time the scene is played, and so aware on so many levels, that everything outside the intense, subjective sphere of the character's reality recedes from consciousness. He or she can no longer worry about remembering lines or whether anyone is watching.

Experience this intense state of focus for yourself by trying some of the improv work in Chapter 22. Maintaining the same focus while acting a text takes more discipline, especially when shooting multiple takes and angles that stretch out into a whole day of movie work. To see Rod Steiger's work emerging in the dailies while working on Ken Annakin's film noir *Across the Bridge* (1957) was a revelation—I had never seen acting of such intensity, nor could I imagine anybody maintaining their character and German accent off camera. Steiger did both, and of course he did wonderful reaction shots.

COMPARING THEATER AND FILM ACTING

Among your actors will be ones whose whole experience is theater, and whose performances remind you uncomfortably of seeing theater productions recorded for the screen. Some quality in the acting, even in acclaimed productions, makes the performances ring false on the screen. In fact, it's mostly a psychological matter and concerns where actors get support for what they do. The theater actor works symbiotically with the pulse of the audience, and does what connects in a theatrical setting. Film actors have no such support. They must work wholly from what their character is thinking, feeling, and doing—just as we do in normal life. No enlarged action or voice projection is needed, for the camera captures every twitch of an eyebrow and every note in the voice. A theater actor must approximate this naturalness for an audience seated at a distance, so he or she must speak louder and make his or her actions a little bigger. Theater training is unparalleled, but acting on camera for the first time can leave actors feeling alone and self-doubting. It is the same for the untrained actor because all of us in unfamiliar situations depend on the sense of approval from those around us. Crew members cannot become an audience; they must remain remote and impersonal as they concentrate on their work, or the actors will start playing for their approbation. And then, all of a sudden, you have a theatrical performance on film!

The film actor's only audience is you, the director. It's your job to draw the actor into an intimate, internalized way of sustaining belief. Clearly, you will need special approaches to support your cast, especially when that cast contains differing levels of experience.

Here are some well-known books on acting. They provoke very partisan followings, but those I find most helpful are Robert Benedetti's concise and accessible *The Actor in You: Sixteen Simple Steps to Understanding the Art of Acting*, 5th ed. (Pearson, 2011), Benedetti's *The Actor at Work*, 9th ed. (Allyn & Bacon, 2004), Uta Hagen and Haskel Frankel's *Respect for Acting* (Wiley, 1973), Charles Marowitz's *The Act of Being: Towards a Theory of Acting* (Taplinger, 1978), and Sanford Meisner's *Sanford Meisner on Acting* (Vintage, 1987). Eric Morris and Joan Hotchkis, *No Acting Please* (Ermor Enterprises, 1995) is particularly appropriate for film work. Several of these texts are old, and may even be difficult to obtain (look for used copies at www.abebooks.com). Acting is an old craft, however, and some vintage texts explain it more concisely and appropriately for film than others do.

CHAPTER 20

DIRECTING ACTORS

DIRECTOR IN RELATION TO ACTORS

Unlike you and your crew, actors have no equipment to stand behind, and nowhere to hide. Their work is intense, exposed, and difficult. This means they are vulnerable, easily discouraged, and quick to compare themselves negatively with other actors. It's important that you and every director do some acting so you experience this for yourself. Actors seldom need challenge or authority—they usually have all that working inside them, and then some. What they work for is recognition, and you, as their director and sole audience, are the only one who can confer it. All directions and all approval come from you, and you alone (Figure 20-1). Everyone in the film unit,

FIGURE 20-1

Whether you're a student director (*left*, Felix Thompson shooting *Bedford Park Boulevard)* or an experienced and celebrated director (*right*, Mira Nair shooting *Hysterical Blindness*) actors look to you for feedback, recognition, and leadership to give their best performance.

and every visitor, must be briefed *never* to make critical comments about the actors' work, and no actor may criticize other actors. Any suggestion or comment, however useful, must be confidentially routed through you, for you to decide whether it should go further.

Good directing is really about good leadership, something you can find in all walks of life.

MAKE CONTACT

Human contact matters most of all to actors. Their handshakes, hugging, and greeting kisses are an important rite having little to do with sexuality. Quite simply, they are sensitive people whose work makes them vulnerable. They depend on each other and even more they depend on you. The harrowing nature of their work makes them need constant reminders that you respect and like them. Make a point of responding in kind with whatever makes a mutually acceptable expression of warmth and liking. Bear in mind that you are an authority figure who must treat all equally and without condescension.

BUILD TRUST AND AUTHORITY

An actor needs to know that the person guiding their performance and putting it on film can be trusted to show them at their best. It's important that you establish your credibility as the director from the onset:

- Know the script and its characters thoroughly and be able to articulate all your impressions.
- Be accessible, and don't bury yourself in technical or logistical issues (a temptation for beginners). Nothing dispirits actors in need of direction more than a director who hovers around the camera crew. You must be there for your actors.
- Direct inductively by asking questions and truly listen to the answers. Often they have ideas that enrich their characters and interactions; other times you may be drawing your cast into discovering what you already know. Whatever people discover for themselves, they never forget. Avoid reeling off instructions—it's confusing and can seem overly authoritarian.
- Don't waste their time. Being late or unprepared, or making actors wait while you deal with problems unrelated to their predicament all show a lack of respect.
- Actors will test you, so be ready for challenge and resistance, especially if you have to modify or supersede earlier instructions. Along the way, your cast will catch things you missed, because each actor carries responsibility for only one character. This makes learning a two-way street.

DIRECT POSITIVELY AND EQUABLY

Your feedback is so vital to actors that most feel under-recognized most of the time. The larger the cast, the less time you have for each actor, and the more this is true. Be ready to meet with anyone in real difficulties and listen carefully to their problems. Not doing so can send them spinning out of control. Set up with the cast that "one-on-ones" are problem sessions and by request, otherwise actors may think you are giving someone else special attention. As you direct, avoid favoring any one cast member, and avoid humiliating anyone in front of his colleagues. Every role is important, so every actor must be treated with equal respect. Never, *ever* get romantically involved with a cast member during production!

Try to remove all fear and comparison in your cast by using positive, constructive phrasing. What springs to your lips as, "Tony, make the next take less wild and rambling," should emerge as, "Tony, see if you can keep the intensity in the next take, but try to get her attention by becoming dangerously quiet." Rather than barking commands, try saying, "I wonder if you could try..." "Maybe you could let me see..." It's your right to ask for alternatives, and to choose from what your actors offer. Often you will get back something better than you could imagine.

Say as little as you can to get actors working toward what you want. Don't intellectualize or think aloud—that's an indulgence and only clogs the actor's mind with verbiage. Concentrate on giving short, practical, actable directions. That is, help actors find things to do: do not ask them to feel feelings or produce particular effects. Actors cannot summon feelings or results; they can only do actable things to which feelings come attached. If you do specify an effect ("look more contemptuous"), an actor must find an actable way to get there. Out of panic, fatigue, or lack of on-the-spot ideas, you have tempted the actor to short-circuit the search process, and so she winds up "indicating"; that is, trying to communicate an idea instead of being inside her character.

At the end of every work session, thank cast members—individually if possible, but collectively if not. Even if things have gone poorly, put an optimistic spin on your comments. People work best for those who expect well of them.

Facing so many unfamiliar pressures, you would do well to work with a small cast to begin with, and capitalize on the most successful relationships by using the best of them again in subsequent productions.

COMMON PROBLEMS

Actors seldom need special techniques, arcane information, or devious tricks from their director. Mostly they need practical help in casting off the layers of self-consciousness and insecurity in order to simply *be*. Performing, by its nature, is self-conscious and self-judgmental. In adverse conditions, the actor may start to act from the head, signaling ideas, and indicate. This is because he has lost touch with the heart and mind of the character, or has never found them. Your job is to find and undo the log jams of tension so the actor can resume the flow of mental and emotional focus. Sometimes the problem will lie not with the actor's ability, but with the script or blocking (your choreography of actors and camera). Occasionally a simple rewording of dialogue or a freer physical movement is enough to clear the obstruction.

LACK OF FOCUS AND RELAXATION

Note the circumstances when an actor loses focus. It will show as a loss of conviction and clarity in their lines, and as uncertainty in their body language. How it shows will vary from person to person, so you must figure out where each actor carries his tension, and whether it shows most in shoulders, face, hands, walk, or voice. There is always a reason. The actor may have been "thrown" (become uneasy because of what somebody did or said), and now needs your help to remedy the difficulty. Often you can lower anxiety by redirecting an actor's attention or by mentioning something they just did that was effective. Confidence, focus, and relaxation go hand in hand: we regain confidence when someone we respect reminds us of what we do well.

When an actor repeatedly loses focus at the same point in a scene, note it without stopping the scene. Usually the actor is aware and has ideas about the source. Maybe a turn feels wrong, or bending down to pick something up makes costume shoes pinch distractingly. Most often it happens because they doubt the meaning of a line. Through sympathetic questioning, you can locate the cause and address it.

MIND-BODY CONNECTION MISSING

Are you convinced by what you see in the bodily actions, gestures, and tone of what your cast members do? This is a hard one, because you *want* to be convinced, you *want* to feel that the cast is successful. So you, too, must be relaxed enough to let the cast have (or *not* have) an effect on you. Only freedom from tension will allow you to have the same sensations and reactions that an audience has. You, after all, are the actors' first audience.

Instead of making binary "either/or" judgments, try to keep an internal barometer going that registers highs and lows throughout the scene. Use your recall to retrieve the high points of the scene—the places where things were really cooking. You start by mentioning these to the cast. Then by subtraction, you can now turn to what was less successful. By reporting where you were convinced and moved, and where your attention lapsed and you felt distanced, you hand initiative to the cast. They will recall their states of consciousness and extract the problems and likely causes. Nearly always, the problem is fuzzy acting objectives. By asking the cast to solve problems, you encourage them to put their artistic process to work, which they will love. Your job is to structure, encourage, and make choices so the process keeps moving. You must also ensure that all the solutions remain within the spirit of your cinematic intentions.

ANTICIPATING OR NOT ADAPTING

Watch carefully for the quality of each character's adaptation: if the actor has the character's interior life going, if he or she is listening and watching, then adapting to obstacles will be as realistic as it is in life. Some reactions take thought; others should be automatic. After all, you don't stop to think when someone throws a punch at your head.

Whenever a character anticipates or lags, you know the actor is working from prepared ideas. Get him to articulate, line by line, what the other characters are implying, and tell him to work off the clues the other characters are sending him. Concentrating on these means his character is working to perceive—correctly or incorrectly—what's around him. A suitor may, for instance, mistake pride and independence as indifference, and wrongly assume he is rejected. The actor who short-circuits this process will react ahead of time, or, by faking thought, react in a calculated yet dead way. The cure is for you to get him or her to voice an interior monologue, and to base it on moment-by-moment clues coming from the other characters—just as we do in daily life.

ACTING IN ISOLATION

Uptight players preprogram their reactions when in fact they should decide their reactions at the very moment the reactions become necessary. When you see a player insulated inside preconceptions, take him or her aside for a private talk. The actor needs to let go, to live in the moment, and to trust that the text will somehow happen. This level of trust and comfort may not come easily, but it's important to find it. Until he feeds into the communal flow, and receives from it, that actor is failing to draw support from the rest of the cast or to give it in return.

You can create this interaction by involving the whole cast in a short and playful improv but don't use it unless you have played in and directed it, and feel confident enough to handle the process. Consider those laid out in the Chapter 22 table under "Improv Exercises," especially Projects IMP-5 and IMP-13. With players you don't yet know well, use improv cautiously in case someone feels threatened or thinks it beneath their dignity. Once your cast is relaxed and trusts you, improv can be wonderfully silly, refreshing, and helpful at unlocking phobic anxieties.

Now return to the scripted scene, and ask everyone to (a) feed small, special intentions into their playing; (b) read specifically what is coming from the other characters; and (c) deliberate before reacting to them. Run the scene more than once, asking for changed nuances. The players will have fun trying to really listen and react. Now everyone will see periods of deliberation as highly charged moments rather than the dread moment when they hold the hot potato.

Communion makes a scene become alive and real, and after it's established, simply alert the cast whenever you see it lagging. Is there a particular reason, or are they simply getting fatigued? Is there a hole in someone's understanding that is making him retreat?

MISSING INTERIOR LIFE

Trained actors sometimes let their character's interior life wither, whereas untrained actors haven't encountered the idea, or don't know how to keep one going. I once directed a cast of very mixed experience. Some had never acted and gave their lines without conviction; worse, the timing of their reactions was all over the map. Taking them aside, showing them how to silently maintain interior monologues, they were able to give transformed performances and consistent timing. You may only be able to do this with untrained actors—your trained players may think you patronizing.

If a two-person scene is stumbling, ask each actor to improvise the thoughts of his or her character in a low "interior" voice before and after every line. Explore this by using the interior monologue exercises in Chapter 22 (IMP-18: "Blind Date" and TXT-3: "Improvising an Interior Monologue"). Coach your actors to find all the dimensions their character can be aware of. When they next play their scene, it will become complex and interesting.

MISSING SUBTEXTS

During rehearsal, nail down every part of the text by making sure, especially when anyone loses focus, that each cast member can articulate whatever their character is trying to get, do, or accomplish at any given moment. Each line, each look or glance, each action, must arise from a defined objective; the actor must know to whom it is addressed and whether he gets his needs met or not. Each definition, as we said in the previous chapter, should contain (a) a first-person active (not passive) verb, (b) a person (or thing) he is acting upon, and (c) an intended effect that will either be fulfilled or not. Work to improve each objective's definition when you see it's necessary. Language really matters: the more striking the actors' objectives, the stronger and clearer their performances. It would, for instance, be weak to say, "My objective is to ask my manager to tell me who took money from the till." Stronger would be, "I'll make my manager admit right now who stole from the till." *Make* is stronger and more playable than *ask*, and *admit* is stronger than *tell*. *Stealing* is more loaded than *taking*.

Your characters must know what they want, from whom they want it, and whether they succeed or not. Help them build urgency into their intentions. By sharpening objectives, your actors *raise the stakes* for their characters. He or she then has more to gain and more to lose. Don't be afraid to ask at a weak moment, "Can we raise the stakes here?" and let the cast figure out how.

THE GENERALIZED INTERPRETATION

Less experienced actors sometimes try to play all of their character's characteristics at once. Called "acting in general," the actor is trying to indicate an abstract character description to the audience. Applied like a color wash, it produces a fuzzy scene whose characters fail to progress, when they should instead move forward in sharp, forceful increments.

Well-trained actors know that acting is sequencing one clear intention after another, one clear and appropriate action after another, one clear demand after another. Rectify generalized interpretations in one of two ways: clarify the unfolding action by breaking it into steps, one moment and one objective at a time. Or, ask the actor to speak their character's interior monologue in a low voice aloud (see p. 228).[1] This helps you ensure the actor is in the moment and listening to other players because his interior monologue will reflect it.

DISTANCING AND INDICATING

Actors commonly give too much (voice, actions, emotions, movement). Fearing they are not reaching the audience, that they are not "good enough" or "big enough," they drive home their character's intended personality. Watching and grading themselves, they are severed from their character. You can also center this actor by asking for an interior monologue. Try asking them, too, to withhold their character's feelings from other characters' knowledge, as we do in life. This gives the actor (and the audience) interesting work to do, and lends dramatic tension.

Intellectualizing also causes distancing. This can be a problem when you and the cast have done too much objective script analysis. Insist that your cast personalize: whenever someone speaks of their character as "her" or "she," gently insist they use the first person. Speak to her as though she *is* the character, not a technician operating a puppet. Immediately convert anything said in passive voice (*she is being made to look for…*) to its active equivalent (*I am looking for…*) so the actor has something more immediate and playable to work with.

---

[1] Exercise TXT-3: "Improvising an Interior Monologue" serves as a good model for this.

INTENSITY, INTIMACY AND LIMITING AN ACTOR'S SPHERE

Actors' interactions must be contained and purposeful, not florid and "actory." You know this is happening when an actor makes unmotivated movements, paces, and flails his arms. Characters gain in power and intensity when gestures and movement are minimal. In Michael Caine's video *Acting in Film* (1989), he demonstrates how much more centered a character seems when the actor overcomes the impulse to blink. In a hilarious "blink count," David Letterman showed Nancy Pelosi, in her first appearance as Speaker of the House, listening to a State of the Union address while standing alongside the basilisk Dick Cheney and blinking no fewer than 29 times to his once.[2]

To be meaningful, actions must be purposeful, minimal, and take place in a small compass. Anyone watching at a distance might imagine that nothing was happening. As a young cutting room assistant in a big film studio, I sneaked onto the set to watch at a respectful distance while the unit shot a close-up. It all seemed very static: after some mumbling from the actors and the assistant director calling "Cut," I thought, "Huh, nothing happened—the camera can't have been rolling." Next day on the big screen, I saw a scene electric with tension in which *everything* happened. The scene had taken place inside an intense bubble of space that the camera had captured completely. Even a whopping Panavision camera is a perfectly intimate voyeur, and reveals the minuscule tightening of a jaw muscle or the waver in a parting glance.

Your cast, particularly when used to working in the theater, will need a great deal of reassurance over this. Tell them that if they are inside their character, and experience their character's thoughts and feelings, the camera does the rest. Redirect an actor who's playing too large by saying, "Visualize a bubble of space only large enough to enclose you and your partner. Talk only to him, here and now. There is no one else, no camera present, just you two." The magnified voices and gestures will stop, and scene intensity will climb.

TACKLING STUBBORN ARTIFICIALITY

You cast someone for a small part, and then find that their concept of acting comes from TV commercials. Valiantly, your homemaker projects a wacky TV mom personality. Were she playing a stage mom, this might do, but now it's terrible. Hamming and indicating come from enacting an *idea* of one's part rather than doing the work to imagine one's way into your character's consciousness. Take your homemaker aside and get her to talk through her character's thoughts and interior monologue. Ask her to recall someone she knows and upon whose image she can model herself. This can be a very successful way to anchor a part. Once she is busy maintaining her character's interior processes, she can no longer stand outside and see herself acting, which is at the root of the problem. Now your homemaker fully inhabits her character, speaks and acts from an authentic consciousness, and the difference is like night and day.

When an actor continues to force feelings and fails to create the character's interior resources, you have a severe problem. As a last resort, clandestinely tape some of the unnatural acting, then show it privately in comparison with grabbed footage of the actor having a normal conversation. He will be shocked and depressed to see himself on the screen in this way. Tell him supportively

---

[2] Do a web search for "Dick, Nancy, Blink Count, Letterman" to find this clip.

that you want him to *be*, not to act. At desperation's door, he may now open up to your coaching. With an incurable voice projector or anyone habitually artificial, the best solution may be to bang yourself over the head and recast. This can badly shake up the rest of the cast, who fear that they, too, may be so bad that you will fire them next.

HOW MUCH REHEARSAL IS ENOUGH?

Actors often express the fear that a scene will be over-rehearsed. If it means drilling to a master plan, this is a real enough anxiety. You must learn to recognize when the actors have "nailed it," meaning they are truly inhabiting their characters and each dramatic moment. Often actors tire during rehearsal, so it's important to refresh them by moving on and returning later.

Never rehearse without plans and objectives in mind, or the cast will sense this and resent their time being wasted. During preparatory work, decide which scenes are pivotal, and use the ensemble's growing ability to focus on problem areas and discover solutions. For the actors, digging deeply for meaning, developing perceptions that flow back and forth between the characters, and creating links and resonances with other parts of the script are all highly productive. It also habituates them to improvising so that you can ask for changes on the set without fazing them.

DON'T OVER-DIRECT

Over-directing can mean rehearsing beyond the point of improvement, or trying to micromanage the cast. Often it is the sign of the director who doesn't trust their instincts and over-intellectualizes. Also, many moments in a film are just simple. Sometimes, getting into a car is just getting into a car, closing a door is just closing a door. Not every moment requires intense sense memory work, digging for subtext, or extended rehearsals. Choosing which scenes require rehearsals and which can be developed during the shoot is a time and energy saving skill a director learns along the way.

A director must also be able to recognize scenes in which the emotional connection is so delicate that to rehearse them extensively might drain spontaneity out of the moment. In these cases, working individually with each actor in the scene during rehearsals and saving the first ensemble performance for when the cameras are rolling can preserve the freshness of the moment. A good example is the café seduction scene in Sarah Polley's second feature film *Take This Waltz* (2011) which tells the story of Margot (Michelle Williams), a contentedly married woman who becomes sexually attracted to Daniel (Luke Kirby), an artist who lives across the street. In order to produce for the camera the tantalizing risk and electricity of the moment when Margot and Daniel's harmless flirtation crosses over into outright seduction, Polley decided not to rehearse the scene.

> We had an exhaustive rehearsal process before shooting the film, but this was the one scene we actually didn't rehearse. So Michelle had never heard those words and Luke had never had to say those words in front of Michelle before.[3]

---

[3] *Sarah Polley: On Love, Desire and the Female Body.* Interview with Melissa Block, NPR's "All Things Considered" (radio broadcast, July 6, 2012).

Although this scene was carefully scripted, the result was a moment that had the spontaneity and element of surprise of an improvised encounter where the non-verbal reactions from both actors are even more emotionally revealing than the dialogue (Figure 20-2).

SOME DO'S AND DON'TS

- *Set limited, positive goals*: Say, "See if you can open the door softly this time"—not, "This time don't make such a racket with that closet."

- *Direct the actor's attention to a particular kind of action*: Say, "I'd like to see you try to figure out what he meant as you turn away." Make the suggestion specific, and locate it in a particular moment. Generalized suggestions that could apply anywhere aren't helpful.

FIGURE 20-2

In her 2011 film *Take This Waltz*, director Sarah Polley provoked complex and subtle reactions from actress Michelle Williams by saving the very first performance of a seduction scene for when the cameras were rolling.

- *Suggest a different subtext*: such as, "Try closing the door on him with finality rather than regret."

- *Remind cast members where their character has just come from*. Wind them up to each scene with a reminder: "You've just come from the stock exchange and seen your father's savings vanish." This is vital while directing, because films are shot in small, out-of-order increments, and actors need constant orientation.

- *Remind actors that nobody is present*: Ask actors to ignore the crew's presence, act as they do when alone in real life, and never to look at the camera. This helps them avoid the temptation to play to an imagined audience.

- *Never demonstrate how you'd like something played*: This implies you are an actor and want a copy of yourself. But you are not an actor, and what you want is unique to that actor. Ask the cast for *their* solutions.

- *Never give line readings*. A line reading means the director reads the dialogue with the emotional inflection they wish the actor to provide and then tells the actor to "say it like that." This is insulting for an actor and reveals a director's lack of imagination.

- *Never say, "Just be yourself"*: This sets actors worrying: "What did he really mean? How does he see me? Which me does he want?" Focus your actor instead on aspects of her character's experience.

- *Never ask for something "smaller"*: An actor takes this as a barbed criticism. Ask for the same intensity but with more intimacy, or for anything else that sounds like development rather than censure.

Learning More

A good further resource is Judith Weston's *Directing Actors* (Michael Wiese Productions, 1999). It's usefully prescriptive and never loses sight of the actor's perspective. Theater oriented and concise is Lenore DeKoven's *Changing Direction: A Practical Approach to Directing Actors in Film and Theatre* (Focal Press, 2006). Acting is better understood in the theater, and better respected, so everything you learn there applies also to film. Film people are apt to want immediate results, whereas theater people know that truthful results only come from immersion in the right kind of processes, which take time and work.

CHAPTER 21

REHEARSALS

Plays grow out of rigorous rehearsal, but fiction films are usually denied it. Producers argue that rehearsal damages spontaneity, and rehearsing wastes money because actors can learn their lines just before shooting. Screen actors as accomplished as Dustin Hoffman, Meryl Streep, and Gary Sinise disagree. They prefer to study and rehearse intensively, and it's no accident that directors famed for their meticulous work at building ensemble acting—Ingmar Bergman, Robert Altman, Ken Loach, and Mike Leigh, as we said earlier—have produced exceptional results and commanded great loyalty from their casts. If top professionals prefer rehearsal, anyone using a cast of mixed experience needs it even more. Let's be clear: film equipment does not produce, as many beginners think, an alchemy whose techniques turn lead into gold. Filming merely magnifies, so that what is good looks better, and what is bad looks worse.

Shaping your ensemble before filming gives your actors a shared history. Your cast has had time to fully enter the world of the script and its characters, whose relationships must become as authentic as those between the actors. The quest for all this is channeled through the sensibility of the director, who becomes coordinator, midwife, and first audience.

THE DIRECTOR PREPARES

Before coming together, the actors and their director thoroughly study the text. This ensures checks and balances so that when actions, motivations, and meanings come under scrutiny, everyone can be usefully partisan. Each actor sees the world of the text mostly from the perspective of his or her own character. Thus, the viewpoints of the different actors often spark new ideas. Not all may be compatible, so the director leads the process of coordinating and reconciling them. You will need to be even-handed, holistic, and speak for the best interests of the project and its general audience.

Actors seek clarity and decisiveness from their director, as well as short, clear, and detailed feedback on their work. Be warned: they feel they never get enough of this. The director who is alive to what each actor is giving, who can describe it accurately, is like the maestro conductor who can tell the fourth cello what intonation works better. Nobody is born with this skill—you have to work mightily to acquire it. Doing your homework—studying drama's sources in life, and analyzing the script—lays the foundation.[1]

SCENE ANALYSIS, SUBTEXTS, AND DEVELOPING THE AUTHORITY TO DIRECT

As a director, you must remain several steps ahead of your cast. The work you've already done breaking down the script is a beginning (see Chapter 17), but now you must break down each scene and decide what drives each step forward for each character within each dramatic unit. You will learn much from the work your actors have done on their own, but they will assume that you understand their parts well. From intense preparation, you have decided what the piece is about, and what you want to do with it. From this comes your authority to direct, something that actors will often subtly contest until you prove yourself. Analyzing a screenplay—as described in Chapter 4 and below in "Scene Breakdown Sessions" (p. 249)—reveals like nothing else how tight or loose its cabinetry is, and what you and your actors must do to fix it.

CONFLICT

The engine of drama is conflict, so you must know how each conflict initiates, develops, comes to a head, and resolves. For conflict to even exist, you must define and heighten the pattern of oppositions so you can orchestrate them well. Conflict between individuals is like a fencing match—much strategic footwork and mutual adaptation leading to strikes. With each strike, the balance of power changes. That moment of altered consciousness is probably a **beat**, and thus holds heightened significance for at least one character. Each beat is a moment of "crisis adaptation," and there may be one or several per scene.

HEIGHTENING DRAMATIC TENSION AND THE CRISIS POINT

The cast is inside the drama looking out. You are on the outside looking in, as the audience will do, so you alone are responsible for dramatic shaping. By relating each beat to plot needs, character attitudes, or characters' feelings, you can focus how it needs to be played for maximum tension. By consolidating the scene's trajectory, clarifying the development of a character's will, you help shape what effect a scene has on the audience. Generating tag titles helps to clarify this and avoid unwanted reiteration. Your aim is to keep the audience involved and guessing all the time. One of the beats in a scene will be its **crisis point**, the major turning point for which the whole scene exists. Confirm the identity of this moment by mentally subtracting it to see whether the scene could survive without it. Your directing has achieved focus when each scene's crisis point is distinct and palpable.

---

[1] This section details what directors bear at the outset of rehearsal, but actors also have their own regimen. I have included a document on the actor's preparation on the book's companion website www.directingbook. com (under "Miscellaneous"). For inexperienced players, you may want to download this document and hold a supportive discussion before they go to work.

NAMING THE FUNCTION OF EACH SCENE

Like a cog in the gears of a clock, each scene has its optimal place and function. Defining how the piece gathers power, scene by scene, enables you to interpret each scene confidently and to define what momentum it feeds into its successor. Define your scenes with a tag title that names its function and lets you accurately communicate its nature to cast and crew. Charles Dickens' chapter titles from *Bleak House* make good examples: "Covering a Multitude of Sins," "Signs and Tokens," "A Turn of the Screw," "Closing In," "Dutiful Friendship," and "Beginning the World." From charged descriptors like these, ideas flow effortlessly about mise-en-scène and scenic design.

DEFINING THE THEMATIC PURPOSE

As director, keep your eye on the authorial thrust, or *theme* of the whole work (see p. 69). Remember that, as an artwork, your film is a delivery system for ideas and convictions and not just a mirror held up to particular people doing wonderfully realistic things. For a film to deliver on its theme, you must get everyone behind it, and your interpretation must clearly be integral to the screenplay or your cast may reject it. The thematic core is important because it's where every cast and crew member returns to decide their creative options—so you must be able to articulate it convincingly.

Your authorial statement will be strongest when it embodies a simple principle that implies profound consequences. Examples: "Sometimes marriage between two good people is not practical and everyone suffers," or, "He is most inflexible and dangerous to those that love him." When you can get small truths right, larger truths of wider resonance follow.

SETTING UP THE REHEARSAL SCHEDULE

Once parts are cast, your assistant director (AD) logs everyone's availability and works out a schedule of rehearsal times. Everyone should get a script if they have a major part, or perhaps only "sides" (selected scenes) if they play a minor character. The AD should assemble and distribute a list of cast and unit contact information, such as email addresses and cell phone numbers. Ask the whole cast to attend the first meeting with their ideas and a detailed biography (sometimes called backstory) for their character. Be absolutely clear that nobody should learn lines until asked. Lines learned too early can fix the actor's initial understanding, after which he may be inflexible to change.

Detailed scheduling may best follow the table reading (below) which tends to confirm which scenes need the most work. Aim never to keep anybody waiting around during rehearsals: actors are generally busy people, and using their time well establishes your respect and professionalism.

Plan enough rehearsals for understanding to really evolve; a rule of thumb is to invest one hour of rehearsal for every minute of screen time. A demanding three-minute scene thus needs at least three hours of rehearsal time. For any scene where a utilities man does nothing more than read a meter, no rehearsal is called for. Use your judgment.

Actors tend to lose concentration after about an hour of intense work, so keep sessions short and take breaks. Doing unfamiliar work is particularly tiring for the inexperienced. Mental fatigue will impair you even more than the cast.

After every rehearsal, someone must remind each actor of the date, time, and place of the next meeting and make sure they have a current schedule.

REHEARSAL SPACE

It's good to rehearse in the actual locations, but usually rehearsal takes place in a large, bare space that is borrowed or rented. With tape on the floor and whatever chairs and tables you have to hand, you can indicate the location of walls, key pieces of furniture, doors, and windows. Minimalist rehearsals have the advantage of giving the cast nothing but the text and its characters to focus on with few distractions. Locations and setting become more important once your rehearsals go "off book" and blocking begins.

REHEARSALS WITH THE BOOK

THE TABLE READING AND INTRODUCING THE PROJECT

It's important to establish a sense of collaborative cohesion and energy by having the entire cast assembled for introductions and the **table reading**, when actors first read their parts out loud together. They want to feel they are working on something special, worthwhile, and even beautiful; so aim to start the first meeting by lifting everyone's spirits. At your very first meeting, speak of your enthusiasm and love for the project, and say why you chose it and what it means to you. Given the natural anxiety that everyone feels at first, your commitment and excitement will help raise morale. The first work is with the **book,** that is, reading from the script. Seat the cast around a table so everyone can see everyone else. Ask the ensemble to read their parts in neutral, not "acted," readings and get the AD to read the stage directions. You are looking for meaning at this stage, not who can act best. Go through the script without stopping, and have a list of fundamental questions to ask during the discussion that follows. Encourage the cast to dig into the piece and explore what kind of person each character is, and what subtexts and themes they are detecting in the film. For any untrained actors present, you will have to relay your expectations in non-technical language.

Now relax and really listen. You begin to see what each cast member brings to the framework that you have set in your motivational opening remarks. Actors like their director to treat them as partners in problem solving, which is at the heart and soul of creativity. They, not you, must develop what motivates their characters, if they are to have a stake in clarifying everything that lies behind the script. Dedicated actors love this approach. Each as an advocate for a single character will contribute new insights. Gently insist that cast members personalize (that is, speak and think in the first person) whenever they talk about their character.

The table reading establishes how each actor sees the piece and how well the nascent characters are fitting together. Expect to get glimpses of where your biggest problems will lie: in particular scenes, in particular actors, or both. Keep an eye open for anyone who seems unduly insecure and might need special support. You will start getting an idea of how your conception of the characters matches the cast's. If there are discrepancies at this stage, express your thoughts and ideas, but do not press for total agreement. Goodwill disagreements provide a creative tension that spurs closer examination during the next phases of work.

At the end, shake hands with everyone and thank them cordially for their good work. Reiterate that nobody learns any lines yet—not until interpretations, meanings, and characters have been thoroughly explored and agreed on.

MEETING ONE-ON-ONE WITH ACTORS

Early on, try to meet with everyone alone, even minor parts, for maybe half an hour. Much of the part's future direction can take flight from the private expectations you set during this initial session. As usual you should mainly listen. Plumb the actor's approach and establish a personal and supportive attitude. The actor may well confide his or her insecurities, which you take note of so you can give the right support. This is a good time to get any of the actor's further ideas, and to encourage, develop, or redirect. You can also get the actor to discuss how the character sees his past, the other characters, and how they see him. The actor will need to give his character defenses and justifications to handle these.

SCENE BREAKDOWN SESSIONS

You are now ready to begin developing the piece and testing your ideas through close readings, one scene at a time. Prepare by making a scene breakdown (if you need a refresher, review the essentials of drama in Chapters 3 and 4). Director and actors should read the whole screenplay and do a scene breakdown alone before meeting to discuss what they understand. The object is to *use active, present tense language to describe what each character is trying to get, do, or accomplish in relation to the others*. Work from the micro toward the macro levels.

- *Lines and action*
  - Give an action verb **tagline** to each line or action that defines its subtext. ("I want you to take me seriously.") Subtexts and their taglines should build logically toward the beat.
  - Subtexts often go unperceived or misperceived by the characters. This helps to inject conflict into their situation, and to charge it with tension.
- *Beats*
  - Determine where the **beats** are for each character; that is, at what point does each character have an irreversible change in consciousness of his or her situation? Remember, there may be only one or multiple beats in a dramatic unit.
  - In the script margin, as in Figure 21-1, bracket each beat to enclose its beginning escalation, and end, naming the beat with a tagline (such as, "I want you to admit that you don't love me").
  - Define what **adaptation** the character makes by characterizing what he or she does following the dramatic beat. ("Because I see you're not going to admit what you did, I'm going to tell your father.")
- *Dramatic units*
  - Divide the scene into **dramatic units**. If it has three major beats, it may have three dramatic units.
  - Title each with a distinct dramatic function. ("Lynn sends Olivia on an errand so she can get Terry alone," "Lynn corners Terry and confronts him in the greenhouse," etc.)

- *Scene crisis*
  - Designate the scene's **crisis point** (or turning point). It is usually the last dramatic beat.
  - Determine what the **result** of this crisis point is—what the new direction the character, conflict or narrative takes.
- *Through-lines.*
  - As you work through one scene at a time, you should be able to detect the longer and more internal character motivations that follow from scene to scene—the character's **through-line**. Like objectives, through-lines are expressed in the first person, using an active verb, and have an immediately assessable result in mind. (Example, "Guillermo wants to earn his son's respect.")

As an example, Figure 21-1 is the first page of a scene in which husband and wife get lost while driving in a city's outskirts. They argue because Tod, typical guy that he is, won't stop the car to look at the map. The page contains a single dramatic unit with its beat typically marked up in handwriting. The beat comes at the pivotal moment when Tod realizes that he must act differently because Angela is now seriously upset. Each character takes several steps on the way to this moment, and you decide these by extracting their subtexts. The subtext steps ramping up to the dramatic beat are also annotated, each with an interpretative tag. See if you agree that:

- Angela's first three lines escalate the same subtext, "I'm afraid we're really lost."
- Realizing they are indeed lost, her subtext changes to, "We've got to get help."
- Tod downplays her anxiety, pitting his will against hers.
- The dramatic beat comes when he realizes he's let things go too far.
- A significant action usually accompanies the dramatic beat. Tod's is to stop the car.
- A new dramatic unit begins.

Trained actors know this work, but the rest of us seldom have the first idea. As a director, work tactfully with your actors until they have planned their character's intentions and adaptations, moment to moment. This work matters because:

- Effective analysis sets you up to direct the action as a set of clear, actable steps.
- Each new dramatic unit is a new course of action fueled by a new volition and emotion.
- The steps in a character's consciousness are like a melody that can extend in time only if the notes are sounded in sequence, not all at once.

REHEARSAL ORDER AND PRIORITIES FOR SMALL GROUPS

At the beginning of rehearsals address only the major problems, or you burden actors with too much information and blur priorities. Later, others of secondary significance, such as lines or actions lacking credibility or nuance, will move to the top of the heap and claim attention. The rehearsal process is thus an archeological dig of continuous discovery and refinement. When every aspect of the piece becomes thoroughly familiar, you will be able to adopt a plan of convenience,

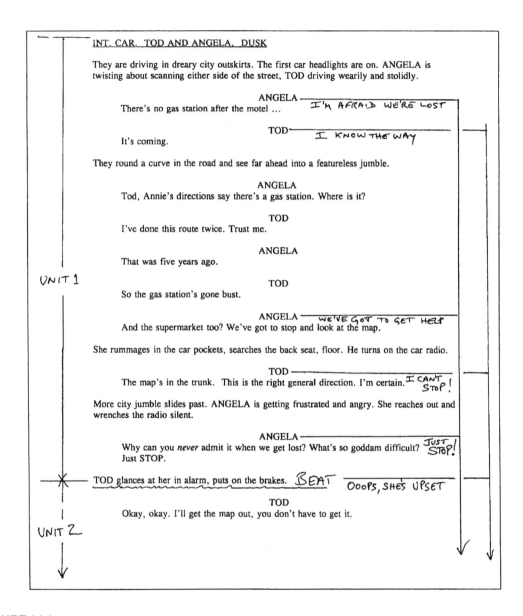

FIGURE 21-1

Doing a scene breakdown to identify the subtext, beats, and dramatic units of a scene helps focus the direction given to actors.

and work in smaller groups and around people's schedules. For the time being, give priority to your key scenes and those presenting special problems.

At first, rehearse significant scenes in script order. Every actor in every scene must know from moment to moment what his or her character is trying to get, do, or accomplish. Actors must know what their character expects as the outcome of his beat—and when the result is success, failure, or the unexpected, he should know how to form the new objective that starts the next dramatic unit. This way, the actor moves through the chain of cause and effect and gains a progressive understanding of the motivations of his character.

CONSOLIDATING CHARACTERS' FORMATIVE EXPERIENCES

Try making use of Chapter 22, Exercise IMP–12: "Make Your Own Character." Using this exercise, the ensemble questions each main character, probing the formative influences in their life, but avoiding the period covered by the film. The actor addressed should answer in character, inventing answers and saying what he or she may think of the other characters. This challenges each actor to fully inhabit his or her part and to know his or her past. It will also deepen everyone else's sense of the character. Try this with all the major roles.

ENCOURAGE PHYSICAL MOVEMENT

Blocking movements will be determined once the cast is "off book" (see p. 253), but encourage the cast to get up and move whenever the scene requires it. Holding a script will inhibit this, but the emphasis on movement plants the need to act using the whole body, not just the voice and face. Each cast member should begin to develop the specific actions that reflect his or her character's internal, psychological movement, especially at the beats.

For example, a man secretly engaged to marry is being questioned by his possessive mother. He decides now may be the time to confess. The text describes what he says, but its degree of significance will only emerge from what he does—and the screenplay does not specify. Maybe he can start drying the dishes, handing items to his mother so her hands are never empty? Let's try the two of them to see how this works. As she becomes especially probing, he goes silent, so maybe he could let the water out of the sink and watch it drain away. When it has gurgled away, he turns and blurts out his secret. Handing off the family china and letting the water run away combine into credible action for the pressure he feels to act on a "now or never" decision. Spontaneous invention usually produces clichés at first, so the director must keep demanding fresh and less predictable action until you see something you like.

While hampered by holding the book and unable to fully interact, actors' readings will remain inadequate, so content yourself with rough sketch-work at this stage. Once you are satisfied that your cast has got the characters, motivations, and ideas for action right, ask them to learn their lines for a scene.

NOTES, FEEDBACK AND ESTABLISHING A WORKING RHYTHM

It's tough to retain the mass of fleeting impressions you get during rehearsals, especially as fatigue descends. Late impressions erase earlier ones, and sooner or later, you find yourself facing an expectant cast with a near-empty mind. Avoid this by carrying a large scratch pad on which to keep notes. Be sure to tell the cast when you are pleased with progress, and characterize your impressions as you go. Be careful about chastising a whole group: the hardworking and blameless will feel particularly hurt by the lash of your tongue. Even when a rehearsal has disappointed you, find positive things to say, such as, "Well, we dealt with some tough stuff today, but it's definitely coming together. Here's where I think we need to go next...!"

If any of your actors have training and experience, be careful what developmental technique you use in case they deem it unnecessary or patronizing. Watch, listen, and question. Let your actors get as far as they can with minimal directing. They are getting to know each other and each other's methods. When problems arise, produce whatever technique breaks the logjam.

CHARACTER COMPLEXITY AND "NEGATIVE" CHARACTERS

It's a cliché, but no less true, that strong people always have an Achilles' heel, the beautiful have an ugly streak, and bright people occasionally do really dumb things. Such faults make them human, fascinating, and contradictory, and this is why acting can be such profound work. Encourage your cast to find the fault lines in their characters, the irregularities that make them special.

Be ready to deal with actors wanting to parlay some unpopular ("negative") trait in their character's makeup into something, well, more likable. Help your actors see that truth is neither positive nor negative, but simply human and part of the job. The Roman dramatist Terence described his artist's responsibility thus: "Nothing human is alien to me." Try telling the actor that unpleasant people, or people who do unpleasant things, don't think of themselves as bad. They always have an explanation, a good reason for their actions, and this lets you work with the actor to create his character's explanation—to himself and to the world—where it may be lacking in the script. Even a villain, in his own eyes, is a good person with unpleasant tasks to perform. Few real-life torturers feel remorse; it was a job the authorities said must be done—for national security.

Actors have problems with all sorts of things, often quite justifiably. Be very careful, however, not to let an actor start rewriting his part. Other actors will see this as a privilege that they should also have. Encourage the actor instead to identify the root of the problem and to suggest several alternative solutions that he can implement. Have him try them out, and select one if you like it. If nothing is convincing, say you need to think about it, and could he keep on with the present text for the moment. Here, you must use your judgment. Either work with the actor to develop approaches that he is more comfortable with, or if you feel that the script is fine and the issue lies with the actor, you must work to get your actor around to feeling better about the part as written.

REHEARSING WITHOUT THE BOOK

When "going off the book," anxiety about remembering lines may temporarily disrupt the actors' flow in rehearsals. Should an actor keep saying he's unsure of the lines and must have the book just *one* more time, take the book away and ask him to improvise. It's more important in any case to play the meaning and spirit of the scene—lines can always be tightened later.

TURNING THOUGHT AND WILL INTO ACTION

From the first off-book rehearsals onward, encourage the cast to move as their character needs. Meaningful dialogue acts on the person addressed and energizes action in him. Actors and directors together develop the pressures within the characters that produce their physical and verbal action (that is, dialogue). Are your characters acting upon each other consistently? Track the psychic ebb and flow of each character's volition. It should be like watching a fencing match in slow motion in which swordsmen parry, thrust, retreat, and advance as they try to get past each other's defenses. This is the actors' responsibility, and the director's job is to spot and correct breakdowns.

Whenever a character's actions and words fail to grip or move you, something is probably lacking from the actor's understanding. Having to will yourself to understand or feel something is a sure symptom of a problem you need to solve.

Expect discussion and even disagreement over the nuances of motivation behind the action and dialogue. Occasionally you will have to rein in disagreement and decide what the cast must work with. This you try to do firmly and pleasantly. Disagreement need not be a subversion of your authority; it can be the heady, untidy excitements of discovery. The elements of each character are now important because their actions should build consistently from scene to scene.

A CHARACTER'S INNER MOVEMENT

There is, as Stanislavski said, no interior state without an outward expression, so you should demand fresh, subtle actions that manifest what each character is experiencing within, particularly at beats. When an actor loses contact with the inner life of his or her character, the symptoms are that he or she:

- Seems to have no credible thought process.
- Comes to life only when there is something to say.
- Goes fixed or blank while waiting for the next cue.
- May actually be visualizing the script page—certain death for movie acting.

You can shift an actor out of this mode by requesting an out-loud voicing of thoughts between lines, as in Chapter 22, Exercise TXT-3: "Improvising an Interior Monologue." This will dig out skewed understandings and expose why an actor loses focus.

REACTIONS

Only better actors can bring reaction shots alive, and that's because he or she is keeping their character imaginatively active. When an actor's reaction shots are clichéd and disappointing, help them change what they are doing within. Avoid having the script supervisor feed lines for reactions; try always to have the necessary actor off-screen.

MONITORING SUBTEXTS

Stretching your attention simultaneously among your needy cast is exhausting. Staying on top of what is being expressed subliminally is even more so. You can monitor subtexts in two ways: decide whether what you expect is present, or simply identify what arises. The latter is more fertile. When subtexts are off course, you'll have to question and redirect the actors concerned. By now they are both midwife and advocate for their characters, and developing what sustains the flux of their individual character's behavior and words. They will be sensitive to what doesn't work and needs changing. This you encourage with feedback while trying to deal even-handedly with the whole cast so nobody feels neglected.

CUING AND PACING

Your job is to set and maintain each scene's dynamics and pacing. In the theater, characters' lines can overlap, but for film scenes that will be constructed through editing (meaning, not single take scenes) lines must usually remain discrete. The editor can create desirable overlaps, but only if there are no overlaps during the shoot and if the general pacing supports it. With enough coverage (separate shots to intercut), the editor can smooth most ills, but cannot disentangle voices stacked in a shot nor change the basic line pacing. Comedy, for instance, usually needs to be a third faster than straight drama. Taping and editing rehearsals, to be described below, will show whether you're on target or not.

SPONTANEITY

A scene that seems to unfold spontaneously, without strain or anxiety, has crossed the threshold of credibility. The actors are now confident that the scene will always happen, and so can listen and watch each other without worrying about their lines. Now they have attention to spare, you can raise the stakes by asking them to move in particular ways. You can feel the intensity, spontaneity, and scene tension rising. It's a very satisfying feeling.

BLOCKING AND USING SPACE EXPRESSIVELY

How characters move through space is significant since space is territory, and territory denotes who's in command, who's advancing or losing ground, who is dominant and who is under threat, and so on. The space between people tells a lot about their intimacy, whether they feel threatening or threatened, and whether they are isolated or close.

Initially, you encouraged the cast to freely develop movement and action—where and when they moved arose from their characters' evolving needs. You assist this now by **blocking** the action, which means moving and positioning actors and camera in relationship to each other. With repeated work, this organic and experimental development settles into a tacitly agreed pattern of business and movement that expresses the characters' perceptions, thoughts, feelings, and will. Actors should be encouraged to make use of what's in each location, whether it is a kitchen, library, bike repair shop, or battlefield.

Keep in mind, rehearsals are only the beginning of the blocking process. During production both director and actors face the reality of the actual location space and the placement of production gear. Blocking is a process of mutual accommodation, and any component may change along the way. Lighting, microphone, or set restrictions all tend to dictate organic changes during shooting, so actors should become used to blocking remaining fluid and not fixed. Unless actors are used to this, they can find changes irritating or even threatening.

LOCATIONS, ENVIRONMENTS, AND RESEARCH

Once rehearsals go off book, it's good to try to rehearse at the actual locations—but in film, where locations are either rented by the day or being constructed and dressed during rehearsals, this is often impossible. Try to indicate important detail in the intended location in your rehearsal space. An advance visit can help you tape the rehearsal space floor with the positioning of walls and furniture. Showing actors pictures of locations, rooms, furnishings, costumes that you have in mind will give them distinct mental images that help set the atmosphere and trigger associative memories.

Plan research trips for your cast to observe the real places where the activities in your film take place. If you're doing a cop film, arrange to spend the day at a local police precinct. If your film takes place at a restaurant, try to obtain permission to observe the activity on an average night: on the floor with the waiting staff and host, in the kitchen with the cooks, and behind the bar with the bartender. Research helps actors imagine the kind of people they must become, and is beneficial to directors as well. For his 2010 film *Black Swan*, Darren Aronofsky not only interviewed ballet dancers, both working and inactive, about their experiences in the ballet world, but spent time backstage with the Bolshoi Ballet at the Lincoln Center to get a sense of what the activity and energy was like for an elite ballet troupe during a performance.[2] Lead actress Natalie Portman spent a solid year conditioning her body to look and move like a ballerina, and took classes and trained with professional ballerinas. Her award-winning performance reveals how all this paid off. Although a dance double performed the most difficult dance passages, Portman was able to execute many of the moves and to be utterly convincing in her role (Figure 21-2).

FIGURE 21-2

Thorough research by both actors and directors can yield informed, believable acting, as it did in Aronofsky's *Black Swan* with Natalie Portman.

---

[2] *'Black Swan' Director Darren Aronofsky on Ballet, Natalie Portman and Lesbian Kisses* by Eric Ditzian MTV News (August, 2010), (www.mtv.com/news/articles/1646763).

THE DIRECTOR AS ACTIVE OBSERVER

Now that interpreting the characters and developing their action are well advanced, it's time to plan their presentation on the screen. Habit makes you want to sit as you observe, but this is dangerous. Unconsciously, you have become a theatre goer who sits in a fixed seat; this will make you unconsciously choreograph the action for a static camera placement. To counteract this, stay on your feet during rehearsals, move around, and keep adjusting your viewing position. By looking for the Storyteller's best viewpoint for each phase of the scene, you are seeking the camera angles that best reveal it. Your cast will become accustomed to mobile observation and won't form the habit of relating to you as an audience in a known place. They are also more likely to play to and for each other—as things happen in real-life relationships. When it comes time to break the action into separate shots, it should all proceed with few conceptual problems.

FORM: SEEING IN AN UNFAMILIAR WAY

During rehearsals, you first occupied the position of the observer; now, assuming the active storytelling role, you are developing the Storyteller's POV. How the Storyteller must act on the audience gives you further ideas about how the story should be accentuated. Like an actor playing a part, you create a distinct Storyteller identity that is distinct from yourself. Your initial ideas came from interrogating the script: What exactly do the story and its times call for? Could it be a comic book style with brightly colored figures? A film noir shot at night in a rainy cityscape? Should the story take place in nightmarishly distorted spaces in the Expressionist style? Should it be fast-paced, or slow and shot in long takes? You answered all those larger questions, but further ideas keep coming as you take a larger view of the story's purpose.

SHOOTING REHEARSALS

Now the cast is off book and reasonably confident, cover rehearsals with a handheld video camera using an observational (or cinéma vérité) documentary style. You and your crew will benefit greatly from reviewing rehearsal coverage, but the cast should not see it (see below).

Instruct a competent camera operator (preferably your cinematographer) to shoot off-book rehearsals with a continuous take using a handheld camera, moving close for close-ups, and backing away, panning, or tracking as the action requires. You do not direct this camera, but stay focused on the cast. The camera treats the rehearsal as a spontaneous happening to be recorded without intervention. Its dailies need no editing because the camera takes pains to be in the right place at the right time. Making this record brings particular advantages. You and the crew can:

- Privately or together review rehearsals.
- Keep a check on running times. The actors' business makes scenes appear faster but they run longer in real time.
- Judge what works from seeing it on the screen.

- Get early warning of mannerisms, clichés, and trends, as well as subtleties that would otherwise appear only in dailies or postproduction.
- Cut together the best rehearsal takes and get a first glimpse of the entire movie.

During taping, the actors can:

- Move freely as their characters demand because the camera is so mobile and attentive.
- Know that the camera serves their process, and won't make them puppets by leading or controlling them.
- Get to know and trust key crew members.
- Become comfortable with the presence of the camera and open their actions to it instead of avoiding it, as sometimes happens when formal shooting starts.

While taping, the crew can:

- Seek each scene's optimal form in terms of camera angles, movement, lenses, lighting, and sound coverage.
- Discover how to cover action appropriately and efficiently.
- Anticipate sight lines and movements from the imperceptible signs each actor gives when he or she is about to move or speak.
- Begin asking for compromises in actors' speed or destination to overcome camera or microphone problems.

By the time formal shooting begins:

- The film benefits from being shot for the second, not the first time.
- Everyone is at ease with each other and their roles.
- Camera placements and movements are known, not theoretical.
- Shooting is based on a living reality, not the static, heroic concepts of the storyboard.
- Dealing with the unexpected is easier because everybody knows the foundations.

By documenting your rehearsals and evolving the camera coverage, you are rehearsing to capture elegantly in production what your cast produces.

DON'T SHOW ACTORS THEIR WORK

If the cast wants to see the taped rehearsals, tell them that in professional circles it's considered too destabilizing. You (but not necessarily your cast) should know that,

- Actors are normally appalled to see themselves on-screen, and this feeds their insecurities.
- Seeing themselves with the imagined judgment of other cast members makes it harder to stay inside their own character's thoughts and experiences.

- Actors who depended on your judgment may now apply their own corrective actions, giving you new problems.
- Untrusting actors—often those who think themselves superior—can begin to direct not only themselves but each other.

If your actors request to see the rehearsal videos, simply tell them the truth—that it's standard procedure in film work not to let actors see any footage before a late stage of editing because it is needlessly unsettling. Say you will show them their work in a fine cut later.

CHECK TIMINGS

As rehearsals proceed, keep a running check on scene timings. Everything looks shorter, but the timings usually reveal it's running longer. Stay poised to review, edit, or tighten pacing as you go. Axing material always seems impossible, but one shooting script in a thousand has already been pared to its working minimum. Taping rehearsals is another excellent way to spot the redundant— by cobbling together a trial movie.

A LONG JOURNEY

The piece will deepen and grow stronger as you and your cast stumble upon yet more meanings and interconnections. This continues long past the point where there seems nothing can be left to discover. With a little luck, you will have an exhilarating sense of shared discovery and closeness that everyone will recall nostalgically years later.

CHAPTER 22

ACTING EXERCISES

IMPROVISATION EXERCISES

Every director needs some firsthand experience of acting, and you can learn the basics most enjoyably by playing "improv" theater games—the subject of this chapter. For books, try John Hodgson and Ernest Richards' *Improvisation* (Grove Press, 1994) and Viola Spolin's *Improvisation for the Theater: A Handbook of Teaching and Directing Techniques,* 3rd ed. (Northwestern University Press, 1999). The latter text was integral to the founding of Second City, the Chicago improvisational school that spawned many actors, comedians, and directors.

Some film directors—notably Ingmar Bergman, John Cassavetes, Ken Loach, and Mike Leigh—use improvisation as a source for drama. Don't assume that this is any easier than working from a script, though. With improvised scenes entirely in the hands of the actors, pacing and development can be fascinating, uncertain, or maddening. Often the players circle a problem repeatedly and sometimes you'll see them, out of frustration or panic, force their character to manipulate a solution. The same can happen, albeit more subtly, when actors work from a text, so the thrills and spills you experience doing improv will set you up to understand all acted situations.

Most exciting is to see that anyone can act—anyone at all—once the armor is laid aside and the actor feels free to play. Do some acting yourself, and directing others becomes a matter of diligently and empathically spotting the keys that unlock each individual's difficulties. The exercises in this chapter establish that:

- Learning that is embedded in shared experience is something you never forget.
- The few major acting principles take repetition to absorb.
- You can't think ahead in improv, so it's very scary at first.
- Players learn to adapt (that is, adjust in a lifelike way to unforeseen obstacles), to take the initiative, and through communion become an ensemble.
- Everything can go hilariously wrong, so people learn without humiliation.
- Like jazz, everyone knows when a piece is "cooking."
- Courageous failures are really successes.

ACTING AND DOING

Acting has a solidly practical theory behind it, but it's something you can only learn through doing, for it requires insight, much concentration, and a certain amount of courage. Wear loose, comfortable clothing that you don't mind getting dirty. Change partners from exercise to exercise so you work with unfamiliar people. Try to play people whose characters, ages, and circumstances are well removed from your own. From improv, expect to learn:

- What it feels like to be closely watched
- What trust or distrust from other actors feels like
- How liberating it is to be silly and enjoy it
- Common hang-ups and situations that actors get into
- What being manipulated by another actor feels like (see below, "Acting Exercises with a Text")
- That the actor who seizes control is as insecure as the one who relinquishes it
- That each actor either acts on others or cedes his character's share of input
- That improvs often get stuck, and the actors have to unstick the piece so it can develop
- That each actor must seize opportunities the other actors make available
- That acting with people you trust takes away competitiveness and insecurity
- That failure is the pathway to success
- That anybody can deal with the unexpected once they can relax
- That you feel great getting a round of applause after taking risks
- That everyone works for recognition.

THE DIRECTOR'S ROLE DURING IMPROVS

Directing an improv may seem like a contradiction in terms, but the director is really the surrogate for an audience. Most of these exercises need nothing beyond your initial explanation and seeing that the actors understand and keep to the ground rules. The more advanced exercises need a director to select and coordinate cast ideas and take spot decisions, or the piece won't start and stop in a timely way. All exercises will benefit from your feedback so the cast can work on specific problems in subsequent versions.

Good directors know a lot about acting and about each actor in their cast. They learn to sense when an individual isn't living up to potential and how to help them eliminate the blockages. From directing improvs, you can expect to discover:

- How clearly you communicate and how you need to improve
- How each actor needs his own kind of communication

- What it feels like when an actor doesn't trust your judgment or challenges you
- How much actors depend on your feedback in their work
- How actors either accept or avoid responsibility in a scene
- How to challenge a passive actor into becoming an active one
- How to start an interior monologue in an actor whose character lacks interior life
- How divisive personalities function and how to avoid being manipulated by one
- How each actor has limiting habits, mannerisms, and patterns
- What a director can do when actors think they are at their limit
- How guilty you feel when actors give their best and you don't like what you see
- How best to earn the trust of actors and crew (each director does this differently)
- How it feels to take someone over a threshold, and how good you both feel.

DISCERNING BEATS AND DRAMATIC UNITS

The director's major responsibility is to understand the characters' development and changes in relation to the expectations of an improvisation or text. Throughout the upcoming exercises, you should work hard at seeing beats—whether actual or latent. Beats, you'll recall, are those special moments when characters change consciousness after working toward a goal. To further refresh your understanding, see "Beats" in Chapter 3, but you can go beat-spotting wherever people are trying to do something. Standing in a post-office line, you can spot the beats while a clerk and a foreign customer negotiate the postal rate for a parcel. Beats are the respiration of life; they are everywhere.

THE ACTOR'S ROLE DURING IMPROVS

Most of all, have fun and enjoy flying by the seat of your pants. The allure of acting is the call to live dangerously and completely, with nothing held back, and to get audience recognition for it. Most actors are shy people who took up acting in order to make major changes in their lives. Your time has come!

MAKE YOUR AUDIENCE SEE

Use no props; instead, use your imagination to "see" your surroundings and the things you handle. Do it with complete conviction, and your audience will see, believe, and be captivated. Once, while serving in the Air Force during my youth, I sat up in bed, hardly out of a dream I'd been having, and pointed across the barrack. "What's the matter?" those present asked a little nervously. "A spaceship, over there, on the wall," I said with complete belief. They all turned to see it. Afterward, they told me that for a few moments they had been scared and completely believed me. To see is to make others see too.

STAYING FOCUSED

The biggest initial challenge will be to achieve and maintain focus; that is, to:

- Think your character's thoughts.
- See your character's physical and mental images.
- Experience your character's feelings as they spontaneously happen.
- See and hear the other characters and react to what they are giving you, here and now.

Improvisation constantly faces the actor with surprises, so you are repeatedly flushed out of your hiding places. It need never cause you to lose focus and fall out of character.

AUDIENCE ETIQUETTE AND IMPROV DURATION

In a class or shooting situation alike, there is always an audience of sorts. Etiquette demands that crew and onlookers be absolutely still and silent, avoid eye contact with the players, yet contribute every iota of their attention in respectful support of the players. Each person in any ensemble supports and appreciates the others, particularly when it involves pushing limits. Either the instructor can call, "Cut!" or, as confidence develops, audience members give a show of hands as they feel that a piece has run its course. From this, actors get used to satisfying audience demands, and student directors can see how closely their judgments parallel those of an audience. To stop a piece by common accord is to go to work immediately on its problems.

ASSESSMENT AND DISCUSSION

During an exercise, a director looks for the combination of spontaneity and intensity that comes when actors fully accept the demands of their role. Reward improv actors with a round of applause at the end of the piece, and follow with brief and concentrated assessment. Here are suggested discussion points, but don't hesitate to follow the natural train of conversation. During feedback:

- Describe what was communicated, avoiding all "good" and "bad" valuations.
- Avoid intellectualizing. Academic discussion drains momentum.
- Describe what stages the piece went through (its structure).
- Say what each stage made you feel (what it delivered).
- Say what particularly struck you (impact), being as specific as possible.

Listen attentively to feedback and don't argue or justify what you did. Learn from your audience.

IMPROV EXERCISES AND EXERCISES WITH A TEXT

The acting exercises in this chapter suggest that all acting takes place between two people, but of course it's equally likely that an actor acts alone or in a large group. Allowing for this range would produce unreadable English, so I have treated the duo as the standard. The theater games that follow, both improv and with a text, are terrific for building skills, and each is described by purpose, activity, and discussion. Sometimes they incorporate a degree of premeditated structure, and sometimes the actor has no prior guidelines. Some exercises also make useful tools when actors get hung up during rehearsal or shooting. In alphabetical order, the main acting principles explored by the improvisation (IMP) exercises are as follows:

IMPROV EXERCISES: IMP-1 THROUGH IMP-20

Action, maintaining while speaking	IMP-11
Adaptation	IMP-5, IMP-12, IMP-16, IMP-17
Communion	IMP-5
Conflict, inner	IMP-19
Conflict, working with	IMP-8
Emotion, developing toward an	IMP-14
Emotion, sublimating	IMP-20
Emotions, bridging between two	IMP-15
Ensemble, creating within an	IMP-13
Focus	IMP-1
Givens, developing character from	IMP-6, IMP-10
Imagination	IMP-2
Inner life	IMP-7
Interior monologue	IMP-18
Observation	IMP-5
Partnership equality	IMP-4
Subtext	IMP-7
Tactile defensiveness	IMP-4
Trust	IMP-3, IMP-4
Voice and body as expressive instruments	IMP-9

Exercise IMP-1: See or be Seen

Purpose Explore the idea of focus as an antidote to self-consciousness. This exercise lets everyone experience just how disturbing it is to have someone watching you when your mind is susceptible to self-consciousness.

Activity Half the class is the audience and remains seated. The other half, the performers, stand in a row facing the audience looking above their heads. Audience members carefully study the faces and body language of the performers.

- The instructor tells the performers to empty their minds and concentrate on simply being themselves.
- After a minute or two, the instructor tells the performers to mentally visualize a room they know well and everything in it.
- After another minute or two, the instructor tells the audience and performers to switch roles and repeats Steps 1 and 2 with the other half of the class.

Discussion

1. Performers: How did it feel to focus on "being yourself"?

2. Audience: How did the performers' feelings show in their behavior and appearance?

3. Audience: What did you see when the performers switched from "being themselves" to visualizing?

4. Performers: What kinds of work can an actor legitimately undertake to avoid feeling self-conscious?

Exercise IMP-2: Domestic Appliance

Purpose   To become in spirit something you are not.

Activity   Study a domestic appliance in its full range of action. In class, announce what you have been assigned to do, then give a full impersonation using your whole body and vocalized sound effects. Try to convey the appliance's spirit as well as its shape, actions, and sounds. The class should choose something for the instructor, who breaks the ice by going first (more than once, I have been asked to become a flushing toilet). It is quite normal to feel foolish and painfully self-conscious. Use what you learned from Exercise IMP-1 to maintain focus.

Examples that can be assigned:

• Coffee percolator	• Washing machine cycling	• Garbage disposal
• Overfilled garbage bag removed	• Upright vacuum cleaner	• Rusty door lock
• Toilet flushing	• Toothbrush at work	• Steam iron
• Cold car engine that will not start	• Electric toaster	• Photocopier
• Electric can opener	• Nutcracker	• Blender with lumps
• Tomato sauce pouring	• Honey pouring	• Clock radio coming on
• Rubber plunger opening drain	• Coffee grinder	• Cell phone on vibrate
• Dripping faucet	• Corkscrew	• Knife chopping onions

Discussion

1. When and why was the actor self-conscious?

2. Where in his or her body could you locate tension from self-consciousness?

3. Did he or she get into focus, and if so, when?

4. Which part of the impersonation made you see the real thing?

Exercise IMP-3: Flying Blind

Purpose   Exploring trust and choosing to be dependent.

Activity   The rehearsal space is made into a disordered jumble of obstacles. Divide into pairs. One person is blindfolded and disoriented by spinning him several times. He now walks as fast as he dares—with his partner not touching him, but whispering instructions on which way to move. As a variation, the seeing partner can guide through touch. After a few minutes, switch roles on the instructor's command.

Discussion
1. Actor: How did it feel to be so utterly dependent on another person?
2. Who mostly took the initiative?
3. Instructor/audience: What did body language tell you about different people's reactions to dependency?

Exercise IMP-4: "Timber!"

Purpose Explore trust, equal partnership, and tactile defensiveness.

Activity Using pairs (same sex or different), one person is a piece of timber, and the other must try to balance the timber upright. You can use any part of your body—*but not your hands*—to catch and steady the falling timber. After a few minutes, swap roles on command. In any acting situation, each must share control equally, being ready to "catch" a partner or be caught, yet neither taking more than momentary initiative. Neither player should fall into a habitually dominant or a submissive acting relationship. This is good for breaking habitual boundaries since actors must be able to make physical contact—and even play love scenes—with people they may neither know nor find attractive.

Discussion
1. What were your thoughts and feelings, being in bodily contact with someone you do not know well?
2. How free and true to gravity was the timber? (How much did he or she protect the two of you by making it easier?)
3. How willing was the timber: To trust you to catch him or her? To fall backward and stay rigid?
4. Did one partner tend to control the situation?

Exercise IMP-5: Mirror Images

Purpose Close observation and moment-to-moment adaptation without anticipating.

Activity You arrive at the bathroom mirror, come close to its surface, and go through your morning routine. Your partner is your image in the mirror, doing everything you do but inverted as a mirror image inverts. Swap roles after a few minutes.

Discussion

1. How successful was the mirror at replicating the actions, without anticipating or lagging?

2. Did the person and image each stay in character?

3. How frank and complete was the person's routine? Who took risks and was therefore self-revealing?

Exercise IMP-6: Who, What, When, and Where?

Purpose   Immediate character and situation development from givens and without props.

Activity   Instructor designates an actor, then asks successive people to supply a who, what, when, and where. The actor then carries out some appropriate action, in character, for a minute or two. The instructor calls "Cut!" when the action is long enough or if development levels off. The class reports what it saw happening and what was communicated. The actor then says briefly what he or she intended. Example:

Who [is present]? Mary Jo Sorensen, 35

Where [is she]? In an airport lounge

When [is this]? Christmas Eve, late at night

What [is happening]? She is waiting for her parents and must tell them she has lost her job.

Discussion

1. What seemed to be going on inside the character?

2. What was convincing, and what sounded false notes?

3. What intentions did not come across as natural?

4. Did the actor carry out all of the assignment?

5. Did he or she remember to interact with the environment?

6. Was there a significant change or development?

Note: From this exercise onward, each class member can vote by silently raising their hands. The director stops the piece when enough of the audience thinks the dramatic development is past its peak.

Exercise IMP-7: Solo, No Words

Purpose   Use unremarkable, everyday action to communicate something of the inner thoughts and feelings of a character whose life is quite unlike that of the actor.

Activity   From an action (the *what*) and using no props, invent a *who*, *where*, and *when* to sustain your character sketch for three minutes. An actor must be able to carry out everyday actions and make them interesting, so avoid storytelling or high drama.

Suggestions
- Alone in someone's house (whose?), where you explore: (a) the refrigerator, (b) the owner's bedroom
- Unwrapping a long-awaited parcel
- Waiting in the dentist's office
- Trying on a new article of clothing
- Taking medicine
- Wrapping a gift
- Cleaning shoes
- Watching something (what?) out the window
- Finding a box of your childhood toys you haven't seen for many years
- Overhearing an interesting conversation in a store
- Caring for a pet
- Taking a bike out after the winter
- Cleaning out your parents' attic
- Waiting for a phone call
- Dividing up the laundry
- Watching a sport

Discussion
1. In a particular performance, what was interesting, and what did it make you see?
2. Could you see not only the character, but also the environment?
3. When did the player break focus and why?

Exercise IMP-8: Duo, No Words

Purpose To communicate through interaction something of the inner thoughts and feelings of two characters, using an everyday action that involves some element of conflict.

Activity From an action (the *what*) and using no props, invent a *who*, *where*, and *when* to sustain your character sketch. Avoid storytelling or high drama, and use action with minimal or no dialogue. Try these:
- Handing a newborn baby to the mother and back again
- Playing pinball
- Making a double bed
- Putting up a tent

- Buying a forbidden magazine
- Photographing a model
- Maneuvring heavy furniture through a doorway
- Washing the best dishes after a special meal
- Carrying a heavy garbage bag
- Washing a child's hair
- Pulling a sliver out of a finger
- Watching a TV show: one likes it; the other doesn't
- Waiting in a doorway for a heavy rainstorm to ease
- Inspecting car damage after a fender bender

Discussion Did the actors create:
1. Two distinct character identities (*who*)?
2. A believable and recognizable environment—country, area, city, place, or room—and use it (*where*)?
3. A distinctive period and time of day (*when*)?
4. A believable tension?
5. A situation in which speech was not called for?
6. An interaction in which neither was controlling the overall movement of the sketch?
7. Did you see communion and adaptation?

Exercise IMP-9: Gibberish

Purpose Using the voice as an expressive nonverbal instrument and using one's body and voice quality as tools of communication. Too often, actors with lines to speak cease to act with the whole body. This exercise simulates speech, but de-emphasizes verbal meaning in favor of underlying intention.

Activity Using the examples in Exercise IMP-8, carry out an activity with a conflict, using gibberish as the characters' language.

Discussion As in Exercise IMP-8
1. How did the actors handle the gibberish conversations?
2. Did they become natural?

Exercise IMP-10: Solo, with Words

Purpose To create a character, employing *who, where, when,* and *what*, and using both actions and speech.

Activity   In creating your character, remember to develop him or her through actions. Do not sit still and rely on a monologue. Here are some suggestions:
- A difficult phone conversation (maybe with a defective cell phone!)
- Reconstructing a painful conversation
- Writing the opening remarks of an important speech
- Rehearsing in front of the bathroom mirror for a traffic court appearance
- Getting ready to tell someone of your betrayal or infidelity
- Working up to approaching your boss for a raise
- Rehearsing the way you will evict a needy relative who came for a short visit and has long overstayed
- Explaining to your employer why you must start a new job in a gorilla costume
- Your head is stuck between the railings enclosing a war memorial. Someone has gone to call the fire department, and you are trying to figure out an explanation
- A practical joke has misfired, and you must calm the irate victim

Discussion   Did the actor:
1. Create a believable character?
2. Keep up a developing action?
3. Make the situation develop?
4. Make you see all the physical objects and surroundings?

Exercise IMP-11: Duo, with Words

Purpose   To maintain conversation and a developing action at the same time.

Activity   Each of these sketches requires both a conversation and accompanying physical action, which should be purposeful. Do not take it too fast, and don't feel you must keep talking all the time. Examples to try:
- Demonstrating a kitchen appliance to a family member
- Washing the best dishes after a special meal
- Eating a meal and discussing a prearranged topic
- Asking for some money that you are owed
- Maneuvring heavy furniture through a doorway
- Showing someone they have not done a good job
- Discussing your son's or daughter's rotten grades
- Teaching a friend to drive
- Asking for something embarrassing from a pharmacist
- Teaching someone a dance step

Discussion   Did they:

1. Keep both topic and actions going?
2. Keep the physical world they created consistent?
3. Listen to and work off each other?
4. Share the initiative equally?
5. Allow the piece to develop spontaneously?
6. Develop interesting characters?

Exercise IMP-12: Make your Own Character

Purpose   To place the actor, as a character, in the hands of the audience.

Activity   Go before the class, in an item or two of costume, as a character based on someone you know who made a powerful impression on you. The class finds out about you by asking questions that probe your identity and values, to which you answer in character. Each character should be onstage for about 10 minutes, and two or three performances per session is the maximum—the interaction can be very intense.

Discussion   Undertaken sincerely, this exercise can be really magical, a powerful exercise in portrayal that tells much about the actor's values and influences. There may be little need for discussion if the exercise goes well. Play it by ear.

Exercise IMP-13: Ensemble Situations

Purpose   To engage the whole group in a collective creation.

Activity   In these situations individual characters contribute to a whole. The *where* and *when* must be agreed on beforehand. The aim is to keep up your character while contributing to the development of the piece. Sample situations:

- A tug-of-war
- Dealing with an obstreperous drunk
- Someone is hurt in the street
- A person faints in a crowded train
- Surprise party
- Party is interrupted by protesting neighbor
- Bus driver stops bus because a passenger refuses to pay
- Airline clerk announces delay to irate passengers
- Lone cop tries to arrest person at demonstration; crowd argues
- Teacher tries to calm down classroom of first graders

Discussion
1. How many subordinate actions were going on during the main action?
2. Did everyone stay in character? (The temptation is to lose focus unless you are important.)
3. How did the piece develop?
4. What compromises did people make to sustain the whole?

Exercise IMP-14: Developing an Emotion

Purpose Two or more actors are asked to improvise a scene culminating in a given emotion in one or more of the characters.

Activity Try this exercise only after the class has developed considerable rapport and experience. The players must invent characters and a situation, then develop it to the point where the specified emotion is reached. The class can stop the sketch when the emotion is reached or if the piece is not going anywhere. Emotions one character might feel include Anger, Suspicion, Sympathy, Relief, Jealousy, Condescension, Rejection, Love, Regret, Disbelief, Friendliness, Release, Superiority, Inferiority, Empathy.

Discussion This asks that actors build to a known conclusion, and it's very tempting to escape by manipulating the situation. All the prior criteria apply, but important considerations here are:
1. Was the interaction credible?
2. Did it arrive at the specified emotion?
3. If not, why not?
4. Was the development even or uneven?
5. Was the initiative shared equally?

Exercise IMP-15: Bridging Emotions

Purpose To make a credible change from one emotion to another.

Activity Same as Exercise IMP-14, except that the players start in the middle of one emotion and find their way to the next. Start with two emotions, and then, if you want to make it truly challenging, specify three.

Discussion Same as Exercise IMP-14

Exercise IMP-16: Surfing the Channels

Purpose To involve a group in immediate and unpremeditated invention.

Activity Divide the class into players and audience. The audience is watching a TV program; the players are actors in TV shows. When the designated situation ("facing death," say) is running out of steam, an audience member may seize the "remote" and "change the channel," announcing what the new program is. The players must now develop "facing death" in the new program format, until someone changes the channel again. After a while, students swap roles. Suggested situations:

- Persuasion
- Confronting authority
- Trapped
- Avoiding commitment
- Returning home
- A life-changing interview
- Facing death
- Cheating on a friend

Discussion

1. How inventive were the players?
2. How authentic were the situations compared to actual TV programs?
3. How quickly were the players and the audience able to make the change?
4. How equally were roles distributed?
5. Did some actors fall into controlling or passive roles?

Exercise IMP-17: Video Convention

Purpose Same as Exercise IMP-16.

Activity Same ideas as Exercise IMP-16, except that the situation is a huge video dealer's convention offering unsold video programs at deep discounts. The audience is composed of potential buyers at a stand where everything imaginable on video is on sale. These are unsold, third-rate, and full of genre clichés. When the audience votes to see a new sample, the director calls out the title of the new video:

- Do-it-yourself kitchen rehab
- Nature films
- 1950s comedies
- Slasher films
- Biology lessons
- Sales motivation
- Teen romances
- Beauty procedures for people over 50

Discussion   Similar to Exercise IMP-16. Accent is on spontaneity and speed of adaptation. Did the cast contribute equally?

Exercise IMP-18: Blind Date

Purpose   To work with interior monologue. This exercise takes great concentration from all concerned, but is a lot of fun. It shows what happens when an actor takes time to listen to his character's interior voices. Listening to those voices consistently brings a new richness and ambiguity to any part. Remember, *the real action of any part is the interior action* going on behind the character's outward words and physical actions.

Activity   A man and a woman have been set up by friends on a blind date. They meet in a bar and discuss how to spend the evening together. Each of Character A's conflicting personality traits are voiced by several class members who sit behind him playing his thoughts (see suggested list below). As the conversation between the couple slowly proceeds, each of the thoughts-voices chimes in, speaking its biased reaction or tendentious thought. Character A listens to his or her "thoughts," and chooses one to act on. Character B, who cannot hear the voices, reacts only to whatever Character A says or does. Character A may initially get a chorus of "inner voices," or there may initially be none. The voices may overlap and argue with each other. Character A should remain in character and take all the time needed to assess and react to them, while B waits as though nothing is amiss. The personality traits (with a voice for each) could include any four of:

- The need to be liked
- The need to be unique
- Fear of rejection
- Fear of being manipulated
- Worry about expense
- Guilt (feeling bad about something you've done)
- Shame (feeling bad about who you are)
- The need to make a conquest
- The need to be normal
- Pride

Discussion
1. How did Character A handle all the input?
2. What were his or her most noticeable influences?
3. Where did Character A break character?
4. Did Character B provide a good foil?
5. What were the most interesting and convincing interior actions?

Variation   Characters A and B go through the scene again, but this time Character A imagines the interior voices for himself instead of hearing them. Usually the scene becomes strikingly different, and shows what riches true inner conflict brings to an actor's work.

Exercise IMP-19: Inner Conflict

This exercise was inspired by Richard Nixon's famous "I am not a crook" speech.

Purpose   To portray a character's contradictory tensions, but never directly reveal them.

Activity   The character is anyone prominent in the news who wishes to be correctly understood. He or she begins with the sentence, "Because I think you may have the wrong idea about me, I'm going to tell you what most people don't know." After the character has spoken for a while, the audience, playing journalists, ask pointed questions.

Discussion
1.   When was the character sincere? When was he or she contrived?
2.   When was he/she suppressing the truth?
3.   How did you know?
4.   What was interesting? What was less so?

Exercise IMP-20: Thrown Together

Purpose   To explore the idea that in life we seldom express what really weighs on our minds; instead, we sublimate our unsolved issues through the situation at hand.

Activity   Put two incompatible characters together in a credible work situation. Each follows his or her usual agenda in relating to other people. The actors should take the time to keep up an interior (and silent) monologue. No issues are ever named; the needs and reactions of the characters must be expressed through the work they are doing together. Whether they finally get along or find mutual accommodation should not be predetermined.

Discussion
1.   Did each character develop?
2.   Did each find a way to play out his or her issues through their work?
3.   Did each choose a credible path?
4.   Did they stay in focus and in character?
5.   Did they find a believable way of cooperating?
6.   Did you believe the outcome?

7. Did either or both find satisfaction, and did one "win"?

8. What was the obligatory moment in the scene, and what made it so?

Variations   Play the scene again, this time with each actor adding his or her character's thoughts in an undertone. Then play the scene as before, with silent, interior monologues.

Discussion   Did having to improvise thoughts change or improve the scene? Can you see using this method to solve a problem in a scripted scene?

ACTING EXERCISES WITH TEXT: TXT-1 THROUGH TXT-10

These exercises, which develop important skills at interpreting texts, are intended to be applied to your rehearsals *after* you've done the initial dramatic beats breakdown (see p. 249).

Each exercise can serve as a resource to help solve common problems during rehearsal or production. Its "medicine chest" utility is provided under the heading "Useful when." In alphabetical order, the main acting principles explored by the exercises with text (TXT) are as follows:

Actors' intrinsic characteristics, using	TXT-1
Beats	TXT-2
Beats, action at	TXT-5
Beats, characterizing	TXT-4
Character's inner life, spot-check for	TXT-8, TXT-3
Dramatic units	TXT-2
Emotions, overconstrained	TXT-6
Improvisation, translating scene into	TXT-10
Indicating	TXT-7
Interior monologue	TXT-3, TXT-8
Isolation, acting in	TXT-9
Textual analysis	TXT-2

Exercise TXT-1: What the Actors Bring

Useful When   The director wants to make thorough use of what each individual cast member brings.

Purpose   To make decisions about the special qualities and characteristics of the actors for use in your thematic interpretation.

Activity   After the read-through:
1.   Make private notes capturing the intrinsic quality of each actor. This, for example, concerns an actor called Dale:

Dale has a slow, quiet, repressed quality that masks a certain pain and bitterness. He is watchful, highly intelligent, intense, and his first reaction is often a protective cynicism; really, it matters to him very much that he be liked. He reminds me of a stray cat, hungry and cold but cornered and defiant.

2.   Develop ideas about how the actors' qualities can legitimately be used to polarize the performances, and how this will affect your thematic interpretation of the piece. For example:

Dale has the quality of honorable victimhood, and this stacks the cards interestingly against the father, who we assume has practiced subtle or overt violence against his son in the distant past, without Dale's mother caring to know.

Exercise TXT-2: Marking Beats in a Text

Useful When   An actor fails to analyze a text satisfactorily.

Purpose   To fully understand how the script functions and how to act it by locating the fulcrum points of emotional change, the beats (see "Scene Breakdown Sessions" (p. 249) and review "The Dramatic Units" in Chapter 4). Beats and dramatic units will also be important to your mise-en-scène (the combination of acting, blocking, camera placement, and editing that produces the dramatic image on film).

Activity   Director and actors should separately study the scene looking for the beats. These are primarily the actor's concern, whereas dramatic units are mostly the director's. A beat may be triggered by dialogue, an action, or incoming information such as a phone call. There may be one beat, or there may be several in a scene. All may belong to both characters or to only one, who may or may not be conscious of shifts in the other. The audience should be able to detect any important changes.

Discussion   In rehearsal, agree where the beats are and what causes them.

Exercise TXT-3: Improvising an Interior Monologue

When an actor says he's got an interior monologue going, but his performance lacks evidence of it, ask for an out-loud inner monologue as a sure way to upgrade a so-so performance. Because it supplies a repeatable interior process, the inner monologue also helps stabilize a performance's timing. This is work that actors may evade or forget, but the mere possibility that you may ask for an out-loud version in front of other actors usually keeps them working at it.

Useful When   A text refuses to come alive, and you need a powerful method of getting actors to externalize their understanding. Also good in rehearsal for unlocking intransigent trouble spots. Usually the problem lies with the actor's understanding, but sometimes it's with the writing itself.

Activity   At a troublesome part of the text, have your actors improvise their characters' interior monologues. Ask them to use a full voice for the "out-loud" line, and a soft voice for the "thoughts voice," or interior monologue. The cast may find this hard or baffling at first, and the scene will go at a snail's pace. But having to create publicly and on the spot always yields deeper understandings, and a high degree of commitment is unavoidable.

Discussion
1. Do the inner monologues show that your actors are on the same wavelength?
2. What did you (the director) learn from the actors?
3. What did you learn about your actors?
4. What do you think your actors learned about you and your approach?

Exercise TXT-4: Characterizing the Beats

Useful When   You need to clarify and energize a scene or a passage that is muddy and lifeless.

Purpose   To give each dramatic unit and its beats a clear intention and identity, which in turn sharpens each beat and fulcrum point. Also, to focus attention on subtext and on the actor's body language, movement, and voice range.

Activity
1. Ask the actors for their taglines for the steps leading toward each beat. Make sure each tag expresses volition. (Examples: "Leave me alone!"; "I need you to notice me"; "You're not going to hoodwink me again.") Correct any tag that is not in the active voice ("Let me go to sleep"—not, "I am being kept awake") so it expresses active will even when the character is being victimized. Each tagline should contain an element of "I want."
2. The actors play the actions and movements of the scene, but speak only the tags as their dialogue. A character may have to say, "I need you to notice me" half a dozen times, developing the possibilities of the tag through bodily action and intonation, so they ramp up to the angry or desperate beat point. Where the text relied on verbal logic, they can now only use action, voice, and body as instruments of will. Shifting from verbal to physical and emotional expressiveness causes interesting developments in the actors' range of expression, with a corresponding increase in power.
3. Now have the actors play the scene as scripted, keeping the body and vocal expression developed previously—and marvel at the difference.

Discussion   What did you learn:
1. About the actors from the movements they used this time?
2. About how they extended their emotional range?
3. About their communion once the exercise had forced it into continuous existence?

Exercise TXT-5: Actions at Beat Points

Useful When   A scene seems monotonous, wordy, and cerebral, and actors are playing the scene "in general," that is, with intellectually correct but generally applied ideas. An actor must build their scene from behaviorally authentic blocks, each made of a single, clearly defined emotion in a sequence of human striving. A scene in which one character shows several emotions will be effective only if he or she builds each separately and sequentially.

Purpose   To focus and physicalize the beats, and differentiate the behavioral phases of the scene. This technique shines a spotlight on turning points.

Activity   When the beat points are located and tagged, ask the actors to devise several possible actions for their character at each beat, or change of awareness. When actors invent from their own emotional range, the action becomes authentic to both actor and character. Actions can start out multiple and exaggerated so the director and actor can locate which feels best, then focus it at an agreed level of subtlety.

Discussion
1. Could you see what is at stake for each character at each beat?
2. How much interpretational leeway is there at important beats?
3. What is the range of options in terms of behavior that could be appropriate?
4. Of the range presented, did the director choose the most telling? If not, why not?

Exercise TXT-6: Give Me Too Much!

Useful When   One or more of your actors is constrained, and the scene is stuck in low gear.

Purpose   To release actors temporarily from restrictive judgments they are imposing and give them permission to overact.

Activity   Tell the actors that you feel the scene is bottled up, and you want them to reach for the same emotions but exaggerate them. Exaggeration gives actors permission to go to emotional limits they fear would look absurd.

Discussion   You can now tell your cast what to change and at what new levels to pitch their energy and emotions. Often exaggeration alone clears a blockade. When actors switch from dabbling fearfully in the shallows to leaping with abandon off the top diving board, they often find they can let go of a specific fear and do the elegant dive.

Exercise TXT-7: Let's Be British

Useful When   A scene has become over-projected, artificial, and out of hand. Actors are indicating like crazy, and now feel that the scene is jinxed and will never work.

Purpose   To return the actors to playing from character instead of striving for effect.

Activity   Ask your actors to play the scene in a monotone, with emotion barely evident, but fully experiencing their character's bottled-up reality underneath the reticence.

Discussion
1.   Did a scene that had turned into sound and fury return to basics?
2.   Did repressing emotions heighten them?
3.   How did the actors feel about it?

Exercise TXT-8: Spot-Check

Useful When   A line or an action repeatedly fails to ring true.

Purpose   To probe an actor's process at a particular moment. This exercise is like a breathalyzer test, jolting the actors into keeping up the inner lives of their characters for fear you will pull them over. Use sparingly.

Activity   Simply stop a reading or an off-book rehearsal at the problem point, and ask each actor what his or her character's thoughts, fears, and mental images were at that moment.

Discussion
1.   Did this flush out a misconception?
2.   Was the actor making a forced emotional connection?
3.   Did the actors' concentration change afterward?
4.   What other effects did this exercise produce?

Exercise TXT-9: Switching Characters

Useful When   Two actors seem stalemated and unaware of each other. This can arise when a defensive actor's over-preparation precludes communion, or when actors distrust or feel incompatible with each other.

Purpose   To place each actor temporarily in the opposite role so later he or she can empathize with another character's predicament and achieve an interesting duality.

Activity   Simply ask actors to exchange parts, without regard for sex, age, or anything else. Then have them return to their own parts to see if the reading changes.

Discussion
1.   Actors: Say briefly what you discovered about the scene from playing the other role.
2.   Actors: What revelations did you have about your own part?
3.   Director: What did you notice after the actors resumed their own parts?

Exercise TXT-10: Translating a Scene into an Improvisation

Useful When   The cast seems tired and unable to generate emotions the scene calls for. Keep improv scenes up your sleeve for any scene that may give trouble. Actors may initially resist your request, but they usually come to enjoy the refreshment after a scene has turned oppressive and immobile. Most will be impressed when you whisk out an alternative approach like this. This exercise can also release the malaise built up from repeated failures with the formal text.

Activity   Take the main issue in the scene, or the one causing a problem, and translate it into two or three analogous scene subjects for improvisation. If, for example, you are having trouble in a scene of conflict between a daughter and her suspicious and restrictive father, you might assign analogous improvs on:

- A scene between an officious nurse and a patient who wants to leave the hospital
- A bus driver and a rider who wants to get off the bus before the next stop
- Two customers in a long supermarket checkout line, one of whom, having only two items, wants to cut into the line

Each of these situations has a built-in conflict hinging on rights and authority, and tackling them rapidly one after another will generate a wider emotional vocabulary that will flow back into the original scene. A variation on this is to let the actors themselves invent analogous scenes. Further mileage is available by doing the improvs again with roles reversed.

Discussion
1. Which improv worked best?
2. What came of switching roles?
3. What were the differences when the cast returned to the text?

CHAPTER 23

PLANNING THE VISUAL DESIGN

Conceiving a film's visual design begins when you first analyze the screenplay and start imagining your film's aesthetic and visual style. During preproduction the director is tremendously busy: while you develop dramatic content and logic with your actors in rehearsals, you are also working with the principal creative crew at developing the film's visual design. This means deciding in detail for every scene the style and look of the settings, lighting, and camerawork.

We explored the broad aesthetic principles of naturalistic or stylistic approaches in Part 4: *Authorship and Aesthetics*, and now concepts must be turned into the practical. To precisely create an expressive and coherent visual world, the crew needs specific visual choices and instructions. Your principal collaborators are the **production designer** (sometimes called the **art director**) and the **director of photography** (**D.P.**, also called **cinematographer**). The production designer as head of the **art department** is responsible for creating the look of the physical environment where your scenes take place. This includes the visual qualities of the locations and sets, set dressing (furniture, wall coverings, ornaments, colors, etc.), **properties** (or **props**, objects handled by the actors) costumes and make-up. The **cinematographer** as head of the camera department is responsible for the photographic look of the film, which includes designing the lighting, compositions and camera angles, and choosing the shooting format, lenses, exposures, and focus.

Together, these principal creative collaborators help the director turn the visual interpretation of the script into a motion picture. All the visual details under their respective areas make up the mise-en-scène of every shot in your film, and therefore make a profound impact on the tone, mood, characterizations, and ultimately the meaning of your movie (see Chapter 12).

The production designer and cinematographer, who started planning the look of a film from first reading the script, aim for a design that is visually eloquent about the script's characters, settings, predicaments, and moods. This involves designing a complete world with all its characters, costumes, settings, furniture, properties, and lighting and color schemes.

VISUAL DESIGN QUESTIONNAIRE

The process starts with broad questions about what aesthetic qualities the screenplay and the director's interpretation suggests (tone, mood, era, and so on) and then, as refinement, moves into a scene-by-scene visual analysis. Here are questions to ponder when you meet with your production designer and cinematographer:

- What is the film's premise and its theme(s)?
- What are its mood progressions?
- What genre does the film fall into?
- Who are its characters (age, economic status, occupation, living situation, self-presentation, etc.)?
- What kind of location should each scene have? (Use photos to focus the discussion.)
- What contribution should each location make toward (1) the meaning of the scene, (2) the film's premise?
- In what season or seasons does the film take place? Does each add a different meaning and require different visual elements?
- What kind of environments do the characters live in and what sort of belongings do they keep around them?
- What kind of props does the narrative require? What can add to characterization?
- What kind of clothes does each character wear, and what should their clothes tell us?
- What color palette and progression would promote the film's thematic development?
- What is the ruling image or visual motif in each scene?

Now break down each scene to determine how the following mise-en-scène elements can support its emotional tone, understanding of character, and narrative meaning:

- Locations, set dressings and props
- Amount and distribution of light
- Color tonality
- Costuming and hairstyles.

VISUAL RESEARCH

You and your collaborators should extensively research and discuss these questions. To do so, analyse films of a similar genre, or ones that take place in similar locations or time period, or that visually establish a similar tone. Use old catalogs, photojournalism, fashion histories, and painting or documentary photography for the look and feel of a period. Photograph locations, make sketches and collect drawings, paintings, photographs, objects, anything at all that addresses aspects of your film's design. Collect and post your images in a single location and soon you and your collaborators will see patterns emerging that lead you to the film's ultimate visual design (Figure 23-1).

FIGURE 23-1 ————————————————————————————————————

Crafting the visual design of a film involves bringing together various sources of visual inspiration. Pictured is a portion of the "visual wall" constructed during pre-production on Guy Moshe's *Bunraku* (2010).

EXAMPLES FOR DISCUSSION

Consider three very different films, each of strong design and a different milieu: Stanley Kubrick's *Barry Lyndon* (1975), Sam Mendes' *American Beauty* (1999), and Darren Aronofsky's *The Wrestler* (2008).

Kubrick's adaptation of William Thackeray's *Barry Lyndon* tells the story of an 18th-century opportunist rake who, believing he has killed a man in his Irish hometown, goes on the run and encounters a lawless world (Figure 23-2). He becomes a soldier and then with alluring charm and humor robs, cheats, and lies his way up the social ladder until he establishes an honorable place as the husband of Lady Lyndon. Kubrick directed the actors to behave entirely naturally, so there's none of the posturing self-consciousness common in period movies. Roy Walker and Ken Adam, art director and production designer, chose authentic architecture inside and out, and characters

FIGURE 23-2

Kubrick's attention to every detail in the production of *Barry Lyndon* resulted in a completely believable period film.

wear their costumes and wigs as naturally as people today wear sunglasses and jeans. The characters' behavior, their leisure, their treatment of each other, their facilities and resources, all make the film feel like a lavishly made documentary captured during a bout of time traveling. Much of this is due to John Alcott's photography, which pioneered special lenses to shoot without artificial light. Night interiors, which have a golden glow, were shot using nothing but candlelight. Candlelit evenings promote storytelling and long meals, and candles and open fires make interiors smoky and grimy. Travel by coach or horseback is a messy, uncertain business and threatened by highwaymen—the muggers of the 18th century. Clothing and wigs were none too clean unless you were wealthy, and animals and people lived in close proximity. All this makes a fascinating setting for a timeless story about ambition pursued with diligence.

Sam Mendes' *American Beauty*, a sardonic fable set in suburban America (Figure 23-3), charts the downward spiral of Lester Burnham's mid-life crisis. He starts looking candidly at his failing marriage, the abusive nature of his job, and at the empty materialism of the social class to which he belongs. The film's upper-middle class suburbs are as repressed, indulgent, and standardized as only the American suburbs can be. Depressed that his beliefs have proved hollow, Lester decides it's because he's had no beauty in his life, and so becomes fixated on a cheerleader, his daughter's best friend Angela.

Naomi Shohan and David S. Lazan, production designer and art director, have made a deadly compendium of everything that wealthy suburbanites cram into their lives. Clothes, cars, furniture,

FIGURE 23-3 ——

The production design, costumes, and cinematography in Mendes' *American Beauty* deftly reflect the flaws and inner conflicts of the family at the center of its suburban drama.

gadgets, and sexual partners are the signifiers by which the characters represent their values and achievements—to themselves and to each other. At first hilarious, their world grows tawdry because of an encroaching spiritual darkness. Visual design is at the heart of this highly critical film, and the naked girl spinning in the rose petals stands for the enticing, impossible object of Lester's fantasies.

Shot by Conrad Hall (Best Cinematography Oscar winner for the film) the photography maintains cold, impersonal blue tones for Lester's workplace. Daylight scenes seem unnaturally clean and vivid. But this contrasts with the murky evening scenes, especially toward the end, during which shadows bring dark impulses into the domestic spaces. The only respite from the harsh daytime and gloomy nights are Lester's fantasies of Angela, shot in bright, soft lighting.

Aronofsky's *The Wrestler* (Figure 23-4) is a painfully naturalistic look at an aging professional wrestler's struggle to rebuild his life after a career-ending heart attack. Fighting before a handful of local fans in high school gyms and VFW halls, Randy "The Ram" Johnson is long past his prime. Production designer Tim Grimes creates the irony of Randy's environment through carefully selected locations, set dressing and costume. Randy's steroid-enhanced body, his long blond hair-extensions, and his glitter tights all reflect the highly theatrical core of his métier, yet here he is eking out a living fighting in colorless small-town community centers and working part time at an utterly banal supermarket. Equally bleak is his living situation, a trailer home crammed with memorabilia from his "glory days." He escapes only through occasional visits to the local strip club, which is equally theatrical, gaudy and dreary.

Cinematographer Maryse Alberti pursues the naturalistic tone and tawdriness of Randy's environment by shooting mostly under available light: the sickly fluorescent lighting of the wrestling venues and supermarket where he works, and the overcast New Jersey winter skies for the exteriors. Early in the film, when "The Ram" is locked out of his trailer for unpaid rent and forced to

FIGURE 23-4

The naturalistic approach to the selection of locations, set dressing, lighting, and costumes gives Aronofsky's *The Wrestler* a gritty, realistic look and feel.

sleep in his van after a match, Alberti shoots him peeling athletic tape from his joints and popping handfuls of pain medication with nothing more than a flashlight.

THE IMPORTANCE OF THE PALETTE

The art and camera departments can have a profound impact on a film by choosing the range of colors for their palette. Kubrick's film is rich in golds, browns, and dark reds like an old master painting—and research into genre paintings evidently played a large part in the design and lighting of the whole film. Mendes (who comes from a theater background) worked with his crew to use the loud, discordant colors typical of the suburban, nouveau riche.

Allied to the visible palette are the choice and processing of film stock, lighting effects produced with color gels, and special use of the digital camera's settings for color effects. Obviously a close and enthusiastic working relationship must exist between the art director, cinematographer, and director.

LOCATIONS AND SETS

Films shot mainly on location—the norm for student and independent filmmaking—must strive to find locations close to the needs of the script and which express the tone and approach of the Storyteller's point of view. Finding just the right locations is no less important than finding the right cast, and should be approached with equal commitment, rigor, and discernment.

In *The Wrestler*, Randy "The Ram" tries to re-connect with his estranged daughter Stephanie and to get back in his daughter's good graces. She is resistant because he's been such a neglectful parent, so he takes her to the Jersey shore where he can conjure a few memories from when he was a better father. For this tentative reconciliation, a ruined structure that was once a palace of fun is an ideal setting. It is a place of forgotten history as old and dilapidated as Randy, who calls himself "an old broken-down piece of meat." Like Stephanie, it too has been neglected and abandoned. Set anywhere else, the film would lack much of the deep resonances that this perfect location offers (Figure 23-4, *bottom*).

Most "real" locations, especially interiors, need some degree of fixing up to look exactly right onscreen. This, called **set dressing**, includes: rearranging, adding or removing decorations, objects or furniture; painting or hanging things on walls; installing a specific window dressing, and so on. "The Ram's" trailer is a perfect location, its interior meticulously carefully dressed with posters, stacks of cassette tapes (!), beer cans and other personal detritus that visibly reflects the character of the man who lives there.

SCOUTING LOCATIONS

Settling where to shoot requires location scouting. Not unlike casting, it means you must visit a number of location possibilities in search of those that work best, expressively and logistically. Ideally, the director scouts locations with the cinematographer and production designer, evaluating the visual potential and technical assets of each. If you are recording extensive sync-sound dialogue in a particular location, then the sound recordist should be present to assess the location's aural qualities and suitability.[1] Here are a few considerations when location scouting:

Aesthetics: Obviously, whether or not the look is appropriate for the script is of prime importance, but see what else the location can contribute to the tone and theme of the film. Look in detail at the architecture, backgrounds, light quality, colors, and so on. Consider with your experts the potential to dress the location.

---

[1] On this book's companion website, www.directingbook.com ("Forms and Logs") you can download a location scouting form, which will help you note location qualities.

Logistics: A film location must also have production functionality. Is the location safe for people and equipment? Is there enough power and access to electricity, should you need to use artificial light? Is it large enough to contain your crew, equipment, and cast? Can everyone get there? Are there bathrooms?

Access: Is the location available for your project. What are the terms? If rental is involved, can you afford it? Is it available on the days, nights, and hours when you need it? Are there are any strings attached, any hostile neighbors poised to call the police?

Sound: Is the location quiet enough for sync sound. Do you hear air-conditioners, kids playing at an adjacent playground, the traffic noise of a nearby highway? How appropriate is the ambient noise for the scenes you're shooting? How controllable is the sound environment? How are the acoustics of the location? See p. 377 for more detail on location scouting for sound.

BUILDING SETS

When your conception of the script calls for a location so specialized that you cannot easily find it (even through dressing an existing location) you may need to construct it. To build a set, whether on a sound stage or at an empty location, requires **set design**. The art department draws sketches like building plans, and once approved by the director, they build that set, a process using carpenters and painters, which can be elaborate and expensive, or simple and affordable.

For his student thesis film *Occult: The Ghosts of Dunkirk*, set deep behind enemy lines during World War II, director Andrew Knudsen shot mostly at locations that could pass as similar places in Germany. He used some woods in New Jersey and an old civil war fortress in Queens, New York. For a scene requiring two Nazi soldiers inside a Tiger 1 tank, Andrew found an enthusiast who built perfect scale models. A brief close-up of the scale model provided the establishing shot they needed, and for its interior, Andrew's art department built a simple, entirely functional set from plywood (Figure 23-5). It created an enclosure with view similar to what a tank commander might see, and incorporated an existing building wall lined with old piping. The shots were kept tight, the lighting appropriately dark, and the film's absolutely convincing tank interior was completed with a little atmospheric smoke.

MOODS AND VISUAL DESIGN

By scanning your script solely for its moods, you and your team can cadence the movie by color and lighting design in step with the mood of the story and characters. If possible, alternate interiors with exteriors and day with night, so that your film breathes in and out. Each change contributes its own contrasting mode of feeling. By combining these with color and image designs, a very large statement lies in the hands of the production designers. A comparison between the hard edged and vivid imagery in *American Beauty*, which falls increasingly into darkness; and the muted, dull tones in *The Wrestler*, which occasionally gives way to the gaudy, theatrical colors of the fight ring and the strip club, reveals very different views of two middle-aged men seeking to reinvent themselves.

FIGURE 23-5

A simple set design was used to successfully recreate the inside of a World War II German tank in Knudsen's thesis film *Occult: The Ghosts of Dunkirk*.

WARDROBE, MAKEUP, AND HAIRDRESSING

Consider clothing as a coded projection of its owner's social status, self-image, and intentions. Think through what personality and mood each character manifests at different times, and how their clothing might contrast with that of other characters. Think not of color and design alone, but of overall tone in relation to surroundings. Very light-toned costumes may be too reflective, whereas dark tones, especially in night exteriors, may disappear altogether. The size and fit of clothes, the way they are worn, the accessories that go with them, can express volumes about the wearer. In *American Beauty*, Lester starts out wearing conservative business suits and by the end is wearing tee shirts and exercise clothing (Figure 23-6). His apparel—including his Mr. Smiley's uniform—neatly reflects the trajectory of his reversion back to rebellious teenager.

Additional meaning can be expressed through makeup and hairdressing. In *Barry Lyndon*, some of the most affected characters have a chalk-white makeup, fashionable in the 18th century, which gives them a peculiar, corpselike presence. This contrasts with the titular character who, appropriate for a rogue interloper penetrating the aristocracy, almost never powders his face. This, too, is part of the design.

As in real life, hairstyles tell us much about a character at first glance. The marine shipping off to war, the conservative banker, the California surf bum, the TV news anchor are all roles suggesting different hairstyles. Randy "The Ram's" long, cheap, blond hair extensions in *The Wrestler* are perfect for someone whose cultural identity never made it out of the 1980s, that era of long-haired rockers like Quiet Riot.

Does anyone really look like those people in your imagination? The real world is far richer than imagination can ever be. What kind of makeup and hairdos will you really find among ladies who play bingo once a week or gamblers at the racetracks? A research trip will enrich you.

FIGURE 23-6

Careful costuming can reveal volumes about a character's personality and evolution, as seen in Mendes'
American Beauty.

THE SCRIPT BREAKDOWN SHEET

The **script breakdown sheet** is the form used in film production to keep track of all the mise-en-
scène details necessary to each scene, including atmosphere (rain, fog, smoke), set dressing, hand
props, costumes, and makeup. Every scene needs a breakdown sheet where everyone can see at
a glance what details it requires. The first version is generated by the assistant director (or production manager) on reading the screenplay and logging every mise-en-scène item mentioned.
Then the production designer double-checks the list, adding details as the visual design evolves.
Though the screenplay includes "a 12-year-old with the demeanor of a Wall Street trader," it is the
art department who assign him a leather briefcase and an iPhone to pull off the effect. You can
download a script breakdown form from the companion website, www.directingbook.com (under
"Forms and Logs").

CINEMATOGRAPHY

During preproduction and production stages, the cinematographer and director collaborate closely on the visual interpretation, starting from broad aesthetic concepts. Their realization for each scene eventually visualizes every detail and composition for every shot. This involves choosing:

- Film stock or video format
- Choice of lens and filtration
- Composition details (depth, perspective, treatment of space)
- Camera movements (type and method)
- Coverage strategy for shooting and editing
- Image design
- Lighting aesthetic (naturalistic or stylized)
- Lighting designs and setups for each scene
- Colors and image tonality.

The cinematographer, expert in the storytelling capability of the image, is in charge of capturing it all. At all levels of film production, from student short to large budget commercial films, the collaboration and creative energy between the director and cinematographer are vital to the film's success. Discussing his collaboration with Danny Boyle on *Slumdog Millionaire* (2009), cinematographer Anthony Dod Mantle said, "He'd have an idea for a picture and I'm there to help him as a visually trained composer of images—that's my job."[2] Cinematographer Roger Deakins (*No Country for Old Men, Revolutionary Road*), says that "... the cinematographer's role is to act as the director's visual 'right hand' [...] on balance, it is evenly technical and creative. With a more visually orientated director the role may be skewed toward one of technique, how to get what the director wants. Conversely the role can be one of much greater creative responsibility."[3]

Because of the broad range of creative detail involved in the director/cinematographer collaboration, this discussion is spread out over three separate chapters. More specific information is in the following chapters: 11, 24, 27.

DESIGNING A WORLD

Each film projects the specifics of a way of life, and each by design expresses a point of view on the enclosed world it presents. Everything is involved: locations, casting, lighting design, furnishings, clothes, props, music, sound design, and even the weather. Each film could be represented by a painting or style of painting—Gainsborough, Hopper, and Renoir, say, and this is not far from what happens. Cinematographer Guillermo Navarro, writing about *Pan's Labyrinth* (2006), mentions as his influences the painter Francisco de Goya; the directors James Whale, George Romero,

---

[2] From *In Contention.com* by Kristopher Tapley, January 14, 2009.
[3] From *The Role of the Cinematographer*, posted 4/24/08 on www.deakinsonline.com

and David Cronenberg; the cinematographer Mario Bava; and the illustrator Arthur Rackham, whose drawings, redolent of opium dreams, disturbed me as a child and were first seen in the 1907 publication of *Alice in Wonderland*.[4]

PROVING THE DESIGN

If you are building sets, drawings must be as specific as architectural blueprints. Sets must be large enough to accommodate the action and camera equipment, and flexible in construction, with removable walls that allow the camera access to relevant parts of the set. The production design team's work may result in formal storyboards, but try to work with an art director who can sketch the ideas as you discuss them. Storyboard computer programs typically fall short when they generate a suitable collection of human images from which to choose your characters. There's no substitute for artist's sketches when it comes to imagery that fires the imagination.

Use a digital still camera to record your characters in their costumes against a limbo background or at the proposed locations under varying lighting conditions. Working with Adobe Photoshop™ or another digital imaging program, make a storyboard of sorts, then experimentally change the image characteristics. By roughly lighting the set and manipulating the contrast, hue, and brightness of the image in your computer, you can produce a set of pictures that relays what you like to the cinematographer and production designer.

---

[4] Interview with Navarro, *American Cinematographer*, January 2007.

CHAPTER 24

COVERAGE AND THE SHOOTING SCRIPT

The specific shooting and editing strategy you employ for each scene in your film is called **coverage**, and it describes the number of shots, angles, and style of shooting you will use to "cover" the scene. There are no right or wrong answers to the question of coverage—how you shoot a scene is at the center of the director's art. The type and amount of shots depend on a number of interlocking factors, principally the scene's dramatic importance and shape, your visual conception, and the time and financial resources available to shoot it. When devising coverage, remember that what you gather in the field determines the success of your editing.

The director and cinematographer decide on coverage, but if you've already shot rehearsals documentary-style, you will have evolved a good sense of optimal camera positions and movements. These tapes, reviewed and dissected, show what visual moments and camera movements worked well, and what strategies can be derived from them. The ultimate goal is to create the shooting script, which is the version of the screenplay you take into production. The **shooting script** indicates every shot required to cover each scene (see fig. 24-4).

GENERAL COVERAGE CONSIDERATIONS

To ensure some stylistic cohesion first imagine the coverage strategy for your whole film before you specify coverage for any individual scene. This does not mean covering every scene in the same way—indeed the methods below can be mixed and matched depending on each scene's needs—it simply means you're first striving to establish a broad aesthetic and tonal approach to your film. If you haven't already done so, read Part 5(especially Chapter 15) which introduces essential coverage strategies. Here are some major choices of approach:

Master scene method: Master scene shooting technique (part of the continuity system) is an extremely flexible, reliable, and common method (see Chapter 15). Practically speaking, this technique involves shooting the scene in a master shot, then changing the placement of the camera to reshoot closer shots of one character, then changing set ups again to shoot the reverse shots of

FIGURE 24-1 ——

Master scene method gives you flexibility to shape the dramatic emphasis of a scene, a technique used master-fully in von Donnersmarck's *The Lives of Others*.

the other character, and so on. With each change in angle, actors repeat moments to create over-lapping action where the editor can make edits. It's not uncommon to shoot the same moment in a scene from two or three different angles and shot sizes (see *The Artist* example in Chapter 15, Figure 15-4). Master scene technique takes time and continuity coordination, but being able to choose between several angles of the same moment gives you great flexibility in shaping the rhythm, dramatic arc, and narrative emphasis of the scene later in the editing.

Despite all the cutting and new angles involved in master scene technique, this style remains remarkable invisible. Applied simply and appropriately, it can be used to support the dramatic intentions of the director while never distracting the audience with overt stylization. This tech-nique is used in the vast majority of films, but here are some worth studying for their precision and simplicity: Alexander Payne's *Sideways* (2005), Reitman's *Up in the Air* (2008), and Florian Henckle von Donnersmarck's *The Lives of Others* (2006, Figure 24-1), which looks at the covert surveillance of a celebrated playwright by an East German Stasi agent before the fall of the Berlin Wall. In this film, cuts to new angles not only establish dramatic emphasis and character POV, but also reveal internal states of mind like dread, compassion, fear, confusion, and so on.

The long-take method: This allows actions to play out over extended periods, sometimes in only one shot per scene. Generally, though not always, this requires a mobile camera and intri-cate blocking of both camera and actors to avoid a flat, stagy appearance. The benefits to long-take shooting are an immediacy and emotional momentum uninterrupted by cuts to new angles. Some actors thrive with this method, preferring the unbroken emotional continuum of a long take over the need to repeat brief moments for different angles. For a superb example of fluid camera control and blocking in long takes, see Rodrigo Garcia's *Nine Lives* (2005), Cristian Mungiu's *4 Months, 3 Weeks, 2 Days* (2007), and Jacques Demy's masterpiece, *The Umbrellas of*

FIGURE 24-2 ————————————————

Jacques Demy's *The Umbrellas of Cherbourg* uses fluid camera movement and long takes that preserve the unity of time, space, and emotional momentum.

Cherbourg (1964, Figure 24-2). A story of lovers in a small French town when the upheavals in Algeria took recruits off to war, it is an operetta in which all dialogue is realistic, yet sung, not spoken. Surprisingly, this works very well. Even if you find it sentimental, the film is a model for frame and color design, camera movement, and blocking.

Note that, using the long-take method, you cannot cut around any acting or camera problems, so it requires virtuoso control by actors and technicians and any error consigns the entire take to the trash can. Another risk shows up only in the first assembly: without control of individual elements within each scene, the editor cannot rebalance their rhythm, performances, or pacing in the story.

The short-take method: In short-take coverage generally, shots are edited together to create rhythm, juxtaposition, and tension, but the audience must expend considerable mental energy on interpreting the cuts. The material is more evidently manipulated, and at MTV's frenetic extreme (borrowed by many action films such as the entire *Bourne* series), the viewer is bombarded with fragments of action from which to infer a whole. It's nearly impossible to sustain this style over long periods without exhausting your audience, but used judiciously in select scenes the short-take method can infuse energy and panache into critical moments of your film.

Rather than rely on overwrought editing, many directors choreograph their mise-en-scène as individual shots containing complex blocking. They shoot safety coverage in case longish takes are flawed or their otherwise inalterable pacing falters.

FIXED VERSUS MOBILE CAMERA

A camera on a tripod is able to hold a steady shot, from longs shots to extreme close ups, without physically crowding the actor. On the other hand, camera moves from a fixed position are restricted to pans and tilts, so the camera cannot move to a better vantage point unless you mount it on a dolly or crane. This allows smooth movement through a preplanned cycle, but requires precision from crew and cast, who must hit chalk marks on the floor if composition and focus are to hold up. Here, the benefits are smooth and dynamic moves that engage audiences by bringing them through the spaces of the film, but the casualty is performance spontaneity and setup time.

If you need to shoot a semi-improvised performance and shoot fast, then intelligent handheld camerawork may be the best solution. In the right hands, it can solve most problems and become a dynamic statement. In the hands of someone inexperienced, however, you can lose hours and end up

FIGURE 24-3

Robby Müller's expert handheld camera technique complements the fractured, chaotic life of Bess (Emily Watson) after her husband is paralyzed in an accident in von Trier's *Breaking the Waves*.

with sloppy footage. Cinematographer Maryse Alberti (*The Wrestler*), after honing her camera handling skills as a documentary filmmaker, is one of the best at handheld techniques. Another is Robbie Müller who shot Lars von Trier's unsettling *Breaking the Waves* (1996, Figure 24-3). Entirely handheld, its purposefully lunging, urgent camerawork complements the way that the headstrong Scots village girl Bess deals with the disaster of her husband becoming paralyzed and unhinged by an oil-rig accident.

SUBJECTIVE OR OBJECTIVE CAMERA PRESENCE

The two kinds of camera presence—one studied, composed, and controlled; the other mobile, spontaneously reactive, and adaptive to change—imply quite different observing presences. One feels subjective and susceptible to the action; the other suggests a more settled objectivity. Camera-handling alone may thus alter the voice of a film and make it more personal and vulnerable, or more confidently general in outlook. Maintaining either mode too long may become dull, whereas shifting justifiably between them can be very potent.

RELATEDNESS: SEPARATING OR INTEGRATING BY SHOT

Composition and framing can also greatly alter what a scene feels like. Isolating two people, each in their own close shots, then intercutting them, produces a different feeling than intercutting two over-the-shoulder shots. The close-ups' relationship in space and time is mediated by the filming process, whereas the people in over-the-shoulder shots are visibly related to each other in time and space. In the over-the-shoulder shots, the observer relates to them as a pair, but in the single shots is always alone with one or the other. Such isolation in cinema is the exception since frame limitations usually compel one to use precious screen space by packing it, and demonstrating the spatial relationships between everything and everybody.

In scenes containing multiple characters, shoot alternate angles and plenty of reaction shots so that the editor can abridge material that is overlong, or cut around problems involving dialogue and simultaneous movement. Backgrounds and foregrounds also count because they, too, permit one to juxtapose ideas. If a character is depressed and hungry, there is a nice irony in showing a huge Ronald McDonald behind her bus stop. Unobtrusively, the composition highlights her dilemma and suggests she might blow her bus money on a large fries. Deciding what part background must play in relation to foreground is a lens-choice and camera-positioning issue. The subject may also be placed in the foreground, background, or middle ground—imagine a prisoner, bars in foreground, cellmate in background at back of cell, for instance. These different planes in the image are compositional elements that help create the all-important sense of depth in

2D photography (see Figure 12-3 in Chapter 12 for a precise and meaningful juxtaposition of foreground and background). As 3D becomes more common, some aspects of composition will need rethinking.

THE CAMERA AS A REVEALING AND OBSERVING CONSCIOUSNESS

Often the camera sets out to reveal not just the subject, but the subject's context, and an attitude to both. Looking down on the subject, looking up at it, or peering between tree trunks, all suggest different contexts, and different ways of seeing—that is, experiencing—the action central to the scene. While you can use Eisenstein's dialectical cutting to make us see that riot police are near a nice bed of tulips, how much more subtle and effective to make the point in a single well-composed frame?

Making the location a meaningful environment and responding to the actions and sight lines of participants in a scene creates a more vivid, spontaneous sense of the scene's dynamics unfolding. Why? Because we are sharing the consciousness of someone intelligent and intuitive who picks up the characters' underlying tensions and ironies. Too often, in routine coverage, the camera placement and editing end up like the limited reactions of someone who merely turns, as dogs do, toward whatever moves or makes a noise. Instead, regard your camera as an astute observer, and imagine how you want to use its material so that an entertaining Storyteller personality can emerge. If you have a scene in a turbulent flea market, it makes no sense to limit the camera to carefully placed tripod shots. Make the camera into a wandering buyer by going handheld and peering into circles of chattering people, looking closely at the merchandise, and then swinging around when someone calls out. However, if you are shooting a church service with its elaborate rituals, your camera placing should be rock steady because that is how anyone present experiences such a situation. Where does the majority of the telling action lie? With a newcomer? The priest? The choir or the congregation?

POINT OF VIEW (POV)

Controlling point of view may remain an elusive notion. As we said, it is not only "what so-and-so sees," though this may comprise one or two shots. Rather, POV sets out to convey more holistically how a character in the film is undergoing particular events. Top priority is to ask whose point of view the scene favors, and a great many of your decisions about composition, camera placement, and editing will flow from this. Decide POV by asking who the Concerned Observer is likely to watch and why. Answers come from the logic of the script and from your instincts. If there is no overriding determinant, the editor will have to decide later, based on the nuances of the acting and whether you've shot enough coverage.

How do you show a man who is being watched by the police get into his car and start it up? Should the audience see our man being watched by police from the policeman's point of view, or from the POV of one more omniscient (that is, the Storyteller)—in which the audience, but not the man, notices the cop? You will probably decide this on plot grounds, but *what the characters seem to experience* should drive your coverage, as happens when you choose whom to watch in a real life situation. You are always trying to guess what the person you are watching is trying to get, do, or accomplish.

Now imagine a more complex scene in which a child witnesses a sustained argument between his parents. How should point of view be handled there? First, what does the argument represent? Is it "child realizing he is a pawn," or is it "parents too bitter to care what their child sees"? It's your choice that matters most—whether we share what the child sees, or whether we see from some distance how the dispute acts upon him.

Issues like this determine whether the scene is really the boy's, the father's, or the mother's. The scene according to all its acting variables can be shot and edited to polarize our sympathetic interest in any of these directions at any given moment in the scene. Making *no* choice would produce faceless, expressionless filmmaking—technical filmmaking with no heart or soul.

There remains a more apparently detached way of observing events, that of the Omniscient Storyteller. Intuition during editing tells you to occasionally resort to this cooler point of view. Probably it's to relieve pressure on the audience before you ramp it up again. Sustained and unvarying pressure is self-defeating since the audience becomes armed against it, or tunes out. Even in his darkest tragedies Shakespeare intersperses scenes of comic relief. His audiences must have shown him the necessity.

THE HEART OF DIRECTING: THE STORYTELLER'S POINT OF VIEW

David Mamet[1] protests that too much fiction filmmaking consists of following the action like a news service. Do you want to document happenings like a dutiful Observer, or tell them with flair like a Storyteller? The first is surveillance, and the second involves inflection; that is, having an active and critical eye for contradictions and ironies, raising questions, and implying a critical mind and heart at work. What identity will you give your Storyteller? What singularities does your Storyteller want us to notice in your characters and their situations? These are not easy questions, and you certainly won't find answers if you wait until shooting or editing.

The key lies in the *attitude* that the storytelling mind, intelligence, and heart take. It should be the psychic lens through which your audience experiences your story. How would you describe the attitude of your Storyteller? What are the ironies and humor in his or her way of seeing? How will you make these evident? Your ideas should have formed while you moved around during rehearsal. If you shot documentary coverage of rehearsals, you watched these newborn characters living salient pieces of their lives on the screen. You watched and identified according to a pattern that began in the intentions behind the writing, and that arises now more completely from the chemistry of personalities and situation. Review your impressions. Use your mind to examine your heart.

To create the Storyteller, you have to bring alive not only the facts of the tale, but also the telling—that is, you must give the narrative the integrity of a quirky human mind that sees, weighs, wonders, feels, and supposes while the story unfolds. Your Storyteller's attitude must infuse every possible aspect of the movie. This means implying puzzlement, doubts, enjoyment, censure, opprobrium, delight, distrust, regret, or fascination. Whatever grips your Storyteller's heart and mind must be implied through the way the Storyteller displays the tale. Do this successfully, and your work will have the humor and intelligence of work that has a human character.

---

[1] *On Directing Film*, David Mamet (Penguin, 1992).

In the struggle for high-concept plotting, filmmaking's factory processes trample the humanity out of their work. Few films have any soul, but when they do, audiences universally respond. This takes a director with a clear, strong identity—one not overwhelmed by the people and the procedures. You might want to review Chapters 9 and 16 for a closer look at the perspectives of the Concerned Observer and the Storyteller before you tackle your shooting script.

CREATING THE SHOOTING SCRIPT

As mentioned earlier, the **shooting script** is the version of the screenplay that you take into production. Camera angles, shot sizes, and camera moves are marked right on the script copy itself and express the director's shooting strategy for each and every scene. The shooting script is distributed to the core creative team (cinematographer, art director, sound mixer) so that they can work out what technical resources they will need. Further, the producing team (producer, production manager) devises the logistics of scheduling for the production process from the shooting script. Considerable time, effort, collaboration, and creative attention go into making it, since the shooting script functions as both the creative and the technical blueprint for the entire shoot.

EXPLORING COVERAGE SCENE BY SCENE

A scene's specific coverage is based on its intended function in the script, your gut feelings about it, the energy that the actors are bringing, and any limitations built into the filmmaking process (such as locations, equipment, budget, crew size, and so on). Obviously, it does you no good to imagine a swooping helicopter shot if you cannot afford a helicopter. But more subtle is to know that some scenes require more shots for their coverage, and others fewer; that one short camera move, perfectly placed, can be more powerful than a relentlessly mobile camera; or that a visual juxtaposition works better within a single frame than two shots edited together. Be careful not to over-determine small moments with too many shots, but by the same token, plan sufficient shots for critical scenes so that they can elevate dramatically.

By the end of this process, you should have determined *all* the specific shots to cover *every* scene in your script. Here some of the basic diagnostic questions for you and your cinematographer to ask:

Dramatic context:

* What is the scene's function in the script?
* What is the ruling mood or emotional tone?
* Who learns and develops, and how does this affect POV?
* Where is the scene's turning point? (For complex scenes we often plan the optimal shot for this moment, then devise other coverage leading up to, then away from it).

Environment:

* What must the scene show to establish the environment satisfactorily?
* Does this orientation come early, or is it delayed for dramatic reasons?

- What is the relationship between the subjects and their environment?
- How will I establish this relationship visually—in one shot? Through shot juxtaposition?

Point of view:

- At each significant moment, whose point of view (POV) are we sharing?
- Whose global POV predominates in the overall story? In the scene? (Subjective? Objective?)
- When and why does POV change?
- How will I make evident the Storyteller's attitudes to the events in this scene?

Eyelines:

- What are the significant eyelines in the scene?
- Where do eyelines change?
- How should the camera be aligned in relation to an eyeline?

Space and character movement:

- Can I use space between characters to indicate relationships (who dominates, and who retreats)?
- What is the appropriate visual perspective on the scene? (see "The Expressive Capacity of the Lens" in Chapter 27).
- What is the relationship of the off-screen space to the visible frame?
- At which points do characters move, and why?
- How will I show it? (Use a wider shot? Moving camera?)
- Should I follow a character with a moving camera, or hold on another?
- What axis does the character follow at each stage of his or her movements?

Camera movement:

- When, how (type of movement), and why (motivation) should the camera move?
- What feelings do its movements create?
- Does the camera movement reveal or conceal narrative detail?

Compositional relationship and isolation:

- What elements should be juxtaposed visually (within the frame) or conceptually (by editing shots)
- When and how to show significant relationship? For instance:
  - A sleeping character who is supposed to be catching a plane, framed with a clock in the background.
  - An argument played in tight, single shots to emphasize the adversarial, isolated feel of the relationship.

- Who or what might legitimately be isolated from surroundings? For instance:
  - A misfit boy is frequently shown alone, but the gang members who tease him appear as a pack.
  - A phone refusing to ring for someone waiting on tenterhooks for a call shown as a single shot.

Rhythm:

- How do the rhythms of the shooting and editing support the rhythms of the scenes and performances?
- How do the rhythms of this scene relate to the rhythm of scenes which come before and after?

It's important for the director to be prepared with clear and communicable ideas, particularly concerning the film's central tone and premise, and to be able to explain their relation to each scene's dramatic context and concept. This will greatly assist the cinematographer who ideally serves as, in the words of Anthony Dod Mantle from p. 293, "the visually trained composer of images." As the two of you reach a mutual understanding about visual style and coverage, the cinematographer is devising the technical approach to pulling it off.

COVERING IMPORTANT ASPECTS IN MORE THAN ONE WAY

Be prepared to cover vital story points or important emotional transitions in more than one way; that way you have choices later and can exercise maximum control in the cutting room over the telling moment. If during a family reunion the mother accidentally breaks a glass from her wedding set, your beat is her moment of realization and grief. Prepare to give it additional poignancy by shooting reactions from others present. Her son shows anger at her clumsiness, her daughter is surprised, her husband amused because he thinks it's just a minor accident, and her daughter-in-law fears she has cut herself. You are unlikely to use many of these reactions, but having them allows you to find the best inflection for the scene in its finished state. Covering this spectrum of reaction allows for a variable richness in defining the moment, and follows our oft-mentioned principle of generating more than strictly necessary so you have options. In the same spirit, if a line is so understated that it risks being unintelligible, shoot two or three versions. This is not compromise but survival; only foolish optimists take a two-day water supply to cross a two-day desert.

INSERTS AND CUTAWAYS

Shoot safety coverage such as reaction shots, cutaways, or insert shots for every sequence so you can bridge shots that don't match. The saying in the industry used to be, "When in doubt, cut to seagulls." An **insert shot**, such as the coins a character glances at in his hand, magnifies the detail within an existing shot, while a **cutaway** shows detail outside the pertinent shot. A cutaway might show a man who, as he crosses the road, fleetingly catches the attention of our main character who is waiting for a bus.

THE FLOOR PLAN AND SHOOTING SCRIPT

Floor plans (also called **overheads**) are schematic drawings from a bird's eye perspective of the scene. They include physical location details (walls, furniture and so on), character positions and movements, and planned camera angles. The floor plan is an important pre-visualizing tool to help determine coverage and create the shooting script.

Figure 24-4 is a scene from a script, and Figure 24-5 is its floor plan. The latter consolidates your intentions for blocking, and helps you plan the fewest and most effective camera angles.

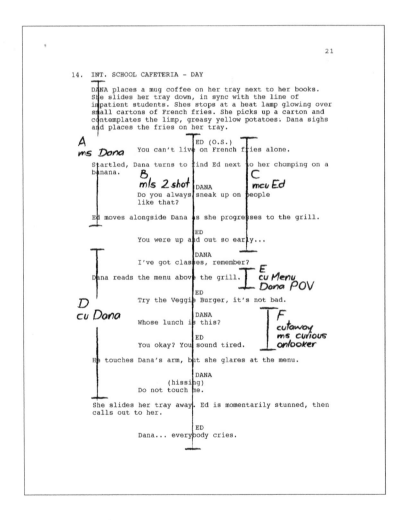

FIGURE 24-4 ───

A bracketed shooting script shows the intended coverage for every scene.

Using it you can precisely indicate the essential axes of action and dramatic tension, the characters' movements, and the camera angles necessary for the edited version. This diagram, growing out of the blocking developed during rehearsals and modified by location realities, helps plan both the shooting and editing, and enables the cinematographer to plan lighting placement and camera movements.

Here is a common method to create a shooting script and floor plans in tandem.

Concerning the Shooting Script (Figure 24-4):

1. *Number every scene* in your screenplay starting at Scene #1. A scene is a dramatic unit which has integrity of time and place. If the script moves to a new location, it's a new scene; move from day to night, another new scene. Since each new scene should already have a new scene heading (see p. 80), all you should need to do is number them sequentially.
2. *Read through the scene,* analyzing it using the questions above and imagining how the scene should unfold visually. Some scenes may need but one shot, others may require all the shots

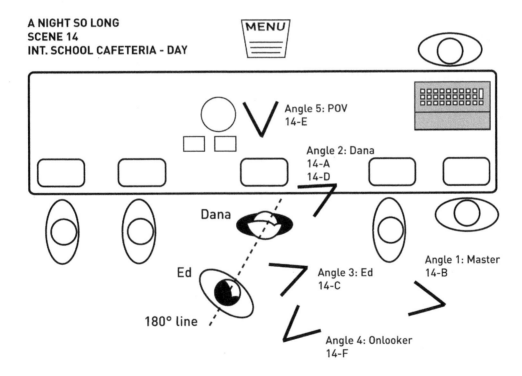

FIGURE 24-5

The floorplan for the cafeteria scene in Figure 24-4. A floor plan is essential for visualizing the placement of the camera and actors.

which make up a typical continuity scene (see p. 179). Still other scenes may require more angles or a moving camera… whatever. This is your show.

3. *Bracket each intended shot* on the script, drawing a vertical line through all of the dialogue and activity that the particular shot covers. This line shows where in the script each shot begins and ends. Remember to give good overlaps between shots so the editor has a range of options for cutting from one shot to the next. The most useful editing overlaps occur on strong actions (such as rising from a chair or turning to leave the room).

4. *Designate each lined shot with a capital letter* starting with shot A, shot B, shot C, and so on. Now every camera setup has a unique shot number. In the case of the scene in Figure 24-4 (Scene # 14 in the script) we are covering it with six shots: 14-A, 14-B, 14-C, 14-D, 14-E, and 14-F.

5. *Give each shot an abbreviated shot description* (see "Common Shot Sizes," p. 160). For example, shot 14-A is MS for medium shot, 14-B is MLS 2 shot (medium long shot, two shot), 14-C is MCU for medium close up, and so on. You can designate over-the-shoulder shots (OTS) and point of view shots (POV) as well.

6. Once you have a bracketed script, anyone can see at a glance how you mean to cover the action and what editing alternatives your coverage permits. Make sure that every line of dialogue and every action has at least one line running through it—that means it's covered by at least one shot. Pay particular attention to where one shot begins and another ends: this is an edit point. Forever keep in mind that for smooth and seamless editing, *the best place to make a cut is always on a strong physical movement* and make sure to overlap those areas (meaning duplicate the action in each shot). For example, the moment Dana turns to find Ed behind her is a strong action to cut on. We can cut from 14-A (the MS shot of her) to 14-B (MLS 2 shot) or 14-C (Ed's MCU). Without this forethought, the editor cannot create smooth action match cuts in postproduction (see *The Artist* example on p. 184).

Concerning the Floor Plan (Figure 24-5):

1. *Make a floor plan* of the intended scene showing walls, doors, windows, and furniture, and indicating the characters' movements and stopping points. This is informed by the blocking worked out in rehearsals and greatly assisted by shooting them. Each scene gets its own floor plan labeled with its scene number.

2. *Mark each camera position* you need to get the shots you've planned in the shooting script. Some shots can be taken with a different lens from the same camera position. Mark each camera position, "Angle #1 on Dana," "Angle #2 on Ed" and so on, and mark which shots in the shooting script are taken from each angle. When several shots can be taken from the same camera position (as in 14-A and 14-D) they will be scheduled back to back before you move the camera and adjust lighting for another position.

The shooting script and floor plans now contain most of the information you need to determine shooting order. Wide (or establishing) shots are shot first because they set performance levels, take most lighting resources, and set lighting patterns. Closer shots must then appear to match both the acting and the lighting logic of the master shot. There is considerable latitude—called **cheating**—for close-ups and over-the-shoulder shots that follow, with reaction shots, inserts, and cutaways done last. In fact, many inserts and cutaways (such as the POV of the menu) can be accomplished after the talent have left for the day and are "off the clock" (see "Location and Shot Order" p. 316).

STORYBOARDS

Another pre-visualization tool used to develop the shooting script is the **storyboard,** a shot-by-shot rendering of a scene from the perspective of the camera and visualized in editing order like a comic strip. Storyboards are drawn in frames that duplicate the aspect ratio of the shooting format and reflect, as precisely as possible, the shot sizes, perspectives, camera angles, characters, and camera movement. On a tightly planned production, the art director may make storyboard sketches for each angle in scenes that involve complex coverage or movement as in Figure 24-6, *bottom.* Storyboard software such as FrameForge Previz Studio 3 can help you generate a professional-looking storyboard, but you may feel underwhelmed by its stock characters. Large-budget films often hire storyboard artists whose visual sensibility closely matches the intended style of the film, but others simply make do with quick, basic sketches. Even inexpert sketches using stick figures are good enough to work out compositions that are interesting and relevant.

CAMERA PLACEMENT

Placing the camera can seem like an industrial decision based on lighting or other technical considerations, but your work will have no soul unless technique helps to reproduce human awareness at work during each dramatic encounter. This is why the decision-making process concerning camera placement is often referred to as "directing the camera." Let's see how this works.

Using Lines of Tension

Consider the camera's relationship to the scene axes, or lines of tension. These are the invisible lines of strong feeling you would draw between the most important people and objects in a scene. Often they are also sightlines and have great dramatic potential (changes of eyeline, for instance), because they justify particular camera angles, and imply the emotional connections (and therefore POVs) associated with particular characters.

Look at the floor plan for a child's view of a mother–father argument (Figure 24-6, *top*). The dotted-in sightlines are the likely lines of psychic and dramatic tension. One axis is that between the mother and father who dominate the scene, but others exist between the silent boy and each parent. These lines of tension suggest possibilities for establishing the POV of the scene. We could, for example, take the preponderance of shots along the father–mother axis, and that would favor the perspective of the adults engaged in the argument. But let's go another way. Let's say we want to put the emphasis on the boy's distress at what he is witnessing. To favor the child's POV, we consider the axes between the boy and the parents, which immediately suggest camera positions.

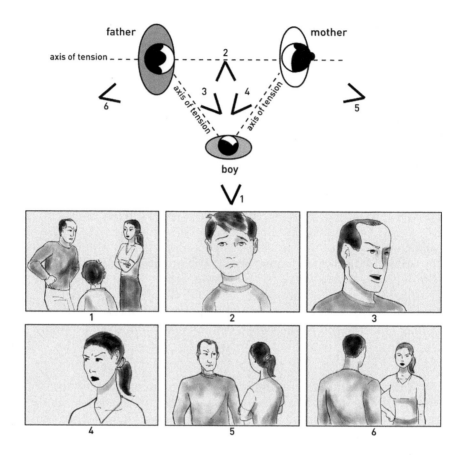

FIGURE 24-6

Drawing lines of tension between characters can guide the placement of the camera to imply a particular subjectivity or relationship; storyboards help further visualize these connections.

What each camera angle covers is shown in the storyboard sequence (Figure 24-6, *bottom*). The master shot (angle 1) is from over the boy's shoulder, which already places the audience along the same visual perspective as the boy, encouraging identification with him. Angle 2 (MCU boy) is the boy's looking shot, which, when used with the boy's POV shots (Angle 3 and Angle 4) create an even stronger sense of POV—we see what he's seeing. Angles 5 and 6 are taken along the father–mother axis and will allow us to shift the POV if we want to. These medium over-the-shoulder shots are fairly neutral, so provide an objective POV. If we were to take these shots tighter, CU singles, they would suggest the POV of each parent (which we don't want in this interpretation of the scene).

Given this coverage, I can edit the scene to give a strong sense of the boy's POV. The scene is not about how the parents feel, but about how the boy feels. But Angles 5 and 6 allow me to modulate this identification with the boy and perhaps present salient moments of the argument in a slightly more objective way.

SUBJECTIVE AND OBJECTIVE

No matter whose point of view you favor, POV in human transactions is apt to migrate. Changes in lines of tension and fluctuations in scene intensity are your prime clues. Let's recall how an onlooker's consciousness moves around when observing two people in conversation. The Concerned Observer's view represents the average, relatively detached movement of human perception, and we can use it as a model for how the camera and editing move our attention around within a scene. Together, camerawork and editing mimic the way an observer's ears, eyes, and psychological focus migrate within an environment, whether quiet or busy.

Angle and shot changes are suggested by stimuli from the scene, but they also arise from a narrative agenda as the Storyteller pursues a line of inquiry. Indeed, perception is often shaped by the predispositions of the Storyteller. Salient observation can be that of a character in the film or of a Storyteller who directs our attention from outside. The mood may start relatively detached, and then grow involved with the predicaments and personal qualities of the characters, or it can happen in reverse order. A film, just as you or I would in any gripping situation, will "breathe" in and out between extremes. The difference can be dramatized by recalling the experience of watching a tennis game (see "The Actor and the Acted-Upon" p. 197).

Notice that *the closer the camera is to a line of tension, the more subjectively involved the audience will feel*. When complementary angles are used, the audience is switched rapidly between each protagonist's subjective experience, so the aggregate effect may be to enter the fray without identifying with one contestant or another. This depends on the balance of editing, as well as, less measurably, the power in each actor's characterization.

We can vary the Observer's relationship to the axes, and vary his or her closeness to what is observed. A close shot is both a magnification of compelling detail (a surprised expression, say) and the psychologically driven exclusion of other, irrelevant detail. You can juxtapose subjects in an antithetical relationship to each other (cat and canary, say) by editing shots of them together— or, more subtly and compellingly, by blocking them together within a single shot.

SHOW RELATEDNESS

How are the protagonists to be spatially related? Showing the couple arguing in the same frame, but the boy separated in a close-up, reinforces his separation from his parents. Relating boy and mother in one frame to father alone in another suggests a different configuration of alliances. There could be other factors—using foreground and background, the sides of the frame, different camera heights, and different levels of lighting—any combination of which might predispose the audience toward interpreting the scene in a particular way or from a particular POV. You learn this by distilling your own guidelines from life experience and well-made movies.

THERE ARE NO RULES, ONLY WHAT FEELS RIGHT

There are no hard-and-fast rules here because human judgment arises from a multiplicity of clues. What matters is the sensibility and rationale by which each shot is composed, lit, blocked, and acted. Compositionally, you are always showing the specifics of relationship between person and object, object and object, or person and person. By relating them, you imply the relationship of one idea, principle, personality, or judgment to another. You can achieve a similar effect through editing or story construction. Using parallel storytelling, for instance, you might intercut a boxing match with a lover's feud. Try out such an idea, and judge from what you see and feel, rather than relying on theory.

REGROUPING AND RESET TRANSITIONS

In scenes where characters move, they often regroup to face in new screen directions. At the very least, this means that early and late reaction shots cannot be interchanged, and the scene cannot easily be restructured in the cutting room if so desired. *Movements that lead to regrouping must be shown on-screen.* Regard them as **reset transitions**, each establishing a new axis of action and tension, and a new compositional phase of the scene. When rehearsing a scene, you avoid letting people mill around; instead you choreograph movements and compose group configurations strictly for their new importance. Movements nearly always carry dramatic significance, and so you limit them in order to make them important.

PLANS AND PRUDENCE

Plan your coverage, but try to foresee potential difficulties. Though you intend to show only one character onscreen during an intense exchange, it may be wise to cover both. This allows you abundance—a necessary fallback if your plans fail.

Every situation imposes its own camera positioning, and movement demands and limitations. The latter are usually physical: windows, pillars or awkward backgrounds in an interior that restrict shooting in one direction, or an incongruity to be avoided in an exterior. A wonderful Victorian house turns out to have a background of power lines strung across the sky, and must be framed low when you had wanted to frame high. Filmmaking is always serendipitous, and so often your vision must be shelved and energy redirected to solve the unforeseen. For the rigid, linear personality, this constant adaptation is frustrating; but for others, it poses interesting challenges. Nonetheless, you must plan, and sometimes plans even work out.

WORK WITHIN YOUR MEANS

Dollying through the noise and confusion of a newsroom in *All the President's Men* (1976) is dramatically justified, but dollying, craning, helicopter shots, and other budget busting visual treatments are beyond the low-budget filmmaker's means. However, few impressions cannot be achieved in simpler ways, especially as whole films have been successfully made with a camera on a tripod. See any of Yasujiro Ozu's masterpieces (Figure 24-7) or see films made with an entirely

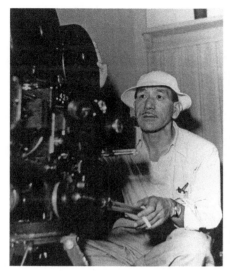 

FIGURE 24-7

It is not necessary to have expensive equipment or complicated shots to tell an effective, compelling story; most of Yasujiro Ozu's (*left*) masterpieces, including *Tokyo Story* (*right*) used a static camera and minimal coverage.

handheld camera, such as *Breaking the Waves* by von Trier, mentioned earlier. Decades of classic cinema were shot with quite limited equipment, and you can do excellent work using the simplest techniques that serve the film's artistic intentions. Resist your crew's desire to experiment with "better" equipment. Fight for simplicity—simple is strong; less is more.

STUDY THE MASTERS

For ideas on how best to shoot a problem scene, study the way the best filmmakers have handled similar situations. Learn from them, but always be informed by your growing perception of life. Find the simplest solutions that answer your perceptual needs. To help you study the masters, use the film analysis exercises at the companion website for this book: www.directingbook.com under "Projects." Analysis Project 5-2: *Editing Analysis* is a film-study project to help you assess how a director embodies choices and intentions.

CHAPTER 25

LINE PRODUCING AND LOGISTICS

Along with all the creative activity during preproduction (script development, rehearsals, and visualization) much needs deciding in relation to the practical aspects of filmmaking: the organization of time and personnel; coordinating locations, props, equipment, and costumes; dealing with film labs and other vendors; working with budgets, contracts, payroll, and insurance; and so on. Coordinating the practical dimension of film production is called **line producing.** It is the domain of the producing team (producer, line producer, and unit production manager), and you cannot make a movie without them.

Good line producing undergirds the production crew and protects the director from logistical issues that would intrude upon the all-important creative aspects of filmmaking. When all goes well, everything necessary to carry out the creative preproduction planning, from locations and sets dressing to equipment and personnel will be there and ready to go as production time comes round.

The director meets regularly with the producing team to elaborate the needs of the project and plan the production period so that everyone is on the same page when the camera starts rolling. At the final meeting before production—actually the culmination of many planning sessions—you lock down arrangements before shooting. By now, everyone heading a department has visited locations and brings their respective breakdowns. Participants include the producer, unit production manager (UPM), director, assistant director (AD), script supervisor (also known as continuity supervisor), director of photography (DP), art director, and head of sound. Now it's time to coordinate everyone's efforts and make last-minute corrections.

SCHEDULING THE SHOOT

Scheduling is normally decided by the UPM and the AD and double-checked by the director and principal crew members, especially the script supervisor and DP. Higher-budgeted productions may use a line producer who works directly with the day-to-day production details on behalf of the UPM.

137	137	EXT	STREET /Neil waiting for car outside	Day	0 1/8 pgs.	3
138	138	INT	JEANNIE'S CAR/Jeannie, Neil talking about Richard being	Day	1 0/8 pgs.	3, 4
96	96	EXT	STREET /Neil walking into bldg	Day	0 1/8 pgs.	3
97	97	INT	DEP'T OF AGING/Neil filing application for senior help,	Day	0 6/8 pgs.	3, 7
			- - - END OF DAY 27- - - Monday, July 20, 2012		2 pgs.	
122	122	EXT	STREET /Neil, Jonas meeting	Night	0 1/8 pgs.	3, 6
123	123	INT	BAR /Neil, Jonas mischevious	Night	1 7/8 pgs.	3, 6, 13
188	188	INT	NIGHTCLUB /Neil talking into cellphone, set up for gig,	Night	0 6/8 pgs.	3
163	163	INT	BAR /Neil visiting the bar, hocking up w/ Amanda	Afternoon	0 2/8 pgs.	3, 13
37	37	INT	BAR /Richard drinking, watching woman walk by	Night	0 5/8 pgs.	1
133	133	INT	BAR /Richard being confronted/almost fighting in bar	Night	0 7/8 pgs.	1, 14
			- - - END OF DAY 28- - - Tuesday, July 21, 2012		4 4/8 pgs.	
8	8	EXT	STREET /Richard walking to car, picking up newspaper	Morning	0 1/8 pgs.	1
9	9	INT	RICHARD'S CAR /Richard turning on car	Morning	0 2/8 pgs.	1
10	10	EXT	STREET /2ND UNIT Richard's car driving off	Morning	0 0/8 pgs.	

FIGURE 25-1

Scheduling programs (like Jungle Software's *Gorilla*, pictured here) can easily generate stripboards and make changes to a film's production schedule.

Good scheduling software (see box on p. 320) helps you distil information from the script, and enables you to schedule (and re-schedule if necessary) actors, props, and other necessities accordingly. It generates scheduling charts and stripboards that show at a glance which scenes and characters must be shot at each location (Figure 25-1). Any competent UPM or AD should be able to use this software with ease.

Aim to set the shortest practicable schedule because the number of working days translates directly into costs (see below, "Under- or Over-scheduling"). The logistics of travel, time to build and to strike sets, and time allowed for contingencies like bad weather, illness, or equipment breakdowns must all be factored in. However, scheduling always involves making educated guesses because no film is quite like any other. Anyone using the available scheduling and budgeting software available can do a thoroughly professional job, as we shall see. Take into account any or all of the following:

- Availability of actors and crew
- Availability of locations
- Locations and travel requirements

FIGURE 25-2 ———

Student director Patrick Ng consults with his AD Lauren Brady about the shooting schedule for the day.

- Costs involved at each stage if hiring talent, equipment, crew, or facilities
- Scenes involving key dramatic elements that may be affected or delayed by weather or other cyclical conditions
- Availability and special conditions attaching to rented equipment, including props— slow-motion scenes, for instance, may require a special camera that might be scheduled according to its optimal hire period.
- Complexity of each lighting setup and power requirements
- Time of day, so available light comes from the right direction (take a compass when location scouting!)

LOCATIONS AND SHOT ORDER

Normal practice is to shoot in order of convenience for locations and availability of cast and crew. Since lighting setups and changes take the most time during a shoot, a compact schedule avoids relighting the same set.

All scenes having a common location are shot on the same day(s) regardless of their order in the script. If there are three INT. CLASSROOM scenes (one in each Act) we'd schedule them all for the same production time so we visit and light the classroom set only once.

As mentioned earlier, wide shots are scheduled first: they establish the spatial relationships and blocking, the lighting logic, and performance intensity. If time becomes tight, you might get away with not shooting a close-up or a detail, but master shots usually cover the most territory in the scene and so are indispensable. Closer shots follow because their lighting and performance pitch must match the master shot. Cutaways and inserts usually come last because they can often be shot after the actors have left or can be picked up by a smaller 2nd unit crew at some other time. Other factors sometimes affect a normal shooting schedule, such as the availability of actors, crew, equipment, and locations.

Rehearsal now really pays off because director and cast can move confidently between the different script junctures and their associated emotional levels. Even so, the non-sequential nature of film shooting can throw many actors off. A director's principal duty on the set is to keep reminding actors where they are in the script, where they have just come from, so they are in their character's correct emotional frame when the camera rolls.

SHOOTING IN SCRIPT ORDER

Certain types of films may need shooting in script order, particularly if director and cast are inexperienced. Here are examples:

- Those depending on a graduated character development—like the king's decline into insanity in Nicholas Hytner's *The Madness of King George* (1995).
- Films using a high degree of improvisation. You shoot in script order to maintain control over an evolving story line.
- Those taking place entirely in interiors and that have a small, constant cast. Here, there may be little advantage to shooting out of scene order, and shooting sequentially benefits acting and continuity.

KEY SCENES AND SCHEDULING FOR PERFORMANCES

Some scenes are so important that, should they fail, no film is possible. Perhaps your film requires its young heroine to fall deeply in love with an emotionally unstable man. It would be folly to shoot too much until you know that your actors can make a difficult and pivotal scene work. Key scenes must be filmed neither too early (when the cast is still green) nor too late (when failure might void weeks of work). If the scene works, it will give a lift to everything else you shoot. If the scene bombs, you will want to work out the problems in rehearsal and reshoot in a day or two. Until the problem is solved, however, you cannot risk shooting the bulk of the film.

Problems of performance should show up in rehearsals, but when shooting starts, camera nerves often kick in, especially in demanding scenes. Filming is occasionally better than the best rehearsal, but particularly at first it is quite often a little inferior. The cast may feel more deeply during the first takes of a new scene, but strong feeling is no guarantee of control or character development. Some actors, realizing they must sustain a performance over several takes per angle and several angles per scene, instinctively conserve energy. You can minimize this by predetermining how you want to edit so you shoot less extensively. Knowing how much or little to shoot, drawing a line between adequacy and wastefulness, is hardest for the new director. Err on the side of caution, and be sure to give your editor enough coverage.

EMOTIONAL DEMAND ORDER

Be aware of the steep demands some scenes make upon the actors. A nude love scene, for instance, or a scene in which two characters become violently angry, should be delayed until the actors are clearly comfortable with each other and the crew. Schedule such scenes late in the day's work because they are so emotionally draining. For nude scenes everyone possible leaves the set.

WEATHER AND OTHER CONTINGENCY COVERAGE

Make contingency shooting plans whenever you face uncertainties. Schedule exteriors early in case they are delayed by unsuitable weather, and arrange for **cover sets**, which are interior locations standing ready as standby alternatives. This way you will not fall behind schedule.

ALLOCATION OF SHOOTING TIME PER SCENE

Depending on the amount of coverage, the intensity of the scene in question, and the reliability of actors and crew, you might expect to shoot anywhere between two and four minutes of edited screen time per 10-hour day. Traveling between locations, elaborate setups, or relighting the same location will greatly slow the pace. It's fairly standard practice to allot setup time for the mornings. While the crew is busy setting up, the director rehearses the cast.

UNDER- OR OVER-SCHEDULING

A promising film may also be sabotaged by misplaced optimism. Consider the following:

- Work may be alarmingly slow at first because the crew is still figuring out efficient working relationships. Schedule lightly during the first three days of any shoot.
- You can always shorten a long schedule, but it may be impossible to lengthen one too short.
- Most nonprofessional (and some professional) units expect to shoot too much screen time in too short a schedule. Be realistic.
- A dog-tired crew and cast work progressively slower. Tempers and morale deteriorate, and artistic commitment evaporates.

- An average shooting day should be 10 hours. Occasionally, you may need to schedule 12-hour days. Beyond that, the law of diminishing returns kicks in—a cast and crew working 14-hour days will make sloppy errors. Worse, fatigue compromises safety on the set.
- The standard turnaround for a crew (the time between the end of one shooting day and the start of another) is 12 hours, and 10 hours is the minimum.

Without resolute progress-chasing an inexperienced crew tends to delay hitting its stride. Any shoot can fall seriously behind if the AD and producing team do not keep the unit on schedule. Crew responsibilities are detailed in the next chapter.

THE CALL SHEET

The production manager and assistant director are responsible for translating the shooting schedule into day-by-day **call sheets**. These, distributed to the entire crew (and posted on the project's Facebook page), detail: (1) what portion of the script is being shot on a specific day, (2) who needs to be on the set, (3) when each person needs to be there, and (4) how to get to the set. Arrival times allow for setup by the crew and makeup and rehearsal times for the cast. For short film projects, you can download blank call sheets from this book's website (www.directingbook.com under "Forms and Logs"), or you can generate you own with one of the popular film scheduling software packages that integrate all scheduling functions (see box p. 320).

BUDGETING THE FILM

In a broad sense, the **budget** of a film is essentially how much money (and other resources) one has available to make a movie. It is not something that one attends to "down the road": you must know what financial resources you have before you begin production or you will experience serious sticker shock.

An ideal approach is to start with the script, cast breakdown, and visual design, and then raise the funds sufficient to make it happen. After that, budgeting means deciding what specific expenses you face and how available funds will be distributed across the various needs of the project.

Budgeting is primarily the domain of the producing team (producer, associate producer and line producer), but the film budget has enormous consequences for the director. Often the director must strategize to make the best film possible on the available money, and must balance interpretive aims (rehearsal schedule, visual design, coverage, and so on) against what is available. A detailed budget includes a price line for every item or service, and lays out how much your film will cost and where the money will go. Use pessimistic figures because the total for a film can be a mortal shock. Better face the music while you can still adapt, and be ready to rewrite scenes that incur more expense than they merit. Approaching production, you and your production crew must consider:

- How much does the production have in the bank?
- What is still to come?
- What "in kind" resources are available?
- What will the film cost using the projected shooting schedule?

- Are there enough funds to cover projected costs?
- Are more funds needed?
- Where can savings be made?
- Can any shooting be delayed until funds have been assembled?

Broadly speaking, budget expenses divide into above-the-line and below-the-line costs. The line itself is the division between preproduction and beginning production. Thus:

Above-the-line costs:

Story rights
Screenplay
Producer's fee
Director's fee
Principal actors' fees.

_____ "The Line"

Below-the-line costs:

Production unit salaries
Cast, stand-ins, extras
Art department costs (sets, props and costumes)
Studio or location rentals
Film stock or media
Camera, electrical, sound, and other equipment (purchase and rental)
Laboratory fees (processing and transfers)
Special effects
Catering, hotel, and living expenses
Transportation
Legal costs and production insurance
Miscellaneous expenses
Music rights and composition
Postproduction expenses (sound mix, color grading, mastering, and other services)
Distribution copies and publicity materials
Festival entry fees and travel to festivals.

All movie budgets should also include a contingency percentage, usually four percent or more of the total budget. This is your Murphy's Law surcharge; it allows for equipment failure, bad weather, reshooting, and other hidden costs.

INSURANCES

A large line item that novices tend to avoid is production insurance. It is not an area to skimp, indeed consider it a necessity for all film shoots, regardless of size, scale, and budget. Accidents happen: an actor falls and breaks an arm, a grip truck has an accident on the way to the set, a $10,000 lens lands on the sidewalk… Without production insurance, any of these scenarios could easily shut you down. Union actors cannot work unless you provide proof of insurance to their union, and many equipment rental houses and locations require proof of insurance. Film workers too are often union members, and their union stipulates what coverage is necessary when they are hired.

If you're a student, your department should have information about where and how to acquire production insurance. If you're an independent filmmaker, the Independent Feature Project (IFP) website is a good place to start your search for affordable insurance (www.ifp.org). Insurance is complicated territory, so be sure to research exactly what kind of policies your project requires. Depending on the expense and sophistication of your production, you may need to carry some or all of the following: preproduction indemnity; workers' compensation; film producer's indemnity; consequential loss; errors and omissions; negative insurance; employer's liability; public, or third-party, liability; third-party property damage; equipment insurance; sets, wardrobe, props insurance; vehicles; fidelity guarantee; union and other insurances. Special insurances are also generally necessary when working abroad under unusual health or other conditions.

Budgeting and Scheduling Forms

For short film projects you can use the budget form, breakdown form, and call sheet blanks available for download from this book's companion website (www.directingbook.com, "Forms and Logs"). If you mean to approach anyone in the professional filmmaking world, all paperwork must use recognized budget and scheduling software. The industry favorite is Movie Magic™, an expensive but all-encompassing software package. Less pricey, and good for the lean independent, is Gorilla™ from Jungle Software. Either will help you break down the script, turn it into a schedule, and arrive at a detailed, properly laid out budget based on all the variables that you supply. The beauty of dedicated relational databases is that any change you enter in the budget, coverage, or scheduling shows up immediately everywhere that it matters. The software will also generate scene breakdowns, call sheets, contact lists, and organize locations and storyboards. Most new users will need training to make full use of their purchase, but properly used, the software even monitors daily cash flow, so there need be no unpleasant surprises lurking in the accounts department.

DRAWING UP AN EQUIPMENT LIST

CAUTION: OVER-ELABORATE EQUIPMENT

Getting over-elaborate is tempting for the technician trying to forestall problems by insisting on the "proper" equipment—always, of course, the most complicated and expensive. Beware of strong-minded cinematographers out to pad their sample reel with nifty techniques from nifty toys. Early in your directing career, you and your crew will be hard put to master basic techniques and gear, so it's wise to foreswear advanced equipment and the time it takes to become proficient with them. This can also be a safety issue: a film production is not the place for on-the-job training in potentially harmful gear, especially when it involves electricity. In experienced hands, however, sophisticated equipment may save time and money. Expect the sound department in particular to want a large inventory. They are often asked to quickly adapt to changes in lighting set-ups, shot sizes, blocking or other circumstances and cannot comply without reserve equipment.

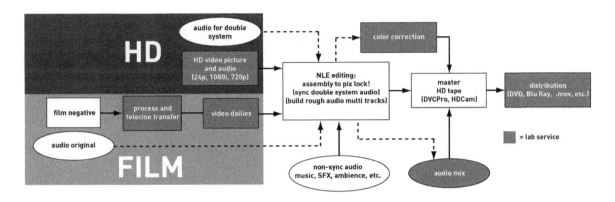

FIGURE 25-3

It is essential to understand the technical process of your workflow before you shoot. Above is a common workflow for film or HD projects that finish on broadcast HD formats. Go to www.directingbook.com to download this and other workflow charts.

WORKFLOW AND EQUIPMENT

One essential factor that a filmmaker (especially a student or independent filmmaker) must research from the beginning of every new project is **workflow**. This is the format path and processes your project must follow. Workflow includes the image shooting and sound gathering formats, the editorial format, the finishing process, the mastering and distribution formats (Figure 25-3). At the present juncture in film production history, workflow varieties are myriad, and each can make a significant impact on the budget of the film, the technical processes, and the range of exhibition possibilities. Filmmakers who lose their way often face expensive consequences. Careful research and cross-checking from the very beginning will go a long way toward minimizing ugly surprises.

Preproduction meetings with your cinematographer, production sound mixer, editor, and postproduction lab (if you require lab services like color grading) are the forum for discussing what formats to adopt for recording both sound and image, and *everyone in the crew must be on the same technical page before a single frame has been shot.* Regarding workflow, there are four basic questions to settle for each new project:

1. *What is the shooting format?* Film, HD video (720p, 1080i), uncompressed or RAW video?
2. *How are we editing?* Format, codecs, frame rate, resolution?
3. *How do we want to finish and master the movie?* Film, HD video (720p, 1080i), uncompressed media files, (2K, 4K)?
4. *How do we want to exhibit and distribute the project?* Broadcast HD format (720p, 1080i), Blu-ray, DVD, web, or a combination? Or high end theatrical projection like 35 mm film, or Digital Cinema? (See p. 325.)

Within these general questions are many arcane and ever-evolving details that you must reconcile if you are not to waste inordinate time, money and energy. Most directors need considerable education in these ever-evolving questions, so a cinematographer, sound mixer and editor are more than creative collaborators—they need to be technologically up to date or your project won't make it through to completion successfully.[1]

SHOOTING FILM OR DIGITAL?

Whether to shoot on film or digitally has two major facets: the first is creative—what look can I get from each production format? The second is budgetary—what will each format cost? Both then involve additional choices: film shooting can be 35 mm or Super 16 mm format, and digital shooting can be done in HD broadcast standards (720p, 1080i) or at 2K or 4K resolutions (uncompressed video files).

Nobody should believe that shooting digitally is inherently cheaper than shooting film. Michael Mann's *Public Enemies* (2009), shot digitally, cost around $100,000,000. You can however use digital video to produce aesthetically beautiful, professionally polished films for less than using film. Add to this recent developments in RAW and uncompressed video shooting, enlarged image sensors, and a full range of superior, interchangeable lenses and you have a very promising medium. With the highly sophisticated digital cameras like the RED Epic and Arri Alexa, digital video can be every bit as visually expressive as any 35 mm film production.

The major expense with film shooting, apart from cost of the film stock, is the unavoidable involvement with a film lab and the expense of its services for film processing, transferring, intermediate prints, effects, optical track masters and possibly distribution copies too. A digital cameras, on the other hand, uses reusable record media like SD or SxS cards or hard drives, and its output is wholly handled by computers.

Given the dramatic increase in the quality of today's lenses, their responsiveness to light, and relatively lower cost, it's no wonder that few students or independent filmmakers now make film their production format. So clear is this trend that the major film camera manufacturers (Panavision, Arriflex, and Aaton) are regularly rolling out the new digital rigs, and are no longer developing new film cameras.

DIGITAL ACQUISITION

Digital video has spawned an explosion of competing formats and compression codecs (see below), and they change and proliferate at an alarming rate. Luckily for filmmakers, this means the capabilities of digital video increase every year, while the price/quality ratio gets ever more advantageous. There will always be high-end gear beyond the reach of filmmakers on a low budget, but the image quality of the lower price cameras is nothing short of astonishing.

Directors generally choose their cinematographers by the quality of their previous work, their creative judgment, and their ideas regarding the project at hand—but at some point you will need to have "the discussion" about shooting technology. What are we going to shoot on?

---

[1] If you'd like a more detailed introduction to all these technologies, try *Voice & Vision: A Creative Approach to Narrative Film and DV Production* by Mick Hurbis-Cherrier (Focal Press, 2012).

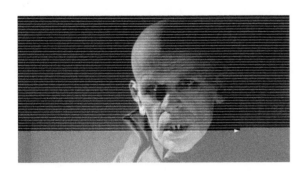

FIGURE 25-4 ————————————————

Progressive scanning renders a complete frame of video (from top to bottom) 30 times per second.

Broadcast HD, formats, and scanning

In the United States, **high definition** (**HD**) broadcast resolution conforms to the frame rate, aspect ratio, and resolution standards established by the consortium of engineers, communication companies, and policy makers of the **ATSC** (**Advanced Television Systems Committee**).[2] Of principal interest to filmmakers are the HD formats:

- *1080i HD* records 1,920 pixels×1,080 lines at a frame rate of 30 interlaced frames per second.
- *720p HD* records 1,280 pixels×720 lines at 30 or 60 progressively scanned frames per second.
- *1080/24p HD* records 1,920 pixels×1,080 lines at a frame rate of 24p (resembling film).

Aspect ratio expresses the width of the frame in relation to its height, and is the same for all these standards, 16:9. At this ratio, HD approximates the cinema format of 1.85:1, and is now the preferred aspect ratio for HD television (see pp. 155–156).

Frame rates and scanning: Because of differing electrical supplies, American frame rate standards are based on 30 fps (frames per second), and the European PAL system is 25 fps. Which you use depends on where you live. ATSC standards create the frames in each of its 30 fps formats using two strategies. One is **progressive scanning** (Figure 25-4), meaning that all of the 720 horizontal lines of video information that make up the image are scanned (drawn on your image sensor or monitor screen), from top to bottom, 30 times per second. Progressive scan formats are indicated with the designation "p" while the "i" designation stands for **interlaced scanning.** Here the entire video frame is scanned twice from top to bottom. First the odd lines of information are scanned (lines 1, 3, 5, 7, etc.) and then the even lines of information are scanned (lines 2, 4, 6, 8, 10, etc.). Each scan is called a **field** and these two fields (the odd field and even field) are interlaced to create a full frame. The interlaced system, therefore, scans each field every 60th of a second and achieves the full frame of two interlaced fields every 30th of a second (Figure 25-5).

Resolution: Most important for the director, however, is the issue of resolution, because it has a direct impact on image quality. Resolution refers to the format's ability to reproduce visual detail, sharpness of line, subtlety and degrees of luminance, and accuracy of color. Video resolution is affected by several factors: scanning type, lens quality, the number of sensor pixels, sampling bit rates, chroma subsampling, and data compression.

———————————————————————————————————————

[2] Canada and Mexico also use the ATSC standard, however, there are three other digital TV systems around the globe. DVB-T (Digital Video Broadcasting—Terrestrial) used in Europe, Russia, Australia, and nations throughout Asia and Africa; ISDB-T (Integrated Services Digital Broadcasting—Terrestrial), used in Japan, Brazil, and most of South America; and DTMB (Digital Terrestrial Multimedia Broadcast), used by China and Hong Kong.

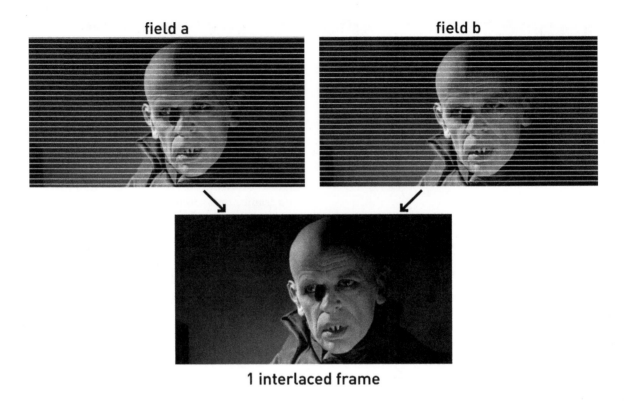

field a   field b

1 interlaced frame

FIGURE 25-5 ──

Interlaced scanning creates one frame from two separate fields (60 alternating fields per second) that combine to produce 30 frames per second.

One principle factor of image resolution is the **pixel count.** A video image is created by hundreds of thousands (sometimes millions) of tiny capacitors lining the face of a video sensor or video monitor. These are called **picture elements** or **pixels** for short. The camera lens focuses light on the pixels of a camera sensor. This is commonly a CCD or CMOS chip which in turn translates those light values into digital information. In your video monitor the reverse process happens, but similarly, the more pixels there are, the better the rendering of image detail, light, and color.

The ATSC resolution standards (720 and 1080) are determined by the number of pixels in each format. We can determine the pixel resolution by multiplying the vertical lines by the horizontal pixels. So, the 720 format contains 921,600 pixels per frame and 1080 contains 2,073,600 pixels per frame—more than twice the information, which means twice the resolution.

Picture compression: With so many pixels capturing so much detail and generating so much data, the camera, postproduction equipment, and television transmitters all have to process a

FIGURE 25-6

HD cameras with interchangeable lenses (like the Canon C300 pictured here) and larger sensors (left) can produce images that approximate the visual characteristics of 35 mm film.

torrent of digital information. However, since much in each frame repeats information from that preceding it, engineers have invented compression **codecs** (short for compression/decompression). Like shorthand, they reduce what gets "written" to the recording medium. A high-compression, "lossy" codec will, however, visibly intrude its economies onto the screen, particularly during image movement.

There are *many* different codecs, most of them proprietary by manufacturer. Sony HD cameras for example use MPEG-2 long GoP and Panasonic uses AVC-Intra. The H.264 codec is popular in many DSLR cameras that shoot video. At this juncture, rather than disappear down the rabbit hole of formats and codecs, you only need to know that your shooting format and codec must be supported by your editing system and by your postproduction lab—should you need their services. Thus, in preproduction your DP, editor, and lab must all talk with each other.

Sensor size: The size of the image sensor inside the camera also greatly affects the aesthetics of the final image, and is thus important when choosing a camera. There are two issues at play: one, larger sensors render finer detail because they can contain a greater pixel density (more or larger pixels). Two, lenses and depth of field are involved because small video sensors tend to create images of great depth of field, so controlling this important compositional element becomes difficult. Professional camcorders utilized fairly large sensors (usually measuring ½", or ⅔"—about the size of a 16 mm film frame). Recent developments have greatly increased sensor size and HD cameras now often have sensors near in size to a 35 mm film frame. Using interchangeable lenses, these cameras achieve the same quality, perspective, and DOF control as 35 mm film production (Figure 25-6). See Chapter 27 for detailed information about depth of field and the creative impact of lenses.

High End Digital Shooting: Uncompressed and Raw

Broadcast quality HD is always recorded compressed, transmitted compressed, and then decompressed for display. Ultra high-end digital camera's, like the Arri Alexa, Aaton Penelope Δ, and RED Epic now record full resolution, 12-bit uncompressed video (or RAW files) and have light sensitivity and image quality easily matching 35 mm negative film (Figure 25-7). Known as **2K** (2048×1080) and **4K** (4096×2304) after their approximate number of horizontal pixels, these ultra-high resolutions far exceed the ATSC HD standards because they're not intended for HDTV broadcast (Figure 25-8). As you might imagine, their video sensors are of exceptionally high quality and *large*. Most have a single, huge sensor (CCD or CMOS) the size of a 35 mm negative

FIGURE 25-7

A new slate of ultra-high end HD cameras like the RED Epic are capable of shooting uncompressed, high resolution video with light sensitivity and dynamic range that match film.

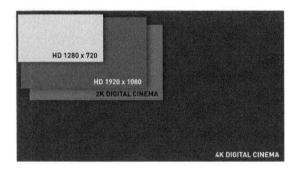

HD 1280 x 720

HD 1920 x 1080

2K DIGITAL CINEMA

4K DIGITAL CINEMA

FIGURE 25-8

The resolution of ultra high-definition cameras, at 2K and 4K, easily surpass ATSC standards for HDTV broadcasting.

frame, and shoot at 24 frames per second, the standard frame rate for both motion picture film and digital camera projection. These high end formats are destined for large screen theatrical projection.[3] The 2K and 4K shooting resolutions correspond to the **Digital Cinema** (**D-Cinema**) standard, a high-resolution digital theatrical projection format established by the **Digital Cinema Initiative** (**DCI**) (see p. 421). Of course, high image quality is still welcome even if your project is never picked up for theatrical release. To review a basic workflow chart for high end shooting and finishing, go to this book's companion website www.directing-book.com under "Workflow Charts."

Consumer Cameras

Given their notoriously small imaging chips (which produce an unmanageably large DOF), poor quality factory lenses, and lack of manual controls for focus, exposure, and so on, low-end consumer camcorders are inappropriate for most—but not all—narrative film production, which demands control over all visual aspects of the image. Some filmmakers, however, have used their small size and "low-tech" aesthetic to advantage; notably Thomas Vinterberg with *The Celebration* (1998), Spike Lee with *Bamboozled* (2000), and Rebecca Miller with *Personal Velocity* (2002). So, never say never. If camera limitations become an advantage, use the technology that delivers it. Besides, technology never made the filmmaker. As these films attest, an aesthetically limited camera in the hands of a powerful filmmaker is always better than a powerful camera in the hands of someone aesthetically impoverished.

---

[3] During the writing of this edition there was much chatter in the industry about achieving resolutions of 5 K and 6 K... so stay tuned.

FIGURE 25-9 ⎯⎯⎯⎯⎯⎯⎯⎯⎯⎯⎯

Director Shanti Thakur shot her film *Red Tulips* (2012) on Super 16 mm film, and finished it as a 2K video master on HDCam SR. A common workflow for festival-bound films.

FILM ACQUISITION

What film camera equipment to use depends on your chosen format, such as 35 mm or Super 16 mm (16 mm widescreen). Superior image quality is associated with 35 mm film because it uses lenses with a usefully limited DOF, and can be shown in any cinema in the world. Furthermore it can be transferred to any video format—at a price. It takes heavy funding up front to buy stock, and is vastly expensive to process and print. Anybody experienced enough to light and shoot in film will probably know where to get the equipment and how much it will cost. A feature with a $1 million budget for film acquisition is considered cheap.

Super 16 mm shoot: This widescreen format is a less expensive and more mobile way to shoot features on film, but get advice from someone who has successfully (and recently) completed your preferred chain of production (Figure 25-9).

35 mm shoot: You will need the appropriate camera support systems and a dolly on rails if you shoot in 35 mm, especially Panavision. Any handheld shots will need either one of the newer shoulder-mounted, short-run 35 mm cameras or, if you intend a more gliding motion, a Steadicam™ operated by someone very strong and very experienced at using it.

The workflow from 35 mm or 16 mm film acquisition always requires lab work to process the original film negative and transfer it to a digital video format for editing using the telecine pull-down process. The additional lab services required to finish to a film print or D-Cinema master are also complex, expensive, and require much consultation with a film lab.

DIGITAL SOUND

Address all questions about sound to the **sound recordist** (also called the **production sound mixer**), who heads the field sound team. This usually includes a **boom operator** and sometimes a **cable wrangler**. To decide sound equipment, consider how sound will be recorded. Through the camera and on the same recording media as the picture? Or on a dedicated and separate sound recorder? The first option is called **single system sound**, the second is **double system sound** recording. Serious narrative film projects are nearly always shot double system for two good reasons: one, the audio components built into digital cameras are usually inferior to those in a professional digital sound recorder. Two, since a field sound recordist must constantly monitor and adjust audio levels, he

FIGURE 25-10 ———————————

Slates provide an easy way of synchronizing double system image and sound during postproduction (a smart slate with timecode is pictured here).

or she cannot keep intruding on the camera operator to do so, nor can the camera operator attend to audio levels either.

So professional production uses double system sound, and since picture and sound are on separate media, they must be brought together in sync during post-production. This is where the **slate** or **clapper board** comes in (Figure 25-10). Its use has several functions: to place a positive visual identification at the head of every take (including scene, shot, take, and sound number), to verbally identify the shot and take, and to create a one-frame, easily identifiable reference "moment" by which to align picture and sound in postproduction. That moment is either the sharp snap of the slate sticks recorded by both camera and the audio recorder at the beginning of every take, or it can be a timecode reference number when using a "smart slate" generating visible time code. Either reference makes syncing sound with picture in postproduction a straightforward procedure.

Planning to shoot location sound poses a number of questions:

- Single system or double system?
- How many channels will you need to record?
- Will you need a portable mixer?
- How will you mike each different situation? (Boom? Planted mikes? Radio lavaliers?)
- If you are using radio mikes, will you carry wired mikes as backup? (You should)
- What kind of slate will you use if you're shooting double system (regular or timecode)?
- What effects or ambient sounds are not obvious in the script, and should be recorded during location shooting?

Conferring with your sound recordist should answer your questions and provide all the information you need to make an accurate estimate for the budget.

POSTPRODUCTION

Whatever acquisition medium you use, you will need a non-linear editing system, from a Mac computer (around $2,000) equipped with Final Cut Pro ($300) at the low end to a $60,000 Avid DS postproduction system at the high end. The length of the movie, amount of coverage, whether special effects will require extensive rendering (computer processing), and whether you'll need lab services will affect the postproduction schedule and budget profoundly. Remember to budget for plentiful hard drive storage, including for the audio phase when the final track is mixed using a Pro Tools™ software suite.

The sound studio may be housed in a large theater, and cost hundreds or even thousands of dollars per day. Budget for project mastering, music rights, color grading, pressing DVDs, and for otherwise making distributable copies. Depending on whether you aim for release on television, Webcast, DVD, or a theatrical Digital Cinema venue, you must know your workflow and have consulted with others who have followed a similar path. The postproduction stages and processes are covered in more detail in Part 8.

PRODUCTION STILLS

It may seem a small matter, but get high resolution production stills taken on your shoots. A really striking production still can give your film immense credibility, so give thought to what compositions will represent the thematic issues in the film, the personalities of the players, and any exotic or alluring situations that will draw an audience.

When production starts, set a policy so everyone knows to freeze on command for a production still. Then the director or DP asks the actors to take up representative moments and juxtapositions from a scene just shot. Ideally you employ a good still photographer, but you may have to designate someone in the crew with a good eye for composition. Often this person is the continuity supervisor. Good stills become vital when you prepare posters and publicity packages for festivals and prospective distributors.

AWFUL WARNINGS…

Make "test and test again" your true religion. Leave nothing to chance. Make lists, then lists of lists. Pray.

Golden Rule #1, be prepared for the worst: Optimism and filmmaking are bad bedfellows. One blithe optimist left the master tapes of a feature film in his car trunk overnight. The car happened to be stolen—and because there were no copies, a whole production was transformed instantly into so much silent footage.

Imagination expended darkly at predicting the worst makes you carry particular spares, special tools, emergency information, first-aid kits, and three kinds of diarrhea medicine. A pessimist never tempts fate and, constantly foreseeing the worst, is tranquilly productive compared with your average optimist.

Golden Rule #2, test it first: Whoever checks out equipment should arrive early, and assemble and test every piece there and then. Never assume that everything will be all right because the equipment comes from a reputable company. Murphy is waiting to get you. (Murphy's Law: "Anything that can go wrong will go wrong.") Expect him to lurk inside everything that should fit together, slide, turn, lock, roll, light up, make a noise, or work in silence. The whole Murphy family hides out in every wire, plug, box, lens, battery, and alarm clock. Make no mistake: the whole bloody clan means to ruin you.

PRODUCTION PARTY

Once you've engaged crew and actors, throw a production party as an icebreaker. One of the lovely aspects of the film business is that, being an itinerant industry, you work with the same people from time to time throughout your working life. Because everyone is freelance, everyone is happy to work. Production parties are thus festive and optimistic occasions that lower the tensions in time for shooting to begin.

PART 7

PRODUCTION

PART 7-1 ———

Slating a shot for double system sound production on the set of the student film *Arsenic and Pink Lace.*

PART 7-2 ———

Lighting and camera set-up on the set of student director Catrin Hedström's *They Call us Animals.*

CHAPTER 26

DEVELOPING A PRODUCTION CREW

This chapter is titled "developing a crew" rather than "choosing" because even when experienced technicians are available, you must know their work and do some trial shooting before production begins. Especially with a small unit, crew members' temperaments affect your actors, so cast your crew for personal maturity as well as technical capabilities. In film school and beyond, filmmaking is an extended village, so check a potential crew member's reputation with key figures in their prior workplaces. Everyone enjoys recommending good people, and when someone's work was problematical you may either be told so outright, or can guess from the diplomatic silence.

DEVELOPING YOUR OWN CREW

Communication: An excellent way to mutually work out communication and collaboration issues is, as we said earlier, to shoot rehearsals using a documentary style of observational coverage (see "Shooting Rehearsals" in Chapter 21). Rehearsals become a lab where you not only develop the acting and ideas about camera coverage, but also a terse and unambiguous language of communication while shooting. One camera operator's close-up, for instance, may be another's medium shot. You get to know each other's expectations and values, and find out what developments (or outright changes) you may require in key crew members. You see how expertly crew members handle equipment, and the crew develop an organic understanding of the cast, the piece, and your intentions. Even so, expect to evolve standards and communication all through production. That's one of filmmaking's great pleasures.

Commitment, ideas and values: Everyone you recruit must understand and accept your commitments to the project and to the significance of drama, and ideally, those you choose should share your values. Assess potential crew members' technical expertise and experience, of course, but ask about favorite films, books, plays, hobbies, travel experience and interests too. Naturally, this matters more in a DP and a production designer than in a grip or assistant editor, but a low-budget enterprise needs optimal unity because much will be done by few. Tech deficiencies can be remedied, but immaturity and negativity cannot. Belief, enthusiasm, and morale really matter (Figure 26-1).

Team qualities: A low-budget film crew is small, perhaps six to 10 people. The crew's aura of commitment and optimism can easily be undermined by a single misfit with a bad attitude. Human

FIGURE 26-1 —————————————————

Putting together a compatible creative team that supports the director's vision is essential. Pictured at left is student director Sarah Sellman shooting her film *Hold Your Arms Out*.

problems come in many forms: you might need to apply pressure to someone likable whose concentration wanders. More seriously (and this usually emerges under pressure when far from home) someone may become unbalanced and regress into bizarre hostilities. This is like having a black hole swallowing up energy, enthusiasm, and morale. Truffaut's *Day for Night* (1973) dramatizes such a breakdown in a cast, but crews are susceptible too. What you want apart from relevant craft experience and enthusiasm for films is warmth, a nurturing temperament, sociability, and a lively sense of humor. Filmmaking is all about details. You want a can-do, low-key realism toward problems, and someone reliable who can sustain effort and concentration over long periods in order to get things right.

Avoid anyone who has only one working speed (usually slow, and who under pressure gets confused or goes to pieces); has a short attention span; forgets or modifies verbal commitments; talks too much; habitually overestimates their abilities; fails to deliver on time; thinks they are doing you a favor (and may use you as a stepping-stone to something better, usually in mid-shoot).

THE CREW'S ATTITUDE AND ACTORS

A well-functioning crew, under the benign but watchful leadership of the DP, makes a huge contribution to the morale of the actors, some of whom may be in front of a camera for the first time. Their exposure makes them hypersensitive to judgments, both real and imagined, and the crew's interest and implied approval is a vital supplement to that of the director. Actors notice any team member's detachment or disapproval.

Warn your team that actors may privately seek their opinions on their work. This is flattering, but a potential morass. Any crew member must react with extreme diplomacy. Be generally supportive, which is mainly what actors seek. If an actor enlists agreement for negative attitudes or wants to communicate something to the director, the crew member should react neutrally then discreetly report the situation up the chain of command. Crew and staffers, on or off the set, should never voice criticism that can weaken anyone else's authority.

Warn the crew to keep any disagreements completely out of public view, since actors find the spectacle of dissent among those they depend on very disturbing. Actors' work makes them vulnerable to all emotional currents, and their attention must remain with their work.

For more on this subject see "Set Etiquette" on p. 345.

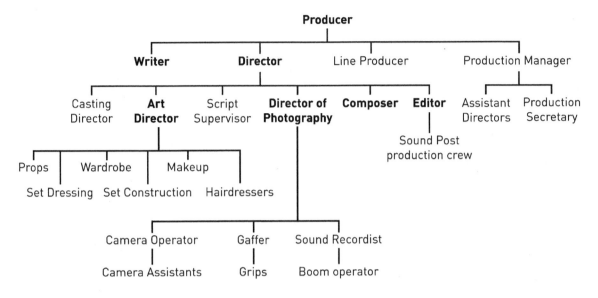

FIGURE 26-2

Lines of responsibility in a small-feature crew, with department heads in bold type. Lines of accountability vary according to the actual unit.

PRODUCTION CREW ROLES

AREAS OF RESPONSIBILITY

Lines of responsibility: No team functions well unless roles and responsibilities are established and each chain of command clearly defined. Contingencies make this all the more important. Everyone should know that when the director is occupied with the cast, the DP normally leads the crew and makes necessary decisions. In most cases, crew members should take queries first to their leader, who takes it to the DP, not the director. The line producer, assistant director(s), unit production manager (UPM), and DP are also there to take unnecessary burdens from the director, whose entire energies must lie with the cast and the DP.

Start formal: When first working together, and for a long time after, stick to the agreed structure of working relationships. Figure 26-2 shows the customary lines of responsibility in a small film unit. Everyone should concentrate on their own responsibilities and refrain from commenting on those of others. As experience teaches trust, that protective formality can be relaxed by cautious and mutual consent.

Other roles: In time, cast and crew fall into additional roles such as prophet, diplomat, visionary, navigator, earth mother, scribe, nurse, and strongman. Every crew develops its own inside jokes, and someone always becomes the all-important jester or clown.

FIGURE 26-3 ⎯⎯⎯⎯⎯⎯⎯⎯⎯⎯⎯⎯⎯⎯⎯⎯⎯⎯⎯⎯⎯⎯⎯⎯

Student director Felix Thompson shooting his short film *Bedford Park Boulevard*.

Synergy: Working well as a group is exhilarating and energizing, especially during crises. A team of determined friends is unstoppable.

ROLE DESCRIPTIONS

Judging from end credits, feature films are made by an army with a bewildering number of roles. Low-budget films also have lots of names because so many can only contribute a day or two of service. The following role descriptions, organized under a large feature unit's customary department structure, represent the modest core for a low-budget shoot. Outlined are each crew member's responsibilities and desirable personality traits, backgrounds, strengths, and vulnerabilities that you can expect to find.

DIRECTION DEPARTMENT

Director

Answers to the producer.

Although films are inherently collaborative endeavors, the unifying vision of the director guides most decisions made during preproduction and production (Figure 26-3). For a complete description of the role, responsibilities and characteristics of the director, see Chapter 1.

Script Supervisor

Answers to the director.

Responsible for understanding what coverage is planned for every scene; making sure it gets shot; and during shooting monitoring the exact words, actions, props, and costumes in use from shot to shot. Assists the director by ensuring adequate coverage for each scene, and by suggesting what economies are possible when time or resources run low. Shooting digitally, or shooting film with a video assist, means shots can be reviewed and checking a shot's contents is simple, if time-consuming. Shooting on film without video assist, however, leaves no visible record until the dailies viewing, so the script supervisor must be eagle-eyed and record every variable, no matter what. Digital stills, volumes of notes, and specialized script supervision software (like ScriptE) all help. See Chapter 30 for more detail on the role and range of responsibilities.

Personality traits are a fierce concentration and formidable powers of observation and memory; thorough understanding of editing; ability to know a script and see how it will construct as a film; fast and accurate typing and ability to produce reports an editor can depend on. Student films often have no script supervisor available, but the editor may be able to do the job. The motivation is certainly there to do it well.

Assistant Director (AD)

Answers to the director in many cases, but belongs under the production department, depending on his or her main function (see full description on p. 338).

PRODUCTION DEPARTMENT

In the United States, where the producer's role is primarily fiscal and logistical, the producer heads the production department. This department, in order to maintain control over all the activities and resources in play, has grown with the increasing complexity of production.

Producer

Answers to executive producer, investors, or studio heads.

Responsible for assembling and administering the necessary funds, and overseeing the project as a whole. Traditionally, the producer has ultimate say in an artistic dispute between, for example, a principal actor and the director. Because each may have status conferred by track record, fame, or success, the power relationship may be delicate, and producers sometimes have to arbitrate. In Europe the producer is more likely to be an artistic entrepreneur, putting together the creative triangle of writer, director, and producer to initiate a project.

Personality traits: The ideal producer concentrates on being an enabler who is firm and authoritative in rationing vital resources. To this end, planning, scheduling, and accounting should be a producer's strengths. Producers of experience and taste are also important arbiters of the film's artistic progress, especially since they normally maintain some distance on day-to-day production. The ideal producer is a cultivated, intelligent, and sensitive businessperson whose goal in life is to nourish good work by unobtrusively supporting the artists and craftspeople hired to produce it.

And here—God help us—is where it can all go wrong. In control of money, producers have power—and some, especially the inexperienced, assume that since artists and technicians are subordinates, their work and values must be too. A dilettante producer often tries to organize the creative, organic process of filmmaking like a construction project, and they have much difficulty trusting their experts. Usually the film suffers as much as its makers.

Probably all producers yearn to control the artistic identity of the work, but the wise ones sublimate their impulses and retain respect for those whose artistry has taken many years to mature. Like anyone else in the business, a producer should have a track record—so you can check their reputation through the grapevine. Never believe you will be treated differently or better than others in your position. Anyone with access to money can call himself a movie producer and get away with it.

Unit Production Manager (UPM)

Answers to the producer.

Responsible for day-to-day logistics and money disbursement. A necessity in the smallest crew, the UPM is the producer's delegate and closely concerned with preproduction and production. As business manager, he or she is based in an office (with the line producer, if there is one), and manages all the arrangements for the shoot, which include:

- Issuing crew, cast, and other contracts.
- Booking rented equipment to the specifications of camera and sound departments.
- Locating accommodation, restaurants, and toilet facilities near each location.
- Making catering, travel, and hotel arrangements.
- Making up (with the AD and director) a shooting schedule.
- Arranging for the dailies to get to and from the laboratory or to the cutting room for digitization.
- Monitoring cash flow and paying bills.
- Incubating plans in case of bad weather or other contingencies.
- Being the liaison for the outside world.
- Hustling and preparing the way ahead.

The UPM's work lightens the load for the rest of the crew, and helps them keep up the pace of shooting without distractions.

Personality traits: The good UPM is organized, methodical, and an able negotiator; trained in business practices, as well as computerized scheduling and budgeting; a compulsive list keeper; socially adept and diplomatic; able to multitask, delegate, and juggle shifting priorities; able to make quick and accurate decisions involving time, effort, and money; and unintimidated by officialdom. Good UPMs often become producers, especially if they have developed the requisite contacts, cultural interests, and knowledge of the film industry.

Line Producer

Answers to the Producer.

Responsible for preparing the budget in preproduction (principally below the line), and adjusting the budget according to actual expenditures over the course of production. Watches over day-to-day expenses, prepares cash flow reports, and provides updated budgets to the UPM. May negotiate with vendors. Low-budget films often merge the roles of UPM and Line Producer into a single position.

Personality traits: Same as UPM's.

Assistant Director (AD)

Answers to the UPM or the director, depending on his or her main function.

Responsible for all the legwork and logistical planning of the production. A feature shoot may have first, second, and third ADs. They seldom become directors because their skills are organizational, and lean toward production management. Their jobs include:

- Helping schedule for shoots
- Arranging locations and permits
- Getting the right people to the right place
- Coordinating props, wardrobe, hairdressing, and makeup personnel
- Contacting, reminding, acquiring information
- Calling and managing artists
- Directing extras and crowds, and barking orders in a big voice for the director
- Often responsible for overseeing health and safety issues.

Sometimes, in the director's absence, the first AD will rehearse actors, but only if he or she has a strong grasp of the director's intentions. An experienced AD may direct the second unit, but more often this falls to the editor.

Personality traits are to be organized and have a good business mind; have an encyclopedic knowledge of guild and union working regulations; a nature both firm and diplomatic; and a voice that can wake the dead.

Craft Services

Answers to the production department.

Responsible for servicing the other departments, protecting the set, and keeping light refreshments at the ready, especially high-octane coffee. Catering is usually handled by contractors who provide a full meal every six hours or so. Food and drink keep the troops human and happy, so skimping can be a bad mistake. Craft services should know any special dietary needs, food allergies, or religious restrictions of cast and crew.

Personality traits are to be watchful, helpful, and take a personal pride in nurturing the army that marches on its stomach.

Production Assistant (PA)

Answers to whoever employs him or her. PA is a good starting position from which to see behind the scenes, but the work can be literally anything.

Responsible for tasks delegated by directors, producers, UPMs, celebrities, overburdened actors, script development departments, agents, and publicity people—all of whom use PAs.

Personality traits are a sunny, can-do temperament (or a good imitation thereof); the loyalty of a St. Bernard; sealed-lips discretion under all circumstances; the ability to organize and juggle priorities, with mind reading and clairvoyance an advantage. On a low-budget production, a PA may carry considerable responsibility and will need the initiative to see where help is needed, and the diplomacy to stay out of trouble.

CAMERA DEPARTMENT

In general, camera crew members should have a keen visual sensibility and have a background in photography or fine art. They should be good with the theory and practicalities of equipment and techniques; observant of details found in people's surroundings; team players; decisive; practical, inventive, and methodical; and dexterous. Depending on the weight of the equipment, they may also need to be robust since handholding a 20-pound camera for most of an eight-hour day is not for the delicate, nor is loading equipment boxes in and out of transportation. The job is dirty, grueling, and at times intoxicatingly wonderful.

The best camera people seem to be those who do not ruffle easily. They are knowledgeable and resourceful, and take pride in improvising solutions to intransigent technical and logistical problems. What you hope to find is the perfectionist who still aims for the best and simplest solution when time is short.

Rather alarmingly, some quite experienced camera personnel isolate themselves in the mechanics of their craft at the expense of the director's deeper quest for themes and meanings. Although it can be disastrous to have a crew of would-be directors, it can be equally frustrating to find isolated operatives in your crew. A narrow tech education is not good enough for anyone in a film crew.

Director of Photography (DP)

Answers to the director.

Responsible for all aspects of cinematography. Also known as the **cinematographer**, the DP is the most important crew member after the director, and responsible for the look of the film. He or she must collaborate closely with the director and make all decisions about camera, lighting, and equipment that contribute to the camerawork (Figure 26-4). The DP is also:

FIGURE 26-4 —————————

The director of photography is responsible for the overall look of the film. Here the DP takes a handheld shot while the AC pulls focus.

- Responsible for specifying the lighting and camera equipment, lenses, and film stock, or their video equivalents
- Leader of the crew's work while the director concentrates on the actors
- Responsible for selection (and, on a low-budget film, the testing and adjusting) of the camera and lighting equipment and knowing its working principles
- When the crew is small, responsible for scouting each location in advance with the gaffer to assess electrical supplies and lighting design

- The person who decides and supervises the placement of lighting instruments
- Supervisor of the camera and lighting crews.

No important work should ever be done without the DP running tests as early as possible to forestall Murphy's Law, which is inexorable in filmmaking.

Camera Operator

Answers to the DP.

Responsible for every aspect of handling the camera, that is, deciding on camera positioning (in collaboration with the director) and physically controlling framing and all camera movements such as panning, tilting, zooming in and out, and dollying.

The operator should be quick to notice the behavioral nuances that signal when each actor is going to speak or move. In improvised fiction, as in documentary, camera work is often "grab-shooting," so the operator must be able to make dramatically correct decisions over what to shoot in a busy scene. Even in a highly controlled shoot, actors going wide of their marks can pose a compositional conflict that the operator must instantly resolve if the take is to remain useful.

Whereas the director sees content happening in three dimensions in front of the camera, the operator sees the action in its framed, cinematic form. The director may redirect the camera to a different area, but without a video assist, only the operator knows what the action will look like on the screen.

FIGURE 26-5 ⸻

The first assistant camera, or AC, is responsible for maintaining the camera in prime condition and ready to shoot at all times.

Assistant Camera (AC)

Answers to the camera operator.

Responsible for everything concerning the camera. The first AC stays beside the camera and is responsible for keeping the camera optics and the film gate clean, for lens changes and settings, for focus, and for setting camera speed (or frame rate). The second AC maintains the slate (or clapper), sets actors' marks in association with the first AC, and may load the camera if there is no third AC to do it. ACs and gaffers manhandle the camera from place to place between setups.

Their main requirements are to be highly organized, reliable, and zealous at maintaining the camera in prime condition, whether film or digital. Because their responsibilities are almost wholly technical, they must be good and diligent technicians (Figure 26-5, *left*).

Gaffer (Also Grips and Best Boy)

Answers to the DP as the head electrician. **Gaffer** is Old English for grandfather, singularly appropriate for one who must know every imaginable way to skin the proverbial cat.

Responsible for rigging lights and knowing how to handle anything (including the camera) that needs to be fixed, mounted, moved, pushed, lifted, or lowered. Gaffers must understand mechanical and electrical principles, and be able to improvise wherever no special equipment exists. Because a good gaffer must grasp the intentions behind the DP's lighting instructions, he or she understands lighting instruments and the principles and practice of lighting itself. The **best boy** is the gaffer's chief assistant (Figure 26-5, *right*).

Grips should be strong, practical, organized, and willing. The **key grip** rigs lighting according to the gaffer's instructions. He or she also has the highly skilled and coordinated job of moving the camera support (dolly, crane, truck, etc.) from mark to mark as the camera takes mobile shots. Under the key grip is the best boy grip. On a minimal crew, grips may double up to help with sound equipment and camera assisting.

Personality traits are resourcefulness and patience since their work involves moving and maintaining large varieties of equipment, of which there never seems enough. While they work, production waits; while production is in progress, they wait. When everyone else is finished, they tear down their masses of equipment, stow it, and haul it away, ready to set up again for the next day's shoot. All this must be good for the soul, for they are often highly resourceful and very funny.

SOUND DEPARTMENT

Sound Recordist (Also Boom Operator and Cable Wrangler)

Every sound problem has multiple solutions, so knowledge of available equipment and interest in up-to-date techniques is a great advantage. In an interior setup, lighting and camera position have to take precedence, and the sound recordist is expected to position mikes without their being seen or causing shadows, and still to capture prime sound quality. The art of recording has little to do with recorders, and everything to do with the selection and placement of mikes—and being able to hear the difference. Sound recordists listen not to the meaning of dialogue but to sound quality, so they must be able to listen analytically and hear any buzz, rumble, or edginess that the uninitiated unconsciously screen out. No independent assessment is possible apart from the discerning ear, and only musical interests and, better still, musical training seem to instill this ability in sound recordists.

Answers to the DP.

Responsible for quality sound, often the casualty in an inexperienced crew. Capturing clear, clean, and consistent sound is very specialized, and extraordinarily important. The **recordist** is responsible for setting up sound equipment, monitoring levels and quality, and solving problems as they arise (Figure 26-6). The **boom operator**'s job is to place the microphone as close to sound sources as possible without getting it in the shot or creating shadows. In a complicated dialogue scene, this requires following the script and moving the mike in time to catch each new speaker. When shooting requires a mobile camera, sound equipment must also be mobile. It takes skill

FIGURE 26-6

The basic sound crew consists of a sound recordist and a boom operator, who are responsible for capturing the cleanest sound possible during production.

and agile, quiet footwork to keep the mike close to, but not in the edge of, the camera's field of view.

On complicated sets, especially with highly mobile actors on camera, a **cable wrangler** may be added to the sound team to manage cables during takes or to serve as second boom operator.

Personality traits are patience, a good ear, and the maturity to accept being low man on the totem pole. Even professionals turn into frustrated mutterers whose mantra is that standards are being trampled. Sound can at least be reconstituted later in the cutting rooms, but camerawork and actors' performances, once shot, are immutable. The recordist is routinely kept inactive and then suddenly expected to "fix up the mike"—so sound people need to think ahead. The least effective only come to life as shooting gets close. The best watch the shooting situation unfold and adapt quickly. They are unruffled specialists whose knowledge of equipment and techniques is extraordinary.

ART DEPARTMENT

Production Designer (Also Art Director)

Answers to the director.

Responsible for designing everything in the film's environment to effectively interpret the script. This means overseeing props and costumes, as well as designing all aspects of sets and locations. If the film is a period production, the **production designer** will research the epoch and its social customs to ensure that costumes and decor are accurate and make an impact. On low-budget movies production designers often do their own sketching and set dressing, whereas, on a larger production, there will be drafts-people, and set dressers under the supervision of an **art director** who oversees the construction of sets and location details. If sets must be built, the art director oversees the various **construction specialists** (carpenters, plasterers, painters, electricians, and riggers).

Personality traits: A production designer needs: a fine arts, design, or architecture background; the ability to sketch or paint fluently; a lively eye for fashion, tastes, and social distinctions; a strong interest in the social and historical background of these phenomena; a flair for the emotional potential of color and its combinations; the ability to translate the script into a series of settings with costumes, all of which heighten and intensify the underlying intentions of the script; managerial abilities and good communication skills since the art director works as a project manager overseeing the, props, set dressers, wardrobe personnel, and set construction.

Special Effects Personnel

Answer to the art director.

Responsible for making explosions, fires, bridges that collapse, or windows that a stunt artist can safely jump through. (The *Lord of the Rings* cycle is a veritable dictionary of special effects, from Middle Earth rock kingdoms to creatures that crawl, prowl, and fly.) At one time, special effects specialized in models for ships sinking or cars blowing up, and process shooting in which a live foreground was married to a preshot background. Now since computers and robotics, and the market for exotic spectacle, special effects people cover everything from saurian family life to space travel. If the script says it's wanted, then it's a point of honor that they can make it, using every imaginable principle—electrical, mechanical, computer, robotic, biological—to provide a working answer. They also handle anything that involves danger and stunt people.

Personality traits: Tenacious, inventive, resourceful, with a love of impossible challenges. Stunt people have a Houdini relationship with danger: they are attracted to it and like cheating injury and death. Their profession embodies survival of the fittest.

Wardrobe and Props

Props and wardrobe departments must be completely organized: each scene has its special requirements, and the right props and costumes must appear on time and in the right place, or shooting becomes a logistical nightmare.

Answer to the production designer.

Responsible for locating, storing, and maintaining costumes and properties (objects such as ashtrays, baby toys, or grand pianos that dress the set). Must keep master lists and always produce the right thing at the right time, and in working order. When no wardrobe person is available, each actor becomes responsible for his or her own costumes. Under these conditions, the assistant director (AD) double-checks what clothes each actor must bring next scene so today's costume is not left in the actor's laundry basket.

Personality traits: Highly resourceful and able to develop a wealth of contacts among antique, resale, theatrical, and junk shop owners. Very practical—because things borrowed or rented must often be carefully operated, maintained, or even restored to working order. Costumes, especially the elaborate or antique, take expertise to keep clean and functional, and often need temporary alterations to fit the particular wearer.

Makeup and Hairdressing

Answer to the production designer.

Responsible for the appropriate physical appearance in face and hair, often with careful attention to period details. A hidden part of the job is catering to actors' insecurities by helping them believe in the way they look. Where the character demands negative traits, the makeup artist may have to work against an actor's resistance. When makeup is tricky, tests are mandatory to ensure that it is credible and compatible with color stock and any special lighting.

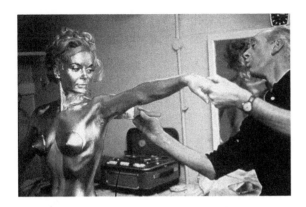

FIGURE 26-7 ————————————

Makeup artist Paul G. Rabiger applying the notorious gold paint in *Goldfinger*.

Personality traits: Diplomacy and endurance. My father Paul G. Rabiger was a makeup man and they have to arrive ahead of everyone, preparing actors when elaborate beards and whiskers are required hours ahead of shooting. Apart from character or glamour preparation, his work included the bizarre, such as putting a black patch over the eye of Fagin's dog in David Lean's *Oliver Twist* (1948), applying gold paint to Shirley Eaton in Guy Hamilton's *Goldfinger* (1964, Figure 26-7), and inventing ghoulish effects for Hammer horror films. One such was flesh melting from a corpse's face to leave eyeballs staring out of bony eye sockets, for which he built a wax face on a skull with a heating element underneath. These challenges he enjoyed, but less so having to placate the neuroses of aging idols or foul-tempered alcoholics at dawn. After the early rush, makeup and hairdressing often have to sit idle on the set, keeping a sharp eye out for when their handiwork needs repair.

SET ETIQUETTE[1]

A film set is an exciting, intense, and pressure-filled environment filled with energetic and driven people who are usually working with limited time and resources. It is tempting in this atmosphere to cut corners to get the job done. Some shortcuts prove counterproductive, others downright foolish and dangerous. The following sections cover essential set etiquette and safety issues so that your project is safe, productive and rewarding. For everyone's happiness and safety make sure your whole team knows these rules.

A director sets the tone and energy of the film set. Everyone deserves respect, and this is not just a top-down issue (i.e., producers respecting the grips), but goes for all crew members toward each other. Leave your ego at the door, as they say in the business. Respect on a film set has three dimensions: respect for the project, for the people on the project, and for ourselves by doing good work.

Do your own job to the best of your ability. Films are created by a coordinated group of individuals: one person slacking off throws everyone off and places an unfair burden on someone else. Lulls in activity are not invitations to go wandering off to get snacks, or make personal phone calls. You never know when the set will suddenly come alive, and you are AWOL when needed.

---

[1] Excerpted and abridged from Mick Hurbis-Cherrier, *Voice & Vision: A Creative Approach to Narrative Film and DV Production* 2nd ed. (Focal Press, 2012).

Always be on time, which means be early! The film industry places a very high premium on promptness. Being late shows a phenomenal lack of respect toward others who arrive on time and ready for work, and whose valuable time you waste. The film industry is a village: anyone who gains a reputation for unreliability (even at the film school level) won't be asked to work.

Maintain a positive "can-do" attitude. Filmmaking involves lots of problem solving. A production thrives with people who love a challenge and are innovative when it comes to solving or working around less than ideal circumstances. Become one of these.

Respect the team structure. No matter what the size of the production team—from four students to 34 paid professionals—a film crew is organized, specialized, and interdependent. Everyone has a specific job to do and people they report to. Know and respect the chain of command, the division of labor, and the areas of the other people on the team.

Stay tuned at all times: Unless using a work-related app (like a DOF calculator), smartphones should be stowed away. All cell phones should be turned off during work hours on the set unless making a project-related call.

Treat everyone with courtesy. Treat people well, and they will treat you well too. Give praise where praise is due and never take credit that is not yours to claim. Don't criticize negatively or humiliate people when they make mistakes—which we all do sometime. Crude comments, jokes, or raucous behavior are simply not appropriate and throw everyone's concentration off. Stay cool, calm, focused—in a word, be professional.

Keep personal animosity out of it. You will surely work occasionally with people you don't like. You have a job to do, so behave like a professional and do your work regardless of personalities.

RESPECT THE PUBLIC'S SPACE

Beyond courtesy between cast and crew is the issue of relations with the public. You will often be shooting in public places like parks, sidewalks, neighborhoods, and coffee shops. These places are not your private film set so you must treat the public with respect and try not to disrupt their lives too much. Keep a low profile by not making excessive noise, not parking in such a way that it obstructs other people's access, and by being conscientious about litter and not taking up more space than necessary.

RESPECT THE LOCATION

Making movies often involves renting or borrowing locations that are ordinarily not film sets. The unwritten rule is that you leave a location in the same or better condition when the shoot is over. This is important if we are to maintain the good faith of those kind people who open their homes, shops, restaurants and property for the sake of our movies.

FOOD AND BREAKS

Twelve-hour work days are not unusual on a film production. Well-timed breaks for food are essential to maintain morale and physical stamina among actors and crew alike. Meal breaks make people happier, healthier and more productive. Do not expect people to work long if you delay or withhold food and refreshments.

A **food break** means all work stops to allow cast and crew to sit, relax, and eat; it does not mean sandwiches on the run. Film work is strenuous and sets can get hot, so have plenty of water on hand to keep your personnel hydrated, and make sure bathrooms are available near the set. Part of preproduction is securing (or renting) the necessary facilities.

PRODUCTION SAFETY AND SECURITY

Nothing in this book means anything if your project is not a safe one and a catastrophe occurs. These guidelines are to alert you to major production issues concerning safety and security. These will help all your team members avoid bad reputation, arrest, equipment loss and damage, law suits, project collapse, injury or even death. This is not a comprehensive discussion however. Be sure to thoroughly research the risks and safety contingencies of your particular project, and check with all applicable labor union, state government, local government, location, and school safety regulations and procedures before you start rolling camera.

THE COMMANDMENTS OF FILM PRODUCTION SAFETY

- Every filmmaker has a moral and legal obligation to keep their cast, crew, and the public, safe. Lack of funds is never an excuse for poor safety practices.
- Safety is everyone's responsibility. You are first responsible for safety in your specific department, but if you see something dangerous or excessively risky anywhere on the set you must mention it. If you see something, say something.
- Learn and follow all safety regulations and guidelines that apply to your specific project (union, government, school, location).
- Acknowledge that, like all of us, you are capable of poor judgment and therefore must remain vigilant, stay smart, follow rules, heed warnings and listen to others who have the experience and expertise when they tell us how things should be done and when we're being unwise and reckless.

PREPARE FOR SAFETY

Much of what makes for a safe production happens in preproduction. Don't believe that your project is so small or so blessed by the gods that you can avoid these steps. Research, study, and follow all the safety guidelines and regulations that apply to your specific project. Anticipate guidelines from state or local governments; law enforcement; regulations at the location where you are shooting; safety requirements by the unions representing your cast and crew; safety guidelines established by your school or department, as well as the production parameters set by your instructor in the syllabus, or verbally for the class.

Someone on the production team should be assigned the role of **safety coordinator**. This can be the UPM or AD, on small shoots, and on larger ones with multiple locations and safety challenges, it should be a dedicated position.

Location scouting must include looking for and noting safety concerns such as traffic, electrical capabilities, structural condition, hazardous materials, potential fire hazards, weather exposure, and the proximity of high voltage lines. Note emergency exits, fire extinguishers and access points. Hold **safety meetings** with the department heads so that each department can anticipate and address specific safety concerns at that location before the shoot occurs.

Everyone must always have emergency contact information, so *put emergency information for every location on all call sheets.* This includes contacts for the police, fire department, ambulance, and the address of the nearest hospital. I have seen what happens when this information is missing and someone is lying unconscious from electrocution.

Consult (or hire) the appropriate safety specialists if you plan to do anything with fire, automobiles, stunts, prop weapons, or water. A little money in the budget for this will pay off with a safe, trouble-free and dramatically convincing production.

Allow enough time for the crew to rest between shooting days so they can do their jobs thoroughly and thoughtfully (see Scheduling The Shoot, p. 313). So, *schedule reasonable hours.*

Everyone must know how to operate their gear, especially large, potentially dangerous items like dollies and generators, before they arrive on the set. Watching a "how-to" video on YouTube does NOT constitute training, so DO NOT rent or attempt to use equipment for which you are not qualified, and DO NOT attempt procedures or equipment use that require a trained and certified technician. Specifically, do not try to use large trucks, cranes, generators, high wattage lights, unless you're trained, qualified and licensed.

Insure your production (see "Insurances" p. 319).

MAINTAIN COMMON SENSE

Most accidents on the set happen because people forget to use common sense. Do not, for example, ask a camera operator to climb up a steep rooftop to get a panoramic shot. This is a wilful, dangerous lack of common sense—negligence in fact. Think safety in what you're doing at all times and don't take shortcuts. Avoid (or ban) all possible set distractions such as pets, visitors, iPods, and the reigning king of all distractions, the smartphone.

The next point is obvious, but must be stated in no uncertain terms. *No alcohol or drugs on a film set.* That means not just illegal substances, but all medications, prescription or otherwise, that cause drowsiness or fuzzy thinking.

Keep your set neat and orderly, tape down cables where people walk, and leave room for movement. Use your staging area, put things away that are not being used. Don't leave gear where people can trip on it and never, never block emergency exits with equipment.

SPECIAL CIRCUMSTANCES CAN BE RISKY

Weather: The entire production team must watch for weather-changes and dress appropriately. Wear extra clothes in cold conditions, since standing around for hours in cold weather lets the cold eventually seep in. In extreme conditions, an exterior location should always have a heated, sheltered area nearby where cast and crew can warm up. In a remote area, this might be a tent or shed with a portable heating unit.

In extremely hot weather, lots of drinking water is crucial and if you're outside, protect your crew from sun exposure. Provide sunblock and rig shade in the form of tarps and umbrellas (which also protect equipment from direct sun).

Finally, don't shoot in hostile weather just to stay on schedule. Ice storms, rain storms, heavy snow, gale force winds not only make for a miserable experience and compromised footage, but are simply dangerous. Reschedule, and don't risk injuring personnel or damaging equipment.

Risky locations: Thoroughly check during location scouting, long before you arrive to shoot, that your location is safe (see p. 289). If you discover a location is structurally insecure, or there are hazardous materials on the site (asbestos, flammable or toxic compounds) or the electrical wiring is not up to code, then simply look for another location. Avoid dangerous locations like steep cliffs, soft riverbanks, busy highways, etc.

Picture vehicles: Automobiles often feature in films, so use *extreme* caution around them. Anyone driving in a distracted state—as anyone is when acting—is prone to cause accidents. Anyone doing their job near vehicles cannot pay full attention to personal danger. At Pinewood studios a continuity supervisor on a racing-car film was crushed against the camera dolly and permanently disabled. In the few moments, when nobody was paying attention, a life was ruined.

Car camera mounts must only be rigged and tested by trained specialists, and should never be driven on public roads without a permit. Even the "simplest" car stunt is dangerous; chases, screeching tires, and fast driving are suicidal folly. Most stunt-related deaths and injuries involve vehicular accidents, so even driving fast must be accomplished by trained precision drivers at the wheel of prepared picture vehicles. All this is simply out of reach for students.

Weapons: Never use a real weapon in a movie: NO real guns, and NO real knives, ever. Use prop weapons: knives that are blunt and often made of plastic, and prop guns. These come in three flavors: guns made of heavy rubber material; non-firing "function" guns made of metal and with working parts, but unable to fire; and blank-firing guns that make a bang and produce a flash from the barrel. All of these require permits and insurance to use on a set. Blank-firing prop guns can injure or kill when used improperly.

If you have a prop gun in your film (non-firing or blank-firing):

- Review all state and federal laws concerning theatrical weapons' use.
- Always rent from a certified and reputable prop weapons rental house.
- Those handling the gun (actor and prop master) must be trained in its use.
- Treat every gun, even a non-firing prop, as though it's loaded and dangerous.
- No one else may touch the prop weapon or blanks.
- Store prop guns and any ammunition blanks in a secure place when not in use. They are designed to look real so must never be taken off the set.
- Notify the local police about your intention to use a prop weapon whether indoors or outdoors and arrange for police supervision.

It does not matter if you are shooting on a sidewalk or an interior scene on private property. Any passer-by or neighbor glimpsing someone pointing a gun at someone else will call the police.

Some of our students were terrified when six Chicago police cars responded to this situation. They could have lost their lives. For more prop weapon safety information, go to www.moviegunservices.com/mgs_safety.htm.

Fire and open flames: Fire is unpredictable and flames of any size can quickly get out of hand. Always have a fire extinguisher on the set in case of electrical or other fires. Bring your own or locate the nearest available one in public buildings, whether you're using open flames or not.

If your film has birthday candles, or a match lighting a gas stove, designate someone armed with a fire extinguisher as flame watcher. Many schools and locations absolutely forbid open flames of any sort, so check all regulations. If your film absolutely must have a fire of any size (like a campfire), and you are legally allowed to have one, then have a trained, bonded, and insured pyrotechnics expert on the set. The same goes for any type of fireworks, even legal ones.

Stunts: In a comedy scene, a woman races her cart down a grocery store aisle, turns the corner and knocks over the store manager. This can be funny, but it's a stunt because it can cause injury. For simple ones like this, cast a performer in good physical shape and who knows how to fall safely. Protect the actor with body pads (elbows, knees, etc.) and floor mats off-screen. Rehearse until the actor is comfortable with the fall.

Any stunt more dangerous than falling from a standing position requires professional stunt doubles and stunt coordinators. If your film requires someone to, say, jump or fall down a short flight of stairs, you cannot do this with a regular actor. No matter how well padded they are, you stand a good chance of injuring them. Also an actor won't give a convincing fall because they don't know how. Professional stunt people are worth the extra expense and insurance precisely because they know how to do stunts safely and in a dramatically convincing way.

Water: Electricity + water = electrocution. When shooting scenes involving water, such as bathtubs and swimming pools, try to use available light. If you must use lighting, say in an interior bathroom scene, never set up lights where they could fall into the water. In fact, it's best to bounce light from a unit set up outside the bathroom itself. To maximize safety, station a grip at each lighting unit.

ELECTRICITY

Shooting often requires lights using thousands of watts of power, which means harnessing a great deal of electricity. Electricity is dangerous stuff; it can kill and must be treated properly. When lighting with more than a portable lighting kit, hire a professional gaffer. As head of the electrical department, the gaffer is a certified electrician, and will oversee the proper and safe use of all movie lights and anything electrical on the set. They also understand how to manipulate lights and gels for creative lighting effect. In a book about directing, it only possible to touch upon what one needs to know about electrical safety on a film set, but check out Harry Box's superb *Set Lighting Technician's Handbook*, 4th ed. (Focal Press, 2010). Written by a professional DP, gaffer, and lighting technician, it covers the duties of the gaffer and electrical department thoroughly, including exhaustive information on the proper and safe use of movie lighting equipment and electricity.

KEEP THE SET SECURE

The security of people, equipment and personal belongings is important when you are shooting, especially in public locations were theft is particularly common. Set up a secure **staging area** for equipment and where actors can safely store their personal belongings while they are on set and in costume. Usually you need someone to guard, or even lock away people's belongings. Never leave anything, valuables or equipment, in a car since they get broken into all the time. Losses are particularly common on messy, disorganized sets, or when set strikes are rushed and things get left behind. Gear gets stolen, also, when too few people are loading or returning equipment. One person must watch the vehicle while others take equipment inside.

Additional Safety Information Resources

There is much more pertinent information to your project's safety not covered here. For more information, start with the **CSATF** (Contract Services Administration Trust Fund). Its Industry Safety Committee is composed of guild, union, and management representatives active in industry safety and health programs. It publishes bulletins and guidelines concerning industry-safe practices for film and television and its *General Code of Safe Practice for Film Production* is a basic summary of safety standards, and a *must read* for everyone involved in film production. Download this either from this book's companion website www.directingbook.com (under "Miscellaneous") or the CSATF website: www.csatf.org/pdf/GenCodeoSafePractices.pdf.

The CSATF *Safety Bulletins* are more detailed safety recommendations for specific issues and circumstances, such as the use of prop weapons, stunts, animals, cold weather, etc. See bulletins at this link: http://www.csatf.org/bulletintro.shtml.

Also valuable is the *Safety Guidelines for the Film and Television Industry in Ontario* published by the Ontario Ministry of Labour. Wherever you are shooting, this is a well-researched, cogently organized, and highly informative production safety publication. You can find a .pdf of these guidelines on this book's website www.directingbook.com

CHAPTER 27

THE DIRECTOR AND PRODUCTION TECH

For the most part, the director relies heavily on the production crew for their technical expertise and creative ability. A director can't possibly know everything necessary to make the film, especially as these days keeping up with changes in production technology is a full-time job. A good DP, AC, gaffer, or sound recordist will stay abreast of changes in their field and bring their experience from working on many films a year. They will always know more about their particular craft than you do, but the more you know about technological basics, the more you can anticipate the creative capacity and flexibility of the tools you depend on to tell your story.

The three major areas of expressive importance a director uses are *lighting*, *camera lenses*, and *sound recording*. You will need some familiarity with their essential technology, processes, and terminology.

BASIC LIGHTING APPROACHES AND TERMINOLOGY

Every aspect of lighting carries strong emotional associations that can be employed in drama to great effect. Directors asking for particular lighting effects and wanting to discuss lighting must use the terminology a DP understands.[1] The technique and the terminology that describes it are therefore powerful tools in the right hands. Here are some basic concepts, terms and approaches:

THREE ESSENTIAL QUALITIES OF LIGHT

The three essential qualities of light that are of immediate and aesthetic concern to the filmmaker are intensity, hard versus soft, and color temperature.

---

[1] The fundamentals of lighting are well explained in Alan J. Ritsko's *Lighting for Location Motion Pictures* (Simon & Schuster, 1980) and Kris Malkiewicz's *Film Lighting* (Fireside, 1986).

Light intensity refers to the strength of the light being emitted by a source. Sunlight, is a very intense source of light, although its intensity is variable given different times of the day or cloud coverage. With artificial light, intensity is determined by the wattage of the lamp (500 watts, 1,000 watts, 2,000 watts, etc.), the efficiency of the reflector system behind the lamp, and the subject to lighting distance. Obviously the closer a lighting unit is to the subject, the more intense it will be, but how much? Without going into the physics of light, the general rule of thumb says that if you halve the distance between the subject and the lighting unit, say from 16 feet to 8 feet, you increase the light intensity four times from the original position. Conversely, if you double the distance between the lighting unit and your subject, the strength of the light will be only one-fourth the intensity compared to the original position.

Hard light is any light source—a glowing filament or other effectively point source—which throws a highly directional beam and is called **hard light**, because it creates sharp-edged shadows. The sun, a studio spotlight, and even a candle flame are all hard light sources. Many movie lighting units, in order to maximize their intensity, use a polished reflector system to augment their hard, directional light throw. You can tell that Figure 27-1, *left* is lit by hard light by its deep and distinct shadows.

Soft light is that from a light source which, for one reason or another, sends light scattered in many directions. Soft light sources create soft-edged shadows or an even relatively shadowless image, as in Figure 27-1, *right*. Soft light sources are, for example, fluorescent tubes or sunlight filtered through clouds in an overcast sky. You can soften the light from a hard lighting unit by reflecting it off a matte white **diffuse surface**, like a white reflector board or white wall, or by placing heat resistant **diffusion media** (like tough frost or tough spun) in front of the light source that scatters the light rays.

FIGURE 27-1

Hard light (*left*) is highly directional and produces sharp shadows, while the scattered rays of soft light sources (*right*) produce shadows with soft edges. Notice the difference in the nose and collar shadows. Also note how the thin shadow caused by the glasses is nearly eliminated.

Color temperature refers to the different color biases in the light sources we use. The varying mix of colors that comprise each different "white" source light is expressed in degrees **Kelvin** (**K**). This scale is based on a theoretical black body being progressively heated so that it gives off the colors of the light spectrum (starting from the cool end: infrared, red, orange, green, blue, indigo, violet, ultraviolet). A domestic incandescent lightbulb gives an orange-biased light of around 2,800 K. Noon daylight is "cooler" (that is, more blue) and is rated around 5,600 K, whereas the light on mountaintops is very cool indeed and might be 10,000 K. The most popular movie lights, which use halogen tungsten bulbs, are rated at 3,200 K, which is "warmer" (or more orange) than average daylight.

The human eye adapts effortlessly to these changes and generally sees a white object illuminated by these different sources as white. But film and video cameras (or the lighting instruments themselves) must be adjusted for the prevailing lights color temperature if white objects are to render accurately on-screen.

Filmmaking has a common problem: take 5,600 K daylight coming through a window and try to augment it with studio lights (3,200 K), and you get very unnatural lighting effects. The cure is to filter the minority source to make it match the majority, and to adjust white balance, or camera filtering, to match your working color temperature.

Only then will all colors be rendered faithfully.

COMMON LIGHTING FUNCTIONS

The basic lights used in a lighting setup are called the **key light**, the **fill light**, and the **backlight**. Once you understand what each lighting type does, and their basic position, you can combine them to achieve a variety of lighting designs and styles.

Key light is the primary source of illumination in the scene. This is not necessarily an artificial source, since it can be the sun or a bonfire. The key light is usually a **motivated** light, meaning that its presumed source is understandable and believable in the world of the film, even if it's not visible on-screen. For example, if we have a man and woman talking at the kitchen table, the key light motivation might be an overhead light fixture (perhaps off-screen), or a candle on the table between them. If the scene takes place during the day, it might be sunlight streaming in through an unseen window. In all these cases, artificial light will be used to actually illuminate the scene, but its angle and color will mimic its ostensible source. Using an unmotivated key light strongly suggests a more stylized aesthetic approach.

The key, often a relatively hard light, is the light that creates the shot's intended shadows: these in turn reveal the angle and position of the supposed light source. Figure 27-2 is a scene from Jon Amiel's *Creation* in which Darwin goes to a church to pray for his dying daughter. The key light is coming from frame left, slightly higher than camera level, and the supposed source is a church window.

Fill light is used to control illumination in shadow areas. Usually it is a soft light that fills in the shadow areas cast by key light to give the appropriate look. Fill light is often thrown from the direction of the camera because this hides the additional shadows behind the subject and renders them invisible. Fill lights do not have to be motivated by a source since their function and positioning are fairly invisible.

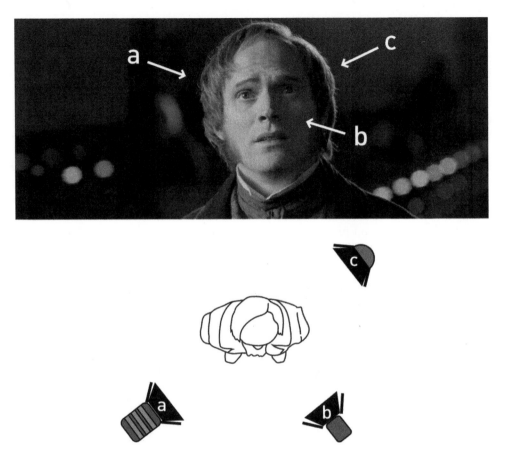

FIGURE 27-2

The classic combination of a key (a), fill (b), and backlight (c) creates a textured look designed to make characters stand out in the shot, as in this example from Amiel's *Creation*.

In Figure 27-2, fill light is illuminating the side of Darwin's face opposite the key, allowing us to see some detail in what would otherwise be a dark nose shadow.

Backlight is that thrown upon a subject from behind—and often from above as well. A common technique is to use backlight opposite the key, throwing a rim of light around a subject's head and shoulders to separate them from the background. Since backlight sources can easily be deduced, they are usually motivated lights as well. In Figure 27-2, the backlight is in its traditional position and its supposed source is the door to the church behind Darwin.

Note that rain, fog, dust, and smoke all show up best when backlit.

FIGURE 27-3

Practicals (any lights appearing in the frame as part of a scene) are often used to motivate concealed sources of light, like the small artificial light hidden behind the cake in this scene from Mendes' *Revolutionary Road*.

Practical: This is any light appearing in the frame as part of the scene: a street light, a table lamp, a chandelier, overhead fluorescents, or flashlight, for example, or, as in Figure 27-3 from *Revolutionary Road* (Mendes, 2008) the candles on a birthday cake. Practicals seldom provide much or any real illumination, but serve as the motivation for a higher wattage key light or backlight positioned off-camera mimicking and greatly augmenting the light from the practical. In this scene DP Roger Deakins has placed a small artificial light (called a "special") behind the cake, duplicating the angle of the candlelight.

Available and mixed light: Just as it sounds, available light is that occurring naturally at the location. It could be the sun or the light from a store window for exterior locations, or overhead fluorescents in a drugstore, or sunlight streaming into greenhouse windows. Often, scenes that use only available light must be carefully choreographed to keep people near windows and light sources. Kelly Reichardt's *Wendy and Lucy* (2008) was shot almost exclusively with available light.

Using available light provides a strong sense of naturalism, but is difficult to sustain if a film has night scenes or interior locations. Most available light sources simply cannot produce an acceptable image, and pushing (force developing) film stocks or maxing out the sensitivity of your video sensor degrades the image.

Very often, especially on lower budget shoots, you'll often see a mix of available light sources augmented by a few carefully placed artificial lighting units. This is **mixed lighting**. Ever more sensitive video sensors and film stocks are making mixed light shooting easier and easier (Figure 27-4).

FIGURE 27-4

Mixed lighting situations involve using available light augmented with artificial lighting sources, as in this scene from De Niro's *A Bronx Tale* (1993), where sunlight from outside appears to provide illumination inside the bar.

TYPES OF LIGHTING STYLES

High-key lighting is that in which fill light approaches the intensity of the key light, filling in practically all the shadows, creating a bright overall look with small or nonexistent areas of shadow. A high-key scene is often associated with a dramatically light tone, as in comedies (see Figure 11-1, bottom on p. 136), but is also commonly used to establish a tone of cold alienation or irony. Beyond these facile associations, high-key lighting can also be used simply because it's appropriate for the location—such as a scene in a supermarket lit by fluorescent fixtures (Figure 27-5, *left*).

Low-key lighting is that in which little or no fill light illuminates the image's shadow areas. The shot looks dark overall with few highlight areas, although the highlights can be quite bright. The predominance of shadows can give low-key images a dark, even sinister, tone (Figure 27-5, *right*, also see Figure 11-1, top on page 136) especially as the shadow areas are as prominent as what is illuminated. There are of course many interiors or night shots in which low-key lighting is natural rather than ominous.

Graduated tonality characterizes the image that has neither bright highlights nor deep shadows, but instead consists of an even, restricted range of mid-tones. This might be a flat-lit interior, like an airport lounge, or a misty morning landscape.

FIGURE 27-5 ——

High-key lighting (*left*, from Romanek's *One Hour Photo*, 2002) produces a bright overall look with few shadows, while low-key lighting (*right*, from the Quays' *Institute Benjamenta*, 1995) results in an image dominated by shadows and high contrast.

TYPES OF LIGHTING SETUP

When lighting a scene, the first consideration is usually, where to put the key light. This requires working out its motivation and then deciding its relationship to the subject, since both factors determine the angle at which the key light hits the subject. Once the key light is in position, we can then decide what other lights are necessary in the set up and where to place them.

Frontal key lighting is close to the camera-to-subject axis so that shadows are thrown behind the subject and out of the camera's view, rather like using a flash on a still camera (Figure 27-6, *top left*). Only slight shadows are visible so the effect is a very flat image. One never needs a fill light because there are no shadows to fill.

¾ **frontal key** is when the light source is positioned at 45 degrees to the camera-to-subject axis—a common position for a key light (Figure 27-6, *top right*). Notice how the shadows cast by this light are at 45-degree angles. This light position is often also raised vertically by 45 degrees as well. To soften shadows created by the key light, use fill light along the camera to subject axis.

Side key (or **sidelight**) is a setup that throws key light directly at the side of the subject (at a 90-degree angle to the camera axis). This illuminates one side of the subject and allows the other to fall into shadow. Sidelight maximizes both shadows and texture. Again, fill light will allow you to control how much detail we see on the shadow side of the subject. Compare Figure 27-6, *bottom left* (which uses no fill) with 27-2 which uses substantial fill.

¾ **back key** illuminates much of the side of the subject farthest from the camera, but we do see bright highlights around the "hidden" side of the subject. This is a position typical for backlight, but you can create a very deep and dramatic image when the key light is placed here. The amount of fill light is critical because we usually need to see some detail on the dark side of the subject, but not so much that the effect is lost (Figure 27-6, *bottom right*. See also figure 11-1 top).

FIGURE 27-6

The placement of the key light can fundamentally set the tone and look of a scene. A frontal key (*top left*) from Boe's *Allegro*, 2005. A ¾ frontal key (*top right*) from Potter's *Orlando*, 1992. A side key (*bottom left*) from Melville's *Le Samouraï*, 1967. A ¾ back key (*bottom right*) from Von Donnersmarck's *The Lives of Others*, 2006.

Back key is when key light comes at 180 degrees across from the camera, illuminating the subject's back. The camera sees only a sliver of illumination around the top of our subject, as the front falls completely into shadow. This, too, is a common position for a backlight (called a rim light), but when used as a key light, the effect is highly dramatic. In Figure 27-7, *top* the back key accentuates the falling water and fill light ensures that we can see some detail in the subject's face.

Key off subject: Though the key is the primary source of illumination, nothing says it must always fall on the subject. With the key light positioned to illuminate, say, a wall behind the subject, the subject is outlined against the light as a silhouette. Like the back key, this is a fairly unusual treatment of a key light (Figure 27-7, *bottom*).

LIGHTING APPROACHES AND EXPOSURE

Lighting approaches are closely linked to exposures—which is a function of the lens. Together they create the final aesthetic impact of the lighting design. The topic of exposures is covered in some detail in the next section on the expressive capacity of the lenses (see p. 367).

FIGURE 27-7

Uncommon key light positions: a back key (*top*, from Amiel's *Creation*) results in a dramatic look that accentuates the falling water. A key placed completely off the subject (*bottom*, from the Coen's *No Country for Old Men*) effectively silhouettes the characters.

THE EXPRESSIVE CAPACITY OF THE LENS

A camera **lens** is a collection of glass elements that gathers light reflecting from a scene and focuses it onto an imaging device which might be celluloid film or a video imaging sensor.

Lenses allow precise control over three essential aspects of the image: **perspective**, **focus** and **exposure**. All three variables have a critical impact on image composition and ultimately on what your shots communicate. While a director could leave the issue of lens selection up to the cinematographer, the impact lenses have on the expressive power of the image is so significant that a director must know the fundamentals of this critically creative tool. Some people find this forbidding, but you don't need a physics degree to use lenses intelligently and expressively. Invest some time reading what follows, and relate it step by step to the accompanying illustrations, and you will acquire an important degree of understanding and control over cinematic art.

FOCAL LENGTH: MAGNIFICATION AND FIELD OF VIEW

One way lenses are classified is by their **focal length**, which is the measurement between the lens' **optical center** (the point in the lens where the image is inverted) and the **imaging plane** (the place in your camera where the image is focused on to the film frame or video sensor). Focal length, measured in millimeters, determines the ability of a given lens to magnify (enlarge) or de-magnify (shrink) the image (Figure 27-8).

The standard against which lens magnification is compared is the **normal lens**, which approximates the perspective of the human eye. By perspective we're talking about the size of near and far objects, and the perception of the distance between them along the z-axis (depth) and also the field of view along the x-axis (horizontal) and y-axis (vertical). You use a normal lens when objects and distances should look "natural," that is, neither enlarged nor reduced compared to what the human eye is used to seeing.

The focal length for a normal lens varies according to the shooting format in use. The larger the format's recorded image, the longer will be the focal length for "normal." A normal lens in the 16 mm film format is 25 mm, but that for a 35 mm imaging plane (35 mm film or 35 mm C-MOS chip) is 50 mm. For the common ⅔ inch CCD chip in a video camera, "normal" is 20 mm and for a ¼-inch CCD chip it is 8 mm.

Lenses with focal lengths *longer* than normal are called **telephoto** (or **long**) lenses. Like a telescope, they magnify the image: the longer the focal length, the greater a lens' magnification

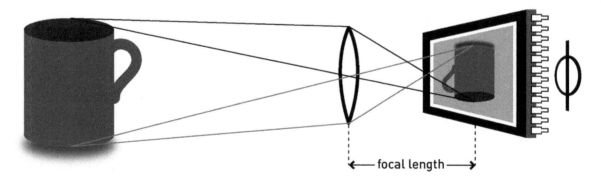

FIGURE 27-8

One way to classify lenses is by focal length, measured as the distance, in millimeters, between the lens' optical center and the imaging plane.

power. Conversely, lenses with focal lengths *shorter* than normal will de-magnify the image. As focal length gets shorter, more of the scene is included in the shot and objects become smaller in the frame. These lenses are called **wide-angle** (or **short**) lenses.

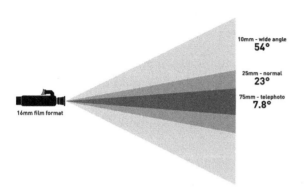

FIGURE 27-9 ————————————

The range visible along the x and y axes of the frame, or field of view, is directly related to a lens' focal length.

FIGURE 27-10 ————————————

Prime lenses only have one focal length (*top*) and tend to be shorter in size than telephoto lenses, which offer a range of focal lengths (*bottom*).

It follows that altering focal length changes the **field of view**; that is, the range along the x-axis and y-axis visible in the frame (Figure 27-9). There are some inverse relationships to absorb here: wide angle lenses broaden the field of view when lens focal distance becomes shorter, while the narrow field of view of the telephoto lens becomes more so as its focal length is made longer.

Prime lens versus zoom lens: Lenses with only one focal length (for example, a 25 mm lens) are called prime lenses (or fixed lenses). Those providing a range of focal lengths in a single lens (a 12 mm—120 mm lens, say) are called zoom lenses (or variable focal length lenses) (Figure 27-10).

Cinematographers covet primes because they use fewer glass elements, are lighter, and **faster** (meaning they allow more light to pass through to the imaging device). They introduce fewer optical and color aberrations than zooms and generally take a sharper image—something especially noticeable in large-screen projection. Prime lenses however take time to change when you need a different focal length, and limit you to their specific focal lengths.

Zoom lenses are wonderfully convenient, because you can use any focal length within their range. Their multiple glass elements however make them bulkier and generally **slower** than prime lenses—meaning they transmit less light because of all the glass the image must pass through. Recently, however, the advent of HD video has seen a parallel development in fast and accurate zoom lenses that are more than adequate for many shooting situations.

SHOT SIZE, PERSPECTIVE AND LENS SELECTION

Important when considering the relationship between lens selection and frame composition is **perspective**. As mentioned earlier, the axes of visual perspective include the two dimensional field of view along the x-axis and y-axis, plus the third or depth dimension, perceived as the distance along the z-axis.

When we first imagine a shot, our initial consideration is often shot size (close-up, medium shot, long shot, and so on). However, framing parameters do not take account of the impact that lens choice makes on composition. A close-up taken with a wide angle lens looks very different from the same framing taken with a telephoto lens. Look at the two medium close-ups from Darren Aronofsky's *Requiem for a Dream* (Figure 27-11). The left-hand frame was shot with an approximately normal lens and reveals the displeasure on Sara Goldfarb's face as she reads the details of a highly restrictive weight loss diet. The right-hand frame is however shot with an extreme wide angle lens placed close to the performer. The distortion created by the lens suggests the altered mental state of someone who has taken far too many diet pills and is starting to hallucinate.

Notice how all compositional axes are affected. Not only do we see more of the room in the wide angle shot, but the perception of depth along the z-axis is greatly exaggerated. Same shot size (MCU), yet something very different is communicated simply through lens selection. This is why you must understand how lenses affect shot composition. Simply asking for a close-up does not entirely describe the shot you may have in mind.

Focal Length, Camera Placement, and Perspective

We can achieve a specific shot size in two ways: change the camera-to-subject distance (move the camera closer for a tight shot or further away for a long shot) or alter the magnification of the scene by changing focal length (telephoto for a tight shot and wide angle for a long shot). Which approach we take profoundly affects the compositional perspectives of the shot, and therefore the "feeling" of the image. Look at the examples in Figure 27-12.

FIGURE 27-11

Lens selection can have a dramatic effect on the look of your image. Both of these shots are medium close-ups; however the left frame was shot with a normal lens and the right frame was shot using an extreme wide angle lens (from Aronofsky's *Requiem for a Dream*).

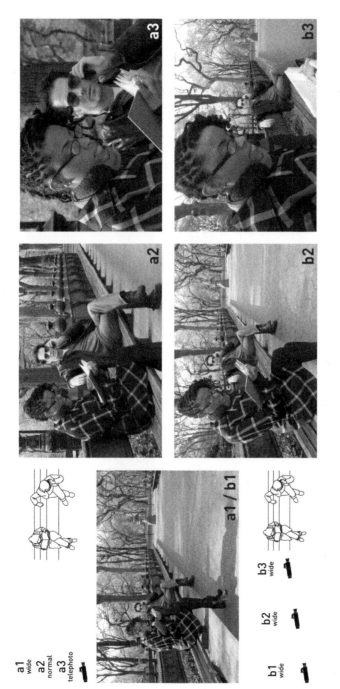

FIGURE 27-12

Focal length and its effect on perspective: a1, a2, and a3 were taken from a single camera position using wide, normal, and telephoto lenses, while b1, b2, and b3 were all taken with the same wide-angle lens and placing the camera increasingly closer to the subjects.

The *"a" series of shots* (a1, a2, a3) in Figure 27-12 were taken from a stationary camera position about 15 feet away from the actors and result from changing the lens focal length: (a1) LS—wide angle, (a2) MLS—normal, and (a3) CU—telephoto. The *"b" series of shots* (b1, b2, b3) in Figure 27-12 were all taken with the *same wide angle lens*, but their shot-size differences were achieved by moving the camera position: (b1) LS—15 feet, (b2) MLS—9 feet, and (b3) CU—2 feet.

As you can see, leaving the camera stationary and changing focal length alters the x-axis and y-axis field of view (narrower or wider), and substantially changes the visual information in the frame (photos a1, a2, and a3). Also, compare the two medium-long shot examples (photos a2 and b2): the shots are the same size (MLS); however, the shot taken with the wide-angle lens and camera closer (shot b2) includes the planter at the right of the frame while the MLS taken with the normal lens does not. Notice too how much we see along the y-axis (tree tops and walkway) in the same two shots.

In the two close-ups (a3, b3) the field of view differences become even more pronounced. Notice how much greater the field of view is with the wide-angle close-up versus the telephoto lens taking the same shot size.

Changing focal length to achieve a specific shot size alters the field of view range (telephoto = narrower, wide angle = broader), while changing only the camera-to-subject distance to achieve a specific shot size maintains the same field of view (planter is visible in every wide angle shot).

The other perception radically affected by focal length and camera placement is that of depth, that is, the apparent sizes and relative distances of objects along the z-axis. As mentioned earlier, a normal lens replicates the same perception of depth as the human eye. The subjects in this example are about 4 feet apart, and shot a2, taken with a normal lens, replicates this distance fairly faithfully. However, as you see in shot b2 (same shot size taken with a wide-angle lens and camera closer) the two subjects feel further apart. The close-up shots (a3 telephoto and b3 wide angle) alter the depth perception differences even more.

Wide-angle lenses tend to exaggerate the depth along the z-axis, especially when close to the subject. They make the space between objects appear greater because of the relative distances between the camera and the objects along the z-axis. For example, examine the three images taken with a wide-angle lens from three different camera positions (b1, b2, and b3). The z-axis perspective in shot b1 doesn't seem exaggerated; but as we move closer with the wide-angle lens (b2 and b3), the distance between them appears to grow wider and wider. This is because the distance between the subjects becomes greater in relation to the camera-to-foreground distance. In shot b3, the camera is only about a foot and a half away from the woman in the foreground, and the distance between the subjects is now four times greater, causing these objects to appear far from each other. The wider the angle of our lens, the more it will exaggerate depth in this way.

The converse is true for telephoto lenses which, given the same frame size, have the effect of compressing space along the z-axis—compare a3 (telephoto at 15 ft.) with b3 (wide angle at 2 ft.). As the focal length increases, one is forced to move the camera farther away to achieve the same shot, thus increasing the camera-to-subject distance relative to the distance between subjects. However, notice that the perception of depth doesn't change in the three shots from the stationary camera (a1, a2, and a3) despite the change in focal length. This is because only magnification changed, not the relative distances.

LENSES AND THE DIRECTOR'S STYLE

Figure 27-12 shows how dramatically a lens choice can influence the composition and visual impact of an image. Indeed, entire films often adopt a visual strategy capitalizing on the "look" of specific focal lengths. Many directors use a fairly consistent repertoire of lenses with which they are comfortable, and that become part of their visual style.

> Ang Lee has his choice of lenses. Usually he will do a master shot with a 27 mm; medium shots will be 50 mm; close-ups, 75 mm. I tried to propose in a certain part of the story going more with a long lens... He liked the idea, but when we were shooting, it would always be the same lenses, and that's just his way of working.
>
> — Rodrigo Prieto, ASC[2]

Terry Gilliam is known as a short lens director because he prefers wide-angle (28 mm and shorter) lenses that give deep frames and dramatic perspectives. Wide-angle lenses define his distinct visual style (Figure 27-13).

> The wide-angle lenses, I think I choose them because it makes me feel like I'm in the space of the film, I'm surrounded. My prevalent vision is full of detail, and that's what I like about it ... The other thing I like about wide-angle lenses is that I'm not forcing the audience to look at just the one thing that is important. Some people don't like that because I'm not pointing things out as precisely as I could if I was to use a long lens where I'd focus just on the one thing and everything else would be out of focus.
>
> — Terry Gilliam[3]

FIGURE 27-13 ———————————————

Terry Gilliam's visual style is characterized by his preference for using wide-angle lenses, as in this scene from *Brazil* (1985).

LENSES AND EXPOSURE CONTROL

Closely related to the issue of lighting design explored at the beginning of this chapter is the creative variable of **exposure**. When a lens gathers light reflecting off a scene and focuses it onto the imaging surface (film frame or video sensor), an "exposure" is made for the duration which light hits the sensitive imaging surface of your recording format. For celluloid film, that surface is the **emulsion** in which photosensitive **silver halide crystals** are suspended; for digital video there are hundreds of thousands of light sensitive photodiodes called **pixels** (short for **picture elements**) that comprise

[2] From *Cinematography for Directors: A Guide for Creative Collaboration*, Jacqueline B. Frost (Michael Wiese Productions, 2009) (original J.B. Frost interview, 2007).
[3] From interview by David Bianculli. Gilliam's "Imaginarium" Surreal and All-Too-Real, *Fresh Air*, National Public Radio, December 22, 2009.

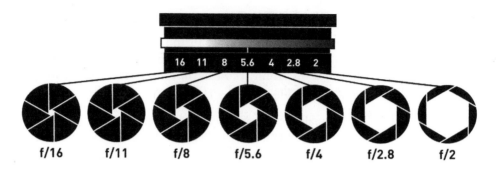

FIGURE 27-14

Lenses are equipped with an iris mechanism that controls the size of an aperture. The opening, calibrated in f-stops, determines the amount of light that passes to the imaging plane.

the **image sensor** (CCD or C-MOS). In either case, variations in the image's light intensity create comparable variations in exposure in order to render an accurate record of the light values from light to dark in your scene.

All adequate film camera lenses have an adjustable **aperture ring** that controls the overall amount of the light passing through the lens. This aperture control activates a mechanism called the **iris,** and like the iris of your eye it opens and closes to create a variable circular opening through which all light passes. This opening, called the **aperture,** has its size calibrated to the **f/ stop scale**. The smaller the f/stop number, the larger the aperture, and the more light strikes the image plane. Conversely, the larger the f/stop number, the smaller the aperture, and the less light passes through (Figure 27-14). In fact, f/stops are a fractional index. Each **stop** change represents a doubling (opening up) or a halving (closing down) of light transmission.

The aperture's most basic function is to control the amount of light in order to get a "properly" exposed image. Too much light would produce an overly bright, washed out, **overexposed** image; too little, a dark, **underexposed** image. However, the issue of exposures is more complex and nuanced than this. Often we must shoot scenes that contain a wide range of light intensities from light to dark, but we can set our aperture at only one f/stop. Here creative choice comes into play because there is no single "correct" exposure for any given scene and the director and cinematographer must decide what in the frame should be exposed correctly and what areas of a scene are better left under- or overexposed.

Figure 27-15 shows three approaches to shooting a relatively dark interior space with subjects seen against a much brighter exterior background. In the left frame (from *Breathless*, 1960) director Jean-Luc Godard and cinematographer Raoul Coutard exposed for the subjects in the interior space, allowing the background to overexpose (by using a larger aperture). In the right frame (from *Vivre Sa Vie*, 1962) Godard and Coutard exposed for the exterior illumination and let subjects indoors fall into underexposure (by using a smaller aperture). In the middle shot (from *Masculin, Féminin*, 1966) Godard and cinematographer Willy Kurant set the f/stop to an aperture

FIGURE 27-15 ————————————————————————————————————

Most scenes have a range of brightness factors. Setting your f/stop determines what will be exposed correctly and what will fall into over- or underexposure. Here are three options for exposing subjects against a bright background: expose for the subjects (*left*), expose for the background (*right*), and a compromise exposure (*center*).

that compromised between those for inside and outside light values. The result is a slightly under-exposed subject and a slightly overexposed exterior. These exposure decisions are no accident; each was calculated to yield specific visual results.

Exposure control allows a director and cinematographer to create a specific tone and mood in tandem with lighting. In the still from *Institute Benjamenta* (Figure 27-5, *right*) cinematographer Nicholas Knowland's careful lighting illuminates the walls of the staircase at different intensities, but the subject's face is intentionally under-lit. The selected aperture exposes the walls correctly and allows the subject to fall into underexposure. This lighting and exposure strategy not only creates a deep frame, but also establishes a tone of foreboding and suspense.

Other times you may want to keep a subject obscured through underexposure, as in this shot of Dr. Gibarian from *Solaris* (Soderbergh, 2002). Here a dead space station crew member appears to his friend Dr. Chris Kelvin in what may or may not be a dream (Figure 27-16, *left*). The under-exposure suggests it could be a preternatural incarnation emerging from Dr. Kelvin's subconscious.

For the shot of Sherriff Ed Tom Bell as he investigates a drug-related shootout in the desert from *No Country for Old Men* (2007, Figure 27-16, *right*), the Coen Brothers and cinematog-rapher Roger Deakins chose to expose for the Sherriff's face which is under the shadow of his hat brim. This choice causes the rest of the frame, bathed in direct sunlight, to overexpose—in a good way. The slightly bleached-out environment makes us feel the heat and intensity of the brutal desert sun.

As a director, you must become familiar with the flexibility and aesthetic impact of exposures. They are a creative image variable, and one size does not fit all: a "proper" exposure might also be a bland one. Other factors that figure in creating exposures—such as format sensitivity and con-trast range, object reflectivity, shutter speed, and lens filters—are technical matters that can be left to your camera crew.

FIGURE 27-16

Conveying tone and mood through exposure control: underexposure in Soderbergh's *Solaris* (*left*) and overexposure in the Coen Brothers' *No Country for Old Men* (*right*).

FOCUS

Focus is determined by the distance between the **focal plane** (or **image plane**, represented by the symbol ϕ on the body of a camera) and the **plane of critical focus**—the place where we set our focus, usually the subject of the shot. The focus ring on the lens gives a range (in feet or meters) that allows the user to precisely set **focus distance** (Figure 27-17). But there is more to the concept of image focus than measuring, setting the focus ring, and shooting. What is in or out of focus guides the viewer's attention and plays a role as a storytelling tool.

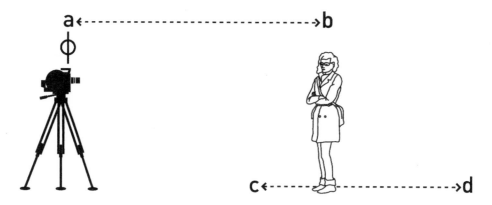

FIGURE 27-17

Focus is measured from the film plane (a) to the subject (b). However, for every given focusing distance, f-stop, and focal length, the actual range that will *appear* to be in focus (from c to d) will vary. This variable range of focus is called depth of field.

FIGURE 27-18 ⎯⎯

Selective focus as an expressive tool. Webb's *500 Days of Summer* (*left*) encourages the audience to concentrate primarily on Tom's (Joseph Gordon-Levitt) reactions by keeping sharp focus on him. In Fleck's *Half Nelson* (*right*), Dan (Ryan Gosling) is purposely thrown in and out of focus to convey drug-induced disorientation.

Figure 27-18 shows two common applications of intentionally **selective focus** for expressive purposes. The *left* still, from Marc Webb's *500 Days of Summer* (2009), is from a pivotal scene when Summer Finn tells deeply personal stories to Tom. She does all the talking, but focus is on Tom because the point is to see how he interprets her stories. Selective focus supports the dramatic perspective of this moment: Tom is assuming that her openness proves he is more than just a casual acquaintance—that she regards him as her boyfriend.

The *right* frame is from Ryan Fleck's *Half Nelson* (2006). Here, the dedicated and talented middle-school history teacher Dan Dunne is caught by one of his students smoking crack cocaine in the school bathroom. Intentionally wayward focus throughout this scene thrusts us deeply into Dan's perspective: allowing him to literally come in and out of focus reflects his drug-altered perception and the mental struggle it takes to pull himself together when he hears a student approaching.

Pulling Focus

Pulling focus simply means changing lens focus while the camera is shooting, a common practice for which there are several reasons. One is to maintain sharp focus on a subject moving along the z-axis (toward or away from the camera). If your subject walks from 35 feet to 10 feet from the camera, and you want to see her clearly, you'll need to adjust the distance setting on your lens to maintain focus. This is called **follow focus** and is usually a fairly invisible adjustment. Typically the camera crew mark the floor at critical distances (say 30 ft., 20 ft., and 10 ft.) and the 1st assistant camera (AC) adjusts the focus ring as the actor passes each mark during the take (Figure 27-19).

Another reason to pull focus is to shift visual emphasis from one subject plane to another by adjusting which area along the z-axis is in focus. You can, for example, shift the plane of critical focus (and the attention of the audience) from a subject in the foreground to a detail in the background. This, called a **rack focus**, can be a particularly revealing visual device. At one

FIGURE 27-19 ———

Follow focus involves maintaining a subject in sharp focus as she approaches or moves away from the camera, by manually shifting the focusing ring as previously marked distances are crossed.

especially dramatic moment in Mike Nichols' *The Graduate* (1967), Benjamin tries to explain to his girlfriend Elaine who the "unnamed older woman" was that he formerly went out with (Figure 27-20). Elaine isn't concerned about some meaningless fling in Benjamin's past; but before he can blurt out the whole truth, Elaine's mother, Mrs. Robinson, arrives on the scene (out of focus in the background, *frame a*). As Elaine turns to acknowledge her mother, there is a rack focus from Elaine in the foreground to her mother in the background that reveals Mrs. Robinson's distressed, guilt-ridden face (*frame b*). The narrative connection is made vividly, efficiently, and visually. When Mrs Robinson retreats in shame, Elaine turns back to Benjamin and the camera takes a full eight seconds to bring her back into focus using a slow rack focus from background to foreground (*frame c*). The effect suggests Elaine's thought process as it slowly dawns on her—*Benjamin was having an affair with my mother!* When, at last, all is clear to her, sharp focus is restored on her face and she furiously throws him out of her room.

DEPTH OF FIELD

Earlier we defined focus as the measurement from the imaging plane to the plane of critical focus (usually the subject). Setting focus distance on the lens is precise—'20 feet' means objects 20 feet from the camera's imaging plan are in focus. However, the resulting shot usually has more objects in focus along the z-axis than simply those at 20 feet distant (Figure 27-21). Some shots, in fact, have background details in focus as far as the eye can see. Why is that?

FIGURE 27-20

Rack focus shifts the visual emphasis between subjects in a shot as in this example from Nichols' *The Graduate*.

FIGURE 27-21

Depth of field is the range of apparent focus in front of and behind the actual focus distance. This allows objects along a variable z-axis range to appear in focus, as shown in this example from Jeunet's *Amélie*.

FIGURE 27-22

Shorter focal lengths (wide-angle lenses) produce deeper depth of field (*top*, from Jeunet's *Amélie*), while longer focal lengths (telephoto lenses) produce shallow depths of field (*bottom*, from Amiel's *Creation*).

In fact, setting focus means that only objects at that exact distance are *optimally* in focus, but most shots include a range along the z-axis (extending in front of and behind the plane of critical focus) where objects *appear* in focus. This is because the degree to which they are out of focus is imperceptible. This *range of apparent focus* along the z-axis is called **depth of field** (**DOF**).

Importantly, DOF is not fixed, but controllable. It, too, becomes a creative image composition tool. The four interrelated factors that determine DOF for a given shot are:

Focal length: The shorter your lens (wide angle) the deeper your DOF. And the longer your lens (telephoto) the shallower your DOF will be (Figure 27-22).

Focus distance setting: The farther the plane of critical focus, the deeper your depth of field will be. The closer you set focus, the shallower the DOF.

FIGURE 27-23

Smaller apertures (*left*) produce deeper depths of field. Larger apertures (*right*) yield shallower depths of field, but lighting has to be reduced (often with the use of neutral density filtration).

Aperture: The smaller the aperture (larger f-stop numbers), the deeper your DOF. But the larger your aperture (smaller numbers), the shallower your DOF. To get a deeper DOF, add light to your scene and reduce the aperture; for a shallower DOF, reduce lighting, or use special filters called neutral density (ND) filters that, like sunglasses, reduce the overall light entering the lens. These can reduce light transmission by one, two, three or more stops (Figure 27-23).

Shooting format: Small shooting formats (film frame or video sensor size) give a deeper DOF; larger shooting formats yield shallower. Thus 35 mm film yields a shallower DOF than 16 mm film. Large format video sensors (some as large as 35 mm film frames) mean that the old issue of video having "unavoidably deep DOF" is a thing of the past (see Figure 25-6).

Determining Depth of Field

DOF guides calculate the precise depth of the z-axis within which focus is acceptable. Publications like *The American Cinematographer's Manual* provide DOF charts for most shooting formats and lenses and you can print them free from websites like DOFMasters.com. Some smartphone apps let you enter the variables (format, focal length, focusing distance, and aperture) to get an instant DOF reading. Some are free like Kodak Cinema Tools (film formats only) or inexpensive like DOFMaster (film and DV formats).

The Utility and Creativity of DOF

Two considerations go into controlling DOF—one functional and the other expressive. If your film has a great deal of movement, and you wish to shoot lengthy and continuous takes with a hand-held camera, you would want a deep DOF. You get it by choosing very sensitive film stock, bright lighting (allowing for small apertures), and wide angle lenses. All these choices might add up to a very deep DOF (say from five feet to infinity) that allowed characters to move freely without the need to pull focus. As long as your subjects stay over five feet from the camera, they will always be in focus. This is one reason why director Mike Figgis became fond of small format digital cameras: he disliked the artificiality of making actors hit focus marks while performing:

> One of the characteristics of digital cameras that I particularly like is that they have such deep focus. With most film cameras depth of field is limited and so focus becomes crucial in respect of the actor's movement … Most digital cameras, though—certainly when they are on their wide-angle mode—have such depth of field that you don't really have to worry about focus.[4]

Other directors feel that deep focus provides a plethora of irrelevantly sharp background and foreground detail that drowns out the subject. The important thing for the director is to understand the visual aesthetic of both approaches, know how depth of field can be controlled, and then use it to creative advantage.

The frames in Figure 27-23 illustrate the difference DOF can make to a composition. The deep DOF in the left frame allows the viewer to clearly recognize the location in addition to the character, and to see how this character is waiting near a fountain. The shallow DOF in the right frame (achieved by using ND filters to allow for a more open aperture) changes the texture of the shot entirely. The character is now isolated from the background and the shot emphasizes her face and expression.

LOCATION SOUND

This section assumes that your production will be using double system sound—although most of the principles here certainly apply to single system sound recording as well (see "Digital Sound" p. 327).

Particularly in film-school filmmaking, sound recording is the neglected stepsister. Because dialogue replacement is usually too expensive for low-budget films, their effectiveness depends on getting good original dialogue tracks. This takes thought, preparation, skill, and accommodation by the director to help the location sound crew.

It is a costly assumption that location sound can be skimped because it can all be "fixed in the mix." Though true to a degree, this is damaging when practiced wholesale, for re-creating dialogue using **automatic dialogue replacement** (ADR—also known as **looping**), is damaging to your drama and vastly expensive in time and effort. See below for explanations.

In a fine article full of information and examples from a raft of feature films, sound designer Randy Thom contends that most directors give no attention to sound design, and relegate location sound recording to lowest priority (see his article in http://filmsound.org/ —a most informative website for all sound information).

Good handbooks are Tomlinson Holman, *Sound for Film and Television*, 3rd ed. (Focal Press, 2010); and Lewis Yewdall, *The Practical Art of Motion Picture Sound*, 4th ed. (Focal Press, 2011).

---

[4] From *Digital Filmmaking* by Mike Figgis (Faber and Faber, 2007).

For an enthusiastic and engagingly eccentric source for everything concerning sound, visit Film TV Sound (www.filmtvsound.com). Its discussions and articles are a mine of reliable information on the principles, practice, and equipment of a film sound department.

SOUND THEORY

Sound reflectivity in different environments is logical enough to anyone who has ever watched the behavior of billiard balls. Of course, there's more to sound theory than how sound bounces off surfaces, but even the relatively limited knowledge that follows will help you choose film sound environments wisely.

Sound perspective is the aural sensation of distance we get from acoustic changes, such as in a voice when someone moves around. Partly it's due to changes of subject-to-mike distance, and partly it's the changing relationship of the voice to its acoustic environment.

Psychoacoustics represent the most potent aspects of sound for film. The term refers to an audience's psychological perception of sound and sound's emotional and cultural connotations. The doyen in this area is the French sound expert Michel Chion, whose *Audio-Vision: Sound on Screen* (New York: Columbia University Press, 1994) explains the ideas he has been developing over several decades. His concepts are far from simple, and require you to learn a specialized vocabulary.

SOUND EXPERTS SHOULD SCOUT EACH LOCATION

When your film relies heavily on sound recorded synchronously with the image, you should invite the sound crew to scout locations with you so you get their assessment of the aural suitability of each location.

The first thing a sound specialist does in a new location is to clap her hands, once and loudly. She listens intently for what follows the "attack" of the hand clap. Ideally, it is an equally rapid decay. If the room is live (reverberant), there is an appreciable comet's tail of sound being reflected and thrown around the room. This concerns her greatly. The composition of surfaces in a location can make the difference between sound that is usefully "dry" (that is, nonreverberant), and that which is unworkably "live" and reverberant.

A reverberant room is one whose hard, facing surfaces reflect and multiply the original, or source, sounds. Because reverberations have traveled farther, they are fractions of a second behind the original—and thus muddy the clarity of their source, or original, sound. Reduce sound reflections by laying sound blankets (soft, sound-absorbent material) on hard floors, and hanging blankets in front of any walls that are out of camera sight.

A resonant room is one that has a "note," within the range of speech, to which the room resonates. You'll know this phenomenon from singing in your shower, and finding one note (or frequency) at which the room joins in, augmenting your song with a note of its own. Resonances are bad news to sound recordists, but their effect can to some extent be tuned out in postproduction. If the room is small, your sound crew may recommend mocking up the desired small space within a larger one, to avoid a boxy acoustic quality.

Test a dubious sound location by shooting some sample dialogue from representative microphone positions. Edit the results together and in no time you have the measure of your problem. The sound crew will be concerned with:

- Reflectivity of ceiling, walls, and floor (drapes and carpet greatly reduce this).
- Whether there are, or can be, soft furniture or irregular surfaces to break up the unwanted movement of sound within the space.
- Whether actors can walk and cameras can be dollied without the floorboards letting out a chorus of tortured squeaks.
- Ambient sound, and sound penetrating from the outside.
- Intermittent sound intrusions like: a nearby railroad, construction sites, schools and playgrounds, refrigerators, and central air-conditioning.

Locations spring all sorts of other sound problems. Autumn leaves sound like swishing cornflakes when actors do walk 'n talk. Sound from an expressway minimal at 2pm rises to a dull roar by 5pm, when rush hour begins. Overhead wires turn into Aeolian harps. Dogs bark maniacally. Garbage trucks mysteriously convene for bottle-crushing competitions, and somebody starts practicing scales on a trumpet. Some of these sonic disasters the astute location spotter can anticipate, some not.

SOUND EQUIPMENT

Most professional sound teams travel with their own equipment. Here are the major pieces of gear in a sound team's arsenal.

FIGURE 27-24 ———————————————

Most professional sound crews are equipped with portable digital sound recorders that record to flash memory or hard drives, often coupled with mixers that can control the input of multiple microphones.

Sound recorders: All sound recorders these days record digitally. Some use removable memory media (like compact flash or SD cards), some record to hard drives, and still others record to both. A sound team usually has multiple recorders: a main recorder (Figure 27-24), having anywhere between two and six microphone inputs, a backup in case the main recorder malfunctions, and a very small, handheld portable recorder for use in extremely tight locations or for portability during dynamic shots.

Sound recorders usually offer many recording variables that affect audio quality, including: file format, sample rate, and bit depth setting. The sound team will strive for the best possible quality audio they can achieve, but beware—these settings are also part of your project's workflow, so it's important for the sound team to reconcile their choice with the camera department, the editor, and possibly the sound mix studio so their settings will be compatible with the picture and editorial workflow. The most common audio settings for high-quality film production audio are 48 kHz sample rate and 16-bit depth settings. Two formats of audio file type are popular: WAV sound files (PC standard format), and AIFF (Apple Mac standard). Your editor and sound mixer will determine which is appropriate.

Microphones: Film recording is done using a variety of microphones, sometimes using multiple types at a time. The sound team's ability to choose the right mike for the situation, and to place it where it will unobtrusively capture a clean recording, often requires great ingenuity and is the principal measure of their skill. Unlike the camera and lighting crew who can pretty much set up their gear wherever they want, the sound team are the last to set up and must work around the art department, camera setup, and lighting pattern. A moving mike can cause serious shadow problems.

A director should also understand something about what a microphone's **reception pattern** is, and thereby understand what each mike can and cannot do (Figure 27-25).

An omnidirectional mike picks up sounds from all directions equally. These mikes produce the most natural voice recording, but are seldom of use in dialogue situations because they pick up so much additional **off-axis sound,** such as that which is reverberant or ambient. However, they work well when recording ambient sound on its own.

A cardioid, or *directional mike,* which gets its name from its heart-shaped pickup pattern, discriminates against off-axis sound (that is, it inhibits sound coming from the sides or behind). By suppressing sound from unwanted directions, cardioids have an enhanced **signal-to-noise ratio.** That is, the desired source sound is relatively louder than the accompanying ambient and reflected sound. Cardioids are the microphone of choice for dialogue scenes, but require getting the mike

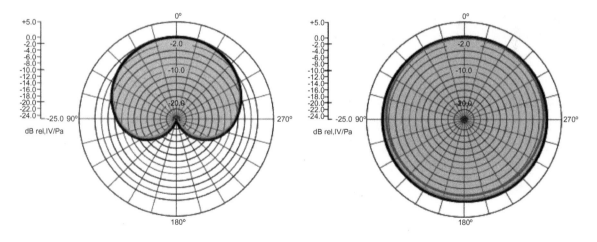

FIGURE 27-25

A microphone with a cardioid pickup pattern (*left*) is more sensitive to sounds coming from the front but less to sounds from behind, while a microphone with an omnidirectional pickup pattern (*right*) records sound from every direction at an equal level.

quite close to the talent. They work wonderfully when shooting close-ups, but if you're shooting a wide (LS) master two-shot, you will not be able to get the mike close enough.

The hypercardioid, or *shotgun, mike* does the best job of discriminating against off-axis sound because of their narrow **angle of acceptance**. This means it picks up sounds well on axis, and discriminate strongly against off-axis sound, but at some cost to naturalness of reproduction. However, hypercardioids can be positioned somewhat further away from the talent than regular cardioids, so you can use this mike in the case of a wide (LS) master two-shot.

The lavalier, or *body mike* is an omnidirectional microphone clipped to the actor's clothing at chest level and connected to a small personal radio transmitter. These produce a good and constant voice level with a low ratio of ambient sound. They do, however, have some quirks:

FIGURE 27-26

A solo sound recordist fully equipped with a sound recorder, boom pole, microphone, and headphones can handle simple sound recording situations.

- Unless you obtain top-rate wireless systems, radio transmission sometimes fails or unexpectedly pulls in taxi and police messages.

- They pick up digestive sounds and clothing rustles (so scenes with a lot of movement are tricky to mike this way). Make sure your cast wears natural fiber clothing because man-made fiber generates static electricity, and sounds like thunder on a small scale.

- Lavaliers lack sound perspective. By remaining at a constant distance from the speaker and picking up so little reverberant coloration, a lavalier removes all sense of the speaker's movement or perspective changes. These must be emulated later in the mix (live now, pay later...). Other mikes have various advantages and disadvantages, but basically there is no substitute for a quiet background and a good mike close to each speaker.

Boom poles, also known as **fishpoles** are telescoping, lightweight poles on which to mount microphones so they can be placed as close as possible to the talent (either above or below) while remaining out of the camera frame (Figure 27-26).

Portable mixers are a standard part of any sound recordist's gear (see Figure 27-24). Since camcorders and location recorders may have too few microphone inputs, a scene requiring multiple mikes will need a **mixer**. These offer a number of microphone inputs (usually from four to eight) and allow each mike's input be controlled individually while outputting a mono or stereo mixed audio signal to the sound recorder.

Headphones should be ear-enclosing to cut out external sounds, and are critical for monitoring all recorded sound. Audio levels are checked and adjusted using VU or peak meters on the mixer and recorder respectively, however, headphones let the boom operator and sound recordist detect when the microphone strays off axis or if unwanted noise is being picked up. Holding recordings below peak sound levels is critical with digital recorders, since they distort far more readily than their more forgiving analogue forebears.

TYPES OF LOCATION SOUND

Location sound is any that is recorded in the same environment as the images, and it breaks into two categories: the first is **synchronous sound** (sync sound), which is audio recorded simultaneously with the image so sound and picture correspond to each other on a frame-by-frame basis; and **wild sound** (also called nonsync sound) that is any recorded independent of picture.

Dialogue is almost always sync audio, although off-screen dialogue might be recorded wild at the same location without the camera even being present. Also, when an actor flubs a line or when some extraneous sound punctuates dialogue, the alert sound recordist asks for a wild, voice-only recording immediately after the director calls "Cut." The actor then repeats the compromised line just as he spoke it during the take. Since the recording is in exactly the same acoustic situation, the words can be seamlessly edited in, and a new take avoided.

Ambient sound: This is sound inherent to the location, whether interior or exterior: a backyard may have a distant traffic accompaniment; a riverside location may have the hum of a power station a quarter mile off. Every room you record in will have its own ambient sound that is noticeable only during silences. It may be a faint buzz from fluorescent fixtures, the hum of voices from an adjacent office, or birdsong and trees rustling from outside.

Before calling for a wrap at any location, interior or exterior, the sound department always records an **ambience track** (also known as *room tone*, *presence track*, or **buzz track**) in a simple procedure: on the heels of the last scene, before anybody leaves the set or changes anything, actors and crew freeze. For a solid minute, using the same mike setup, the sound crew makes a recording of the particular quality of silence at that location. This, duplicated to create as much track as needed, becomes the all-important sound filler for gaps in edited dialogue tracks.

Wild sound: A sound recordist will also be on the lookout for recording wild tracks (audio recorded while camera is not running). **Wild sound effects** (**SFX**) are nonsynchronous recordings of sounds that might be useful to augment the sequence's sound design later. A car door slam that sounded meager in the wide shot can be re-recorded (after the camera has moved on) with a much closer mike for a richer sound, then synced to the shot later, or perhaps you need to record the sound of footsteps coming up a wooden staircase for off-screen sound.

Ambience tracks (**Atmospheres**) are also often recorded as wild sound and can be useful to use later as additional background noise, especially if they are native to the locations, but not present when you were shooting. A children's playground, the squawk of crows in the trees, or a nice clean track of crickets at night can all be useful in postproduction. A shot of pristine woodland may be ruined by the sound of a nearby cement factory, but substitute an early morning ambient track recorded five miles away, and your problem is solved. A good recordist is always collecting good "atmos" tracks.

RECORDING REQUIREMENTS

Direct and reflected sound: In dialogue sequences, the sound crew aims to get clean sound that is "on mike." This is dialogue spoken near a microphone and into its most receptive axis. Ideally it is sound relatively uncolored by reverberant sound reflecting off walls, ceiling, floor, or other hard surfaces such as tables and other furniture. Sound bouncing off surrounding surfaces before finding its way to the microphone travels by a longer route and arrives fractionally after the source sound. This appreciably muddies the clarity of the original, but you probably won't realize this until you edit different mike positions together as you must with any well-covered dialogue sequence. In a reverberant location, each microphone position has different acoustic characteristics determined by the differing mike distances from the speakers, differing mike directions, and different admixtures of ambience and reflected sound. Just when dialogue should sound seamless, editing different mike positions together makes the seams glaringly evident. This is always a challenge to the sound editor, to say the least.

Shadows and multiple mikes: Getting microphones close enough to actors without causing visible shadows takes cooperation and compromise between sound and camera specialists, and the director. Often it will require placing multiple mikes and feeding their inputs into a mixer. Location sound like this must be mixed, because every mike left open needlessly records its own share of ambient, source, and reflected sound. All the channels joined together can produce a chaotic set of problems. A multichannel recorder can be used so that each mike is recorded separately, keeping their contributions discrete for a later mix-down of the best coverage. If mixing must be done on the spot, the recordist really must know what he or she is doing, for once mixed, the omelet cannot be unscrambled. Verify results before proceeding.

Source-to-microphone distances: Keeping boom-mounted microphones close enough to do a good recording job when actors are on the move is a rare skill. The boom operator's main task is to stay close to whoever speaks, on their axis, yet remaining at all times just out of frame. Failure to do so means a mike in frame, or sound levels plummeting as the mike-to-subject distance increases. Ambient sound levels, however, remain constant which means that the ratio of source to ambient sound can vary a lot. Adjusting playback levels afterward can make the speaker's voice constant from angle to angle, but the cuts reveal telltale changes in ambience levels. This too creates problems for the sound editor later.

Photography trumps sound: Because the sound crew must keep their microphones out of sight and fit around the needs of lighting and photography, the director can mitigate their difficulties by stabilizing speakers during a dialogue sequence. Alternatively, by getting creative with set dressing, that nice potted plant on a dining room table can conceal a strategically placed mike. Good dialogue recordings pay large dividends later.

Seeking More Technical Detail

This chapter on the essentials of lighting, lens, and sound technology only touched on what a director should know. For a more thorough overview of technical aspects of lighting, lenses, and the nature of sound and sound recording techniques, see *Voice & Vision: A Creative Approach to Narrative Film and DV Production* 2nd ed. by Mick Hurbis-Cherrier (Focal Press, 2012).

CHAPTER 28

ON SET: PRODUCTION BEGINS

BEFORE THE CAMERA ROLLS

The lion's share of work on a film project happens in preproduction. Actors are rehearsed, visual designs determined, shot coverage planned, and locations, props, set dressings, equipment are secured, and so on. All this activity is meant to ensure that everything and everyone you need to make the film is in place when production is ready to go: this is the film set. So many resources, people, and money converge during a relatively compressed period of time that everything must be well prepared. The days you have to shoot your film are the most precious in the life of the project.

THE DIRECTOR'S ROLE

A director is like an orchestra conductor whose challenge is being aware of many people's work simultaneously. It's a period of high concentration as everyone tries to do their best work. A supportive, enthusiastic cast and crew will endure and triumph together, but under the best of conditions, work will be stressful. For you, it is a time of unremitting pursuit of perfection shot through with occasional euphoria or despair.

Directing a film means starting out with a detailed movie in your head. You have broken it into its components, and now you maneuver the cast and crew into creating each part as you want it. But obstacles and opportunities intrude along the way, so the movie in your mind must constantly evolve and adjust. Crew and cast know this, and when they turn to you expectantly after a shot, they are asking, "Did you get what you wanted?" One way or another, you must be able to answer. And not just answer; you must lead.

Helpful in this is, when you first direct, to make brief **crib notes** on index cards as reminder lists so you don't forget any of your intentions in the hurly-burly of the set. Defining the beats and story points you must make, and nailing down what you intend for each sequence, means you are directing from a plan instead of waiting to recognize success if it should appear. When fatigue sets in, and memory and imagination shut down, crib notes become a lifesaver (Figure 28-1). Later as you gain in experience and confidence, you may not need these shopping lists any longer.

```
Scene 23: TONY RETURNS HOME AFTER 5 YEARS SILENCE

Metaphor: Return of the prodigal son      (Time: 3.5 min)

Tony Wants to:
      Get his mother's photo from father
      Evade specifics about the past
      Convince his father he's not a failure
      Avoid showing how much he missed and loves his father
Dad Wants to:
      Keep his wife's photo
      Keep Tony at an emotional distance
      Deny he had anything to do with Tony leaving
      Convey that Tony hurt him
      Get Tony to come back again
Scene Must Convey:
      Tony guards his status as an independent man
      Father is afraid of being left alone
      Mother's death is the root of their turmoil
```

FIGURE 28-1 ————————————————————————————————————

Having crib notes detailing the beats and story points of each scene is a good way for the director to keep focused in the controlled chaos of a film set.

DAILY ORGANIZATION

A smoothly running organization signals professionalism to cast and crew. This is particularly vital if low-paid (or unpaid) people are to maintain confidence in your leadership. Your unit should provide the following for every shooting day:

- A contact list with everyone's (cell) phone numbers in case of emergency
- Printed call sheets for cast and crew well in advance (with a map to the location and emergency information in case of illness or accidents) (p. 318)
- Daily scene and shot list from the production schedule (p. 313)
- Scene coverage thoroughly worked out with the director of photography (DP) and script supervisor (Chapter 24)
- Floorplans for camera crew (p. 304)
- A pre-established lighting design worked out by the DP from the floorplans

- Appropriate props and costumes ready to go (Chapter 23)
- Your assistant director (AD) should carry lists of everything so that you carry nothing in your head, and nothing gets forgotten.

GETTING TO THE FIRST SHOT: AN OVERVIEW CHRONOLOGY

1. **Preparing the set:** Art department arrives at the location first, to **prepare the set**. On location, this includes moving or bringing in furniture, painting walls, placing set dressing details and props, and so on. The art department is usually one step ahead of the production unit, preparing the next location while you shoot.

2. **Load in:** The camera and sound departments arrive and "load in" equipment to the **staging area**, the place on the set where equipment and their containers are neatly kept. It must be out of the way of the set, near enough to be convenient, and secure against theft.

3. **Rigging the stage:** Camera and electrician **rig the stage**, meaning they rough in the camera placement and lights based on the floorplans and DP's lighting designs. As mentioned earlier, wider master shots are usually shot first (see p. 316). An art department person will be on hand in case any setting adjustments need to be made. As this proceeds, the sound team is working out their miking strategy for the scene.

4. **First line up:** After rigging lights, placing props and furniture, and anticipating the action, the crew asks for the precise setup from the director, who confirms framing with the director of photography (DP), and what is or isn't in shot. The director outlines what the characters are going to do; the camera is set in place, and the operator can frame what's expected.

5. **Blocking and tech rehearsal:** The actors will be asked to do a walk-through in the actual space. Final blocking is determined and focus points are marked on the floor and on the camera as necessary (see p. 371). During the tech rehearsal walk through, actors repeat their lines in a relaxed manner and move in stages under the director's instruction to the points where they will stand or sit during the scene. At each stage, director and DP review final framing and lighting (Figure 28-2).

   The sound crew takes a close interest in the placement of lighting, which direction the characters face as they speak, and work out how to best cover the scene for sound. If coverage presents undue difficulties, they may ask for blocking or lighting compromises. This is often the first time the actors are in the actual environment of the scene, so they are familiarizing themselves with the space (see "Tech Rehearsals" p. 399). After the walk-through, the actors go to wardrobe and makeup while the crew establish the final lighting set up. Lighting can be a long, slow business, especially if there are two or more characters with elaborate movement paths. This may require multiple key lights and a great deal of planning and adjustment. To test the effect of their work, the DP and crew use **stand-ins** (people of similar size and build to the actors) who walk through while the actors get ready. In a small crew, a spare crew member of the right height will become the necessary stand-in.

FIGURE 28-2

Director Martin Scorsese (*center*), DP Michael Ballhaus (*left*) and Jack Nicholson (*right*) do a run-through for lighting, framing and blocking during the shooting of *The Departed*.

6. **Wardrobe, makeup:** While the camera crew finalize lighting and practice camera moves, the cast go into wardrobe and makeup. If the sound department plans to use wireless microphones for the scene, they will plant the microphones on each actor while they get into costume.

7. **Rehearsals:** While lighting is going on, director, cast, and script supervisor do last-minute work on the scene. If an actor is missing, the script supervisor will read their lines (called **running lines**) or provide action cues so the scene can be worked over (Figure 28-3). Some directors make it a policy to have all cast members present for such rehearsals.

8. **Dress rehearsals:** Actors and director now return to the set. They are first walked through the scene again, for their own benefit and that of the DP, camera operator, and sound team. Their hair and makeup may need touching up by makeup and hairdressers (Figure 28-4). Next comes the **dry run**—a full rehearsal in costume and makeup, but without running the camera. The cast does this at low intensity to conserve energy until the camera is running. This helps internalize what they must think and do to make their lines and action coincide with the precise needs of the camera, its movements, and attendant lighting. Any problems with

costumes will show up and can be fixed. At this time, the members of the sound crew are checking sound levels and settling optimal boom positions. The script supervisor takes a scene timing as a benchmark for the shots about to follow.

9. **Take the shot!** When all cast and crew feel ready, you can roll camera.

The first shots of any production always seem to take an eternity to line up and light, and the assistant director (AD) must be on hand to apply judicious pressure and report as soon as the set is ready. For the first production day it's wise to schedule a light shoot. Remaining on schedule while the unit finds its rhythm lets everyone feel accomplished and energized for the rest of the production.

ROLL CAMERA

As it comes time to roll camera, the script supervisor makes a last check to see that actors are correctly costumed, the right props are at hand, and that nothing on the set has been forgotten or misplaced.

The assistant director (AD) marshals everyone to their starting positions, ensures that doors and windows seal out exterior sounds, and calls for silence on the set. There is a last hair and makeup check, and the DP confirms that all lights are on. If you are using a film camera, the assistant camera (AC) has inspected the film gate for debris, something that must be done regularly and without fail.

Distances have been measured out, and the focus puller is ready to adjust the lens in perfect synchronization with the actors' movements, all according to the marked tape on the

FIGURE 28-3

While the crew finalizes the lighting, the director does last-minute work with the actors, getting them emotionally into the scene. Student director Andrew Knudsen gives performance notes to his actor on the set of his short *Occult*.

FIGURE 28-4

Makeup and hair are constantly checked and retouched as needed in preparation for a new take.

lens focus ring (Figure 28-5). The script supervisor confers with the AC concerning the next slate number, which we will assume is Scene 14, shot C, take 1. Only by correctly slating each shot can

FIGURE 28-5 ──────────────────────────

Before a take, focusing distances are measured and marks are placed on the ground and on the lens, according to the actors' movements.

you know what you have covered, and be able afterward to organize it in the cutting room. This information is scrupulously recorded in the camera, sound, and continuity logs. These are vital information sources as the footage piles up—so vital, in fact, that we must pause to establish how marking systems work.

SHOT AND SCENE IDENTIFICATION

Shot identification is based on, and must remain coordinated with, the shot labels indicated on the shooting script and floorplans (see p. 304). Let's say we're shooting the scene from the shooting script on p. 304, Figure 24-5. The **scene** and **shot identification numbers** are 14-A, 14-B, 14-C, 14-D, 14-E, and 14-F. These setup numbers will be written on the slate and recorded in the logs when each new shot is attempted. The **take** number simply refers to the number of times we try each shot before we get it right and can move on to the next (14-C take 1, 14-C take 2, 14-C take 3, and so on). Once we get what we want in a shot, the director calls out "circle it." and you can move on to the next shot on the shot list (see "Another Take, Circle, or Keeper" p. 392). Often best actions or performances will be found in an amalgam of takes.

The Slate

At its simplest a **slate** or **clapper board** is a basic information dry-erase board with a hinged bar (Figure 28-6). Banging the bar closed creates a visual and aural reference point for syncing picture with sound. The person responsible for updating the slate between takes and operating it is called the **slate loader** (usually the 2nd assistant camera). The slating or clapper-board ritual has three main functions:

- Visually, the slate identifies the production, scene, and take number at the head of every shot. Useful for syncing, in postproduction, and for the film laboratory, the slate board may also carry a **color reference chart** (or **chip chart**) to help with color correction.

- Aurally, the slate operator's scene announcement identifies the scene and take number on the soundtrack for sound transfer personnel.

- The closing clapper bar provides an exact picture frame against which to align the *bang!* in the recorded track. This is vital when sound and picture are recorded separately and must be synchronized for viewing and editing.

There are fancier, more automatic film-marking systems, such as the "smart slate." This is a clapper board containing a timecode display that comes on when the bar is opened and whose timecode freezes at the point where the clapper bar is closed (see Figure 25-10). This makes syncing sound to its timecoded picture easy, and is especially handy for grab-shooting when voice announcements may have been impractical. However, camera and sound recorder must be compatible. Every morning, technicians must jam-sync (synchronize) the timecode generators because their clocks drift apart over a period of time.

Having a "clapper" as sync reference becomes vital whenever you shoot **double system** (picture and sound recorded separately), but no aural "clapper" is needed when recording **single system** sound (sound and picture on the same record media). With either system, you must however identify every shot and take visually before the director calls action, or face chaos later in the cutting room.

FIGURE 28-6 ————————————

A slate contains information that identifies each shot and provides an aural and visual reference point for synchronizing sound in post.

Scene, Shot, and Take Numbers

There are two methods for slate numbering.

Method 1: The scene/shot/take system, favored in the Hollywood fiction film system, bases its numbering on the script scene number, for example: Scene 14, Shot C, Take 3 (written "Scene 14-C, take 3"). Hollywood makes big, highly supervised productions, and needs lengthy factory part numbers. For the small, flexible production however, this may be overkill. The more elaborate your system, the more susceptible it is to breakdown as you depart from first intentions or people get tired.

Method 2: The cumulative setup/take system is preferred for documentaries and features in Europe. Shooting simply begins at Slate 1, with as many takes as you require. Each new camera setup gets the next slate number, and Take 1. Slate 142, Take 2 would be the 142nd camera setup, second take. For the overstretched small crew this is the preferred system since it requires no liaison to coordinate numbers with the script, and no flustered adaptation when the inevitable script departures come up. All the script supervisor must do is record the setup and take number against its scene in the master script, or into a database.

SHOOTING LOGS: CAMERA AND SOUND

A film shoot requires various logs and it's crucial, especially for the arduous processes of syncing and organizing footage in postproduction, that they remain coordinated with each other and the slate (Figure 28-7).

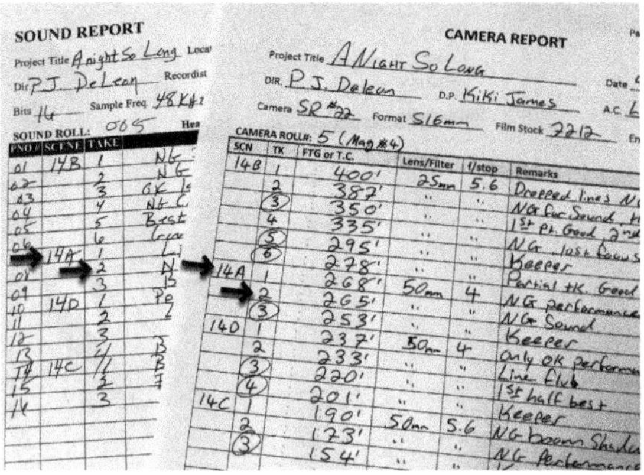

FIGURE 28-7 ——————————————

Camera and sound logs must be assiduously maintained and coordinated with the information on the slate (see Figure 28-6). Download camera and sound logs at www.directingbook.com ("Forms and Logs").

A **camera log** (or camera report), kept by the AC, records each film magazine's content by shot, take, and footage or timing. Each film magazine, video tape, or media card gets a **roll number**. The camera log also notes critical technical information, like f/stop setting, lens type, and any filtration. This information comes into play during processing and later in editing. A day-for-night scene, for example, might be shot using a blue filter to give it a moonlit look: but without the relevant documentation, the film lab might easily treat the filtering as an error needing color correction in the transfer.

A **sound log** (or sound report) kept by the film sound recordist, records scene and take numbers and whether each track is sync or wild (nonsync voice, effects, or atmos recording). Sync or wild is important to whoever must sync the rushes and transfer the wild audio into its correct place in the editing system.

A less obvious function of logs is to record (by serial number) which piece of equipment made which recording. Should a strange hum appear in the sound, or a consistent scratch turn up on a film negative, the offending machine can be quickly withdrawn for examination.

COUNTDOWN TO "MARK IT," THEN "ACTION"

The director, satisfied that all is ready for a take, nods to the AD, and so begins an unvarying ritual that gets everything rolling:

> **AD** (loud voice): "Okay, quiet everybody—we're about to roll."
> *Silence descends. The 2nd AC (clapper loader) takes a position holding the slate in front of the first actor, at a height where it is clearly visible. On close shots, the camera operator will sometimes direct its placement to ensure that the all-important number and clapper bar are in shot.*
> **AD:** "Roll sound."
> *The sound mixer turns on the recorder and waits a few moments until able to report that the recorder's mechanism has stabilized.*
> **Sound Mixer:** "Speed."
> *The camera operator now turns on the camera, which comes up to speed almost instantaneously.*
> **Camera Operator:** "Mark it."
> **2nd AC:** "14-C, Take 1."
> *BANG!—the clapper closes, and the 2nd AC scuttles out of shot and settles quietly off frame.*
> **Director:** "Action."

The magic word "Action!" can be said in a variety of ways, depending on what you want to convey: excitement, mystery, surprise, dread, routine. It's the director's last prod, and as the scene begins, the script supervisor starts the stopwatch.

If, during the scene, a car horn is supposed to sound from Johnnie waiting in the road, the script supervisor will call out, "Beep, beep" at the right place, and a character will respond with, "Aha, there's Johnnie. I gotta go." Other scripted cues, such as a voice calling "Nancy!" from the alley below, or a plane going overhead, will be cued in the same way.

Starting Without a Slate

Sometimes, when the setup is so tight that the slate cannot get into shot, or when you are shooting spontaneous material and don't want to alert everyone, you quietly signal camera and sound recorder to start rolling. After the action is complete, and while the camera is still rolling, the slate is brought into shot by the AC, but upside down. The AC calls out the scene number and says, "Tail slate" or "Board on end" then announces slate and take number and claps the bar, after which the director calls "Cut." In the cutting room, the person syncing the material should find a note in the log and continuity sheets warning that the material was tail-slated.

CREW RESPONSIBILITIES

Every crew member has something to monitor during filming:

- The camera operator watches through the viewfinder for focus, composition, framing, movements, and whether the mike is edging into shot. Film cameras have an oversize viewfinder, so the operator can see anything about to encroach before it enters the masked-off film area.
- The director of photography is watching the lighting as the actors move from area to area.
- The camera assistants watch for focus, stock running out, and that the camera gate or image chip is clean.
- The script supervisor watches how each physical movement is accomplished, listens for departures from the scripted dialogue, and notes it all down for every take (see Chapter 30).
- The director watches every aspect of the scene for its emotional truth and intensity. What is being expressed? Is the scene emotionally focused? Does it deliver what it's meant to deliver? How was this take different or special?
- The sound recordist listens for dialogue quality, background, noises-off intruding, and whether the actors' lines are on axis and clear of any footsteps, set noises, or audible body movements.
- Assistant directors watch to see if actors hit their marks, and make sure all is quiet on the set.
- Makeup and hairdressers watch to see if their work is wilting under the lights.

- Electricians are watching to see that all lights stay on.
- Grips are watching to see that the rigging they have done remains firm, that lights are staying up, that scenery is firmly anchored, and that the camera hits its marks during tracking shots.

The scene proceeds until the director calls "Cut."

WHO CAN CALL "CUT"

Sometimes you'll let an unsuccessful take run its course to avoid chopping actors short during the middle of a difficult scene. Nobody may call "Cut" unless they have previously established their right to do so with the director. Someone else might be allowed to abort the take if:

- The camera operator sees a hopeless framing mistake or that an actor went wide of the mark and veered out of frame.
- The sound mixer decides that if for some reason sound is unusable.
- A stunt supervisor sees a situation of imminent danger or failure.
- Very occasionally, a prestigious actor may call "Cut."

Directors never want the cast to start deciding which aspects of their work are usable. A big-name actor might be accorded that privilege, especially if the director is of lesser status, but ordinary mortals must keep the scene going until released by the director. Even though someone flubs a line, the director may know that this part of the scene is to be covered in another shot, and that a momentary glitch is unimportant.

ANOTHER TAKE, CIRCLE, OR KEEPER

If the director needs another take, it will be: "Cut, let's go for another." Then, as the slate and logs are updated for another take, the director will have a quiet word with the actors, saying what she is looking for, and from whom. But if the director feels that a take was completely successful and there is no need to go for another try, then she will say, "Cut!... Good for camera?" If Camera confirms that all was good, the director will check with the sound recordist, and if all was good for sound, then the director will say "Circle that," and the unit will move on to the next camera setup. A **circled take** means that there is useable material in that take and when shooting film it also means that the director wishes those takes to be transferred to video for editing. Particularly if a scene is long, there may be two or three takes circled, with accompanying notes such as "Use the first part of Take 4 and the last part of either Take 6 or 7." The director must inform the script supervisor what is usable in each take. To conserve money you do not need to have labs transfer takes that are obviously poor—only circled takes.

With digital shooting and editing, there is no need for such on-the-spot choices because no extra expense is involved in digitizing everything into the editing computer. Because of this the lingo for indicating the last successful take is changing. Some directors will still say "Cut!... circle that," or even the older school version "Cut!... Print it!" But on digital shoots I've heard directors refer to the last, good take as a "best take" or "keeper take," as in "Cut!... that's a keeper," and I've heard directors simply say, "Cut!... we got it. Let's move on to the next set up."

CLOSER SHOTS AND REVERSE SHOTS

Once the master, establishing shot is "in the can," the camera will be moved in to get a variety of closer shots according to the coverage plan in the shooting script. Each new setup gets a new slate number; each new attempt becomes a new take. Different camera positions may use different lenses or different camera heights to alter the sense of space and perspective. The backgrounds may be **cheated** (adjusted but not so that it shows) to contain enough of something significant in the frame as a juxtapositional comment. Lighting too will be cheated since wide-shot lighting only sets the general mood and closer shots are routinely adjusted for contrast or to achieve a better effect. The key lighting must still come from the same direction, and the shot must still intercut with the master shot, but within these parameters, there is plenty of latitude for poetic license.

SHOT OR BLOCKING CHANGES

Occasionally, while you are shooting, new ideas for coverage emerge. Perhaps the MLS and MS of one character can be merged into one longer shot? Or you noticed a nice moment in the master shot and decide to add a new close-up to capture it. The script supervisor confers with the director over the changed coverage so there are no ghastly omissions.

Sometimes, when you change blocking, it's fatally easy to **cross the line**. This of course means that the camera has strayed across the scene axis (see "Crossing the Line or Scene Axis" in Chapter 4). It will cause alarm and despondency in the cutting room and may make an assembled scene look truly awful.

Here's where resorting to your floorplan and storyboards is a lifesaver, for they show unequivocally who should look in which direction. If a scene is to cut together well, each participant must maintain their particular screen direction, either looking screen left or screen right, no matter where the camera is placed. If people move, you must show the group taking up their new positions, and then maintain the new logic of screen directions that result from their change.

RETAKES AND PICKUP SHOTS

Sometimes a take is excellent except for a couple of lines or a movement. Then and there, the director will retake that section without even stopping the camera. Calling "Keep rolling" to camera and sound, the director will say to the cast, "Go back and do the section about the storm again." The script supervisor will call a beginning cue, and the scene will resume until the director calls "Cut." Director and script supervisor then confer about whether to shoot extra cutaway shots of listeners so the new section is thoroughly covered. These shots will get appropriate numbers, and their function will be noted in the continuity sheets.

Another way to cover the inserted section would be to move the camera and shoot from another character's angle—and in editing, bounce the section off a close shot of this listening character so the scene becomes her point of view.

Anything not in the shooting script is considered a **pickup shot**. Perhaps during an exterior shoot, the director notices a neat line of birds perched along a power line. It's a lovely image that might have a place in establishing the scene or as a cutaway. The DP grabs the shot and the logs will then label that shot with the scene number and the designation PU for pickup (14-PU1, 14-PU2, etc.).

IMPORTANT: SHOOT AMBIENCE TRACK

When the materials for a scene have been shot, and the editor has everything needed, it's time to **strike** the set—meaning dismantling everything and restoring the location to its original state. But wait, the sound department must first record an **ambience track** (also called **presence**, **buzz track** or **room tone**). A voice yells, "Everyone stand still!" In eerie silence, the unit stands like statues, uncomfortably aware of their own breathing and of the little sounds in the room. After one minute of recording room ambience the sound recordist calls "cut" and the crew can now break down the set. That minute of room tone is crucial when it comes to editing dialogue tracks.

CONTINUITY SHEETS

For a feature shoot, the script supervisor produces reports that are often masterpieces of observation. Each setup has its own sheet to record the following:

- Production, personnel, and date
- Slate and take number
- Script scene number
- Camera and lens in use
- Action and dialogue variations
- Successes and flaws for each take
- Which takes are to be printed by the film lab (big-budget films use the camera reports to request selective printing)
- Any special instructions from director or script supervisor to the editor.

  (See Chapter 30 for more detail.)

IT'S A WRAP

After the sound team has recorded the ambience track, the AD yells "It's a wrap!" and pandemonium breaks out as everyone starts their winding-up responsibilities:

- Electricians lower all the lights and roll up cables while hot lighting fixtures cool.
- Grips strike the set and collect their clamps, stands, and boxes.
- Props collect all the properties and stow them for safety, marking them off in an attendance list.
- Camera people take their equipment apart and stow it in its many travel boxes.

- Precious tapes or memory cards are carefully grouped and marked for delivery. They represent a whole day's work.
- Stuff accumulates in piles on the floor: all the C-clamps here, all the sandbags there, all the cables in the corner.
- Sound equipment goes into its boxes.
- Makeup cleans off the actors, who change into their street clothes.
- Hairdressers collect wigs, mustaches, and sideburns for overnight repairs and cleaning.
- Wardrobe collects costumes for cleaning and repairs.
- The AD hands out call sheets for the next day, plus some script revision sheets photocopied on different-colored paper. Several people groan at the sight of changes still coming in.
- The director, in close conversation with the actors, thanks them. Then, to the unit, the director calls out: "Thanks for a good day's work, everyone."
- The AD or craft services check there is no damage to the location and that everything is left clean and tidy.
- The caterer or **gofer** ("go for this, go for that" person) unexpectedly produces coffee and sandwiches, and a low sigh of relief among the famished goes up.

On a small crew, those with little equipment to wrap help those with much (lighting, for instance). Like all human organizations, a film crew can personify divisions of rank. As general of your troops, you must be concerned for the whole army's welfare. If appropriate, pitch in and help with the donkeywork. You need everyone's respect and loyalty, and carrying things shouldn't be beneath your dignity.

Make sure that everything in a borrowed location has been replaced exactly as found. Attention to someone else's property signifies concern and appreciation, and helps ensure a welcome should you want to return. Initial reluctance to accept a film crew's presence often arises because people have heard horror stories about cavalier treatment of property.

Doors open and close as weary, exhilarated people schlep the equipment out to the transport, munching as they go. The camera assistant is checking the lens and camera gate or carefully labeling tapes, record media, or film cans while the recordist and continuity supervisor are finishing reports. The latter is filling out a daily progress report for the line producer or production manager, who will be anxious to know how many pages of script were covered and, if it's film, how much stock was consumed. Engines start up, and the circus moves on its way. Tomorrow, it will reconvene at the next location.

CHAPTER 29

DIRECTING ON THE SET

DIRECTING THE ACTORS

While the actors are publicly working their way through a labyrinth of strong feelings, the director must suffer in stoic silence. The cast endows you with their trust, so in return you become the all-caring, supportive, and quietly confident parent figure. Inside, you are probably racked with uncertainty about whether you have the authority for the job. How can you, when you feel like a fraud? So you play the role of being confident—a role the whole unit wants to believe. Fake it till you make it, actors say. It helps to limit the area you oversee, by being better prepared than anyone else, and by keeping everyone busy.

Your major responsibility is always to the cast; the actors' respect rests on how accurately and briefly you can reflect what each just did, and where in detail each should aim next. You are the conductor directing your instrumentalists, so divest yourself of anything impeding it (Figure 29-1).

Cast and crew may test your patience and judgment. Leaders usually have their powers challenged, yet behind what seems like a sparring and antagonistic attitude may lurk a growing respect and affection. The unaccustomed parental role—supporting, questioning, challenging—may leave you feeling thoroughly alone and unappreciated. You are authority, and creative people are often refuseniks who maintain their most active and ambivalent relationships with authority figures.

For each member of your cast, "my director" and the other actors are temporarily the most important people in their life—allies with whom to play out complex and personal issues that involve love, hate, and everything between. This is a legitimate path of exploration for an actor or any other artist, and you are the arbiter of their success, and the guide when things go wrong. For you, finding a productive working relationship with the subtle personalities of each actor is really discovering how best to harness their temperaments and yours as you create something bigger than all of you together.

With crew and cast, keep the roles of friend and director separate. A friend may be forgiving and understanding, and not hold anyone's feet to the fire. But a director must uphold the purpose of the project, not least because it involves so many people's work and so much money. Standing at the crossroads, you do what it takes to keep everyone intent on the common enterprise.

There is no set way to handle this except to demand that everyone concentrate on their own area of responsibility and remain fiercely loyal to the project. Your dedication is a model of

FIGURE 29-1 ——————————————

A director must oversee many interlocking opera-
tions and never lose track of the actors' needs.
Pictured is a student unit at work on Andrew Van
Beek's *Jack-o-lanterns*.

leadership here, and professionals understand
this—though the rest may not. Human relationships under stress are always different and
evolving, but if you have to choose, aim to be
respected rather than liked. Later, after things
have turned out well, admiration and liking
will come.

ACTORS' ANXIETIES AT THE BEGINNING

Whatever level of performance was achieved
in rehearsal now comes to the test. Actors feel
they are going over Niagara Falls in a barrel, so wise scheduling puts the least demanding material early as a warm-up. Actors suffer
maximum jitters and minimum confidence just
prior to first shooting. Take each aside and tell
him or her something special and private. It
should be sincere and supportive. Thereafter,
that actor has a special understanding to maintain with you. Its substance and development
will reach out by way of the film to the audience, for whom you are currently the surrogate.

In the first day or two, there will be a lot of tension, either frankly admitted or displaced into
one of the many behaviors that mask it. Try not to be wounded or angered; if someone is deeply
afraid of failing a task, it is forgivably human to pick quarrels or demote the work's importance.
It does not mean, as many film technicians secretly believe, that actors are a childish breed. They
are normal, often shy, people who sometimes succumb to agonies of self-doubt. Your appreciation
and public recognition given for even small achievements—and your crew's astute diplomacy—
will work wonders to restore morale.

Why filming takes so long is incomprehensible to the uninitiated, so warn actors unused to making
movies that filming is invariably s-l-o-w. Tell them to bring books, playing cards, or crossword puz-
zles—anything to fill the inevitable periods of waiting while the crew sets up each new camera angle.
Even a professional feature unit may shoot only one to four minutes of screen time per eight-hour day.

Anxieties subside as the process establishes its rhythms. As the cast falls in with the pace
and demand of shooting, each player begins to take pride at being one of a team. Performances
improve so much that you wonder about the usability of the earlier material.

DIVIDING YOURSELF BETWEEN CREW AND CAST

A student director is often using an untried crew and wants to personally monitor everything the
crew does. Desist. You won't direct your cast adequately unless you let the DP and AD lead the
crew. Know what you need from your cast, and work unceasingly to get it. This will take all your
attention, and then some.

DIRECTING ACTORS DURING A SHOOT

During the shoot there are multiple opportunities for you to rehearse and direct the actors (Figure 29-2).

Tech rehearsals: Although tech rehearsals are mostly for the crew to get their bearings, the cast is usually also becoming familiar with the details of the location (if you haven't rehearsed there). Help them understand and exploit the space, the specifics of its sets, the furniture and anything they will be handling. If it's a kitchen scene in which they open a drawer and pull out some silverware, decide where the forks and spoons will be. Runthroughs allow them contact with *their* space before the camera rolls, and you want them to naturally and entirely inhabit their environment and character. Tech rehearsals are also your opportunity to tweak the blocking and give reality to the location.

FIGURE 29-2

Your major responsibility is always to the cast; they need your guidance. Student director Auriel Rudnick blocking a scene for her short *Fitted*.

Lighting set-ups: While the crew set up the next camera angle, take your cast aside and cue each actor on his character's recent past and emotional state as he enters this scene. This is both informing and motivating, and may need refreshing before every setup—and sometimes before every take. The prior scene may not yet have been shot, or was shot some time ago, and now you alone know its emotional content. Only you can judge whether today's scene will graft naturally onto tomorrow's.

Your AD will quietly tell you when the setup is ready so actors can start with the minimum of waiting. Actors now take their positions.

Walk-throughs: With the lights, camera, and full crew now present, the walk-throughs are your opportunity to get the actors into the emotional space they must inhabit for the scene. If the scene is complex, keep them at half intensity until the crew is completely ready for a take. Don't squeeze the freshness out of a scene by asking for full performance levels while the AC is adjusting focus marks and the boom operator is figuring out where to mike the scene. However, runthroughs allow you to see the scene getting to the point where a take may very well "nail it," and that's when you decide to roll camera. Remember, the magic word "Action" can be said 50 different ways—urgent, thoughtful, gentle, questioning, challenging, abrasive, singsong, or fearful.

"Action!" can be a directing cue all by itself.

Between takes: Immediately after calling "Cut!" you must decide whether the take was a "keeper" (acceptable take), or whether you are going for another. From this the actors know whether their work was on target. If the take was lacking in some way, you must clarify what you want next. It may have been a framing or lighting problem, or you may briefly give the actors new, actable adjustments and goals that you want from them. Be clear about what worked and what didn't during the take, but make it relatively quick and nonjudgmental, because you want to shoot before the collective intensity dissipates. Momentum is everything, so avoid unnecessary discussion.

CHANGING GOALS

Your new goals may require something different from each actor in a group scene. From one, you want the same good level of performance; from another, a different emotional shading or energy level. Each actor must know what you expect. Avoid asking anyone for the same thing again. This is baffling because the actor is inside his instrument and doesn't know what you saw that you liked in the previous take. Part of him thinks, "If she liked what I did, why do I have to do it again?" He may understand that you want him to reproduce an effect. So give even the satisfactory players objectives that will keep them building rather than trying to repeat a result.

Actors sometimes feel they can do better, and will ask for another take. You must decide whether or not that's necessary. Your competency is now under scrutiny, because either the actor noticed something you missed, or he is blowing something out of proportion. Which is it? The cast should always be allowed to improve, but an actor who keeps asking for just one more take may be luxuriating in an anxiety fetish or manipulating directorial decisions. If you were paying full attention and saw nothing wrong, you may need to simply say that the last take was fine and that the unit must move on. If the actor convinces you that another take will yield pure magic, then give him a shot. After only one or two of these episodes you will have a good sense for whether the actor is sincere or playing a head game. Actors' insecurity has a thousand faces.

DEMANDS AND FEEDBACK

Often the director's Achilles heel is a passive, gullible tendency to accept what actors give as the best they can do. As an audience of one, you feel tremendous guilt and uncertainty. All these people doing all this... for little old me! You want to please them, to thank them, to be loved by them. And you mustn't even react while they perform, to tell them how grateful you feel. You are mirroring their need for approval with your need to be liked and forgiven... It's an uncomfortable, squirming kind of experience to begin with.

Try to adopt the confident artist's creative dissatisfaction. Treat each scene as a seeming beneath which hide layers of significance that only greater skill and aspiration can lay bare. Never grade your players from "good" to "bad" but instead concentrate on telling each in a few words *what they communicated*, which will vary from take to take. Say what you would like in the next shot, and if possible give separate, additional input to individual players. Sometimes you can discreetly seek confirmation of your impressions from the script supervisor, who also monitors performance shadings. But you must develop trust in your own instincts, and that can only happen if you clear the mental and emotional space for your instincts to operate.

Pushing for depth means expecting at the right times to be moved by the actors, and when your cast members deliver real intensity, you will feel it—no question. You and they are creating as you go, not simply placing a rehearsal on record. But watch out when you find yourself *trying* to feel what you should feel naturally. This comes from guilt: the cast is trying so hard, and you are the hard-to-please pasha. This is something that must be resisted, or you will not be able to react like an unattached audience member—as you should. If the performance works, it works; if it doesn't, it doesn't. Accept it and move on to asking yourself and your cast why. Is it fatigue? Repetition? Tell your cast diplomatically what you felt. Often one actor knows something that can help you sort out what went wrong. Sometimes all it takes is to re-work an awkward line of dialogue, or a bit of blocking to help them find their focus. If this is what they are pointing out, then listen to them.

When a scene begins sagging into comfortable middle age, it's usually because the cast is on autopilot and not listening to each other. Remind your players to listen, or take each aside and privately suggest some small but significant change that will impact other cast members. By building in little stresses and incompatibilities, by making sure cast members are working off each other, you can restore tension when it has languished.

SIDE COACHING AND REACTION SHOTS

When a scene goes static and sinks to a premeditated appearance, try **side coaching** to inject tension. This means you interpolate at a quiet moment in the scene a verbal suggestion or instruction, such as, "Terry, she's asking the impossible—she's laying a trap." Your voice injects a new interior process in the character addressed, and the scene moves off in a new direction. This won't work if your actors are unfamiliar with side coaching and react in surprise. So introduce this technique in rehearsals and warn them not to break character should you use it. Side coaching is most useful when directing simple reaction shots. The director provides a verbal image for the character to spontaneously see or react to, or an idea to consider, and you see an immediacy of reaction.

Usually the best reactions are to something actual. If a character must go through a complex series of emotions while overhearing a whispered conversation, make the other characters do a full version of their scene even though they are off camera. If, however, your character must only look through a window and react to an approaching visitor, her imagination, with a bit of side coaching, should provide all that is necessary.

Reaction shots are enormously important because they lead the audience to infer (that is, cocreate) a character's private, inner life. They also provide the vital, legitimate cutaways that allow you to combine the best takes during editing.

Never dismiss cast and crew from a set without first covering all likely reactions, cutaways, and inserts for that scene.

FOR THE NEW SHOT

As soon as you have an acceptable take, brief the DP about the next shot, then turn to the cast. Give any brief, positive feedback necessary about the last shot and give preparation for the next. The AD may decide to take the actors aside to rest them if the crew is roaring into action changing the camera, set, and lights. Previously, the cast were royalty—now they slip into obscurity while the crew goes to work. Actors can sometimes feel quite insignificant, given all the attention the equipment and its technology gets from the crew. No wonder they usually prefer acting in the theater.

CHALLENGING YOUR CAST

You and your cast are working in a highly allusive medium, so your audience expects metaphorical and metaphysical overtones. To draw us beyond externals and surface banality, to make us see poetry and conflict beneath the surface, you must challenge your actors in a hundred interesting ways. Your demands should reinforce their own sense of always being capable of something just a little better. This creative dissatisfaction is as it should be, but be ready for an undertow of complaining. Emphasize the positive, and regard the grumbling as the noise in the rigging of a ship pushed to capacity. Don't imagine for a moment that you should be able to make everyone feel good.

EVERYONE NEEDS FEEDBACK

Actors learn from their schooling and theater work to depend on audience feedback. Now they are being filmed and you are their only audience. During a take you cannot signify approval, amusement, or anything else. When the camera stops, your job is to briefly make each actor feel the sense of closure he used to receive from a live audience.

Actors are not fooled by empty gestures. Your brain has been running out of control trying to factor in all the editing possibilities that might make the last performance usable, and now you must say something intelligent to your trusting players, each of whom is (and must be) self-absorbed and self-aware. You manage to say something approving, and the cast nods intently.

Now your crew needs you, and the actors are asking, "What are we doing next?" The production manager is at your elbow demanding confirmation for the shooting at the warehouse next week. The warehouse people are on the phone, she says, and they sound testy. So there you have it: you wanted to direct, but the glamour of directing turns out to be walking around faint from lack of sleep, answering an avalanche of questions, juggling countless egos, and feeling your head is about to explode.

CRITICISM FROM THE CAST

Be prepared for personality problems and other friction during shooting. Any preferences or criticisms expressed by actors during rehearsal may surface more vehemently under duress. There will be favorite scenes—and scenes the actors hate. Professionals should handle both with aplomb. There will be scenes that involve portraying negative characteristics that the actor finds odious, and certain lines upon which an actor becomes irrationally fixated. In serious cases, you can parry by allowing the actor to use alternative wording. But don't offer this until all other remedies have been exhausted—and do it as a one-time-only concession, or your cast may all want to start writing alternatives.

Most things you don't have to decide on the spot. Be ready to take things in; think about them, and delay making changes until you are sure. When critical suggestions are incompatible with the body of work already accumulated, say so as objectively as you can. Remaining open-minded does not mean swinging like a weather vane. You will get well-meant but impractical suggestions, so be ready to deflect them by being well prepared and so full of interesting demands that everyone is too busy to become critical. This shouldn't deter genuinely thoughtful and constructive ideas.

As knowledge of each other's limitations grows, actors can become critical or even hostile to each other. Occasionally two actors who are supposed to be lovers take a visceral aversion to each other. Here, only loyalty to the project and commitment to their profession can avert disaster.

Filming makes intense demands on people, and a director must be ready to cope with everything human. You will learn hugely about the human psyche under duress, and this will make you a better director—and maybe even a better human being. If this sounds scary, take heart. The chances are good that you and your cast will like each other and that none of these horror stories will happen to you—yet.

USING SOCIAL TIMES AND BREAKS

During the shooting period, spend time (outside the actual shooting) with your cast. However exhausted you become, it is a mistake to retreat from the neuroses of your cast to the stoic understanding of the crew. Try to keep cast and crew together during meals or at rest periods. Frequently, while lunching or downing a beer after work, you will learn something that significantly complements or changes your ideas. New ideas and perceptions can generate that precious sense of shared discovery that binds crew and actors together in an intoxicating feeling of adventure. Work becomes a joy.

DIRECTING THE CREW

As we have said, beginning directors want to oversee the whole crew's work. A check of composition, as we shall see, is absolutely necessary, but the director must cede control to their senior production personnel. For their part, those people must be fully aware at all times, and take the appropriate initiative without waiting for explicit instructions. Here are the most important things a director can do for their crew:

- Communicate the concept, story, and purpose of the film to the entire crew, and show them why you love this story. This establishes your personal investment in the project and what you expect from them.
- Have a thorough shooting script and floorplan ready to clearly indicate the coverage for each scene.
- Communicate any blocking or lighting requirement or changes precisely.
- Don't make frivolous changes or unreasonable demands.
- Bring energy, a sense of mission, and passion for the project to the set.
- Listen to suggestions (which should all be filtered through the DP or AD).
- Respect their expertise and let them do their job.

COMMUNICATING

Before shooting begins, each crew member should have read and questioned the script and contributed ideas in his or her own area of specialty. A director should, in turn, understand the rudiments of each technician's craft and be able to communicate in the craft's special terms. That's why this book wants you to know so much about the whole production process. From you or your delegates, the crew needs positive, concise directions with as much advance warning as possible. Your technical team won't rise to cope with genuine crises if things that could have been foreseen have gone unattended.

Avoid thinking out loud, especially when the pace heats up. Instead, arrive at conclusions so you can produce brief, practical instructions in wording that cannot be misinterpreted. Without being condescending, get people to repeat instructions of any complexity so you are sure they understand. Anything that needs to be in writing should be.

The assistant director (AD) and the director of photography (DP) should deal with all production and technical questions, or you won't do your own job properly. You are there to *answer the needs of the actors and concentrate on building the film's dramatic content.* Your script supervisor will be an important ally, although this person cannot always judge performance quality since script supervision demands a fierce concentration on the details of words, actions, and materials. Do not fail to confer over coverage, especially if you make changes.

LOOK THROUGH THE CAMERA

When a new shot has been set up, *you must look through the viewfinder* to ensure that you are satisfied with the framing at the start and at the conclusion, as well as with other key compositions on the run-through. When there is a lot of moving camera coverage, you will need to agree with your operator on compositions, angle, size of the image, and so on (Figure 29-3). Walk the actors (or stand-ins) through the take, freezing them at salient points to agree with the operator on what should appear in the frame. To stabilize these decisions, your crew will need to make chalk marks on the floor for both actors and the camera dolly. Everyone may have to hit particular marks at specific moments in the scene.

Precision separates the experienced from the inexperienced in cast and crew, but trying to impose too much control on an inexperienced ensemble may be an exercise in futility and wreck cast morale. Because framing, composition, lighting, and sound coverage are the formal structuring that translate a live world into cinema, the director must keep the strongest possible contact with the outcome on the screen. When shooting digital video (or film with a video assist), you can watch the whole take on the monitor during recording and know immediately what you have. Be aware that retreating to a video monitor may make the actors feel abandoned because you are not beside the camera and physically present for them.

FIGURE 29-3 —————————————

The director should check the framing before a take to ensure she is satisfied with the composition of the shot. Student director Samantha Sanders checking the frame on her thesis film, *Gypsy Blood*.

With film and no video assist, the results remain in doubt until the dailies return from the laboratory. All the director can do is to clearly brief the technical crew through the DP, and then stand close to the camera so you sense what it sees. With a little practice, you can see whether the operator is in sync with the action from their movements.

MAKING PROGRESS

Shooting is stop-start work, with many holdups for lighting or camera setups. A crew can easily slow down while everyone waits. Nobody can say quite who is holding things up. In fact, everyone is waiting for the notorious and elusive A.N. Other, a Murphy relative who bedevils the tired and disorganized. The good AD is, among other things, a sheepdog constantly looking for bottlenecks and barking everyone into action the moment that shooting can continue.

WHEN YOU AND YOUR CREW ARE ALONE

If you have a fairly small and intimate crew, encourage them, when you are alone and the actors elsewhere, to discuss their impressions of the shoot. Some members—such as grips, electricians, and ADs—do their work before shooting, and then stand observing during the actual take. What they notice may usefully complement your sense of what is really happening. You, after all, have goals from rehearsal to fulfill, but they are seeing the action for the first time and have an audience-like reaction.

The work of other crew members—camera crew, and sound recordist in particular—demands such localized attention to quality that they cannot reliably register the dramatic. You will therefore get a very mixed bag of observations, some of them way off track. Encourage all views, but do not feel you must act upon or rebuff ideas that imply criticism of your work. If, however, most members of the crew find fault with a main character, take serious notice.

WRAPPING FOR THE DAY

At the end of a working day, thank each actor personally, and the crew collectively. Respectful appreciation affirms that you take nobody for granted. By implication, you demand that respect in return. Under these conditions, people will gladly cede you the authority to do your job.

No wrap is complete without a careful reiteration of the next day's arrangements by the AD and the unit production manager (UPM). If you are shooting exteriors, someone must keep abreast of weather reports and have contingency shooting ready as bad-weather alternatives. Call sheets should be issued to cast and crew, and rented equipment should be returned, batteries charged, and film dailies delivered to wherever they must go.

SHARE DAILIES WITH THE CREW BUT NOT THE CAST

Dailies are the raw unedited footage generated by a film production. They're called dailies because after wrapping, directors and principal crew review all footage shot the previous day. That way they can monitor the consistency of their footage and correct any problems before leaving the location.

Actors want to work with a director of vision whose methods they trust. Their greatest pleasure comes from working with one who gets more from them than they had realized possible. For the same reason you forbade your actors to see rehearsal tapes, you don't let them see their dailies. Actors are like the rest of us, and hate what they see of themselves on the screen. By trying to cure perceived faults, each begins to self-direct instead of listen to you. By innocently letting them see themselves, your perfectly good footage becomes part of their struggle with their demons.

The crew, however, must see each day's work. It's an important evolutionary process for everyone. If the cast finds this discriminatory, tell them it's standard practice, and promise them a viewing of the first cut to assuage their natural curiosity. By then, they will have already given their performances, and thus cannot compromise what they do (see "Dailies: Reviewing and Evaluating Footage" p. 425).

CRITICISM FROM THE CREW

Student crew members are sometimes unwise enough to let those in earshot know how much better they could direct than the director. This is intolerable and must be immediately squelched. Nothing diminishes your authority faster than actors feeling they are being directed by a committee. Directing a film effectively is not, has not been, and never will be democratic.

Guard against anarchy by making sure all territories are clearly demarcated before shooting starts. Anyone who strays must be told, privately and very firmly, to tend his own area and no one else's. A crew member with a legitimate complaint should, as we have said before, address it to the DP. It may not even require your attention.

There will be occasions when you have to make a necessary but unpopular decision. Make it, bite the bullet, and do not apologize. Like much else, it is a test of your resolve, and the unpopular decision will probably be the one everyone knows is right.

MORALE, FATIGUE, AND INTENSITY

Morale in crew and cast tends to be interlocked. Giving appropriate credit and attention to each member of the team is the best way to maintain loyalty to the project and to each other. Everyone works for recognition, and good leadership trickles down. Even so, immature personalities will come unraveled as fatigue sets in or when territory is threatened. Overworking the crew is a key factor here. Under severe fatigue, people lose their cool, and work becomes sloppy.

Keep morale up by taking special care of creature comforts. Your production department must keep people warm, dry, and ensure that they have food and drink, bathrooms to go to, and somewhere to sit between takes. Avoid working longer than four hours without a break, even if it's only a ten-minute coffee break. From these primal attentions, cast and crew infer that "the production" cares about them. Most, when they feel valued, will go to the ends of the earth for you.

YOU AS ROLE MODEL

You are the director, and your seriousness and intensity set the tone for the whole shoot. If you are sloppy and laid back, others will outdo you. If you demand much of yourself and others, but are appreciative and encourage appropriate humor, you will run a tight ship. Convert every negative criticism into a positive request for an alternative. Your vision and how you share it will evoke respect in the entire team. People will follow an organized visionary anywhere.

CHAPTER 30

MONITORING CONTINUITY AND PROGRESS

A director's recurring nightmare is to discover, when crew and cast have departed, that a vital angle or shot has been overlooked. When a film's story proceeds by a series of images, or when the narrative is carried by nonverbal actions, directing and keeping track of what you have covered are relatively simple. Mistakes and omissions occur more frequently when scenes involve several simultaneous actions, such as crowd or fight scenes with many people in frame whose relativity must match from shot to shot. Even complex dialogue scenes, especially those with characters moving around, can spring unpleasant surprises when shooting crosses the axis or if reaction shots get forgotten. Fatigue and last-minute changes raise the odds of error in all situations, and this is most likely to happen in low-budget filmmaking, where too few people cover too many tasks. Working fast and hand to mouth, intentions must often be modified, and crossing intended shots off a list can easily go awry. The checklist may be so rife with changes that the list itself becomes a hazard. However, if the script supervisor and cinematographer really understand editing, their attention or that of the editor (standing in for the script supervisor) can provide vital checks and balances as shooting progresses.

During production, the **script supervisor** (or continuity supervisor) works hardest and longest of anyone and is in some ways the person closest to the director during the process of shooting (Figure 30-1). It is many years since I worked with one, so I am indebted in this chapter for the gold mine of procedures and methods in Pat P. Miller's *Script Supervising and Film Continuity*, 3rd ed. (Focal Press, 1999).

The script supervisor's key role is guarding against omissions or mismatches in the production, and to keep track of every shot that has been covered and all issues concerning continuity. If you lack a script supervisor on your project, try using the editor. They have more reason than most to get things right.

THE SCRIPT SUPERVISOR PREPARES

The script supervisor is going to monitor the continuity of costumes, properties, and characters' words and behavior—something that otherwise falls haphazardly to director, actors, and crew. He

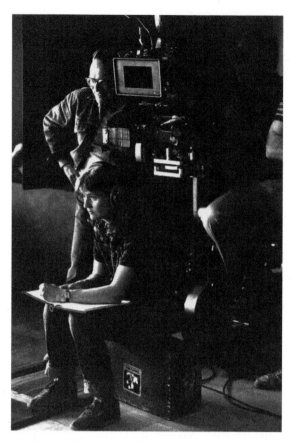

FIGURE 30-1

The script supervisor keeps track of coverage and continuity and maintains close communication with the director during production. Pictured is Martha Pinson with Sidney Lumet on the set of *Power* (1986).

or she is also going to watch that everything planned in the coverage is shot, and if variations and additions arise, keeps extensive notes on what they are.

Script notes: As soon as a finished script exists, continuity work begins by making a close reading for a list of locations and of characters in the first breakdown. Very important are their names, characteristics, physical attributes, overt actions, and their entries and exits. The script supervisor then must read, analyze, break down, and reread the script until its every need is committed to memory. He or she makes a breakdown of the type shown in Figure 17-2 (see Chapter 17) to lay out the scenes in order, each with their location, time of day, characters, chronological data, script pages, and length. This note-taking culminates in one or more sheets per camera setup, records that provide guidance during the shoot and after it, when they are used intensively by the editor.

Chronology: The script supervisor also makes a thorough chronology for the story. If the story is told out of order, or has flashbacks or flash-forwards, this may have profound consequences for the age or condition of the characters, and thus for their makeup and costuming. Continuity must at all times know where the story is, spatially and temporally, as well as what has befallen the characters before we see them, and where they go afterward.

Coordinating and communicating: As coordinator for many important details, the script supervisor gets specifics from wardrobe, props, and makeup, and makes sure the production manager has the right details for each scene. The production office will issue the daily *call sheet* specifying scenes, actors, costuming, properties, equipment, transport to locations, and any other special provisions for the next day's shoot, including emergency contacts in case of illness or injury.

MONITORING COVERAGE AND TIMING

The script supervisor must also be intimately familiar with the coverage plans in terms of editing and shooting strategies. He or she understands how every dramatic beat should be covered and can anticipate edit points where continuity from shot to shot is especially important, and updates the shooting script as changes occur. After each shot has been successfully accomplished, the script supervisor marks a solid line through all of the actions and dialogue recorded by the shot to indicate that it was covered, how it was covered and how many takes it took. Occasionally the solid line is interrupted by a squiggly line, indicating action or dialogue that occurred during the shot, but was not visible to the camera from that particular angle (therefore not covered). Detailed notes, including shot timings and number of takes, are also written along side each shot. If the director decides on any changes to the planned coverage, say merging two shots into one with a camera move, then this too is recorded in the supervisor's script markings and notes. Script supervisors thus need to understand editing and coverage principles because both may be in flux during shooting (Figure 30-2).

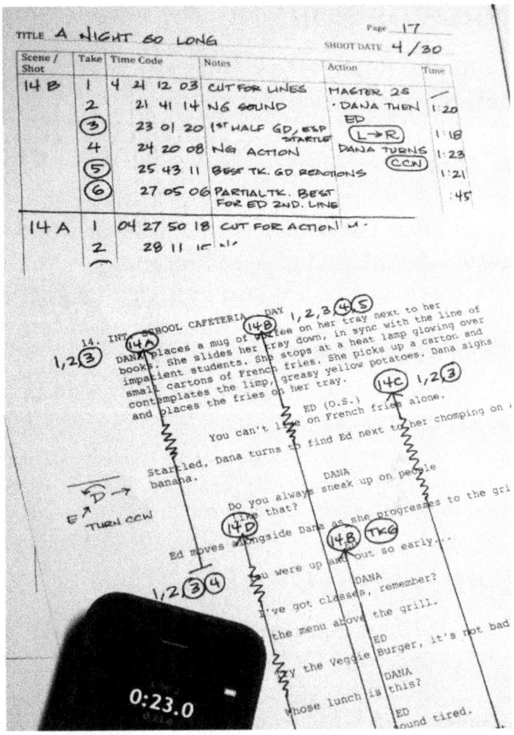

At the end of the shooting day, the script supervisor has a record of what was actually shot, down to variant dialogue lines. Anyone can see at

FIGURE 30-2

Script supervisors constantly update the shooting script by crossing off shots as they are taken, timing every shot, and noting any changes to the coverage.

a glance how the scene was covered and what dialogue or actions remain yet to be covered.

Script supervisors use a stopwatch to keep track of scene timings, since scenes persistently running over length will lead to an overlong film. This leads to dropping whole scenes in the cutting room, and an irate producer demanding why you wasted money shooting them in the first place. How long each scene should last is predicted by a page count, one page normally lasting one minute of screen time, and scene length being specified to the nearest eighth of a page. Master scenes yield the first overall timing, and every take of every shot in every scene is logged by its timing.

Keeping track of script pages shot per day, and screen time completed lets the unit know its progress. The producer can know if the film is lagging its schedule or exceeding its intended length.

TYPES OF CONTINUITY

Continuity implies the simple match of details from one scene to the next, and even one cut to the next, but if a chronologically late scene precedes an earlier one, continuity must be back-matched to preserve the logic of compatibility. There is also direct and indirect continuity:

Direct continuity is when one shot or one scene follows another. A character cannot change jackets while stepping from one room to another, for instance.

Indirect continuity is that between scenes separated by time or other scenes. If a man goes carousing and we next see him many hours later, this is indirect continuity. Although he is in the same clothes, they are now rumpled and stained, and his face shadowed with stubble. During parallel storytelling, we might intercut two stories, so indirect continuity must hold good in all the A segments and all the B segments.

The script supervisor's job is to watch for everything that an alert audience will ever notice. Sometimes this takes research—otherwise someone will inevitably point out that Slender Willow cigarettes were not produced in China until five years after the period of the film and the Yellow-Crested Jub-Jub *never* makes its mating call in September.

MONITORING CONTINUITY

Normally, the script supervisor sits beside the camera in order to see what it sees, but might otherwise watch a video feed. Often the monitor's acuity won't be good enough, or, if it's an exterior location, the screen will be washed out by daylight. Events also start to happen off camera before they appear in frame, so the wider awareness of sitting next to the camera is preferable. Between takes, you'll often find the script supervisor right at the elbow of the director, confirming what has been shot, what's up next, and discussing the prognosis for finishing all the setups in the allotted production time.

WARDROBE AND PROPERTIES CONTINUITY

The script supervisor must know wardrobe details from scene to scene, and keep a hawk eye on the continuity of costumes, hair, makeup, and properties. There are three classes of property:

Hand props, such as a comb or diary, which the characters handle.

Stage props, such as a lava lamp or princess bed, which are part of an environment and may be related to one of the characters.

Breakaway props, such as a pottery figure or a foam cup, which get broken or used up in some way and for which replacements must be on hand for subsequent takes.

PHYSICAL CONTINUITY

The continuity supervisor must know if a character's beer glass was full or half finished, how a jacket was buttoned, or a scarf tied. A cake with two slices taken in one scene cannot appear later complete but for one piece eaten. If a character picks up a glass of wine with her right hand in the master shot, but her left in closer shots, the editor has a problem. Similarly, if a character rises during a line in a medium shot, but after that line in the long shot, there will be wailing and gnashing of teeth in the cutting room.

Continuity's job is to alert everyone to continuity lapses and inconsistencies in camera movements or timing, to get them corrected or to know what options exist as alternatives. This means being very prepared and very observant, *all* the time. Taking digital snaps of characters or sets before and after each take helps keep tabs on what people wore, how they wore it, and how their hair and makeup looked. Shooting on video makes some of this less necessary, but it's amazing how sure an actor can be that his jacket was unbuttoned—until video footage proves otherwise.

MONITORING DIALOGUE

From take to take, the script supervisor logs all the words that the actors use. The supervisor records variations that may create problems in editing. Plot information is often embedded in dialogue, so it would be disastrous to settle for a take in which the detective gave the wrong name as the suspect. The script supervisor may also note the relative pacing, subtext, and feeling from take to take.

MONITORING YOUR OWN PROGRESS AS DIRECTOR

DRAMATIC AND TECHNICAL QUALITY

There are various levels of oversight to monitor dramatic quality, which is top of the list so far as your future audience is concerned. Primarily, you want consistency and conviction in the performances, credible action, mood-enhancing lighting, responsive camera movements and compositions, and clean dialogue tracks, but you can only concentrate on the actors and camera movements.

Screening takes on the set: Whether shooting digitally or on film with a video assist system, evaluating video can be very helpful, but also very time consuming if it becomes a nervous habit. As we have said, don't allow actors to watch their work on the set—they can easily become impulsively critical and start directing themselves. On one of my films I allowed a lead actor to watch what I thought was a fantastic performance, imagining it would give him a confidence boost, but as we were watching the take he furrowed his brow and muttered to himself, "C'mon Jim, you've got lazy mouth." After that, I had to struggle to calm his over-active jaw and excessive articulation.

Screening dailies: If at all possible, get your transferred video dailies back from the lab and screen them—without sync sound if need be. A feature unit must see dailies, so any reshooting can be done before the set is struck, or before lighting becomes too difficult to reconstruct. Even a dog-tired unit can summon enthusiasm for seeing its own work. As we have said, you must politely but firmly exclude the actors by saying it's a technical check for the unit only (see Chapter 32).

Screening scene assemblies: Because computerized editing is now possible anywhere, the editor can accompany a location unit and digitize video dailies as they become available. Once material is captured, a day's work can be assembled in an hour or two. The unit then sees its latest work in rough outline before the set is struck. Many mismatches show up only in edited form—such as inconsistencies in acting, lighting, framing, sound, or continuity. These, once known, may be improved or corrected in subsequent shooting. Most importantly, the director can see whether performances are consistent and pitched right and whether stylistic intentions are working out. Because the editor can be continuously assembling and revising the whole film as its parts become available, a rough assembly of the whole movie should be available within days of the end of shooting. If the editor cannot be at the location, they can always post scene assemblies online through a video sharing service like YouTube or Vimeo.

FULFILLING YOUR AUTHORSHIP INTENTIONS

Directing film actors means getting the precise aims of the characters to show in both their interior and exterior lives. You watch like a hawk to see that your cast maintains the detail and clarity of performance you expect. This is extremely taxing, and you can easily become distracted. Keep nothing in your head that can instead be dumped onto paper as a checklist. Lists save your life when that fatal fog descends during sustained shooting and you are too tired to think or feel. Check your crib notes (see p. 283) so you waste no energy ransacking memory for your goals. Make them the night before shooting, check them at the start of the scene, and check them again at its conclusion. Did you cover every item in your notes? Are there fresh consequences for scenes that follow?

Fatigue and the oblivion that comes with it are the director's biggest hazard. During the comforting industrial rhythms of production, it's fatally easy to let your attention lapse. The big question you should be asking, which may seem blindingly obvious, is: Am I fulfilling my authorial intentions? You are haunted by another, though: Do I have a film? (Figure 30-3). Success is hard to measure except in fuzzy, subjective terms, but it's helpful to break your intentions down into more specific areas of examination.

Dramatic clarity: The sign of effective performances is that, standing by the camera, you spontaneously feel what the audience is going to feel. An effective human presence on the screen is deceptively simple: when actors truly feel what their character is feeling, you and the audience will feel it too. When it's real, it takes you over. If you are searching for what you expect, something is missing, and you must take action. If the actors are failing or faking, you must lead them psychically to a new place where they reconnect with their characters' thoughts, actions, and emotions. This is usually different from actor to actor, and your best clues come from the rehearsal history.

Subtext: All takes on all angles of all scenes remain unpredictable of outcome, which is why you have to maintain such high concentration and sensitivity if you are to interpret nuances accurately. A director who looks only for the expected, or who allows his or her attention to wander, misses the boat.

FIGURE 30-3

Despite the logistical and technical distractions inherent in film production, a director must maintain steady progress toward his original creative goals. Student director Carl Boles discusses a framing with his DP Habib Awan on his short film *Never Dream, The Beginning*.

Here are typical internal responses to two takes of a scene set in a bus station when, late at night, two stranded passengers start a desultory conversation. The action and dialogue in each take are identical, yet each take elicits different responses from anyone alert. One suggests two losers unenthusiastically sizing each other up. The other shows two depressed, disgruntled people wondering whether they can be bothered making conversation. When you ask yourself what truth was played out—the answer arising from one take is that "you despise someone with your own shortcomings" and from the other, "alienated people in social situations tend to isolate themselves." You look for analogies to illuminate each. One is that "two neutered cats circle each other." The other, "two exhausted convicts decide it's not worth cooperating to break rocks." These answers reveal that, quite spontaneously, different subtexts emerged in the playing of each take. Only if you are alert to the nuance of the moment do you catch these differences, which are actual and ephemeral, never intellectual and theoretical.

Scene dialectics: With repetition, scenes can fall into a mesmerized, singsong state, and if you are fatigued you may go along with it. Make sure, therefore, that the dialectics in each scene are well evidenced. By this I mean the opposing polarities of will and opinion that set person against person, movement against movement, idea against idea, and the parts of a person against himself or herself. These are the insoluble and irresolvable pressures and tensions that stand out like spars in a majestic bridge construction.

Interrogating your psyche is the only way to break into that sealed room where your intuitive self lives, the part of you that has already registered the scene's underlying qualities and meaning. Once you access what it knows, you can set about remedying any shortfall between intention and execution.

At each juncture, assess whether you have won or lost. This is hard and lonely work because what you see taking place before the camera is often underwhelming. Just when you expected to feel creative, you suffer gnawing doubts—doubts that you can share with nobody.

The dailies invariably reveal more on the screen than you saw at the time. There is a negative aspect to this: a bravura performance seen live comes across as hamming it up on the screen. If you suspect this while shooting, call for more takes, and direct the actors to seek more contained and sincere emotion. The less convinced you feel, the more you should cover yourself with alternatives for editing later.

RESOURCES AND COST REPORTS

As the director, you handle the human, the spiritual, and the ineffable. But your decisions all translate into bills, changing costs, rates, and schedules. No matter what order you shoot in, your line producer or production manager (PM) should compute from day to day where the production stands in relation to its projected budget. Every day you should be told whether the production is near or over budget. If you've overspent, what will you do? Modern budgeting software makes this easier to decide. Knowing early that a complicated sequence has consumed more resources than intended will signal that you must either raise more money, economize to get back on track, or be ready to drop the least vital scenes. Maybe you can shoot the last scene without the crane...

Many first shoots are liberally covered in the early stages and stretched perilously thin toward the end, and then the late coverage may be editable only one way, if at all. To counter this, budget your production and monitor its resources as you expend them, or your shoot will be like an expedition that leaves home eating steak—and then boils its shoes in the wilderness to stay alive.

When shooting ends, your role at last eases up. The toll on your psyche is far more severe than you yet know. At the end of a demanding shoot, many directors get low in spirits or even physically ill for a week or two. Think of it as postpartum depression.

AT THE END OF THE PRODUCTION

You had an icebreaker party before shooting began—now have a get-together at the end of shooting to thank and congratulate everybody. If money's low, have a potluck in which everyone brings their favorite dish, or brings drinks or desserts. Someone should coordinate this, so you don't get five pasta salads and no dessert. Notice how much freer everyone is together after their shared journey with its battles and fellowships. Which of these people would you like to work with again? What ideas might take shape for the next story?

PART 8

POSTPRODUCTION

PART 8-1 —————————————————————————————————————

Editor Thelma Schoonmaker during the editing of Scorsese's *Hugo* (2011).

PART 8-2 —————————————————————————————————————

Director Todd Haynes reviewing footage.

CHAPTER 31

POSTPRODUCTION OVERVIEW

Editing is the transformation of chance into destiny.

——Jean-Luc Godard

Postproduction is the phase in which the sound and picture gathered in production are transformed into the film seen by the audience. The editing suite is thus the crucible of filmmaking, and editing—or working with an editor—will teach you more about your directing than anything else. Most filmmakers edit their early work, and this is as it should be; later you will want a creative editor as a collaborative partner.

So important is the art of editing that no director can remain uninformed of its language, creative capacity, and flexibility. Provided with adequate coverage, the editor can make an enormous creative input to the tone, rhythms, and credibility of your story, so it's true what they say: "Editing is your second chance at directing." Editing can't of course transform a poor individual performance, but film is so malleable a medium that editors regularly perform miracles at the narrative level, where sheer momentum can obscure many a passing blemish.

THE POSTPRODUCTION TEAM

Those who make up the postproduction team may include the **editor, assistant editors, sound designer, sound/music editor, composer, sound-mix engineers,** and **colorist.** Overseeing the whole team, from first assembly to final lab processes and mastering, is the editor, whose qualities provide leadership and focus to the whole crew.

THE EDITOR

The editor answers to the director during the director's cut, but to the producer if changes are demanded for the producer's cut. The editor is responsible for making all the practical and aesthetic decisions while building the movie from its raw materials gathered during production (sound and picture) and postproduction (sound effects, atmospheres, music). The good editor is patient, highly organized, willing to experiment endlessly, and diplomatic about trying to get his or her own way. The nature of the work allows editors to think in deep and sustained ways, which is part of their value. Assistant editors and sound personnel echo these qualities.

Editors read the screenplay for reference, but no editor can follow its design unless the actual footage supports this. They must always make the best film possible from the materials supplied, and this means making responsible, subjective judgments. Even in a tightly scripted fiction film the editor needs the insight and confidence to know when to advocate alterations to the original intentions that better serve the film's needs.

Editors can be private and uncommunicative while at work, obsessed with detail, and unable to leave well enough alone. The film industry saying, "Never trust an editor with a tan," implies that good editors seldom leave their work. The accomplished editor works closely with the director, who often arrives from the production process exhausted or even depressed. Blinkered by their intentions and all the effort it took to achieve particular shots or scenes, directors are often wedded to material that is better rearranged or left out entirely. The editor, not present at shooting, and arriving with an unbiased eye similar to that of the audience, is ideally placed to reveal to the director what possibilities or problems lie dormant in the raw materials. Often they find unglimpsed possibilities in actors' performances or in balancing narrative pacing and structure. Understanding the power of visual juxtapositions, they will argue for a reordering of material where meaning can be augmented.

The editor's work used to begin once shooting was complete, but today in the digital age editors often find themselves reviewing raw footage and producing rough cuts of scenes during shooting. Editing is not just assembly, as Hitchcock mythology suggests, but more like coaxing a brilliant musical performance from a set of imperfect, overlapping, and incomplete scores. Postproduction includes a range of interpretive developments that include: reworking story order, determining scene emphasis and rhythm, controlling POV and tone through picture editing and sound design, and polishing the visual look with color timing. All this requires you the director to see, listen, adapt, think, and imagine while your editor tries to liberate the best from your film's potential.

So important is the director/editor collaboration that most established directors have a favorite editor who accompanies them from film to film. There are celebrated and long-term collaborations between Martin Scorsese and Thelma Schoonmaker, Jane Campion and Veronika Jenet, Francis Ford Coppola and Walter Murch, as well as Stephen Frears and Mick Audsley—to name just a few (Figure 31-1).

DIRECTOR-EDITORS

In low-budget movies, the director is sometimes a director-editor and called a hyphenate. Trying to control both fields is risky, and insecure personalities feel under attack and field criticism with pain and difficulty. Even among accomplished feature directors, some of the slackest films come from wearing too many hats. See *Dances with Wolves* (1990) at 183 minutes, then quake at the thought that Kevin Costner—star, director, and producer—saw fit to issue a director's cut of 224 minutes.

FIGURE 31-1

Director/editor partnerships are some of the most enduring in film. Steven Spielberg has worked with editor Michael Kahn since 1977 (*left*). Thelma Schoonmaker (*right*) has been Martin Scorsese's editor since 1967.

Every film is meant for an audience, so yours during its creation will need the steadying and detached point of view of an editor as an audience proxy. Lacking the tension of this partnership, directors seldom get sufficient distance on their intentions or upon the actuality of their material. Commonly, directors who edit fall prey to love or hate and will axe in disgust what may work perfectly well, and then cling obsessively to "darlings," those unjustly favored moments or scenes that film folklore says you must kill. A good editor's cool advocacy helps produce a tough, balanced, and effective film—more in fact than anyone can deliver alone.

TECHNOLOGY, WORKFLOW, AND THE DIRECTOR

The technology of film shooting and postproduction remains in a constant state of accelerated evolution. New shooting and editing formats, new codecs (compression formulae), and new nonlinear editing (NLE) systems, processes, and procedures arrive monthly. Shooting on film is quickly fading, along with the complex process of film-to-tape transfers, but a staggering number of new digital formats are emerging to pose ever more complex postproduction challenges. The resulting options in shooting and editing are mindboggling, and clearly a book on directing cannot cover their technology. But since knowledge is power, you do need to know the rudiments of the technology you depend on, especially while editing your own films. It's best to seek out the most detailed and current publications, websites, and discussion boards pertaining to every postproduction technology you must rely on. Further, every new film you undertake will probably need a new technology and require fresh research from the most current resources available.

WORKFLOW

We explored the idea of workflow on p. 321 "Workflow and Equipment," but a quick refresher is appropriate here. **Workflow** includes the stages and format path your film project will take from production to exhibition. It includes the production formats for picture and sound, the format setting you use for editing, the formats used during the various finishing processes (color grading and sound mixing), the mastering format, and the distribution formats.

Format options are many and constantly evolving so a filmmaker can easily lose their way. Keeping up with workflow options and practices is a full-time job; so from the very beginning, you must consult with the people whose job it is to stay abreast of the state of the technology: your cinematographer, production sound mixer, editor, postproduction sound mixer and postproduction

---

PostProduction Technical Resources

This list of print and web resources should help you research the necessary workflow and postproduction technology that accompanies every new project. Be sure you are using the newest print edition and that it covers your specific formats and tech situation. Online sources come and go but keep your eye out for the websites that maintain robust discussion boards and interesting associated blogs.

A non-product based overview of workflow, formats, and editing procedures can be found in *Voice & Vision: A Creative Approach to Narrative Film & DV Production* 2nd ed. by Mick Hurbis-Cherrier; Focal Press.

NLE editing systems:

Start with the product manual and then...

- *Avid Editing: A Guide for Beginning and Intermediate Users.*
  Sam Kauffmann; Focal Press.
- *Apple Pro Training Series: Final Cut Pro.*
  Diana Weynand; Peachpit Press.
- *Visual Quickpro Guide: Avid Express Pro.*
  James Monohan; Peachpit Press

Color correction:

- *Color Correction Handbook: Professional Techniques for Video and Cinema*
  Alexis Van Hurkman, Peachpit Press

Postproduction sound:

- *Sound Design: The Expressive Power of Music, Voice and Sound Effects in Cinema*
  David Sonnenschein; Michael Wiese Prods
- *Audio Post Production for Television and Film, 3rd ed.*
  H. Wyatt and T. Amyes

Web resources:

- *http://ace-filmeditors.org*
- *www.filmsound.org*
- *www.studentfilmmakers.com*
- *www.hdforindies.com*
- *www.creativecow.net*
- *www.artoftheguillotine.com*

lab in preproduction before you shoot. By the time you reach the postproduction phase of your project, you should know from where you came and where you are going:

1. *Shooting format:* Film, HD video (720p, 1080i), uncompressed or RAW video
2. *Editing format:* frame rate, codecs, and resolution
3. *Finishing and mastering formats:* Film, HD video (720p, 1080i), uncompressed media files (2K, 4K)
4. Exhibition and distribution format: Broadcast HD format (720p, 1080i), Blu-ray, DVD, web, or a combination? Or high end theatrical projection like 35 mm film, or Digital Cinema. Just a quick aside, **Digital Cinema** (or **D-Cinema**) is the industry wide standard for digital theatrical projection. Established by the *Digital Cinema Initiative* (DCI) in 2002,[1] the standards are essentially 2K and 4K resolutions (jpeg2000 codec). D-Cinema is quickly replacing 35 mm film as the theatrical projection method.

To review a basic workflow chart for 2K, 4K shooting and D-Cinema finishing, go to this book's companion website www.directingbook.com ("Workflow Charts").

THE POSTPRODUCTION STAGES

This section is far from comprehensive and concentrates on the stages in which the director can assert some creative and interpretive control. Postproduction includes a number of stages, each involving a range of both technical and creative tasks, and many that call for close collaboration between director and editor. The basic postproduction steps are:

1. Processing and film-to-tape transfer (when celluloid is the shooting medium)
2. Transferring, logging, organizing, and syncing footage
3. Reviewing and evaluating footage (screening dailies)
4. Inputting comments and marking up the editing script
5. Editing and reviewing a first assembly
6. Editing picture and primary sound
7. Evolving from rough cut into a fine cut
8. Picture lock
9. Gathering sound elements:
    - Recording narration, Foley, ADR and score music if necessary[2]
    - Locating pre-recorded hard effects, ambience, and music if necessary
10. Constructing multitrack sound design (dialogue, ambient sound, sound effects, music)

---

[1] More information about D-Cinema can be found at www.dcimovies.com.
[2] Narration, Foley and ADR (for Automatic Dialogue Replacement) are post-synchronized voice and sound effect recording.

11. Sound mix: equalization and mix-down of multi-tracks into stereo master
12. Adding titles, graphics, and visual effects
13. Color correction
14. Mastering the final program (with post lab if necessary)
15. Duplication and multi-format distribution (HDCAM, DVD, Blue-ray, mov, etc.)

The chapters that follow give an overview of the conceptual and artistic processes, as you can expect to encounter them, stage by stage.

CHAPTER 32

EDITING BEGINS: GETTING TO KNOW THE FOOTAGE

TRANSFERRING, LOGGING, AND ORGANIZING FOOTAGE

In postproduction, organization is critical. The editor and, if you have them, assistant editors receive footage in digital form. If the shooting format was digital, they receive footage straight from the camera on recording media like SSD, P2 or SxS cards. If the shooting was done on film, they'll receive the footage from the lab after the film has been processed and transferred to a digital format (usually HDCAM or DVCPRO HD).

In either case, the editorial staff will **transfer** (or **ingest**) the footage into their non-linear editing system (NLE).[1] While doing this, they will identify each individual shot as a unique, separate media file called a **clip**. All media clips are organized in the NLE system's **project window** inside media folders called **bins.** These each correspond to a scene (film bins were once used to organize celluloid footage). Sound files from the location sound recordist are similarly identified, and each bin should wind up containing all the materials you need to edit that particular scene. In this way, every shot is identified and easy to locate. This process of labelling every shot and organizing them by bins and scene numbers is called **logging** (Figure 32-1).

Organizing footage matters because hard drives can be duplicated and shared. The director and editor may each have one so they can then still discuss options when each is on a different coast. Though it's unusual to change editors during a project, well-organized footage allows someone else to step in and take over.

SYNCING DAILIES

As we mentioned earlier, most narrative film productions, whether shot on film or digitally, utilize double system sound for sync sound shooting—that is, the camera records the picture while

---

[1] Currently, the term "transfer" is used for ingesting footage from record media cards and "capturing" is used for tape based media sources.

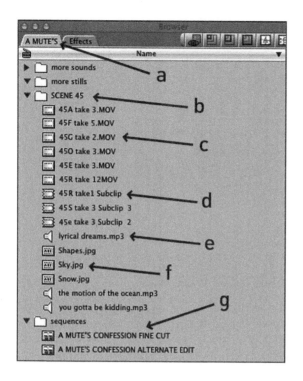

FIGURE 32-1 ————————————————————

Organizing your material is crucial for every project. In Final Cut Pro the project folder (a) contains all project files including the bin folders (b) that hold all necessary elements for each scene including master clips (c), subclips (d), sound files (e), and graphics files (f). Sequences (g) are also found in the project folder.

a sound recordist independently captures the audio onto separate recording media. The next step after ingesting and logging is to sync all takes involving sync sound to create **sync clips**. The clapper board is used to align picture and sound in perfect synchronization so they merge into a single clip with sync sound. The manual for your specific non-linear editing system will explain the syncing procedure step-by-step. It is a fairly simple and routine process, but only if the slating (clapper board) procedure was done correctly during production.

MARKING THE SCRIPT

When logging the footage is complete, the editor prepares the **editing script,** so that its pages look like Figure 32-2. To "mark up" the script, view all the material for one scene, viewing one camera setup at a time. You represent each setup as a line bracketing what that angle covers. Note that a change of lens is treated as a new setup; although the camera may not have physically moved, the framing and composition will be different. Shots that continue over a page break are indicated by an arrow. Leave a space in the line, and neatly write in the scene number and the briefest possible shot description. Note also which chosen takes the director designated as keepers (or circled takes) during the shoot, and include problems on botched takes ("Fluffed line," "Cam framing NG," etc.). Detailed information is then quickly available in the continuity reports or dailies book (see below). Though the editor's mark-ups appear to duplicate the shooting script (see Chapter 24, Figure 24-4), they are based on actual footage and chosen takes—footage that definitively exists—and so at times may differ markedly from the script. If the script supervisor has done their job well and provided the editor with a clearly marked supervisor's script and production notes (see Chapter 30), the editor can certainly use that after checking it against the actual footage to ensure accuracy.

From this process in which the editor scrutinizes all the footage for the first time comes a script that shows at a glance what angles cover every moment of every scene, and which takes contain the best moments in each angle. This way the editor can look at the marked up script and get an immediate sense of all its inherent editing options.

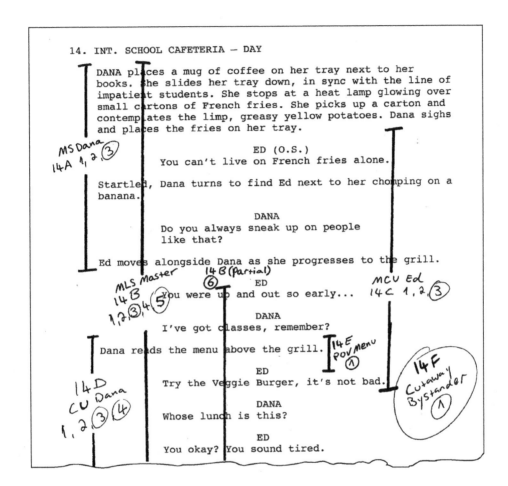

FIGURE 32-2

The editor's marked script indicates the actual footage taken, including circled takes.

DAILIES: REVIEWING AND EVALUATING FOOTAGE

Dailies (aka **rushes**) are the raw unedited footage generated by a film production. They're called dailies because directors and principal crew aim to review all footage shot the previous day. That way they can correct any problems, reshoot scenes, or simply monitor the consistency of their footage before leaving the location. Short films or films shot on a tight time schedule may not allow the luxury of reviewing footage so frequently, but it is critical to review raw footage in case you need to schedule reshoots.

The traditional rite of viewing raw unedited dailies has changed somewhat now that digital technology provides edit-ready footage instantly. During the shoot, individual takes are reviewed regularly on high-definition field monitors, and editors are expected to transfer, log, and sometimes edit footage to provide roughly edited **scene assemblies** on the spot. This way, key personnel can monitor the performances and scene coverage during production, as well as the consistency and quality of the footage. Low-budget film economics (and inherent time limitations) sometimes prevent cutting until everything is shot, but feature films that can afford it normally employ the editor from the start of shooting.

CREW VIEWING SESSION

View dailies at the best available quality, either projected large or on an HD monitor. If you take notes during this screening, try never to let your attention leave the screen, because you will assuredly miss important moments and nuances. This means making large, scribbled notes on many pages of paper or using the voice recorder on your smartphone. After a crew screening, there is usually a debate over the effectiveness, meaning, or importance of different aspects of the material. Participants often have differing feelings about the credibility and motivation of the characters. Listen rather than debate, for these represent the possible reactions of a future audience. Keep in mind, however, that crew members are disproportionately attuned to their own discipline, and may overestimate its positive or negative effect. They also develop their own subjective relationships with the actors and the filming situations.

THE EDITOR AND DIRECTOR VIEW DAILIES

During shooting and after, editor and director see the dailies seated next to each other. A marathon viewing in particular will highlight the relativity of the material and expose the problems you face in the piece as a whole. You might discover that certain mannerisms arise repeatedly in one actor and must be cut around if he is not to appear phony. Or you might discover that one of your two principals is more interesting to watch and threatens to unbalance the film. If, during the dailies viewing, you find yourself reacting to a particular character with, "She seems unusually sincere here," write it down. In fact, note any unexpected mood or feeling. Several takes may have no usable footage at all (and become **outtakes**) but you might also discover that an outtake contains a magical moment that might prove useful in the edit. If so, note it down. Sit through everything—outtakes, false starts, aborted takes—because there always may be something that you'll need later.

THE DAILIES BOOK

As the director and editor find issues that arise—good or bad, large or subtle—they take careful, shot-by-shot notes in what will become the **dailies book**, an important reference of first impressions. It records anything good and useful in each take, and also what is problematic. Gut feelings often seem unfounded, so you may be tempted to ignore or forget them. However, they are seldom unrepresentative; what triggered them is embedded in the material for any first-time audience to experience. Later when inspiration flags and memory glazes over, these notes will be a lifeline back to first impressions.

FIGURE 32-3

Comments on every shot can be entered right into the NLE system for quick reference.

Essential information and impressions can also be entered in the "**clip notes**" function of your NLE system where they can be reviewed every time you scan through your various clips (Figure 32-3).

Next, view all the material, one scene at a time. Dailies already digitized can easily be called up in scene order. Run each sequence looking for possible edit points, and stopping to discuss its problems and possibilities. The editor will need the dailies book to record the director's choices and note any special cutting information.

THE ONLY FILM IS IN THE DAILIES

The sum of the dailies viewing is your window on the movie's potential and deficiencies, and provides a notebook full of choices and observations. Now you must confront the raw material—and change hats. You are no longer the instigator of the material: now (with your editor) you are the surrogate for your audience. Empty yourself of prior knowledge and intentions since the only film possible is hiding in the dailies, and your editor may discern it more quickly than you do. Nothing beyond the dailies has any relevance. The script is a historic relic, like an old map to a rebuilt city. Stow it in the attic for your biographer.

PARTNERSHIP

Once shooting is over, the editing staff begins full-time work with the director. He or she is usually fatigued, and often anxious and uncertain until the film begins to prove itself. Many directors suffer a sort of postpartum depression following the sustained momentum of shooting, and most, however confident they may appear, are morbidly, even grotesquely, aware of their material's failures. If the editor and director do not know each other well, they will usually be formal and cautious. The editor is taking over the director's baby, and the director often carries mixed and potentially explosive emotions.

Relationships between directors and editors vary widely according to the chemistry of their temperaments and standing. The director will discuss any further intentions behind each scene and give any necessary special directions and then leave the editor to make the assembly, which is the first raw version of the film. The wise director leaves the cutting room so he or she can return with a fresh and constructive eye. The obsessive director sits in the cutting room night and day, watching the editor's every action. Whether this is amenable depends on the editor: some enjoy debating their way through the cutting process, but most prefer to be left alone to work out the film's initial problems in bouts of intense concentration over their logs and equipment.

In the end, nothing escapes concentrated discussion; every shot and every cut is scrutinized, debated, weighed, and balanced. The creative relationship is intense, and often draws in all the cutting room staff and the producer. The editor must often exert delicate but sustained leverage against the irrational prejudices and fixations that occasionally close like a trap around the heart of virtually every director. Ralph Rosenblum and Robert Karen's book *When the Shooting Stops... the Cutting Begins* (Da Capo Paperback Series, 1986) tells just how crazed this relationship can become.

THE FIRST ASSEMBLY

The **first assembly edit** simply means stringing together all the shots of each scene, end to end, and all the scenes and sequences together in their broadest and most basic shape. Though just a messy first draft, the first assembly is exciting—for the film is starting to reveal itself. Don't worry about length, balance, or finesse at this stage. To get there, you should:

- Review the dailies book for the impressions on each shot and take.
- Figure out how the coverage might initially be assembled. Use mostly master shots, and leave until later any close-ups or cross-cutting (repeatedly cutting between, say, two speakers when a single angle would adequately relay the action). Don't worry about finessing continuity or

cutting on action, and don't use any lap (overlap) cutting (for example, a speaker's outgoing dialogue overlaps a shot of the listener before the listener replies). Don't worry either about transitions (dissolves, fades, etc.).

- Assemble the simplest version that is faithful to the script and reflects the reality of the footage. Don't bother trying to cure anything questionable, such as changes in actors' pacing.

- Include two versions of anything when both seem equally viable. You can choose later in the widest possible context.

Of course, you will be longing to go to work on favorite sequences, but to fix details would be to avoid confronting the film's overall identity and purpose. View the whole assembly as soon as possible in long, loose form.

FIRST ASSEMBLY VIEWING

When you initially screen the first assembly, run it without interruption of any kind. Make no notes, because this will take your attention from the screen. Your job is to take in the film as any super-attentive audience would. From this viewing come important realizations about the character, dramatic shape, and best length of the film. You will get a handle on all the performances and know what overall control you need to exert. Fundamental issues are now out of the closet: maybe the film is slow and some scenes include unnecessary exposition, start slowly, or hang on beyond a good ending point. You may have two endings, one false and one intended, or a minor character who is unexpectedly stronger than a major one. A sequence you shot in miserably cold conditions by a river at night turns out to stall the story's advance and needs to be dropped. Kill your darlings, but keep them in a dead darlings bin in case you need to resurrect anyone.

The first assembly is the departure point for the denser and more complex film to come. As a show, it is long and crude, yet despite its artlessness it can be affecting and exhilarating.

THE SECOND VIEWING: DIAGNOSTIC QUESTIONING

Now run your movie again to see how your original impressions stand up. Following further discussion with your editor, list your major aims for each sequence, arranging them strictly by priority. You and your editor can tackle some fundamental issues:

- Does the film feel dramatically balanced? Place a moving and exciting sequence in the middle, and the rest of the movie may seem anticlimactic.

- Does the film circle aimlessly before it starts to move?

- When is there the momentum of a story unfolding, and when not? Asking this will help you locate impediments in the dramatic arc's development.

- Which parts of the film seem to work, which not?

- Which parts drag, and why? Some acting may be better than others, but the problem may be that a scene is either wrongly placed or repeats the dramatic contours of one previous.

- Which of the characters most held your attention, and which the least?

- Was there a satisfying alternation of types of material, or was similar material clumped indigestibly together?
- Were there effective contrasts and juxtapositions? Are there more to be made?
- Sometimes a sequence does not work because the ground has not been properly prepared, or because there is insufficient contrast in mood with the previous sequence. Variety matters as much to storytelling as it does to dining. What metaphorical allusions did you notice your material making? Could it make them more strongly? That your tale carries a metaphorical charge is as important to your audience as a water table is to pasture.

To question the imprint your story has made and predict a likely audience response, try always to view the film as if for the first time. After seeing an assembly, list memorable material. Glance at the script to see what left no particular impression. The human memory discards what it does not find meaningful, so all that good stuff you forgot simply did not contribute. That does not mean it never can—simply that it's not doing so at present. Right now, your project is in its crudest form, so deal only with your dominant reactions. Here are some common problems with their solutions.

TABLE 32.1 Assembly problems and their solutions

Problem	*Possible Solutions*
The writing is poor in comparison with other sequences.	Cut the whole scene? Shorten? Rewrite and reshoot?
Acting is at fault. Dramatic rhythms are too predictable, or actors are not in character or in focus.	Help, but not a cure, is available in further editing. Very often, reaction times are wrong and convey the wrong (or no) subtext. Rebalancing these can help.
Scene outcome is predictable.	Scene structure is at fault? Too long or too slow? Maybe the scene is in the wrong place?
Two or more sequences make a similar point.	Repetition does not advance a film's argument unless there is escalation in dramatic pressure. Make choices and ditch what's redundant.
Dramatic intensity plummets. A useful analogy is the idea of a rising or falling emotional temperature. To see material in its context is to see correct relative temperatures more clearly.	If your film is raising the temperature, then inadvertently lowering it before the intended peak, the viewer's response is seriously impaired. Sometimes transposing one or two sequences works wonders.
The viewer is somehow set up by the preceding material to expect something different.	We read film by its context; if the context gives misleading signals or fails to focus awareness in the right area, the material can fall unaccountably flat.

These are only a few areas of dramatic analysis. Dig deeply into your instincts by acknowledging how you feel about the dramatic outcome of your material. Just as a playwright routinely rewrites and adjusts a work based on audience feedback, so the filmmaker makes a vast number of adjustments, large and small, before admitting that a work may be finished. Later, when you have a fine cut and the material becomes showable, you will call in a few people whose reactions and tastes you respect.

RESOLUTIONS AFTER SEEING THE FIRST ASSEMBLY

Once you have seen and discussed the whole ungainly epic, you and your editor can make far-reaching resolutions about its future development. These may involve performances, pacing, parallel storytelling, structure, or overall meaning. Remember that your editor is massively uninterested in whatever you originally intended—that's ancient history.

It's always a temptation to tinker with the attractive stuff, like dialogue or continuity detail, but at this stage you must prioritize your tasks. Arrange your problems by hierarchy and deal with the major issues first. If the story's structure is awry, reorder the scenes and run the film again without making any refinement to individual scenes. If there is a serious problem of imbalance between two major characters, go to work on bringing forward the deficient character. After each running, correct only the major problems.

LENGTH

Most beginners' films are agonizingly long and slow, and advice about slashing their running time is painful but necessary. If you can recognize early that your movie should last, say, 20 minutes at the most, you can get tough with that 40-minute assembly. Films have a natural span according to the richness and significance of their content, so look to the content of your film itself for guidance over length and pacing. The hardest and most impressive achievement in any art form is having the confidence and ability to say a lot through a little. You and your writer felt you'd cut the script to the bone: now you see all the other places you should have cut. Nonlinear editing can preserve each of your cuts, and during the film's evolution, you can always look back to see whether there's anything in an earlier version that you actually prefer. Commit all these versions to DVD, perhaps, for your private amusement later in life.

STRUCTURE

Most of all, you need to find the best dramatic structure if the movie is to feel like a well-told tale. A good screenplay never guarantees a great film because the cast, production, and editing all introduce new emotional shading and development. These, not the original intentions, are what the audience experiences and these, as they become apparent, are what you must address. Understandably, the director is always the one most encumbered by the film's history.

LEAVE THE EDITOR TO EDIT

Having decided the next round of changes, leave the cutting room until summoned back. Not all editors or directors can work this way, but you must try because both editor and director lose objectivity after long exposure to the footage. So, a director returning with a fresh eye is better able to tell the editor where changes are working or still needed.

Everyone in the postproduction crew must constantly struggle to rid themselves of prior expectations and conditioning in order to function as a surrogate for a first-time audience. It takes Zen mastery to let go of your deep familiarity with the footage and clearly see "what is" rather than "what was" or "what should be."

CHAPTER 33

THE ROUGH CUTS

You get to contribute so significantly in the editing room because you shape the movie and the performances ... You help the director bring all the hard work of those who made the film to fruition. You give their work rhythm and pace and sometimes adjust the structure to make the film work—to make it start to flow up there on the screen.[1]

—Thelma Schoonmaker

After you've reviewed all the footage, created the first assembly, thoroughly critiqued the film's basic structure, and more or less determined the best takes to use for each scene, you can begin the rough cut process. A **rough cut** is a version of the film in which the full range of material and storytelling techniques are used to implement the goals decided after scrutinizing the assembly edit. No sequence is yet fine tuned, but the editor tries to make each scene occupy its right place and succeed dramatically. Do not be tempted to waste time finessing edits and sweating the ultrafine points yet.

Rough cuts are edited with picture track and audio essentials only. If your scenes involve dialogue, then the editor will cut picture and dialogue together. If voice-over drives certain sequences, then cutting will include picture with voice-over. For passages where music dominates, the editor cuts picture to temporary music (called a **scratch track**) that conveys the "feel" expected of the final music. Lose no time placing sound effects or layering soundtracks—it's needless effort that is likely to be undone along the way.

You will usually go through several rough cut versions, tightening and improving the film with each. The number depends entirely on the footage, the goals, and any deadlines limiting the editing period. Screening rough cuts systematically with a critical eye ensures that each new version is an improvement, not just a different version with the same problems. After the director and editor have reworked some rough cuts on their own, they screen the latest for a small audience to get fresh perspectives and feedback to help them onward to a fine cut (see Chapter 34).

---

[1] "The Last Temptation of Thelma" by Lan N. Nguyen (ivillage.com March 15, 2005).

EDITING PRINCIPLES

The rough-cut stage is the heart and soul of editing. Here you determine the integrity and structure of the story, and its tone, dramatic arcs, scene and character dynamics, subtexts, and themes begin to emerge in their true cinematic form. Here is where editors employ all their editing skills. It is important that a director fully understands (and therefore trusts) the storytelling principles, potential, and flexibility of editing. We have already discussed the basics of juxtaposing and editing patterns in Chapter 15, so what follows are a few more principles that build on that discussion.

EDITING MIMICS AN OBSERVING CONSCIOUSNESS

In a dialogue scene, as discussed in Chapters 15 and 16, we cut between speakers based on whatever would make an observer shift his attention. Watch how eye contact and eye-line shifts function in real life, for these are the outward signs of attention shifts. Edit according to attention and eye-line changes, and you'll be working from human behavior rather than from disembodied theory. The veteran editor Walter Murch says, "The blink is a momentary and unnoticed cessation of vision, which I believe we use unconsciously to punctuate the phrases of our thoughts."[2] He uses eyeblinks as a key to dialogue editing, as you can read in his *In the Blink of an Eye*, 2nd rev. ed. (Silman-James, 2001).

FIGURE 33-1

In *Nashville*, as in his other films, Robert Altman includes a dense, layered soundtrack that conveys the lifelike feel of group situations.

When film was silent, it had to juxtapose shots and scenes to imply continuity, development, relatedness, or contrast. The audience guessed the relational associations and much of our enjoyment still comes from imagining, hypothesizing, and guessing subtexts as we follow the narrative. Counterpointing visual and aural impressions today only takes farther what was called "montage" in film's earliest days. Counterpointing sound against action, rather than using sound to accompany or illustrate, came relatively late and was probably developed by documentary editors trying to compress lengthy materials drawn directly from life. Robert Altman among fiction filmmakers—particularly in *M*A*S*H* (1970), *Nashville* (1975, Figure 33-1), and *Gosford Park* (2001)—places great faith in the audience's ability to interpret densely layered dialogue tracks.

---

[2] Interview by Kiran Ganti at the Film and Television Institute of India, Pune, April 2004, www.folkbildning. net/%7Ee-kurs/sound/interview-with-walter-murch.htm. More interviews and articles on Murch can be found via http://filmsound.org/murch.

EYE CONTACT

Imagine two diners holding a romantic conversation across a restaurant table. Inexperienced players gaze soulfully into each other's eyes as they speak, and the results are embarrassingly phony because they are playing *an idea* of how people converse, not what really happens in life. Do some discreet people-watching at a restaurant to find out, and what you'll see is more subtle and interesting: often neither person makes eye contact more than fleetingly. We reserve the intensity of eye contact for special moments—that is, to:

- Check what effect we have just had.
- Get information from the other person's expression so we know how next to act on him or her.
- Use eye contact to apply additional pressure on the other person.
- Interpret from the person's body language or expression what is meant when he or she is acting on us.

In subtle ways, each speaker is either acting, or being acted upon, and only at crucial moments does one search the other for facial or behavioral enlightenment. Much of the time, the listener's gaze rests on isolated or neutral objects while he or she mentally focuses inwardly on gleaning what the other person may want or mean. These objects in film can often be made to hold symbolic or other meaning.

Hearing is different, for it may be totally focused on the other person for the duration of the conversation. But it, too, can wander. Eyes and ears move their attention independently, but always working in tandem to feed their separate streams of information into the overworked brain.

Play the Concerned Observer while you watch a couple in conversation, and monitor how and why your eye line shifts between the speakers. Notice how,

- You are often following the shifts in their eye lines, wanting to see what they are looking at, and involuntarily switching your gaze from subject to object.
- Each eye-line change causes you to hypothesize a new subtext or motivation.
- There is a rhythm to your eye-line changes that is controlled by the shifting contours of the conversation itself.
- You made an instinctive judgment about who and what to look at, often on the basis of something on the periphery demanding a closer look.

Observing yourself in the act of observing is the best editing teacher you will ever have. Independently, your center of attention switches back and forth, cued by the conversing pair's action and reaction, their changes of eye line, and their physical actions. However (and this is very important) you also begin to make directional choices *based on your evolving thoughts*. That is, watching becomes thinking, and thinking develops possible meanings, for evidence of which you then search. Making a hypothesis is like shining a light ahead in the dark. Unconsciously, the Observer uses their developing insight to search out the most telling information.

CAMERA ANGLES AND CUTTING REVEAL PSYCHOLOGY

To reproduce on film what you have just seen, you would need to cover each speaker from the viewpoint of the other, and add a third viewpoint to encompass them both as you, the Observer, see them. For good measure, you'd add complementary over-the-shoulder angles and close-ups. The Observer's point of view (POV) is outside the enclosed consciousness of the two speakers, and because it shows them in a more detached, observational way, it implies the Storyteller's POV. Now you have a complete model for basic movie coverage (see Chapters 16 and 24).

Film, as we have said, has difficulty relaying people's interior life, but wherever a person directs their attention strongly suggests to the onlooker what she is thinking and feeling, even though she may try to hide it. Editing is thus a powerful tool to *imply inner life and inner character contours*. This ability to move viewpoint allows the film to mold what the audience sees, and to structure whose point of view and whose state of mind the audience shares at any given moment. It is a probing, cinematic way of seeing that is modeled on the way we unconsciously delve—visually, imaginatively, and logically—into any event or human process that attracts our attention.

OBSERVER INTO STORYTELLER

According to the charisma of your actors and the choices you made in shooting and editing, your audience will identify with one or other of the characters, or with the more embracing perspective of the invisible Storyteller/Observer. While Character A talks, the film might allow the audience to look detachedly at either A or B, to share the perspective of either one upon the other, or to look at them both in a longer shot. The Concerned Observer turns into a Storyteller whenever faithful, thoughtful watching becomes active and critical telling. This implies that the Storyteller has ideas about the characters and their world, and wants you to guess who they are and what they are trying to get. Instinctively we recognize this from struggling ourselves to understand pivotal figures such as our parents, employers, and life partners, any of whom could deserve a lively and partisan account. When the film's level of involvement holds distinct and critical expectations of the characters, their agendas, and what they represent in the tapestry of life, this is a real Storyteller at work, full of zest to tell gripping tales.

EDITING TO INFLUENCE SUBTEXTS

ALTERING PERFORMANCE RHYTHMS

For any scene adequately acted and shot, much dramatic control now rests in the cutting room. This concerns not only who or what is shown at any particular moment, but *how much time each character takes to process what he sees, feels, or hears*. This timing originated with the actors, but can be adjusted whenever the editor has sufficient coverage. Reaction time—the inner process that precedes outward action—contributes hugely to the power and consistency of a scene's subtext. Inexperienced film actors, learning lines and repeating them in numerous takes and angles, tend to drop into a shared, set rhythm. This homogenizes their characters' inner lives to a monotonous shared average. It will show up in an early cut, and is deadly. Now the scene rhythms must be retuned in editing to recover the changeableness and unpredictability when people are truly thinking on their feet.

To define what is at stake here, imagine a two-person, interior scene where a man asks a simple question of a woman who is visiting for dinner: "Do you think it's cold outside?" Depending on the context and on her nonverbal reaction, we might sense several subtexts. He could be saying:

- "Since we're about to leave, do you think I need warmer clothes?"
- "Let's not go to the party after all."
- "Do you want to stay the night with me?"

What makes the audience choose the likely subtext? Surely, it's not only how the lines are said, but how the listener reacts to the speaker. An easy and unreflecting "No" is very different from one delivered after a momentary silence, or after one that is long delayed by internal debate. Not only do such timing differences and behavioral nuances direct what we imagine, but prior events (such as, the man has just visited the doctor) also condition the subtext we apply. Thus, *the order of material in a film and the amount of apparent thought each character devotes to each part of their interaction can imply different subtexts.* This is turn can lead the audience to generate a whole new set of open questions. You want this because it raises dramatic tension by suggesting the complexity of real life.

In a scene where performances are indifferent, and particularly when they are uneven, editing that is sensitive to subtexts can drive up the stakes so the scene acquires more intensity and a more defined point of view. By exerting fine control over the rhythms of reply, eye-line changes, actions, and reactions, the scene can become a unified entity that nobody could quite have foreseen.

MAKING OR ALTERING SUBTEXTS

No editor can change a character's rate of speech or reaction times in a single, unbroken take, but much potential opens up when the scene is covered from more than one angle. Look at Figure 33-2. Version A is a representation of the master shot (two shot), a timing that the actors reproduced in all subsequent takes. The diagram shows picture and sound as separate strands, much as you see them on an editing program timeline. Cutting to a close up for the response "Let's just go home" simply preserves the actors' original timing (though by merely using a CU the audience feels greater significance in his reply). But cutting to a new angle provides myriad opportunities to manipulate the rhythm of the exchange. Version B uses overlap cutting (see the following section for extended explanation) to make his reply come as quickly as possible. A clipped response like this can add a whiff of impatience or dismissiveness to the moment. Version C, on the other hand, doubles his reaction time by adding together the pauses from both master and CU shots. Adding extra time before his response could add weight to his words because they appear to have come after some deliberation. If you have additional reaction shots to cut to, you could double them up, cutting back and forth between them to extend the time between question and response even further!

This is a small example of the interpretive flexibility editing provides. Careful rebalancing of performance reaction times can add massively to the credibility of the characters' inner lives. This

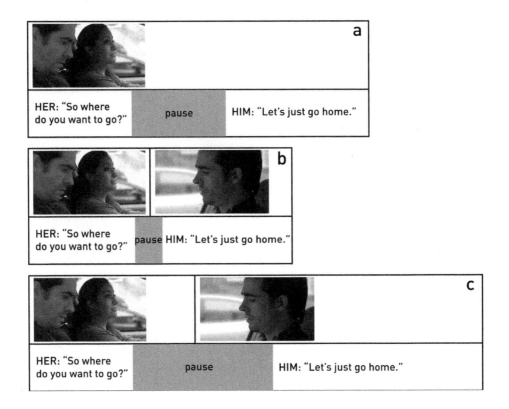

FIGURE 33-2

Altering the rhythm of dialogue exchanges can change the subtext of a scene. *Version a* shows the timing in the unedited master shot. Trimming pauses when cutting to a new shot speeds up the timing (*version b*) and combining pauses between two juxtaposed shots increases the timing of a response (*version c*).

deepens the internal moments that compel each into action or speech, and contributes greatly to the overall impact of the film. New rhythms are now aiding and abetting performances and creating the grounds for us to infer greater thought, feeling, and reaction.

VISUAL AND AURAL EDITING RHYTHMS: AN ANALOGY IN MUSIC

The interplay of editing's rhythmic elements needs some further explanation. Though everything in editing takes place in minutes, seconds, and frames, you can no more make dramatic decisions from script or stopwatch calculations than music can be composed with a metronome.

Rhythmic interplay: Let's examine what an edited conversation between two people really is. We have two different but interlocked rhythms going. First, there is the rhythmic pattern of their voices in a series of sentences that ebb and flow, speed up, slow down, halt, restart, and continue. Set against these rhythms, and taking their rhythmic cues from the vocal rhythms, is the visual tempo set up by the complex shifts of visual choice, outlined previously and evoked in the interplay of cutting, camera composition, and movement. The visual and aural streams proceed independently yet are rhythmically related, like the relation between music and the physical movements of two dancers.

Harmony: When you hear a speaker and see his face as he talks, sound and vision are allied like a melody with its harmony. We could, however, break the literalness of always hearing and seeing the same thing (harmony) by making the transition from scene to scene into a temporary puzzle.

Counterpoint: Suppose we cut from a woman talking about her vanished husband to a shot panning across tawdry seashore hotels. We start with the speaker in picture and sound; then while she is still speaking, we cut to the panning shot, allowing her remaining words to play out over the hotels shot. The effect is this: while our subject is talking about her now fatherless children and the bitterness she feels toward the absent husband, we glance away and our mind's eye imagines where he might now be. This film treatment implies the mental (or even physical) imagery of someone present and listening. The speaker's words counterpointed by the image lets loose our imagination so that we ponder what he is doing and what is happening behind the crumbling façades of the hotels. Counterpointing words against an unrelated image could simply be used to illustrate. We might for instance cut to the hotels when she says, "… and the last I heard, he was in Florida…" This would probably signal a new sequence in a new location.

Many an elegant contrapuntal sequence in a feature film is the work of an editor trained in documentary and now using their skills to raise the movie above a pedestrian script, as Ralph Rosenblum relates in *When the Shooting Stops … the Cutting Begins* (Da Capo Paperback Series, 1986). Directing and editing documentaries has contributed importantly to the screen fluency of Robert Altman, Michael Apted, Lindsay Anderson, Carroll Ballard, Werner Herzog, Krzysztof Kieslowski, Ken Loach, Louis Malle, Alain Resnais, Martin Scorsese, and Haskell Wexler, to name but a few of the better-known fiction directors.

Dissonance: Another editing gambit exploits discrepancies. For instance, while we hear a salesman telling a new assistant his theory of dynamic customer persuasion, we see the salesman listing the virtues of a hideaway bed in a monotone so dreary that his customer seems bored into a trance. This discrepancy, to pursue the musical allusion, is a dissonance because it spurs the viewer to create a resolution. Comparing the man's beliefs (heard) with his practice (seen), the viewer is driven to conclude, "Here is someone who does not know himself."

TRANSITIONS AND TRANSITIONAL DEVICES

The transitions we make in life—from place to place, or from time to time—are either imperceptible because we are preoccupied, or may come as a surprise or even a shock. Stories replicate these differences either by hiding the seams between sequences or by indicating and even emphasizing them. An action match between a woman drinking her morning fruit juice and a beer drinker raising his glass in a smoky dive contrasts the scene shift by contrasting the act of drinking. A dissolve from one scene to another would signal, in rather creaky language, "and time passed." A simple cut from one place to the next leaves the audience to fill in the blank. However, imagine a teenager singing with the car radio on a long, boring drive, then suddenly interrupted by flash images of a truck, screeching tires, and the youngster yanking desperately at the steering wheel. The transition from comfort to panic is intentionally one of shock, and reproduces the violent change we undergo when taken nastily by surprise.

Sound can also be used as a transitional device. Hearing a conversation over an empty landscape can draw us forward into the next scene (of two campers shivering in their tent). Cutting to a shot of a cityscape while we still hear the campsite birdsong gives the feeling of being confronted with a change of location while the mind and heart lag behind in the great outdoors. Used like this, transitional devices can imply an emotional point of view.

Each film transition, like the literary phrase, "and then...," is a device signaling the progression between discontinuous story segments, and each transition's style implies an attitude or point of view emanating from either the characters or the Storyteller.

THE OVERLAP CUT AND TRANSITIONS

The **overlap cut**, also known as a **lap cut** or **L cut**, is a contrapuntal editing device useful for blurring the unnatural seams between shots. It works by bringing a speaker's voice in before his picture, or vice versa, and this removes the level cuts that reduce editing to staid and predictable blocks of action.

Figure 33-3, *top* is a straight-cut version of a conversation fragment between an aging father and his impatient son, who is trying to get the father to go to the hospital. Whoever speaks is shown on the screen, and before long this pattern becomes predictable. You could alleviate this by slugging in some reaction shots (not shown).

Now look at the same conversation using overlap cuts (also called lap cuts or L cuts). In version A, we cut away from the father to the son early, while the father is still saying, "You don't tell me what to do." Bringing the son in like this privileges his reaction and an implicit POV starts to creep into the scene—we're connecting with the son's perspective. In version B, we reverse this character emphasis by bringing the father's picture in *twice* while his son is still speaking; once while the son is saying "We've got to go now," (we will see the father's rising anger that his son is ordering him around) and again "...but listen to the doctor," (seeing his disdain when the word "doctor" is uttered). This strategy, allowing the audience to trace the father's reactions, now favors the father's perspective. With the same material we can greatly alter the perspective of the scene—provided that the scene coverage from production is there to work with.

How to decide when you need overlap cuts? Let's return to our trusty editing model: human consciousness at work. In a conversation between two people, you turn your head from one to the other. Seldom will you turn at the right moment to catch the next speaker beginning; only an omniscient being could be so accurate. Or perhaps you hear an incendiary remark and quickly turn to the listener to catch his reaction. Editors who make neat, level cuts between speakers tend to give a prepackaged, premeditated look to their work. Such omniscience destroys the illusion of watching something develop spontaneously. If a film is to convince us that a dialogue sequence

straight cuts

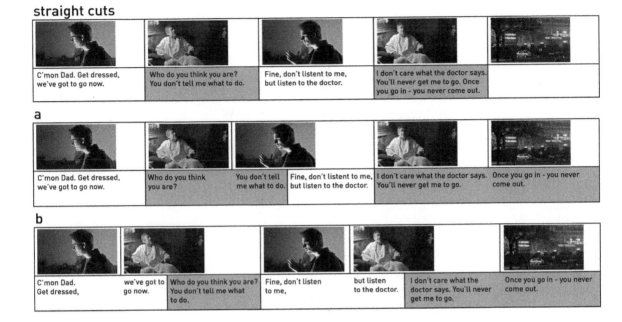

FIGURE 33-3

Three versions of the same scene using the same footage, but simply by using overlap cuts the POV of the scene can shift radically.

comes spontaneously from real life, its editor must replicate our attention as well as the disjunctive shifts when our eyes follow our hearing, or our hearing (that is, concentration) catches up late with something we have just seen.

Effective editing is always grounded in the unfolding consciousness of the story's characters. Added to this is what the involved, opinionated Storyteller wants us to notice. Not only does the Storyteller hear and see what each speaker say, (which is nothing special), but is hinting at what is happening inside each protagonist by showing us clues in their actions and reactions. Where the Concerned Observer notices evidence, the Storyteller imposes ideas about the characters' attitudes, significance, contradictions, and even about their place and time. Thus a film that truly entertains you does so by putting you in the company of an astute, witty critic who savors human nature and lets you see as much as possible that is telling about the characters.

For filmmaking and editing in particular, the message is clear. To take the audience along with the astute subjectivity of the Storyteller, the editor often makes sound and picture changeover points as staggered cuts, for these replicate an agile human consciousness shifting and adapting in the moment.

SEQUENCE TRANSITIONS

In the most banal scene transition, a character exits the frame leaving an empty set, then cuts to another empty frame before our character reappears and moves into the scene. This is really proscenium arch theater, a kind of clumsy scene shifting that puts a huge hiccup in a film's momentum. Inexperienced directors often engineer scenes to start and stop this way, but a savvy editor quickly looks for ways to axe the dead footage. Just as there are dialogue overlap cuts, so there are live transitions from one sequence to another by using the lap cut.

Notice how, in the straight-cut version in Figure 33-3, if we wait for the conversation to be over before we transition to the next scene, the image of the hospital just sort of hangs out there on its own. But if we execute a tidy little lap cut (Figure 33-3, version A) we not only get a much smoother transition, but also a very revealing juxtaposition by bringing the shot of the hospital right over the line "Once you go in—you never come out."

Keep in mind, we easily could go the other way with this lap cut as well. For example, we could bring in the doctor's line "I'm glad you came in to see me, Mr. Donato" while the image rests on the resistant figure of the father from the previous scene. Then, after the doctor's ironic line, we cut to the corresponding picture from the doctor's office in the hospital.

SOUND EFFECTS AS SCENE ELISION

You have seen this overlap technique done with sound effects. It might look like this: the schoolteacher rolls reluctantly out of her bed, and as she ties up her hair, we hear the increasingly loud sound of a playground until we cut to her on duty at the school door. Because our curiosity demands an answer to the riddle of children's voices in a woman's bedroom, we do not find the location switch arbitrary or theatrical. This, called **anticipatory sound**, drags our attention forward to the next sequence.

Another type of overlap cut makes sound work another way: we cut from the teacher leading kids chanting their multiplication tables to the same teacher getting food out of her refrigerator at home. The dreary class sound (called **holdover sound**) subsides slowly while she exhaustedly eats some leftovers.

In the first example, anticipatory sound draws her forward out of her bedroom, while in the second, holdover sound persists after she gets home. This lets the Storyteller show how the din exists in her mind: both cases imply that she finds her workplace burdensome. Overlap cutting can thus do more than soften transitions between scenes: it can imply what dominates our schoolteacher's inner consciousness.

Quite different would be to let the silence of her home trail out into the workplace. In this scenario, she is seen at work with her bedroom radio still playing softly before its sound is swamped by the rising uproar of feet echoing in a corridor. At the end of the day, her TV sitcom could displace her voice giving out the dictation, and we cut to her relaxing at home.

By using sound and picture transitions creatively, we can transport the viewer forward without cumbersome optical effects such as dissolves, fades, or other still worse intrusions that are foreign to human experience such as the ripple-dissolve. We are also able to scatter important clues about the characters' subjective lives and inner imaginings, something film cannot otherwise easily do.

THE PROBLEM OF ACHIEVING A FLOW

Run your evolving cut a few times, and it will strike you more and more as a series of clunky blocks of material, with a distressing lack of flow. Dialogue scenes, centered upon showing each speaker, seem especially cumbersome. First, there is a block of this speaker, then a block of that speaker, then a block of both, and so on. Even the sequences transition from one to the next in a blocky way, like watching train boxcars pass, each discrete and hitched to its fellows with a plain link device. This kind of editing I think of as boxcar cutting.

How do you achieve the effortless flow seen in the cinema? To move in this direction, we must return to how human perception functions at points of transition.

COUNTERPOINT IN PRACTICE: UNIFYING MATERIAL INTO A FLOW

Counterpoint means bringing together the sound from one shot with the image from another, as we have said. To return to my example of the salesman with a great self-image and a lousy performance, you could show this on the screen by merging two sets of materials: one of him talking to his assistant over a coffee break (Sequence A), and the other of him in the salesroom making a pitch to clients (Sequence B). We can edit the materials into juxtaposition. The conservative, first-assembly method would alternate segments as in Figure 33-4A: a block of explanation, then a block of sales talk, then another block of explanation and another of sales, and so on until the point has been hammered home. After a few cuts, both the technique and its message become as predictable as a boxer slugging a punching bag. Let's instead integrate the two sets of materials as in Figure 33-4B. Start Harold explaining his sales philosophy (Sequence A) during the salesmen's coffee break. While he's showing off to the younger man, we begin fading up the sound from the salesroom (Sequence B) in which we hear Harold's aggressive greetings. As he reaches full volume, we cut to the salesroom picture (Sequence B) to see that he has trapped a reluctant customer and is launching unstoppably into his sales pitch. After this is established, we fade up the coffee-break conversation again (Sequence A). We hear the salesman say how he first fascinates the customer. When we cut to Sequence A's picture,

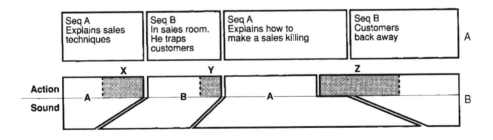

FIGURE 33-4

Counterpointing the content of one sequence against another. Sequence A assembles material in blocks with straight-cut sound, whereas Sequence B takes advantage of overlap editing and counterpoint.

we find that Harold has moved uncomfortably close to his junior. Harold tells him how you must first make the customers admit they like the merchandise. During this, we cut back to the salesroom (Sequence B) picture, only to see the customer backing away angrily. We bring up Sequence B's sound as the customer says she only came to buy a pillow.

Notice that in the overlap areas (X, Y, and Z) of Figure 33-4B, picture from one sequence is counterpointed against sound from another. Instead of having description and practice separated as discrete blocks of material, description is now laid against practice, and ideas against reality, to make a much harder-hitting juxtaposition. The benefits are multiple. Talking-head conversation is kept minimal, whereas the behavioral material—the salesroom evidence against which we measure his ideas—now predominates. The audience must reconcile the gap between the man's self-image and what he is actually doing. Counterpointing the essentials allows you to pare down the combination of materials to a muscular, spare version that you never get when film writing is conceived as theatrical dialogue.

Counterpoint editing cannot be worked out beforehand in scripting since entry and exit points depend on the nuances of playing and camerawork. But if both scenes are shot in their entirety, one becomes parallel action to the other. The resulting sequence is worked out from the materials themselves, and will reliably and effectively compress the two. You will find a shooting/editing project to practice these skills on the companion website www.directingbook.com under "Projects." Look for Project 2C: Vocal Counterpoint and Point of View. This adds a vocal counterpoint to action, but you might want to try improvising the salesman scenes, and fusing the two by editing them in counterpoint.

THE ROUGH-CUT VIEWING

Each rough cut gets a similar degree of scrutiny, but especially with the early versions it is important to deal only with the largest-scale problems first. As you work your way through multiple versions, your critique becomes increasingly concerned with finer points. Initially, though, your concerns revolve around:

Exposition:

- Is there adequate, too little, or too much expository detail?
- Is exposition integrated with the action, or does the film pause to inform the audience?
- What exposition, if removed, could the audience still infer?
- What exposition could be delayed (always better to make the audience wonder and wait if you can)?

Momentum and tension:

- Does the film maintain momentum throughout?
- Is every scene moving the story forward?
- Is dramatic tension sustained?
- Where do momentum and tension falter, and why?

Duration:

- What sequences feel long, and what material redundant?
- How does the film duration feel as a whole—long, short, or about right?

Characters:

- How logical and satisfying is the development of each major character?
- Is anything misleading or alienating about the characters?
- Is each established before he or she becomes dramatically necessary?

Balance:

- Does the film breathe so that, like music, each movement feels balanced and inevitable, or is there a misshapen, unbalanced feel to some parts?
- Is there a satisfying balance between interior scenes and exteriors? (This often means dealing with any unintentional claustrophobia the film generates. Well-balanced films alternate between intensity and release, much as a person must alternate intimacy with solitude, indoors with outdoors, family with work, day with night, and so on).

Theme and meaning:

- What is the film's present thematic impact?
- Who or what is delivering it?
- Where is the intended impact failing?

As each successive rough cut gets closer to the mark, you'll find yourself asking more localized and detailed questions, such as:

- Which sequences would benefit from later in-points and/or earlier out-points? (Most scenes are better entered or left in movement rather than in stasis.)
- What needs to be done so each character exerts maximum impact, and in which sequences?
- Which sequences cry out for special attention to rhythm and pacing?
- Is every word of the dialogue necessary? Are there any you could cut?
- Are there places where a reaction shot can replace words?
- Does the dialogue editing produce dramatic tension, flow, and subtext?
- How little exposition can you get away with?
- How effective is the ending?
- Are there still false endings before (or worse, after) the true one?

Again, ask the editor to fix only the major faults before you schedule another viewing.

DRAMA TAKES PLACE IN THE AUDIENCE'S IMAGINATION

By creating a texture of sound and picture that invites interpretation, a film juxtaposes antithetical elements with great economy, and kindles the audience's involvement in developing whatever explanations might resolve the story's dialectical tensions. Now the audience is no longer passively identifying and submitting to the controlling will of the movie, but is living an imaginative and critical inner life in response to the film's prompting. Such active, critical awareness was what Bertolt Brecht, striving to arrest the audience habit of passively identifying, set out to accomplish in the theater.

THE AUDIENCE AS ACTIVE PARTICIPANTS

A demanding texture of word and image thrusts the spectator into a critical relationship and encourages active rather than passive participation. The Storyteller has developed an understanding with the audience that promises not just diversion but a challenge to interpret, a chance to weigh what is seen against what is heard and to balance an idea against its contrary. The film will now sometimes confirm and other times contradict what had seemed true. As in life, the viewer must use critical judgment when, as in our example of the salesman, a man's self-image turns out to be an unreliable guide to his character.

Interesting ways to use juxtaposition and counterpoint always emerge when the basic coupling of sound and picture on the screen is broken. For instance, you might show an interior with a bored teenage girl looking from a store window at people in the street. A radio somewhere off-screen is broadcasting the report of a dog show as she watches a boy and his mother having a violent argument outside, but the girl is too abstracted to notice the counterpoint. Though we see the mother and child, we hear the commentator detailing the breeds and their traits. There is an ironic contrast between all the different planes of consciousness, a family argument is raised to the level of a public spectacle, but our main character is too naïve or inward-looking to notice. Very succinctly and with not a little humor, both her unconsciousness and a satirical view of mother and child relationships have been compressed into a 30-second shot. Now that's economy!

SUMMARY

In the examples above, we have established that human consciousness can probe and process its surroundings,

- Mono-directionally (eyes and ears on the same information source)
- Bi-directionally (eyes and ears on different sources)

so that,

- Ears can pull eyes forward to see a new setting.
- Eyes can pull ears forward to hear a new setting.

Using these techniques, film imparts the sensations of a character's shifting planes of consciousness and association. A welcome bonus from overlap cutting is that you can use it to completely dispense with optical transitions such as the fade or dissolve.

CHAPTER 34

GETTING TO FINE CUT AND PICTURE LOCK

After weeks or months of sustained editing and several rough-cut versions a debilitating familiarity sets in. You lose objectivity and the ability to make judgments on behalf of an audience. Every version begins to look the same, and all look too long. You have become obsessed with particular faults in your footage, and curing them seems overwhelming. Not unusually, you want to hang on to a sequence or a minor character that the editor and others think is redundant. These are your darlings, and you must kill them if the film is to be consistent and work well.

This disabling condition is most likely to overwhelm the hyphenate, the director-editor who has lived too closely and too long with their intentions and footage. But this staleness can also infect whole editing crews. Now you must now call upon outsiders' reactions to the piece. Typically a feature film will have at least two **rough-cut screenings** to elicit reactions and feedback. However, before you arrange this, you need some preparation.

DIAGNOSTICS

MAKING A FLOWCHART

Before showing a rough cut to outsiders, help yourself spot anomalies by making an abstract of your film in the form of a block diagram. The storyline analysis form (discussed in Chapter 17, Figure 17-3) will speed the work of analysis and can be downloaded from the companion website www.directingbook.com, under "Forms and Logs."

Translating anything into another form helps you see it differently. Statisticians, for instance, make the meaning of their figures visually evident through a graph, pie chart, or other proportional image. You need similar help with film, because it's a slippery, deceptive medium whose mesmerizing present-tense detail continually blocks one from achieving a sense of overview. A flowchart will give you a fresh and more detached perspective on your work, and from it you will fix some problems easily because the act of diagramming alone brings revelations and new ideas.

To best see what the audience sees, do this work from the screen, not from memory and certainly not from the script. To begin, run your film one sequence at a time and:

1. Fill in each sequence's content briefly (characters and main action) in a box and note its timing.

2. Make tag-titles describing what each sequence is supposed to contribute to the film's development. It might be expository information, or introduce a new setting, character, or mood. It might introduce a character whose function develops later in the film.

3. Now examine the flowchart you have made from your film. It has limitations because film sequences are not like a succession of soloists, each singing a self-contained song, but more like the delayed entries of parts in a choral work. Each entering voice joins and cross-modulates with those preceding, and some foreshadow or set up references that will only make sense later.

4. Draw and annotate lines indicating any special relationship that exists between each new sequence and those before or after. Doing this may reveal, for instance, that in parallel story-telling one sequence is too far away from its counterpart.

5. Assess each sequence's length in relation to its contribution, and give each an audience impact rating to help you assess how the film's dramatic pressures evolve.

Analyzing your work like this forces you to acknowledge what is on the screen, and to translate amorphous sensations into hard-edged statements. What does the progression add up to? As with the first assembly, you will find some of the following:

- The film lacks early impact or has an unnecessarily pedestrian opening that makes it a late developer (fine for 19th-century Russian novels, but fatal for a film that may live or die on TV).

- The main issues are unclear or take too long to emerge (a writing problem, but you may be able to reposition a scene earlier, even ahead of titles, to commit the film to an interesting line of development).

- The type and frequency of impact is poorly distributed over the film's length (dramatic feast or famine).

- There is an erratic development of basic, necessary information about characters, backstory, and environment, including:
  - Omissions
  - Duplication
  - Redundancy
  - Expository information positioned too early so audience forgets it
  - Insufficient expository information or information placed too late

- The film makes the same dramatic statement in several ways. (Three consecutive scenes reveal that the hero has a low flashpoint. Choose the best, and reposition or dump the others.)

- A favorite sequence or character fails to contribute to the thrust of the film. (Another darling. Close your eyes and swing the axe.)

- The film's resolution emerges early, leaving the remainder of the story tediously inevitable. (Rebalance or withdraw indicators in the movie to keep resolution in doubt. That way the audience stays interested and working.)
- The film appears to end before it actually does. (False or multiple endings—a common problem.)

Naming each ailment leads to its cure, and when you implement each remedy you will sense the improvement rather than see it. It is like resetting a boat sail; everything looks the same, but she surges under new power. Preparing flowcharts brings one more huge benefit. Knowing now what every brick in your movie's edifice is supposed to uphold, you are excellently prepared to test the film's intentions during a trial screening with a small audience.

THE ROUGH CUT TRIAL SCREENING

Your **trial audience** should be a half dozen or so people whose tastes and interests you respect. You're seeking from them a fresh, first-time viewer's perspective, so you can't include anyone who knows the project, least of all the cast, crew, or screenwriter. In fact the less the audience knows about your film and your aims, the better. You should however try to find people familiar with the critique and feedback process, especially those who can make allowances for a work in progress. The uninitiated tend to perceive the rawness of a rough cut (sparse, provisional soundtrack, inconsistencies in color and exposure, choppy continuity editing, and so on) as mistakes. What you seek is a fresh look from people who understand how to look critically and constructively, and these are usually peers—editors, directors, producers, programmers, professors—but they can also be creative writers, architects and visual artists, anyone who understands the process of critiquing drafts. Here are a few other tips:

- Give your movie a working title. It forms part of the viewer's "contract" with the film by signaling the story's purpose and identity.
- Check sound levels and adjust them in your software, or you will get misleadingly negative responses. Even film professionals will misjudge a movie whose sound elements are inaudible or overbearing.
- Once you have your audience in its seats, warn that the film is a work in progress and still technically raw. Also warn that you will call out a brief description of any important missing elements such as music and sound or visual effects.

LISTEN CLOSELY, GUIDE DISCUSSION, DO NOT EXPLAIN

Asking for critical feedback must be handled carefully, or it can be a pointless exercise. Your job now is to listen and interpret what people get from the screen. After the viewing:

- Ask for impressions of the film as a whole.
- Keep quiet and take notes. Your film must stand or fall on its merits, so concentrate on everything that your audience may be telling you.

- Avoid the temptation to explain. It's pointless to fill in missing information or say what you intended. This only confuses and compromises the audience's perceptions, and can even imply that they are inept viewers.
- Focus and direct your viewers' attention, or you may find the discussion moving away from your needs.

Since you must often guide the inquiry into useful channels, here are some further open-ended questions that move from large issues toward the component parts:

- What is the story really about?
- What are the major issues in the film?
- Did the movie feel the right length, or was it too long?
- Were there any parts that were unclear or puzzling? (Wait, then list whatever you suspect made no impression. Audiences often forget whatever passed over their heads.)
- Which parts felt slow?
- Which parts were moving or otherwise successful?
- What did you feel about ___ (name of character)?
- What did you end up knowing about ___ (situation or issue)?

By using targeted inquiry you can test the function you assigned each sequence. Depending on your trial audience's patience, you may only be able to survey dubious areas, or even get liberal feedback on most of your film's parts and intentions. Occasionally someone insists on talking about the film he would have made rather than the film you have just shown. Diplomatically redirect the discussion.

POST SCREENING REFLECTION

Absorbing reactions and criticism is an emotionally draining experience, and especially tough when the screening is your film's showing to an audience. It is quite usual to feel threatened, slighted, misunderstood, incompetent, and to come away with a raging headache. Feeling so beleaguered, it is fatally easy to miss important feedback, so it may help to make an audio recording that you can revisit later in peace.

Balancing different views: Dealing with criticism means absorbing multiple views, and when the dust settles, guessing at how audience members could arrive at such varying impressions. You and your editor can now watch the movie with the eyes of those who never understood that the messenger was the workmate seen in an earlier scene. You find a way to put in an extra line, or insert a close up and, without compromising the film, the problem is solved.

Before rushing to fix anything, take into account the number of people reporting any particular difficulty. Make allowances, too, for the subjectivity and acuity of individual critics. Comments from different audiences may in any case cancel each other out, and no action be called for. However, comments that cluster around a particular area, even though they do not agree, should throw up a red flag that something is amiss.

Make changes cautiously: Change nothing substantial without very careful reflection. Remember, when you ask for criticism, people try to make their mark on your work. You will never be able to please everyone, nor should you try.

Hold on to your central intentions: Never let your central intentions get lost, and never revise them unless there are overwhelmingly positive reasons to do so. Act only on suggestions that support and further your central intentions. This is a dangerous phase for the filmmaker—indeed, for any artist. If you let go of your work's underlying identity, you can lose your direction, so try to keep listening and to think deeply about what you hear. Don't let strong emotions make you carve into your film precipitously. It may take you a week before your contradictory passions settle.

The uses of procrastination: Whether pleased or depressed by your film, try to stop working on it for a few days, or even a few weeks, and do something different. When you pick up the film again after a lapse, its problems and their solutions will no longer seem overwhelming. If such anxiety and depression is new to you, take comfort; you are deep in the throes of the artistic experience. It is the long and painful labor before birth.

TRY, TRY AGAIN

A film of any substance demands a lot of work in the editing room, so expect to make several rounds of alterations and to try the film on several new audiences. It will all seem unconscionably slow to the novice. You may eventually want to show the last cut to the original trial audience to see what changes they report. As a director with a lot of editing in my background, I have seen, times without number, how a film really evolves in editing. Magic and miracles appear from the footage, yet even film crews seldom appreciate this. Putting a year of part-time work into a 30-minute film is nothing unusual for a new director determined to make their work live up to its potential.

THE FINE CUT

The revisions you make after each rough-cut screening should get you closer and closer to the mark. Once you're satisfied with your film's basic editing and all your scenes have the placement and dynamism you've been seeking, you will sense there are no more big changes needed. This means you have arrived at the fine-cut stage. The **fine-cut** process involves three principal tasks:

1. Finessing all the edits one by one. This is where the editor makes all those small edit adjustments like trimming or adding a few frames to sharpen the timing of a reaction shot or to get a cut on action to match perfectly.

2. Together, the editor and director make the final decisions on the type and duration of scene transitions (dissolves and fades) and visual effects.

3. The editor, with the postproduction sound team, begins building the multi-track sound design, one layer at a time. This includes:
   - Cleaning up all dialogue tracks of unwanted noise
   - Constructing and smoothing out the ambient sounds (background atmospheres) for every scene
   - Laying down music tracks and building the sound effects tracks.

During this process the editor must often tweak edits here and there to keep everything perfectly in sync. We will look into the process of creating the sound design in more detail in the next two chapters.

KNOWING WHEN TO STOP

Avoid setting deadlines for editing. Instead, look for compelling evidence that your film's development is coming to a standstill. Some directors go on fidgeting and fiddling beyond the point of usefulness, and some even spoil their work. It comes from the fear of letting go, and is like admitting that your child is now an adult and doesn't need you anymore.

PICTURE LOCK!

When, at last, you've reached the end of the editing process, when all the creative editing decisions have been made, and not another frame needs to be changed, you have arrived at **picture lock**. Now the sound design team goes to work adding music, placing sound effects and layering tracks in perfect sync with the picture (which is deemed inalterable). Building the sound design is now another opportunity for the director to exert some creative and interpretive influence on the tone and authorial point of view of the film.

CHAPTER 35

WORKING WITH MUSIC

In extreme youth, I was an assistant editor on a dozen feature films. With each the editing crew would become jaded from living for months with the project, and then adding music would take us on a whole new journey into the story and its characters. This was always a thrilling revelation.

SPOTTING SESSION

Spotting for music is the process of viewing the fine cut, deciding where it needs music, and deciding, too, where that music will come from. Some may be popular music chosen to create the atmosphere of a particular time or place. If so, you must acquire its copyright. The rest of the music will need a film composer, which will be covered later. In any case, as you identify where music should start and stop, and decide the nature of that music, the editor will be making detailed notes in a **music cue sheet.** This is the same whether you are using pre-recorded music or working with a composer, or both (see p. 456).

MUSICAL CHOICE AND SCRATCH MUSIC

To decide what type of music works, try a variety of recorded music against key sequences. This is called using **scratch music**. As with so much else, you only know things work when you see them working. Of course, it's easy to be obvious and use Beach Boys for surfboarders, ethnic accordions for European holidaymakers, or cancan for anything French. Even quality orchestral music will seem clichéd if it's already too familiar to the audience.

Original score music has many advantages and is usually composed after editing is completed. You edit in the meantime by laying in scratch music taken from music that is readily available. It should resemble in mood and associations the music that you hope to have composed later. When the composer delivers, you can then swap out the scratch tracks for your composed music.

Playing against the obvious can yield fresh insights. Better than illustrating, which means duplicating the visual message, is to counterpoint the visible with music that provides an unexpected emotional offset. Take the climactic battle scene, for instance, in Terrence Malick's *The*

FIGURE 35-1

Terence Malick and composer Hans Zimmer go against genre expectations with their musical score for the battle scenes in *The Thin Red Line*.

Thin Red Line (2006, Figure 35-1). It is when the American forces finally overtake the Japanese stronghold at Guadalcanal, a bold and bloody assault. Malick eschews using high-energy music that would indicate heroic struggle and patriotic victory, and instead composer Hans Zimmer underscores the scene with a slow, brooding and emotionally intense soundtrack. This encourages the viewer to consider the surreal brutality of war in general, rather than identifying with the particular struggle and its outcome. Because there is no uplift in this American victory, the music asks us to feel the deeper implications of the violence that humans inflict on one another.

A well-judged score can supply the sense of integrity or melancholy in one character, and the jagged interior impulses that direct the actions of another. Music can enhance not only the givens of a character, but indicate invisible motives or foreshadow significant actions. Structurally, music can supply needed phrasing to a scene, or help create demarcations by bracketing transitions in scenes or between acts. Short "stings," or fragments of melody, can also be good if they belong to a larger musical picture. Even an uninspiring sequence may suddenly come to life because music lends it a fresh and surprising subtext that accelerates its forward movement.

USING PRE-RECORDED MUSIC

Many films use pre-recorded music as both score and source music, but this invites limitations and risks. First, given that the music was not written specifically for the film after picture was edited, the editor feels obligated to cut picture to the rhythms and pacing of that music. Second, if you are using popular music, viewers may bring strong associations and prejudices to particular songs

Filmscore Series: Dramatic Orchestra vol. 1	Track list/Preview	12	19	$99.95	P 🛒
Filmscore Series: Dramatic Orchestra vol. 2	Track list/Preview	10	61	$99.95	P 🛒
Filmscore Series: Epic Battles	Track list/Preview	10	26	$99.95	P 🛒
Filmscore Series: Horror	Track list/Preview	14	68	$99.95	P 🛒
Filmscore Series: Thrillers	Track list/Preview	12	58	$99.95	P 🛒
Flamenco	Track list/Preview	10	60	$99.95	P 🛒
Funky Guitars	Track list/Preview	9	9	$99.95	P 🛒
Funny Animations	Track list/Preview	13	18	$99.95	P 🛒
Gangsta vol. 1	Track list/Preview	12	31	$99.95	P 🛒

FIGURE 35-2

There are many online film music services offering pre-composed music for a fee. Pictured are only a few of the many options at Neosounds.com.

or styles of music that could work against your intentions. Most serious of all is that using pre-recorded music imposes the burden of obtaining rights.

Never assume that recorded music you want to use will be available when you get around to inquiring. The very worst time to negotiate with the lawyers representing composers, performers, publishers, or performing rights societies is when they intuit that your film has come to depend on a particular recording. You are now in the weakest possible position, and those with a nose for such things will try to suck you dry.

Obtaining music rights, like most legal issues, is complicated. The particularities of your project (length, story context, company policies, etc.) will dictate what strategy you should employ to secure the music you want. Thomas A. Crowell's *The Pocket Lawyer for Filmmakers*, 2nd ed. (Focal Press) is a good first step toward understanding these issues.

MUSIC LIBRARIES

There are many royalty-free music libraries online where you pay a fee per music file. A resource like www.neosounds.com sells fully composed music as well as mix-and-match music loops for you to build your own music tracks (Figure 35-2). If you're on a budget and want to enhance car chases, high-tension mountaineering, or need general feel-good music, you may be in luck. Otherwise, the chances of finding something suitable for drama of any originality are slim. If your film can be classified as "non-commercial" you usually pay a nominal fee, but if you secure any sort of distribution or broadcast deal, then you're obligated to pay a much larger "mass use" license.

COLLABORATING WITH A COMPOSER

Commissioning original music obviates the difficulty of negotiating and paying for copyright clearance on recorded music. Hiring a composer can be costly, but it leaves you free thereafter to use the music as you wish. To choose a composer, closely examine his or her prior work—in other media, not only film—to assure yourself that he or she works in the idiom you need. To get a rough idea whether their musical identity fits your story, place existing music experimentally against your film. Then, before you commit yourself, talk with whoever has previously worked with your composer to be sure there are no tastes, work habits, or preferences that may become problematic.

An experienced composer likes to take six weeks or more to compose about 15 minutes of music for a 90-minute feature film—but to be ready for the recording session, they may have to do it in three, with a flurry of all-night music copyist work at the end.

BEGINNING WORK

Film composers are hired late, and generally have to work under pressure. However, the more time you allow them, the better their work. For much of what follows, I am indebted to my son Paul N. Rabiger (http://paulrabiger.com/en/index.html) who makes film music in Cologne, Germany. Like many, he works largely with synthesizers, and uses live instrumentalists when the budget allows. The sequencing software favored by many composers includes Steinberg Cubase and Apple's Logic Pro, programs that permit many tracks, and integrate **Musical Instrument Digital Interface** (**MIDI**) with live recording. They also support video in QuickTime format so the composer can build music to an accurate video version of the film.

Ideally, the composer reads the screenplay and sees the first complete cut. He or she avoids coming in with preconceived ideas, and probes what the director wants the music to accomplish. He or she then mulls over the film's characters, settings, and overall content, and develops basic melodic themes. Next comes deciding, within the budget, what instrumental texture works best. Particular characters or situations often evoke their own musical treatment, or leitmotif (recurring theme), and this is always best worked out with some time in hand, especially if research is needed because the music must reflect a particular era or ethnicity.

In common with sound designers, composers sometimes get maddeningly cerebral requests. Try to be concrete by describing what you want the audience to feel at particular points, or what the characters feel but don't show. Avoid intellectualizing or thinking out loud, because this can paint a confusing picture. Don't pretend to know more about music than you do, and be ready to say what you feel in response to a musical example. Bring as many recorded excerpts as you need to illustrate whatever can't be put into words—which is usually almost everything. This is a precious time when you and your composer explore each other's minds. Often composers bring revelations about your film—things you didn't even know were there, and which music can now accentuate.

WHEN THERE IS SCRATCH MUSIC

The scratch music that nobody expected to keep can now confront the composer with a problem. Perhaps it's a stirring passage from Shostakovich's *Leningrad Symphony* or Jimi Hendrix in full cry. Certainly this indicates what you'd like, and what mood, texture, or tempo you'd prefer, but it also raises a barrier. The hapless composer must now extract whatever you find valuable, and then try to outgun the scratch examples with his or her own musical solutions.

In short, use scratch tracks when editing to explore musical possibilities, but ask your composer whether or not to include them in viewings and musical deliberations.

DEVELOPING A MUSIC CUE SHEET

Once the film's content is more or less locked down, it is screened by the director, editor, and composer for the music spotting session. Ideally, the screened version has timecode burned into the lower part of the screen: this functions to display a cumulative timing at any place in the movie. You discuss where music seems desirable and what kind seems most appropriate, and you have the time code as references.

Typical composer's questions center on the nature of the music (the tone, the tempo, its function and its relationship to the picture) and how time is supposed to pass. Some music sections may serve as an emotional counterpoint to the action, others to shore up a weak scene or two.

Music start points often begin from visual clues (car drives away, say, or a poignant reaction shot). Dialogue clues provide other start points: ("If you think I'm happy about this, Mister, you've got another think coming" CUE MUSIC).The director and composer find agreement on where each music section starts and stops, and on the general style and tone of the music itself.

During these discussions, the editor and composer create the **music cue sheet** which, like the sound-effects spotting sheet in Figure 36-1 (Chapter 36), uses timecode to specify the beginnings and endings of every music segment and contains cue notes written next to each. Music, like other addictions, is easy to start but difficult to end. That is, you'll have no difficulty starting a music segment, but ending one so the audience doesn't feel deprived will take some subterfuge. A common practice is to conclude or fade out music at the entry of something new and more commanding. You might for instance take music out under the first seconds of a noisy street scene or conclude it just before the dialogue in a new scene. To develop your own guidelines, study films that integrate music with the genre and kind of action your film contains.

The goal is for the composer to leave with a music cue sheet in hand, a full set of notes, and a copy of the film (DVD or QuickTime file with visible time code) to compose to. He or she will either create a traditional score to be performed and recorded, or will work with computers and MIDI-controlled synthesizers that produce music directly. In the course of hands-on composing like this, music cues are occasionally added, dropped, or renegotiated when ideas meet actuality. Poorly placed or unjustifiable music may prove worse than no music at all.

Sometimes a composer will start from simplicity and develop to a complex musical destination. In Joseph Losey's *The Go-Between* (1970), Michel Legrand's superb score starts in the main character's Edwardian boyhood with a plangent and slightly ominous Mozart theme. While a visitor at an aristocratic home, the boy finds he is being used as a go-between, carrying messages in a forbidden love affair. The music gathers in complexity as a terrible conflict develops in his loyalties. Gradually, we realize that the dessicated older man making present-day inquiries is the boy grown up. As the tragedy unfolds, the theme deepens into a full and tragic voice for its elderly subject—a man atrophied from emotional trauma in boyhood.

WHEN TO USE MUSIC, AND WHEN NOT

Music is commonly a transitional device, a filler, or something to set a mood. Better is to use it to suggest what may be hidden, such as a character's withheld expectations, interior mood, or burgeoning feelings. The classic example is Bernard Herrmann's unforgettable all-violin score for Alfred Hitchcock's *Psycho* (1960), with its crescendo of jabbing violins that scream as the pressures within the outwardly amenable Norman Bates rise to the intolerable. Music is natural to melodrama, but perhaps hardest to write tastefully for comedy.

When its job is to set a mood, the music should do its work and then get out of the way to return and comment later. Sometimes at a moment in the screening the composer will point out just how effective, even loaded, a silence becomes. The rhythms of action, camera movement, montage, and dialogue are themselves a kind of music, so you need not paint the lily.

Music effectively foreshadows events and builds tension, but should never give the story away, nor should it ever "picture point" the story by commenting too closely or merely enhance what's already visible on the screen. Walt Disney was infamous for "Mickey Mousing" his films—an industry term for fitting scores closely to the minutiae of action. The first of his true-life adventures, *The Living Desert* (1953), rendered its extraordinary wildlife footage banal by making scorpions square-dance and by playing trills or percussion rolls for anything that dared move. Used like this, music becomes controlling and smothering.

A related problem is simply using too much music, and burdening the film with a musical interpretation that blocks the audience from making its own emotional judgments. Hitchcock's *Suspicion* (1941) and many a film of its vintage are marred in this way. Far from heightening such a movie, wall-to-wall music flattens it by maintaining an exhausting aura of perpetual melodrama. Happily, fashions change, and less is now considered more. A rhythm alone, without melody or harmony, can sometimes supply the uncluttered accompaniment that a sequence needs.

In a 40-minute film, there may be 30 music cues—from a sting, or short punctuation, to a passage that is extended and more elaborate. There will be music for a main plot, but there may also be musical identities for subplots. Keeping these discrete during cross-cutting can be problematic, and their relationship, particularly in key, is important. So many factors are involved in producing an integrated score that music cues, once decided, should never be changed without a compelling reason.

CONFLICTS AND COMPOSING TO SYNC POINTS

An experienced musician composing for a recording session will write to very precise timings, paying attention to **spot effects** such as a tire screech or a dog barking. The choice of instrumentation must not fight dialogue, so the arrangement cannot be too busy during dialogue or foregrounded effects. Adding music to an already loaded track forces the audience to expend too much mental energy interpreting it, but sometimes music can entirely replace a diegetic soundtrack that is too thick. Musical punctuation, rather than a welter of naturalistic sound effects, can also be effectively impressionistic.

When the composer must work around dialogue and spot effects, supply a well-advanced version of the soundtrack, not the simple dialogue used during editing. This is particularly true for anything destined for a cinema setting, where the sound systems can be powerful and sophisticated, and everything in the track will be fully exposed.

When a written score is to be recorded to picture, it is marked at key points with the cumulative timing. Music is normally recorded to picture as a safeguard, and the conductor can keep a running check that sync points line up. The composer might put a dramatic sting on the first appearance of the pursuing motorcycle at 27 seconds, and on the appearance of the revolver at 01:16, for instance. This is only a problem when the score is played by live musicians. When it is made using MIDI computerized composing techniques, the composer builds the music to a QuickTime scratch version of the film and music fitting is done at source.

MUSIC EDITORS AND FITTING MUSIC

Because a live recording session is too expensive to produce exactly fitting music, the editor attends each session and confirms whether necessary shot adjustments are possible—usually just a few frames here and there. **Music editors** specialize in cutting and fitting music, and may play a large role in finding the period music to create the right atmosphere in, say, a coming-of-age feature film set in the 1970s. Sometimes they work closely with a composer, making sure during the fluid late stages of editing that the composer's intentions are maintained. Sometimes they work as hatchet man for the director, cutting and splicing to make film and music come together.[1] Often they have formal training in an instrument or in composition, and their expertise is vital to a musical, where much of the film is shot to playback on the set.

---

[1] See Jason Gross's *Online Music Magazine* interview with David Slusser www.furious.com/perfect/slusser.html.

CHAPTER 36

THE SOUND MIX

FINALIZING SOUND

SOUND, PSYCHOACOUSTICS, AND SOUND'S NARRATIVE CONTRIBUTION

Sound is an incomparable stimulant to the audience's imagination, and only rarely gets its due. Ideally, everyone would be alert to sound composition possibilities from scripting onward, but often it becomes a late, mop-up operation. To combat this, note down every idea anyone has for sound along the way, and don't leave it all to an audio-sweetening session. (That, by the way, is an expression I detest. It suggests that sound is sour and needs sugaring. Sound design, sound editing, and sound mix are the more direct and respectful terms.)

Finalizing sound is a computer operation that usually uses Pro Tools and a first-rate speaker system approximating a theater sound environment. Though few movie theaters come close to being "state of the art," good sound—as Dolby cinemas have shown—is also good business, so sound may yet get its day.

Any good sound editor will tell you it's not quantity or complexity of sound that makes a good soundtrack, but rather, the psychological journey that sound leads you on while you watch. This is the art of psychoacoustics. Effective sound is usually simple sound rather than complex, and specific and narratively focused rather than generic realism. Although film sound is made of different elements—music, dialogue, ambience, effects—it is a mistake at the ultimate compositional stage to put them in a hierarchy and think of them separately. Walter Murch, the doyen of editors and sound designers, makes a practice of watching a film he is editing with the sound turned off, so he can imagine what the sound might properly be. Listed in Randy Thom's "Designing a Movie for Sound" (www.filmsound.org/articles/designing_for_sound.htm) are less obvious and often overlooked functions of sound, which can supply narrative information and not just mood. It can:

- Indicate a historical period
- Indicate changes in time or geographic locale
- Connect otherwise unconnected ideas, characters, places, images, or moments

- Heighten ambiguity or diminish it
- Startle or soothe.

SOUND EFFECTS (SFX) AND THE SOUND SPOTTING SESSION

Before the sound editor goes to work splitting dialogue tracks and laying sound effects, there should be a roundup discussion between editor and director about the sound identity of the whole film and how each sequence fits in. This is the SFX **spotting session** during which you decide where the film needs sound effects, ambient sound, or music. Especially if you have monitored and directed the sound treatment throughout, the sound spotting session will be a special and even exhilarating occasion. This session determines where,

- Dialogue problems may require special EQ or dialogue replacement (ADR). If sound got low priority during location shooting, rough dialogue tracks will disrupt the dreamlike quality that a good film attains, so curing dialogue inequities is now worth a lot of your attention.
- Sound effects are needed. **Spot effects** sync to something on-screen, such as a door closing, a coin placed on a table, or a phone being picked up. Offscreen (OS) effects are non-sync and come from beyond the parameters of the visible frame.
- Foley effects (specially recorded SFX—footsteps, for example) will be needed. Each sound must sound convincing and be the right perspective. Usually these must be specially shot to picture.

As you work through the film, note every sound-effect decision (and its exact location by time-code) on an **SFX spotting sheet** (Figure 36-1). This is the sound-effects equivalent of the music cue sheet. Agree on known sound problems and on a strategy to handle each. This is a priority because dialogue reconstruction—if it's needed—is an expensive, specialized, and time-consuming business, and no film of any worth can survive having it done poorly.

POSTSYNCHRONIZING DIALOGUE (ADR)

Postsynchronizing dialogue means ensuring that each actor who recreates his speech tracks is in lip-sync with an existing picture. In this extremely laborious operation, also called **looping** or **automatic dialogue replacement** (**ADR**), each actor watches himself on the screen and rehearses before getting the OK to record. Long dialogue exchanges will be broken into perhaps 30-second increments.

This is a process to avoid like the plague because ADR often sounds flat and dead in contrast to live location recordings. It's not only lack of background presence and changing sound perspectives, and it's not even a lack of location acoustics—these can be reconstituted. It's the artificial situation actors find themselves in. They are reproducing dialogue in snippets and feel completely in the hands of whoever is directing each few sentences. The process drags down the actors' performances, so they hate ADR sessions with a passion.

THE FOLEY STAGE AND RE-CREATING SYNC SOUND EFFECTS

Many sound effects shot **wild** (non-synchronously) on location, or in a special sound studio can be fitted to picture and will work just fine. The **Foley studio** was named after the intrepid inventor

POST AUDIO SPOTTING SHEET

TITLE: ___The Mute's Confession___   DIRECTOR: ___P. Delgado___   SND DESIGNER: ___K. James___

RERECORD MIXER: ___B. Seery___   COMPOSER: ___----___   FOLEY: ___----___

☐ MUSIC   ☒ HARD EFFECTS/AMBIENCE   ☐ FOLEY   ☐ ADR/VO

Cue#	T.C. IN	T.C. OUT	Description
1	00 : 01 : 58 : 23	00 : 03 : 54 : 11	Diner ambience (busy until cue # 6)
2	00 : 02 : 08 : 06	00 : 02 : 19 : 16	Motorcycle starts, revs, peels out (O.S.)
3	00 : 02 : 22 : 01	00 : 02 : 31 : 13	Police sirens approach, stop (O.S.)
4	00 : 02 : 36 : 21	--- : --- : --- : ---	Bell above diner door tinkles
5	00 : 02 : 36 : 21	00 : 04 : 14 : 22	Police radio chatter (belt radio)
6	00 : 03 : 54 : 11	00 : 04 : 14 : 22	Diner Ambience dips, almost out
7	00 : 04 : 14 : 22	00 : 04 : 20 : 18	Ext. street ambience
8	00 : 04 : 14 : 22	00 : 04 : 20 : 18	Police radio chatter (Cruiser radio)
9	00 : 04 : 20 : 18	--- : --- : --- : ---	Police cruiser door SLAMS shut (echo)
10	00 : 04 : 20 : 18	00 : 05 : 00 : 24	Police Radio chatter (Int. car)
11	00 : 04 : 20 : 25	00 : 05 : 00 : 24	Police Siren starts up and continues (Int. car)
12	00 : 05 : 00 : 24	00 : 06 : 02 : 03	Int. County Jail Ambience
13	00 : 05 : 25 : 10	00 : 05 : 30 : 12	Voice yells down hallways (o.s.)(reverb)
14	00 : 05 : 33 : 06	--- : --- : --- : ---	Cell door slams shut (o.s.)

FIGURE 36-1

A sample spotting sheet for SFX and ambience. The same form can be used for music spotting as well. Download this form at www.directingbook.com ("Forms and Logs").

Jack Foley, who in the 1940s discovered that you could mime all the right sounds to picture. A Foley studio has a variety of surfaces such as concrete, heavy wood, light wood, carpet, linoleum, gravel, and so on. Foley artists bring many pairs of different footwear and may add sand or paper to modify the sound of their footsteps to suit what's on the screen. They are ready to improvise any situation: baking powder in a plastic bag, for instance, makes the right scrunching sound for footsteps in snow, and a punched cabbage can be made to sound like someone being hit over the head. One of my tasks on a thoroughly forgettable Jayne Mansfield comedy, *The Sheriff of Fractured Jaw* (Raoul Walsh, 1958), was to make horse footsteps with coconuts, and steam engine noises with a modified motorcycle engine. It was great fun.

Sounds shot to fit a repetitive action—such as knocking on a door, shoveling snow, or footsteps going up a flight of stairs—can be re-created by recording the actions wild and a little slower. In the cutting room, you then cut out the requisite frames before each impact, quite easy on a computer. More complex sync effects (two people walking through an echoing quadrangle) will have to be postsynced just like dialogue in a Foley session, paying attention to the different surfaces their feet pass over (grass, gravel, concrete, etc.). The echo can then be added at the sound mix stage.

A grueling week or two of postsync sessions makes you understand how invaluable is the location recordist who can procure good original recordings. For the low-budget filmmaker, where and how you record sound effects is unimportant; it only matters that they sound authentic and are in sync with the action. Sometimes you will find what you want in sound libraries, but never assume that any sound is right until you've proved it against picture. To locate libraries, enter "sound effects library" in a search engine. Some will let you listen to or even download low resolution SFX to try them out. Try Sound Ideas at www.sound-ideas.com/bbc.html.

Start hunting sound effects well ahead. Many libraries are top-heavy with stuff shot in the Dark Ages. Effects tracks may come with a heavy ambient background or system hiss. This is inaudible with noisy, exotic sounds such as helicopters or elephants rampaging through Malaysian undergrowth. Unfortunately it's the nitty-gritty stuff—footsteps, door slams, dog growling, and so on—that proves hard to get right. You can and should shoot your own, but sound effects can be authentic in origin, yet sound otherwise. At one time there were only six different gunshots used throughout the film industry. When my unit tried recording authentic new ones, they sounded like pitiful cap-gun noises.

Another caution: sound effects can easily be overdone. A cat in a kitchen only needs to meow if it's seen demanding breakfast. At www.filmsound.org/cliche/, there's a hilarious list of sound clichés: all bicycles have bells, car tires always squeal on corners, storms start instantaneously, wind always whistles, doors always squeak… and much more.

PREPARING FOR THE SOUND MIX

After all soundtracks have been laid, editing culminates by preparing and mixing the component soundtracks. Entire books have been written on this preeminent subject alone (see p. 420), so what follows are some essentials and some tips. The mix procedure determines the following:

- Relative sound levels—between a dialogue foreground voice track, say, and a factory scene background (if, and only if, they are on separate tracks).

- Equalization (EQ)—the filtering and profiling of individual tracks to match others or to maximize intelligibility for ear comfort. A voice track with a rumbly traffic background can, for instance, be much improved by "rolling off" the lower frequencies, leaving the higher voice frequencies intact.

- Quality consistency—two mike positions on two angles covering the same speaker need careful EQ, level, and ambience matching or one will not flow seamlessly into the other.

- Level changes—fade-up, fade-down, sound dissolves, and adjustments for new track elements such as narration, music, or interior monologue.

- Sound processing—adding echo, reverberation, telephone effect, and so on.

- Dynamic range—compression squeezes the broad dynamic (loudness) range of tracks meant for a cinema movie into the narrower range favored for TV transmission. Limiting leaves the main range untouched, but holds peak levels within a preset ceiling.

- Perspective—equalization and level manipulation can mimic perspective changes; this helps create through sound a sense of space and dimensionality.

- Multichannel sound distribution—different sound elements must go to different channels to create space and horizontal spread on stereo or surround-sound playback.
- Noise reduction—Dolby and other noise-reduction systems minimize the system hiss that would intrude on quiet passages.

You are ready to mix tracks into one master track when you have:

- Finalized content of your film
- Fitted music
- Split dialogue tracks. This means grouping them by their EQ and other needs:
  - A separate track for each microphone position in dialogue sequences
  - Possibly a different track for each speaker, depending on the EQ needs for each mike position on each character
- Filled-in backgrounds (missing sections of background ambience, so there are no dead spaces or abrupt background changes)
- Recorded and laid narration (if there is any)
- Recorded and laid sound effects and mood-setting atmospheres
- Finalized Pro Tools timeline contents.

MULTI-TRACK LAYERING

The overall goal of the sound mix is to bring all tracks into acceptable compatibility, given that the viewer will expect slightly different levels and sound perspectives according to camera distances. Modern sound-editing programs permit a virtually unlimited number of audio tracks—a situation of plenty that can pose its own hazards—and they allow editing with surgical precision, even within a syllable (Figure 36-2). During the rough-cut stage, however, you edited only the soundtracks necessary to make dramatic decisions, and used perhaps just dialogue tracks and occasional scratch music. There is now a lot of layering and planning required to produce the smooth stream of aural consciousness familiar from feature films. Although we shall discuss soundtrack hierarchy as though dialogue was always foremost, this may vary. Depending on dramatic requirements, music or sound effects might be faded up to the foreground, and dialogue played almost inaudibly low.

DIALOGUE TRACKS AND THE PROBLEM OF INCONSISTENCIES

The variety of location acoustic environments, different microphones, and different mike working distances all play merry havoc with voice consistency and the proportions of voice levels to their background atmosphere (sometimes called signal-to-noise ratio). When these disparate tracks are cut together in the assembly, the viewer can barely focus on the characters and their story because of the stress caused by unmotivated and irrational changes in sound levels, perspectives, and room acoustics. Suddenly you appreciate the effortless, seamless sound continuity of feature films. This is achieved by skillfully adjusting sound levels and **equalization** (**EQ**) at the mix stage, and can only

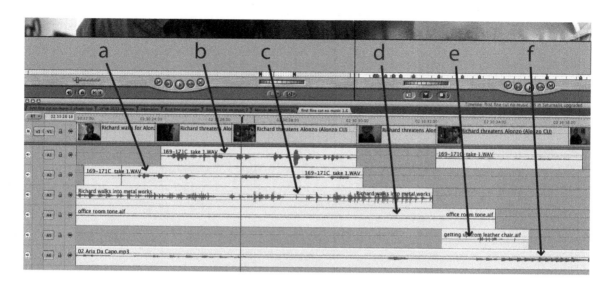

FIGURE 36-2

NLE systems can layer upward of 99 tracks of audio. A typical distribution of sound tracks used during the final stages of editing includes several dialogue tracks (a and b); ambience track (c); production room tone (d); sound effects (e); and music (f).

be accomplished if the tracks are first intelligently laid for the purpose. This is a painstaking, specialized, and labor-intensive process.

Splitting dialogue tracks: these are split (grouped on separate tracks) according to the scene coverage's mike positions. In a scene shot from two angles, say, and having two mike positions, all close-shot sound will go on one audio track, and all medium-shot sound on another. This minimizes cut-to-cut EQ adjustments since one setup will cover multiple cuts. A scene with six camera setups and six mike positions may call for six audio tracks, and these may additionally be split by character because each voice needs its own special EQ and level treatments.

Inconsistent backgrounds: background tracks must be cleaned of extraneous noises such as creaks, wind-rumble, mike-handling sounds—anything that doesn't overlap dialogue and which can be removed. The resulting gaps are filled from presence tracks shot on location. When backgrounds fail to match from angle to angle, the sound editor must augment the quieter ones to match the noisier. Because the ear registers a sound cut more readily than a graduated change, changes in ambience are often made through sound dissolves rather than cuts. Difficult background changes can often be masked by a commanding foreground sound in which the audience's attention is distracted.

LAYING MUSIC OR EFFECTS TRACKS

Cut the track in just before the first modulations so its arrival isn't heralded by studio atmosphere. Arrow A in Figure 36-3 represents the ideal cut-in point; to its left is unwanted presence, or hiss.

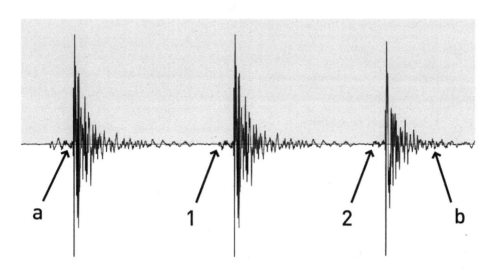

FIGURE 36-3

Sound modulations: attack, three bursts, and decay. Arrows 1 and 2 indicate the possible cutting points.

To the right of arrow a are three attacks in succession leading to a decay to silence at arrow b. This attack-sustain-decay profile is typical for many sound effects (footsteps, for instance), so this editing strategy has many uses. By removing sound between 1 and 2, we could reduce three drumbeats or footfalls to two, or speed up their rhythm. Some cuts, actions, and camera movements may need minor rebalancing so they synchronize with the music. If you cannot, then lay the music so that no sync relationship seems intended.

NARRATION, VOICE-OVER, AND PRESENCE

Even the most professional actor can seldom read narration and make it sound spontaneous. Consider improvising, by giving the actor a list of points to be made, and then let him or her improvise a thoughts voice in character. By judicious side-coaching or interviewing, you can get a quantity of entirely spontaneous material. When you lay narration or interior monologue, you will need to record "presence" to fill the gaps between sections so the track remains "live" during a quiet sequence.

AMBIENT SOUND

Ambient sounds are those that "naturally" occur in the scene's location and help define its aural environment. They create a mood (birdsong over a wood, or hammering over the exterior of a carpenter's shop), but can also mask ambience inconsistencies when you cut together original sync recordings (Figure 36-4). Ambience can powerfully infuse a scene with emotion without recourse to score music. One of my films contained a scene of a suburban man who returns home and receives some unsettling news from his neighbor. I added an ambient track of cicadas buzzing

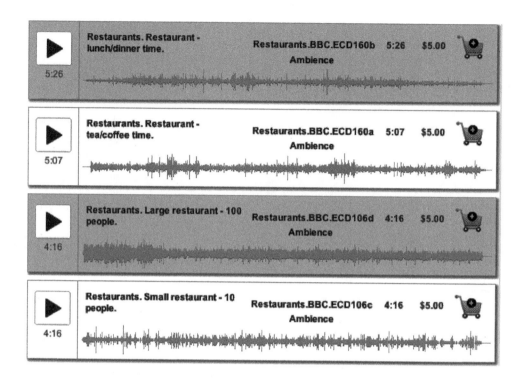

FIGURE 36-4

Online and CD sound effects libraries offer many thousands of SFX and ambience tracks for you to choose from. Pictured are three different restaurant ambience tracks from the BBC collection at Prosoundeffects.com.

annoyingly (from a SFX CD library), a sound appropriate for the location and unnerving, thus reflecting the main character's frayed nerves.

SOUND-MIX TIPS

DIRECTING THE MIX

Though you may not know how to achieve a particular effect, you must say what each sequence should sound like, and explain specifically what you don't like or would prefer for a particular section. According to your requests, and depending on what the sound editor has laid in the soundtracks, the mix engineer will offer alternatives from which you can choose.

PREMIXING

A busy exterior in a feature film may comprise 30 or more soundtracks, and these usually require premixes. Do them in an order that reserves control over the most important elements until last.

Because intelligibility depends on dialogue remaining audible, retain control over the ratio of dialogue to everything else by keeping it to the very last stage of mixing.

APPROVE SECTIONS, THEN LISTEN TO THE WHOLE

During the mix, you and your editor approve each stage and each scene in the process. At the end of this scene-by-scene process, be sure to return to the very beginning and listen to the whole film without stopping. Your time will surely be rewarded by finding an anomaly or two.

MAKE SAFETY COPIES AND STORE THEM IN DIFFERENT LOCATIONS

A sound mix is a long and expensive process, so it is professional practice to immediately make safety or backup copies. These are stored in multiple buildings in case of loss or theft. Do the same with film negative and video originals; keep masters, safety copies, negatives, and internegatives (copy negatives) in different places so you won't lose everything should fire, flood, revolution, or act of God (or those claiming to act on His behalf) destroy what otherwise fits so nicely under your bed.

CHAPTER 37

THE FINISHING TOUCHES

With your picture lock edit and mixed soundtrack in hand, you are ready to take the film across the finish line. The biggest creative decisions are now behind you, and many of the coming tasks are purely practical. There are however one or two significant areas where a director can still make more aesthetic and interpretive contributions to the film. Finishing your film includes:

- Color correction.
- Adding titles and credits.
- Mastering the final program.
- Duplication for multi-format distribution.
- Promotion and distribution.

COLOR CORRECTION

Many NLE systems incorporate a standard color correction tool called a **three-way color corrector**. Using this, a filmmaker has the capacity to control **color** (**hue** and saturation) and **luminance** (**brightness**) in three areas of the image—blacks, mid-range, and whites (Figure 37-1). The three-way color corrector is not a superficial accessory but a powerful image correction tool. Color correction itself is used to accomplish four goals.

1. Correct exposure problems and color temperature discrepancies.
2. Match color and brightness values across all clips in a single scene.
3. Enhance colors to create subtle tonalities for a specific "look" or mood.
4. Create color effects, like stripping an image of all but one specific color.

The process of manipulating image characteristics in postproduction is called **color grading** and allows one to adjust for inconsistencies in exposures and color temperatures from shot to

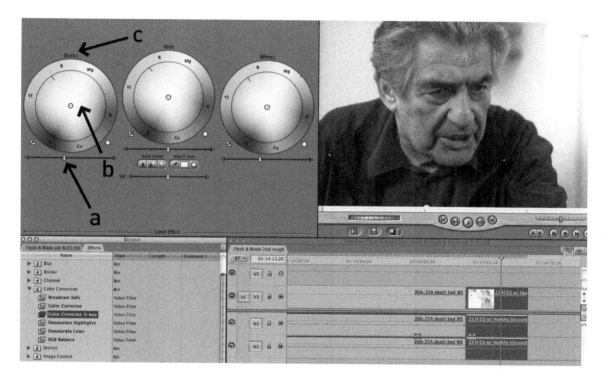

FIGURE 37-1

The three-way color corrector in Final Cut Pro. (a) The luminance slider; (b) the color balance controls; (c) the color correction control range (blacks, mids, or whites). The shot selected in the timeline is brought up in the viewer for color correction.

shot. You can also add a subtly expressive color tinge to a scene, a facility that is, remarkably, just a user's guide away. But be careful: it's tempting to jump in and fiddle with the color wheels and sliders without understanding how it all works. Suddenly skin tones look greenish in one scene, and pasty yellow in another. Shadows turn blue and bright areas clip into pure white blotches. Like many visual effects, color grading can easily be overused, and it takes someone with restraint, and aesthetic sensibility to give your film a consistent, professional visual polish. That person is a called a **colorist**. Like a sound mixer, colorists generally work with tools that are far more power-ful than those bundled with an editing package (Figure 37-2).

The creative capabilities of color grading have increased exponentially in recent years, and what was formerly left to the editor or cinematographer is now considered by many directors to be an essential and creative step that they supervise with the cinematographer. The result is a fine control over the tone, mood and visual impact of the film. Jean-Pierre Jeunet used digital color grading extensively in films like *Amélie* (2001) and *Micmacs* (2009, Figure 37-3) to enhance the image with the warm, lush, and painterly color tones essential to his nostalgic, hyper-real visual aesthetic.

When working at higher resolutions, color grading is also commonly referred to as the **digital intermediate** process (**DI**). It works with huge uncompressed video files called **DXP** (digital picture exchange) files. Once these are fully color graded, they are used to perform a **film out** to a digital film recorder that scans the final picture on to 35mm celluloid for film distribution. If your film is destined for Digital Cinema projection, then color grading is performed on uncompressed video files then saved as uncompressed video on a **Digital Cinema distribution master** (**DCDM**). The lab then compresses all your project's video and audio files using a standard codec to make up the **Digital Cinema Package (DCP)** that goes to theaters for projection. As more commercial theaters make the switch to digital projection, the film out process will eventually fade away (see "High End Mastering" on p. 474).

TITLES AND CREDITS

Every film acquires a working title, but the final one is often plucked late and in an agony of indecision. It must be short, special, and epitomize your film's allure. Festival programs and TV listings seldom have space to describe their offerings, so your work's title may be its only chance of piquing an audience's curiosity.

FIGURE 37-2 ————————————

Professional colorist Nichole Kizer at Copper Post using a DaVinci Resolve during a color grading session for *Queens of Country* (2012).

FIGURE 37-3 ————————————

Jeunet uses digital color grading extensively in films like *Amélie* and *Micmacs* (2009, above) to create a unique, hyper-real visual style.

Most titles and credits, once chosen, can be successfully generated by most NLE software systems. If, however, your film requires titling beyond the basics—such as mixed or customized fonts, more spacing options, or better resolution—then you can always use third-party graphics software like Adobe After Effects, and import the files to your project.

Title style: Be conservative since overambitious front titles tend to promise more than the film may deliver. Make legibility your priority, and decide your titling and its placement according to the background composition. Take films of comparable length and subject as models.

Overladen credits: Credits should be brisk, and the same name should not crop up in multiple key capacities. Avoid fancy logos or visionary company names. Let your film, not its packaging, do the talking.

Contractual or other obligations: Obey contractual obligations when you use union actors—or live to regret you were ever born. Often contracts stipulate size and wording of title credits. Since many favors are granted in return for a screen acknowledgment, honor your debts to the letter, and double-check you've left nobody out. Funding or college degrees may also prescribe special wording, so review and triple-check all those commitments you made months earlier.

Spelling: Have spelling checked scrupulously, particularly people's names; misspelling connotes indifference to the very people who have given you their all.

MASTERING

After your film is picture locked, sound mixed, color corrected, and includes titles and credits, you are ready to take it out of the computer and send it into the world. The first step is to master your film. **Mastering** simply means outputting your project at the highest quality possible and saving a master copy on a stable recording format. This is the conclusion of your project workflow, so the specific format and recording media will depend on source and delivery formats. Consult with your editor, cinematographer, and postproduction lab if you are using one. Here are some generalities:

Do your homework: Plan out the remainder of your workflow, from shooting format to mastering format, and make sure all experts agree.

Master to the most robust record media possible and make multiple masters: Masters are used to archive and make multiple distribution copies so they need to be as robust as possible.

Do not master to DVD or **Blu-ray**: these are distribution, not mastering formats.

Master to the same format that you shot with (if possible): This ensures you lose no image quality from acquisition to output and also that all of your elements, raw footage and program master, are in a common format.

High end mastering: Even if you envision distribution on 35mm film or as a Digital Cinema Package, do not incur the expense of a film out or creating the DCP. Simply master on HDCAM SR, which is fine for making film festival copies. If a distributor buys your film, *they* will foot the bill for these expensive lab procedures (see p. 325 and p. 473).

DISTRIBUTION COPIES

From your program masters come distribution copies. Today there are many distribution outlets, and you therefore face another thicket of formats and codecs. In broad terms, distribution breaks down into tape, discs, and the web. Plan distribution copies for all possible outlets.

Screening dubs are copies generated from one of your master sources at a professional facility. Many film festivals and cable/broadcast programmers require submissions on particular tape formats such as DVCAM, HDCAM or DVCPRO HD. Check the submission requirements carefully and remember—*never, ever send your master!*

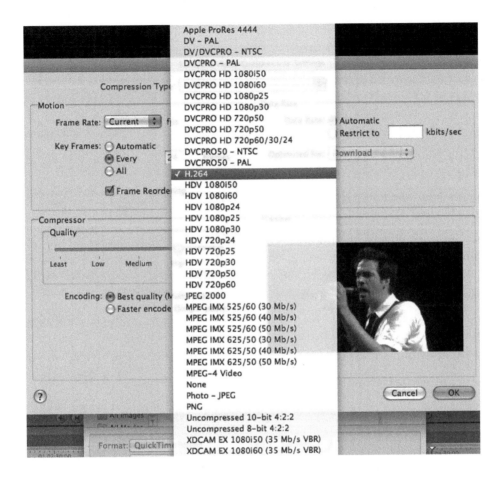

FIGURE 37-4

Most NLE systems offer a huge range of output options depending on your intended distribution avenues.

Exporting your film for disc authoring and web distribution: Most NLE systems offer a huge range of output options depending on your intended distribution avenues (Figure 37-4). You can:

- Export your movie as an uncompressed QuickTime movie file (or MPEG 4[1]). This can be used by professional DVD (standard definition) and Blu-ray (high definition) pressing services, and can also be used for distribution over the web. Video hosting websites (like Vimeo and YouTube) have their own compression specifications, but you can run a QuickTime movie file through any number of programs to accomplish the compression you need.

---

[1] H.264 is a very common web upload codec for video hosting sites.

- Output an MPEG 2 file for DVD authoring in programs like iDVD or DVD Studio Pro which let you create your own DVDs on recordable media. A professional service usually requires you to make a 250-disc minimum order, which is not always practical. Check any DVDs you send out rigorously. It's heartbreaking when a festival has to abandon an excellent project because your DVD froze.

- Save multiple copies: This is the digital age—so make multiple copies of everything you've exported and tuck them away on server grade hard drives. Your movie will always be there when you need a copy.

PROMOTIONAL MATERIAL

Publicity: Study other people's methods of promotion, and adapt whatever seems effective. Most filmmakers hate stepping forward to publicize their work, and do a shoddy job. So hoist up your pants and learn how to launch a publicity blast. You will need large, appealing posters to go up wherever your film will be shown, as well as a **publicity folder** whose materials should be on high quality paper and contain:

- An informative "teaser" description that makes people want to see the film. Include a synopsis and brief narrative of production.
- Evocative production stills of a quality high enough to use on a poster or on your website (see p. 329).
- List of festival awards and selected screenings.
- Positive press reviews.
- Cast and principal crew names and their prior accomplishments.
- Contact information: your phone number, email, website, Facebook address.
- Your business card.

Social media: these are promotion tools that no emerging filmmaker can ignore. The advent of such as Facebook and Twitter provide enormous opportunities for you to promote yourself, build an audience beyond the festival circuit, and connect with a potential audience and the larger film community. A regular presence and carefully devised updates will help you maintain a broad and receptive public.

Website: If you can't do it yourself, pay someone to set up a website and teach you how to update it. Websites allow people to find you, see samples of your films, read press reviews, download press packets and stills, and make contact easily. See filmmaker Ramin Bahrani's website as an example: www.raminbahrani.com (Figure 37-5).

Screeners: DVD or Blu-ray discs that you send to festivals or to programmers for consideration are called **screeners**. A polished and professional disc package (disk with extras, printed

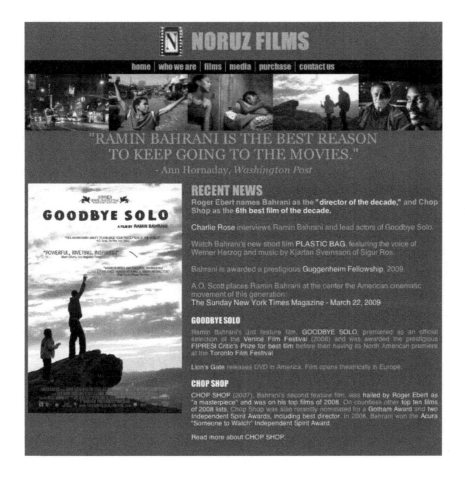

FIGURE 37-5

Ramin Bahrani's website serves as a good example of an effective filmmaker's site. Go to www.raminbahrani.com.

covers, and a plastic case) will best represent your film. Often you will include your publicity packet with the screener.

MAKING FESTIVALS AND SCREENINGS WORK FOR YOU

Festivals: Enter your work in every festival that might further your artistic and commercial identity. Go to them all if you can afford it, because the ultimate rite of passage is seeing your work with a paying audience. Reactions can be thrilling or chastening, and will differ from audience to audience. From this baptism of fire you will emerge knowing what film to make next.

Personal contacts: Almost everything of value seems to happen through person-to-person contact, so learn to work the crowd at festivals and conferences. Research who's who; pleasantly introduce yourself by name and film to anyone that matters; look them in the eye; give them your business card, and tell people how much you'd like them to see your film (as a target, I know this really works). Hand them a flyer specifying the screening's time and place.

Filmmaker's comments: Rehearse so you can introduce your film briefly and graciously in public. Give credit to others, and signify openness to comments of all kinds—in person or via email. At question time afterward, get things started by telling the audience what you'd like to learn from them. In your replies, don't ramble: be brief, informative, modest, and stay in learning mode. If anyone asks what film you want to make next, pitch your best one or two ideas in 30 seconds each.

After the screening, shake people's hands by the door and thank them for coming. Give out your business card, and ask for honest comments by email. If there's a bar or social area, hang out till closing time—but stay sober so you can chat people up, collect information, and make new friends. Collaborators, associates, employers, supporters, and backers all seem to materialize through social occasions like these.

And now for something completely different...

So, what *are* your ideas for the next movie? Only when you finish a film, and empty yourself out completely does another project begin to form in the vacuum. That's how the artistic process begins all over again.

FILMOGRAPHY

(films listed in alphabetical order)

4 months, 3 weeks, 2 days. Dir. Cristian Mungiu. Mobra Films, 2007. (DVD: IFC Films)

8 Femmes. Dir. François Ozon. BIM, 2002. (DVD: Universal Studios)

400 Blows, The. Dir. François Truffaut. Les Films du Carrosse, 1959. (DVD: The Criterion Collection)

500 Days of Summer. Dir. Mark Webb. Watermark, 2009. (DVD: 20th Century Fox Home Ent.)

2001: A Space Odyssey. Dir. Stanley Kubrick. Metro-Goldwyn-Mayer, 1968. (DVD: MGM/UA Home Video)

Across the Bridge. Dir. Ken Annakin. Rank Org., 1957 (DVD: Shanochie Ent. Corp, British Film Collection)

Alive in JoBurg. Dir. Neil Blomkamp Spy Films, 2006.

All the President's Men. Dir. Alan J. Pakula. Warner Bros., 1976. (DVD: Warner Home Video)

Allegro Dir. Christoffer Boe. AlphaVille Pictures, 2005. (DVD: Koch Lorber)

Alphaville. Dir. Jean-Luc Godard. Athos Films, 1965. (DVD: The Criterion Collection)

Amélie. Dir. Jean-Pierre Jeunet. Victoires Prod., 2001. (DVD: Miramax Home Ent.)

American Beauty. Dir. Sam Mendes. Dreamworks SKG, 1999. (DVD: Dreamworks)

Artist, The. Dir. Michel Hazanavicius. La Petite Reine, 2011. (DVD: The Weinstein Company)

Atonement. Dir. Joe Wright. Universal Pictures, 2007 (DVD: Universal Studios Home Ent.)

Badlands. Dir. Terrence Malick. Warner Bros., 1973. (DVD: Warner Home Video)

Ballast. Dir. Lance Hammer. Alluvial Film Co., 2008 (DVD: Kino Video)

Bamboozled. Dir. Spike Lee. 40 Acres & A Mule Filmworks, 2000. (DVD: New Line Home Video)

Barry Lyndon. Dir. Stanley Kubrick. Hawk Films Ltd., 1975. (DVD: Warner Home Video)

Beginners. Dir. Michael Mills. Olympus Pictures, 2010. (DVD: Universal Studios Home Ent.)

Big Lebowski, The. Dirs. Coen Brothers. Working Title Films, 1998. (DVD: Universal Studios Home Ent.)

Black Swan. Dir. Darren Aronofsky. Protozoa Pictures, 2010. (DVD: 20th Century Fox Home Ent.)

Blade Runner. Dir. Ridley Scott. The Ladd Company, 1982. (DVD: Warner Home Video)

Blue Velvet. Dir. David Lynch. De Laurentis Ent. Group, 1986. (DVD: Sony Pictures Home Ent.)

Bonnie and Clyde. Dir. Arthur Penn. Warner Bros. Seven Arts, 1967. (DVD: Warner Home Video)

Brazil. Dir. Terry Gilliam. Embassy Inter. Pictures, 1985. (DVD: The Criterion Collection)

Breaking the Waves. Dir. Lars von Trier. Zentropa Ents., 1996. (DVD: Artisan)

Breathless (*À Bout de Souffle*). Dir. Jean-Luc Godard. Impéria, 1960. (DVD: The Criterion Collection)

Bringing up Baby. Dir. Howard Hawks. RKO Radio Pictures, 1938. (DVD: Warner Home Video)

Bronx Tale, A. Dir. Robert De Niro. Tribeca Productions, 1993. (DVD: Universal Studios Home Ent.)

Bunraku. Dir. Guy Moshe. Picturesque Films, 2010. (ARC Entertainment)

Cabinet of Dr. Caligari, The. Dir. Robert Wiene. Decla-Bioscop AG, 1920. (DVD: Kino Video)

Celebration (*Festen*)*, The*. Dir. Thomas Vinterberg. Nimbus Film, 1998. (DVD: Universal Studios)

Chelovek s Kino-Apparatom (*Man with Movie Camera*). Dir. Dziga Vertov. VUFKU, 1929. (DVD: Kino Video)

Chop Shop. Dir. Ramin Bahrani. Noruz Films, 2007. (DVD: Koch Lorber Films)

Cléo from 5 to 7. Dir. Agnès Varda. Rome Paris Films, 1961. (DVD: The Criterion Collection)

Clockwork Orange, A. Dir. Stanley Kubrick. Warner Bros., 1971. (DVD: Warner Home Video)

Close Up (Nema-ye Nazdik). Dir. Abbas Kiarostami. Kanoon, 1990. (DVD: The Criterion Collection)

Code Unknown (Code inconnu): Récit incomplet de divers voyages. Dir. Michael Haneke. Canal+, 2000. (DVD: Kino International Corp.)

Come and See. Dir. Elem Klimov. Mosfilm, 1985 (DVD: Kino Video)

Constant Gardener, The. Dir. Fernando Meirelles. Potboiler Productions, 2005. (DVD: Focus Features)

Crash. Dir. Paul Haggis. Bull's Eye Ent., 2004. (DVD: Lions Gate Films Home Ent.)

Crazy, Stupid, Love. Dirs. Glenn Ficarra. John Requa. Carousel Productions, 2011. (DVD: Warner Home Video)

Creation. Dir. Jon Amiel. Recorded Picture Company, 2009. (DVD: Icon Home Ent. (UK))

Crouching Tiger, Hidden Dragon. Dir. Ang Lee. Good Machine, 2000. (DVD: Sony Pictures Home Ent.)

Dancer in the Dark. Dir. Lars von Trier. Zentropa Ent., 2000. (DVD: New Line Home Video)

Dances with Wolves Dir. Kevin Costner. Majestic Films, 1990. (DVD: MGM Home Ent.)

Dark Knight, The. Dir. Christopher Nolan. Warner Bros., 2008. (DVD: Warner Home Video)

Days of Heaven. Dir. Terrence Malick. Paramount Pictures, 1978. (DVD: Paramount Home Ent.)

Distant Voices, Still Lives. Dir. Terence Davies. BFI Films, 1985. (DVD: British Film Institute)

District 9. Dir. Neil Blomkamp. Wingnut Films, 2009. (DVD: Sony Pictures Home Ent.)

Diving Bell & Butterfly, The. Dir. Julian Schnabel. Pathé Renn Productions, 2007. (DVD: Miramax Home Ent.)

Dogfight. Dir. Nancy Savoca. 1991. (DVD: Warner Home Video)

Dr. Mabuse . Dir. Fritz Lang. UCO-Film, 1922. (DVD: Kino Video)

Easy Rider. Dir. Dir. Dennis Hopper. Columbia Pictures, 1969. (DVD: Sony Pictures Home Ent.)

Edward Scissorhands. Dir. Tim Burton. 20th Century Fox, 1990. (DVD: 20th Century Fox Home Ent.)

El Mariachi. Dir. Roberto Rodriguez. Columbia Pictures, 1992. (DVD: Columbia Tristar).

Election. Dir. Alexander Payne. Paramount Pictures, 1999 (DVD: Paramount Home Video)

Erin Brockovich. Dir. Steven Soderbergh. Jersey Films, 2000. (DVD: Universal Studios Home Video)

Eternal Sunshine of the Spotless Mind. Dir. Michel Gondry. Focus Features, 2004. (DVD: Universal Studios Home Video)

Everlasting Moments. Dir. Jan Troell. Götafilm, 2008. (DVD: The Criterion Collection)

Fahrenheit 451. Dir. François Truffaut. Enterprise Vineyard Prod., 1966. (DVD: Universal Studios)

Ferris Bueller's Day Off. Dir. John Hughes. Paramount Pictures, 1986. (DVD: Paramount Home Video)

Fighter, The. Dir. David O. Russell. Relativity Media, 2010. (DVD: Paramount Home Ent.)

Fisher King, The. Dir. Terry Gilliam. Columbia Pictures Corp., 1991. (DVD: Columbia Tristar Home Video)

Following. Dir. Christopher Nolan. Next Wave Films, 1998. (DVD: The Criterion Collection)

Frozen River. Courtney Hunt. Harwood Hunt Productions, 2008. (DVD: Sony Pictures Home Ent.)

Full Metal Jacket. Dir. Stanley Kubrick. Stanley Kubrick Productions, 1987. (DVD: Warner Home Video)

Gainsbourg: A Heroic Life. Dir. Joann Sfar. One World Films, 2010. (DVD: Music Box Films)

Gasman. Dir. Lynne Ramsey. Holy Cow Films, 1998. (DVD: The Criterion Collection)

Gladiator. Dir. Ridley Scott. Dreamworks SKG, 2000. (DVD: Dreamworks Home Ent.)

Go-Between, The. Dir. Joseph Losey. EMI Films, 1971. (DVD: Optimum)

Godfather, The. Dir. Francis Ford Coppola. Paramount Pictures, 1972. (DVD: Paramount Home Video)

Goldfinger. Dir. Guy Hamilton. Eon Prods.,1964. (DVD: Sony Pictures Home Ent.)

Gone With the Wind. Dir. Victor Fleming. Selznick Inter. Pictures, 1939. (DVD: Warner Home Video)

Goodbye Solo. Dir. Ramin Bahrani. Noruz Films, 2008. (DVD: Koch Lorber Films)

Goodfellas. Dir. Martin Scorsese. Warner Brothers Pictures 1990. (DVD: Warner Home Video)

Gosford Park. Dir. Robert Altman. Sandcastle 5 Prod., 2001. (DVD: Universal Studios)

Gospel According to St. Matthew, The. Dir. Pier Paolo Pasolini. Arco Film, 1964. (DVD: Legend Films)

Graduate, The. Dir. Mike Nichols. Embassy Pictures Corporation, 1967. (DVD: MGM DVD)

Groundhog Day. Dir. Harold Ramis. Columbia Pictures Corp., 1993. (DVD: Sony Pictures Home Ent.)

Haine, La. Dir. Mathieu Kassovitz. Canal +, 1995. (DVD: The Criterion Collection)

Half Nelson. Dir. Ryan Fleck. Hunting Lane Films, 2006. (DVD: Sony Pictures Home Ent.)

Havre, Le. Dir. Aki Kaurismäki. Sputnik Oy, 2011. (DVD: The Criterion Collection)

Hiroshima Mon Amour. Dir. Alain Resnais. Argos Films, 1959. (DVD: The Criterion Collection)

Hope and Glory. Dir. John Boorman. Nelson Ent.,1987. (DVD: MGM Home Ent.)

Hours, The. Dir. Stephen Daldry. Paramount Pictures, 2002. (DVD: Paramount Home Ent.)

Hurt Locker, The. Dir. Kathryn Bigelow. Voltage Pictures, 2008. (DVD: Summit Home Ent.)

Hysterical Blindness. Dir. Mira Nair. HBO, 2002. (DVD: Home Box Office Home Video)

I'm Not There. Dir. Todd Haynes. Killer Films, 2007. (The Weinstein Company)

Inland Empire. Dir. David Lynch. Studio Canal, 2006. (DVD: Rhino Ent. Company)

Insomnia. Dir. Christopher Nolan. Section Eight, 2002. (DVD: The Criterion Collection)

Institute Benjamenta Dirs. Brothers Quay. Image Forum, 1995. (Distribution: Zeitgeist Films)

Into the Wild. Dir. Sean Penn. Paramount Vantage, 2007. (DVD: Paramount Home Video)

Intolerance. Dir. D.W. Griffith. Triangle Film Corp., 1916. (DVD: Kino Video)

Iron Man. Dir. Jon Favreau. Marvel Studios, 2008. (DVD: Paramount Home Ent.)

Jetée, La (short). Dir. Chris Marker. Argos Films, 1962. (DVD: The Criterion Collection)

Jules and Jim. Dir. François Truffaut. Les Films du Carrosse, 1961. (DVD: The Criterion Collection)

Kes. Dir. Ken Loach. Kestrel Films, 1969 (DVD: The Criterion Collection)

Kid with a Bike, The. Dirs. Dardenne Brothers. Les Films du Fleuve, 2011. (DVD: Sundance)

King's Speech, The. Dir. Tom Hooper. See-Saw Films, 2010. (DVD: Anchor Bay Ent.)

L'Arroseur Arrosé. Dir. Francis Doublier. Lumière *1895*. (DVD: Kino Video)

Lives of Others, The. Dir. Florian Henckel von Donnersmarck. Arte, 2006. (DVD: Sony Pictures Home Ent.)

Lolita. Dir. Stanley Kubrick. MGM, 1962. (DVD: The Criterion Collection)

*M*A*S*H* Dir. Robert Altman. 20th Century Fox Film Corp., 1970. (DVD: 20th Century Fox Home Ent.)

M. Dir. Fritz Lang. Nero-Film AG, 1934. (DVD: The Criterion Collection)

Mabaroshi. Dir. Hirokazu Koreeda. TV Man Union, 1995. (DVD: New Yorker Video)

Madness of King George, The. Dir. Nicholas Hytner. Close Call Films, 1994. (DVD: MGM Home Ent.)

Man Push Cart. Dir. Ramin Bahrani. Noruz Films, 2005. (DVD: Koch Lorber)

Man Who Knew Too Much, The. Dir. Alfred Hitchcock. Paramount Pictures, 1956. (DVD: Universal Home Video Inc.)

Margin Call . Dir. J.C. Chandor. Before the Door Pictures, 2011. (Lionsgate)

Masculin/Féminin: 15 faits précis. Dir. Jean-Luc Godard. Argos Films, 1966. (DVD: The Criterion Collection, 2005)

Meek's Cutoff. Dir. Kelly Reichardt. Evenstar Films, 2010. (DVD: Oscilloscope Pictures)

Memento. Dir. Christopher Nolan. I Remember Productions, 2000. (DVD: Sony Pictures Home Ent.)

Men of Honor. Dir. George Tillman Jr. State Street Pictures, 2000. (DVD: 20th Century Fox Home Ent.)

Messenger, The. Dir. Oren Moverman. All the King's Horses, 2009. (DVD: Oscilloscope Pictures)

Metropolis. Dir. Fritz Lang. UFA, 1927. (DVD: Kino Video)

MicMacs Dir. Jean-Pierre Jeunet. Epithète Films, 2009. (DVD: Sony Pictures Home Ent.)

Nashville. Dir. Robert Altman. American Broadcasting Co. (ABC), Paramount Pictures, 1975. (DVD: Paramount Home Video)

Neighbours (short). Dir. Norman McLaren. National Film Board of Canada, 1952.

Never Again, Forever. Danae Elon and Pierre Chainet (1997)

Nine Lives. Dir. Rodrigo Garcia. Mickingbird Pictures, 2005. (DVD: Sony Pictures Home Ent.)

No Country for Old Men. Dirs. Ethan & Joel Coen. Paramount Vantage, 2007. (DVD: Miramax Home Ent.)

Nosferatu. Dir. F.W. Murnau. Jofa-Atelier Berlin-Johannisthal, 1922. (DVD: Kino Video)

Notorious. Dir. George Tillman Jr.. State Street Pictures, 2009. (DVD: 20th Century Fox Home Ent.)

Old Boy. Dir. Chan-wook Park. Egg Films, 2003. (DVD: Tartan Video)

One Hour Photo Dir. Mark Romanek. Killer Films, 2002. (DVD: 20th Century Fox Home Ent.)

Orlando Dir. Sally Potter. Adventure Pictures, 1992. (DVD: Sony Pictures Home Ent.)

Out of the Past. Dir. Jacques Tourneur. RKO Radio Pictures, 1947. (DVD: Warner Home Video)

Pan's Labyrinth. Dir. Guillermo del Toro. Estudios Picasso, 2006. (DVD: New Line Home Cinema)

Paris, Texas. Dir. Wim Wenders. Road Movies Filmproduktion, 1984. (DVD: The Criterion Collection)

Personal Velocity: Three Portraits. Dir. Rebecca Miller. IFC Productions, 2002. (DVD: MGM Distributing Corp.)

Piano, The. Dir. Jane Campion. Jan Chapman Productions, 1993. (DVD: Miramax Lionsgate)

Power. Dir. Sidney Lumet. Lorimar Productions, 1986. (DVD: Warner Home Video

Promesse, La. Dirs. Dardenne Brothers. Eurimages, 1996. (DVD: New Yorker Films)

Psycho. Dir. Alfred Hitchcock. Shamley Productions, 1960. (DVD: Universal Home Ent.)

Public Enemies. Dir. Michael Mann. Universal Pictures, 2009. (DVD: Universal Studios Home Ent.)

Puffy Chair, The. Dirs. Duplass Brothers. Duplass Brothers Productions, 2005. (DVD: Netflix)

Quattro Volte, Le. Dir. Michelangelo Frammartino, Invisible Film, 2010. (DVD: Kino International)

Raging Bull. Dir. Martin Scorsese. Chartoff-Winkler Productions, 1980. (DVD: MGM Home Ent.)

Raiders of the Lost Ark. Dir. Steven Spielberg. Lucasfilm Ltd., 1981. (DVD: Paramount Home Video)

Rashomon. Dir. Akira Kurosawa. Deiei Motion Picture Co., 1950. (DVD: The Criterion Collection)

Ratcatcher. Dir. Lynne Ramsey. Holy Cow Films, 1999. (DVD: The Criterion Collection)

Rear Window. Dir. Alfred Hitchcock. Paramount Pictures, 1954. (DVD: Universal Home Ent.)

Red Tulips (short). Dir. Shanti Thakur. Lucida Films, 2012. (DVD: Lucida Films)

Repulsion. Dir. Roman Polanski. Tekli British Productions, 1965. (DVD: The Criterion Collection)

Requiem for a Dream. Dir. Darren Aronofsky. Artisan Ent., 2000. (DVD: Lions Gate Films)

Revolutionary Road. Dir. Sam Mendes. Dreamworks, 2008. (DVD: Paramount Home Ent.)

Rome Open City. Dir. Roberto Rossellini. Excelsa Film, 1945. (DVD: Kino Video)

Rope. Dir. Alfred Hitchcock. Warner Bros., 1948. (DVD: Universal Home Ent.)

Run Lola Run. Dir. Tom Tykwer. X-Filme Creative Pool, 1998. (DVD: Columbia TriStar Home Ent.)

Russian Ark. Dir. Aleksandr Sokurov. Egoli Tossell Film AG, 2002. (Wellspring Media)

Samouraï, Le. Dir. Jean-Pierre Melville. TC Productions, 1967. (DVD: The Criterion Collection)

Samson and Delilah. Dir. Warwick Thornton. CAAMA Productions, 2009. (DVD: Trinity)

Schindler's List. Dir. Steven Spielberg. Amblin Ent., 1993. (DVD: Universal Studios Home Video)

Se7en. Dir. David Fincher. New Line Cinema, 1995. (DVD: New Line Home Video)

Separation, A. Dir. Asghar Farhadi. 2011. (Sony Pictures Classics)

Seventh Seal, The. Dir. Ingmar Bergman. Svensk Filmindustri, 1957. (DVD: The Criterion Collection)

Sex, Lies, and Videotape. Dir. Steven Soderbergh. Outlaw Productions, 1989. (DVD: Sony Home Ent.)

Sheriff of Fractured Jaw, The. Dir. Raoul Walsh. 20th Century Fox, 1959.

Shining, The. Dir. Stanley Kubrick. Warner Bros., 1980. (DVD: Warner Home Video)

Sideways. Dir. Alexander Payne. Fox Searchlight Pictures/Michael London Prod., 2004. (DVD: 20th Century Fox)

Silence of the Lambs. Dir. Jonathan Demme. Orion Pictures Corporation, 1991. (DVD: The Criterion Collection)

Sling Blade. Dir. Billy Bob Thornton. The Shooting Gallery, 1996. (DVD: Miramax Home Ent.)

Slumdog Millionaire. Dirs. Danny Boyle & Loveleen Tanda. Film4, 2008. (DVD: 20th Century Fox Home Ent.)

Social Network, The. Dir. David Fincher. Columbia Pictures, 2010. (DVD: Sony Pictures Home Ent.)

Solaris. Dir. Steven Soderbergh. 20th Century Fox, 2002. (DVD: 20th Century Fox

Sortie des Usines Lumière à Lyon, La. Dirs. Lumière brothers. Lumière, 1895. (DVD: King Video)

Soul Food. Dir. George Tillman Jr.. Edmonds Ent., 1997. (20th Century Fox)

Star Wars. Dir. George Lucas. Lucasfilm, 1977. (DVD: 20th Century Fox Home Ent.)

Still Life (Sanxia haoren). Dir. Zhang Ke Jia. Xstream Pictures, 2006. (DVD: New Yorker Video)

Story of Adèle H., The. Dir. François Truffaut. Les Films du Carrosse, 1975. (DVD: MGM World Films)

Stroszek. Dir. Werner Herzog. Werner Herzog Filmproduktion, 1977. (DVD: Anchor Bay Ent.)

Submarine. Dir. Richard Ayoade. Warp Films, 2010. (DVD: Anchor Bay Ent.)

Sunshine. Dir. Istvan Szabo. Channel Four Films,1999. (Paramount Classics)

Suspicion. Dir. Alfred Hitchcock. RKO Radio Pictures, 1941. (DVD: Warner Home Video)

Sweet Sixteen. Dir. Ken Loach. Sixteen Films, 2002. (DVD: Lions Gate)

Sweetie. Dir. Jane Campion. Arenafilm, 1989. (DVD: The Criterion Collection)

Syriana. Dir. Stephen Gaghan. Warner Bros., 2005. (DVD: Warner Bros. Ent.)

Take This Waltz. Dir. Sarah Polley. Joe's Daughter, 2011. (DVD: Mongrel Media)

Taste of Honey, A. Dir. Tony Richardson. Woodfall Film Prod., 1961. (DVD: BFI Video)

Ten. Dir. Abbas Kiarostami. Abbas Kiarostami/Key Lime/MK2 Productions, 2002. (DVD: Zeitgeist Films)

The Enigma of Kaspar Hauser. Dir. Werner Herzog. Werner Herzog Filmproduktion, 1974. (DVD: Anchor Bay Ent.)

Thelma and Louise. Dir. Ridley Scott. MGM, 1991 (DVD: Sony Pictures Home Ent.)

Thin Red Line, The. Dir. Terrence Malick. Fox 2000 Pictures, 1998. (DVD: 20th Century Fox Home Ent.)

THX-1138. Dir. George Lucas. American Zoetrope, 1971. (DVD: Warner Home Video)

Tiny Furniture. Dir. Lena Dunham. Tiny Ponies, 2010. (DVD: The Criterion Collection)

Tokyo Story. Dir. Yasujiro Ozu. Shochiku Films, Ltd., 1953. (DVD: The Criterion Collection, 2003)

Touch of Evil, A. Dir. Orson Welles. Universal International Pictures, 1958. (DVD: Universal Studios Home Video)

Traffic. Dir. Steven Soderbergh. USA Films, 2000. (DVD: Focus Ent.)

Treeless Mountain. Dir. So Yong Kim. Parts and Labor, 2008 (DVD: Oscilloscope Pictures)

Trial of Joan of Arc, The. Dir. Robert Bresson. Agnes Delahaie Prods., 1962. (DVD: Pathé)

Two Friends. Dir. Jane Campion. 1986. (Image Ent.)

Umberto D. Dir. Vittorio DeSica. Rizzoli Films, 1952. (DVD: The Criterion Collection)

Umbrellas of Cherbourg, The. Dir. Jacques Demy. Parc Film, 1964. (DVD: Koch Lorber Films)

Up in the Air. Jason Reitman. Paramount Pictures, 2009. (DVD: Paramount Home Ent.)

Vivre Sa Vie Dir. Jean-Luc Godard. Les Films de la Pléiade, 1962. (DVD: The Criterion Collection)

We Need to Talk About Kevin. Dir. Lynne Ramsey. BBC Films, 2011. (DVD: Oscilloscope Pictures)

Weekend. Dir. Jean-Luc Godard. Comacico, 1967. (DVD: New Yorker Video)

Wendy and Lucy. Dir. Kelly Reichardt. Film Science, 2008. (DVD: Oscilloscope Pictures)

Where is the Friend's House. Dir. Abbas Kiarostami. Kanoon, 1987. (DVD: Facets Multimedia)

White Ribbon, The. Dir. Michael Haneke. X-Filme Creative Pool, 2009. (DVD: Sony Pictures Home Ent.)

Wild Child, The. Dir. François Truffaut. Les Films du Carrosse, 1969. (DVD: MGM World Films)

Wings of Desire. Dir. Wim Wenders. Argos Films, 1987. (DVD: MGM/UA Home Ent.)

Wizard of Oz, The. Dir. Victor Fleming. Loew's Inc., 1939. (DVD: Warner Home Video)

Wrestler, The. Dir. Darren Aronofsky. Protozoa Pictures, 2008. (DVD: 20th Century Fox Home Ent.)

Young Adult. Dir. Jason Reitman. Paramount Pictures, 2011. (DVD: Paramount)

PHOTOGRAPH AND ILLUSTRATION ACKNOWLEDGEMENTS

Cover:*(top)* Reproduced by permission of Capri Releasing Inc. and Mongrel Media Inc., *(bottom)* See Saw Films/The Kobal Collection; **Figure 1-1** Courtesy Alcon Entertainment/Section Eight Ltd/The Kobal Collection/Mcewan, Rob/Art Resource; **Figure 1-2** Courtesy State Street Pictures; **Figure 1-3** Courtesy Noruz Films; **Figure 1-4** (*left*) Courtesy Anglo Enterprise/Vineyard/The Kobal Collection/Art Resource; **Figure 2-3** Courtesy Don Harwood/photo by Jory Sutton; **Figure 2-4** (left) Courtesy Nimbus Film/The Kobal Collection/Art Resource; **Figure 9-3** Courtesy Usa Films/Capitol Films/Film Council/The Kobal Collection/Tillie, Mark; **Figure 11-7** (*left*) Courtesy Decla-Bioscop/The Kobal Collection; **Figure 11-7** (*right*) Courtesy Warner Bros/The Kobal Collection/Art Resource; **Figure 18-2** Courtesy of Virginia Dutton; **Figure 20-1** (*left*) Courtesy Buffalo Picture House, (*right*) Courtesy Blum Israel/Hbo/Karuna Dream/The Kobal Collection/Art Resource; **Figure 20-2** Reproduced by permission of Capri Releasing Inc and Mongrel Media 2008; **Figure 21-2** Courtesy Fox Searchlight/The Kobal Collection/Art Resource; **Figure 23-1** Courtesy Picturesque Films; **Figure 23-5** Courtesy Andrew Knudsen; **Figure 24-2** Courtesy Parc Films/Madeleine Films/The Kobal Collection; **Figure 24-7** (*left*) Courtesy The Kobal Collection/Art Resource; **Figure 25-2** Courtesy Patrick Ng; **Figure 25-6** Courtesy Canon USA; **Figure 25-7** Photo by Htat Htut; **Figure 25-9** Photo by Larry Kamerman; **Figure 25-10** Courtesy Buffalo Picture House; **Figure 26-1** Courtesy Sarah Sellman; **Figure 26-3** Courtesy Buffalo Picture House; **Figure 26-4** Courtesy Buffalo Picture House; **Figure 26-5** Photo by Htat Htut; **Figure 26-6** Courtesy Andrew Knudsen; **Figure 26-7** Courtesy Danjaq/Eon/Ua/The Kobal Collection/Art Resource); **Figure 27-24** Courtesy Andrew Knudsen; **Figure 28-2** Courtesy Warner Bros./The Kobal Collection/Art Resource; **Figure 28-3** Courtesy Andrew Knudsen; **Figure 28-4** Courtesy Catrin Hedström, photo by Zac DeZon; **Figure 28-5** Courtesy of Nicole Haddock; **Figure 29-1** Courtesy of Jacqueline Reyno/Photo by Rachel Jones; **Figure 29-2** Photo by Htat Htut; **Figure 29-3** Photo by Jane Kim; **Figure 30-1** Courtesy Martha Pinson; **Figure 30-3** Courtesy of Carl Boles; **Figure 31-1** (*left*) Courtesy Columbia/The Kobal Collection/Art Resource) (*right*) Courtesy Thelma Schoonmaker; **Figure 33-1** Courtesy Paramount/The Kobal Collection; **Figure 35-2** Courtesy Neosounds.com; **Figure 36-4** from Prosoundeffects.com; **Figure 37-2** Courtesy Nichole Kizer/Photo by Ken Easley; **Figure 37-5** Courtesy Noruz Films. **Part 1** (*top*) Photo by Htat Htut (*bottom*) Courtesy of Patrick Ng; **Part 2** (*top*) Photo by Sunina Khargie (*bottom*) Courtesy Jared

Stanton, Photo by Daniel Waghorne; **Part 3** (*top*) Courtesy Hannah Janal (*bottom*) Courtesy Andrew Knudsen; **Part 4** (*top*) Courtesy of Nicole Haddock (*bottom*) Courtesy Andrew Knudsen; **Part 5** (*top*) Courtesy of Jacqueline Reyno/Photo by Kathryn Ferrara (*bottom*) Courtesy of Top Gun Productions/The Kobal Collection/Art Resource; **Part 6** (*top*) Courtesy Tyler Perry Company and The Kobal Collection/Art Resource. (*bottom*) Photo by Htat Htut; **Part 7** (*top*) Courtesy Jennifer Kim (*bottom*) Courtesy Catrin Hedström, photo by Zac DeZon; **Part 8** (*top*) Photo by Marc Ohrem/Marc Ohrem-Lecelf/Leclef Photo Inc. (*bottom*) Courtesy Killer Films/The Kobal Collection/Art Resource

    Additional Photography by Mick Hurbis-Cherrier and Gustavo Mercado
    Illustrations by Gustavo Mercado

INDEX

Page numbers in **bold** refer to illustrations